Studies in Church History

15

RELIGIOUS MOTIVATION: BIOGRAPHICAL AND SOCIOLOGICAL PROBLEMS FOR THE CHURCH HISTORIAN

RELIGIOUS MOTIVATION: BIOGRAPHICAL AND SOCIOLOGICAL PROBLEMS FOR THE CHURCH HISTORIAN

PAPERS READ AT
THE SIXTEENTH SUMMER MEETING AND
THE SEVENTEENTH WINTER MEETING
OF THE
ECCLESIASTICAL HISTORY SOCIETY

EDITED BY

DEREK BAKER

PUBLISHED FOR
THE ECCLESIASTICAL HISTORY SOCIETY

BY

BASIL BLACKWELL · OXFORD

1978

ISBN 0 631 19250 6

Printed in Great Britain
by Crampton & Sons Ltd, Sawston, Cambridge

PREFACE

The present volume of *Studies in Church History* is the fifteenth to be produced by the Ecclesiastical History Society and the sixth to be published by the Society itself in collaboration with Basil Blackwell. 'Religious motivation: biographical and sociological problems for the church historian' was the theme of the sixteenth summer meeting of the Society, held at the University of Oxford, and of the seventeenth winter meeting. The thirty-three papers included in this volume are a selection from those read at these two meetings.

The Society is grateful to the British Academy for generous financial assistance in the production of this volume.

Derek Baker

CONTENTS

CONTENTS

CONTENTS

CONTRIBUTORS

JOHN McMANNERS (*President*)
Regius Professor of Ecclesiastical History, University of Oxford

G. V. BENNETT
Fellow of New College, Oxford

HENRY CHADWICK
Dean of Christ Church, Oxford

ROGER HIGHFIELD
Fellow of Merton College, Oxford

COLIN MATTHEW
Student of Christ Church, Oxford

HUGH TREVOR-ROPER
Regius Professor of Modern History, University of Oxford

BRYAN WILSON
Reader in Sociology, University of Oxford, and Fellow of All
Souls College

DEREK BAKER
Lecturer in History, University of Edinburgh

W. D. J. CARGILL THOMPSON
Late Professor of Ecclesiastical History, University of London,
King's College

RICHARD CARWARDINE
Lecturer in American History, University of Sheffield

FRED A. CAZEL, JR
Professor of History, University of Connecticut

EAMON DUFFY
Lecturer in Ecclesiastical History, University of London, King's
College

GILLIAN R. EVANS
Lecturer in History, University of Reading

CONTRIBUTORS

ANTHONY FLETCHER
Senior Lecturer in History, University of Sheffield

JOAN G. GREATREX
Associate Professor of History, Carleton University, Ottawa

BERNARD HAMILTON
Senior Lecturer in History, University of Nottingham

CHRISTOPHER HARPER-BILL
Lecturer in Medieval History, St Mary's College, Strawberry Hill, London

JOHN HENDERSON
University of London, Westfield College

R. F. G. HOLMES
Magee Professor of Christian History and Doctrine, the Presbyterian Colleges, Belfast

M. D. LAMBERT
Senior Lecturer in History, University of Bristol

EMMA MASON
Lecturer in History, University of London, Birkbeck College

COLIN MORRIS
Professor of Medieval History, University of Southampton

RICHARD MORTIMER
University of London, King's College

DUNCAN NIMMO
Research Fellow, Department of Educational Research, University of Lancaster

W. B. PATTERSON
Professor of History, Davidson College, North Carolina

STUART PIGGIN
Lecturer in History, University of Wollongong

ANDREW PORTER
Lecturer in History, University of London, King's College

xii

GEOFFREY ROBSON
Senior Lecturer in Religious Education, Westhill College,
Birmingham

DAVID M. THOMPSON
Lecturer in Modern Church History, University of Cambridge

A. F. WALLS
Head of Department of Religious Studies, University of
Aberdeen

W. R. WARD
Professor of History, University of Durham

HADDON WILLMER
Lecturer in Theology, University of Leeds

W. N. YATES
City Archivist, Portsmouth

INTRODUCTION

Not all motives are avowed or avowable, not all are present in the conscious mind and, sometimes, motives are claimed or ascribed to mask self-interest or to persuade and manipulate. The biographer continually faces these problems; some are insoluble, some are capable, if not of solution, at least of clarification in the light of modern psychological and medical knowledge, but most are susceptible of what might be called 'half-way explanations'. Through an exposition of the nuances, careful attention to chronological development, a sympathetic attitude and a literary style that can combine sympathy with irony and criticism, the reader can be brought to a half-way position where, even if nothing is proved, he can at least understand; he can say 'that's what I would have done', or 'there but for the grace of God go I', or 'it's odd how curiously the human mind works'.

Problems of motivation will, more especially, haunt the ecclesiastical historian, for 'religious' motivation can be overwhelmingly irrational, its manifestations can be ambiguous, and hypocrisy and self-deception are proverbially found in their most extreme form in the religious context. There is, however, a further problem for the historian who works in the field of ecclesiastical biography, for the religion of an age inevitably takes forms – liturgical, literary, artistic, institutional and, even, moral and mystical – which reflect the economic and social climate of the times. By what standards should we judge? Do we think of religion as some pure essence (which we ourselves and our circle have defined, here in our own time), or do we accept it as the average conformist minds of that day saw it? What of the blind spot of a saint who lacks a social conscience over some great issue? What of the 'vocations' of aristocrats who automatically expect that they will walk into bishoprics, of monks who live scholarly lives, better than their contemporaries, but well below their own proclaimed ideals, of church leaders who espouse political causes we now regard as cruel or reactionary or futile?

As historical studies have developed in our own generation, there is yet a further ramification of the problem of motivation. History has become sociological, and religious manifestations of every kind have been subjected to statistical analysis. These manifestations can be shown to flourish in certain geographical areas, in certain social classes, in certain family groups and not in others, they rise and fall under the

INTRODUCTION

pressure of changing historical conditions. How do we explain these differences? In the search for explanation a multitude of new questions arises. How do we distinguish 'practice' from 'fervour'? What is the place of religious inspirations coming from outside the institutional religious groups, maybe from unbelievers or anticlericals? When a religion reforms itself or is reformed, where is the core of its original identity? How deep do mass conversions go, and what is the precise nature of the conversion of the individual? Is religion caught, taught or merely inherited? And, for ourselves, if we believe, to what extent are we prisoners of the past? in matters of religion, can we ever start again?

CONVERSION IN
CONSTANTINE THE GREAT

by HENRY CHADWICK

THE study of church history, in a degree perhaps unparalleled among the various branches of historical study, combines both the analysis of flux and change and also the continuities and constants that somehow remain through the vicissitudes and disasters of human history. Without needing to have any prefabricated pattern imposed upon it, in Marxist or other style, church history discloses startling continuities, so that to talk about Constantine or Origen or Augustine is somehow not to indulge in antiquarianism but to be talking about issues which (despite vast changes in the intellectual framework within which the debate proceeds) remain alive for the living community of the church now. The sweat drips from our brows as we make the effort to preserve impartiality and detachment. My subject is Constantine's conversion and the shift that this brought to the intellectual and religious history of Europe. If we put the story back into its historical context and try to look at it with the eyes of a contemporary, the shift may not seem exactly the kind of shift that at first the modern historian thinks he sees.

The old Oxford tradition did not feel comfortable with the secularised trinitarianism of Cambridge, where history has long been divided into ancient, medieval, and modern; a threefold division with those deep echoes of Joachim of Fiore or of the radical sects of the seventeenth century who felt sure that now had come the true and final manifestation of the Paraclete, and that all previous history could be dismissed as a back number. At Oxford, while it is true that in 'Greats' ancient historians are not encouraged to study much after the time of Hadrian, the school of modern history boldly solves the problem of periodisation by beginning with Diocletian and Constantine. Of course all periodisation is nonsense. But it can be useful nonsense, and Diocletian's reorganisation of the empire after the fearful crisis of the third century makes a good starting point. There is also the fact that, after a yawning gap in the third century (for which, except for Herodian's novelettish work only taking us to 238, much of our information is derived accidentally from Christian sources like Cyprian

I

and Eusebius),[1] from the beginning of the fourth century our sources
suddenly become voluminous, to a degree to which ancient historians are
unaccustomed. The empire's transition from paganism to Christianity
looks so like a major watershed in the history of the Mediterranean
world that it is also necessary to remind oneself that in its main fabric
and structure ancient society did not change when Constantine was
converted. The Greek and Latin languages continue to be dominant,
and those outside the ethnic and linguistic unity (or rather duality)
of the Mediterranean culture are 'barbarians'. Constantine and his
Christian successors enact a number of laws in which Christian
influence can be discerned.[2] But these laws do not affect the continued
validity of the entire tradition of Roman law inherited from the past.
Among these old laws there were many that were obsolete and others
that were conflicting, remarks Ammianus Marcellinus.[3] In the time
of Diocletian about 297, a jurist of the imperial chancery named
Gregory made a vast collection of imperial edicts classified under
various titles, an endeavour which looks as if it were at least in part
intended to sort out some of the anomalies. Twenty years later another
chancery jurist named Hermogenianus produced another collection,
parts of which survive.[4] The conversion of the emperor to Christianity
made no difference whatever to the continued validity of the corpus of
legal enactments, under which society was governed.

What kind of a caesura did the change of religion mean? We may
speak (with the emperor Julian) of the Constantinian 'revolution': yet

[1] On the crisis of the third century see Geza Alföldy, 'Die heilige Cyprian und die Krise
des römischen Reiches', *Historia* 22 (Wiesbaden 1973) pp 479–501; 'The Crisis of the
third century as seen by contemporaries', *Greek Roman and Byzantine Studies* 15
(London 1974) pp 89–111. Some interesting reflections on the identification of 'Late
Antiquity' as a period are offered now by René Martin, 'Qu'est-ce l'antiquité
tardive?' in *Aion: le temps chez les Romains*, ed R. Chevallier (Paris 1976) pp 261–304.
[2] On Constantine's legislation, A. Ehrhardt, 'Constantin d. Gr. Religionspolitik und
Gesetzgebung', *ZRG, RAbt* 72 (1955) pp 127–289, argues that the Constantinian laws
preserved in the Theodosian Code are mere summaries made by chancery lawyers not
all of whom were sympathetic to his beliefs. Walter Ullmann, 'The Constitutional
Significance of Constantine the Great's settlement', *JEH* 27 (1976) pp 1–16, interprets
Constantine's adhesion to Christianity in terms of a bid to harness Christian virtues to the
rebirth of the empire, with a consequent incorporation of the church within Roman
public law (that is, religion and the civil service). This paper has rich bibliographical
notes. See also his book, *Medieval Foundations of Renaissance Humanism* (London 1977)
pp 42–3.
[3] Ammianus xxx, 4, 11.
[4] On Gregorius and Hermogenianus see F. Schutz, *History of Roman Legal Science*
(Oxford 1946) p 287 where his date, 291, for the publication of the codex Gregorianus
should, I think, be amended to 297.

Conversion in Constantine the Great

an essay could easily be written to show how closely Constantine resembles what went before and how very similar Diocletian and Constantine are in their general character and policies. Of course they were both Illyrians, inclined to look down on the softness and lack of energy of Italy.[5] (A passage in Ambrose contrasting the prosperity of orthodox Italy with the sad fate in his time of Arian Illyricum is no doubt a reflection, in theological form, of the Italians' reply.)[6] Their concept of government is remarkably similar. Lactantius says that Diocletian wanted his eastern residence at Nicomedia in Bithynia to rival old Rome;[7] did he thereby sow the seed of Constantine's New Rome? At least Diocletian gave Constantine the notion of a capital in the east which would be a centre of gravity for the Greek half of the empire. Constantine made it a Christian city adorned at its highest points by churches, not temples. But the antithesis to old pagan Rome is surely a subordinate motive in the foundation of Constantinople. Its opening dedication was celebrated by a festival of the Tyche of the city with prayers offered by Christian clergy which looks like reunion all round. A colossal statue of Constantine (on the 'Burnt Column') with the features and insignia of the sun-god[8] was soon venerated with candles and incense.[9]

---

[5] *Paneg Lat* 10(2), 2; compare 11(3), 3.

[6] Ambrose, *de fide* ii, 139–42. Compare the letter of the usurper Maximus to Valentinian II, *Avellana* 39 (*CSEL* 35, p 88), written about easter 386, observing that the barbarian invasion of Illyricum and the obliteration of the city of Mursa (the great stronghold of western Arianism) are a divine vengeance which should warn Valentinian from encouraging Arianism at Milan. Compare my remarks in *Priscillian of Avila* (Oxford 1976) pp 117–18.

[7] Lactantius *MP* 7, 10 'Ita semper dementabat Nicomediam studens urbi Romae coaequare'.

[8] Chron Pasch pp 284–5 (*PG* 92 (1865) cols 708B–12A = Mommsen, *Chronica Minora* i, 233–4); Malalas XIII, 321 (*PG* 97 (1865) col 480). Lydus, *de Mensibus* 4, 2 (pp 65 *seq* Wünsch) says Praetextatus the hierophant and Sopater also took part in the dedication of the Tyche of Constantinople. Compare *Scriptores Originum Constantinopolitanarum,* ed T. Preger (1901) p 56. According to Socrates, *HE* i, 17, 8, followed by the tenth century *Patria* of Constantinople (ed Preger, p 174), the radiate crown on the statue was formed by the nails of Calvary (similarly Zonaras 13, 3; iii p 183 Dindorf; the story is known to Gregory of Tours, *Gloria Martyrum* 6, *PL* 71 (1879) col 711).

[9] Philostorgius, *HE* 2, 17; compare Theodoret, *HE* 1, 34. Compare F. J. Dölger, *Sol Salutis*² (Münster 1925) p 67; Jean Ebersolt, *Sanctuaires de Byzance* (Paris 1921) pp 72–3; R. Janin, *Constantinople Byzantine*² (Paris 1964) p 79. T. Preger, 'Konstantin-Helios,' *Hermes* 36 (Berlin 1901) pp 457–69, argued that Constantine intended the statue to be interpreted syncretistically. This opinion is opposed by I. Karyannopulos, 'Konstantin der Grosse und der Kaiserkult,' *Historia* 5 (1956) pp 341–57. The texts of Philostorgius and Theodoret demonstrate that, whether or not it was Constantine's intention, the statue was soon venerated with lights and incense in the manner of pagan emperor-cult.

Above all, the crisis of the third century, in which the empire simply disintegrated with civil wars and barbarian invasions, seemed to Diocletian to require not only military and provincial reorganisation but also a return to the old gods by whose favour the empire had prospered. Therefore, Diocletian is a moral and religious conservative. His edict issued at Damascus on 1 May 295 forbidding marriages within prohibited degrees is likely to have some bearing on the prevalence of brother/sister marriages in Mesopotamia.[10] It expresses great fear that if incestuous unions are not stamped out, the 'immortal gods cannot be expected to be propitious to the Roman name'. Only those marriages are allowed which conform to Roman law. 'So the majesty of Rome will be brought to greatness by the favour of all the gods.' The language is remarkably like that which Constantine will use when confronted by the threat of church disruption in the Donatist schism in Africa.[11] The sources plausibly represent Galerius as prime mover in the Great Persecution and Diocletian as most reluctant to persecute until finally moved by an oracle of Apollo at Didyma.[12] This is very like Constantine's reluctance to hear the Donatist dispute, eventually leaving the Donatists to the judgement of God, a decision whose weakness Augustine deplores.[13]

After the fearful insecurity of the preceding half-century Diocletian realised that his reconstructed imperium needed an ideological theory. He called himself Jovius, the earthly representative of Jupiter; his colleague Maximian he called Herculius, as representative of Hercules.[14] As the practical authority of the emperor seemed to weaken, so the divinity of the Roman emperor took ever stronger expressions (a phenomenon for which ecclesiastical historians will find other parallels). Ammianus once comments that whereas former emperors were simply saluted as judges, Diocletian introduced the foreign custom by which those admitted to the presence were required to

---

[10] *Mosaicarum et Romanarum Legum Collatio* vi, 4. I discuss this document in a paper on 'The Relativity of Moral Codes' in the volume of essays in honour of Robert M. Grant (1978).

[11] For example, his letter to Aelafius, perhaps *vicarius Africae* (313), in Optatus, App III (ed Ziwsa), expressing fear lest contentions in the church may move the highest God 'not only against the human race but against me personally to whose care he has committed by his celestial assent the rule of all earthly affairs.'

[12] Lactantius *MP* 10–11. On the role played by the oracle at Didyma near Miletus at this period see L. Robert in *Comptes rendus de l'Académie des Inscriptions et Belles Lettres* (Paris 1968).

[13] Augustine, *ad Donatistas post gesta* 31, 54; 33, 56 (*CSEL* 53 pp 156, 158).

[14] Aurelius Victor 39, 18; Lactantius *MP* 52, 3; *Paneg Lat* 8(5), 4, 1; 10(2), 11, 6. The titles also appear in inscriptions: Dessau *ILS* 621–3, 634.

Conversion in Constantine the Great

venerate the purple.[15] Before the emperor's audience hall special veils were hung which surprised even the officials controlling access to the imperial presence (so the panegyric on Maximian of 291).[16]

From 293 Diocletian created the tetrarchy: two supreme augusti, each with an adjutant entitled caesar who would have the expectation of becoming augustus and coopting his own caesar to replace him.[17] The very tetrarchy itself was given a mystical justification: According to a panegyric delivered at Gaul in 297 in the presence of the caesar Constantius, fourness is of the very nature of things.[18] There are four elements, four seasons of the year, four corners of the earth, four horses drawing the chariot of the sun. The argument is that used over a century earlier by Irenaeus to explain why the number of canonical gospels must necessarily be four.[19] According to Cornelius Labeo, Zeus, Hades, Helios and Dionysius are four seasonal names of the one sungod who is also called Iao (the God of the Jews).[20] The justification of the imperial tetrarchy is that it corresponds to something inherent in the structure of the cosmos; and this is a theme that in one form or another is entirely characteristic of the world of classical antiquity, with its assumption, for a time questioned by the sophists in fifth-century Greece but much too tough to be destroyed by such lightweight characters, that the political order somehow corresponds to nature, that law and order in society do not depend on some human contract or convention but reflect the law and order of the seasons, the vegetation, the stars and planets;[21] that the place of kings in society is vindicated by the social harmony of bees under their 'king' (the ancients took it for granted that the royal sex was male);[22] and so on. The fourth eclogue of Vergil offers a classic statement of this belief in the essential harmony of man and his environment. And one has only to recall psalm 104 to be reminded that something of this sense of

[15] Ammianus xv, 5, 18.
[16] *Paneg Lat* 11(3), 11, 1–3.
[17] See W. Ensslin in *PW* 7A, *sv* Valerius (142), col 2436.
[18] *Paneg Lat* 8(5), 4, 2.
[19] *Adv Haereses* III, 11, 8.
[20] Macrobius, *Sat* i, 18, 18 *seq*; 19, 15. Compare Dio Chrysostom 36, 39 *seq* on the Iranian myth of the four horse chariot of the god of time. Nigidius Figulus' fourth book 'On the Gods' (cited by Servius, *ad Ecl* iv, 10) attributed to Orpheus the association of Saturn, Jupiter, Neptune, and Pluto with the four seasons (A. Swoboda, *P. Nigidii Figuli Reliquiae* 1889, reprinted Amsterdam 1964, p 83). These texts are brilliantly discussed by E. Peterson, ΕΙΣ ΘΕΟΣ (Göttingen 1926) pp 241–53.
[21] Dio Chrys I, 42 *seq.*
[22] Seneca, *de Clementia* i, 19, 2–4. For the bees as a model for human society see Celsus in Origen, *c. Cels* iv, 81. It lies in the background of Vergil's fourth Georgic.

5

harmony between man and nature can be at home in the biblical tradition. Accordingly, the panegyrist of 297 stands in a very ancient tradition when he looks for a political theory that will justify the tetrarch's authority in cosmic terms. It would not be difficult to collect passages from fathers of the church after the time of Constantine in which the position of the emperor is justified as part of the immutable order of the nature of things.[23]

When Eusebius of Caesarea came to write his own political theory for Constantine's monarchy, in the third and fourth books of the *Vita Constantini* (which I regard as an undoubtedly authentic work from Eusebius' pen), he saw monotheism as having its earthly counterpart in loyalty to a single supreme emperor, and simultaneously in the one revealed truth given to the church. St Paul had written of 'one Spirit, one hope, one Lord, one faith, one baptism, one God and Father of us all' (Eph. 4, 4–5). The 'One God' formula appears to have been an apotropaic formula of jewish exorcism, which spread widely to become a formula of acclamation.[24] Cyprian of Carthage already expanded the Pauline formula to be one God, one Christ, one bishop.[25] In the letters of Ignatius of Antioch it is a frequently repeated theme that the single bishop of the local church represents the monarchy of God, a correspondence taken to such realistic lengths that Ignatius sees in the silence of bishops a particularly divine characteristic in that 'Silence' is a name of God in mystical and gnostic speculation.[26]

The political theory which made the emperor (whether Diocletian or Constantine) the earthly counterpart of a God cannot have been irrelevant to Diocletian's systematic exclusion of the old senatorial families from real power either in the army or in the administration.[27]

[23] There are excellent remarks on these themes by A. Dihle, 'Antikes und Unantikes in der frühchristlichen Staatstheorie', in the transactions of the sixth international congress of classical studies at Madrid 1974: *Assimilation et Résistance à la Culture gréco-romaine dans de monde ancien* (Bucharest/Paris 1976) pp 323–32. Much material is collected in F. Dvornik, *Early Christian and Byzantine Political Philosophy* (Washington, D.C., 1966).
[24] E. Peterson has argued to this conclusion.
[25] *de Unitate* 4–5; *Ep.* 43, 5.
[26] H. Chadwick, 'The Silence of Bishops in Ignatius', *HTR* 43 (1950) pp 169 *seq.* Iranian cult of the god Silence is mentioned by Ammianus Marcellinus xxi, 13, 4.
[27] Compare Lactantius *MP* 8, 4 (Maximian's purge of senate); 17, 2 (Diocletian's unpopularity on his brief stay in Rome). Detailed examples are given by M. T. W. Arnheim, *The Senatorial Aristocracy in the Later Roman Empire* (Oxford 1972) pp 39 *seq.* Mr O. P. Nicholson points out to me how both Maxentius and, at least in his early days, Constantine bid for the support of the Roman senate by emphasising the status of old Rome.

No doubt Gregorius' juristic collection underlined the truth that the emperor is now the one source of law; the old senatusconsulta will give way to imperial rescripts. We are on the way to Justinian's doctrine that all past enactments are invalidated unless included in his codex: that is, the emperor's ratification is the sole fount of authority. Ruler cult gave place to a high doctrine of the divine right of kings. In the mid-fifties of the fourth century both Athanasius and Ammianus, from very different points of view, find occasion for highly critical comments on Constantius II's estimate of himself as the exclusive embodiment of law.[28] Themistius gives formal expression to the doctrine that the emperor is the living embodiment of the law, so that the emperor is both the source of all law and standing above it.[29]

But beside the theme of the emperor as cosmic order, there is another theme derived from Jewish-Christian eschatological hope, a very unconservative and radical theme which speaks of the ending of the existing order. St John of Patmos saw in his vision a new heaven and a new earth, with a heavenly Jerusalem descending as a bride adorned for her husband (Rev. 21, 1 *seq*). The reader of the *Divine Institutes* of Lactantius is inclined to take the first six books as mild apologetic tracts advancing views not likely to be very startling to most of his pagan contemporaries. But the seventh book is an eschatological tractate: the advent of a Christian emperor heralds an 'almost golden age' (7, 24 and 26), which calls all men to live righteous lives to prepare for the imminent establishment of God's kingdom. Like Tertullian before him,[30] Lactantius sees the continued existence of Rome as the one barrier to the disintegration of things (7, 25). So the empire has a positive role to play in averting the rule of Antichrist. But what is needed is a revolution to sweep away the moral corruption of the old fabric and to bring in a new, Christian society.

In his commentary on St Matthew Origen remarks that the doctrine of Christ's second coming on the clouds of heaven is taken in a literal sense by simple believers, and educated believers are often distressed by this article of the creed. It speaks the language of symbol: it may mean either the universal extension of the Christian gospel to all

---

[28] Athanasius, *Historia Arianorum* 33, proves his thesis that the Arians have no king but Caesar by quoting Constantius II's claim that the emperor is also the source of authority for canon law, an opinion for which Constantius could appeal to 'the Syrian bishops'. Compare Ammianus xv, 1, 3; 6, 37; he has a notable comment at xvii, 12, 17 on some who believed that Fate can be overcome by an emperor's will.

[29] I, 15B; V, 64B; XVI, 212D; XIX, 228A.

[30] Tertullian, *Apol* 32, 1; 39, 2; *ad Scapulam* 2, 6.

nations of the world, or that inward coming of Christ to the individual soul in a mystical union so intense that the soul becomes one Spirit with the Lord.[31] If Origen himself was evidently more attracted to this latter view, many Christians would certainly have thought the former interpretation more immediate and accessible.

In the second century a famous passage of Melito of Sardis sees the *pax Romana* as a providential means of spreading the peace of God throughout the world to facilitate the Christian mission.[32] In his reply to the pagan Celsus Origen takes up the same theme.[33] Long before Constantine Christians hoped and prayed for the miracle of the conversion of the emperor.[34] About 180 Celsus knows of a Christian dream of uniting all peoples of the world, both Greeks and barbarians 'even at the furthest limits' under one law, an ideal which Celsus regards as an additional example of utterly unrealistic Christian fantasy. Origen's reply makes it clear that he too thinks the ideal unlikely to be realised in this world; but it will be in the world to come and, meanwhile, Christians strive towards that end to produce at least an approximation.[35]

Up to this point I have sought to sketch the conservatism of Constantine—the degree to which he continued to talk and act as other men had done before him, whether as pagan emperors or as Christian apologists. But now the question can be put: wherein then lies the revolution which both Julian and Eusebius or Lactantius associate with his conversion?

The question of Constantine's conversion used to be seen as a debate between the secularist and the ecclesiastical standpoints—between the cynical portrait of Burckhardt's Constantine who adopts Christianity because he calculates that the church will support his rise to world power, and the idealised or hagiographical picture of Constantine[36] stemming from Eusebius' panegyrics, in which the

[31] Origen, *in Matt comm series* 70, ed Klostermann-Benz, 2 ed U. Treu, 1976, p 165.
[32] Eusebius *HE* iv, 26, 8.
[33] Origen, *c. Cels* ii, 30 compare *Selecta in Psalmos* xii p 332 Lommatzsch.
[34] Tertullian, *Apol* 21, 24 'Sed et Caesares credidissent super Christo, si aut Caesares non essent necessarii saeculo aut si et Christiani potuissent esse Caesares'. Origen, *c. Cels* vii, 71.
[35] *c. Cels* viii, 72. Lactantius (*Div Inst* 5, 8, 6–11) says that if polytheism were ended and God alone worshipped, the acknowledgement of universal brotherhood would end wars and dissensions; knowledge of divine law would end sedition, fraud, robbery, sexual immorality; indeed, laws themselves would become unnecessary.
[36] See the Greek office in the Menaion for 21 May; or Severus of Antioch's hymn, edited and translated by E. W. Brooks in *PO* 7, 5 (1911) 663-4.

emperor, miraculously converted by his vision, is the thirteenth apostle, the very model of a most Christian monarch, so that no greater compliment could be paid, either to a Byzantine emperor or to a converted Frankish king from whom the church expects support than to call him a New Constantine.[37]

Refuting Burckhardt has become an easy game. It is simply done with the observation that the church was nothing like numerous or influential enough to be a source of political power. In 300, it remained a small minority group, especially in the west. It had ambitions to influence the course of world history because of its eschatological expectation of a triumph of God over the evil in the historical process. And there were certainly Christians in high places as is demonstrated by Cyprian's astonishing epistle 80, disclosing that, from his intelligence service at the court, he has received the terms of a new imperial edict ordering fresh persecution of the church well in advance of the receipt of this document by the proconsul of Africa. There was evidently a dedicated Christian near the top. But the church was in no sense an impatient political pressure group that could look useful to a Machiavellian, power-hungry young man on the make. Nevertheless the burying of Burckhardt does not, I think, justify us in eliminating all political dimensions from Constantine's religious beliefs. His contemporaries thought his conversion fraught with consequence, not a private matter between the emperor and his Maker. The fourth-century Christian sources see Constantine's conversion as a miracle. The pagan sources naturally do not. They offer two motivations for his change of religious allegiance. On the one hand Julian, Eunapius, and Zosimus say he fled to the church to obtain cheap forgiveness for his dreadful crimes—especially that of 326 when his son Crispus and his wife Fausta were murdered, according to gossip, on suspicion of having had a stepson/stepmother, Hippolytus/

---

[37] After Themistius' oration for Jovian of 1 January 364 (*or.* V, 70 D) this became a ceremonial greeting for Byzantine emperors; compare the acclamations for Marcian at the council of Chalcedon (*Act Chalc* vi, 5, *ACO* 2, i, p 336) or at the accession of Justin I in 519 (Constant Porphyrog *de Caerim* I 93, *CSHB* p 430). At the eighth session of the second council of Nicaea (787), Constantine and his mother Irene are acclaimed as New Constantine and New Helena: Labbe-Coleti, *Concilia* 8, cols 1243-4. In the West Gregory of Tours hails Clovis as a New Constantine (*HF* ii, 31); Pope Adrian I similarly greets Charlemagne (*ep* 60, *PL* 98 (1862) col 306B). The Genoese annals say that after the recovery of Constantinople in 1261 Michael Palaeologus was styled New Constantine; see D. J. Geanakoplos, *Emperor Michael Palaeologus and the West* (1959) p 121. It would be surprising had it not been so.

9

Phaedra affair.[38] Libanius on the other hand (Or. 30.6) says Constantine
was converted because he needed a lot of money: he had to take gold
from the temples to finance his costly new capital at Byzantium.[39]

It is noteworthy that both these pagan explanations agree in giving
a late date to the conversion—after the fall of Licinius in 324 and his
rise to sole power. Now it is certain from Constantine's letters on the
Donatist controversy, and from his role in the first stages of the Arian
controversy and at Nicaea in 325, that his identification with
Christianity, his allegiance to the Deus Christianorum, is earlier.
Nevertheless our pagan sources may offer a signpost to the truth that
only after he had become sole emperor was there some change in his
public attitude to pagan cult which had practical consequences.
Libanius says that he did not stop pagan worship: he simply took the
gold.

Since Norman Baynes' British Academy lecture of 1929 (reprinted
1972) Constantine's conversion has been seen in a different light from
either Burckhardt or the more idealistic view: in 312 before the
battle at the Milvian Bridge in which he eliminated his rival Maxentius,
he invoked the supreme God of the Christians; and his military
success, in a battle in which the cards were stacked against him,
imparted to Constantine a sense of being called by God for a mission
in which the destinies of the church and empire were bound together.[40]
His later letters can apostrophise the Lord with the sudden claim
'I am your man'. Baynes rested his argument on the authenticity of
the letters of Constantine preserved in Eusebius. Subsequent investigations (especially A. H. M. Jones' identification in 1951 of the London
papyrus as containing one of the documents preserved in the Vita
Constantini) have vindicated this view. At the same time a wider gap
than Baynes explicitly allows for has been discerned between

[38] Julian 336AB; Zosimus ii, 29; the refutation of this pagan thesis is in Sozomen, HE i,
5, and Evagrius, HE iii, 40 seq. Compare F. Paschoud, 'Zosime, 2, 29 et la version
païenne de la conversion de Constantin', Historia 20 (1971) pp 334–53. The evidence
for the poisoning of Crispus at Pola in 326 is examined by P. Guthrie in Phoenix 20
(1966), 326–31; he thinks Constantine's motive was to be rid of a bastard son (by the
concubine Minervina) and so to preserve the legitimate dynastic succession on his
death. It would then remain obscure why he needed to be rid of Fausta.
[39] Libanius, or 30, 6. Julian (335B) also thinks Constantine wanted money to spend on
the gratification of himself and his friends. Compare Ammianus xvi, 8, 12:
Constantine first excited the avarice of his followers, but Constantius took their greed
further.
[40] See J. Straub, Vom Herrscherideal in der Spätantike (Stuttgart 1939); and his paper
'Konstantins christliches Sendungsbewusstsein,' Regeneratio Imperii (Darmstadt 1972)
pp 70–88.

Conversion in Constantine the Great

Eusebius' idealised picture of the most Christian emperor and Constantine's pro-Christian policy as expressed in these letters. Baynes was certainly correct that we can accept the authenticity and inward sincerity of Constantine's adherence to Christianity from the Milvian Bridge onwards. What has remained obscure is whether, or in what sense, and from what date, Constantine understood his conversion in an exclusive, absolutist sense of involving an active rejection of the polytheistic tradition which should and could affect his public policy.

The third century had seen possibilities of rapprochement between Christianity and higher paganism. The polytheistic tradition had become markedly more monotheistic in tone under the parallel influences of neoplatonic philosophy and of the cult of the unconquered sun. Solar monotheism does not only appear in the panegyric mentioning Constantine's vision of Apollo in the temple at Autun in 311, but in representations of the sungod on Constantine's coinage as late as 325, and in the statue of Constantine at Constantinople with the sungod's insignia mentioned above. Nothing justifies us in supposing that for a decade or more after the Milvian Bridge Constantine thought of Christian faith as necessarily involving total rejection of all the higher forms of pagan religious philosophy or even practice. He could have found much that would be congenial in the mildly theosophical tracts containing revelations of Hermes Trismegistus.[41] We know for a fact that he held the Sibylline oracles in high regard.[42]

Moreover his attitude before and at the council of Nicaea is profoundly unsympathetic to the exclusive rigidities of any one party within the church. The Nicene creed itself derived much of its success from its ambiguity or (if you prefer the kinder word) comprehensiveness. The creed was supported by the emperor because he saw that it could be somehow accepted by almost everybody and excluded almost nobody. Eusebius of Caesarea's letter to his church explaining how after much midnight oil he had reconciled his signature with his conscience shows that the signatories embraced 'a wide spectrum of theological opinion'. No doubt the creed had not been intended by its drafting committee to contain ambiguities. The happy accident

---

[41] This suggestion was made by H. Kraft, *Konstantins religiöse Entwicklung* (Tübingen 1955). See also H. A. Drake, *In Praise of Constantine: A Historical Study and new translation of Eusebius' Tricennial Orations*, University of California Publications, Classical Studies 15 (1976) pp 46–79.

[42] See Constantine's letter to Arius in Athanasius, *de Decretis* 40, 19 (ed Opitz) and *Oratio ad sanctos* 18 and 21.

11

HENRY CHADWICK

that it did contain some enabled Constantine to send round the magister (officiorum?) Philumenos with the biblion at the end of the council and to obtain the signatures of 218 out of 220 present. The two Libyan bishops who refused to sign objected less to the creed than to the sixth canon subjecting Libya to Alexandrian jurisdiction.[43] His policy of union by comprehension in the church is consistent with a desire not to draw hard and fast lines in his relation to pagan beliefs.

What then of Constantine's wish to keep doors open? The 'Edict of Milan' agreed with Licinius in 313 grants to Christians and to all men free choice of worship 'that all the divine powers may be propitious'.[44] The words closely echo those of Galerius' edict of toleration of 311.[45] Traditional Roman policy was to allow all cults, unless seditious or immoral, as to the advantage of Roman power. Each local tribe worships its own god, but the Romans have been rewarded with rule over the entire world because they worship all gods.[46]

But when Constantine comes to write his Letter to the Provincials[47] his position is altogether sharper: Christianity is true, idolatry false; yet paganism is to enjoy full toleration because true religion cannot be compelled. The pagan neoplatonist Sopater, friend of Iamblichus, was still influential at court.[48] But we need not regard Constantine's toleration as externally imposed upon him by his sense of political realities while being out of line with his real inner convictions.[49] It is not necessary to have weak beliefs to be tolerant of religious diversity. Toleration does not logically require the epistemological scepticism of Porphyry, Symmachus, or Themistius.

[43] H. Chadwick, 'Faith and Order at the Council of Nicaea', HTR 53 (1960) pp 171–95. To the evidence there adduced on the Alexandrian struggle to control Libya I should have added Basil, ep 61, on Athanasius' excommunication of a civil governor of Libya; and on the final victory there is explicit seventh-century evidence in Sophronius, PG 87 (1865) col 3548.
[44] Eusebius HE x, 5, 4; Lactantius, MP 48, 2.
[45] Eusebius HE viii, 17.
[46] Minucius Felix 6; Augustine de Consensu Evang I, 12, 18–19.
[47] Eusebius VC ii, 48–60.
[48] Eunapius, VS 5, 1, 5, p 458; 6, 2, 1 p 462; compare pseudo-Julian, epp 184–5 Bidez; Zosimus ii, 40, 3.
[49] This is implied by A. Alföldi in JRS 37 (1947) p 14. When Eusebius (VC iv, 62) reports Constantine as saying in his last sickness that his deferment of baptism has been motivated by a desire to be baptised in Jordan but there is now to be no 'hesitation' (amphibolia), I take the hesitation to be exclusively his fear of post-baptismal sin, not a hesitation about the faith. Compare Greg Naz or 40, 26 on the desire to be baptised in Jerusalem as an excuse for postponement of baptism. On liberty of conscience in the fourth century compare my article 'Gewissen' in RAC (1978).

Conversion in Constantine the Great

In his youthful *Soliloquies* (i, 13, 23) Augustine said that wisdom is not approached by only one way; each man according to his capacity grasps the one God, just as eyesights may differ in power to see a bright light. In the *Retractations* (i, 4, 3) he criticises this sentence as implying that 'there may be a way other than Christ'. The doctrine of the incarnation does not easily lend itself either to the vindication of coercion or to the sceptical relativism of Porphyry and his pagan successors. In another passage of his *Retractations* (i, 14, 2) Augustine asks in what sense a believer in Christ has attained truth in this life when we see only puzzling reflections in a mirror (1 Cor. 13, 12). He comments that the truths we can see apart from faith do not bring *beata vita*. In short, it is possible to believe in the incarnation, that is that God has so involved himself in love to his own creation that he has made his own a particular human life in Jesus Christ, without at the same time thinking it right or morally fitting to compel men to associate themselves with the community of believers. Paradoxical as it may seem, Constantine may have understood that better than the late, illiberal Augustine.

Christ Church
Oxford

HERLUIN, ABBOT OF BEC
AND HIS BIOGRAPHER

by CHRISTOPHER HARPER-BILL

THE *Vita Herluini*, composed by Gilbert Crispin, abbot of Westminster, has long been recognised as the most important source for the foundation and early history of one of the greatest of the Norman religious houses. It formed the basis of Porée's account several years before it was first edited in its entirety by Armitage Robinson.[1] The significance of the text is more than local or hagiographical, for it covers a crucial period in Norman ecclesiastical development. When Herluin first determined to adopt the monastic habit, the reconstruction of religious life in the duchy was far from complete. When Gilbert wrote the *Vita*, some time after the elevation of Anselm to the see of Canterbury, Norman prelates, many of them sons of Bec, were urgently engaged in the reformation of the church in William the Conqueror's new kingdom. Gilbert Crispin's interpretation of the religious vocation was very different from that of the founder. He wrote as a man experienced in ecclesiastical government and as a theologian of moderate distinction;[2] he had grown to maturity in the cloister and had experienced no crisis of conversion. His outlook was certainly coloured by his own experience and preoccupations. The *Vita* is the interpretation by a man raised in a flourishing and learned community of the motivation of an uneducated knight who had experienced spiritual rebirth in a world where religious values were far less certain. The form and emphases of the *Life* are perhaps worth some consideration.

The authenticity of the picture presented by the *Vita* is guaranteed by the intimate connection of the Crispin family with the political vicissitudes of the duchy and with the development of the abbey of Bec from the time of Gilbert's grandfather, who like Herluin had been a subtenant of Gilbert of Brionne. The account of Herluin's secular career provides a valuable insight into early eleventh-century Norman

[1] A. A. Porée, *Histoire de l'Abbaye du Bec* (Evreux 1901); the *Vita* is printed by [J.] Armitage Robinson, [*Gilbert Crispin, Abbot of Westminster*] (Cambridge 1911) pp 87–110. I am indebted to professor R. Allen Brown for many discussions of this topic.
[2] Armitage Robinson, caps 4–5; R. W. Southern, 'St Anselm and Gilbert Crispin, abbot of Westminster', *Medieval and Renaissance Studies* 3 (London 1954) pp 78–115.

society from the point of the subtenant. He had grown up as a *tiro*, an apprentice knight, in the household of count Gilbert. The text makes it clear that he held lands of the count, which were confiscated after Herluin's refusal to act as his emissary to the duke in a cause which he felt to be unjust. He must, however, have possessed other lands, probably allodial estates; his first withdrawal from the count's service must have involved the reunciation of any fief held of him, yet Herluin was still able to command the service of twenty knights who, according to Gilbert Crispin, were hand-picked from among his own men. Yet if Herluin had a measure of independence, he still continued as a mature man to frequent the count's household and to render him the service of arms and counsel.[3]

Gilbert Crispin constantly emphasises the nobility of Herluin. His hero was proficient at all the accomplishments befitting elevated birth, including warfare, although the biographer was constantly at pains to stress that this military activity was conducted with honour and was in accordance with the will of God; he was held up as an example of fidelity to his lord, which was mitigated only by his overriding concern for the principles of justice. He was a model of Christian lordship, more concerned for the fate of his impoverished dependants than for his own; 'he averted his mind from anything dishonourable and spent all his energy on those honourable activities practised by the great men at court.' Herluin was, in short, the ideal secular *miles Christi*. His life as a knight, however, was recorded 'not so much as an example of the pursuit of military glory as of the keeping of faith,'[4] and such a secular life was far from the ideal. Gilbert went on to elaborate the conventional story of the *vir Dei*, the stereotype which had originated with Athanasius's *Life of St Antony*.[5] Herluin is cast in the same mould as so many early medieval saints who abandoned an honoured position in society to adopt a regular life, and after their conversion advanced to a position of spiritual authority, culminating in an edifying death. Herluin experienced, according to Gilbert's account, a spiritual crisis, and for a long period struggled to reconcile his secular existence with the practice of true Christianity; he was as an Israelite preparing for the flight from Egypt.[6] He abandoned the luxurious life of the court for a regime of private austerity, and yet continued to serve the count,

[3] *Vita* pp 87–90.
[4] *Ibid* p 88.
[5] See D. Baker, '*Vir Dei*: Secular Sanctity in the Early Tenth Century', *SCH*, 8, pp 41–53.
[6] *Vita* p 89.

16

performing his missions mounted on an ass rather than on a warhorse, an object of ridicule to his companions-in-arms. Eventually came the final crisis which led to the realisation that such dual standards could not be maintained. 'As soon as the cause of his heavenly lord demanded it, he broke forthwith the bond by which he was bound to the service of his earthly lord.'[7] He opted for the religious life 'in a land where it was considered a marvel for a knight of unimpaired ability to lay down his arms and become a monk.'[8] The reason for his long delay was apparently the desire to devote not merely himself, but his possessions, to the service of God, and he sought the release of his fief by the count. The age was still far distant when the noble convert was prepared naked to follow the naked Christ.

The life thus far is perhaps less than entirely credible. It was written by a man who as an oblate had known the venerable abbot and who was soaked in the tradition of Bec, and one should not discount out of hand the opinion of Orderic Vitalis, who held the abbey and monks of Bec in the highest esteem, but who believed that Herluin had made his profession as the result of a vow made to the Virgin when in danger of his life during a skirmish.[9] Orderic did not believe that such an entry to the religious life was in the least shameful or reprehensible, so long as the vows were conscientiously fulfilled, and he gave an honourable mention to many monks of St Evroul who had spent most of their lives in the pursuit of arms. Gilbert was anxious, however, to emphasise the rejection by Herluin of the cynical convert to religion. Rodolf Pinellus, who replied to the abbot's criticism of his life by saying that when he had had his fill of wordly gratification and was tired of fighting he would become a monk, was struck down the same night, carried off by demons and denied any chance of redemption.[10]

Gilbert gives no explanation of Herluin's conversion other than religious enthusiasm. He was illiterate, and so had not earlier in his life had to face the decision which confronted Ralph 'ill-tonsured', son of Giroie, and Robert de Grandmesnil, both men of high intellectual accomplishments from their youth who first chose a military career and subsequently entered the cloister.[11] There is no reference to any

[7] *Ibid* p 90.
[8] *Ibid* p. 87.
[9] [*The Ecclesiastical History of*] O[*rderic*] V[*italis*], ed M. Chibnall (Oxford 1969–) 2 p 12.
[10] *Vita* pp 94–5.
[11] *OV*, 2, pp 40, 74.

contact with monks before his conversion, such as that experienced by
those knights of Maule who discussed speculative matters with the
religious, and many of whom adopted the monastic habit on their
deathbed,[12] or to any strong influence like that of Gerold of Avranches,
chaplain to Hugh of Chester and subsequently abbot of Tewkesbury,
who prompted a group of knights to become monks of St Evroul.[13]
There is no mention of a physical disease or wound which might have
hastened his decision, as did the blinding and castration of William
Giroie, the genital disease of Robert Goel or the festering wound of
Richard of Heudicourt.[14] We do not even know if Herluin was
married and like Ansold of Maule needed to seek the permission of his
wife to adopt the religious habit.[15]

Once he had determined to abandon the secular life, Herluin
withdrew to a hermitage which he constructed with his own hands,
and spent much of his time acquiring the elements of literacy. The
'new esquire of Christ' diligently trained in religious exercises as he
had hitherto trained in arms. Herluin's lack of education may explain
a strange incident in Gilbert's account. He states that Herluin toured
the duchy in search of an established community which he might
enter, and found all the houses which he visited to be sadly lacking in
grace; from one of them he was physcially ejected by an arrogant
monk.[16] While Gilbert Crispin may not have appreciated the merits
of the Norman episcopate, who despite their many achievements were
typical products of the unreformed church, he must have been aware
of the spectacular success of William of Volpiano, who had by 1034
inaugurated the revival of monastic life in Normandy, and whose
successor John of Fécamp was a model of abbatial spirituality. Less
than twenty miles from Bec lies Bernay, founded under the auspices
of St William, the architectural precocity of which testifies to a
flourishing spiritual life in the 1030s;[17] not much further distant is
Jumièges, to which the Grandmesnils subsequently turned for the
first abbot of their own foundation; Thierry's subsequent career is
testimony to the excellent spiritual and intellectual training provided
there in the same period. It is possible that Herluin, still barely literate,

[12] Ibid 3, p 206.
[13] Ibid p 226.
[14] Ibid 2, p 14; 3, p 208; 2, p 132.
[15] Ibid 3, p 196.
[16] Vita pp 91-2.
[17] A. W. Clapham, English Romanesque Architecture after the Conquest (Oxford 1934) pp 4-5.

was not considered a suitable candidate for the religious life in houses modelled on the Cluniac pattern. If so Gilbert, determined to emphasise the spiritual merits of the founder of a learned community, had to disguise the fact. He applied dual standards; the disturbances in the cloister which Herluin witnessed elsewhere were presented as an indication of declining standards, whereas the furore at Bec which marked the consecration of the third church in 1077, when the doors were broken down by an enthusiastic throng, was regarded as a symptom of exuberant piety.

Gilbert's main concern was the development of the community at Bec as he had known it in its heyday. The *Vita* belongs to what Southern has called 'the commemorative pattern', a type which originated in the various lives of the abbots of Cluny. This form of hagiography 'avowedly subordinates the display of supernatural powers to the display of activity directed towards a practical end.'[18] Gilbert's life of Herluin was a memorial to the community as much as to the founder, a *liber memorialis* from which those who followed could learn of the ethos of Bec in the earliest days. The 'miracles' of Herluin were really nothing of the sort, as Gilbert, despite his *apologia*, undoubtedly realised, and this surely accounts for the fact that Herluin, although venerated as blessed, was never canonised.[19] In the place of marvels, Gilbert gave an account of the regime of the monastery. Written by one who as a young man must have talked to some of the earliest monks, this is invaluable. Yet some caution is advisable; he was attempting to portray the ideal abbot, and the passages in which he recounts Herluin's attempts to restrain murmuring among his monks and his endeavours to adapt his governance to the individual characteristics of each of his brethren are pure echoes of the *Rule* of St Benedict, and are paralleled by Orderic's description of the administration of abbot Thierry.[20] Perhaps the most significant passages for Gilbert were those in which he described the growth of the material prosperity of the abbey and the extension of its influence through the merits of its sons.

The advent of Lanfranc was crucial to the material and scholarly development of the abbey, and one of the most notable features of the *Vita* is the attention devoted to the future archbishop of Canterbury.

[18] R. W. Southern, *St Anselm and his Biographer* (Cambridge 1963) p 323.
[19] E. W. Kemp, *Canonisation and Authority in the Western Church* (Oxford 1948) p 105.
[20] *Vita* pp 93, 104; *OV* 2, p 20; *The Rule of St Benedict*, ed J. McCann (London 1952) cap 2.

There can be few works of hagiography in which the subject has to share the stage to such an extent with one of his contemporaries. Unlike his kinsman of the next generation, Milo Crispin, Gilbert did not set out to write a eulogy of Lanfranc,[21] and his account of his years at Bec is the more reliable because he omits the legendary material which was included by Milo. Occasionally there is disagreement between the sources—Milo, for example, stated that monastic discipline had broken down at Bec when Lanfranc arrived, and that it was due to his efforts that it was restored, while Gilbert merely implies that Herluin was overburdened and needed assistance. Nevertheless, the *Vita Herluini* ascribes a crucial role in the development of Bec to Lanfranc.

Every religious institution undergoes changes in its aims and institutions, but at Bec this process, which normally extends over a century, was conflated and took place within the lifetime of the founder and first abbot. Leclercq has emphasised the fact that every religious order has a second founder—Bernard for the Cistercians, Bonaventura for the Franciscans—who effects a radical change in the aims and ethos established by the original founder.[22] Normally the founder is in his grave long before this change occurs, but at Bec Lanfranc exercised this radical function during Herluin's lifetime, without apparent conflict. Herluin had been unable to find satisfaction within the monastic pattern of the duchy, which was strongly influenced by Cluny, and had retired to pursue the life of a hermit, until the influx of companions had made it imperative for the ecclesiastical authorities to establish a conventional form of monastic government. The community survived, but achieved no great distinction until the arrival of Lanfranc, who was the catalyst which transformed Bec into a learned body integrated into Norman society, favoured by the duke and constantly expanding due to its spiritual and intellectual excellence.

This transformation is worthy of note. Bec in its origins was quite distinct from other Norman houses, which were endowed by the ducal or one of the great aristocratic families and conformed to the pattern established by William of Volpiano. The main preoccupation was the liturgy, which in houses modelled on Cluny developed into a continuous round, relieved by work in the *scriptorium*. It was harsh

[21] *Vita Lanfranci, auct. Milo Crispin, PL* 150 (1880) cols 19–98.
[22] J. Leclercq, 'A Sociological Approach to the History of a Religious Order', in *The Cistercian Spirit: A Symposium*, ed M. B. Pennington (Shannon 1970) pp 134–43.

economic necessity which led Herluin and his companions to labour in the fields and to construct their own buildings, and these activities represent a break with the aristocratic features of contemporary monasticism. It is noteworthy that Gilbert, despite the changes wrought at Bec by Lanfranc, does not denigrate this interpretation of the *Rule*. He presents Herluin as the ideal of the active life and Lanfranc as the ideal of the contemplative life.[23] Yet unlike the Cistercians of the early twelfth century, Gilbert clearly distinguished between the two modes of life and did not regard them as interchangeable. There is certainly no evidence that Lanfranc engaged in manual work, and this is in marked contrast to the view of St Bernard, who envisaged that the ideal monk would be at the same time a scholar and a toiler in the fields.[24] There is a clear indication that at Bec the original lay spirituality of the founder became clericalised, a change which is emphasised by a comparison of Gilbert's account of the early years with Lanfranc's constitutions for Christ Church Canterbury, which represent a return to the aristocratic tradition of Benedictine monasticism.[25]

Gilbert, who had known Lanfranc in the later years of his priorate at Bec and had followed him to Canterbury, without doubt approved of the changes which he had brought about; a scholar himself, he owed his intellectual training to the school of Bec, where he had sat at the feet of two great masters. As the head of a great Anglo-Norman religious corporation, however, he could appreciate too the administrative gifts of Herluin. 'The abbot was expert in resolving controversies arising in worldly matters, and skilled in all things concerning the external relations of the monastery; in the work of construction and the procurement of the necessary materials he could not, within the limits of his religious calling, have been more far-sighted and efficient . . . Expert in the laws of the duchy, he acted as a safeguard to his monks against wicked predators.'[26] In the early years, at the head of an impoverished community, he had managed by constant vigilance to ensure the survival of his foundation; the arrival of Lanfranc and the foundation of a monastic school which attracted widespread patronage and spread abroad the fame of the house

---

[23] *Vita* p 96.
[24] See C. J. Holdsworth, 'The Blessings of Work: the Cistercian View', *SCH* 10, pp 59–76.
[25] *The Monastic Constitutions of Lanfranc,* ed M. D. Knowles (London 1951) especially p 82, n 1.
[26] *Vita* p 96.

provided the resources which completed the transformation of Herluin from a hermit fleeing from the world into a Benedictine abbot of the traditional style, superintending widespread landed estates. Gilbert himself was enthusastic about this transformation. 'In its early years the monastery did not possess enough ground for its essential buildings, now within a few years its demesne extended for miles. What shall I say of the crops, pools, thickets, farmlands and vineyards which were accumulated for the use of God's servants? There was no abbey more amply endowed with everything necessary to sustain the life of man.'[27]

The ease of this transformation, and the lack of apparent conflict between Herluin and his prior, is all the more notable in view of the obvious tension at St Evroul. There prior Robert, brother of Hugh de Grandmesnil, opposed abbot Thierry in every way; 'he preferred to lead rather than to follow, and to command rather than to obey . . . he often secretly criticised the holy abbot, his father, because he was more concerned with spiritual than secular affairs. At times he openly attacked him and disparaged some of his decisions which were a little unwordly.'[28] Orderic was uneasy in his treatment of this obvious conflict; he criticised Robert as prior, and indulged in a eulogy of his qualities after he became abbot.[29] Gilbert had no such problems; the only competition between Herluin and Lanfranc was in piety and humility. The fusion of their talents gave Bec its unique character.

The logical climax of the *Vita* was the consecration of the third abbey church, which was closely followed by the death of Herluin. Gilbert indeed describes with enthusiasm the great concourse of prelates and nobles who were lavishly entertained by a community which thirty years before had been struggling for survival, and he dwells upon the edifying death of the founder. Yet even here it is Lanfranc who occupies the centre of the stage.[30] It was he who years before had persuaded Herluin to move the site of the house. He now obtained from the king-duke permission to consecrate the church and returned from England to perform the ceremony. Herluin was prepared to face death only after he had seen his spiritual son. 'Lord, now lettest thou they servant depart in peace, for mine eyes have seen.' For Gilbert, one may feel, it was Lanfranc who symbolised the spirit of Bec.

---

[27] *Ibid* p 98.
[28] *OV* 2, pp 64–6.
[29] *Ibid* p 74.
[30] *Vita* pp 105–8.

Herluin, Abbot of Bec and his Biographer

After his arrival at Bec, Lanfranc became central to Gilbert's account; after his departure, which was soon followed by the conquest of England, the scope of the *Vita* widened. It ceased to be an internal history of the abbey and became a brief commentary on the ecclesiastical life of the Anglo-Norman realm. The *Life* of Herluin gave way to a glorification of the impact of the Norman church, and particularly of Bec, upon England, where Gilbert himself had spent his most productive years. The recovery of the church of Canterbury under Lanfranc was treated with as much enthusiasm as the growth in the material prosperity of Bec itself. 'He enriched the see with extensive landed endowments and with gold and silver, and fulfilling the command in Exodus "Honour thy father and thy mother, that thy days may be long upon the land" he showed himself generous in all things to his spiritual father and mother, the church.'[31] The role of the archbishop as primate of the British Isles and apostle of the island race was emphasised. The treatment of Lanfranc as archbishop is in fact a literary expression of his own claims within the British church.

Gilbert's own view of the significance of the role of Bec is epitomised by the vision which he ascribes to Herluin on the eve of Lanfranc's departure to become abbot of St Etienne, Caen.[32] He dreamed that he had in his orchard a particularly fine and fruitful apple tree, which the king demanded to have transplanted in his own garden; he unwillingly acquiesced in his lord's demand, but all the roots could not be pulled up, and from what remained new shoots sprang forth and developed into luxuriant trees, so that both king and abbot were delighted with the fine crop which they harvested. Gilbert explained the significance of the dream; the orchard was the church of Bec, whose greatest tree, Lanfranc, by his example and teaching bore fruit in all the churches of Normandy. When the Conqueror was intent on implanting the ordinances of holy religion among the English, Lanfranc went unwillingly and Herluin was loath to command him to go; but the fruit borne by the transplanted tree resulted in the continual improvement of the state of religious observance in England. The monastic order, which had deteriorated to the level of a lay institution, had been completely reformed; the clergy had been compelled to live under a canonical rule, and the people, forbidden the vanities of their barbarian observances, had been instructed in the correct norm of life and belief. Yet in the abbot's own orchard of Bec the shoots flourished; many men

[31] *Ibid* pp 99–100.
[32] *Ibid* p 100.

trained under Lanfranc reached the heights of spirituality, intellectual distinction and ecclesiastical authority. Gilbert specifically mentioned Anselm, William abbot of Cormeille, Henry abbot of Battle, and Arnost and Gundulf, bishops of Rochester.[33]

Gilbert's estimate of the influence of Bec would be echoed by modern historians. If Herluin's foundation became the most prominent house of the duchy, this was the result not of direct colonisation, but of the recruitment of her sons to preside over many Norman and English houses, and even more of the excellence of the monastic school, which inculcated in many men destined for high office what has been termed 'a doctrine of the monastic life' in which the positive virtue of charity replaced penitential mortification for the sins of the world as the prime purpose of the life of a monk.[34] Early monastic life at Bec had been introspective; the founder and his companions had made a virtue out of their poverty and had attempted, consciously or not, to recreate the balanced self-sufficiency of early monasticism. 'Those whom he received to rule, he ruled strictly in the manner of the early fathers . . . none wasted his bread in idleness.'[35] There is no hint of the missionary zeal which characterised the career of William of Volpiano. Herluin had renounced a world in which he had achieved social and military success, but in which 'there was scarcely any guidance or signpost on the right road . . . priests and bishops were openly living in a married state and carried arms as if they were laymen; people still lived according to the ways of the Danes of old.'[36]

By the time of the founder's death an ecclesiastical revival had transformed the religious life of the duchy and Bec had been instrumental in the transplantation of these new standards to the conquered kingdom. There can be little doubt that the impact of Bec upon England was of prime importance to Gilbert Crispin, and was one of the reasons for the composition of the life. The *Vita* is a story of triumph. The material and spiritual success of the monastery was symbolised by the consecration of the third abbey church, but even more significant was the journey made by Herluin to England, which occupies a disproportionate amount of the text.[37] There the abbot saw

[33] *Ibid* p 103.
[34] J. Leclercq, 'Une doctrine de la vie monastique dans l'école de Bec', *Spicilegium Beccense: Congrès International de IXme Centenaire de l'arrivée d'Anselme au Bec* (Paris 1959) pp 477–88.
[35] *Vita* p 93.
[36] *Ibid* p 89.
[37] *Ibid* pp 100–2.

that his dream of the transplanted tree had become reality; it had borne
abundant fruit. For Gilbert, the great glory of Bec was that it had
developed from a humble hermitage into a great seminary producing
rulers for the world from which Herluin had fled. After half a century
of vigorous reform, the biographer perhaps had little sympathy for the
motives which had spurred Herluin to rejection of the world, but felt
himself compelled to recount those providential events which had
transformed the ecclesiastical life of three provinces.

Take note of the rewards which the bountiful hand of God
bestows upon his servants even in this life. He who was once held
in contempt by all because he assumed the poverty of Christ now
had to honour him the primate of the whole realm of England
and all those committed to his charge. This reward by God's
munificence Lanfranc received also, for if he humbled himself to
the man to whom he had once surrendered his freedom to enter
the service of God, he saw prostrated at his feet magnates and
indeed the whole kingdom, dependant upon him according to the
strictures of ecclesiastical law.[38]

St Mary's College
Strawberry Hill

[38] *Ibid* p 102.

A CHANGE OF MIND IN
SOME SCHOLARS OF THE ELEVENTH
AND EARLY TWELFTH CENTURIES

by GILLIAN R. EVANS

UIBERT of Nogent gives a number of examples of a change
for the better (*bonae mutationis exempla*)[1] in the lives of his
contemporaries. He evidently considered conversion to be a
subject of strong topical appeal to his readers, as well as a matter of
importance in itself, and he gives as many examples as he can. He has a
double sense of the word *conversio* in mind. He often refers to the
decision to enter a monastery which was the common meaning of the
term in his day, but he also understands by it something closer to the
larger sense of 'conversion'. Evrard of Breteuil, he says, turned from his
pride to examine the wretched state of his soul, and began to look
about him for a way of life in which he might live more worthily.[2]
He followed the example of Theobald of Champagne, who came to
dislike the profession of arms: *inter ipsa rudimenta militiae arma
despiciens,*[3] and made himself self-supporting as a charcoal-burner.
One Simon, count of Valois, 'enriched the religious life of our day by
the outstanding example of an unexpected conversion': *mirabili nostri
temporis religionem inopinae mutationis claritate ditavit.*[4] Such a conversion was often—as Guibert relates it—sudden and irreversible in
the change of direction it brought about. For St Bruno, his
conversionis initia was something to which he, and others, could later
look back with certainty as the moment when he began to live a
different kind of life.[5]

Guibert's intention in describing these individual conversions is
two-fold. He suggests that, as a direct result of the example such men
set, others were encouraged to join them in pure and energetic living
of the monastic life. These conversions led to others until the whole

---

[1] Guibert of Nogent, *De Vita Sua,* ed G. Bourgin (Paris 1907) p 22.
[2] *Ibid* p 25.
[3] *Ibid.*
[4] *Ibid* p 28.
[5] *Ibid* p 30.

complexion of the religious life of the times was changed. They gave rise, in other words, to a revival. And secondly, as he shows in the case of his mother's conversion and his own, he recognised the experience of conversion as something which works inwardly upon the soul.

Guibert's main purpose in these chapters is to show how a converted man sets an example. That example is likely to be more telling if his conversion can be seen to have brought about dramatic changes in his way of life. All the examples he gives are of noblemen who have stood out in the past because of their personal excellence or their military efficiency—or else their savage pride. They are men in the public eye, and when they cease to behave as they once did, the change is noticed. When they commit their lives to voluntary poverty they bring a freshness and energy to the reform of the lukewarm practices of the monasteries of the day which again provides a necessary contrast. It would scarcely serve Guibert's purposes to describe the conversion of an insignificant man who had not previously been noticeably irreligious, who decided to follow a vocation to the religious life in a spiritually sound and thriving house, simply because there would be nothing startling in the change, or in the effect it has had. He intends his words to act upon the consciences of his readers rather as the lives of these men have done on those who have actually seen their example at work. These conversions are described in terms which are intended to increase still further their fruitfulness in the world at large.

Consequently we hear little from Guibert of subsequent adjustments and nothing of the taking of hands from the plough. He does not go at any length into the long-term working out of the inner process of conversion—except in the case of his mother and himself. He does not ask how lasting it has been in Evrard's case or that of Bruno, though he himself, as he frequently acknowledges, has turned away from God and been brought back to him again and again. He recognises that his own adolescent piety was short-lived, and that it was not for long that he preferred to go to services rather than to be on time for meals.[6] It serves his purposes as a writer of edifying history to show the enduring results of sudden and irreversible changes of direction in individuals upon the attitudes of society.

It is never satisfactory to judge an experience of conversion without reference to the circumstances in which it took place. Nock's classic work on conversion is concerned with the special problems which

[6] *Ibid* p 18.

arise when we ask what the Christians of the first centuries recognised as 'conversion'.[7] A rather different set of criteria presents itself if we attempt to identify experiences of conversion in more modern times. In each case, a meeting of different background conditions and some spiritual experience which is arguably common to the converted in any age, has produced a view of conversion which is, in some respects, peculiar to its period. Several men of the eleventh and early twelfth centuries recognise explicitly that they have themselves undergone not only a change of heart, but also a change of mind. Because they are articulate, they, unlike the majority of their contemporaries, have something to say about the event from within. They place an emphasis on the intellectual aspects of the change conversion has brought about in them which stamps their experience with the mark of its time.

In Guibert's day it was acceptable to be a Christian in every sphere of society. We are not dealing here with the conversion of intelligent men who may have to face some ridicule from their friends if they declare themselves Christians, as Augustine's contemporaries did, and as is frequently the case today. But a creed which enjoys full intellectual respectability may nevertheless be more or less apathetically believed by many; it is a noticeable feature of the sermons of St Bernard and Alan of Lille that they seek to stir up feeling and awaken a more lively quality of faith in their listeners. We are concerned for the most part, not with conversion from unbelief, but with conversion from half-hearted belief to full commitment. That is as true for scholars as for unlettered men.

There is another kind of conversion about which much is said by twelfth-century writers, and that is conversion from mistaken belief. The twelfth century was an age of polemical theology. Dialogues between Christians and jews, Christians and philosophers, Christians and pagans, were written in some numbers soon after the turn of the century. Some of these are clearly artificial exercises. Others may represent the polished versions of real conversations, particularly those with the jews.[8] Later, Alan of Lille wrote a four-part defence of the

---

[7] [A. D.] Nock, [*Conversion*] (Oxford 1933).

[8] Gilbert Crispin's *Disputatio* between a Christian and a jew is a case in point. See the edition of B. Blumenkranz (Antwerp 1956), and compare Gilbert Crispin, *Disputatio Christiani cum Gentile de Fide Christi*, ed C. C. J. Webb, *Mediaeval and Renaissance Studies* 3 (London 1954) pp 55–78, and Peter Abelard, *Dialogus inter Philosophum, Judaeum et Christianum*, ed R. Thomas (Stuttgart 1966).

faith against cathars, Waldensians, jews and muslims.[9] But even within the faith itself there were firmly-held differences of opinion, some of them of long standing. Anselm wrote his *De Processione Spiritus Sancti* to refute the Greeks' view of the procession of the Holy Spirit, and his *Letters on the Sacraments* to explain some differences of usage in the celebration of the eucharist.[10] Peter Abelard was accused of heresy by his fellow Latin Christians. Whether we look for conversions from one faith to another, from one sect to another or from mistaken belief within a single sect to what is accepted there as the correct view, we find evidence of energetic missionary activity on every side among academic theologians. A sense of a responsibility for converting those in error is frequently obvious.

This is worth mentioning if only because its importance in twelfth-century thinking about conversion draws attention to the question of the intellectual content of the conversion experience. William James once listed the features of conversion as 'a passion of willingness and acquiescence, which removes the feeling of anxiety, a sense of perceiving truths not known before, a sense of clean and beautiful newness within and without and an ecstasy of happiness.'[11] All this has to do with emotional and spiritual changes, except for the 'sense of perceiving truths not known before', where some element of intellectual assent enters in. Thinkers of the eleventh and early twelfth centuries are rarely forgetful of the existence of a relation between intellectual conviction and emotional assent, but they also set a high value upon the exercise of the intellect itself. Even learned men are not converted only in their rational minds, but they are likely to require that their reasons are satisfied.

It is not often that writers of the day consider the possibility of any of their readers having a serious intellectual difficulty in believing in God. (Conversion involves of course far more than that, but there can be no conversion which does not rest upon that belief). In the commentaries upon and references to Romans I: 19–20 which discuss that evidence for the existence of God which is present even to pagans in the very structure of the created world, the emphasis is rarely placed upon the proof of God's existence in itself. It is far more usual for the

[9] *PL* 210 (1855) cols 305–430, see, too, [M. T.] d'Alverny, [*Textes inédits d'Alain de Lille*] (Paris 1965) pp 156–62.
[10] *Anselmi Opera* [*Omnia*, ed F. S. Schmitt], 6 vols (Edinburgh/Rome 1938–68) 2, p 178, line 3, p 224, line 12.
[11] Nock, pp 7–8, see W. James, *The Varieties of Religious Experience* (London 1907) pp 189, 209.

commentator to beg the question of God's existence and to ask what may be deduced about God from his creation, and what can be known only by revelation. Peter Abelard, for example, says that 'the mystery of the Incarnation could not be grasped by human reason from the visible works of God, as his power, wisdom and kindness may be clearly seen'.[12] This preoccupation with what God is like rather than with whether he exists at all reflects a general assurance about fundamentals. Even now Anselm's ontological argument for the existence of God in the *Proslogion* works best and with a more immediate force for believers, and it is doubtful whether he seriously expected it to have to stand up to the test of a radical atheist's questioning, even though he says that it is intended to provide an independent demonstration that God exists.[13] Aquinas, too, even though he says that the existence of God is not immediately self-evident to everyone, nevertheless appears to see the task of demonstrating the existence of God as little more than an academic exercise; he does not envisage it as one where a man's deepest certainties are being put at risk.[14]

These writers who take so confident a view that the question of the existence of God is proven, commonly give time and thought to the relation between the intellectual and the emotional or spiritual components of assent, as though that were a far more vexed question. There is nothing new in this: Haimo of Auxerre, a contemporary of John Scotus Erigena, says in his commentary on Titus. I, i, that there are two modes of recognition of the truth, that in which religious faith plays a part (*secundum pietatem*) and that in which the assent is purely intellectual (*carens pietate*).[15] Twelfth-century writers have, however, something of a special interest in the problem. There is a recognised element of what Thierry of Chartres calls: *intentionis veritas*,[16] an act of will in assenting to the truth which the intellect perceives. Simon of Tournai cites a frequently-mentioned definition of Augustine's in his *Commentary on the Creed: Credere nihil est aliud quam assensione cogitare*,[17] 'To believe is nothing else than to think with assent'. The

[12] Peter Abelard, *Commentaria in Epistolam Pauli ad Romanos*, ed M. Buytaert (Turnholt 1969) CC, *Cont Med* 11, p 68, lines 725–8.
[13] *Anselmi Opera*, 1, p 93, lines 6–7.
[14] Thomas Aquinas, *Summa Theologica*, I, Question 2, Article 1.
[15] *PL* 117 (1881) col 811.
[16] *Commentaries on Boethius of the School of Thierry of Chartres*, ed N. M. Häring (Toronto 1971) p 517, line 89.
[17] N. M. Häring, 'Simon of Tournai's Commentary on the so-called Athanasian Creed', *Archives d'histoire doctrinale et littéraire du moyen age*, 43 (Paris 1976) pp 152–3, and see Augustine, *De Praedestinatione*, bk 2, cap 5, *PL* 44 (1865) col 963.

intellectual and emotional, or voluntary, components of the experience of certainty of faith are being set side by side for consideration.

Anselm suggests that when we have properly understood the idea of God it will be impossible for us not to believe in him: *Nullus quippe intelligens id quod deus est, potest cogitare quia deus non est.*[18] 'Noone who understands what God is, can think that God does not exist'. He places so firm an emphasis on the component of intellectual understanding here that he seems to be suggesting that it will, if it is sure enough, carry with it the wholehearted assent of any right-minded man. Elsewhere he seems to be saying, as in the famous *credo ut intelligam*, that belief must precede understanding. The interdependence of the two was clear to a good many thinkers of the generations which followed, although the emphasis upon intellectual understanding or upon emotional acceptance varies.

Anselm's discovery of the *Proslogion* argument was not in every respect a 'classic' conversion experience, but it does perhaps exemplify uniquely well the intellectually-based conversion of which the eleventh and twelfth-century scholar speaks so often. He describes, as Augustine does in his *Confessions*,[19] how he suffered from confusion of mind. Even after he had given up the search for the argument because he felt that it was becoming an obsession with him, and that it was interfering with his concentration upon the *opus dei*, he found that he could not put it out of his thoughts: *tunc magis ac magis nolenti et defendenti se coepit cum importunitate quadam ingerere.*[20] 'Then it began to enter into my mind irresistibly, more and more, although I did not want it and I resisted it.' There is something of Francis Thompson's *Hound of Heaven* about this, except that Anselm does not say he felt that God was exerting the pressure he describes, but rather that the argument itself pursued him. There is also some indication that the period of anguished searching achieved in him a receptive and prepared state of mind into which the moment of recognition suddenly fell. At an intellectual level there is all the stuff of a conversion experience here, and many of the characteristic emotional and spiritual concomitants are present, too.

The grasping of the ontological argument set the seal for Anselm on a decade or more of intensive inner searching for a sense of direction. The *Monologion*, the *Prayers and Meditations*, and perhaps some of the

[18] *Anselmi Opera*, i, p 103, lines 20-1.
[19] Augustine, *Confessions*, bk 8, cap 8.
[20] *Ibid* p 93, lines 15-16.

early letters are, in different ways, by-products of this period of internal spiritual and intellectual reorganisation. After he had written the *Proslogion* Anselm was, intellectually speaking, able to see more clearly where he was going. A period of steady productive creative effort followed in which he developed his particular abilities as a writer and as a thinker.

The results of this distinctive conversion experience were not, however, restricted to the intellect alone for Anselm himself, and he was anxious that they should not be so confined for his readers. He worked the *Proslogion* argument into a setting of devotional writing which was designed to evoke in his readers something of the same preparedness of mind which had enabled him not only to recognise the force of the argument when it came to him but also to assent to it with joyous willingness.[21] He encourages his reader to go into a quiet place, empty his mind of all his worries and of all the small matters of business which occupy it, and think about God until he is in a state of receptiveness.[22] The experience, for all its markedly intellectual character, was not merely one of new understanding, and it would be misleading to suggest that it was less fully an experience of conversion because of its unusual features.

Otloh of St Emmeram describes a very different kind of experience of intellectual discomfort in his *Liber de Tentationibus Suis*. He says that he was a clerk given to many vices who, when he had often been warned by the Lord to live a better life, at last made his profession as a monk: *Fuit quidam clericus vitiis multis modis deditus, qui cum saepius a Domino commoneretur pro emendatione sua, conversus tandem venit ad monasticam professionem.*[23] (Otloh uses the word *conversus* here in a context where it may of course convey nothing more than the decision to enter a monastery.) The decision he took would certainly seem to have given him no immediate happiness, since he says that he soon began to be troubled by doubts as to whether he had acted wrongly in taking his decision without the advice of his parents and friends. A long series of temptations beset him; many of them took a problem raised by some scriptural text as their point of entry into his mind. His difficulties were increased by the fact that he had, as he says, begun to study the bible seriously when he entered the

[21] *Anselmi Opera*, I, p 93, line 20.
[22] *Ibid* p 97, lines 4–10.
[23] *PL* 146 (1884) col 29.

monastery. [24] He has described his intellectual struggles, he tells us, so that others 'who desire to read holy scripture when they are first converted' may know that the devil is full of tricks, and that 'he attacks all those who read the bible'. The new reader must therefore trust divine Grace to help him resist the devil and come to a clear understanding:

> Hoc ideo clericus supradictus ideo scripsit, ut his qui in conversionis initio sacram Scripturam legere cupiunt, ostenderet qualiter immensam diabolicae fraudis astutiam, qua omnes eamdem Scripturam legentes impugnare solet, agnoscere et praecavere, qualiter etiam divinae inspirationis gratiam agnoscere et invocare debeant. [25]

After his struggles with temptation Otloh achieved a new confidence, which has something of the same basis in intellectual certainty as Anselm's discovery of his ontological argument, although it is a certainty of an entirely different kind and at quite another level. Otloh, too, writes an account of his findings, and sets it in context for his readers, but his purpose is to warn them of the ways in which an apparent conversion may go wrong unless both mind and soul, both understanding and will, work together in defence against the devil. Anselm's account contains no warning; it is entirely and gladly affirmative. Nevertheless, both writers, looking at the experience of a change of mind, have felt it necessary to emphasise that a change of heart must go with it.

A common image-pattern of Anselm's involves light and vision. The theme is frequently found in contemporary writings, too, and not only among monastic writers. The intellectual vision of the *Proslogion* discovery had an earlier parallel in a vision he had as a boy. Eadmer describes how Anselm dreamed that he climbed to the top of a mountain, where God held court as a great king. He talked to God, who welcomed him kindly and instructed that he be given bread to eat. [26] Neither Eadmer nor Anselm himself has anything more to say about the result of this vision than that it seems to have given Anselm a firm determination to dedicate his life to God [27] There is a loose parallel here with Otloh's initial decision to become a monk. When Otloh acted upon his *conversio* he found that it took him some time to

[24] *Ibid.*
[25] *Ibid* col 51.
[26] Eadmer, *Life of St Anselm*, ed R. W. Southern (London 1962) pp 4–5.
[27] *Ibid* p 5.

A change of mind

work his way through the intellectual difficulties it raised for him. Anselm does not seem to have had so long and bitter a struggle with temptation, although something of his own process of arduous exploration is clearly visible in the early *Prayers and Meditations*. Guibert of Nogent, too, had an early vision—perhaps not of great significance—in which a white-haired old man told him to go to his tutor who would love him.[28] He, too, suffered agonies of temptation in the early days of his monastic life at Fly, and these were at least in part battles of an intellectual kind occasioned by the attempt to make sense of his reading:

> Quaestiones . . . intelligentiae plurimam mihi acrimoniam ministrabant, et objectionum difficultates crebra conjecturarum mearum ruminatione et diversorum versatione voluminum, multiplicitatem sensuum et respondendi mihi efficaciam pariebant.[29]

'[The solving of] questions greatly added to the keenness of my understanding, and the difficulties of the objections [which were put to me] often demanded thought and the turning over of many books. But these things bore fruit in the increase of my powers of mind and in the pertinence of my replies.' The results of all this intellectual and spiritual labour, Guibert asserts, were to his good, although they cost him much effort.[30]

We should, perhaps, expect to find exactly this pattern in the lives of men of learning who underwent conversion. The first seeing or 'vision' of the need to make a commitment to God was likely enough to lead to a man's entering a monastery, especially in the eleventh century. There was, as yet, no hard choice to be made between remaining in the schools, and becoming a monk—a choice which, for Abelard and for Alan of Lille, too, perhaps, was to lead to an unsatisfactory dividing of time between the schools and periods of time spent as a religious.[31] But a man whose tastes naturally led him towards books might then find himself in a position where he had to make a major adjustment to the demands of his intellectual interests. This seems to have been the case for Otloh and Guibert and for Anselm.

[28] *De Vita Sua* p 13.
[29] *Ibid* p 60.
[30] *Ibid.*
[31] On Abelard's times as a monk, see his own *Historia Calamitatum*, ed J. Monfrin (Paris 1967) and J. Sikes, *Peter Abailard* (Cambridge 1932); on Alan's life, see d'Alverny pp 11–29.

At the same time, as each of these writers shows, a nagging sense of sin and general spiritual turmoil attends the process of intellectual adjustment. In many of his early letters Anselm can be seen helping the young monks in his charge to work their way through this period of settling-down into enjoyment of their 'converted' state. Guibert himself describes how Anselm taught him to 'manage his inner man': *qualis interiorem meum hominem agerem*,[32] on his visits to the monastery at Fly, and how he emphasised in particular the importance of applying the power of the reason to the governing of the activities of the body: *qualiter super regimine corpusculi rationis jura consulterem*.[33] The habit of mind which made it natural to look to both intellectual conviction and emotional assent in an act of belief encouraged writers to apply this two-fold process to the working out of the consequences of conversion, too.

Hermann, who wrote *A Little Book on his Conversion* from Judaism, provides a rare opportunity to see into the mind of one of those jews with whom Gilbert Crispin and others argued. In Hermann's case it seems to have been principally Rupert of Deutz who brought about the change of heart. Hermann cannot of course be considered typical of his kind, since he has now become entirely sympathetic to the views his Christian adversaries had put before him. Besides, he is anxious to make it plain that he is not a man who has been easily convinced: *non ea facilitate conversus sum, qua multos saepe infideles*.[34] 'I was not converted so easily as unbelievers often are.' On this count, too, if his words can be taken at their face value, we cannot consider him typical. But if he is speaking the truth he has something to tell us about the intellectual struggle which not only Christian scholars but also converted *infideles* underwent when they were men of learning. Like the Christian scholars whose experiences we have seen at first hand, Hermann found the completing of the process of conversion a long-drawn-out business: 'Now I will explain the process of my conversion as it happened, in order from the beginning,' he says.[35] He, too, had visions, which he later saw as presages of what was to come, as turning-points in his attitude.[36] He, too, describes conversations with others in which he tried to settle his intellectual uncertainties and objections to what he

---

[32] *De Vita Sua* p 66.
[33] *Ibid.*
[34] PL 170 (1854) cols 805–6.
[35] *Ibid* col 807.
[36] *Ibid.*

was coming to believe. He, too, found that the new insight worked slowly upon his mind until he saw its implications: *in ventrem memoriae saepius mecum ruminanda transmisi,*[37] 'I often retired within the chamber of my memory to reflect with myself.' The image Hermann uses here is that of ruminating or chewing something over in the 'stomach' of the mind. Hard thinking is involved here over a considerable period of time, because, like any educated Christian convert, Hermann has had to bring himself to accept his new faith intellectually as well as emotionally.

The argument he seems to have found most telling of all is one which would have appealed to his intellectual pride. It was put to him that the jews were like brute beasts, content with the chaff of the literal sense of scripture, while the Christian, like the rational being he is, enjoys the sweet heart of the grain: *dulcissima paleae medulla,* that is the spiritual sense.[38] The Christian with whom he talked encouraged his curiosity: *at illi curiositati meae congratulantes,*[39] and this can only mean his intellectual curiosity. It was put to him that the image of the cross which he found offensive was used by Christians principally for the benefit of simple men: *propter simplices et idiotas,* because unlike Hermann they could not read the bible for themselves, and this was the only way in which they could understand the work of the Redeemer.[40] The actual arguments which Hermann found convincing are not expounded in any detail in his account; certainly if he talked as long and hard as he says he did, he has recorded remarkably little of what was said. But thoughout his story the emphasis upon the intellectual aspects of the *agnitio veritatis* is a consistent theme. The devil fought back with arguments of his own when he saw Hermann slipping from him.[41] The whole process of conversion for Hermann seems to have operated at this level.

Hermann became a Christian and when he described his conversion we must suppose him to have adopted the conventions we have seen at work in the framing of other contemporary accounts. Perhaps his story tells us no more than that those conventions were quite widely accepted, not only in Guibert's France, but also in Germany and in Europe at large in these decades.

---

[37] *Ibid* col 808.
[38] *Ibid.*
[39] *Ibid.*
[40] *Ibid* col 811.
[41] *Ibid* cols 820–1.

In the nature of things, accounts of what it meant to be inwardly converted and to live out the implications of conversion in the late eleventh and early twelfth centuries can come only from the pens of lettered men. Their awareness of the problems of understanding and of intellectual conviction is a heightened one. There may have been unlettered men, or men such as Guibert describes as having given up the profession of arms to devote themselves to God, for whom the special flavour of the experience of conversion lay in those other aspects which James describes: the 'passion of willingness and acquiescence', the 'sense of clean and beautiful newness within and without', the 'ecstasy of happiness'. But for Otloh, Guibert and Anselm at least, these qualities of their new experience are balanced by an intellectual recognition which, for all its ultimate delightfulness, may have cost them long periods of painfully hard inner dispute and searching. It is not clear whether Hermann enjoyed a pleasure in his new faith like theirs. The 'managing of the inner man' does not consist entirely in the resolving of intellectually inspired inner doubt by any means, but that uncertainty plays a larger part in the experience of the converted in the eleventh and early twelfth centuries than Guibert's account of the lives of Evrard, Thibaut and Bruno would suggest. These and others like them set an example to society because their outward alteration was obvious to all. The example which could be held up by the possessor of such a mind as Anselm's when once he knew what it was he had to say, worked, not on society, but on individual minds—as it still does. The effects of such a conversion, like that of Augustine, have a way of enduring beyond the range of short-term social change.

University of Reading

POPULAR PIETY IN THE LODÈVOIS IN THE EARLY TWELFTH CENTURY: THE CASE OF PONS DE LÉRAS

by DEREK BAKER

IN 1854 the Congregation of Rites suppressed the feast and cult of the 'blessed' Pons de Léras. At its suppression the cult of 'Saint' Pons had been formally part of the liturgy of the diocese of Lodève for a little over a century: there are no records of any earlier popular devotions. The inclusion of Pons in the liturgy of the diocese was the work of Mgr Jean-Georges de Souillac (1732–50), the penultimate pre-revolutionary bishop of Lodève, and the composition of a liturgical office for the feast of the blessed Pons de Léras (18 September) was the work of Souillac's successor Mgr Jean-Félix-Henri de Fumel (1750–90).[1] It is difficult to see a pre-eminent piety at work in this distinguished patronage. Even the most assiduous of recent local historians of the Lodèvois, who makes it plain that he would be glad to see the cult re-instated, is quite clear that the eighteenth-century proclamation of the 'blessed' Pons was *une affaire d'État et non pas d'Église*,[2] owing nothing to papal approval, which was never sought, and confined solely to Lodève.

The spectacle of bishops and patrons seeking to enhance the prestige, reputation, and revenues of their sees and foundations by the judicious encouragment of selected cults is not, of course, uncommon. It would not, however, normally be expected of the eighteenth-century French provincial episcopate, particularly in a diocese whose patron saint, Saint Fulcran, was the most famous, and one of the best documented, of its sons and bishops, and the effective founder of its medieval fortunes.[3] Local patriotism can do curious things, and the much later

1 The most recent account of the diocese of Lodève is [*Un diocèse languedocien: Lodève Saint-Fulcran*, ed Jean] Mercadier (Millau 1975). Pons de Léras is the subject of a study by [V.] Ferras, ['Lodève et le bienheureux Pons de Léras, ermite et cistercien de l'abbaye de Sylvanès (XIIᵉ siecle)'], Mercadier pp 52–64. The bishops of the diocese are surveyed by [G.] Alzieu, ['Le diocèse de Lodève et ses évêques'], Mercadier pp 65–88. See too John McManners, 'Aristocratic vocations: the bishops of France in the eighteenth century', below pp 305–25.
2 Mercadier p 53.
3 For Fulcran and his cult see F. Hebrard, 'Il y a mille ans saint Fulcran . . .', Mercadier pp 11–51. The first *Life* of Fulcran, was written in the twelfth century by Peter de

DEREK BAKER

enhancement of the cult of the shadowy Milo of Benevento comes to mind in this context,[4] but this eighteenth-century French promotion becomes the more curious the more closely the candidate himself is considered. He was a native of the Lodèvois it is true, but his renunciation of the world took him elsewhere. Yet it was Lodève which rediscovered him six centuries later: neighbouring dioceses, the order which he ultimately joined, acknowledged him not at all.

The only approximately contemporary evidence for the life of Pons de Léras is to be found in the *Treatise on the conversion of Pons de Léras, and true account of the origins of the monastery of Sylvanès*, written by Hugh of Sylvanès, chronicler of the abbey, some twenty or thirty years after Pons death. It was printed by Baluze, Colbert's librarian, and professor of canon law in the Collège de France, in his *Miscellanea* in the early eighteenth century, and it is likely that the renewed interest in Pons at Lodève derived from this publication.[5]

The story that Hugh of Sylvanès has to tell of the origins of his abbey, and the life of its 'founder', influenced though it is by the usual Cistercian conventions and polemical attitudes, is brief and descriptive. It is not, however, devoid of interest, nor without difficulty, for though local historians have paid considerable attention to the abbey and its 'founder', particularly in the nineteenth century, their contributions have not always assisted the clarification of the problems.[6] What seems clear, however, is that Pons de Léras was a local-born brigand who preyed upon his neighbours, and upon travellers along the main road north from Montpellier and Lodève at the point, near his 'castle', where it broke out of the valley of the Lergue, and climbed through the dramatic Pas de L'Escalette on to the Causse de Larzac. The Causse itself long continued to have a grim reputation for travellers and pilgrims as the later foundation of La Couvertoirade in the twelfth

---

Milhau, who has been identified as the abbot of Mazan in the Vivarais. If this identification can be accepted then the *Life* of Fulcran is the production of the same milieu which produced the *Life* of Pons de Léras: Mazan was adopted as the mother house when the Cistercian abbey of Sylvanès was constituted from the community of hermits at Mas Théron.
[4] See M. Dunn, 'Milo of Benevento: the making of a myth', forthcoming.
[5] [E.] Baluze, [*Miscellanea: Collectio Veterum Monumentorum quae hactenus latuerunt in variis codicibus ac bibliothecis*], 7 vols (Paris 1678–1715). The life of Pons de Léras is printed, *ex veteri codice MS eiusdem monasterii* [Silvanès], in vol 3 (1680) pp 205–26. There is no editorial introduction: [Incipit] Tractatus [de conversione Pontii de Larazio, et exordii Salvaniensis monasterii vera narratio. Auctore Hugone Francigena monacho eiusdem monasterii.]
[6] See the works cited by Ferras.

40

Popular piety in the Lodèvois

century by the Templars as a fortified refuge indicates, and it is unlikely that Pons was the only brigand operating in the area at the end of the eleventh and beginning of the twelfth century. Neither the date of Pons' birth, nor of his conversion from a life of crime, are recorded. All that can be said is that he renounced the world at some point during the episcopate of Peter I of Lodève (1106?–1142), having first arranged for the entry of his wife and daughter into a nunnery, and of his son into the black monk house of Saint Saviour at Lodève. Peter I, *le Bon Pasteur*, was the first of the able quartet of twelfth century bishops, all drawn from important local families, who governed the see of Lodève and established its independence under the crown.[7] Peter I succeeded to the see after an inter-regnum marked by usurpation and deposition, and by lay intervention in the affairs of the church, and it is quite as likely that it was the vigorous restoration of strong government in the diocese as the pious pastoral example of the bishop which changed the brigand Pons' way of life. At all events Hugh of Sylvanès makes it clear that Peter I was closely involved in Pons' transformation, and the account suggests that the penitent robber's appearance before him on Palm Sunday came as no surprise to the bishop. Naked, with his companions, wearing a wooden collar like a criminal, beaten with rods, Pons presented a written statement of his crimes, and sought public forgiveness from the bishop. This at last reluctantly granted, he departed on penance to Saint-Guilhem-le-Désert where he and his companions received absolution, and then on a lengthy peregrination, perhaps also enjoined, to Compostella, Mont-Saint-Michel, Tours, Limoges, Saint Léonard–de–Noblat, and finally Rodez, where bishop Adémar received them. It was during this stay, according to Hugh of Sylvanès, that various local lords tried to persuade the pilgrims to settle on their lands, but it was, in fact, much further on that they settled, near Camarès, on the lands of Arnold du Pont, 'long-known to Pons and his companions as a benevolent and pious man'.[8] This was clearly no haphazard choice. The road from Vabres l'Abbaye, the old episcopal see in which the pilgrims had chosen to settle, to Lodève passed through Camarès on its route below the southern scarp of the inhospitable Causse de Larzac. Pons and his companions were on home ground again, and if they knew their patron they were likely to know

[7] See Alzieu pp 71–2.
[8] Cognoscebant autem eum ex multo tempore, scientes quia homo erat benevolus et laetus, et ad omne opus virtutis promptus, *Tractatus* cap 14, pp 216–17. For Camarès see A. Andrieu, *Camarès—Mille ans d'histoire locale* (Rodez 1931).

41

the locality. Mas-Théron, the retreat they chose, lay some five miles from Camarès, and less from the valley road, and was in an area of thermal springs. At this point the familiar pattern repeats itself. The hermits became a local attraction; the reputation of their life, and, it is said, of their miracles spread from the Rouergue to the Lodèvois, and many came to join them—to receive their hospitality, to witness the miracles, 'but above all to live with these men of God'.[9] Increased numbers necessitated a change of site, to the valley of Sylvanès, and brought pressure for organisation: the foundation of a regular community and the choice of a rule. Traditionally the settlement at Mas-Théron is dated to 1132 and the formal establishment of a Cistercian community at Sylvanès to 1136.[10] Pons himself, still a layman, was not the first abbot of the house, but died as a monk of the new foundation on 1 August 1140/2. His death preceded the construction of the abbey church, traditionally said to have been begun in 1157, and surviving conventual buildings, but it is reasonably clear that, unlike many Cistercian foundations, Sylvanès was secure and prosperous from its inception. After the initial transfer from Mas-Théron there was no need to change the site, and the relatively early literary activity of Hugh of Sylvanès is another indication of success and achievement. Though they post-date him this southern *Exordium* and the substantial surviving buildings are enduring testimony to the career of the repentant Pons de Léras.

Yet, as so often with these early twelfth-century initatives, it remains in doubt how far the individual example and intention was instrumental or incidental to the final achievement. At Whitby, Molesme, Cîteaux itself; with Gervase of Louth Park, Bernard of Tiron, Robert of Arbrissel, the demands and expectations of disciples, patrons and bishops acted powerfully to mould and direct the spiritual energies which they encountered. It could not be otherwise with Pons de Léras, one of the few laymen to be recorded as the successful director of a popular religious movement apparently acceptable to patrons and ecclesiastical authorities alike, and it is clear that the need for organisation and a rule, as for a change of site, was forced upon the hermits of Mas-Théron by increasing numbers, assisted in all probability by pressure from their patron. It is at this point that the deliberations and

[9] Ferras, Mercadier p 55, compare *Tractatus* caps 15–20, pp 217–21.
[10] See the references collected by Ferras, Mercadier pp 55–6: Hugh of Silvanès gives 1136—Tum primum Salvaniensis Ecclesia in abbatiam surrexit—Tractatus cap 22, p 222. On the name see Dimier 1 p 143.

decisions of the embryo community are of particular interest. According to Hugh of Sylvanès debate as to whether to adopt the Carthusian or Cistercian way of life was followed by the visit of Pons to the Grande Chartreuse, to consult the fifth prior, Guy (1110–37), the great organiser of the order, and it was on his advice that the community applied for affiliation to Cîteaux.[11] It is an edifying story, but scarcely convincing. At this date neither Carthusians nor Cistercians were well-represented in the Languedoc, though Saint Bernard's activities in support of Innocent II during the papal schism would not have passed unnoticed, but it is not difficult to see that indirect knowledge of Carthusian austerity would have made that order more appealing to the hermits of Mas-Théron than the elaboration of developed and militant Cistercianism.

It must on the face of it be more likely that Pons de Léras' visit to the prior of the Grande Chartreuse was to seek affiliation to that house, rather than the prior's advice, and Guy's refusal to accept responsibility for a community as remote as Sylvanès, and apparently headed by a reformed layman with no formal clerical training, however holy, is entirely understandable, and supplies a significantly different context for his recommendation of Cîteaux from that understandably recorded by the Cistercian chronicler Hugh of Sylvanès.

The decision to seek affiliation to Cîteaux made Sylvanès the first Cistercian foundation in the Languedoc: Fontfroide and Valmagne are later creations, and even the 'three sisters' of Provence—Senanque, Silvacane and Le Thoronet—postdate it.[12] Nor was it an easy decision to realise, and the steps by which it was achieved remain in dispute. The nearest Cistercian house to Sylvanès was Mazan, remote in the

---

[11] Tractatus caps 20–1, pp 221–2: the Carthusian prior is not named, and there is virtually no reference to Pons de Léras in Carthusian sources. While the main conflict was between supporters of the Cistercian and Carthusian way of life—Facta est ergo contentio inter eos quis ordinum videretur esse maior—one other possibility was canvassed—quibusdam etiam sanctimonialium virginum monasterium construere dicentibus dignum. This was realised by the foundation of the nunnery of Nonenque (c1146) by Guiraud, third abbot of Silvanès (1144–61).

[12] Fontfroide, founded 1093, Cistercian 1146; Valmagne, founded 1138, Cistercian c1145/53, was one of a number of houses founded by Gerald de Sales, the disciple of Robert of Arbrissel, which later affiliated to Cîteaux (for example, Cadouin—founded 1115, affiliated ? after 1154—and Loc Dieu—founded 1123, affiliated c1162); Le Thoronet, founded 1136, and Senanque, 1148, both daughter houses of Mazan; Silvacane, an eleventh-century foundation, affiliated to Cîteaux c1147; the nunnery of Vignogoul, near Montpellier, founded in the early twelfth century, followed Augustinian customs until compelled to adopt the usages of Cîteaux by pope Alexander III in 1178: affiliation probably followed soon afterwards.

Vivarais, and itself only recently founded from Bonnevaux in Savoy,[13] and it was to Mazan that Sylvanès was affiliated. According to Dimier, whom it is probably safest to follow in the present state of knowledge, Pons gave the site of Sylvanés to Mazan, entered the parent community with his hermit companions in order to learn the Cistercian life, and returned to Sylvanès under its first abbot, Adhémar, monk of Mazan.[14] Local historians would prefer a more direct link with the community at Mas-Théron though, on the whole, they admit the colonisation of Sylvanès by a community sent out from Mazan in the normal Cistercian manner.

Whatever the way it was achieved, however, the establishment of Sylvanès is an important step in the Cistercian penetration of the Midi, and if it is borne in mind that there is no record in Carthusian sources of Pons de Léras' approach to the prior of the Grande Chartreuse, it may represent the first stage in a deliberate policy of Cistercian expansion which can be seen more clearly operative in other cases. Anyone familiar with Cistercian expansion in more northerly and easterly parts of Europe, will find significant differences in the Midi. There, new foundations were remarkably few, and for the most part Cistercian colonisation proceeded by the appropriation and donation of existing communities. Sylvanès, to which the community of Théron had already moved, is a case in point.[15] Valmagne, in the rich and well-watered lands between Pèzenas and Montpellier, founded in 1138 by the viscount of Béziers and Agde, Raymond Trencavel, was transferred to the Cistercian order as a daughter-house of Bonnevaux by the Cistercian pope Eugenius III less than a decade later. The attachment to the white monks of Fontfroide, in a fertile corner of the Corbières near Narbonne (1143), of Senanque (1148), Silvacane (1144) and Le Thoronet (1144), and, further afield, of Robert of Arbrissel's foundation at Cadouin near the Dordogne (1146), and

---

[13] 1120.

[14] A. Dimier, L'Art Cistercien I (2 ed La Pierre-qui-Vire 1974) p 143, following Tractatus cap 21. Other views are summarised by Ferras, Mercadier pp 56–7. Dimier asserts that the first abbot of Silvanès, Adhémar, was a 'moine venu de Mazan'; Hugh of Silvanès implies that he was one of the original community at Mas Théron—'Ex quibus unum virum sapientem et bonum, litteris eruditum, videlicet domnum Ademarum, illis praeposuit [the abbot of Mazan], et abbatem esse constituit, domus curam illi tradidit, et dimisit', Tractatus cap 21 p 222. Adhémar ruled for only six months, ibid cap 28 p 225.

[15] Hugh of Silvanès's brief chapter (21) could be read to imply the establishment of Cistercian facilities at Mas-Théron for the community from the original hermitage to enter after their year's probation and training at Mazan.

Stephen of Obazine's community at Obazine in the Corrèze (1147) are also to be dated to these years.[16] How much can be made of all this it is difficult to say. These were, after all, the great years of Cistercian influence and expansion, with St Bernard widely active under the first Cistercian pope after his labours on behalf of Innocent II during the papal schism of 1130-9. Such transfers of existing communities to the white monks are bound to seem normal in a period which saw the absorption of the order of Savigny itself, and the near-incorporation of that of Sempringham. But it is as well to bear in mind that these are also precisely the years when Henry the monk and Peter de Bruis were active and influential throughout the Languedoc, and when both Peter the Venerable and Saint Bernard found themselves committed to sustaining the cause of orthodoxy there.[17] The later direct involvement by the papacy of the white monks in campaigns against southern heresy is too well-known to require emphasis here, and it would not be altogether fanciful to see the outlines of such a policy being established in the lifetime of Saint Bernard and Eugenius III. For all the antiquity of the churches of the Languedoc they had suffered much from Arian Visigoths, Arab incursion, the aggression of Charles Martel and his successors, and from the uncertainties of changing political frontiers and allegiances, quite apart from the general dilapidation consequent upon the lack of strong government within the western Church as a whole. Centres like Saint-Guilhem-le-Désert and Aniane might have a great reputation, but there is nothing to show that they had anything to contribute to the solution of the new problems posed by popular enthusiasm and heterodoxy, and ultimately heresy, which arose in the twelfth century.[18] Gaucelin Raymond de Montpeyroux was a strong and successful bishop of Lodève for over a quarter of a century (1161-87), and earned praise from Hugh of Sylvanès for his public refutation and conviction of Albigensian heretics,[19] but the example is an isolated one, and there is little indication that dioceses like Lodève and its neighbours had the resources, men or institutions to direct and contain the forces

[16] See above n 12.
[17] For recent treatment of these topics see R. I. Moore, *The Origins of European Dissent* (London 1977); R. I. Moore, *The Birth of Popular Heresy* (London 1976); M. D. Lambert, *Medieval Heresy* (London 1976), and the bibliographies therein.
[18] See Alzieu, Mercadier pp 65-70, and incidental references in the articles by Hebrard and R. Saint-Jean ('Une abbaye de l'ancien diocèse de Lodève: Saint Guilhem-le-Désert', Mercadier pp 114-35) in the same volume.
[19] Alzieu, Mercadier p 72.

represented by Henry the monk and Peter de Bruis, or the popular enthusiasm released by them, and by Pons de Léras.

The career of a man like Pons de Léras is an apt comment on the outlook and attitudes of this society. However much the circumstances of his conversion from a life of crime may be questioned, however generalised and conventional the sparse account of his life of piety thereafter, however great an embarrassment he may have been as the probably illiterate lay leader of a community of hermits at the moment of its transmutation into a Cistercian abbey, there can be no doubt that there was a conversion, that Pons de Léras did display an example and exercise a spiritual influence which captured the attention of prospective patrons and those who came into contact with him, and that he was a leader: unlike the hermit leader Seleth who inconveniently occupied the best site for the Yorkshire abbey of Kirkstall[20] he does not entirely disappear from the scene after he had handed over his hermitage to the Cistercians. Patrons, we are told, competed for the establishment of the hermit and his companions on their lands, and yet apart from his colourful past there is nothing remarkable about him—a comment on hospitality, a vague hint of miracles—nor had he, like so many other better-known wandering hermits, any reputation as a popular teacher. Pons' popularity may have dependend, as much as anything else, on the lack of comparable examples or vocations locally, and some confirmation for such a view may perhaps be found in the absence of similar foundations and cults in the Lodèvois and neighbouring regions during these years.

His popularity is also evidence of the popular appetite for austere example, an appetite not confined of course to the Lodèvois but widely evident in western Europe where, on the whole, it was more generally ministered to. The community at Mas-Théron grew, so Hugh of Sylvanès records, principally because the recruits wanted to live with the men of God. There is an ascetic interest and temperament visible here which the talk at Mas-Théron of becoming Carthusians, if it may be given any credence, emphasises, and which is given unexpected confirmation by the foundation of one of the earliest daughters of Grandmont, Saint-Michel de Grandmont (?1128) less than five miles to the east of Lodève.[21] Though a thirteenth-century bishop of Lodève came to be regarded as the second founder of the house there

---

[20] See *Fundacio Abbathie de Kyrkestall*, ed E. K. Clark, *Thoresby Society* 4 (Leeds 1895).
[21] See R. Saint-Jean, 'Un prieuré de l'ancien diocèse de Lodève: Saint-Michel de Grandmont', Mercadier pp 136–51.

Popular piety in the Lodèvois

is no hint of episcopal involvement in its obscure beginnings, and like Sylvanès it seems to have owed its foundation to the initiative of a secular patron acting independently.

Against such a background, however microcosmic, it is not difficult to understand the attraction of men like Henry the monk and Peter de Bruis, or the impact of Cathar austerity. Equally, the difficulty experienced by the established ecclesiastical authorities in dealing with these new problems comes more clearly into focus. In one of Professor McManner's senses men like the twelfth-century bishops of Lodève, however able, were 'prisoners of the past'.[22] Their energies and resources were fully occupied in overcoming the problems they had inherited, and the local structures of their dioceses, ancient though they might be had nothing to offer in the face of such challenges. The hope lay in men like Pons de Léras. Itinerant, eccentric layman though he was the orthodoxy of his witness never seems to have been in question, and it clearly met a popular need.[23] Yet here, as elsewhere, a Mas-Théron becomes a Sylvanès, and if in the Languedoc an element of ecclesiastical policy conditioned and strengthened the normal patronal pressures towards the institutionalising of piety it can only be suggested that it was a mistaken policy. Elsewhere in the west the crisis forced upon individual vocations by the pressures of society can be appreciated and condoled: in the Lodèvois, as elsewhere in the Languedoc, it is society as a whole which suffers, and there remains a spiritual vacuum and need for Cathars and their heterodox contemporaries and predecessors to fill. Would a Cistercian abbot have had to preside at the sack of Béziers if a Cistercian abbot had not been installed at Sylvanès? Though the question is unreal it is not altogether without point. 'This was the world of the monks, the rim of pallor between day and night. Here they paced, backwards and forwards, backwards and forwards, in the neutral, shadowless light of shadow. Neither the flare of day nor the completeness of night reached them, they paced the narrow path of the twilight, treading in the neutrality of the law. Neither the blood nor the spirit spoke in them, only the law, the abstraction of the average. The infinite is positive and negative. But the average is only neutral. And the monks trod backward and forward down the line of neutrality'.[24]

University of Edinburgh

[22] See above, introduction.
[23] See below, p 55 n 33.
[24] D. H. Lawrence, *Twilight in Italy*, (Penguin Ed) p 36.

47

THE MOTIVES OF THE CATHARS: SOME REFLECTIONS

by M. D. LAMBERT

CATHARISM in the affected regions of Languedoc, especially the eastern Toulousain, Carcassès, part of the Albigeois,[1] where the problem of heresy first reached crisis point for twelfth-century churchmen, affected all classes. This is admitted by Marxist as well as non-Marxist historians. A working hypothesis has been put foward by Griffe to explain why the heresy, which affected a whole series of localities in the twelfth century, built up support more strongly in these areas of Languedoc than anywhere else.[2] Usurpation of tithes, he suggests, predisposed an impoverished rural nobility to support cathar preachers who confirmed them in their hostility to the church by suggesting religious reasons why they should not give up the detained tithes. Disputed allegiances, conflicts and war costs weakened the position of the lords who might otherwise have supported persecution at the early and vulnerable stage of the heresy's development. So preachers were free to gain converts.

Among the nobility, Griffe suggests, women tended perhaps more often in early years to respond fully to the preachers' religious appeal and take the step from patronage to commitment by receiving the *consolamentum* and becoming perfect; husbands, sons or other male relatives tended to follow after.[3] Koch, working independently of Griffe, attempts to tease out the evidence of women's role in Languedocian catharism in order to argue that the force predisposing women of all classes to the heresy was the status given to the perfect, adored by believers and sympathisers, much greater than that available, with few exceptions, in catholicism.[4] What Koch was unable to provide was a full comparison between the outlets open to religiously

---

[1] [E. Griffe], *Les Débuts* [*de l'aventure cathare en Languedoc* (1140–1190)] (Paris 1969) pp 176–7. I am indebted for helpful criticism of points in this paper to Dr Janet L. Nelson, Mr R. I. Moore, Professor D. Burr.

[2] *Les Débuts* pp 166–208; compare [W. L.] Wakefield, *Heresy, Crusade and Inquisition* [*in Southern France, 1100–1250*] (London 1974) pp 65–81.

[3] *Les Débuts* pp 182, 184; [E. Griffe], *Le Languedoc cathare* [*de 1190 à 1210*] (Paris 1971) pp 26–7; see Wakefield, *Heresy, Crusade and Inquisition* p 74; [M. Roquebert], *L'Epopée Cathare* [*1198–1212: l'invasion*] (Toulouse 1970) p 103.

[4] [G.] Koch, *Frauenfrage* [*und Ketzertum im Mittelalter*] (Berlin 1962) caps 3, 7.

inclined women in heresy and orthodoxy in these regions; if the two were put side by side we might better be able to understand what led women to prefer to enter a house of cathar perfect than an orthodox nunnery. Nevertheless, cathar ritual and practice support Koch. Even though a man perfect would lead in the prayers in a mixed gathering,[5] the status of the woman perfect was high. She held precedence over believers and sympathisers, male and female, and was entitled to be adored, that is, receive the *melioramentum* from all.[6] Koch's argument (which is necessarily supposititious) does not, however, logically help with the case of women perfect drawn from the nobility, because they, we may surmise, already had status because of their rank: the gain, through receiving the *consolamentum*, would not have been so remarkable.

There may yet be more to be said about social class, sex and the rise of cartharism. Perhaps in discussing the role of women in catharism, we should look not only at status but also at the function of the perfect's life, giving purpose to the single woman or the widow. Withdrawn as the woman perfect often was,[7] in contrast to itinerant male preachers, her house was a support point to the preacher and her influence a major factor in implanting the heresy within the families of the affected regions.[8] Perhaps, too, discussion of the attractions of status should be widened, so as to include men as well as women outside the ranks of the nobility. All classes participated, but the proportions differed, and differed at different times. Yet Dossat, who has a profound knowledge of the inquisition material, attempting in a sentence to summarise the social composition of the perfect in Languedoc over the course of cathar history, has said bluntly that they were 'for the most part . . . poor peasants or artisans.'[9] The gain in status for neophytes of this rank receiving the *consolamentum* is obvious.

[5] [L.] Clédat, Le Nouveau Testament [traduit au XIIIᵉ siècle en langue provençale suivi d'un rituel cathare] (Paris 1887) p xxii.
[6] [R.] Nelli, La Vie [quotidienne des Cathares du Languedoc au XIIIᵉ siècle] (Paris 1969) p 92; for the role of women in conferring the consolamentum in Italy, see Sacconi's Summa in [A.] Dondaine, [Un] Traité [neo-manichéen du XIIᵉ siècle: le Liber de duobus principiis, suivi d'un Fragment de Rituel cathare] (Rome 1937) p 65 lines 23–4.
[7] Nelli, La Vie p 48.
[8] Koch, Frauenfrage pp 49–70; Griffe, Le Languedoc Cathare pp 77–184 passim; for examples of the importance of women in one noble family see W. L. Wakefield, 'The Family of Niort in the Albigensian Crusade and before the Inquisition', Names 18 (Potsdam, New York 1970) pp 97–117, 286–303.
[9] Y. Dossat, 'The Cathars' NCE 3 p 247, similarly in the same author's 'Les Cathares d'après l'Inquisition', Ca[hiers de] F[anjeaux] 3 (Toulouse 1968) pp 71–104 at p 82; but note the warning on social class in Wakefield, Heresy, Crusade and Inquisition p 79.

The motives of cathars

Northern and central Italy, the other major area of cathar influence, give less openings for socio-economic analysis because of the nature of the documentation of the heresy there. We are better informed about the internal doctrinal history of Italian catharism and worse informed about its social history. Inquisition records give flashes of information in depth on heresy in the towns but we lack the materials for the continuous study of the social composition of the sect in a limited geographical setting, of the kind that is available for parts of Languedoc from the fourth decade of the thirteenth century. If we accept Violante's summary of the Italian situation, there were important differences between catharism there and in Languedoc.[10] Italians seem to have had a more speculative interest in dualism and were more in touch with the Balkan and Byzantine founts of the heresy. The class structure differed. Violante argues that there was no peasant involvement.[11] Whatever theories are evolved to account for participation in catharism must take account of this vital difference between the areas of major settlement. Both in Italy and in Languedoc certain factors inhibited persecution—the political fluidity in Languedoc, tinged with complicity with heresy in some aristocratic families, the flux in Italy, its great church-state quarrels and anticlericalism, the independence of its cities.[12] Beneath the umbrella of tolerance or protection in both areas, preachers and missionaries had time to infiltrate and build up groups of followers without effective counteraction to destroy their work at an early stage, as often happened elsewhere in western Europe.[13]

If we wish to elucidate the motives of the cathars, we must begin with the perfect. Salvation depended on joining their ranks, in life or at the point of death. On their preaching and example success of the movement depended. We can see in the era of its decline in the success of Pierre Autier in the Ariège 1295–1310 what one dominating personality armed with cathar assumptions about perfection could do

[10] C. Violante, 'Hérésies urbaines et Hérésies rurales en Italie du 11e au 13e Siècle', J. Le Goff, *Hérésies et Sociétés [dans l'Europe préindustrielle, 11–18 Siècles]* École pratique des hautes études. *Civilisations et Sociétés* 10 (Paris 1968) pp 171–98.
[11] *Ibid* pp 184–5.
[12] On Italy, see R. Manselli, *L'Eresia del Male* (Naples 1963); E. Dupré Theseider, 'Gli eretici nel mondo comunale italiano', *Bollettino della Società di Studi Valdesi* 73 (Torre Pellice 1963) pp 3–23; A. Murray, 'Piety and Impiety in Thirteenth Century Italy', *SCH* 8 pp 83–106. It is not my intention here to do more than allude to the Italian background.
[13] For developments elsewhere, see [A.] Borst, *Die Katharer* (Stuttgart 1953) pp 89–134.

and we can assume the same process for the ill-documented start of catharism.[14]

Possible attractions of status have been discussed. Is there also, we may ask, a characteristic psychology of the successful or obdurate perfect? Obsessive literalism will occur to us as a feature, demonstrable in the penances imposed for not saying paternosters at the requisite times and in the language of the rituals with their fussy prescriptions. 'When Christians [that is, perfect] encounter a man with whom they must have speech while they are praying to God, if they have said eight prayers these can be counted as a single; if they have finished sixteen they can be accounted the Double . . .'[15] Literalism was reinforced by the tendency to view evil more as a soiling than a positive act of will and by the consequences of their equating of dietary lapses and moral faults.[16] A perfect could forfeit salvation as well by eating an egg as by committing a major crime. Tension was screwed up further by the belief that when the donor of the *consolamentum* fell, all those whom he had consoled forfeited their *consolamentum* as well.[17]

Perfect were semi-vegans. Milk, cheese and eggs were forbidden as products of coition. Fish, which was believed to be the product of water, was allowed; otherwise nuts would be the only major source of protein. The dangers of protein deficiency which may afflict the modern vegan would be accentuated by the fasts on bread and water on Mondays, Wednesdays and Fridays.[18] Coulton once speculated on the links between the low diet and the life and attitudes of the Egyptian hermits.[19] We might do the same for the perfect and ask how far dietary deficiencies facilitated the weaving of fantasies. Some of the

---

[14] J. M. Vidal, 'Les derniers ministres de l'Albigéisme en Languedoc. Leurs doctrines', R[evue des] q[uestions] h[istoriques] ns 38 (Paris 1906) pp 57–107, 'Doctrine et morale des derniers ministres albigeois', RQH ns 41 (Paris 1909) pp 357–409; 42 (1909) pp 5–48. For the dating of the appearance of catharism in Languedoc see the conclusions of R. I. Moore, 'St Bernard's mission to the Languedoc in 1145', BIHR 47 (1974) pp 1–10: his revision of the accepted timetable still leaves a wide gulf between the cathar missionary work of the 1160s and 1170s and the recollections of suspects in the inquisition records of the 1240s.

[15] Clédat, Le Nouveau Testament p xxi; trans by [W. L.] Wakefield, [A. P.] Evans, Heresies [of the High Middle Ages] (New York/London 1969) p 491.

[16] See the characterisation of the ethics of Gnostics and Bogomils in [H. C.] Puech, [A.] Vaillant, Le Traité contre les Bogomiles de Cosmas le Prêtre (Paris 1945) pp 260–79; also [M. D.] Lambert, Medieval Heresy, [Popular Movements from Bogomil to Hus] (London 1977) pp 14–23, 108–13.

[17] Sacconi in Dondaine, Traité pp 69–70.

[18] Borst, Die Katharer p 184.

[19] G. G. Coulton, Five Centuries of Religion 1 (Cambridge 1923) pp 16–17.

perfect were great storytellers, working on an ancient store of scriptural episodes, bogomil and gnostic material to discuss the origins of evil and the fall of man.[20] Satan in the guise of a serpent comes out of the reeds and has intercourse with Eve with the tail.[21] Satan smuggles a most beautiful woman into heaven to seduce the good angels; inflamed with lust for her, they fall from heaven in crowds.[22] Animals are formed from the flesh of foetuses of pregnant women who have aborted with fright at the spectacle of war in heaven.[23] Developed, borrowed, worked up, these were narratives which plainly gave pleasure to the perfect who retailed them and the believers who listened to them. What, we may ask, was their significance, with their strong sexual associations and their gross organic emphasis, for a class of celibates who have renounced all contact with the opposite sex? Does sexuality return unconsciously through words? Or do the stories give vent to an organic disgust characteristic of certain anxious temperaments? A taste for the exotic, perhaps in otherwise humble and humdrum lives, also peeps through in the Italian context in the journeys of cathar leaders to the Balkans to obtain foolproof *consolamentum* in the years following the breakdown of Nicetas's tradition.[24] In the view of these perfect moral perfection and assurance of salvation were not to be found in the known land of Italy but in misty Balkan redoubts. We will be reminded of the role which Tibet played in the imagination of the nineteenth century and of the attempts of Madame Blavatsky, including an ill-recorded journey from India to obtain ancient wisdom from contacts with Tibetan masters.[25]

A perfect is likely to have more imaginative than logical power, and such personalities are likely to be less troubled than contemporary hostile controversialists by logical inconsistencies within dualism, or even by the differences of opinion which led to splits within catharism and the setting up of mutually hostile organisations of heretics.[26] A

[20] Survey in H. Soederberg, *La Religion des Cathares: Études sur le gnosticisme de la basse antiquité et du moyen age* (Uppsala 1949).

[21] R. Reitzenstein, *Die Vorgeschichte der christlichen Taufe* (Leipzig/Berlin 1929) pp 301–2. The story derives from a bogomil apocryphon brought from Bulgaria: for analysis and translation, see Wakefield, Evans, *Heresies* pp 448–9, 458–65, 767–9, 773–6.

[22] I. von Doellinger, *Beitraege zur Sektengeschichte des Mittelalters* 2 (Munich 1890) p 186.

[23] T. Kaeppeli, 'Une Somme contre les hérétiques de S. Pierre Martyr (?)', *AFP* 17 (1947) p 330. The author describes this belief as *unum de suis secretis archanis*.

[24] Lambert, *Medieval Heresy* pp 126–32. For the siting of these meetings see the comment of J. V. A. Fine Jr. in *Speculum* 41 (1966) pp 526–9.

[25] *Dictionary of American Biography* 2 (New York 1929) pp 361–3 and literature given.

[26] R. Manselli, 'Églises et Théologies Cathares', *CaF* 3 (1968) pp 129–76.

school of dualism rested primarily on the personality of a leading perfect with his direct contact with another world and the guarantee of authenticity conferred by his *consolamentum*. The body of creation narratives was their school of instruction. Orthodox churchmen tended to see their enemies in their own terms—faulty sacraments in place of true ones, a rival hierarchy challenging that of the true church, a cathar pope directing the challenge to the faith from some obscure land of dualists, placed perhaps in Bosnia or Bohemia, but in either case certainly non-existent.[27] Because of this frame of thought controversialists tended to see cathars in the light of their own assumptions and to expect doctrinal dissension to damage the enemy cause more than it did. To realise how much conflict and disappointment adherents of such movements can stand we should read Lady Lutyens's account of her experiences in twentieth-century theosophy.[28]

The perfect included few of profound training or much religious culture. An anti-intellectualist strand is discernible. Cathars believed that the church needlessly obfuscated what was in fact perfectly simple. The outburst from the heretical treatise reconstructed from its refutation by Durand of Huesca, 'O senseless men of learning, who hath bewitched you into incomprehension of these things? O full of all guile and of all deceit . . . O blind leaders of the blind, what can be plainer in holy scriptures?'[29] reads like a cry from the heart. To the author dualism seemed the natural inference from the world-renouncing texts of scripture and orthodox exegesis a mere distortion. Italian catharism, though it had a higher intellectual level than that of the Languedoc, was not academically distinguished, as analysis of its best extant product, the *Liber de duobus principibus*, shows.[30]

On these lines one may reconstruct the characteristic temperament of a perfect, or the temperament which might be fostered by the life of the perfect. What emerges is the character of a tense, rather literal-minded perfectionist with a strong determination, imaginative rather than logical power, perhaps with a tendency to organic disgust,

[27] The latest discussion of this 'pope' is in F. Šanjek, *Les Chrétiens bosniaques et le Mouvement Cathare* (Paris/Louvain 1976) pp 107–16. 'Boemia' and 'Boemi' is surely a mistake for Bosnia (*ibid* pp 112, 113) but the site is plainly shrouded in romance and rumour. See further J. V. A. Fine Jr, *The Bosnian Church: a new Interpretation* (Boulder 1975).

[28] Lady Emily Lutyens, *Candles in the Sun* (London 1957).

[29] C. Thouzellier, *Un Traité cathare inédit du début du XIIIe siècle d'après le liber contra Manicheos de Durand de Huesca* (Louvain 1961) pp 104–5; trans by Wakefield, Evans, *Heresies* p 506.

[30] C. Thouzellier, *Livre des deux Principes* (Paris 1973) p 82.

anti-intellectual and not strongly religiously educated. Nevertheless, not all who took up the onerous way of life of the perfect held to it, despite the filtering effect of strict probation with fasting and the care taken to exclude those who seemed unsuitable. Griffe describes an outflow in Languedoc from the ranks of the perfect, the motives for which, if sometimes only to be guessed at, appear to include, besides fear, genuine conversion back to catholicism and the influence of relatives, an element of spontaneous personal decision.[31] The life seemed too hard or ceased to please. A number were perfect who had received the *consolamentum* early in life:[32] family influence that brought them in waned with greater maturity. In practice not all temperaments were suited by the way of life and that fact may recall to us that one reason for catharism's success was not directly connected with its idiosyncratic beliefs at all. The heresy succeeded in some localities simply because it was there and appeared the only vital religious outlet attractive to the minority desiring a personal commitment. It drew to itself all the hopes, wishes and ambitions which cohere round a religion, providing, for example, a limited element of schooling,[33] looking after girls who could not otherwise be provided for,[34] catering through the *consolamentum* on the deathbed for those seeking salvation.[35] All this, and the inflow of the few to the life of the perfect which accompanied accepted status, was the outcome of the patronage of a set of aristocratic families who produce patrons and perfect over three generations. Roquebert shows us among the participants in the attack on the inquisitors' party at Avignonet twelve men who were closely related to each other, in turn linked to nineteen perfect women.[36] The umbrella of support provided by these families kept catharism in being right down to the revolt of Raymond Trencavel in 1240, the aftermath of which destroyed their power for ever.[37]

---

[31] *Le Languedoc Cathare* pp 83, 85, 87, 89, 98, 99, 119, 120, 121, 124, 127, 128–9, 130, 134, 136, 141, 149, 174–5. Cases of double heretication, in which the perfect left but were reconsoled later, are discussed pp 105, 144; see also p 127.

[32] *Ibid* pp 134–5.

[33] *Ibid* p 85; Borst, *Die Katharer* p 107.

[34] Koch, *Frauenfrage* p 28.

[35] For examples of villages where the deathbed *consolamentum* became the norm, see *Le Languedoc cathare* p 91; cemeteries of heretics, *ibid* pp 92, 96, 101, 123, 147, *CaF* 3 (1968) p 80.

[36] *L'Épopée cathare* p 126.

[37] See comment on the dating of the decline of catharism by Wakefield in *Names* 18 (1970) p 303.

One factor which facilitated patronage, in Italy as much as in Languedoc, was the simplicity and flexibility of the cathar church. We are accustomed, and rightly, to looking at this from an idealistic point of view and recognising how the perfect incarnated the twelfth-century desire for wandering preaching in poverty. [38] But there are also practical attractions. Cathars had no religious buildings as such to keep up. Perfect had a low standard of living. Associations of perfect, often related, perhaps working together at a trade or consisting of a group of noble women in a widow's house, in their cheapness, flexibility and the ease with they could be set up and dispersed resembled nothing so much as the catholic beguinage.[39] An informal organisation. consisting of small units, was easily able both to shed its less zealous members and to break and re-form elsewhere in face of persecution,

A major attraction of catharism lay in the moral life of the perfect. Churchmen imply this when they so commonly argue that the orthodox church could defeat the heretics if its clergy were of higher standard. The point is borne out by the self-applied terms for the cathar élite, *bons hommes* and the like,[40] and by the language of their own treatises. *The Vindication of the Church of God* introduces its chapters with a moral claim, made in contradistinction to the catholic church—'This church refrains from killing', 'This church refrains from adultery', and quotes with approval the text of the epistle of St James, 'Whosoever shall keep the whole law but offend in one point, is become guilty of all', confidently asserting that the cathars observed all the commandments of the law of life.[41] Like the heretical preachers described by Everwin of Steinfeld in Cologne in 1143-4[42] the author of the *Vindication* based the claim of the cathars to be the true Christians on the fact that they were poor and persecuted where the Roman church was wealthy and powerful.[43] When the postulant at the rite of the *consolamentum* in its Provençal version was addressed by the *ancianus* he was told that he was being introduced to a pure under-ground Christianity going back to the earliest days of the church.

[38] Grundmann (2 ed) pp 13–38.
[39] *Le Languedoc cathare* p 189. For economic aspects see the observations of E. Werner in his review of Borst, *Die Katharer* in *Byzantinoslavica* 16 (Prague 1955) pp 135–44.
[40] Borst, *Die Katharer* pp 240–53.
[41] H. Venckeleer, 'Un Recueil cathare: le Manuscrit A.6.10 de la 'Collection Vaudoise' de Dublin I—Une apologie', *Revue Belge [de Philologie et d'Histoire]* 38 (Brussels 1960) pp 815–34 at pp 823, 824, 827; trans by Wakefield, Evans, *Heresies* pp 599, 602; Jas 2 10–11.
[42] *PL* 182 (1879) cols 676–80.
[43] *Revue Belge* 38 (1960) p 828.

The motives of cathars

'This holy baptism . . .', the *ancianus* says, 'the Church of God has preserved from the apostles until this time and it has passed from Good Men to Good Men until the present moment . . ."[44] In catharism in its heyday personal ethical life was in accord with office and status in a way in which it was not in catholicism.

Sympathisers who venerated the self-denying life of the cathar ascetic might well have no intention of imitating it themselves. Yet they expected high standards from the perfect who were, in a sense, their proxies before God. In return, the perfect gave their followers their prayers and their counsel, both spiritual and material, perhaps, too, an ultimate assurance that they could keep their more indulgent way of life and still in the end secure salvation.[45] There are affinities here to the attitudes of orthodox patrons to their religious houses.[46] The life of the perfect gave weight to their teaching and, as is well known, superficial likenesses between catharism and contemporary catholicism—scriptural language, ascetic attitudes and practices, apocryphal material, even the use of chains of paternosters in prayer—aided a process of instruction which carried hearers away from orthodoxy.[47] The arbitrary, fluctuating exegesis characteristic of the cathar[48] and his manipulation of ascetic texts was not, however, a teacher's device but a form of interpretation which the élite genuinely accepted. At one point, nevertheless, the teacher made use of a popular feeling which he can hardly have shared. Ekbert of Schönau implies that cathar preachers jeered at the mass, saying that Christ's body must have been as big as a mountain to feed the faithful for so long.[49] Cathars did not reject the mass out of this kind of scepticism: they rejected it because the mass made use of evil matter. Ekbert wrote in 1163 of catharism in the Rhineland. There are other parallels for a cathar use of scepticism later, and in other countries,[50] as part of a process of disillusioning hearers with contemporary orthodoxy as a

---

[44] Clédat, *Le Nouveau Testament* p xvii; trans by Wakefield, Evans, *Heresies* p 489; compare the Latin ritual in Dondaine, *Un Traité* p 159 lines 22–4.

[45] Le Roy Ladurie, *Montaillou, [village occitan de 1294 à 1324]* (Paris 1975) p 541.

[46] Below p 61–75.

[47] E. Delaruelle, 'Le Catharisme en Languedoc vers 1200: une enquête', *Annales du Midi* 72 (Toulouse 1960) pp 149–67.

[48] C. Thouzellier, 'La Bible des Cathares languedociens et son usage dans la controverse au début du XIIIe siècle', *CaF* 3 (1968) pp 42–58; see also this author's fundamental work on the controversies in Languedoc, *Catharisme et Valdéisme en Languedoc à la fin du XIIe et au début du XIIIe siècle* (2 ed Louvain/Paris 1969).

[49] *PL* 195 (1855) col 92.

[50] Borst, *Die Katharer* p 217 n 14.

preliminary to turning them towards more positive heretical beliefs. In a Toulouse inquisition of 1273–6 Ekbert's tag about Christ's body recurs in more than one confession.[51] Reading them one is not very conscious of dualism at all, but of an earthy rationalism reminiscent of English lollards. Bernardus de Soulhaco, for example, ridiculing the host as baker's dough such as he had in his cupboard or insisting that one need confess sins only to God carries us into an English fifteenth-century heresy trial rather than a thirteenth-century inquisition in Languedoc. [52] At the time catharism was in sharp decline, perfect had fled and Waldensians were no longer in evidence. One may wonder whether the views often expressed in this inquisition were the *detritus* of cathar teaching or, as Wakefield suggests, the outcome of a spontaneous rationalism[53] which lay below the surface in various societies, was occasionally brought to light in some inquisition held at a time of tension over heresy but more often lay fallow, available to be used by preachers of various persuasions, and acting as a kind of escalator to carry men away from orthodoxy into varied heresies.

For the village of Montaillou the register of the inquisition of Jacques Fournier provides other evidence of deviant opinions, often with affinities to those uncovered in the Toulouse inquisition, and in a similar fashion not directly attributable to catharism.[54] The historian of Montaillou, Le Roy Ladurie, has suggested a slightly different explanation for them—that the presence of a rival force to catholicism stimulated the emergence of ancient, folk-lore beliefs and other deviations.[55] His detailed study shows us, above all, the cross-currents in a village society, the semi-magical reverence for *bons hommes* in their clandestine circle, and the existence of villagers who wavered between orthodoxy and heresy, as in the case of Pierre Maury who wanted to be a benefactor of both parties because he did not know which of the two beliefs was better. He inclined more to heresy simply because he was in contact more often with heretics.[56]

[51] W. L. Wakefield, 'Some unorthodox popular ideas of the thirteenth century', *Medievalia et Humanistica* ns 4 (Denton/Texas 1973) pp 25–35.
[52] *Ibid* p 27; J. A. F. Thomson, *The Later Lollards 1414–1520* (Oxford 1965); A. G. Dickens, 'Heresy and the origins of English Protestantism', *Britain and the Netherlands*, 2 ed J. S. Bromley, E. H. Kossmann (Groningen 1964) pp 47–66.
[53] *Medievalia et Humanistica* 4 (1973) p 33.
[54] Le Roy Ladurie, *Montaillou* pp 523–42.
[55] *Ibid* p 531.
[56] J. Duvernoy, *Le Registre d'Inquisition de Jacques Fournier Évêque de Pamiers (1318–1325)*, 3 (Toulouse 1965) p 209.

The motives of cathars

Montaillou is, however, a mountain village and its investigations took place in the last years of Languedocian catharism. Progress towards understanding of the heresy in its setting in the south of France will best be advanced by investigations in depth on the same lines, for other sites and earlier periods, such as Wakefield is undertaking for Le-Mas-Saintes-Puelles. We may expect to see from his analysis how heresy fared in a coarse peasant society,[57] and, a vital offset to too much clear-cut generalising, how, as at Montaillou, personal motives affected religious opinion. At Le-Mas a man before the inquisition recalled that twenty years earlier, as a boy, he had been in the company of heretics (his mother was a warm believer) who asked him to come with them and they would make him a good scholar. His duties, herding cows, prevented him at first from doing so. Finally he went to join them, in a house at Le-Mas. But his mother came and, believer or not, pulled him out by his hair, beating him.[58]

University of Bristol

[57] See Roquebert, *L'Épopée cathare* p 122.
[58] I owe this account to the kindness of professor W. L. Wakefield, formerly of State University College in Potsdam, New York. For his source, Toulouse, town library, MS 609, see Y. Dossat, *Les crises de l'inquisition toulousaine* (Bordeaux 1959). The confession is to be found on fol 42ʳ (Petrus Faure) and a corroborating one by Na Mateus, the mother, on fol 29ᵛ.

TIMEO BARONES ET DONAS FERENTES[1]

by EMMA MASON

T HIS sentiment might well have been voiced by any abbot contemplating the ambivalent relationship between his house and its patrons. They expected material, as well as spiritual returns on their investment, and these might well conflict with the best interests of the monastery. Ambivalence, though, was equally reflected in the attitude of religious houses towards their benefactors, as this brief survey of baronial patronage in England, between the late eleventh and the mid thirteenth centuries, indicates.

No real doubt seems to have been held by baronial patrons that benefactions were necessary to their wellbeing in the afterlife, but they were largely guided by the maxim that 'it is the thought which counts', judging from the limited extent of their grants, whether on their own behalf or for the souls of deceased kinsfolk. Could things have been otherwise? They were imbued from infancy with the concept that the integrity of the fief must prevail over all other considerations. Inevitably such conditioning was reflected in their response towards things spiritual as well as towards temporal claims on their loyalties.

The patronal relationship maintained by a baron towards local religious houses was designed at least as much to further his temporal as his spiritual interests, and in particular reflected on the status of his own family in relation to territorial rivals. The continued preeminence of his line was emphasised by the acknowledgment of a neighbouring religious house that successive heads of his dynasty inherited the position of being its patrons and founders.[2] The more strongly this role was asserted, the more the family's superiority over territorial rivals was enhanced.[3]

---

[1] I am grateful to Wendy Ransford and Rosamund Rocyn Jones for helpful discussions on certain aspects of this paper.
[2] [R. W.] Southern, [*Western Society and the Church in the Middle Ages*] (Harmondsworth 1970) p 245.
[3] [*Charters of the Honour of*] Mowbray [*1107–1191*, ed D. E. Greenway], Records of Social and Economic History, ns I (London 1972) p xli.

Religious houses welcomed this aspect of the relationship. They were as much attuned to the hard facts of life as were baronial houses, and welcomed the strongest protector available.

The power and status of the patron was evidently of more concern than the extent of his benefactions. Short of some overwhelming political upheaval, there was unlikely to be any great quantity of land available for new donations by this period,[4] and the patrons of most houses confined themselves largely to making minor gifts and confirmations. In an era when violence was endemic, patrons, whatever their shortcomings, were a necessity of life, and in one sense, the more ruthless they were, the better this served the interests of 'their' religious houses. Great Malvern priory was harassed over a long period by the rival claims of Westminster abbey and Worcester cathedral priory to control it. Accordingly the monks of Great Malvern were glad to acquire Walter de Beauchamp as their protector early in Henry III's reign.[5] Walter's predecessors had shown little interest in the house, but they too had their differences with Westminster and Worcester. He was just the protector which Great Malvern needed, and the chapter subsequently claimed, quite without justification, that his ancestor, the notorious Urse d'Abetot, had been their founder.[6] A menacing neighbour might on occasion be converted by special pleading on the part of an influential friend into becoming the protector of his erstwhile victim, as in the case of Reginald de St Valery and Osney,[7] while a really powerful man could deal out patronage both at first and second hand. The Arrouasians were never popular in England, but when Walter Giffard founded a house of this order at Notley, one of his tenants was induced to found another on his estate at Missenden, while Giffard's influence at court won the royal favour for both houses simultaneously.[8]

Most baronial families concentrated their patronage on houses in the region where they enjoyed preeminence. The Worcestershire Beauchamps, for instance, ruthlessly extended their grip over the rich

[4] Southern p 253.
[5] [The] Beauchamp [Cartulary, ed Emma Mason], P[ipe] R[oll] S[ociety], ns (forthcoming) no 61.
[6] Placitorum Abbreviatio (Record Commissioners, London 1811) p 331; MA, 3, p 447.
[7] [The Letters and charters of Gilbert] Foliot, [ed A. Morey and C. N. L. Brooke] (Cambridge 1967) no 174.
[8] [The cartulary of] Missenden [abbey, ed J. G. Jenkins] (Bucks Archaeological Society, Bucks Record Society and HMSO 1938–62) 3, p xii.

Timeo Barones et Donas Ferentes

lands along the lower Severn and Avon, and their religious patronage, which was by no means lavish, was one expression of this.[9]

The role of hereditary advocate of a particular house was acquired by many barons, as a result of which they enjoyed on a small scale advantages similar in kind to those accruing to the monarchy from its exercise of regalian right.[10] The powers wielded by advocates generally diminished during the period under discussion, although the Ferrars earls of Derby asserted wide claims over the Benedictine priory of Tutbury well into Henry III's reign. They made alterations in its possessions virtually at will, and while the monks were recompensed on these occasions,[11] the inconvenience and sense of insecurity were no doubt considerable. In the course of time, the earls negotiated for the priory a large measure of independence from its mother house, but simultaneously obtained for themselves a major share in the appointment and, occasionally, the deposition, of its priors.[12] The earls retained control over all Tutbury's land transactions; enjoyed rights in its property during a vacancy, and claimed to exact taxation at will. When the monks resisted such demands by Robert de Ferrars, earl of Derby 1254–66, he retaliated by demolishing their buildings.[13] The prolonged and intensive subjection of Tutbury to its advocate is remarkable, and possibly the unrest of the 1260s gave earl Robert an opportunity to revive powers which had lapsed at an earlier date. This is the more likely in that much of the twelfth-century evidence on advocates' abuse of their position dates from the troubled 1140s, when Gilbert de Lacy took possession of the lands of the Augustinian canons of Llanthony Prima 'by seigneury'.[14] Roger de Mowbray asserted his rights as advocate over the Augustinian priory of Newburgh, enjoying custody of its property during vacancies; conferring licence to elect, and claiming rights of assent to the election. He also enjoyed wide proprietary powers over the Cistercian house of Byland during the early years of its existence, presenting the

[9] See my introduction to Beauchamp.
[10] Margaret Howell, Regalian right in medieval England (London 1962). Magnates, as much as the king, prized formal recognition of their rights over 'their' churches. On 16 August 1200, king John granted William Marshall licence to bestow the pastoral staff on successive abbots of Notley (MA 6, p 279, no 5). I am grateful to Margaret Hine for this and subsequent references to Notley abbey, on which she is now working.
[11] [The cartulary of] Tutbury [priory, ed A. Saltman] (HMSO 1962) p 12.
[12] Ibid pp 13–14.
[13] Ibid p 14; nos 94–5.
[14] [W. E.] Wightman, [The Lacy family in England and Normandy 1066–1194] (Oxford 1966) p 187.

63

abbot-elect to the archbishop in 1142, and claiming in 1147 the right to pronounce on the abbey's religious subjection to Savigny.[15] William earl of Gloucester similarly prevented Tewkesbury abbey from holding a free election, whereas his father and grandfather had acknowledged the abbey's rights in this matter, sanctioned as they were by papal authority. Gilbert Foliot, bishop of Hereford, was acting as vicar of the Worcester diocese when the incident occurred, and in admonishing William, he referred to Tewkesbury as *ecclesiam vestram* while denying that the adjective carried jurisdictional connotations.[16]

Later in the twelfth century the role of lay protector could still bring advantage to the patron, rather than to the house under his protection. Battle Abbey had by then lost the interest of its royal patrons, who were in effect replaced by the justiciar Richard de Luci. His oversight remained largely benevolent during the lifetime of his brother, abbot Walter, but following the latter's death, Richard increasingly turned the situation to his own advantage.[17] Kinship between abbot and patron was usually to the advantage of the baronial 'protector', whatever the motive of the chapter in acquiescing in such elections. From the baron's point of view the whole object of exercising his rights in an election was to secure the appointment of an abbot who would serve the interests of his dynasty. This was particularly important to him in unstable frontier societies, such as the Scottish marches, where promotions in houses of the new ascetic orders, supposedly resistant to lay pressures, were frequently influenced by these considerations.[18] A chapter might itself choose a head who was known to be acceptable to the dominant baronial family of the neighbourhood, as with the election at Selby of Elias Paynel in 1143. He was a kinsman of Henry de Lacy of Pontefract who, it was hoped, would protect the property of the house against lesser local landholders. The plan misfired, for this election inevitably identified the monks with the Lacy interest, and attacks on the family's lands easily spilled over into depredations of Selby's property.[19]

In king John's reign the diminishing powers of advocates still carried the practical advantage that they helped keep down the

---

[15] *Mowbray* p xlii.
[16] *Foliot* no 136.
[17] Eleanor Searle, *Lordship and community: Battle abbey and its banlieu 1066–1538* (Toronto 1974) pp 92–3.
[18] Derek Baker, 'The surest road to heaven', *SCH* 10 (1973) p 47; and 'Legend and reality: the case of Waldef of Melrose', *SCH* 12 (1975) pp 81–2.
[19] Wightman pp 76, 233.

expenses incurred in the patronal relationship. Roger de Tosny, for instance, obtained from the prioress of Flamstead an acknowledgment that the nunnery would not have more than thirteen inmates at any one time, nor become subject to any other house. He also obtained recognition that his assent was necessary before any new abbess assumed office,[20] even though this right was in general on the decline. Some forty years later, Robert Grosseteste simply allowed Joan de Sanford the right to order the election of a new abbot of Missenden to proceed, and he placed limitations on her powers to administer the abbey during a vacancy.[21]

In the mid thirteenth century, lesser rights of appointment were sought and obtained. Great Malvern priory, for instance, conceded that the Beauchamp family might nominate one monk in perpetual succession to pray for their souls.[22] The nominee would incidentally be party to deliberations in chapter regarding the priory's material concerns which might affect the interests of his patron's family. On such occasions it would be to their advantage to retain his loyalty in matters secular as well as sacred.

The link with any given house was usually maintained by the territorial successors of its early patrons, since it emphasised the continuity of the baronial line when it had actually changed, perhaps more than once. The Cistercian nunnery of Cookhill, for example, enjoyed the patronage not only of Waleran de Newburgh, earl of Warwick, but also of his Mauduit and Beauchamp successors in the earldom, even though their own gifts were negligible. The chief objective of William de Beauchamp in maintaining the link was apparently to stress the descent of the title from earl Waleran to himself, for his charter of confirmation posthumously bestowed on his mother, the sister of the Mauduit earl, the title of countess.[23] This aspect of patronage was manifested at all levels of baronial society, from successive earls of Gloucester[24] and Hereford[25] to the parvenu family of Du Plessis, which embellished its antecedents by continuing the links with Missenden earlier maintained by their Noers and

[20] *Beauchamp* no 370.
[21] *Missenden* 2, no 31.
[22] *Beauchamp* no 61.
[23] T. Tanner, *Notitia Monastica* (Cambridge 1784) p 624.
[24] [*Earldom of*] Gloucester [*charters*, ed R. B. Patterson] (Oxford 1973) nos 51, 63–4, 117, 139, 166, 178.
[25] [*Charters of the earldom of*] Hereford, [*1095–1201*, ed D. Walker], *Camden Miscellany* 22, C Ser 4, 1 (1964) no 6.

Sanford predecessors.[26] Undoubtedly the new men wanted the
prayers of the monks, but they also wanted recognition of their
ancestry. The religious houses for their part prudently wished to obtain
a confirmation of their property from a new line and, hopefully, to
enlist its interest in their fortunes.

Normally, a monastery could expect to obtain both a confirmation
of its patrimony and, perhaps, new donations, provided the incoming
baron had succeeded to his position by marriage or inheritance.
When he was an intruder, imposed simply by the royal will, the
consequences were unpredictable. Hugh de Laval evidently regarded
himself as the heir of the Lacy family in the honour of Pontefract, and
made generous grants to their religious houses of Pontefract and
Nostell, admittedly of ecclesiastical sources of revenue,[27] but his
successor, William Maltravers, farmed the honour on a short lease, and
his attitude towards local monasteries was miserly.[28] The arbitrary
attitude of the crown in the earlier twelfth century towards the
disposal of fiefs created problems for religious houses even where the
newcomer was inclined to be generous, since his gifts were necessarily
of property to which others had a claim, even though in the eyes of
churchmen the imperfect title of the donor to the property was
outweighed by the fact of donation.[29] A patron in the present was
worth any number in the past. Monasteries were well aware of the
relative pecking order among their local baronage, and were at times
prepared to demote an old benefactor if a newcomer could better
maintain their interests.[30]

Baronial generosity might diminish for various reasons, not all of them
reflecting on the patron's belief in the merits accruing to a benefactor.
Just as the overriding preoccupation of a religious house was with
maintaining the integrity of its patrimony, so a baron's prime concern
was with the integrity of his fief. If this was endangered, he could not
make alienations on any scale until he had repaired his fortunes.[31] New
religious orders appeared more meritorious, and therefore more
efficacious in earning salvation for their patrons, so that Augustinians,

[26] *Missenden* nos 58–62.
[27] Wightman p 67.
[28] *Ibid* pp 69–71.
[29] Pontefract was involved in one such episode (Wightman p 75), and Southwick in
another (See my 'The Mauduits and their chamberlainship [of the Exchequer]', *BIHR*
49 (1976) pp 3, 7, 17–18).
[30] Wightman pp 109–10; Hereford p 9, no 76.
[31] Wightman p 207.

Cistercians and military orders in turn attracted gifts which would have gone to the Benedictines in earlier generations.[32] A tailing-off of benefactions was deplorable enough, but the Tosny family went further, diverting the identical income previously bestowed on older houses to whichever of the new orders had most recently attracted their enthusiasm.[33]

On the other hand, the perils attendant upon a long pilgrimage were liable to provoke a sudden manifestation of benevolence, evinced by Henry de Lacy's abrupt termination of a dispute with Nostell when he decided to visit the Holy Land.[34] In similar circumstances, Waleran de Beaumont, earl of Worcester, was both more cautious and more explicit, expressing his profound trust in the prayers of the monks of Worcester, and his great affection for them, which he intended to demonstrate *if* he returned safely from his pilgrimage to Compostella.[35]

Religious houses gained, as well as suffered, from the violence of the world around them. Their baronial patrons owed their territorial position to a readiness to hit out before others hit them.[36] They had constantly to demonstrate that their wrath was to be feared, yet retained an underlying awareness that their whole approach to life was liable to incur their damnation. In crude terms, they tried to buy off the consequences of their aggression by offering a share of the loot to those whose prayers would hopefully resolve their dilemma. Such a naive attitude cannot, however, be contrasted with any superior spirituality of the cloister, for religious houses were all too ready to cooperate in this cycle. They bemoaned the persecution they endured in time of civil war, but could then overwhelm the offenders with fears of the consequences. In the event, a house might not merely recoup its losses, but also add substantially to its estates, like Nostell, Pontefract,[37] and Leominster.[38]

The *curiales*, owing their influence to their official contacts rather than to their place in a regional hierarchy, had limited scope for committing acts of physical violence, but ample opportunity to divert the course of justice. The material returns could be considerable, and

---

[32] *Ibid* pp 60–2, 82, 109–11, 182–3, 207, 237–8.
[33] See my ['English] Tithe income [of Norman religious houses'], *BIHR* 48 (1975) p 92.
[34] Wightman p 83.
[35] [*The cartulary of*] *Worcester* [*cathedral priory*, ed R. R. Darlington], PRS, ns 38 (1968) p xxv.
[36] *Leges Henrici Primi*, ed. L. J. Downer (Oxford 1972) p 98.
[37] Wightman pp 75, 78.
[38] Hereford no 25.

Sibton was among the houses which gained as a result.[39] There was a general awareness of the spiritual dangers inherent in attendance at court, demonstrated by Peter of Blois, who justified the courtier's activities in that they were useful to the state, and frequently accompanied works of salvation.[40] The courtier's dilemma was that he could not prosper anywhere else, while the consequences of his temporal gains might be painful and eternal.[41] Westminster abbey was a frequent beneficiary of those in this situation. Early in the thirteenth century, for instance, the chamberlain Robert Mauduit made substantial donations in return for which the monks undertook to commemorate him in their prayers, and to celebrate his *obit* in the dignified style accorded to those of their more esteemed abbots.[42] This agreement was the curial equivalent of the understanding reached by a magnate with the most prestigious house in his own locality. Since the courtiers owed their own prosperity to that of the king, they naturally turned to the house which preeminently had his interests at heart. Their work in the exchequer kept the abbey literally before their eyes, while the splendid setting it afforded the divine office would make its prayers on their behalf appear highly efficacious. At the same time, the very existence of this great church at the centre of government served as a reminder that there were other claims on their loyalties besides those of the *regnum*.

By whatever means wealth was obtained, and however tenaciously a baron clung to it, his deathbed was the classic occasion on which neighbouring religious houses might expect him to disgorge this world's goods in their favour, a hope not always fulfilled in the event. Melodramatic gestures were frequent enough, but the nature and duration of the resulting grants was distinctly variable.

The belated repentance of Robert Dispenser, a *curialis* of the late eleventh century, occasioned reparations more spectacular than substantial. He and his brother Urse d'Abetot had conspicuously enriched themselves by appropriating lands of various religious houses in Worcestershire, most of which were retained by the Beauchamp

[39] ['Early charters of] Sibton [abbey', ed R. A. Brown], *A medieval miscellany for Doris Mary Stenton*, ed Patricia M. Barnes and C. F. Slade, PRS, ns 36 (1962) p 67.
[40] P. Dronke, 'Peter of Blois and poetry at the court of Henry II', *Medieval Studies*, 38 (1976) p 195.
[41] Peter of Blois forcefully expressed the dilemma of the *curialis* in his poem *Quod amicus suggeret*', *Ibid*, pp 206-9.
[42] See my 'The Mauduits and their chamberlainship', pp 21-3.

descendants of Urse.[43] Among their victims was Westminster abbey, better able than most to exact redress. Evidently the monks enlarged upon the perils awaiting Robert if he died without returning their land in Comberton, for it was restored with all due solemnity, even though the phrases of the enactment, *in vita sua . . .pro anima sua*, hint that he was suspiciously near his end. In the presence of eminent witnesses and tenants of both parties, Robert's wife, together with Urse, symbolized the restoration by placing on the high altar of Westminster a pair of silver candelabra; a thurible; a pallium and a tapestry.[44] This makeshift restoration was given a more considered aspect in public, being represented as a 'gift' on Robert's part.[45]

The very fact of promising land to a religious house would hopefully ensure the donor's return to health. Later, perhaps much later, he would actually part with what he could comfortably spare when all ambition was spent. It did not always work out like that. During Stephen's reign, John de Chesney vowed during an illness to found a Cistercian house 'on account of the many wrongs he committed, both in time of peace, when he governed the shire, and in time of war'. His condition worsened, however, and his brother and heir was required to fulfill his promise. Not altogether surprisingly, there was a delay of some four years before he did so.[46] The endowment had to be made from what was now the brother's property, and his own spiritual needs were not necessarily so urgent.

Surviving relations were generally distressed at being bequeathed a legacy of unfulfilled vows, convinced as they were that the perjured testators were enduring the fires of hell, but material circumstances influenced their response to the problem. In the mid twelfth century Margaret de Bohun laudably honoured the commitments of various dead kinsmen out of concern for their probable fate,[47] while expressing on her own behalf the hope *ut Deus warentizet me et heredes meos de inimicis et periculis et omnibus malis.*[48] Margaret was a widow who had experienced the death of several children[49] and was not preoccupied with the need to preserve a fief. When that concern was uppermost, even the most moving religious experiences were liable to be discounted. Early in Henry III's reign, the dying Roger de Tosny was

[43] See my *Beauchamp*, introduction.
[44] Westminster Abbey domesday (Muniment book 2), fol 292.
[45] *RR* 2, no 903.
[46] Sibton p 65.
[47] Hereford nos 91, 94–5.
[48] *Ibid* no 109.   [49] *Ibid* p 2.

assailed by ghastly visions of hell. He was given to understand that these also awaited his elder brother Ralf, and that the only way they could escape its terrors was for Ralf to found a house of some ascetic order, the inmates of which must be induced to pray fervidly on their behalf. The horror-stricken Ralf agreed,[50] and on mature deliberation —over several years—undertook to provide the Cistercian abbey of Cumhir with endowments to found a daughter house. However, the meagre lands which he eventually assigned proved quite inadequate for the purpose, and the disillusioned monks of Cumhir undertook to persuade their annual general chapter to absolve Ralf from his vow.[51]

Even the most violently anticlerical magnates made material reparation on their deathbeds, small though the gesture might be in comparison with the extent of the wrongs committed during a life-time of self-aggrandisement. William de Beauchamp requested in his will, drawn up early in 1269, the restitution of whatever he had seized unjustly. The vague wording may have owed something to the prompting of his confessor rather than to any consciousness of particular acts of appropriation, though, for William was precise enough in other clauses. The whole countryside had felt the weight of his power, and accordingly virtually every religious house in the region was to receive a flat-rate donation, by no means lavish. The only houses singled out for more generous offerings were the nunnery of Cookhill, where his wife was buried; the Franciscan friary in Worcester, where he hoped to be buried, and Worcester cathedral priory.[52] This house, more than others, had felt his wrath, and being the most prestigious community in the region, could doubtless make its voice heard where it mattered most.

Donations in less urgent circumstances were often made with an eye to the material wellbeing of the donor rather than to that of the recipient. Ecclesiastical sources of revenue formed a large proportion of the gifts of even wealthy families,[53] while minor landholders could only retain their status of benefactor at all by donating this type of income.[54] Lands were granted sparingly, and where a lucrative manor was bequeathed, it tended to be an outlying estate, the

[50] Matthew Paris, *Chronica Majora*, ed H. R. Luard (*RS* 1872–84), 3, pp 143–5.
[51] *Beauchamp* nos 382–3.
[52] [The] *Register of [Bishop] Godfrey Giffard*, [ed J. W. Willis Bund], 2, Worcs Hist Soc 15 (Oxford 1902) pp 7–8.
[53] Wightman pp 61–2.
[54] Southwick priory register 1, Hants Record Office, Winchester, MS HRO M54(1), fols 2, 22.

administration of which was proving difficult and expensive.[55] Marcher barons wishing to gain the merits due to a benefactor without diminishing their resources were prone to donate lands at the farthermost bounds of their territory, in remote valleys which would be the first to be overrun by the Welsh during their next rising, as with Tosny grants to Cumhir[56] and Lacy grants to Llanthony Prima.[57]

The initial outlay on a new foundation need not be large for a baronial family to establish its position as hereditary patrons. Tenants of the fee could usually be persuaded to make gifts of their own,[58] and subsequent confirmations both of these and of the grants of predecessors were represented as donations of the next generation.[59] Grants by the Mowbrays show that material returns were often expected. The establishment of a Cistercian house contributed to the enrichment of the countryside;[60] properties granted 'in pure alms' might actually be expected to render rent and perhaps forensic service,[61] and rights were occasionally reasserted in churches alienated to religious houses at an earlier date.[62] Robert earl of Gloucester similarly retained rights in land he confirmed to St Peter's Gloucester,[63] while barons of the meaner sort, in both senses of the word, were often known to retain the use of lands which they had supposedly given to religious houses—an abuse which the statute of Mortmain was designed to eradicate.[64]

Aspiring patrons were liable to donate property which was not theirs to give, as with a grant made to Kirkstall by Henry de Lacy of land rightfully belonging to the Bigod earl of Norfolk, but which the house subsequently regarded as a Lacy benefaction.[65] Even the grandest families habitually achieved the status of benefactor at little real cost, and by glossing over inconvenient facts. This led to considerable, and often genuine doubts by religious and laity alike as to what had

[55] Wightman p 60.
[56] *Beauchamp* nos 382–3, and see F. M. Powicke, *King Henry III and the Lord Edward* (Oxford 1947) pp 624, 628–9.
[57] Wightman pp 183–4.
[58] *Ibid* p 61.
[59] *Mowbray* p xli; [*The cartulary of*] *Darley* [*abbey*, ed R. R. Darlington], Derbs Archaeological Soc (1945) nos L4, N7.
[60] *Mowbray* p xlii.
[61] *Ibid* pp xl, xlii.
[62] *Ibid* p xliii.
[63] *Gloucester* no 83.
[64] *Select charters and other illustrations of English constitutional history*, ed W. Stubbs (9 ed Oxford 1966) p 450.
[65] Wightman pp 109–10.

actually been given, and on what terms.[66] It often happened in consequence that two houses believed themselves to be the possessors of the same property, and either or both might obtain metropolitan or legatine confirmations bestowed without full knowledge of the facts.[67]

Patrons did not always have a high opinion of the good faith of 'their' houses regarding the fulfilment of spiritual obligations towards them. Tortuous penalty clauses were imposed on the hospital of St John the Baptist at Lechlade when the executors of Isabel de Mortimer established a chantry for her there,[68] but these stringent terms were at least supervised by the diocesan bishop. William Marshall, donating land to Notley on the understanding that candles would be burned for the souls of his family, stipulated that the performance of this obligation would be judged 'by view of the sheriff and two worthy men of the parish'.[69] Not only the smaller houses found their activities open to suspicious inspection. The monks of Worcester were astounded when William de Beauchamp, earl of Warwick, accompanied by his brothers, invaded their house one night on hearing a rumour that the monks had exhumed the body of their father. They proceeded to break open his tomb, and only called a halt when they had identified his corpse by certain markings.[70]

The episode illustrates one facet of the ambivalent relationship between a religious house and a family to which it afforded burial. The Beauchamps had traditionally been buried in the cathedral priory,[71] yet the earl's father tried to break the pattern in 1269 by requesting burial by the Franciscans of Worcester.[72] The frustration of his wish was probably due to a family feeling that this was unworthy of the father of the first Beauchamp to become an earl, yet the earl himself was later buried in the Franciscan church. The monks plainly regarded this as a slight on the cathedral, and their chronicler wrote disparagingly of the inferior Franciscan burial ground, which was subject to flooding in winter; of the vulgar funeral procession, with the friars triumphantly bearing off the body like victors exulting over their booty, and concluded that the shocking breach of tradition was due

[66] *Worcester* xxxv.
[67] See my 'Tithe income' p 92, and my 'The Mauduits and their chamberlainship' pp 3, 7; Wightman pp 184, 207–8; *Darley*, nos H 5–6.
[68] *Beauchamp* no 78.
[69] Christ Church College, Oxford, charter xxvi.
[70] Worcester annals, *Annales Monastici*, ed H. R. Luard, 4 (*RS* 1869) p 471.
[71] *Ibid* pp 382, 528.
[72] *Register of Godfrey Giffard* 2, p 7.

to unethical pressure from the dying earl's Franciscan confessor.[73] The Beauchamps were probably more concerned to gain by association with the Franciscans than to thwart the Benedictines, but the chronicler would allow no hint that his church had been rejected by the head of the greatest family of the region. Clearly there was some status to be gained from sheltering its tombs, even though the bishop's register reveals that the earl and his father before him constantly encroached on the rights of bishop and monks alike.[74]

Where there was a continuous tradition regarding burials, a religious house could expect repeated material advantages, most obviously in the shape of burial dues, which comprised a large proportion of the deceased's possessions. Clearly the more affluent he had been in his lifetime, and the greater the volume of intercession required on his behalf, the more lucrative a proposition the burial would be.[75] On the other hand, the very fact that a house had afforded burial to a member of a rising family might dispose his more prosperous descendants towards unforseen acts of generosity, typified by Miles of Gloucester's patronage of Llanthony Secunda on the strength of Llanthony Prima's having housed his father's tomb.[76]

A monastic chapter's view of the neighbouring barons was largely conditioned by the attitude which they took towards its house.[77] When an abbey had occasion to feel neglected by certain of its patrons, the chapter might simply omit them from its list of those whom it commemorated.[78] It might, however, take matters further, conveying to posterity its own jaundiced view of the family in question. A monastery kept a chronicle primarily to enhance its reputation and to define its property and privileges. The narrative depicted the house struggling like a hero of contemporary romance against its enemies.[79]

---

[73] Worcester Annals, *Annales Monastici* 4, p 537. The chronicler emphasised the role of the Franciscan confessor, stating that none of the earl's kindred was at the deathbed.

[74] *Register of Godfrey Giffard* 2, p 75. The earl's father was associated with the Franciscans some years before his death (*Beauchamp* no 106), so that belief in their superior merits may well have been his overriding motive for attempting to break the traditional burial pattern.

[75] M. Brett, *The English Church under Henry I* (Oxford 1975) p 227. Greed to obtain burial dues might literally bring about the downfall of religious houses, as Harald Hardrada demonstrated, see Snorri Sturluson, *King Harald's Saga*, transl M. Magnusson and H. Palsson (Harmondsworth 1966) p 57.

[76] Wightman p 184.

[77] B. Meehan, 'Outsiders, insiders and property in Durham around 1100', *SCH* 12, pp 45–6.

[78] Wightman p 111.

[79] Antonia Gransden, *Historical Writing in England c. 550 to c. 1307* (London 1974) pp 269–70, 272.

EMMA MASON

If a local baron proved miserly, or if his actions threatened the interests of the house, he would inevitably feature as the villain of the piece, a menace not only to the house but also to the whole region. Posterity would receive a tendentious account of his political actions and a travesty of his attitude towards things spiritual.

The attitude of patrons towards their houses was undoubtedly ambivalent. They benefitted materially, as well as spiritually, from their relationship with 'their' religious houses, and in their pursuit of things temporal seem often to have lost sight of things eternal. The moral defects were by no means all on one side, though. Religious houses were certainly partners in this scheme of things, conniving both at the keeping of crude spiritual balance sheets, to their own material advantage, and at the maintenance of factions in regional power struggles. They knew very well, if only from the lawsuits in which they were so often implicated, that they were frequently enriched by property to which their self-styled benefactors had no title. Their gains often accrued to them as an indirect result of violence or fraud from which they would recoil in horror if it had been directed against themselves. Their patrons damaged their own spiritual prospects in winning the lands which enriched the monasteries, while the monks did not always maintain for long the spiritual obligations which they owed in return. A shrewd eye for change led a house to determine the moment when former benefactors might be demoted to make way for a more useful patron, and what price the former donor's spiritual account then? The attitude often displayed towards impoverished patrons implied, in effect, that salvation was something to be bought on an instalment plan, and if the payments stopped, so did the benefits. Religious communities, on the other hand, doubtless considered that their overriding obligation was to the maintenance and enlargement of their endowment, held in trust for their patron saint. In pursuit of this they were quite prepared to use spiritual weapons against those who wavered even momentarily in their material commitments towards them.[80]

The ambivalence in the relationship between a monastic chapter and its patron was akin to the unspoken state of tension often existing among members of a family. Chapters were recruited from the kindred of neighbouring landholders, but were largely unsympathetic towards their dynastic aspirations. A tacit element in this underlying hostility

[80] Wightman p 78.

74

was, perhaps, the resentment of landless younger sons towards big brother, rationalised in the form of a struggle to uphold the rights of the religious community into which they had been adopted. A chapter might justify its uncompromising stance on the grounds that patrons were self-seeking, unpredictable and often violent. Monks therefore had good reason to fear the barons even when bringing gifts. The barons might argue, however, that they had equally good cause to be wary of their protégés.

University of London
Birkbeck College

RELIGIOUS AND SECULAR MOTIVES FOR SOME ENGLISH MONASTIC FOUNDATIONS

by RICHARD MORTIMER

ANC autem donationem feci eis pro salute memorati domini mei illustris Regis Henrici et pro salute anime mee et Berthe uxoris mee, et omnium antecessorum et successorum nostrorum.[1] Thus briefly Rannulf de Glanville explains his foundation of Leiston abbey, and we have no reason to doubt his word. This motive is completely conventional and occurs in virtually every contemporary monastic foundation charter, which underlines its validity rather than detracting from it. Perhaps there is no need to look further; but Glanville's is not the only voice to be heard on the foundation of Leiston abbey, and the founder does not answer all the questions we should like to ask. Did he perhaps have other motives? How did he go about choosing a religious order? To these questions we have to find our own answers. We can arrange facts in a suggestive series, and then ascribe more or less simple intentions which explain them. The shortcomings of such a method are obvious, though the results can be plausible and are often the only ones available. The unreliability of the answer is our penance for the temerity of the question.

Rannulf de Glanville is best known as Henry II's justiciar in the 1180s and possible author of the treatise which bears his name. In the early 1170s he founded a house of Augustinian canons at Butley, near Ipswich; this was large and wealthy by East Anglian standards, but relatively few early documents survive from it.[2] Some ten years later, during his period as justiciar, he founded a rather smaller house at Leiston in the same part of Suffolk for canons of the Premonstratensian order, from which we have rather more evidence.[3] At an unknown date he also founded a small hospital at West Somerton near Yarmouth, later under the control of Butley priory.[4] Gerald of Wales, in the

---

[1] Leiston Cartulary (BL MS Cotton Vespasian E xiv) fols 35ʳ/ᵛ. See R. C. Mortimer, 'An edition of the Cartulary of Leiston Abbey', PhD thesis London 1977.
[2] *MA* 6 pt 1 pp 380–1; A. J. Ellis and F. Bickley, *Index to the Charters and Rolls in the British Museum* (London 1900) 2 pp 106–7.
[3] Leiston Cartulary.
[4] *MA* 6 pt 2 p 769; BL Harley Roll N 20.

77

Speculum Ecclesiae, refers to the two main houses, claiming to present us with the founder's thoughts as well as his actions.

Miles quidam nobilis Radulphus, cognato vero de Glanvilla, qui senescallus Angliae summusque justiciarius aliquandiu fuit, firmumque propositum habuit, sicut ipsemet coram familiaribus suis saepe referre consuevit, construendi duas abbatias in terris suis; cumque diutius, tanquam vir prudens et sapiens, de qua religione vel quibus religionibus illas facere vellet secum deliberasset, monachos Cluniacenses ad mentem revocans, illos tanquam ventri prout videbatur nimis addictos, penes se re[c]usabat, respiciens autem ad Cistercienses ipsos, tanquam nimis cupidos et ambitiosos, refutabat. Dicebat enim quia nullius ordinis viros totiens coram ipso in foro publico pro tribunali sedente, super cartis falsis et sigillis adulterinis, super terminis terrarum metisque finalibus dolose transpositis, multisque cupiditatibus aliis valde detestandis, convictos invenit. Ideoque quasi per singula currens, tandem ordinem Canonicum tanquam caeteris juxta suum arbitrium modestiorem, longeque minus seu gulae sive cupidini datum, elegit; duasque domos Canonicas fecit, unam in terra conquestus sui de Canonicis nigris, scilicet triginta vi., altera vero in patrimonio suo de Canonicis albis xxvj., et ecclesias ipsorum, domos, et officinas omnes, sumptibus propriis egregie construxit; et abbatias ambas redditibus amplis, tam in ecclesiis quam in terris, abunde dotavit et ditavit.

Ad domorum quoque suarum honestatem et spiritualem utilitatem prudenter adjecit, ut nunquam terras amplius ullas aut reditus sibi perquirerent, aut quocunque commercio compararent, sed tantum gratis oblata et caritative collata susciperent; ne, propter res scilicet augmentandas pecuniam congererent, et ad hoc reponerent, ut terras aut reditus ubi locum viderent emere possent; et ob hoc hospitalitatem et caritatem, propter quam praecipue post obsequia divina constitutae fuerunt, minuere praesumerent . . . et tam diocesani episcopi quam etiam archiepiscopi confirmationes, super his adquirere curavit.

Mira viri prudentis atque discreti providentia; processu namque temporis accidit, ut propter cupiditatem et ambitionem sic extinctam, caritatemque et hospitalitatem plenius adauctam, spontaneis fidelium largitionibus, ambae domus illae, tam in terris quam in ecclesiis, ultra spem omnem augmentatae fuerint et ditatae.[5]

[5] *Giraldi Cambrensis Opera*, RS 21, 4 (1873) pp 244–5.

Motives for monastic foundations

Under the skilled hand of Gerald of Wales the justiciar's opinions emerge looking suspiciously like Gerald's own. How far is his story borne out by other sources? He is demonstrably wrong in only one particular: Leiston was not founded on inherited land, but on a manor given to Rannulf in 1173 out of the escheated honour of Eye[6] There are doubts about some other assertions—on the later occasions for which we have information Leiston had 11, 14 and 15 canons, not 26,[7] and subsequent donations hardly enriched it *ultra spem omnem*. He is at least right that Glanville founded two houses of canons, one white and one black, though it is hardly likely that the foundations were mooted simultaneously, as Gerald implies. He is quite right about the care taken to obtain confirmations, as is evident from the number in the cartulary, royal as well as ecclesiastical.[8] But it is Glanville's alleged disapproval of the canons amassing money to buy lands and rent which is most interestingly confirmed in the abbey's deeds. In a charter of Henry II dating between December 1184 and May 1185,[9] the king confirms the promise made by the canons to Rannulf *quando eos ibidem fundavit* that they shall buy no land, and shall receive none in pledge or at farm, unless conferred without recompense and in free alms; and that they shall not take away any part of any tenement of the men of the vill, but shall let them hold their lands for the services due. This clause recurs in Glanville's later foundation charter, in Richard I's confirmation, and in some archiepiscopal documents.[10]

So where Gerald's facts can be checked, many, including the most interesting, are abundantly borne out. The archdeacon is not, however, the only source for the foundation of Leiston abbey. We are fortunate in having a detailed account of the foundation by one who took part in it. This was given as evidence in a lawsuit between Welbeck and Durford abbeys in the second or third decade of the thirteenth century, and was copied into the Welbeck cartulary.[11] From this it appears that the justiciar turned first to the abbot of Welbeck; they discussed the appointment of an abbot for the proposed foundation and agreed on Robert, abbot of Durford, whom Rannulf knew and liked. Canons

[6] Leiston Cartulary fols 33v–4r; Pipe Roll 19 Henry II, P[ipe] R[oll] S[ociety] (London 1895) p 132—£10 allowed on honour of Eye account: the full yearly allowance was £20, Pipe Roll 21 Henry II, PRS (1897) p 126.
[7] [H. M.] Colvin, [*The White Canons in England*] (Oxford 1951) p 358. My indebtedness to this work will become clear.
[8] Leiston Cartulary fols 1r–9r, 29r–32v, 39r, 40v–1r.
[9] *Ibid* fols 31r–2v.
[10] *Ibid* fols 34r, 11v, 17v–18r. In some cases it has been erased and rewritten.
[11] Colvin pp 345–8.

79

were taken from both houses, as the founder desired that no tribute (*corporalem exactionem*) should be levied by any superior foundation by virtue of paternity within the order. Glanville wanted to make Leiston the greatest house of its order in England, because it was of his gift and the king's. We are shown the way in which Glanville went about founding his second religious house, and his desire that it should be an impressive institution, not occupying the subordinate position usual for a house colonised from other establishments of an order, though in the latter respect his wishes were not fulfilled.

Why Welbeck? The justiciar must have met many members of religious orders through his legal duties and attendance at court. He could have come to know the abbot of Welbeck in any number of ways, at any time. One possible point of contact is through his brother Gerald, who had married the heiress of the founder of Welbeck, and who granted charters to that abbey.[12] This is the closest connection between Rannulf de Glanville and Welbeck of which we are aware. How, then, did the justiciar come to know the abbot of the poor and rather remote Sussex house of Durford? This too could have happened at any time, possibly when Glanville witnessed a royal charter to Durford which Eyton attributes to 1181.[13] However this chain of personal contacts was made, we know it existed, and it cannot have been the only one linking the justiciar to the religious life of his time. He was in a position to make the kind of judgement of which Gerald tells us: Gerald may be exaggerating, or even inventing, Glanville's attitude to the Benedictines and Cistercians to suit his own purpose, but the justiciar's actions speak louder than the archdeacon's words. We can see what Glanville disliked: aggressive monastic landlordism—putting up rents, saving money to expand holdings; and he thought it advisable to exact a promise from the canons at their foundation to eschew such behaviour, going so far as to write it into his foundation charter, and into the confirmations as well. This is as close as we can come to Glanville's personal preferences. Henceforward we are dependent on inferences from patterns of fact.

Glanville's first foundation, Butley, was an Augustinian house, and here he was following in the footsteps of many an earlier curial official.[14]

---

[12] *EYC* 3 pp 318, 326; BL MS Harley 3640 fol 41ʳ; I. H. Jeayes, *A Descriptive Catalogue of Derbyshire Charters* (Derby 1906) no 1079.

[13] BL MS Cotton Vespasian E xxiii fols 5ʳ/ᵛ; R. W. Eyton, *Court, Household and Itinerary of King Henry II* (London 1878) pp 245–6.

[14] J. C. Dickinson, *The Origin of the Austin Canons and their Introduction into England* (London 1950) pp 126–30.

When some ten years later he founded another house he chose the Premonstratensians. This order of canons had recently been patronised by Robert Mantel and Robert fitz Rannulf, both sheriffs,[15] as well as by Gerard de Glanville's father-in-law Thomas of Cuckney. Family connections are involved here too, for Thomas's other daughter Isabel married a nephew of Agnes of Orby, foundress of the Premonstratensian house of Hagnaby, and Agnes's son John married a niece of Robert fitz Rannulf, founder of Beauchief.[16] Both Hagnaby and Beauchief were dedicated to St Thomas Becket, and both were colonised from Welbeck. John of Orby witnessed one of the foundation documents of Beauchief, and Agnes appears to have been related to the Cuckney family before founding Hagnaby.[17] The Premonstratensian order was thus expanding along family lines before the foundation of Leiston.

The sudden burgeoning of Premonstratensian houses founded by Rannulf de Glanville's relatives was noticed a century ago by Stubbs.[18] Four houses were begun by about 1190: Swainby (later moved to Coverham) by the justiciar's daughter Helewise, West Dereham by his nephew Hubert Walter then dean of York, West Langdon by his son-in-law William d'Auberville, and Cockersand was refounded by another nephew, Hubert's brother Theobald Walter. Family influence is clearly at work here, an impression confirmed by the charters. Henry II's charter to Coverham is witnessed by Rannulf de Glanville and Theobald Walter, and Helewise's purchase of land for her abbey by her father and her cousin Hubert.[19] The formal foundation charter of West Dereham is witnessed by a large family group including the founder's cousin Theobald de Valeines, as well as his uncle Rannulf de Glanville and his brother Theobald.[20] Glanville and his wife Bertha are included among the spiritual beneficiaries in the foundation charter of West Langdon, which is witnessed by Hubert Walter and a number of other relatives.[21] This house was colonised from Leiston. At Cockersand the spiritual beneficiaries included Rannulf de Glanville and the founder's brother and parents.[22]

[15] Colvin pp 101–4.
[16] *Ibid* pp 106–7.
[17] *Ibid* pp 107–8, 343 no 8.
[18] *Chronica Magistri Rogeri de Hovedene*, RS 51 (1868–71) 4 p lxiii n.
[19] *EYC* 5 nos 359, 335.
[20] Colvin pp 348–9.
[21] *Ibid* pp 349–50.
[22] W. Farrer, *The Chartulary of Cockersand Abbey*, Chetham Society (Manchester 1898) 2 pt 1, frontispiece; compare *MA* 6 pt 2 p 906 no 1.

This group provides the most obvious example of family connection between patrons. The Premonstratensian houses that followed exemplify the connection, clearly reinforced in the 1180s, between the order and prominent members of the royal administration. Thus Langley abbey, in Norfolk, was founded by Robert fitz Roger, sheriff of Norfolk and Suffolk, and Torre in Devon by William Briwerre, that 'pillar of the Angevin monarchy in England'.[23] Richard Malebisse, though never a sheriff, was amongst other things an itinerant justice and keeper of the royal forests in Yorkshire in the reign of John;[24] after an unsuccessful attempt to transfer Croxton and appropriate the credit, he founded Newbo abbey in the late 1190s. The Derbyshire house of Dale, begun in religious enthusiasm earlier in the twelfth century, was put on a more business-like footing by William fitz Ralph, sheriff of Nottingham and Derby and seneschal of Normandy.[25] The two main foundations of the thirteenth century, Halesowen and Titchfield, owed their existence to a yet greater figure, Peter des Roches, bishop of Winchester. Finally even the humble William of Wendling, founder of the last English house in his (presumably) native Norfolk village, was an escheator and judge.[26]

The place of the canonical orders should not be exaggerated when considering the monastic patronage of the men who ran Angevin England. Of Premonstratensian founders Peter des Roches showed an interest in the Dominicans, and Theobald Walter and William Briwerre also founded Cistercian houses.[27] Hubert Walter was on the point of converting the college of Wolverhampton into a Cistercian house when he died.[28] Nor were those who made their name as royal servants necessarily devoted to the Premonstratensians: for example Geoffrey fitz Peter, earl of Essex and sometime justiciar, founded a Gilbertine house, Shouldham in Norfolk, but no Premonstratensian one. Nevertheless nearly all the houses founded by Glanville and his relatives and colleagues were either Augustinian or Premonstratensian. Why should their patronage have inclined towards houses of this type?

---

[23] Colvin pp 150–3.

[24] *Ibid* p 165; D. M. Stenton, *The Earliest Lincolnshire Assize Rolls*, Lincoln Record Society (1926) pp xxiv–xxv.

[25] A. Saltman, *The Cartulary of Dale Abbey* (HMSO London 1967) p 4.

[26] Colvin pp 178–89, 191–3.

[27] W. A. Hinnebusch, *The Early English Friars Preachers* (Rome 1951) p 107; Briwerre founded Dunkeswell, Devon (Colvin p 153 n 4), and Theobald Walter Arklow (*MRHI* p 126).

[28] C. R. Cheney, *Hubert Walter* (London 1967) p 154 n 4.

One possibility is that the relatively small size of Premonstratensian and Augustinian houses reduced the cost of a foundation, and the comparatively low endowment necessary per canon ensured that the investment would be, as it were, cost-effective. But we have seen that Glanville did not choose poverty and obscurity for his houses—Butley was the second richest house in Suffolk in the sixteenth century. This may have been a motive with more modest patrons, but not with the justiciar. The theory fits the Augustinians, who seem to have no minimum number of canons, better than the Premonstratensians who required at least thirteen for a new foundation.[29] Cost-effectiveness is harder to assess, as we can rarely be sure of the actual numbers in canonical houses in the twelfth century, and whether the number represents the founder's intention.

It has also been pointed out that the arrival of the Premonstratensians and their expansion coincide roughly with the Cistercian decree of 1152 forbidding further foundations. The coincidence is striking enough, but this transference of patronage may not have been forced; we cannot simply assume that the Premonstratensians' patrons would have founded Cistercian houses instead if they had been allowed to do so—in fact two Premonstratensian patrons managed to found Cistercian houses as well, despite the ban.

Another suggestion is that the canons' claim to live the apostolic life was received more favourably than others' in this period, and that orders of monastic priests were the most appropriate ministers for the parish churches which laymen could no longer feel easy in holding. Whether or not parish churches were served by the canons themselves in the twelfth century, we may well suppose that religious houses were regarded as the most appropriate recipients of revenues from parish churches, though the canonical orders were by no means the only, or even the best endowed, beneficiaries, and some houses had no churches at all. But it is not easy to see exactly what was different about the Premonstratensian version of the apostolic life as practised in late twelfth-century England. Whatever its beginnings, the Premonstratensian order by this time was an enclosed, monastic one. There is no sign that it differed in its ideas from its contemporaries; any distinction was one of degree rather than kind. The early Premonstratensians on the continent seem to have had a reputation

---

[29] Pl. F. Lefevre, *Les Statuts de Prémontré* (Louvain 1946) pp 91–3. *De construendis abbatiis* is part of the earliest legislation.

for austerity,[30] but there is very little evidence that the English houses made such an impression.

The reasons of patrons for choosing the Augustinians will be hard to generalise about, since their foundations are so varied and numerous. The Premonstratensians are an easier subject, because smaller and more closely knit. While there may be some truth in all the above possibilities, none of them takes account of the pattern of patronage we have seen developing. These men were administrators; 'it was only the latest recruit to the ranks of the feudal baronage who needed to build an abbey on his newly acquired estates':[31] they were making their fortune by the old and tried method of royal service, and founding a monastery was an act characteristic of the group to which they aspired. In this way the decision to found resulted from their view of their social position. It was an announcement, and a public act of conformity.

When the originating impulse lay with a secular founder he needed the resources of an existing institution to carry out his intention. In a world without friars, and which the Carthusians were penetrating only with difficulty, the founder was presented with a choice between Cistercians, Benedictines and the orders of canons, just as in Gerald's story. His choice took place against a background of personal contacts which we can barely glimpse, though we can see their consequences: canons are transferred from Nottinghamshire to Suffolk; the abbot of Durford becomes the first abbot of Leiston. Many such personal contacts would also be family ones. Many of these founders are related by blood and marriage, and united in the means they have chosen to make their way in the world. Glanville's action sets the pattern for his relatives and dependants.

As far as we can see, what its founder wanted from Leiston was a house whose size and good behaviour would do him credit. He gave it a firm basis of prosperity; he did his best to secure its independance; he tried to legislate against degrading temporal ambitions in the only way open to him, in his formal charter. Gerald adds the practice of hospitality and charity, and we may well believe these to have mattered to a man of affairs who also founded a hospital. The wish that his canons should renounce their economic advantages is compatible with the desire to found a prosperous house. Undeniably religious motives

[30] Colvin pp 30–1. The evidence cited is rather scanty.
[31] *Ibid* p 38.

are complicated by more secular ones: the practice of virtue at the behest and at the expense of a layman would confer eternal credit on him in this world as well as the next.

University of London
Institute of Historical Research

EQUESTRIS ORDO:
CHIVALRY AS A VOCATION IN
THE TWELFTH CENTURY

by COLIN MORRIS

THE motives of individuals are necessarily conditioned by the expectations of society. Some walks of life are recognised as demanding a high degree of self-sacrifice and noble motivation, as being (in modern terms) vocations. Others are careers worthy of esteem, and yet others are condemned, so that it is supposed that no ethically minded person would engage in them. As the social structure changes there is an adaptation in the pattern of esteem, and an interesting example of this process is provided by the new thinking about knighthood which emerged in the late eleventh and early twelfth centuries. So much has been written about chivalry that a broad review of the subject is out of the question in this paper, but it may be of interest to re-examine it in the light of this theme. An appropriate starting-point is provided by a passage from the history of the first crusade written about 1110 by Guibert of Nogent:

> In our time God has instituted holy warfare so that the knightly order (*ordo equestris*) and the unsettled populace, who used to be engaged like the pagans of old in slaughtering one another, should find a new way of deserving salvation. No longer are they obliged to leave the world and choose a monastic way of life, as used to be the case, or some religious profession, but in their accustomed liberty and habit, by performing their own office, they may in some measure achieve the grace of God.[1]

Guibert's view is startling because he clearly thinks that the preaching of the crusade has brought about, not just a change in human awareness, but a new dispensation: the order of knights once could only hope for redemption by abandoning chivalry and joining the monastic order, but they now may be saved by practising their profession of arms. It is interesting to notice that Guibert regarded knighthood as an 'order', and there is other evidence that at this time it was coming to be so categorised. In 1098 the young Louis, later Louis VI of France, was

---

[1] Guibert of Nogent, *Gesta Dei per Francos* i, *RHC Occ* 4 p 124.

'ordained' a knight, and there is a vernacular parallel in the concept of a *law* of knighthood which is found in the *Song of Roland*: *Adobez sunt a lei de chevalers.*[2]

Recent studies have shown that, to the men of this period, an *ordo* was a reasonably clear conception. It was a way of life blessed by God, within which a virtuous man might tread the path of salvation. The orders provided a structure without which the world would dissolve into licence and chaos. The concept was vividly expressed by Bernard of Clairvaux in an attack on those who did not live according to their order. He based his argument upon saint Paul's prophecy that men shall rise from the dead each in his own order (1 Cor xv. 23):

> When men begin to arise from the dead, each in his own order, where do you think this company will be? If they try to turn to the knights, they will throw them out because they have not shared in their trials or dangers. Similarly with the peasants and with the merchants, so that all the orders of men in turn will drive them away from their borders because they had not taken part in their work. So what remains to be said—except that people whom every order both rejects and condemns will be put in that place where there is no order, but eternal chaos.[3]

The significance of the *ordo* was expressed just as clearly by Gerhoh of Reichersberg:

> For every order, and absolutely every profession in the catholic faith and apostolic doctrine has a rule suited to its quality, and by fighting lawfully under this it will be able to attain to the crown.[4]

The interest of contemporary writers in defining knighthood as an order within which God could be rightly served was related to social changes which were particularly apparent in eleventh-century France. The development of the equipment and skills of the heavily armed horsemen made them a *corps d'élite* on the battlefield and created an

---

[2] Letter of count Guy of Ponthieu to bishop Lambert of Arras, *Recueil des Historiens . . . de la France*, ed M. J. J. Brial, 15 (Paris 1808) p 187: *debeo Ludovicum Regis filium armis militaribus adornare et honorare, et ad militiam promovere et ordinare.* The reference in the *Song of Roland* is specifically to the weapons proper to knights, and not to any wider 'law of chivalry': [J. Bédier, *La Chanson de*] *Roland* (Paris 1937) line 1143.

[3] Geoffrey, *Declamationes ex S. Bernardi sermonibus* 10, PL 184 (1879) col 444 A. Important contributions to our understanding of *ordo* have been made in a number of studies, written from different starting-points, by Y. Congar, M. D. Chenu and M. Mollat.

[4] Gerhoh of Reichersberg, *Liber de aedificio Dei* 43, PL 194 (1855) col 1302 D. Gerhoh makes it clear that he is not referring only to monks, but to all the baptised, *sive divites sive miseri, nobiles ac servi, mercatores et rustici et omnino cuncti, qui Christiana professione censentur . . .*

intense pride in the prowess of the *chevalier*. At the same time a significant shift was taking place in the pattern of landownership. Georges Duby has shown how in the vicinity of Cluny the great estates of Carolingian days had been divided among some forty or more families, who were mostly descended from their Carolingian predecessors. Such families retained a close connection with their lord's household and usually had duties such as castleguard which kept the link very much alive, but in terms of property they had ceased to be household retainers and now formed a lesser aristocracy, free of the seigneurial *haute justice* which bound the population as a whole. It should be noticed that in Germany the equivalent development did not take place until after 1150. In spite of the importance of this social change it would be naïve to conclude that in France the eleventh century saw the emergence of a new knightly class which had to be provided with ethical standards corresponding to its new influence. Things were in fact more complicated than that. The wor ds *milites* and *chevaliers* were applied to a great range of social levels. The highest aristocracy, and indeed the royal families, prided themselves on being *chevaliers*; and the term in addition could describe the new group of substantial landowners and the many landless, violent men who lived by their weapons and who enjoyed no sort of social esteem. Chivalric literature as it remains to us from the twelfth century was, not surprisingly, sponsored and paid for by the great aristocracy, and we do not know how far it was valued by those knights who supported themselves on their moderate holdings. We are dealing, not only or not primarily with the emergence of a new social class, but with a new style of fighting and above all of changing sensitivities.

The definition of knighthood as an order was part of a conscious attempt to win the military classes for Christ, and it was directed against two other ways of thinking about chivalry. On the one hand it represented an abandonment of the insistence that in order to be saved a knight must become a monk. This old negation of worldly occupation was still very much alive at Cluny under abbot Hugh (1049–1109)[5] and is expressed in the donation by Geoffrey III of Sémur to the Cluniac house of Marcigny in 1088:

> I, Geoffrey of Sémur, have heard the Lord say in the gospel, 'unless a man renounce all that he possesses, he cannot be my disciple' (Lk. xiv. 33), and recognise the enormity and the

---

[5] See [H. E. J.] Cowdrey, [*The Cluniacs and the Gregorian Reform*] (Oxford 1970) part 3.

profound abyss of my sins. I have chosen rather to be lowly in the house of God than to dwell in the tents of the wicked, and having taken off the belt of worldly service (*militiae saecularis*) in which I had gravely offended God, to submit myself . . . to the service of God, whose service is perfect freedom.[6]

While affirming the value of true chivalry in God's sight, the new way of thinking also opposed the secular values which were being expressed among the knights. It is scarcely surprising that their thinking was marked by display and arrogance. William of Poitiers linked chivalry and pride, *cavalaria et orgueill*, among the things which he was about to renounce.[7] The warriors had their own standards and way of life, and the poems of the troubadours express a delight in sexuality and, at other times, a love of violence, which were in clear contrast with the accepted Christian ethic. The two professions, knight and clerk, were often contemptuous of each other. Their rivalry was expressed in the discussions whether a clerk or a knight made the better lover, and one suspects that this was a joke which could at times be all too serious. Some people were torn between the two ethics. Guibert of Nogent remembered the time when as a boy he had been drawn to knightly pursuits:

> And I, enjoying a most harmful liberty, began to misuse my power, to ridicule churches, to hate study, to love the company of my young lay cousins devoted to knightly activities, and profaning the sign of the clerical office to announce remission of sins and to indulge in sleep.[8]

Guibert told the story of how archbishop Manasses of Rheims, a great lover of knights, had remarked that the archbishopric would have been a good thing, if only one did not have to keep singing mass.[9] In the late eleventh century there was thus an intensely secular chivalric ethos, hostile to the clergy, and the literature of the twelfth century makes it clear that the conflict of ethics continued, with knights following their professional inclination to make love or war, and to glorify these in song.

The advocates of Christian knighthood were conscious that they were attempting an innovation. We have already seen how Guibert thought that a Christian *equestris ordo* was a wholly new thing, a recent

---

[6] Ed J. Richard, *Le Cartulaire de Marcigny-sur-Loire* (Dijon 1957) no 15, pp 15–17, cited Cowdrey p 140.
[7] Ed A. Jeanroy, *Les Chansons de Guillaume IX* (Paris 1913) no 11 p 28.
[8] Guibert of Nogent, *De vita sua* I. 15, ed G. Bourgin (Paris 1904) p 52.
[9] *Ibid* I. 11, p 31.

Chivalry as a vocation tn the twelfth century

invention of God's. When Bernard of Clairvaux addressed his pen to a similar theme he did so under the title, *In Praise of the New Militia*. The development during the century of military orders, those monk-warriors devoted to the holy war in Palestine and Spain, was a striking innovation, and Bernard's specific purpose was to encourage recruiting for the Templars; but in reality his thought applied more widely, to all knights who truly wished to serve their Lord.[10] A powerful point of propaganda was the insistence that a true knight was necessarily one who was faithful to the teaching of the church; an exploiter of the church and the poor was not a *bad* knight, but had ceased to be a knight at all. This emphasis appeared early in the argument. It is neatly summed up in the slogan *non militia sed malitia*.[11] Urban II is said to have offered to his hearers in 1095 the promise: 'now they may *become* knights who hitherto existed as robbers'.[12] A similar idea lies under the famous line of the *Song of Roland*: '*Fust chrestiens, asez oüst barnet*'.[13] Against the forces of *malitia* the church assembled its formidable yowers of teaching and propaganda, including the visual arts. To take only one of many possible examples, there is at St Benoît-sur-Loire a capital in the transept which re-interprets one of the miracles of St Benedict and shows the saint releasing a peasant from the unjust knight who had captured him.

To true knights, conversely, preachers were eager to make available whatever support they could. Sermons *ad milites* were probably standard practice in the twelfth century. Sometimes the advice shows real perception of the problems which faced a knight in his attempts to be a faithful Christian, as in a remark by the outstanding recluse Stephen of Muret or Grandmont:

> It shows admirable knowledge, and is very pleasing to God, when a man who is involved in an evil enterprise restrains himself from evil. It can be done like this. If a knight is setting out on an expedition for the sake of his secular lord, to whom he cannot refuse obedience, if he wishes to be faithful to God, let him first speak thus in his heart: 'Lord God, I will go on this expedition, but I

[10] There was also however a contrary line of argument. William of St Thierry described St Bernard's father as *vir antiquae et legitimae militiae, cultor Dei, justitiae tenax*, PL 185 (1879) col 227 A.
[11] Anselm ep 86 to contess Adela: *vult dimittere militiam, immo malitiam, quam hactenus . . . exercuit*, ed F. S. Schmitt, *S. Anselmi . . . Opera Omnia*, 3 (Edinburgh 1946) p 211.
[12] Fulcher of Chartres, *Historia Iherosolymitana*, RHC Occ 3 p 324. Some mss read *nunc fiant Christi milites, qui dudum exstiterunt raptores*, but others omit the word *Christi*.
[13] *Roland* line 899.

91

promise that I will be your knight there, wanting nothing in it except to be obedient to you, to eliminate evil and to seek after what is good on every occasion as much as I can'.[14]

Stephen gives some details about how such a man should behave and concludes: 'thus he can be a monk who wears a shield upon his neck'. Serious attempts were made to present to the knights their Christian duties in ways they could readily understand. One of these is perhaps a little unexpected. By the middle of the twelfth century a considerable part of the upper classes had become anxious to achieve a tone of elegance in their way of life, and there was a distinct tendency to present Christianity in terms of good manners. In Chrétien de Troyes (a writer well trained in the schools and concerned about ethical questions) we find many pieces of advice about how to behave nicely as well as how to do one's duty as a knight. This was not an eccentricity of Chrétien, for John of Salisbury thought that courtesy is next to godliness: 'there is nothing more civilised than to follow virtue seriously'.[15] That this was on the right wave-length for at least some of the military class is suggested by a story from the latter twelfth century of a group of knights who invaded a lecture by Alan of Lille at Montpellier, and demanded to know what constituted the highest courtesy, *maxima curialitas*. He replied that it consisted of liberality and beneficence, and proceeded to improve on the occasion by adding that *summa rusticitas* was continually to steal and pillage. 'The knights of our time, who do not cease to take from the poor what is theirs, are the greatest boors of all'.[16] Perhaps we need not wonder too much at this equation of virtue and good manners, for it lies close to another theme of the age: that true nobility is to be found in character and not in accident of birth.

The message which spoke most clearly to the hearts of the military class was however the summons to the holy war. Guibert of Nogent thought that it was the preaching of the first crusade which constituted the new dispensation for the knights, and crusading remained close to the centre of the chivalric ideal. To explore its meaning for the *equestris ordo* would take us through the whole field of crusading ideology, and all that is necessary here is to notice how the preaching of the holy war was expressed in terms which would readily appeal to knights. It is

[14] Stephen of Grandmont, *Liber de Doctrina* lxiii. 1, ed J. Becquet, *Scriptores Ordinis Grandimontensis*, CC (1968) p 33.

[15] John of Salisbury, *Policraticus* viii. 9, ed C. C. J. Webb 2 (Oxford 1909) p 280.

[16] M. Th. d'Alverny, *Alain de Lille. Textes inédits* (Paris 1965) pp 16–17, n 30.

particularly evident in vernacular poems of the twelfth century that knights are being summoned to the service of Christ in language familiar in their ordinary affairs. A recruiting-song for the second crusade presented the holy war as a tournament appointed by God:

Deus ad un turnei empris	God has a tournament decreed
Entre Enfern e Pareis,	Between the power of heaven and hell,
Si mande trestuz ses amis	And says to those who serve him well
Ki lui volent guarantir	And who to his assistance speed,
Qu'il ne li seient failliz.[17]	He will uphold them in their need.

The theme of revenge loomed large in this propaganda. *The Chanson d'Antioche* began with a description of the crucifixion in which, in response to the sympathetic words of the penitent thief, Christ made this remarkable prophecy:

My friend! said he, that people is not born
That shall avenge me with their sharpened swords.
The Franks shall then deliver all the land,
And they that share in that great pilgrimage,
Their souls shall enter to our paradise.[18]

Passages such as this suggest to the modern reader that the demands of Christian ethics were being debased to a level where they had become nothing more than military virtues, or even military vices. Undoubtedly this is part of the truth. When the church attempts to speak in contemporary terms it may discover that it has adopted contemporary standards. The underlying intention, however, was a much larger one: the summons to the knights to put their swords at the Lord's disposal was part of a wider attempt to Christianise society as a whole, and to recognise the value of activities which would once have been regarded as wholly secular. It was associated with attempts to prescribe an ethic for peasants, for merchants and for government officials. No longer was the possession of an order and a rule the peculiar privilege of monks, for as Gerhoh observed every baptised Christian had his rule and his order. The laity had a part in the service of God and even in the protection and reform of the church.[19]

The ideal of a Christian society had two models. One rested upon

---

[17] J. Bédier, *Les Chansons de Croisade* (Paris 1909) no 1.

[18] Ed Paulin Paris, *La Chanson d'Antioche* (Paris 1848) I. pp 10 and 12.

[19] The more radical followers of Gregory VII readily appealed to the laity in order to break the power of the simoniac clergy, and already in the ten-fifties at Milan Ariald was expounding some important views about the lay order. See G. Miccoli, 'Per la storia della pateria milanese', *Chiesa Gregoriana. Ricerche sulla Riforma del secolo XI* (Florence 1966) pp 101–68.

the application to mankind as a whole of the Pauline doctrine of
'varieties of gifts', which was understood in a hierarchical sense. The
structure of human society consisted in the mutual obedience and
command of a series of orders appointed by God. This idea was
certainly not new, but it was a concept on which Gregory VII laid
much stress:

> The dispensation of divine providence ordained that there should
> be different grades and diverse orders, so that when the lesser
> show reverence for the greater and the greater bestow love on the
> lesser, then a single concord may be made out of diversity . . .
> For the whole could not subsist without the support of the great
> order of this diversity.[20]

This striving for right order throughout the world issued in the
attempt to enlist the aristocracy in the service and protection of the
Roman church as *fideles* or *milites sancti Petri*.[21] The concept was
primarily applied to the situation in Germany and Italy, where the
distinctive techniques and ideas of knighthood had not developed as
far as in France, but when it was applied within French society (as it
was most notably in the preaching of the first crusade) it naturally
helped the growth of the idea that the *chevaliers* constituted a distinct
order with its own special duties and obligations.

Side by side with this hierarchical model there was also another idea
of the right ordering of society, whose starting-point was the brotherhood and equality which had marked the life of the church at
Jerusalem in the time of the apostles.[22] This was specially the ideal of
the monks, whose way of life was supposed to be a re-enactment of
that of the apostles, and it was held with special fervour by the
Cistercians. The spirit of primitive communism is evident in the
enthusiastic description of life at Rievaulx which Aelred put into the
mouth of a novice there:

> And what delights me especially, there is no acceptance of persons,
> no consideration of family status. Need alone gives rise to
> differences, only infirmity is a ground for discrimination. For
> what is produced in common by all is distributed, not according

[20] E. Caspar, *Das Register Gregors VII*, MGH Epp Sel 2, VI 35 p 450. The passage is based
ultimately on 1 Cor xii 4–11, but immediately it is an almost *verbatim* quotation from
Gregory I. See P. Ewald and L. M. Hartmann, *Gregorii I Papae Registrum Epistolarum*,
MGH Epp 1, V 59, vol I, p 371.
[21] See the valuable discussion by I. S. Robinson, 'Gregory VII and the Soldiers of Christ,'
History 58 (1973) pp 169–92.
[22] The essential texts, ceaselessly quoted, were *Acts* ii, 42–7 and iv 32.

to the dictates of wordly favour or personal love, but to each according to his need.[23]

Cistercian writers were willing to engage in a conscious polemic against the hierarchical view of society, arguing that men were naturally equal and that obedience had become necessary only as a result of sin.[24] On the face of it we would hardly expect this spirit of equality to have much appeal to the *chevaliers*, with their consciousness of military excellence and their increasing pretensions to aristocratic elegance, but it did in fact influence their understanding of their vocation. The military orders embodied considerable elements of the apostolic ideal, and the Cistercians in particular had an important influence on the emergence of the Templars and the Spanish order of Calatrava. Moreover, participation in holy war was seen as analogous to joining a monastic order. The troubadour Marcabru saw it as a *Lavador*, a new baptism,[25] and the literature of the first and second crusades shows in innumerable references how the participants saw themselves as having become poor for the sake of Christ. They thought of themselves as *pauperes*, were taught by the legate Adhémar of Le Puy to reverence and protect the poor, and swore an oath of brotherhood for their assistance in a time of crisis. The spirit of equality is shown in the rule of the Hospitallers where they were enjoined to dress humbly,

> for our lords the poor, whose servants we acknowledge ourselves to be, go naked and meanly dressed. And shameful it would be if the serf were proud of his lord humble.[26]

The early twelfth century is sometimes presented as the time when a definitive code of chivalry was being formulated. There is a truth in this, but it is a very approximate truth, for there were in reality many contending ideals of knighthood. There were for example the glorification of war and the cult of courtly love. Against them stood the preachers, pastors and canon lawyers who were endeavouring to build up knighthood as a vocation, within which a man might serve God in his military calling. They did not have one single programme for this,

[23] Aelred of Rievaulx, *Speculum Caritatis* ii. 17, PL 195 (1855) col 563 AB.
[24] Bernard of Clairvaux, *Sermones in Cantica* xxiii. 6, PL 183 (1879) col 887 A: *omnes homines natura aequales genuit.* Although hierarchy and obedience were constituted as a result of sin, Bernard still saw them as God-given dispensations which retained their force in this present world.
[25] R. T. Hill and T. G. Bergin, *Anthology of the Provençal Troubadours* (Yale 1973) no 11, I, pp 13–15.
[26] Cited J. Riley-Smith, *The Knights of St. John in Jerusalem and Cyprus* (London 1967) p 41.

since as we would expect in a large enterprise of evangelism, it was fashioned from a number of different sources. We have seen briefly in this paper how the traditional concept of *ordo* was extended so as to bring chivalry within the realm of divine salvation, and how it was influenced also by ideals of service and community derived from the *Acts of the Apostles*. There were other influences, too: the extension of the rewards of martyrdom to those who died in holy war was an important one.[27] In truth one should think less of a code of chivalry than of conflicting ideals of chivalry, and above all of an endeavour to bring many of the vocations of men into the conscious and deliberate service of God.

University of Southampton

[27] An influence which became important from at least the middle of the twelfth century was the ethical teaching of Seneca and Cicero. For the varied estimates of the impact of this, see E. R. Curtis, *European Literature and the Latin Middle Ages* (London 1953) pp 519–37, and E. Neumann, 'Der Streit um das ritterliche Tugendsystem,' *Erbe der Vergangenheit. Festgabe für K. Helm* (Tübingen 1951) 137–56.

THE ELEPHANT OF CHRIST:
REYNALD OF CHÂTILLON

by BERNARD HAMILTON

I T is written in the Koran:
Hast thou not seen how thy Lord dealt with the
army of the Elephant?
Did he not cause their strategem to miscarry?[1]
Historically the Elephant was the Christian king of Ethiopia who
attacked Mecca in 570, but some twelfth-century Moslems considered
that this sura was a prophetic reference to Reynald of Châtillon, who
was singled out as the chief enemy of Islam.[2]

Modern historians do not accord the same importance to Reynald,
but usually treat him as a maverick who did more harm to the
Christian than to the Moslem cause,[3] and even Prawer, who is aware
of the complexity of the issue, admits that he is baffled by him.[4] This
situation is partly the fault of Reynald's only biographer,
Schlumberger, who portrayed him as a romantic hero and made little
attempt to interpret his life in the context of twelfth-century history,[5]
but it is also partly as a result of the character of the source material.
Reynald's career falls into two distinct parts, separated by a long
period spent in a Moslem prison. The first part of his life is well-
documented; his prison life is a total blank; his later life receives very
uneven coverage in Christian sources, because he was a political
opponent of William of Tyre whose work influenced most other
western crusader sources for this period.[6] Much, therefore, of what is
known about Reynald's later life is derived from Moslem writers who
were hostile to him and not always well-informed about the reasons
for his actions.

---

[1] Sura CV.

[2] Letter from Saladin to the caliph in A[bou] C[hamah, *Le Livre des deux Jardins*] *RHC Or* 4, p 233.

[3] It would be invidious to single out particular works. This view has generally prevailed since the publication of Schlumberger's life of Reynald (see note 5) in 1898.

[4] J. Prawer, *Histoire du Royaume latin de Jérusalem*, 2 vols (Paris 1969–70) 1, pp 594–6.

[5] [G.] Schlumberger, [*Renaud de Châtillon, Prince d'Antioche, Seigneur de la terre d'outre-Jourdain*] (Paris 1898).

[6] See the study of the relationship of these sources by M. R. Morgan, *The Chronicle of Ernoul and the Continuations of William of Tyre*, Oxford Historical Monographs (Oxford 1973).

Yet if royal and private documents are taken into account as well
as chronicles, there is enough evidence to enable a more balanced
assessment to be made of Reynald's career. This is a large subject,
which I intend to deal with at greater length elsewhere. In this paper I
shall consider only his motivation as a crusader, and I shall deal chiefly
with the last years of his life. But because of the nature of the sources
some brief consideration of his earlier life is essential.

He was the younger son of a northern French noble family[7] who
came to the east in the reign of Baldwin III and made the misalliance
of the century by marrying the king's widowed cousin, Constance,
princess of Antioch.[8] As prince of Antioch Reynald could not be
described as an asset to the Christian cause: he tortured the latin
patriarch,[9] ravaged Byzantine Cyprus,[10] quarrelled with the other
crusader leaders during an attack on Shaizar so that the campaign had
to be abandoned;[11] was forced to undergo a ceremonial penance by the
emperor Manuel Comnenus in front of the entire diplomatic corps of
the near east whereby, as William of Tyre says, 'the glory of the latin
world was put to shame';[12] and finally, in 1161, was captured by the
governor of Aleppo while cattle-rustling among the predominantly
Christian peasantry of western Edessa.[13]

[7] Schlumberger pp 3-4 argues that he was the younger son of Geoffrey, count of Gien-
sur-Loire, and therefore took his cadet title from Châtillon-sur-Loing. His authority is
[Chronique d']Ernoul [et de Bernard le Tresorier, ed M. L. de Mas Latrie] (Paris 1871) p 22.
[8] He is first mentioned serving Baldwin III as a mercenary knight at the siege of Ascalon.
His marriage caused general astonishment 'that such a famous, powerful and well-born
woman, the widow of such an outstanding husband, should condescend to marry a kind
of mercenary knight.' W[illiam of] T[yre Historia Rerum in partibus transmarinis gestarum,]
XVII, xxi, xxvi, RHC Occ I, pp 796, 802.
[9] This occurred after 1153 and before 1155 when Amalric de Limoges was living in
Jerusalem, Cartulaire de l'Église du St-Sépulcre de Jérusalem, ed E. de Rozière, Collection
des documents inédits sur l'histoire de France, series I, 5 (Paris 1849) no 50 pp 92-3. As
Amalric did not die until 1193, [Chronique de] M[ichel le] S[yrien, patriarche jacobite
d'Antioche (1166-99), ed J. B. Chabot], 4 vols (Paris 1899-1924) XXI, viii, vol 3,
pp 411-12, it is difficult to accept William of Tyre's description of him as sacerdos
longaevus at the time of his arrest by Reynald, WT XVIII, i, RHC Occ I, pp 816-17.
[10] WT, XVIII, x, RHC Occ I, pp 834-5: [John] Cinnamus, [Libri Historiarum, ed. A.
Meineke] (Bonn 1836) IV, 17, pp 178-80.
[11] In fairness to Reynald it should be said that he claimed that Shaizar was traditionally
part of the principality of Antioch, but count Thierry of Flanders, to whom Baldwin III
proposed giving the city when it was captured, refused to do homage to Reynald for it,
WT, XVIII, xvii, xviii. RHC Occ I, pp 847-51.
[12] WT XVIII, xxiii, RHC Occ I, pp 859-61; Cinnamus, IV, 18, pp 181-3.
[13] WT XVIII, xxviii, RHC Occ I, pp 868-9, who gives a precise date, November 23 in
the eighteenth year of king Baldwin's reign. Baldwin was crowned on Christmas Day
1143, H-E. Mayer, 'Studies in the History of Queen Melisende of Jerusalem', DOP 26

The Elephant of Christ: Reynald of Châtillion

He stayed in prison for fifteen years and nothing is known about that period of his life. If the last years of his life are seen simply as a continuation of his wild youth he can be represented as a robber baron preying on harmless Moslem merchants and pilgrims. I do not think that the evidence supports this view, and I shall attempt to show that in the second half of his public life he was sincerely committed to the crusader cause in a way in which he had not earlier been. But his actions can only be justly evaluated if the extent of his influence in the crusader kingdom is recognised: this has been constantly under-estimated, as William of Tyre intended it should be.

Reynald's status did not remain unchanged while he was in prison. His wife died,[14] his stepson came of age and became prince of Antioch, and Reynald was left a landless man.[15] Yet in 1176 his captors demanded the huge ransom of 120,000 gold dinars for him, which his friends at Jerusalem paid,[16] for despite his loss of Antioch Reynald had become more important while he was in prison than he had been before. His step-daughter had become Byzantine empress,[17] his daughter had married the king of Hungary:[18] he thus had international connections such as few crusader leaders could boast. Moreover, he was cousin by marriage to Baldwin IV of Jerusalem.

Baldwin IV was a leper; his death was thought to be imminent; he could not marry and father an heir. His closest male kinsman, Raymond III of Tripoli, was unpopular with some of the nobility and with the

(1972) p 114, therefore his eighteenth year began on 25 December 1160, and Reynald's capture occurred on 23 November 1161. This is confirmed by Kamal-ad-Dîn who places the event in Dou-kidja A.H. 556, that is, 22 November–21 December 1161, [L'histoire d'Alep de] Kamal-ad-Dîn', [trans E. Blochet], R[évue de l']O[rient] L[atin], 3 (Paris 1895) p 533.

14 In c1163, Du Cange, Les Familles d'Outre-Mer, ed E. G. Rey (Paris 1869, repr 1971) p 194.
15 He came of age in 1163. In the interval between Reynald's capture and that year the government was committed to the partiarch Amalric by Baldwin III, WT XVIII, xxx, RHC Occ 1, p 872.
16 WT XXI, xi, RHC Occ 1, p 1025, who places Reynald's release in the second year of Baldwin IV's reign, 15 July 1175–14 July 1176. Reynald witnessed a charter of Baldwin lord of Ramleh in 1176, CGOH no 495. Michael the Syrian states that count Jocelyn's ransom was 50,000 dinars, that of Raymond III of Tripoli, released a few years before, 80,000 and Reynald's 120,000, MS XX, iii, vol 3, pp 365–6. Some value must be attached to these figures because the amount of count Raymond's ransom is independently attested, WT XX, xxviii, RHC Occ 1, p 995.
17 She had married Manuel Comnenus on Christmas Day 1161, WT XVIII, xxxi, RHC Occ 1 p 876; Cinnamus V, 4, pp 210–11.
18 Nicetas Choniates, de Manuele Comneno, V, 8, ed B. G. Niebuhr (Bonn 1835) p 221; Chronica Albrici monachi Trium Fontium a monacho novi monasterii Hoiensis interpolata, ed P. Scheffer-Boichorst, MGH SS 23 (Hanover 1874) p 850.

99

king's mother[19] who found in her brother Jocelyn, and in prince Reynald, both of whom were released from prison in 1176,[20] other members of the royal family to whom the work of government might be delegated. Jocelyn was appointed seneschal of the realm[21] while Reynald was married to the greatest heiress in the kingdom, Stephanie, lady of Outre-Jordan and was also given the lordship of Hebron.[22] He thus became ruler of a great fief in the south and east of the kingdom.

In June 1177 William of Montferrat, the husband of the king's elder sister Sibyl, who was clearly being groomed for the succession, died, leaving his wife pregnant with the future Baldwin V. The king wished, for reasons of health, to appoint a regent, a position which William would naturally have held had he lived. Reynald, who was the king's kinsman, but had no claim on the throne, yet who was an experienced soldier and administrator, was appointed instead.[23] He vindicated the king's trust when, with few troops at his disposal, he defeated a huge Egyptian army led by Saladin at the battle of Montgisart.[24] Saladin considered this so serious a defeat that only his victory at Hattin effaced it.[25]

---

[19] Agnes de Courtenay, daughter of Jocelyn II, count of Edessa. Her marriage to Amalric had been annulled in 1162 at the insistence of the high court of Jerusalem, though the children of the marriage, Baldwin IV and Sibyl, were legitimated. WT XIX, 4, *RHC OCC* 1, pp 889–90; in 1167 Amalric married Maria Comnena, who bore him one daughter, Isabel.

[20] WT, XXI, xi, *RHC Occ* 1, p 1025 states that their release was simultaneous.

[21] R. L. Nicholson, *Joscelyn III and the Fall of the Crusader States 1134–1199* (Leiden 1973) p 73, n 173.

[22] Before November 1177 when Reynald made a grant as 'quondam Antiochie princeps et nunc . . . Hebronensis et Montis Regalis domius,' *CGOH* no 521. Stephanie had been married twice before, to Humphrey III of Toron by whom she bore two children, Humphrey IV and Isabel, and after his death to Miles de Plancy, Amalric I's seneschal. That marriage was childless, and Miles was assassinated in 1174, WT XXI, iv, *RHC Occ* 1 pp 1008–9.

[23] The appointment was first offered to the king's cousin, the count of Flanders, who was visiting the holy land, but for a variety of reasons he declined it. William of Tyre implies that Reynald had exercised the regency before the count of Flanders's arrival in the east: 'Constituit ergo dominus rex, sicut et prius ante comitis introitum fecerat, regni et exercituum procuratorem dominum Rainaldum.' He adds that Reynald was to be 'subject in all things to the advice of the count' (of Flanders), but as the count left for north Syria almost immediately this was not an effective limitation of Reynald's powers. WT, XXI, xiii–xix (specially xiv), *RHC Occ* 1, pp 1025–37.

[24] William of Tyre records Reynald's presence at the battle, but treats the king as commander-in-chief. He adds that the entire Frankish force consisted only 375 men, WT XXI, xxii–xxiv, *RHC Occ* 1 pp 1041–47; Ernoul p 54 praises Reynald's courage in this battle, but does not name him as commander. Moslem writers state unequivocally that Reynald commanded the crusader army, Behâ ed-Dîn, [*The Life of Saladin*, trans C. W. Wilson], *PPTS* (1897) pp 75–6; AC, *RHC Or* 4, pp 188–9.

The Elephant of Christ: Reynald of Châtillion

It is clear from the royal charters which have survived that for the next five years Reynald held a paramount position in the kingdom after the king.[26] His importance was generally recognised: he was employed as an ambassador;[27] he was asked to mediate in ecclesiastical disputes;[28] the prince of Cilicia married his step-daughter;[29] while the king's younger sister, Isabel, was betrothed to Reynald's stepson.[30] During Reynald's ascendancy the widowed princess Sybil married Guy of Lusignan, presumably with Reynald's approval:[31] certainly he remained a constant supporter of Guy, and perhaps saw in him the potential which later came to fruition at the siege of Acre. Reynald was almost certainly involved in the appointment of Heraclius as patriarch in 1180 instead of William of Tyre.[32] The wisdom of this choice is debatable, but it is perhaps not unconnected with William's silence about Reynald's considerable later achievements. It was also during the time of Reynald's ascendancy, in the spring of 1180, that the kingdom made a truce with Saladin, whose lands were suffering from the effects of prolonged drought.[33]

---

[25] 'This is how the Sultan himself spoke . . . of this defeat . . .: "Great though this disaster was, God . . . made it good at the famous victory of Hattin." I would add . . . that that only happened ten years later.' AC, *RHC Or* 4, p 189.

[26] He heads the list of lay witnesses in a group of royal charters issued between 1177 and 24 February 1182: 1177, grant of the heir-apparent, Sibyl, countess of Jaffa, S. Pauli, *Codice diplomatico del sacro militare ordine Gerosolimitano oggi di Malta*, 2 vols (Lucca 1733–7) I, p 63 no lxiii; 1177, charter of Baldwin IV, J. Delaville Le Roulx, *Les archives, la bibliothèque et le trésor de l'ordre de St. Jean de Jérusalem à Malte*, B[ibliothèque des] é[coles] f[rançaises d'] A[thènes et de] R[ome], series 1, 32 (Paris 1883) pp 127–8 no xxxix; 1177, charter of the countess Sibyl, *ibid* pp 129–30 no xli; 22 October 1179, charter of Baldwin IV, [*Tabulae ordinis Theutonici*] ed [E.] Strehlke (Berlin 1869) pp 11–12 no xi; 28 April 1180, charter of Baldwin IV, *CGOH* no 582; 6 February 1182, charter of Baldwin IV, *CGOH* no 625; 24 February 1182, charter of Baldwin IV, Strehlke pp 13–14 no xiv.

[27] He was the only lay member of the delegation sent from Jerusalem to Antioch in 1181 to try to mediate peace between Bohemond III and the patriarch, WT XXII, vii, *RHC Occ* I, p 1073.

[28] He mediated in a property dispute between the abbess of Ste. Marie la Grande and the Abbot of Our Lady of Josaphat, the document is undated. Ch. Kohler, 'Chartes de l'abbaye de Notre-Dame de la Vallée de Josaphat en Terre-Sainte (1108–1291)— Analyses et extraits', *ROL* 7 (1899) no xlv, pp 153–4.

[29] Roupen III, prince of Cilicia, married Isabel of Toron in 1181, Ernoul p 31; Sempad the Constable, *Chronique du royaume de la petite Arménie, RHC Arm* I, p 627.

[30] WT XXII, v, *RHC Occ* I, p 1068–9.

[31] WT XXII, i, *RHC Occ* I, pp 1062–3 Ernoul p 60.

[32] WT XXII, iv, *RHC Occ* I, p 1068.

[33] This was criticised by William of Tyre because it gave the crusaders no advantage, WT XXII, i, *RHC Occ* I, p 1063.

Saladin was then master of Egypt and Damascus and protector of Mecca and Medina, and was at war with the Zengid princes of Aleppo and Mosul. Reynald's lordship of Outre-Jordan, with its string of fortresses, of which the most important were Kerak of Moab and Montreal, commanded the lines of communication between Damascus and Egypt, as well as the pilgrimage routes from Mesopotamia to Mecca and Medina.[34] Saladin had seized the port of Eilat in 1170[35] but had made no serious attempt to capture the other fortresses of Outre-Jordan.[36] It was obviously in his interests to be at peace with the lord of Outre-Jordan so that he would meet with no obstacle in moving troops through his territory in order to pursue his conquests in the north.[37]

Although it might at times be expedient to make a truce, it was clearly not in the interests of the crusaders passively to allow Saladin to become master of much of western Islam. In December 1181 the death of the prince of Aleppo created succession problems there which Saladin might have found advantageous. The sultan was in Egypt and it was sound policy to create a diversion which would prevent him from moving his army to the north. This is what, it seems, Reynald attempted to do. Probably in the early spring of 1182 he set out to attack the oasis of Teïma, 250 miles south of Kerak, on the pilgrimage route to Medina[38] The governor of Damascus intervened and forced him to retreat, but he was nevertheless able to capture a rich pilgrim caravan. This was not, as it is often represented as being, a wilful violation of the truce motivated solely by a desire for plunder, but a calculated attempt to divert Saladin away from Aleppo.[39] Even

---

[34] P. Deschamps, *Les châteaux des Croisés en Terre Sainte. I. Le Crac des Chevaliers. II. La défense du royaume de Jérusalem* (Haut Commissariat de la République française en Syrie et au Liban. Service des Antiquités et Beaux-Arts. *Bibliothèque archéologique et historique*, 19, 34), 2 vols (Paris 1934–9) 2, pp 34–98.

[35] Ibn al-Athir [extract from the Kamel-Altevarykh,] in *RHC Or* 1, p 578. Compare the letter later written by the Cadi el-Fadhel to the caliph detailing Saladin's achievements in AC, *RHC Or* 4, pp 174–5.

[36] In 1171 and 1173 Saladin campaigned in Outre-Jordan but achieved no permanent success because he failed to co-operate with the army of Nureddin. See A. S. Ehrenkreuz, *Saladin* (New York 1972) pp 99–101.

[37] This does not imply that Saladin wanted peace with the Franks as a whole. Possession of a port on the Syrian coast would have speeded troop movements between Egypt and Damascus and Saladin's campaign in Galilee in 1179 can best be understood as an attempt to gain such a port.

[38] Abou Chamah dates this attack A.H. 577, 17 May 1181–7 May 1182. He cites a letter sent by Saladin to the caliph in which the sultan explains that it had been possible to take a cavalry force across the Syrian desert that winter because 'the desert is covered this year with abundant grass'. *RHC Or* 4, pp 213–15.

though it failed, Saladin was criticised for his failure to protect the
haj[40] When Saladin protested to Baldwin IV about the violation of
the truce, Reynald refused to make reparation.[41] This cost him the
king's favour, and Raymond of Tripoli once again became the
dominant figure in the kingdom.[42] Reynald did not attempt to
dispute the king's decision but worked with the count of Tripoli.

Saladin brought his army from Egypt to Damascus that spring
despite crusader attempts to bar his passage,[43] and after some
inconclusive fighting with the Franks that summer[44] went on to campaign in Mesopotamia.[45] In his absence the Franks planned a two-
pronged counter-attack. William of Tyre reports in detail about the
campaign against Damascus led that winter by Raymond of Tripoli
and the king,[46] but it is only from Arab writers that we learn of
Reynald's half of the attack.[47] In the winter of 1182–3[48] the prince, who
had had a number of ships completed in sections,[49] had them carried by

---

[39] Ernoul gives two very similar accounts of Reynald's seizing a caravan during a time of
truce and both seem to refer to this incident, pp 54–6, 96–7. WT XXII, xiv, *RHC Occ* I,
p 1088, makes a brief reference to the seizure of the caravan but not to the projected
attack on Teïma. The chief account is in Abou Chamah cited in n 38.

[40] Abou Chamah quotes from the letter which Saladin sent to the caliph to justify himself.
Although he had taken no direct part in foiling Reynald he was clearly concerned lest
his ability to defend the *haj* should be called in question. He writes: 'We are amazed
that while We are defending the tomb of the prophet (blessings be upon him), and are
solely concerned with its protection, [the prince of Mosul] is disputing the land which
belongs to Us and attempting to seize it unjustly.' AC, *RHC Or* 4, p 215.

[41] Ernoul p 55.

[42] WT XXII, xiv, *RHC Occ* I, pp 1077–9, relates how Raymond returned to court at
easter 1182 through the pressure of barons who were favourable to him. His ascendancy
is reflected in a charter of 27 April in which the king granted tithes at Toron to William
of Tyre. For the first time since 1177 Reynald did not rank first among the lay-witnesses
to a royal charter drawn up when he was present at court, but was listed after
Raymond III and count Jocelyn, Strehlke no 15, pp 14–15.

[43] He left Cairo on 12 May and reached Damascus on 17 June, AC, *RHC Or* 4, pp 217–18.
WT XXII, xiv, xv, *RHC Occ* I, pp 1087–92, is very critical of the way in which the
campaign was conducted.

[44] WT XXII, xvi–xviii, *RHC Occ* I, pp 1092–1101.

[45] This caused great alarm in the crusader kingdom, WT XXII, xix, *RHC Occ* I, pp 1101–2.

[46] *Ibid* XXII, xx–xxii, *RHC Occ* I, pp 1102–9.

[47] Ernoul mentions the expedition but treats it as a voyage of exploration, pp 69–70.

[48] The campaign started after 25 August 1182 when Reynald was with the court at Acre,
G. Müller, *Documenti sulle relazioni delle città toscane coll'Oriente cristiano e coi Turchi
fino all'anno 1531, Documenti degli archivi toscani* 3 (Florence 1879) no 19, p 23, and
el-'Imad says that victory was obtained by the Moslems in the month of Chawal
A.H. 578 (28 January–26 February 1183), AC, *RHC Or* 4, p 230.

[49] Ibn al-Athir says that ships were built at Kerak, *RHC Or* I, pp 658–9. This is unlikely
since there would not have been suitable materials or skilled craftsmen there. Probably
they were built at one of the ports controlled by Reynald's ally, Guy of Lusignan,
perhaps at Ascalon.

camels to the gulf of Akaba, where they were assembled and launched on the Red Sea.[50] Two ships besieged Eilat, probably under Reynald's supervision,[51] while the rest of the fleet attacked pilgrim and merchant shipping and finally landed a raiding-party on the Arabian coast which marched on Medina with the intention, it was said, of seizing the Prophet's body.[52] Saladin's brother, el-Adil, took prompt action, and despatched a fleet from Egypt which raised the siege of Eilat, destroyed the crusader fleet, and caught up with the raiding-party when it was within one day's march of Medina. Some of the Frankish prisoners were sent to Mecca where they were ritually slaughtered, while the rest were publicly executed in the chief cities of Egypt.[53] This was not, as it is sometimes said to have been, a pirate raid, but the most daring part of a concerted campaign in which all the forces of the kingdom joined. Nor was the expedition a total failure: much of Saladin's time in the next two years was spent in trying to capture Reynald who, by his sacrilegious attack on Medina, had called in question the sultan's claim to be the protector of the Islamic religion.

Perhaps Reynald's initiative in 1182 restored him to the king's favour. Certainly in 1183, when Saladin invaded Galilee, it was Reynald's friend, Guy of Lusignan, whom the king appointed as his

[50] AC, *RHC Or* 4, p 231; [E. Blochet, 'Histoire d'Égypte de] Makrizi[, traduction française accompagnée de notes historiques et géographiques],' *ROL* 6 (1898) pp 435–89, 8 (1900–1) pp 165–212, 501–33, 9 (1902) pp 6–163, 466–530, 10 (1903–4) pp 248–371, 11 (1905–8 pp 192–232, 8 p 550; [*The Travels of*] Ibn Jubayr[, trans R. J. C. Broadhurst] (London 1952) p 52.

[51] From the descriptions of the siege it seems probable that the Moslem garrison had taken refuge on the fortified Ile de Graye, facing Eilat, AC *RHC Or* 4, p 231, Makrizi *ROL* 8, pp 550–2. Schlumberger is probably correct in suggesting that Reynald supervised the siege of Eilat and did not accompany the rest of the fleet. This would account for his escape from the Moslem counter-attack. G. Schlumberger, 'Expédition de Renaud de Châtillon contre la Mecque et Médine,' *Récits de Byzance et des Croisades*, 2 vols (Paris 1922) 2 p 147.

[52] The Arab sources agree on the main outlines of the campaign; Ibn al-Athir, *RHC Or* 1, pp 658–9; AC, *RHC Or* 4, pp 230–5; Makrizi, *ROL* 8, pp 550–2; Modjir-ad-Dîn, *Histoire de Jérusalem et d'Hébron*, cited E. Blochet, 'L'histoire d'Alep de Kamal ad-Dîn,' *ROL* 4, p 160, n 1; Ibn Jubayr, pp 51–3. Ibn Jubayr relates the rumour that Reynald's men intended to steal the prophet's body. This is possible. It would have been as useful a bargaining counter to the crusaders as the True Cross later proved to be to the Moslems. Modjir-ad-Dîn's surmise that Reynald wished to re-bury the prophet's remains in Frankish territory and attract the profitable Moslem pilgrim traffic there is less plausible.

[53] El-Fadhel says that 170 prisoners were taken; el-'Imad says that some were executed at Mecca 'like animals destined for sacrifice', both are cited in AC, *RHC Or* 4, pp 231, 235. According to Makrizi only two prisoners were sacrificed in this way, *ROL* 8, p 552. Ibn Jubayr saw some of these crusaders executed at Alexandria in March 1183, p 51.

deputy rather than Raymond of Tripoli.[54] In the autumn, moreover, the marriage took place of Reynald's stepson Humphrey and the king's sister Isabel.[55]

This marriage took place at Kerak and Saladin attacked the castle while it was crowded with wedding guests and when the garrison was undermanned because of heavy losses in the summer campaign.[56] The sultan was later joined by large re-inforcements from Egypt[57] and Reynald was in great danger.[58] Although he sent to ask the king for help at the beginning of the siege it was slow in arriving [59] because Guy of Lusignan's opponents chose this time to persuade the king to depose him from the regency, have the five-year old Baldwin V crowned as co-king, and appoint Raymond of Tripoli as regent.[60] It is reasonable to infer that Guy's opponents chose to attack him when there was no possibility that Reynald, who was his chief supporter, could be present. Only when this business was settled did they march to the relief of Kerak, and Saladin withdrew at their approach.[61] But the respite was slight: in the following summer Saladin raised a confederate army from all over his dominions and again attacked Kerak, but again withdrew when the royal army came to its relief.[62]

Although Reynald can have had little reason to like Raymond of Tripoli he co-operated with him when, after Baldwin IV's death in March 1185, Raymond became virtual ruler for the child-king Baldwin V.[63] In this he showed a greater sense of the need for Christian

[54] WT XXII, xxv, *RHC Occ* I, pp 1116–17. Reynald was certainly attending the king at this time, *ibid* XXII, xxvii, *RHC Occ* I, p 1122.
[55] *Ibid* XXII, xxviii, *RHC Occ* I, p 1124; Ernoul p 103.
[56] One hundred men from the garrisons of Kerak and Montreal were captured or killed in a saracen ambush in the previous summer, AC, *RHC Or* 4, p 243.
[57] Behâ ed-Dîn, pp 91–2. These reinforcements reached Kerak on 22 November.
[58] On November 23 Reynald was forced to abandon the *faubourg* and retreat to the castle. This enabled Saladin to range mangonels on the garrison and to keep up a heavy bombardment. Kamal ad-Dîn, *ROL* 4 p 170; el-'Imad, cited AC, *RHC Or* 4 pp 248–9; WT XXII, xxx, *RHC Occ* I, p 1129.
[59] Saladin left Damascus on 22 October and the crusader relief army arrived on 4 December, Behâ ed-Dîn pp 91–2. Saladin must have reached Kerak at the beginning of November: William of Tyre says the siege lasted *per mensem continuum*, XXII, xxx, *RHC Occ* I, p 1130. The royal army only took three days to reach Kerak from Jerusalem, Ernoul p 105. Ernoul p 104 states that Reynald sent a messenger to ask the king for help when the siege began and lit a beacon on the keep, visible in Jerusalem, to show that he was being attacked.
[60] WT XXII, xxix, *RHC Occ* I, pp 1127–8.
[61] *Ibid* XXII, xxx, I, pp 1129–30; Ernoul pp 105–6; el-'Imad in AC, *RHC Or* 4, pp 245–8; Behâ ed-Dîn p 92; Kamal ad-Dîn *ROL* 4, p 170.
[62] AC, *RHC Or* 4, pp 249–56; Behâ ed-Dîn pp 94–7; Kamal ad-Dîn *ROL* 4, p 172.

solidarity than either Guy of Lusignan had done in the last years of
Baldwin IV's reign, or than Raymond himself was to do in Guy's
reign. It may therefore be assumed that Reynald was party to the four-
year truce which the crusaders made with Saladin in 1185 because of
another severe drought.[64] The Arab historian, Ibn al-Athir, implies
that Reynald also made a private truce with Saladin, allowing the free
passage of Moslem merchants through his lands.[65] The first year of the
truce was uneventful, but in the late summer of 1186 Baldwin V died.
Although the constitutional position about the succession was compli-
plicated,[66] two parties soon formed supporting the rival claims of the
princesses Sybil and Isabel. Self-interest should have impelled Reynald
to support Isabel, who was his daughter-in-law, but he supported
Guy of Lusignan and Sibyl as he had always done[67] and was probably
influential in persuading his stepson, Isabel's husband, to recognise
Sybil as queen, thus depriving the other party of a candidate for the
throne.[68] It is arguable that in this way he averted a civil war.[69]

Soon after Guy's enthronement Reynald siezed a caravan near
Montreal in violation of the truce and refused to make reparation
when Saladin complained to the king.[70] If one holds the traditional

---

[63] He heads the list of lay witnesses in a confirmation of the sale of crown lands issued by
Baldwin V and Raymond of Tripoli at Acre on 16 May 1185, H-F. Delaborde, *Chartes
de la Terre Sainte provenant de l'Abbaye de Notre-Dame de Josaphat*, BEFAR, 19 (Paris
1880) no 43, pp 91–2.

[64] Ernoul p 124; [*L'Estoire de*] *Eracles* [*Empereur et la Conqueste de la terre d'Outremer*],
XXIII, viii, RHC Occ 2, pp 12–13.

[65] Ibn al-Athir, RHC Or 1, p 676.

[66] In Baldwin IV's reign Raymond of Tripoli had only agreed to act as regent for
Baldwin V on condition that should the child-king die before coming of age the
respective claims of his two sisters should be referred to the pope, the western emperor
and the kings of France and England for adjudication. Eracles XXIII, iv, RHC Occ 2,
pp 6–7; Ernoul pp 115–19. Traditionally such a choice belonged to the high court of
Jerusalem.

[67] Reynald addressed the people assembled in the Holy Sepulchre before Sibyl's
coronation affirming that 'ce est li plus apareissanz et li plus dreis heirs dou roiaume.'
Eracles XXIII, xvii, RHC Occ 2, p 28.

[68] Ernoul pp 135–6. Reynald's involvement in this is nowhere explicitly stated. Yet if
Humphrey of Toron had not been in agreement with his stepfather he would not have
made his submission to Sibyl, and this suggests some measure of communication
between Reynald and Humphrey.

[69] With the exception of Raymond of Tripoli, who was, in his wife's right, prince of
Galilee, all the barons of the kingdom made their submission to Guy with varying
degrees of goodwill, Ernoul pp 136–7. It is arguable that Guy and Sibyl, who held the
counties of Jaffa and Ascalon and the cities of Jerusalem and Acre, would not have
given way so readily to Humphrey had he been crowned, and that the kingdom would
have been divided by civil war.

view that Reynald was a robber baron there is nothing mysterious about this incident, but if, as I have argued, he was an experienced and responsible crusader leader, it is more enigmatic. Ibn al-Athir reports, however, that the caravan was 'accompanied by . . . a large armed escort'[71] and I would suggest that Reynald regarded this as a breach of the truce.

Reynald's action proved to be a declaration of war. After a preliminary invasion of Outre-Jordan in the spring of 1187[72] Saladin entered Galilee. Reynald had been one of Guy's chief advisers[73] and it is not surprising that Guy was swayed by his advice about how to conduct the war against Saladin and by that of the Grand Master of the Templars than by the words of his former enemy, Raymond of Tripoli.[74] Reynald's judgment proved to be wrong, the Christian army was defeated, and he left the field of Hattin as Saladin's prisoner. The sultan offered him the choice of apostasy or death, and when he refused to abjure his faith he had the doubtful distinction of being executed by the sultan himself for the honour of Islam.[75]

In Lusignan circles he was treated as a martyr for the faith, and Peter of Blois, who learned of his death from king Guy's brother, wrote a *Passio Reginaldis*.[76] It is strange that Reynald's life reminded Peter of Blois, just as it reminded his Moslem contemporaries, of the

---

[70] Ibn al-Athir dates this A.H. 582 (24 March 1186–14 March 1187), *RHC Or* 1, p 676. Eracles XXIII, xxiii, *RHC Occ* 2, p 34, places it after Guy's coronation. The incident is also reported by el-'Imad, cited AC, *RHC Or* 4, pp 258–9, and by Behâ ed-Dîn p 114.

[71] *RHC Or* 1, p 676.

[72] He initially went to escort a pilgrim caravan in which his sister was travelling and subsequently laid waste the lands around Kerak and Montreal, Behâ ed-Dîn pp 108–9; AC, *RHC Or* 4, pp 261–2.

[73] Reynald heads the list of lay witnesses in three charters issued by king Guy in favour of count Jocelyn on 21 October 1186, Strehlke nos 21–3, pp 19–21. He also heads the lay witnesses in a grant of king Guy for the German hospital of Jerusalem, issued on 7 March, Strehlke no 20, p 18. The document is dated 'MCLXXXVI, indicatione vᵃ' and is dated 7 March 1186 by the editor. This is wrong since Guy was not king then. Clearly a mistake has been made in the transcription, and the document was drawn up on 7 March 1187. This is confirmed by the fact that the fifth indiction ran from 1 September 1186–31 August 1187.

[75] Eracles XXIII, xxxi–xxxiii, xxxv, *RHC Occ* 2, pp 47–50, 52–3.

[75] Ernoul pp 172–4; Eracles XXIII, xlv, *RHC Occ* 2, p 67; Ibn al-Athir *RHC Or* 1, p 687; Kamal ad-Dîn, *ROL* 4, pp 180–1; Behâ ed-Dîn pp 42–3, 114–15; AC, citing various sources, *RHC Or* 4, pp 275–6, 284–5, 298–9, 305.

[76] Both Geoffrey and Amalric of Lusignan were present at Hattin, Peter does not specify which was his source. Peter of Blois, *Passio Reginaldis Principis Antiocheni*, *PL* 207 (1854) cols 957–76.

elephant. He remarks of him: 'As elephants are roused to battle by the sight of blood, so, and more fervently, does the sight of the Holy Cross and the remembrance of the Lord's Passion rouse Christian knights.'[77] Reynald had certainly fought at Hattin to defend the Holy Cross. I would suggest that the last eleven years of his life may best be understood as devoted to a similar purpose.

University of Nottingham

[77] Sicut elephanti animantur ad bellum ostensione sanguinis, sic et fortius animaverat Christi milites vivificae crucis ostensio et memoria Dominicae passionis. *Ibid* col 974.

RELIGIOUS MOTIVATION IN THE BIOGRAPHY OF HUBERT DE BURGH

by FRED A. CAZEL, JR

HUBERT de Burgh was the most powerful man in England during the minority of Henry III, the real ruler of England for most of the decade of the 1220s. In his climb to power, in his exercise of it, and perhaps most of all, in his sudden disgrace and persecution, his biography is dramatic and compelling. One of the factors in his rise and fall was the religious motivation for his acts, a factor which is all too often neglected in modern biography and history. No one doubts that Hubert de Burgh was a Christian, though his lord, king John, flirted with disbelief; but no one has really considered what effects Hubert's Christianity may have had upon his actions. Nor how strong it was by comparison with other motivations.

The most famous action of Hubert—the one immortalised by Shakespeare—was his refusal to allow Arthur to be blinded and emasculated when the prince was in his custody at Falaise in 1202. The original source for this story is the chronicle of Ralph of Coggeshall, a well-informed contemporary, and Ralph makes it clear that Hubert was motivated both by compassion and by policy.[1] The order seemed so cruel that Hubert believed John would repent of it and indeed be angry with anyone involved in carrying it out. Christian compassion was not the only motive in Hubert's decision to save Arthur from harm, then, but policy would not have entered in had it not been for the compassionate belief that John had ordered cruel and unusual punishment.

Not that Hubert de Burgh was a soft man. He was a knight and that meant a soldier, a man of blood. While chivalry rendered warfare relatively safe for knights, others often suffered sorely whether combatants or not. So, Matthew Paris tells us matter-of-factly, Hubert once commanded a troop of soldiers harrying the lands of John's enemies, carrying off whatever they could, destroying whatever they could not carry off, and not even sparing churches.[2] One night during

---

[1] [*Radulphi de*] Coggeshall [*Chronicon Anglicanum*], ed J. Stevenson, RS 66 (1875) pp 139–41.

[2] [*Matthaei Parisiensis*] *Chronica majora*, ed H. R. Luard, 7 vols, RS 57 (1872–84) 3 pp 290–1.

FRED A. CAZEL, JR

this expedition Hubert dreamed that he saw an image of Christ on the cross which spoke to him and said, 'When next you see my effigy, spare me in it, and carry it away and worship it.' Next day, as his troops were devastating the countryside, a priest ran up to Hubert carrying a great cross with such a crucifix. When Hubert saw the image was just as he had dreamed, he dismounted and fell on his knees to adore it and he restored the goods of the church to its priest. To this good deed Hubert attributed his reconciliation with the king in 1234, not apparently because of his compassion for the priest or his parishioners but rather because of the dream and the obedience it required of him. The dream echoes the legend of the conversion of saint Hubert,[3] and perhaps we have to look to his cult for the basis of Hubert's view that by obedience to the dream he had established a credit in heaven sufficiently great to explain his reconciliation with the king. Certainly we do not find here the evidence to generalise the compassion which Hubert felt for Arthur, unless one postulated that unconscious guilt about his troop's devastation caused his dream. But that would be pure speculation.

Hubert's lasting military reputation derived from his command of Dover castle under Louis's sieges in 1216 and 1217 and his command of the English fleet at the battle of Sandwich in 1217. Even Louis was constrained to admire the defence which Hubert and his garrison put up against his full-scale assault and the fidelity and constancy they showed in refusing to surrender after John's death.[4] Loyalty to his lord the king was the cornerstone of Hubert's career and he profited accordingly. But constancy was the word used by Matthew Paris in his chronicle and by the abbot of Prémontré in a letter to Hubert in 1220,[5] and clearly they meant the Christian virtue of long-suffering, of withstanding hardships in the pursuit of a good cause. Was this praise mere flattery, or did his contemporaries find his actions at

[3] The saint was converted by the apparition of a stag bearing a crucifix between its antlers. The incident was clearly borrowed from the life of saint Eustace, whose day was celebrated in the middle ages only a day earlier than saint Hubert's (*ASB, Novembris*, I pp 779–80). The story is not found in a *vita* of saint Hubert before the fifteenth century—L. Van der Essen, *Étude critique et littéraire sur les Vitae des saints Mérovingiens de l'ancienne Belgique* (Louvain 1907) pp 68–70—but the transfer could have been made elsewhere than in the Low Countries where the *vitae* were written. Only two English churches are known to be dedicated to saint Hubert—F. Bond, *Dedications and Patron Saints of English Churches* (London 1914) p 218—and one of these is the church of Hubert de Burgh's manor of Corfmoulin, Dorset.
[4] *Coggeshall*, pp 132–3; *Chronica majora*, 2 p 664, 3 pp 3–5.
[5] Gervase of Chichester in [*Sacrae antiquitatis*] *monumenta* [*historica, dogmatica, diplomatica*], ed C. L. Hugo, I (Stivagii 1725) pp 70–1.

110

Dover religiously motivated? Similarly, at Sandwich the tactics he adopted made possible a stunning English victory, a few against many, and so great was the booty that it was agreed to use a large part to found a hospital at Sandwich dedicated to saint Bartholomew, whose day it was, for only with God's grace and the intercession of the saint could so great a victory have been won.[6] Hubert's fame was memorialised before his patria in Norfolk when a relative built a chapel there dedicated to saint Bartholomew.[7] Again, we are in the presence of a cult, but also the English victory was clearly felt to be not only man's but God's. The war between the king and his barons was represented as a kind of crusade by both sides. The barons called theirs the 'Army of God' while the papal legate promised remission of sins to those who took the king's part.[8] The religious motivation of the participants doubtless varied enormously. With Hubert de Burgh loyalty to the king, national feeling, soldierly pride, comradeship in arms, must all have played a part in his actions at Dover and Sandwich. Yet one can hardly doubt that religion played its part, that his constancy *was* in a cause he believed to be God's as well as man's.

The crusade to the holy land was preached in England pretty much throughout Hubert's life and it is not surprising that he had taken the vow sometime before 1219. When exactly he took it cannot be discovered, just possibly for the Third or Fourth Crusade, but perhaps most likely when the Fifth Crusade was being preached after 1215. In any case his going became less and less desirable for the governance of England and in January 1219 the pope allowed Hubert to be absolved of his vow.[9] In 1232, after his disgrace, he took the vow of the crusade again, more one would suspect for protection than devotion. He was really too old to be a useful crusader and once again he was absolved from his vow, but he had to redeem it. This he did by the gift of his palace in Westminster, which was sold to the archbishop of York for 400 marks.[10] The seriousness of his commitment is

[6] Kate Norgate, *The Minority of Henry III* (London 1912) pp 49–54, provides a good secondary account.

[7] *MA*, 6 pt 1 p 487.

[8] *Chronica majora*, 2 p 586, 3 p 19; compare Walter of Coventry, *Historical Collections*, ed W. Stubbs, 2 vols, RS 58 (1872–73) 2 p 235; *Royal [and Other Historical] Letters [Illustrative of the Reign of Henry III]*, ed W. W. Shirley, 2 vols, RS 27 (1862–66) 1 p 167 (attributing this letter to Gualo rather than Pandulf).

[9] *Regesta Honorii Papae III*, ed P. Pressuti, 2 vols (Rome 1888–95) no 1842.

[10] Westminster Abbey Domesday, fol 347b; PRO Cartae Antiquae C 52/34 mem 1, partially printed in *The Historians of the Church of York*, ed J. Raine, 3 vols, RS 71 (1879–94) 2 pp 160–1. The archbishop then deeded the property to his church: *[Calendar of] Charter Rolls*, 6 vols (London 1903–27) 1 p 284.

indicated by the nature of the redemption, for the purchase price was sufficient to keep a large force in arms for a season's campaign. On the other hand, Hubert had twice taken the vow of the crusade and twice had not gone himself. Clearly he was more like Henry II than Richard, more like Geoffrey fitz-Peter than Ranulph of Chester. His commitment was honourable rather than adventurous, perhaps more intellectual than passionate, the second time almost certainly more self-centered than God-centered. But then the crusade was sold by its preachers as a good bargain, and the surprise is that so many did not take the vow. Those who did and then commuted their vows, like Hubert, had the church's promise of remission of sins duly confessed and that was religious motivation enough.

The church expected men of means to make large gifts to the clergy and especially to the religious; in return, the clergy promised prayers for the salvation of the donors and their designated beneficiaries. Hubert de Burgh made many such donations. In some cases his gifts had aesthetic significance: silken cloths to St Paul's and to St Alban's; a stained glass window to Rochester cathedral; mural decoration of a chapel in Norwich cathedral; an illuminated text bound with a jeweled gold cover for the new Salisbury cathedral on its dedication.[11] In these gifts other motivations can be detected besides the religious: the love of the beautiful, ostentatious display, competitiveness, the seeking of praise. One is reminded of Suger, but not even saint Bernard believed there was no religious motivation in such gifts, just that it was misplaced. Still, saint Bernard should have approved Hubert's earliest donations which were made to the Cistercian abbey of Cleeve in Somerset after he became its patron in 1199.[12] Although Hubert made gifts to religious communities of many kinds,[13] he early favoured the

[11] *Chronica majora*, 6 p 390; William Dugdale, *History of St Paul's Cathedral in London*, ed H. Ellis (London 1818) appendix p 322; *Register of St Osmund*, ed W. H. Rich-Jones, 2 vols, RS 78 (1883–4) 2 pp 43–4; BM MS Cotton Vespasian A XXII (Registrum Ecclesie Roffensis) fol 91^v; at Norwich the decoration of the present Jesus chapel, formerly dedicated to saint Stephen and all the Holy Martyrs, is attributed to Hubert de Burgh since his coat of arms is prominently displayed.

[12] *MA*, 5 pp731–4; *Patent Rolls*, [*Henry III*], *1225–1232* (London 1903) pp 163–4; *Calendar of Patent Rolls, Edward I, 1272–1281* (London 1901) p 442; *Charter Rolls*, 1 p 59.

[13] *MA*, 6 pt 1 p 74; BM MS Cotton Nero E VII (Walsingham Cartulary) fols 91, 140; BM MS Harleian 2110 (Castleacre Cartulary) fol 291; *MA*, 5 pp 555–6; *ibid*, 5 p 326; *Calendar of Charter Rolls*, 4 pp 71, 209; *Calendar of Patent Rolls, Henry VI, 1422–1429* (London 1901) p 453; Norwich Dean and Chapter MS Registrum secundum, 2 fol 39, and Registrum septimum, fol 78; BM MS Additional 5516 (Charters of Saint Sepulchre's, Canterbury) fol 9^r/^{v}; *Early Charters of St Paul's Cathedral*, ed Marion Gibbs, CSer 3 series, 58, p 279.

Premonstratensians. A small house of that order just outside Dover, St Radegund's, Bradsole, was being considered for consolidation with the neighbouring house of West Langdon when Hubert took it under his wing and left St Radegund's well enough endowed to survive till the dissolution.[14] When Hubert founded a house, however, it was a hospital for travellers and pilgrims, the Maison Dieu at Dover, for which he gave or obtained a large endowment.[15] In 1221, the same year that the Maison Dieu was founded, the friars preachers came to England and settled in Oxford. When they wished to establish a convent at London, it was Hubert de Burgh who bought them land in Holborn.[16] Gradually he transferred his chief attention to this newest of religious orders. When his chivalric nephew, Reymond, died in 1230, he was buried in the Maison Dieu, Dover.[17] But when Hubert died in 1243, he himself was buried in the chapel of the black friars.[18] A member of the order was an executor of Hubert's will and the Dominicans received a large legacy.[19] Hubert's choice of beneficiaries for his alms followed the main currents of religious feeling in his day, and the religious motivation for his gifts, the desire for eternal salvation by the prayers of the most religious men of his day, cannot be doubted.

Hubert held the rights of patronage over other churches and religious houses in addition to the ones he founded. Advowsons were economically valuable, and he probably enjoyed the power his patronage gave him to choose the incumbents of churches and to approve the abbots and priors of monasteries. But there is good evidence that Hubert took the responsibilities of advocacy seriously and sought to use his power for the good of the church and its clergy. The best-documented case concerns Tewksbury Abbey, the patronage of which Hubert acquired with the custody of Richard de Clare in

[14] *Monumenta*, ed C. L. Hugo pp 70–1; *MA*, 6 pt 2 pp 939–43; Oxford Bodleian MS Rawlinson B.336 pp 16, 42, 148, 169; Rawlinson B.461 p 29; Gough Kent 18 pp 105b–106; *Close Rolls, 1231–1234*, pp 289–90.

[15] *MA*, 6 pt 2 pp 655–8; *Calendar of Charter Rolls*, 1 pp 48, 78, 126, 191, 141, 315, and see index for other references; *Calendar of Patent Rolls, Henry III, 1258–1266* (London 1910) p 541; *ibid, Edward II, 1313–1317* (London 1898) p 551; *Placita de quo warranto*, ed W. Illingworth and J. Caley (London 1818) pp 330–1b, 353b, 360b.

[16] William A. Hinnebusch, *The Early English Friars Preachers* (Rome 1951) p 23.

[17] Gervase of Canterbury, *Historical Works*, ed W. Stubbs, 2 vols, RS 73 (1879–80) 2 p 128.

[18] *Chronica majora*, 4 p 243.

[19] *Calendar of Liberate Rolls* (London 1917–) 2 p 242; *Calendar of Documents Relating to Ireland*, ed H. S. Sweetman and G. F. Handcock, 5 vols (London 1875–86) 1 p 450 (no 3012).

1230.[20] In 1232 the abbot died and the monks had to obtain their patron's license to elect his successor. According to the monks' account of the proceeding, Hubert gave his license freely, did not interfere in the election, and admitted their choice without demur, only urging the abbot to relinquish the pomp of the world and diligently watch over his house and his monks. Indeed, Hubert presented the elect to the king and tried to smooth his way with the bishop of Worcester, who was angry with the monks of Tewksbury. A similar case, though Hubert was not personally the patron but was apparently acting for the king as patron, involved the long-standing dispute between the monks of Christ Church, Canterbury, and the monks of Rochester concerning the rights claimed by the former over the latter.[21] In May 1229, during the vacancy of the archdiocese, Hubert came to Canterbury with a large entourage and sought to settle the dispute. At the justiciar's instance, the prior and convent of Canterbury remitted all their claims and gave the kiss of peace to the representatives of the monks of Rochester. Then, in September when the king and justiciar came to Canterbury on the new archbishop's receipt of his pallium, the king asked this peace be confirmed by another kiss between the prior of Canterbury and the subprior of Rochester. Some earthly honour may have accrued to Hubert by this display of his state and dignity, but one can hardly deny him due praise for his encouragement of Christian charity among the black monks or doubt his religious motivation in so doing.

When Hubert de Burgh was dismissed from court 29 July 1232, he did not flee the country as so many of his contemporaries had done. Rather, not once but three times he fled to the sanctuary of the church and looked to God and his saints and ministers for protection. Hubert first took sanctuary at Merton priory, where on 22 September he prostrated himself before the high altar until the London mob which threatened his life, was turned back by royal order.[22] Thence going north probably to join his wife and daughter in sanctuary at Bury St Edmunds,[23] he had reached Brentwood in Essex when the king

---

[20] *MA*, 2 pp 79–81.

[21] *Flores historiarum*, ed H. R. Luard, 3 vols, *RS* 95 (1890) 2 pp 196–7, printed from a Rochester source. See also the Dover Annals, BM MS Cotton Julius D V fol 27ᵛ.

[22] *Chronica majora*, 3 pp 224–6; *Annales de Theokesberia*, [*Annales Monastici*], ed H. R. Luard, 5 vols, *RS* 36 (1864–69) 1 p 86.

[23] *Close Rolls*, [*Henry III*], *1231–1234* (London 1905) p 161; *Chronica majora*, 3 p 226; 6 p 64.

sent out troops to capture him.[24] They found him in sanctuary in a chapel there, dressed only in his shirt and again clinging to the altar. He was seized, nonetheless, and taken to the Tower of London, and when the bishop of London secured his return to Brentwood, he was besieged there until in early November he left of his own accord rather than be outlawed. After humiliation before the Londoners, Hubert was imprisoned in Devizes castle.[25] The next summer he became fearful for his life and persuaded two members of the garrison to carry him out of the castle at night into the sanctuary of a church just across the moat. Again he was hauled back into custody and again the diocesan bishop forced his return to sanctuary. Again he was besieged, but this time he was carried away into Wales by an old comrade who was allied with the Marshal in his rebellion. Thus was Hubert saved for the reconciliation with the king which took place the next spring. He had good reason to believe in the efficacy of sanctuary, of prayers, of good deeds, even of miracles. But when he first entrusted himself—and separately his wife and daughter—to sanctuary, he could not know how well things would turn out; he simply trusted in the benignity, the mercy, and the love of God. Wendover says he bore all his trials with equanimity: 'having a clear conscience, as he said, he commended his cause to the Lord.'[26]

His belief in Providence appears also in the one extant letter in which Hubert indicates something of his religious belief.[27] He wrote from Brittany in July 1230 to the chancellor and regent, the bishop of Chichester, about the crossing of the king's expeditionary force in May and its activities since then. Hubert had not favoured this expedition and indeed it caused the first known rift between the old justiciar and the young king who had so long been guided by his minister. But in his letter Hubert is objective about the campaign and hopeful of the king's progress into Poitou which was about to begin, 'the Most High conceding.' No one, he says, is able to triumph over his enemies, unless the Lord of Hosts leads him. Therefore, he begs the prayers of the bishop, that 'you may solicitously and earnestly invoke and cause to be invoked for us the grace of the Most High that He may

[24] *Ibid* 3 pp 226–30; *Close rolls, 1231–1234*, pp 153–5, 161; *Annales de Dunstaplia*, [*Annales Monastici*], 3 pp 129–38.
[25] *Foedera* I pt I pp 207–8; *Chronica majora*, 3 pp 232–4, 249–50, 252–3; *Calendar of Patent Rolls Henry III, 1232–1247* (London 1906) pp 27, 28–30; *Close Rolls 1231–1234*, pp 325–6, 327, 328–9 twice, 350; *Annales de Theokesberia*, p 91.
[26] *Chronica majora*, 3 p 229.
[27] PRO Ancient Correspondence, SC 1/6/101.

direct and order us and our acts.' The letter may well have been written by Hubert's own chancellor, Richard de St John, who wrote to the bishop of Chichester at the same time in a similar style.[28] But in the reference to God as 'the Most High' and in the general tone of the letter one may detect Hubert's own personality. The letter shows him deeply conscious of God's will, firmly believing in the efficacy of prayer, and highly respectful of the clergy's spiritual role.

Hubert's religious education can only be approached obliquely. He was a literate man. A royal record tells us that he had a psalter with him in sanctuary at Brentwood[29] and Matthew Paris further says that Hubert completed a devotion from it for the soul of his old enemy, earl Ranulph of Chester, who died while Hubert was besieged.[30] Hubert must then have had a fair degree of schooling and might well have read more of the bible than the psalter. By 1219 he had employed a chaplain, Luke of Wissant, who had earlier been a chaplain to the king and then to Pandulf, the papal nuncio and legate, and was called his 'venerable friend' by the abbot of Prémontré.[31] Luke was a curialist clerk who became treasurer of the king's household, but he was also canon of London and Salisbury, dean of St Martin's le Grand, and ultimately archbishop of Dublin.[32] So far as he participated in the life of the chapters of St Paul's and of St Martin's as well as the papal curia, Luke can hardly have failed to bring Hubert de Burgh into touch with the thought and feeling of important and influential elements of the church. Hubert's brother Geoffrey and his nephew Thomas de Blundville were clerks who largely by his influence were elevated to the bishoprics of Ely and Norwich respectively;[33] but their own religious training and motivation is less well known than Hubert's and their influence upon him cannot be evaluated. On the other hand, Hubert's knowledge of all the prelates of England must have been very extensive and his contacts with some of them religiously as well as politically important to him. Just association with Stephen Langton alone, Paris theologian as well as cardinal

[28] *Royal Letters*, 1 pp 379–80 (no CCCX).
[29] *Close Rolls, 1231–1234*, p 161.
[30] *Chronica majora*, 3 pp 229–30.
[31] *Rotuli litterarum patentium*, ed T. D. Hardy (London 1835) p 68; *Rotuli litterarum clausarum*, ed T. D. Hardy, 2 vols (London 1833–44) 1 pp 75, 153b, 196b, 387b, 445b; *Patent Rolls, [Henry III], 1216–1225*, (London 1901) p 185; *Monumenta*, ed C. L. Hugo, p 71.
[32] *Patent Rolls, 1216–1225*, p 512; *Patent Rolls, 1225–1232*, pp 104, 178, 232–37; Le Neve, 1 p 423; *Register of St Osmund*, 2 pp 37, 43–4.
[33] *Annales de Waverleia, [Annales Monastici]*, 2 p 301; *Chronica majora*, 3 p 121.

archbishop, can hardly have failed to influence Hubert's view of the universe and thus his religious motivation. Politically Langton stood for the liberties of the church, the rights of subjects, the preservation of property, justice, and peace. If Stephen and Hubert were not agreed fully on the respective rights of subjects and kings, they were both believers in the preservation of peace and cooperated in quieting disturbances in both England and Wales. But Langton's influence on Hubert's religion may have been less important than his mother's training or the values of a respected master in arms, whatever they may have been.

In his role as a governor and a judge, Hubert has been charged with serious shortcomings. Not that he was unable or unwilling to do justice: his seneschalship of Poitou was remembered as a time when justice was done and malefactors hanged.[34] The Londoners hated him because he had brought troops into their city after a football riot in 1222 and had given short shrift to rich and well-connected citizens who had uttered the French warcry.[35] But in 1223 it was complained against him that he did not rule the kingdom 'with equal laws.[36] and the complainants made enough of a case that he had to take the bishops of Bath and Salisbury as colleagues in government for the rest of the minority.[37] No more than Edward Coke or Francis Bacon was he above the receipt of gifts for the exercise of his influence; he acquired a number of rich estates by private gift which were almost certainly bribes.[38] In one case, a man complained after Hubert's disgrace that his friends had given an advowson to Hubert to save the man's life, and a sizeable payment was required then to clear the title.[39] Also, after his disgrace a number of people came forward to complain of 'unjust disinherisons, of exactions, of spoliations', and if the juries of inquest were honest, Hubert or his seneschals and bailiffs were guilty of raiding Naboth's vineyard.[40] He was more successful than the other

---

[34] *Royal Letters*, 1 p 96 (no LXXXI).

[35] *Chronica majora*, 3 pp 71–3; *Matthaei Parisiensis Historia Anglorum*, ed F. Madden, 3 vols, RS 44 (1866–69) 2 pp 251–2; *Annales de Dunstaplia*, pp 78–9.

[36] *Chronica majora*, 3 p 79.

[37] See the attestation of chancery writs beginning 12 December 1223 and continuing into 1226, though the king took on more and more independence during these years.

[38] Winford Eagle, Dorset; Newington-next-Hythe and its outliers in Kent; the honour of Hornby in Lancashire; Wheatley, Notts; Long Compton, Warwickshire.

[39] PRO Curia Regis Rolls KB 26/120 mem 23d; PRO Feet of Fines CP 25(1)/156/63 no 739.

[40] *Chronica majora*, 3 p 223; *Close Rolls, 1231–1234*, pp 163, 173, 177 (compare 209), 179, 191, 196 (compare 223), 208, 218, 230, 242, 248, 362. That Hubert's officials may have been more to blame than he, see PRO Ancient Correspondence SC 1/6/141.

magnates in enriching himself at the expense of the king, both with
grants of lands in fee and of custodies of heirs with their lands.[41]
Modern historians have accused him of avarice, but contemporaries
do not seem to have made the charge. When he was disgraced, he
was charged with many things which even Roger of Wendover thought
were maliciously mendacious, [42] but the key to the king's anger seems
to have been the belief that Hubert had been unfaithful to him in the
receipt and expenditure of royal revenues during his tenure of the
justiciarship.[43] The evidence which his enemies used to convince the
king of his infidelity can no longer be identified, and on the other
hand one might say with Wendover that Hubert made enemies
among the magnates by his very loyalty to the king's interests.[44]
Hubert said that his conscience was clear and despite the evidence of
his enemies which was given in his absence, he may have been less a
sinner than sinned against. At least, the case is moot.

In sum, Hubert de Burgh was a Christian believer whose religion could
move him deeply in the darkest moments of his disgrace, perhaps less
deeply in the case of the crusade, and arguably still less deeply in ethical
matters like justice and property. His Christianity led him to believe in
the clemency and providence of God, in the cult of the saints, in prayer
and ritual, in dreams and miracles; perhaps less important to him was
the confession of sins, contrition and penance, the resolve to sin no
more. Yet, he had a conscience, he could be compassionate, and he
had shown constancy in a good cause more than once. If religion is
known to have moved him at so many points in his life, his biographer
must give sufficient attention to religion in those incidents when his
motivation is unknown. When Hubert opposed the invasion of
France in 1230, for example, was it because he had been bought by the
French court, or was it not that he foresaw profitless conflict and
preferred peace, perhaps looked to that which Henry finally made in
1259? When he built castles in Wales and launched a major effort to
conquer that land, was it only from personal interest or even English
national interests; or might he not have seen conquest as a way of
pacifying that wild land? When he married Margaret of Scotland,

[41] At the time of his disgrace Hubert was almost certainly the richest subject in the land:
not only had he built up an earldom of Kent worth about £1500 a year, but he held
the custodies of the earldoms of Arundel, Clare and Gloucester as well as the rich
baronies of Mowbray, Avrenches, and Briouse of Totnes and the Marches.
[42] *Chronica majora*, 3 p 222.
[43] *Ibid* 3 pp 220–1.
[44] *Ibid* 3 p 221.

was it only for personal ambition or was it also to help seal the peace between England and Scotland that lasted even beyond his period of power? All of which is not to say that Hubert de Burgh might not have sought power and wealth for themselves as well as the good they could do. He was no saint. But his biographer must assess the extent to which his religion moved him towards good.

University of Connecticut

CHRISTIANS, JEWS AND MUSLIMS IN THE SAME SOCIETY: THE FALL OF *CONVIVENCIA* IN MEDIEVAL SPAIN

by ROGER HIGHFIELD

O N I March 1492 the Jews were expelled from Spain.[1] Ten years later the Moorish inhabitants of Castile were offered the alternative of conversion or emigration.[2] The fate of the Moors in the kingdoms of the Crown of Aragon was deferred until the reign of the emperor Charles V.[3] But though he kept the inquisition out of Aragon for forty years, he did not succeed in reconciling his Morisco subjects with their Christian brothers.[4] Philip II failed much more notably. For his policy stimulated the great Morisco revolt of 1568–70. Thereafter they were scattered round the kingdom in a forced diaspora.[5] In 1582 their expulsion was proposed in the council of state.[6] Finally in 1609–10 the government of Philip III, chastened by the twelve years truce in the Netherlands, set about the expulsion of all the three hundred thousand or so Moriscos who remained.[7]

Thus was Christian unformity established in a country which had seen in the early middle ages adherents of the three religions living side by side. At the end of the eleventh century Alfonso VI had prided himself on being emperor of the two laws, Christianity and Islam.[8] When Zaida, widow of the governor of Córdoba, had fled to his court, Alfonso had received her as his concubine[9] and had had her baptised with the name of Isabel. The Cid, who had made himself

[1] *Documentos [acerca de la expulsión de los judíos,* ed L. Suárez] Fernández (Valladolid 1964) pp 391–5.
[2] [M. A.] Ladero [Quesada] *Los mudéjares [de Castilla en tiempo de Isabel I]* (Valladolid 1969) pp 320–4.
[3] [J.] Lynch, [*Spain under the Hapsburgs*], 2 vols (Oxford 1964–9) I p 207.
[4] *Ibid* pp 205, 208.
[5] *Ibid* pp 215–17, and see J. Caro Baroja, *Los moriscos del reino de Granada* (Madrid 1957) pp 57–85; H. Lapeyre, *Géographie de l'Espagne morisque* (Paris 1959) pp 124–5; [P.] Boronat, [*Los moriscos españoles y su expulsión*], 2 vols (Valencia 1901) I pp 291–4, in Lynch I p 209 n 9.
[6] Boronat I pp 291–4.
[7] Lynch 2 pp 44–5.
[8] [J. F.] O'Callaghan, [*A History of Medieval Spain*] (Ithaca 1975) p 207.
[9] *Ibid* p 213.

ruler of the Moorish kingdom of Valencia, had been an enthusiast for Arabic literature.[10] In the thirteenth century Peter III of Aragon regularly witnessed documents in Arabic,[11] while the son of St Ferdinand was buried in a mantle sown with a Muslim design and the Arabic word *Baraka*, blessing, embroidered on it in Kufic characters.[12] Alfonso X himself went one better than Alfonso VI when he recognized the importance of Muslim biblical scholarship and under-wrote the orthodoxy of Jewish law. As Hillgarth has observed, he was closer in thought to a caliph than he was to Louis IX or to Edward I.[13]

Alfonso acknowledged the important part which the Jewish minority played in his kingdom in many ways. For the Jews were doctors, tax-collectors and middlemen in many different trades and professions. For reasons which we need not examine here they had been very well represented in Roman Spain. When the Muslims conquered the Visigoths the conquerors had received a warm welcome from the Spanish Jews who expected to be better treated under the Muslims than they had been under the Christians.[14] And so no doubt they were, since they were held to be equal under the law; nor could they be blamed by the Muslims for the death of Mohammed, as they were by the Christians for the death of Christ. However at the end of the thirteenth century their position in Christian Spain still seemed strong, just at a time when, by contrast, in England and in France agitation was being worked up against them. That agitation culminated in the expulsion of the Jews from England in 1290 and from France soon afterwards. In those countries economic and political factors had worked against them. The story of the fall of good relations between the English Christians and the Jews in the thirteenth century has been well worked out by the late Dr Roth.[15] Here we need perhaps only note two features of that story — firstly the role of the Jews as royal tax-collectors had led them to be particularly vulnerable in periods of financial and economic stress; and secondly, as their position worsened, myths appeared like those connected with the deaths of little St William of Norwich[16] and

[10] R. Menéndez Pidal, *La España del Cid* (Buenos Aires 1939) pp 424–5.
[11] *Ibid* p 421.
[12] A. F. Kendrick, 'Textiles' in *Spanish Art, Burlington Magazine monograph* 2 (London 1927) p 65.
[13] [J.] Hillgarth, [*The*] *Spanish Kingdoms, 1250–1516*], 2 vols (Oxford 1976) I p 220.
[14] O'Callaghan pp 47, 51, 92.
[15] C. Roth, *A History of the Jews in England* (Oxford 1941) pp 38–90.
[16] *Ibid* p 9.

little Hugh of Lincoln.[17] William was said to have been crucified by the Jews of Norwich and Hugh to have been killed by those of Lincoln for ritualistic purposes. Comparable phenomena were to recur in the build-up to the Spanish expulsion.[18]

The height of Muslim influence in medieval Christian Spain was probably reached at the end of the thirteenth century under Alfonso X of Castile. He himself presided over the finest productions of the so-called 'School of Toledo'. There since the end of the eleventh century translations from the Arabic had been undertaken; a centre of studies and a channel had been provided through which Greco-Arabic learning had reached the west. If Alfonso was the author of the *Cantigas de Santa María* ascribed to him, then the king himself wrote poetry in a Muslim form known as the *zejel* and the majority of these *Songs to the Virgin* were cast in a Muslim verse formation. The Moorish jongleurs who sang and accompanied this kind of poetry on lutes were famous. The fourteenth century Castilian poet, the archpriest of Hita, wrote similar songs especially to be sung by Moorish jongleuses. Their singing and playing in churches created something of a scandal; and in 1322 the council of Valladolid forbade it. However we must not overpaint the picture of the interpenetration of Muslim, Jewish and Christian influences or of the peaceful *convivencia* between the three communities. Encouragement of Jewish translators from the Arabic was one thing, effective protection of the minority communities quite another. Alfonso himself inherited a long tradition of Christian restrictions of the Jews as well as one of tolerance; and the *Seven Parts*, his great law code, reflected both traditions.[19] Moreover Islam no less than Christianity was subject to fits of intensified zeal and to bouts of persecution. The most striking period of Muslim persecution of Christians had been in the ninth century. Arabised Christians or Mozarabs had then made a notable exodus to the Christian kingdoms of the north, and they did so again in the twelfth century. In the thirteenth a still greater threat to

---

[17] *Ibid* pp 56–7.

[18] For the history of a Christian boy ritually murdered in imitation of the crucifixion at Saragossa in 1250 and for Berceo's account of a re-enactment by Jews of the crucifixion on a wax figure at Toledo see Hillgarth 1 pp 212–13.

[19] Under it Jews were not allowed to hold public office (*Ibid* p 296). They were to be allowed to live among Christians 'so that they may live for ever in captivity that men may remember that they come from the lineage of those who crucified our Lord Jesus Christ.' [*Las*] *Siete Partidas* [*del rey Alfonso X*], 3 vols, Real Academia (Madrid 1807) VII, xxiv. 1; Hillgarth 1 p 210.

convivencia had developed at the Roman curia. The third and fourth
Lateran councils issued specific restrictive legislation to govern
relations between Christians, Jews and Moors. This legislation aimed
at setting the communities apart physically in Christian, Jewish and
Moorish quarters and in making the Jews and Moors wear distinctive
dress so that they could be recognised. The establishment of the
Dominican and Franciscan orders meant that the papacy had an army
of zealous supporters who wished to further the success of its
intentions in Spain as in the rest of Europe. Nevertheless despite these
developments there is still a striking difference between the world of
Alfonso X and that of Ferdinand and Isabella. How had this
remarkable transformation come about?

Much of the story is well known, thanks in particular to the work of
Hillgarth, who in the first volume of his notable book, *The Spanish
Kingdoms*, has taken the subject from 1250 to 1410.[20] The long
neglected social and economic sides of the downfall of the Jews have
been treated in definitive fashion by Wolff[21] and MacKay.[22] The
special problem of the converted Jews has been the subject of great
debate between the late Américo Castro and Sanchez Albornoz;[23]
Henry Kamen has told the story of the inquisition,[24] while for Islam
the topic has been much illuminated by Southern's lectures.[25] However
considerable problems remain. For when the views in favour of
expulsion of the Jews triumphed in 1492 and for the conversion or
expulsion of the Muslims in 1502 in Castile, these were by no means
favoured by all the Christian leaders. The supporters of these
developments, Torquemada, the Dominican, and Cisneros, the
Franciscan, have taken the limelight.[26] The Jeronimite, Talavera, has
tended to be overlooked. Southern has reminded us, moreover, how

[20] *Ibid* 1 esp cap 5.
[21] P. Wolff, 'The 1391 pogrom in Spain. Social crisis or not?', *PP* 50 (1971) pp 4–18.
[22] [A.] MacKay, ['Popular movements and pogroms in fifteenth-century Castile',] *ibid* 55 (1972) pp 35–67.
[23] Américo Castro, *España en su Historia* (Buenos Aires 1948) trans W. F. King and S. Margaretten as *The Spaniards: an introduction to their history* (Berkley 1971) C. Sánchez Albornoz, *España, un enigma histórico*, 2 vols (Buenos Aires 1956). The controversy is summarised by O'Callaghan pp 18–19, and see now [E.] Benito Ruano, *Los orígenes [del problema converso]* (Barcelona, 1976).
[24] [H.] Kamen, [*The Spanish Inquisition*] (London 1965) and see also [Tarsicio de] Azcona, [*Isabel la Católica* (Madrid 1964)] cap 6.
[25] [R. W.] Southern, [*Western Views of Islam in the Middle Ages*] (Cambridge, Mass., 1962).
[26] For the attitude of cardinal Mendoza see A. Albors, *La Inquisición y el Cardenal de España* (Valencia, 1896) in Azcona p 386 n 51.

in the 1450s another Spanish thinker, John of Segovia, had favoured the method of conference between members of different religions as a means of governing their relations. What did these contrary views amount to? Why were they superceded?

As Wolff, MacKay and Benito Ruano have shown the problem of the Jews in Christian society in Spain became complicated in the fifteenth century by the great numbers of the converted. The civil war in Castile between Peter the Cruel and Henry II was stoked by anti-semitism. The fact that Peter had been particularly well served by Jewish civil servants and taxgatherers enabled Henry to inflame public opinion against the Jews. The pogroms of 1391 were the result. There followed waves of conversion which more or less broke up the Jewish communities in some of the large cities like Seville and Toledo, though the same was not true of the smaller towns. But the *conversos* presented fresh difficulties. For their conversion opened to them appointments to offices and in particular to municipal offices. To quote MacKay, 'Conversion which seemed temporarily to solve many tensions, opened more opportunities to the converted Jew in terms of finance, tax administration and officeholding.'[27] For about half a century it looked as if the *conversos* might indeed be assimilated into Castilian society. John II of Castile, and still more his adviser, Alvaro de Luna, made regular use of Jewish taxfarmers[28] and *converso* administrators, like the royal secretary, Fernán Daíz de Toledo.[29] Members of the family of the *converso* Solomon Halevi of Burgos became learned bishops. He and his son were bishops of Burgos as Pablo de Santa María[30] and Alonso de Cartagena.[31] Other *conversos* intermarried with members of the nobility; thus large numbers of noble families had *converso* relations. Unfortunately other factors were unpropitious—the financial difficulties of the Trastámaras led to a policy of debasement. This in turn accelerated a severe inflation.[32] On top of the existing burdens of taxation[33] a crisis in the supply of grain

[27] MacKay p 42.

[28] [Y. F.] Baer, [*A History of the Jews in Christian Spain*], trans L. Schoffman, 2 vols (Philadelphia 1961/1966) 2 pp 250–1 in MacKay p 42.

[29] Author of the *Instrucción del Relator* in Alonso de Cartagena, *Defensorium Unitatis Christianae*, ed P. Manuel Alonso (Madrid 1943) p 345 in *ibid* p 45 n 2 and see [N.] Round, '[Politics, Style and Group Attitudes in the *Instrucción del Relator*]', *Bulletin of Hispanic Studies* (Liverpool 1923–) 46 (1969) pp 289–319; Azcona p 386 and n 50.

[30] MacKay p 48. Other *converso* bishops were Juan Ortega de Maluenda, bishop of Coria and Gonzalvo García de Santa María, bishop of Plasencia.

[31] O'Callaghan p 607.

[32] MacKay pp 53–4.

[33] *Ibid* p 56.

bore down heavily especially on the towns. Again if the downfall of
Alvaro de Luna in 1453 is compared with that of Peter the Cruel we
find hostility to the *conversos* at least as important a factor as
hostility to the Jews. And in the riots at Toledo in 1449 it was the
conversos who were the main victims.[34] A series of events then broke
out which acted as a pointer to the establishment of the inquisition in
1478–80. In 1449 in a riot at Toledo, Pedro Sarmiento, a rebellious
royal alcalde, issued a decree known as a sentence or statute by which
the *conversos* were to be denied ecclesiastical or municipal office in the
city.[35] There followed a battle of words between a lawyer who
supported Sarmiento and a group of impressive writers who
argued the case for treating the converted like any other Christians.
The lawyer's name was Bachelor Marcos García de Mora.[36] His
opponents included the influential Fernán Díaz de Toledo, already
mentioned, author of a memorandum in favour of the Hebrew
nation[37] which he sent to the bishop of Cuenca. This was Fray Lope
de Barrientos, the champion of the *conversos*. But perhaps the most
striking writer was the *converso* bishop of Burgos, Alonso de Cartagena,
who wrote an important tract in 1449, called *Defensorium Unitatis
Christianae*.

   The defenders of the *conversos* had a cast iron case; but, as has been
seen, this did not stop the downfall in 1453 of one of their and the
Jews' main patrons, don Alvaro de Luna, chief minister of John II of
Castile.[38] And there is no doubt that his favouring of Jews and
conversos played a major role in his collapse. Hostility against them
both thereafter was sustained. Two years later we hear that a Spanish
cardinal, John of Carvajal, had been speaking ill of *conversos* at the
curia. As a result Fernán Díaz de Toledo wrote him a letter in their
defence. In it he raised an interesting and a dangerous point. None of

[34] [E.] Benito Ruano, *Toledo* [*en el siglo XV*] (Madrid 1961) pp 191–6, 96–100; *Memorias de Don Enrique IV*, Real Academia, 2 vols (Madrid 1835–1913) 2 pp 545–51. For an embryonic attempt to establish an inquisition arising from a petition of Henry IV to pope Nicholas V in 1460 see [V. Beltrán de] Heredia, 'Las bulas [de Nicolas V acerca de los conversos de Castilla'], in *Sefarad*, 34 vols (Madrid 1941–   ) 21 (1961) pp 21–47.
[35] The text is in Benito Ruano, *Toledo*, pp 191–6 and see his 'La "Sentencia-Estatuto" de Pero Sarmiento contra los conversos toledanos', Benito Ruano, *Los orígenes*, pp 85–92.
[36] *Ibid* pp 103–32, 'El memorial de los conversos del Bachiller Marcos García de Mora ("Marquillos de Mazarambos")'; A. A. Sicroff, *Les controverses des statuts de 'pureté de sang' en Espagne du XVe au XVIIe siècle* (Paris 1960) pp 33–62.
[37] 'Instruccion del Relator para el obispo de Cuenca, a favor de la nacion Hebrea- ano de 1449', published by Fermín Caballero in *Noticias de la vida, cargos y escritos* [*del doctor Alonso Díaz del Montalvo*] (Madrid 1873) pp 243–54.
[38] [R.] Menéndez Pidal, *Historia de España*, 26 vols (Madrid 1947–   ) 15 (1964) pp 210–11.

the defenders of the *conversos* had any time for *conversos* who were
secret judaizers. Fernán suggested to the cardinal that it might be
necessary to combine protection of the rights of true *conversos* with a
purgation of the undesirable elements among them.[39] This suggests
that one call for an inquisition came from moderate *conversos* anxious
to protect their position as genuine *conversos*. Another stimulus came
from the observant Franciscans. They wrote to the Jeronimites to
invite their common action in a case of an apostate and heretical friar
who had fled to the kingdom of Granada. These seem to have been
some of the events behind the first formal petition of the century for
an inquisition, made in the name of Henry IV of Castile to pope
Nicholas V.[40] The pope was asked 'for the honour and defence of the
Christian faith to allow that with royal agreement two ecclesiastics
should be nominated as inquisitors for New Castile and Andalusia by
Lope de Ribas, bishop of Cartagena and the papal nuncio;[41] and two
more for Old Castile. It is interesting to note that the Castilian Crown
as early as 1460 was reaching forward to the new principle that it
should itself control the inquisition which it requested. In answer to
this petition the pope appointed the papal nuncio as inquisitor general
of the whole kingdom with powers to nominate subordinates.[42]
Perhaps because Nicholas had not given the king what he had asked
for, or more likely because of the political crisis in which Henry soon
found himself, nothing very much seems to have occurred as a result
of the papal response. But that the idea of an inquisition had not been
forgotten was revealed in the heart of that same political crisis, when
the Castilian nobility tried to depose Henry and replace him with
Isabella's brother, Alfonso. In a compromise solution for the problems
of the kingdom, known as the *Sentence of Medina del Campo*, there are
no less than twenty-two articles devoted to the Jewish question and
two concerned with the desirability of the establishment of an
inquisition against those suspected of heresy.[43] This was a request for
the traditional inquisition of the thirteenth century. The *conversos* were
not named but the important point is that the articles show that there

[39] Azcona p 376 and n 25; Round p 290 n 2; P. Sainz de Baranda in Co[lección de] Do[cu-
mentos] In[éditos para la historia de España], 112 vols (Madrid 1842–95) 13 (1848) p 32
n 39.
[40] Heredia, 'Las bulas', pp 21–47 and app 5.
[41] This was Antonia Giacomo Venier, papal collector (Azcona pp 379–80).
[42] *Ibid* p 381.
[43] *Ibid*. For the events which broke out at Toledo in the summer of 1467, culminating in
El fuego de la Magdalena, see Benito Ruano, *Toledo* pp 93–102.

was a steady current of opinion in favour of an inquisition which had been initiated before 1460 and was continued into 1465, long before Ferdinand and Isabella came to the throne or the Spanish Inquisition was established in 1478–80.

A most severe economic crisis, which continued to exacerbate the difficulties of both Jews and *conversos*, occurred between 1465 and 1473. At this stage hostility towards the Jews was revived by the same kind of myth as had appeared in twelfth and thirteenth-century England. We find again atrocity stories surrounding the supposed murders of children. At Sepúlveda in 1468 it was alleged that Jews had performed a ritual murder of a Christian child.[44] Sixteen Jews were punished for the supposed crime. It seems to me very interesting that this kind of myth should have taken the form which it did. For if one asks what is likely to inflame Christians most, the answer would be something involving children and the crucifixion of Christ. If one asks what aroused suspicions against the Jews it seems that the very nature of Judaism marks it off from both Christianity and Islam in that its rituals and services are in large measure closed and secret. This feature laid it open to accusations of secret practices such as ritual murder. Add in the idea of the crucifixion of a child for the sake of magic—itself a very old conception—and you have the atrocity story most likely to cause the maximum effect among Christians. The story of 1468 was to recur on the very eve of the expulsion. In the eighteenth century a special papal commission under cardinal Ganganelli reported that there was absolutely no truth in any of these allegations of ritual murders.[45] Unfortunately that was too late in the day. In fifteenth century Castile the myths were believed; they greatly inflamed public opinion.

Another feature worked in the same direction—the evolution of the concept of purity of blood (*limpieza de sangre*). Perhaps because the Spaniards must be one of the most mixed races in Europe they developed a theory of purity of descent. An instance is provided by the foundation at Salamanca of the college of San Bartolomé by the archbishop of Seville, Diego Añaya Maldonado. His fifteen students had to be suitable in learning, of good report and of pure blood.[46]

The pattern of anti-Jewish and anti-*converso* riots in the 1470s followed that of those at Toledo in the 1440s and 1450s. They were

[44] Menéndez Pidal, *Historia de España*, 15, p 6 n.
[45] See C. Roth, *The Ritual Murder Libel and the Jews* (London 1935).
[46] C. M. Ajo G. y Sainz de Zúñiga, *Historia de las Universidades Hispánicas* (Avila 1957–   ) I p 341.

The fall of convivencia in medieval Spain

popular and they occurred in specific towns. If the riots at Valladolid in 1470 were directed against the Jews, those at Córdoba in 1473 led to the expulsion of the *conversos*.[47] The movement came to a head in Seville in 1477–8 during Isabella's stay in the Andalusian capital. Hostility was inflamed by the preaching of the prior of the Dominican house there—Alonso de Ojeda. His sermons led to a popular demand for an inquisition in Castile.[48] A report on the troubles at Seville revealed that *conversos* were practicing secretly Jewish rites; and this report had the backing of the prior of the Dominican house in Segovia, Thomas of Torquemada.[49] The queen's confessor, Fray Hernando de Talavera, was an opponent of the proposal. He was a Jeronimite and prior of their house at Santa María del Prado,[50] Valladolid. He certainly strongly disliked treating converts from Judaism and Islam worse than Old Christians.[51] If indeed converts became heretics then the proper punishment for them was ex-communication as St Paul had shown.[52] They should certainly not be killed, for as Tertullian had said, no Christian should be the executioner even of his greatest enemies,[53] and St John Chrysostom had declared to condemn a heretic to death is an unpardonable crime.[54] With regard to the forcible conversion of Jews he argued that the fourth council of Toledo (meeting under the aegis of St Isidore) had denounced it in general and in particular recent examples which had occurred under king Sisebut.[55] On the issue of the offering of rewards for conversion he quoted pope Leo IX's canons from the council of

[47] Baer 2 pp 306–8.
[48] Kamen pp 34–5.
[49] *Ibid* p 35.
[50] Mosén Diego de Valera, *Crónica*, ed J. de Mata Carriazo (Madrid 1957) p 123 n 1 (quoting Zurita and MS L); and see [F. Márquez] Villanueva [*Investigaciones sobre Juan Alvaro de Gato*] (Madrid 1960) p 130.
[51] Kamen p 52.
[52] [Fidel] Fernández, [*Fray Hernando de Talavera*] (Madrid 1942). The argument seems to be derived from 1 Cor 5 and perhaps from Rom 16:17.
[53] The most likely passage which Talavera had in mind seem to be Apologeticum 46:15, *Corpus Scriptorum Latinorum Paravianum*, ed P. Frassinetti (Turin 1965) pp 107–8. I owe this suggestion to the kindness of Mr G. Fowden.
[54] Fernández p 173. I have been unable to follow up this author's reference to 'Historia Bibliográfica de Granada', thesis for the Academia Provincial de Bellas Artes de Granada.
[55] HL 3, pt i (1909) p 274, esp canon 57 and the general reference to the council of Toledo in [A.] Gómez, ['De rebus gestis Francisci Ximenii'], in *Hispaniae Illustratae*, ed A. Schott, 4 vols (Frankfort 1603–8) 1 p 959; for a disputed passage of the fourth council see the unedited reply of Lope de Barrientos, bishop of Cuenca to a bachelor, in Fermín Caballero, *Noticias de la vida, cargos y escritos*, app 1, pp 323–42.

Rheims.[56] However the Catholic Monarchs, in what doubtless seemed
to them to have been emergency conditions, decided to yield to the
arguments of the Dominicans; they asked Sixtus IV for an inquisition.
Here was at last the parting of the ways. In Rome the pope granted
the royal request if, like Nicholas V, before him, he seems to have
acted with some reluctance.[57] In fact it does not appear as though
either crown or papacy had a clear idea of what they were about to
create. The Aragonese inquisition of the thirteenth century had soon
died out. The initiative of 1459–60 had come to a standstill. But the
Castilian inquisition, which became the Spanish inquisition, was to last
till the nineteenth century. The fact that it was the child of popular
initiative and that its control lay chiefly in Castilian hands seems to
have been the main reason for its longevity. Justifiable fear of its
effects led the *conversos* of Seville in 1480 to mount a conspiracy in
order to defend themselves. When the plot was discovered its leaders
were burned in the first *auto da fe*, 6 February 1481.[58] Hojeda preached
the sermon before the *auto*. Though he died soon afterwards the
inquisition quickly struck deep roots. Its establishment spelled the
imminent end of *convivencia* between Christians and Jews. In 1483 a
partial expulsion of the Jews from Andalusia was ordered.[59] But for
the moment the Catholic Monarchs were absorbed, first in mounting
and then in executing the campaign against Granada. Jewish financiers,
such as Abraham Senior and Isaac Abrabanel, played a loyal and
important part in helping to finance the war.[60] However war
taxation pressed hard on the Castilian townsmen, especially in
Andalusia. Jewish doctors continued to frequent the court, and the
royal policy of protection for Jewish quarters was maintained, but
fiscal pressure continued to exacerbate relations between Jews and
Christians. Among several signs of increasing pressure may be noted
the fact that the viceroy of Spanish-held Sardinia in 1488 intensified

[56] It is not very easy to see which canons of the council Talavera had in mind. No 2 forbade
the purchase or sale of orders and no 5 the taking of fees for baptism. A ban on offering
rewards for baptism might be deduced from these two canons and that would echo
the same views as were expressed in the *Seven Parts* on offering rewards for conversion,
see HL, 4 pt 2 (1911) p 1023.
[57] 1 November 1478, see Kamen p 35.
[58] *Ibid* p 37.
[59] *Documentos*, p 35 (Córdoba, Cádiz and Jerez); expulsion from Seville followed between
1484 and 1491.
[60] For Abraham Senior see [M. A.] Ladero [Quesada,] *Castilla y [la conquista del reino de]
Granada* (Valladolid 1967) p 221 and *Documentos, passim.* For Abrabanel and the
sources quoted by Azcona see his *Isabel* p 644 no 40.

restrictions against the Jews.[61] They were forbidden to live outside ghettoes or to ride abroad or to transact business on feast days except indoors. Nor might they leave the island or export goods. Meanwhile in Andalusia and New Castile popular outbreaks against both Jews and *conversos* reached a new intensity. Anti-Semitism was whipped up by a scare known as the case of the Holy Child of La Guardia, a place in the archdiocese of Toledo. It was alleged that a Christian child had been crucified and had had its heart cut out in order to create a magic spell, by which Judaism should triumph and Christianity be destroyed. On 17 December 1490 in a paroxysm of hysteria two Jews and six *conversos* of La Guardia were killed.[62]

Two years later, with the city and kingdom of Granada conquered, and with gusts of anti-semitism blowing strongly in New Castile and Andalusia Ferdinand and Isabella abaondoned their role as protectors of the minority; they ordered the Jews to accept conversion or to be expelled.[63] Those orders were given on 31 March 1492. Of a total of between 100,000 and 200,000 Jews the majority preferred exile to conversion and fled to Portugal, Navarre, Aragon, Africa or the Netherlands.[64] Perhaps a quarter of the total remained as *conversos*. Though that was only the beginning of their troubles we must leave them there.

It is worth observing, however, that the fears about the Jews and *conversos* were in no way political. No foreign power was outraged by their expulsion. No one could intervene to protect them. The emotions they aroused were fears for the practice of Christianity, fears of contamination by intermarriage, and jealousy of the success and power in high places of the converted; it was alleged, moreover, that they were not properly converted, but remained secret adherents of Judaism. By contrast with the myths of La Guardia the records of the inquisition recently examined and published by Beinart do strongly suggest that in this last respect the accusations were not without

---

[61] A. Boscolo, 'Gli ebrei in Sardegna durante la dominazione aragonese da Alfonso III a Ferdinando il Cattolico'. *V Congreso de la Historia de la Corona de Aragón*, Estudios, 5 vols (Saragossa 1952–61) 2 pp 9–17. Between 1484 and 1486 there had been increasing pressure on the Jews of Burgos (*Documentos* p 33), on those of Vitoria and other centres (*Ibid* pp 33–4).

[62] Fidel Fita, 'La verdad sobre el martirio del Santo Niño de la Guardia', B[oletín de la R[eal] A[cademia de] H[istoria], 11 (Madrid 1887] pp 7–134.

[63] *Documentos* no 177, pp 391–5.

[64] F. Baer, following Bernáldez, gives a total of 200,000 (*Die Vertreibung der Juden aus Spanien* in Millás Vallicrosa, *Sefarad* 6 (1943) pp 163–88); but the number may be an overestimate, *Documentos* pp 55–64.

foundation.[65] Indeed could it have been otherwise? The Jews have the strongest feelings for the family and for the community. In their hour of need they naturally hung together closely. Again if one is offered the choice between conversion or exile that is only one step better than conversion or death. It is not to be expected that conversion thus effected will be more than skin-deep, even if the ecclesiastical authorities mount a major programme of education of the converted such as later cardinal Cisneros was to seek to do.

Before turning to the Muslims let us consider the legal position in Castile on the subject of conversion. For the great law code of Alfonso X—the *Seven Parts*—had an important section devoted to the problem. It dealt with the Moors especially, but also with the Jews, and it faced squarely many of the practical issues of the living together of Chrstians, Jews and Muslims. Title xxv of the seventh part, law I says that Muslims should live among Christians in the same way as Jews, that is keeping their law and not abusing the Christian. In towns where Christians live Muslims ought not to have mosques nor make sacrifices in public.[66]

Law 2 prescribes that Christians should try to convert Muslims by good words and suitable sermons and not by force nor by offering rewards . . . Anyone who interferes with the legitimate process of conversion of a Muslim should be punished in the same way as a Jew would be who killed a *converso* or prevented a Jew from being converted.[67] Another law of the same title protected Muslims who turned Christian from being dishonoured,[68] and another ensured the safe passage of Muslim representatives travelling to Spain on legitimate business.[69]

As is well known there are many signs that, although Alfonso's code was in itself never fully effective, for long this part of it did correspond to much that went on the field of conversion. Southern has shown[70] how down to the early fourteenth century conversion was still genuinely attempted by disputation as the *Seven Parts* had suggested that it should be. The point is particularly well demonstrated

[65] *Records of the trials of the Spanish Inquisition in Ciudad Real*, ed H. Bienart (Jerusalem 1974) I; see also J. Caro Baroja, *Los judíos en la España moderna y contemporánea*, 3 vols (Madrid 1962) I pp 275-7.
[66] *Siete Partidas*, 3 pp 675-6.
[67] *Ibid.*
[68] Law 3 (*Ibid* p 677).
[69] Law 9 (*Ibid* pp 680-1).
[70] Southern pp 67-74.

The fall of convivencia in medieval Spain

by the career of Ramón Lull. In 1263 there had been a disputation before the king of Aragon in which a Dominican friar had argued with a rabbi.[71] Lull himself had been in close contact with the group of Barcelona Jews from which the rabbi came. Then in 1293 Lull extended his range by going to Tunis to preach to and dispute with the Muslims. One might have supposed that this would have proved rather a hopeless method of procedure.[72] But it is recorded that he had considerable success, and that when he was ultimately expelled some Muslim scholars were ready to be converted and baptised.[73] He must have hoped that if a Muslim scholar of great repute could be converted, or a rabbi, that act in itself might bring over to Christianity a whole following. A similar effort by a Dominican—Ramón Martí—to convert the king of Tunis, must also have aimed at getting that king to set an example to his people, as Clovis or the Anglo-Saxon kings had done.[74] Hillgarth has pointed out Lull's greatest achievement was to have persuaded the council of Vienne to decree in 1311 that pairs of catholic scholars should teach Hebrew, Arabic and Syrian at the curia and at the four universities of Oxford, Paris, Salamanca and Bologna.[75] The only known result of this initiative seems to have been the appointment of teachers of Hebrew and Syrian at Paris and at the curia.[76] But the tradition took time to die away. A contemporary of Lull, much influenced by him was Don Juan Manuel, of the Castilian blood royal, the author of the *Libro de Estados*. Hillgarth has shown that he 'fully shared or even surpassed Lull's spirit of tolerance for Islam and his confidence in the use of reason in theological argument.'[77] The form of the set disputation actually lasted until 1412–14 when a debate was held at Tortosa.[78] But by that

---

[71] Hillgarth p 166. The Dominicans were particularly active. They founded schools for training missionaries in Hebrew and Arabic at Tunis (before 1250), at Murcia (1266) at Valencia and Játiva. The Franciscans founded the college of Miramar, Majorca, None of these schools seems to have survived long.

[72] Ramón Martí seems to have given it up after the 1263 disputation and took to writing his major work—the *Pugio Fidei contra Judaeos*, in which he defended Christianity against the Jews. In it he drew heavily on St Thomas Aquinas's *Summa contra Gentiles*, a treatise on natural theology intended to equip missionaries for debate and argumentation with Muslims' (O'Callaghan p 496); see Hillgarth pp 165–6.

[73] J. N. Hillgarth, *Ramon Lull and Lullism in Fourteenth-Century France* (Oxford 1971) p 26.

[74] *Ibid* p 22.   [76] *Ibid* pp 128–9 n 347.

[75] *Ibid* pp 29, 128 and n 344.   [77] Hillgarth p 225.

[78] However the dispute had been forced on the unwilling Jews by the anti-pope Benedict XIII and was by way of being a forcible instruction of the Jews in the Christian religion, see A. Pacios López, *La Disputa de Tortosa*, 2 vols (Madrid 1957).

date, as Southern has shown, a period of hope was changing into one of disillusionment, and the disputation was now little more than a prejudiced setpiece of propaganda. Nor do the Spanish universities of the late middle ages seem to have contributed much to the study of Hebrew, Arabic or Syrian. However along the frontier between Castile and Granada the practical business of living side by side forced men's hands and minds; there Arabic interpreters were the order of the day. There were also special judges appointed from both Christian and Muslim judiciaries to deal with cases which concerned both Muslims and Christians. There was also a Castilian judicial officer known as the *Alcalde Mayor* of the Moors to whom appeal could be made.[79] There were also two orders—the Mercedarians and the Trinitarians—who had to cultivate Arabic, since they had regular contact with the Moors in their work of rescuing and ransoming Christian captives.[80] As Southern has reminded us, when John of Segovia wanted to get a text of the Koran and a Muslim jurist to interpret it, he had to wait two years after applying to the university of Salamanca and the general of the Franciscan order.[81] He might have done better to have approached the Mercedarians or the Trinitarians or the *Alcalde Mayor* of the Moors. Another reason for the survival of a tolerant concept of *convivencia* was more theoretical. It lay in the fact that although the fifteenth century grew more prejudiced in Castile it also paid more and more attention to the *Seven Parts* of Alfonso X; and they came to be accepted as a text for study[82] and as the basis for the codification of the law, asked for by the cortes in 1433 and again in 1438. Both practical and theoretical influences were thus at work when the conquest of Granada was completed in 1492.

The terms of the capitulation of Granada were, as is well-known extremely generous.[83] They formed the culmination of a series of capitulations with surrendering towns between 1488 and 1492. Ladero has traced the considerable differences between the sets of

[79] See Ladero, *Los mudéjares*, p 23 and n 19. On 17 January 1475 Abraham Jarafe, alfaquí, doctor and member of the household of archbishop Carrillo held this position.
[80] The Mercedarians had been founded by Peter Nolasco. The order had been helped by James I of Aragon to set itself up in the kingdom of Valencia and Raymond Penyafort had drawn up its constitutions, O'Callaghan p 497. The Trinitarians were a French order. Both were founded to negotiate for Christians captured by Muslims.
[81] Southern p 88.
[82] G. Beneyto Pérez, 'Science of Law in Spain of the Catholic Kings', in *Spain in the Fifteenth Century*, ed Roger Highfield (New York 1972) p 282.
[83] M. Garrido Atienza, *Las Capitulaciones para la entrega de Granada* (Granada 1910).

terms.[84] In each case those who did not wish to be converted were offered the alternative of emigration. The crown agreed to provide shipping for the emigrants at Almería and a free passage if they emigrated within a year. They were also allowed to take their goods. An important member of the royal family of Granada (named Yahya) on accepting baptism was assured of property (in the río de Almería area), exempted from the alcabalá tax, freed from billeting, allowed to keep a troop of twenty armed men and given a substantial income. If any of this was promised before baptism, it must have come close to conversion by reward. The capitulations allowed the Muslims to keep their own laws. The position of converts from Christianity, that is, of renegades, was carefully protected. Local uses and customs were to be upheld. Recent Moorish converts (like Yahya) were given important positions in the new administration. He was made chief magistrate of Granada (*alguacil mayor*) under his new name (Pedro de Granada Venegas). Above all the sympathetic count of Tendilla was made captain general and head of the secular government while Fray Fernando de Talavera, bishop of Avila was made the first archbishop of Granada under the new regime. Judging by a memorandum[85] which he drew up for regulating the life of the conquered Moors he was in full sympathy with the lenient spirit of the capitulations and indeed may well have helped to inspire them.

Who was this man who was chosen by Ferdinand and Isabella to raise the standard of the cross over the Torre de la Vela of the Alhambra,[86] and to whom they now entrusted the delicate task of integrating their new subjects into the ecclesiastical framework of Castile?[87] Born about 1430 he was accused by his critics of being of a

---

[84] Ladero, *Los mudéjares* pp 31–53.

[85] Printed in Azcona pp 761–3; he had long been an advocate of the conquest. Sigüenza calls him *el movedor o despertador* of the campaign [Fr. José de] Sigüenza[, *Historia de la orden de San Jerónimo*,] ed J. Catalina García, 2 ed, 2 vols, N[ueva] B[iblioteca de] A[utores] E[spañoles] (Madrid 1907–9) 2 p 300.

[86] M. del C. Pescador del Hoyo, 'Como fue de verdad la toma de Granada.' *Al-Andalus* 41 vols (Madrid 1933–) 20 (1955) p 330. There were three early biographies—by 1) Jorge de Torres, maestrescuela of Granada, 2) by the author of the 'Breve Suma', perhaps Jerónimo Fernández de Madrid, abbot of Santa Fe, and 3) by Alonso Fernández de Madrid, archdeacon of Alcor; the best description of them is in [P. Tarsicio de] Azcona, [*La Elección y Reforma* [*del episcopado español en tiempo de los Reyes Católicos*] (Madrid 1960) pp 243–4. All were written by contemporaries of Talavera. Among modern biographies the more important are P. de Alcántara Suárez y Muñano, *Vida del Venerable don Fray Hernando de Talavera* (Madrid 1866) and cap 4 of Márquez, *Investigaciones*.

[87] The province of Granada was allotted the bishoprics of Guadix and Almería in addition to Granada itself. Following ancient practice Málaga was attached to Seville.

converso family.[88] He was sometimes known as Hernando de Talavera and sometimes of Oropesa,[89] the head of the lands of the lords of Oropesa, which lies some twenty-eight kilometres to the west of Talavera. At the university of Salamanca, however, he was Fernán Pérez de Talavera. He may well have been a kinsman of the lords of Oropesa as he was stated to be by a contemporary. He certainly became their protégé, probably to begin with of García Alvarez de Toledo, the third lord, who died in 1444,[90] and certainly thereafter of Fernán, the fourth lord.[91] Records at Barcelona strongly suggest that Talavera made an agreement there in 1442 to learn the skills of a scribe from a writing-master called Panyules.[92] The art which he learned was to stand him in good stead when he went to the university of Salamanca soon afterwards. For the patronage of the lords of Oropesa for a time ran dry, and we are told that Talavera eked out his funds by teaching calligraphy and making copies himself.[93] From some of his surviving writing we know that he wrote an elegant 'semi-Gothic' hand.[94] While he was a bachelor at Salamanca, as he tells us himself, he translated for the fourth lord of Oropesa Petrarch's *Invectiva contra medicum*.[95] But he was not to turn humanist, nor to remain a scribe or a protégé. After becoming licentiate in theology he was appointed to the chair

---

[88] They may well have been right. His opponents were later to accuse him of being a member of the Contreras family through his mother. The treasurer of the chapter of Granada in his time was Antonio de Contreras, Márquez, *Investigaciones*, p 141 n 138.

[89] Pulgar is the chief authority for calling him Hernando de Oropesa. For the date of his birth see n 97.

[90] P. León Tello and M. T. de la Peña Marazuela, *Archivo de los Duques de Frías*, 3 vols (Madrid 1955–73) 3 (table) and no 29, p 11.

[91] 'Breve Suma', fol 139ᵛ in Márquez, *Investigaciones*, p 141 n 137. Talavera's father is said to have been *muy cercana pariente de la casa de Oropesa*. Another pointer may be provided by the fact that Talavera's nephew was Francisco Herrera, dean of Granada, and one of his nieces was called María Herrera, F. Bermúdez de Pedraza, *Historia Eclesiástica de Granada* (Granada 1638) fol 176ᵛ; she was said to have been the daughter of a certain (*fulano*) Herrera. A member of his household was Gabriel Alonso de Herrera, author of *Libro de Agricultura* (Alcala 1513), and a fellow townsman from Talavera. It has not been noticed that the wife of the third lord of Oropesa was called Juana Herrera.

[92] J. Domínguez Bordona, 'Algunas precisiones sobre fray Fernando de Talavera' *BRAH*, 144 (1959) p 229. He is referred to as '*Fernando de Talavera, habitatori Barchinone, oriundo ville de Talavera, Archiepiscopatus de Tholeta*'. Domínguez lists Talavera's writings.

[93] Azcona, *Elección y Reforma*, p 244.

[94] The following appear to be autograph, Escorial MS b IV 26 'Tratado contra la demasia del vestir' (Domínguez no 7), Escorial MS a IV 29 'Tratado dirigido a las religiosas de San Bernardo de Avila' (Domínguez no 8) and the foundation document of Santiago de la Madre de Dios de Granada, B[iblioteca] Na[cional] MS 6923. Less certainly autograph is BNa MS 9815 'Invectiva contra un medico' (Domínguez no 14).

[95] *Ibid* pp 227–9.

The fall of convivencia in medieval Spain

of moral theology at Salamanca. Years later the traveller, Jeronimo Münzer, was to pay a graceful tribute to Talavera's theological learning.[96] By 1455 he had taken orders [97] and was beginning to look beyond the university to the Jeronimite house of Alba de Tormes not far away. The Jeronimites were an order who had taken their inspiration from the Italian eremites.[98] Confirmed by Gregory XI in 1373[99] they had attracted royal patronage in the succeeding eighty years, and important houses had been founded, as at El Parral, Segovia and at Yuste, where the lords of Oropesa had already played an important role as patrons. The Jeronimites had also refounded the great house at Guadalupe in Estremadura.[100] Under the patronage of the senior branch of the Alvarez de Toledo family, the counts and later dukes of Alba, the house at Alba de Tormes had acquired the reputation of being the most rigid of an order which was probably the least relaxed in Spain. Since the general of the order [101] was also a kinsman of the lord of Oropesa it is small surprise to find Talavera being received into the order on 15 August 1466. He quickly made a name for himself as preacher and confessor. On taking his monastic vows he preached a sermon on the contemplative life of Mary and the active life of Martha in the presence of the countess of Alba.[102] Later he was to write a tract for the countess of Benavente, María Pacheco, half-sister of the first countess of Oropesa, in order to instruct her in how to arrange and occupy her day.[103] In the same spirit of practical

[96] Quoted in Domínguez p 215.
[97] Sigüenza 2 p 290. For the chronology of Talavera's career and his interesting will, see now Q. Aldea, 'Hernando de Talavera, su testamento y sa biblioteca, *Homenaje a Fray Justo Pérez de Urbel, OSB*, 2 vols (Silos 1976–7). I owe this reference to the kindness of professor Russell.
[98] Sigüenza 1 p 26.
[99] *Ibid* 1 pp 27–31; see also A. A. Sicroff, 'The Jeronymite Monastery of Guadalupe in Fourteenth and Fifteenth-century Spain' in *Collected Studies in Honour of Americo Castro's Eightieth Year*, ed M. P. Hornik (Oxford 1965) pp 397–422.
[100] *Ibid.*
[101] For Alfonso de Oropesa (General 29 October 1457–28 October 1468) see Azcona pp 378, 387 and Sigüenza, 1 pp 361–88. He was the author of *Lumen ad revelationem gentium et gloriam tuae Israel* and a life of St John Chrysostom to whom he was especially devoted, *ibid* 1 p 372.
[102] *Ibid* 2 p 291, who calls her 'duchess', but the counts of Alba only became dukes in 1469.
[103] *Escritores Místicos Españoles*, [ed M. Mir], NBAE (Madrid 1911) pp 94–103, Domínguez no 8; this must have been written between 1466 when the countess married and 1485 when Talavera ceased to be prior of El Prado. The countess was half-sister of the second countess of Oropesa who had married Fernán Alvarez de Toledo the second count in 1480. The most likely date for the tract is therefore between 1480 and 1486.

piety is his confessional, the *Breve forma de confesar*[104] but he could
also write religious poetry as he demonstrated in a lyric gloss on the
prayer, *Ave Maria*, to each Latin phrase of which he added a dozen
lines of Castilian verse.[105] His interest in the Jewish question is shown
by a book called the *Impugnación Católica* which he wrote in 1481 as
a riposte to a work in favour of the Jews which he claimed to be full
of a thousand heresies and which circulated in Seville in 1480.[106]
Sometime after 1492 he edited a mystical work, the first volume of a
popular *Vita Christi* by an early fifteenth century bishop of Elne, and
published it at Granada at his own expense in 1496.[107] The esteem
which he enjoyed among the Jeronimites was marked by his appointment as prior of El Prado, Valladolid.[108] Probably through the
influence of cardinal Mendoza he became confessor to queen Isabella.[109]
In this delicate role he certainly showed himself to be a man of
courage. In 1493, for instance, he was not afraid to castigate the queen
sharply. In a letter of that year he roundly condemned the dancing
which he accused her of having allowed to take place between her
ladies and the French representatives who came to witness the peace
treaty of that year.[110] Early in her reign Isabella gave Talavera plenty
of chances to play Martha's role. For she instructed him to keep a
Book of Liveries in which to enter up expenses incurred in discharging
the obligations of her conscience.[111] In 1480 he was given the thankless
task of recovering Castilian revenues according to the resumption of

[104] *Ibid* 1 pp 3–35, Domínguez no 2.
[105] Sigüenza 2, pp 325–9.
[106] [A.] Fernández de Madrid, *Vida [de Fray Fernando de Talavera, primo arzobispo de Granada]*, ed F. G. Olmedo (Madrid 1931) p 123; see [G.] Haebler, *Bibl[iografía] Ibér[ica del siglo xv]*, 2 vols (The Hague 1903–17)] 1 p 303, no 631; Domínguez no 21; this too was written when Talavera was prior of El Prado and after 1480. It was published at Seville c1493 and has been edited by F. Márquez (Barcelona 1961).
[107] Fernández de Madrid, *Vida* p 124; it was printed by Mainardux Ungut and John Pegnitzer, Haebler, *Bibl Ibér* 1 p 346 no 711.
[108] Sigüenza says (*Historia de la Orden* 2 p 293) that he remained prior for sixteen years. Since he became bishop of Avila in 1484 this means that he became prior about 1468. He had resigned his chair at Salamanca by proctor on 5 July 1466 'because he expected to absent himself from the city', *Extractos de los libros de claustros de la Universidad de Salamanca*, Siglo XV (1464–1481), ed F. Marcos Rodríguez (Salamanca 1964) no 208, p 87. Professor Russell kindly drew my attention to this source.
[109] *Ibid* p 295; this was by 1478 [Fernando del] Pulgar, *Crónica [de los Reyes Católicos]*, de J. de Mata Carriazo, 2 vols (Madrid 1943) 1 pp 339–40.
[110] [D.] Clemencín, *Elogio [de la Reina Católica doña Isabel]* (Madrid 1821) pp 359–71.
[111] *Ibid* p 424 and see A. Prieto Cantero, *Casa y Descargos de los Reyes Católicos*, cat xxiv del Archivo General de Simancas (Valladolid 1969). In 1479 he was an envoy to Portugal, *Crónica* 1 pp 404–10.

The fall of convivencia in medieval Spain

them decreed at the cortes of that year.[112] In 1484, though unwilling, he was made bishop of Avila, and at once began to visit and reform his diocese. In this he was interrupted by letters from the pope and from the monarchs urging him to return to the court. On doing so he was to find himself the chairman of the famous commission which investigated the proposition for Columbus's first voyage.[113] Nor was he allowed to concentrate on that. Throughout the Granada campaign he had been a keen supporter of the war and acted as collector of the Cruzada tax.[114] He was present at the capture of Málaga, at the siege of Baza and often intervened at the front to seek to modify some of the harsher incidents. Here he acquired extensive experience of the Moors. This was the man to whom the archbishopric of Granada was entrusted in his early sixties.

One of his first acts was to found a college for twenty-five students aged between fifteen and twenty.[115] They were to wear the Jeronimite habit and acquire Latin grammar, philosophy, music, canon law and theology. They were to learn the third chapter of St Paul's first letter to Timothy and the first chapter of his letter to Titus by heart. In short this was to be a seminary for providing trained clergy for the new province. As a seminary it was to be held up as an example at the council of Trent. As to the Moors themselves Talavera soon patronised a converted Moor who had lived at Granada since before the conquest. This was Fray Pedro de Alcalá, who became a member for the archbishop's household and his confessor. Talavera employed him to compile a grammar which was called the 'art of picking up some knowledge of the Arabic language.'[116] It seems to have been completed in 1501 and was published at the archbishop's expense at Granada in 1505,[117] together with a simple Arabic/Castilian vocabulary consisting of lists of verbs and nouns.[118] In addition we know that Talavera had Arabic translations made of Christian prayers and of the psalms and and copies of them distributed in Granada.[119] He

[112] Clemencín, *Elogio*, p 420; Azcona pp 360–1; A. Matilla Tascón, *Declaratorias de los Reyes Católicos sobre reducción de juros y otras mercedes* (Madrid 1952) pp 15–16.

[113] B. de las Casas, *Historia de las Indias*, ed J. Pérez de Tudela Bueso, 5 vols. B[iblioteca de] A[utores] E[spañoles] (Madrid 1957) I pp 110–14, 118; S. E. Morison, *Admiral of the Ocean Sea*, 2 vols (Boston 1942) I pp 116–19, 131–2.

[114] He was appointed by Sixtus IV in 1482 and continued to act until the city fell, Ladero, *Castilla y Granada*, pp 205–6; see also Pulgar, *Crónica* 2 p 334.

[115] Fernández de Madrid, *Vida*, pp 81–4; Pedraza, *Historia Eclesiástica*, fol 185.

[116] Fernández pp 215–16.

[117] Nicolás Antonio, *Biblioteca Scriptorum Hispaniae Nova*, 2 vols (Madrid 1788) 2 p 166.

[118] Domínguez pp 213–14.

[119] 'Breve Suma', fol 151ᵛ in Márquez, *Investigaciones*, p 117 n 41; Azcona p 762.

certainly set his priests an example by beginning to learn Arabic himself. How much he learned is unclear. One of his contemporary biographers quotes him as having said that he would give one of his eyes to be able to teach in Arabic.[120] An eye-witness tells us that he soon learned to turn to the congregation at the end of Mass and say instead of *Dominus vobiscum, Baraka ficun.*[121] He encouraged his flock to greet the appearance of the Corpus Christi procession in Granada with Moorish dances and the playing of the instrument known as the *zambra*;[122] behind the procession groups of Moorish tradesmen formed up, each under its banner. When he visited remote parts of his diocese like the Alpujarras, and there was no chance of using an organ at mass, again he encouraged the use of the four-stringed *zambra* as an accompaniment. That his priests should learn Arabic made obvious sense if they were to get their message across to their congregations. So no doubt did the archbishop's decision to keep the inquisition at arm's length and away from the kingdom of Granada which was a mission field where it would be out of place.[123] But if Gómez, the biographer of Francisco Jiménez de Cisneros is to be believed Talavera went further than was required by the basic problems with which he was faced. For he and the archbishop of Toledo differed on their interpretation of St Paul. Talavera used the Apostle's arguments in the first book of Corinthians to justify his use of readings in Arabic from the old and new testaments at the night office and at mass in the churches of his province, and of his printing of parts of the gospels in Arabic.[124] Cisneros was, of course, the great patron of the polyglot bible. He believed intensely in biblical studies. But his intention in publishing the bible was, to quote the prologue, that 'every theologian should also be able to drink of that water which springeth up to eternal

---

[120] Domínguez p 213 (quoting 'Breve Suma'); Sigüenza, 2 p 306; Mármol says that he learned enough to teach the ten commandments, the articles of faith and prayers in Arabic and to hear confessions, Luis de Mármol [Carvajal], *Historia del rebelion [y castigo de los moriscos del reyno de Granada]*, 2 vols (2 ed Madrid 1797) 1 p 108.

[121] Transcribed as *Ybara figun*, [K. Garrad, 'The original memorial of don Francisco] Nuñez Muley', *Atlante* (London 1953–) 2 (October 1954) p 215; and see Márquez, *Investigaciones* p 117 and n 41.

[122] *Zambra* from the Arabic *zamr*, see J. O. Corominas, *Diccionario Crítico Etimológico de la lengua Castellana*, 4 vols (Berne 1954) 4 pp 818–19. Corominas mistakenly attributes the description of Talavera in Mármol's *Rebelion* to Cisneros.

[123] Azcona, *Elección y Reforma*, p 258.

[124] Gómez, *De Rebus*, p 961. For certain feast days he had the lessons translated into Castilian 'so that the people could understand them', 'Breve Suma' fol 149^r/^{v} in Márquez, *Investigaciones* p 116 n 40; Pedraza, *Historia Eclesiástica*, fol 186^v.

life, at the fountain-head itself. This is the reason, therefore, why we have ordered the bible to be printed in the original language with different translations . . . Our object is to revive the dormant study of the sacred scriptures.'[125] His eye was on the needs of graduates studying theology. Hence his noble edition of six hundred copies in six volumes—a fine reference work for an academic library.[126] Naturally this was a very different type of publication from Fray Pedro's little dictionary and grammar. And as to readings from the bible in Arabic at mass in the churches of Granada, that said Cisneros, quoting St Matthew chapter seven, was to cast pearls before swine and to place before men who were not yet confirmed in the Christian religion its sacred mysteries so that they would be laughed at and thwarted.[127] In his comment on St Matthew he seems to be following closely the comparable comment on this passage by Tostatus or Alonso de Madrigal, the learned bishop of Avila, whose teaching had predominated at Salamanca in his student days. Tostatus had said 'we ought not to communicate divine things to carnal men of this world who are willful, for such men are like swine and make cheap in their sight everything which is taught them especially if the mysteries are told to infidels and the argumentative'.[128] Cisneros also seems to have been relying on St Paul's first epistle to the Corinthians, in his case on chapter fourteen, where the apostle had written, 'Except ye utter by the tongue words easy to be understood, how shall it be known what is spoken? For ye shall speak in the air . . . wherefore let him that speaketh in an unknown tongue pray that he may interpret.' Or again 'If therefore the whole church be come together into one place, and all speak with tongues, and there come in those that are unlearned, or unbelievers, will they not say that ye are mad?' However sound he might have been on the interpretation of St Paul Cisneros had no patience with the capitulations of 1492. Nor did he approve of a policy of *festina lente*. He believed in mass conversions in the interest of the salvation of souls. Moreover from the moment when he appeared in Granada in 1499 and all through the rebellion which he himself had stimulated he made it quite clear that he wanted to achieve the conversion of the whole of the conquered

[125] J. P. R. Lyell, *Cardinal Ximenes* (London 1917) p 27.
[126] *Ibid* pp 28, 34.
[127] Gómez, *De Rebus*, p 961.
[128] Alfonsus Tostatus, *Commentaria in terciam partem Mathaei* (Venice 1596) p 118.

kingdom.[129] To him it was a glorious conclusion to the capture of Granada. He also made the practical point that so long as there were unconverted Muslims living near the coast this was an open invitation to the Turks or the barbary corsairs to intervene and to join forces with their correligionists. This fear kept recurring right up to 1609. There was reality in it. For if there had been several raids already before 1499 many more were to follow especially in the middle of the sixteenth century when the Turks were attacking Malta.

Cisneros like Talavera came from New Castile. Seven years younger than the Jeronimite he had been schooled by brother Juniper of the Franciscan house at Alcalá de Henares.[130] Thence like Talavera he too had gone to the university of Salamanca.[131] Indeed their time there had overlapped. But after taking the arts course Cisneros had read canon and civil law of which he became a bachelor. He also read theology under Roa.[132] He differed from Talavera in having spent six years at Rome[133]—that was after 1460. He had early shown himself to be single-minded and fearless, notably in not being afraid to stand up to archbishop Carrillo of Toledo; Carrillo had imprisoned him when he pressed his own case for a benefice which the archbishop wanted for one of his minions.[134] Like Talavera he caught the eye of cardinal Mendoza; both men owed their advancement to the key position of royal confessor to an introduction from cardinal Mendoza. Cisneros seems to have gained his ascendancy over the queen after Talavera went to Granada in 1492, and still more after he had himself succeded Mendoza as primate at Toledo in 1495. Our knowledge of his views on conversion is derived in part from a series of letters which he wrote for his own dean and chapter during the years 1499–1501.[135] The salvation of souls stood in the forefront of his endeavours. Moreover he believed that he had the wholesale backing of Ferdinand and Isabella. Two points in his immediate task especially concerned him. He set his mind on converting the whole of the

---

[129] See Ladero, *Los mudéjares*, no 88, p 235, letter of 4 January 1500. 'We believe firmly that no one must remain who is not a Christian . . . we are determined to press our policy forwards and to set aside all else.' Cisneros claimed that Talavera shared this viewpoint.

[130] [C. J. von] Hefele, [*Life of Cardinal Ximenez*], trans J. C. Dalton (London 1885) p 3.

[131] *Ibid.*

[132] Gómez, *De Rebus*, p 932.

[133] Hefele p 4.

[134] *Ibid* pp 6–8.

[135] Ladero, *Los mudéjares*, nos 85, 88–9, 91, 96 and 99.

kingdom of Granada, if need be by mass conversion.[136] In one of his letters he wrote, 'We are hoping in the Lord that there will remain no one unbaptised, but that there will be one faith and one baptism.'[137] Secondly he did not wish the renegades to go scot free as under the capitulations.[138] They were apostates and as such subjects for the inquisition. The Catholic Monarchs recognized that 'between the archbishops of Toledo and Granada there were differences . . . which could be very awkward.'[139] This was particularly true in the field of conversion. For Talavera did not believe in mass conversion. In his confessional, written well before 1492, he condemned those who baptised adults without their having received catechetical instruction for eight months or a time set by a prelate.[140] He considered it positively sinful to baptise many together without necessity, except on the eve of easter or pentecost.[141]

The mental worlds of Cisneros and Talavera had indeed much in common. Though Cisneros was very much of an Old Christian they seem to have come from comparable social backgrounds. Each had read theology at Salamanca. Both were keen biblical students. Both belonged to religious orders with whose reform each had been intimately associated. Talavera held himself to be a devotee of St Francis, as of St Dominic, even if he was still more of St Jerome.[142] He was himself to found a house of Poor Clares at Loja and one of Franciscan friars at Talavera.[143] Both men believed in apostolic poverty and personal austerity and practiced them. In his confessional Talavera accepted the general necessity for the different religious communities to live apart. He describes in his tract the sins which are committed by those who consort too much with infidels. They sin who give a public office to an infidel, such that Christians are made subject to an infidel. Christians sin who serve infidels by being regularly with them in their houses. Christian nurses should not nurse infidel children. Christians should not leave legacies to mosques or synagogues. Christians sin who go to be cured by infidel doctors, especially if they

---

[136] *Ibid* no 88.
[137] *Ibid* no 85. Writing to the dean and chapter of Toledo on 16 January he could report that already 50,000 souls had been converted and 'I hope in Our Lord that all this kingdom will be converted in which there are more than 200,000 souls' (no 89).
[138] *Ibid* no 83.
[139] *Ibid* no 87.
[140] *Escritores Místicos* p 11.
[141] *Ibid.*
[142] Sigüenza p 316.
[143] *Ibid* p 309.

have access to Christian doctors and apothecaries; similarly Christian women sin who patronise Moorish midwives, if Christian midwives are available. Joint bathing between Christians and Moors is a sin. Lords should encourage infidels to wear distinctive dress, not to go out in passion week nor to open their doors and windows on Good Friday.[144] Yet the triumph of Granada reacted on the two men in very different ways. The archbishop of Toledo seems to have been inspired by a kind of Messianic nationalism which spurred him on to more and more energetic attacks on the problem of the conquered Moors. Some might call his onslaught forthright. Harvey has referred to the 'disastrous nature' of 'his blundering intervention.'[145] Certainly there seems little doubt that it was the arrival of Cisneros in Granada in 1499 which directly stimulated the revolt which followed in December of that year.[146] On or about 18 December 1499 a revolt broke out in the Moorish quarter of Granada, known as the Albaicín. The incident which set the flames alight concerned the arrest of a renegade's daughter and seems therefore to have been provoked by a violation of the capitulations.[147] Cisneros found himself besieged in his house. The situation was saved by the intervention of the count of Tendilla and the mediation of Talavera. Far from being dissuaded from his course the archbishop of Toledo set about a series of mass conversions and at some stage effected the arrest and virtually forced conversion of a leading Muslim called Zegrí.[148] News of the revolt rapidly spread to the hinterland of Granada; soon the whole mountainous district known as the Alpujarras was alight.[149] In the opinion of Vallejo Ferdinand was in no doubt whom he should blame for the outbreak and was angry with Cisneros for putting the work of

[144] *Escritores Místicos* pp 4–5.
[145] In a review of Ladero, *Los mudéjares* in *EHR*, 87 (1972) p 363.
[146] Ferdinand and Isabella arrived in Granada in early July 1499, A. Rumeu de Armas, *Itinerario de los Reyes Católicos* (Madrid 1974) pp 254–6. They left for Seville in the first days of December. It seems that it had been on their initiative that Cisneros had been summoned from Alcala to Granada, Hefele p 61; Pedraza, *Historia Eclesiástica*, fol 195.
[147] Gómez, *De Rebus*, pp 959–60. For the date see Ladero, *Los mudéjares*, p 72.
[148] Gómez, *De Rebus*, pp 958–9; it is true that he repudiated the treatment meted out to Zegrí by Dr León, Pedraza, *Historia Eclesiástica*, fol 195ᵛ. For a royal instruction, dated 12 October 1501, ordering copies of the Koran and other Muslim religious books to be burned see Ladero, *Los mudéjares*, no 146, p 72. It is probably to this late date that the famous incident in which Cisneros directed the burning of a pyre of Muslim books in the Plaza de Vivarrambla should be attributed.
[149] Mármol, *Historia del rebelion*, p 124. It had reached the area round Granada by the end of December 1499 and the first few days of January 1500, Ladero, *Los mudéjares*, pp 73–5.

the Granada campaign in jeopardy.[150] Muslim sources tell us that the inhabitants of Granada clearly thought that the Christians had broken their faith over the capitulations. Don Francisco Nuñez Muley, who had been a page to archbishop Talavera, in a memorial written when he was himself very old said, 'the conversion of the said inhabitants of this kingdom was by force and against what had been agreed in the capitulations between the Catholic Kings and Boabdil.'[151] A Muslim imam, writing to a young friend, put the blame on Ferdinand, 'If the king of the conquest does not keep faith, what can we expect from his successors?[152] Myths and rumours spread as wildly on the Muslim side as on the Christian, like that reported by another Muslim writer — Al-Maqqari — that the king had ordered that those who had rebelled against him must be converted or die.[153] Al-Maqqari was certainly right in recognising that the rebellion had altered the attitude of the sovereigns. After it Talavera's policy did not entirely disappear; but it took second place. In July 1501 the monarchs prohibited Muslims from entering the country lest they should disturb the indoctrination of the Moriscos.[154] The same point is made in a different way in a letter which they wrote to the corregidor of Córdoba in September of the same year.[155] 'You write to us that to convert the Moors of Granada it is necessary to offer them some reward. It seems to us that that should not be done lest scandal should arise.' Here the monarchs stood by the *Seven Parts*. But they go on, 'First they should be treated very well with many warnings, that they must understand that their souls will be saved, also that that is what we chiefly want and what would please us immensely and serve us greatly.' But if in the end they are obstinate, you can ask them to leave our kingdoms, for we must not allow there to be a place in them for infidels.' In February 1502 all unconverted Moors were expelled.[156]

Thus for all Ferdinand's resentment at Cisneros's actions it was the Franciscan's views which triumphed in the end. They also had the

---

[150] Juan de Vallejo, *Memorial de la vida de Fray Francisco Jiménez de Cisneros* (Madrid 1913) p 38, and see no 86 in Ladero, *Los mudéjares*, pp 230–2.

[151] *Nunez Muley*, p 204.

[152] M. A. Ladero Quesada, *Granada, Historia de un pais islámico, 1232–1571* (Madrid 1964) p 163.

[153] Al-Maqqari in F. Fernández y González, *Estado social y político de los mudéjares de Castilla* (Madrid 1866) p 202 n 1.

[154] Ladero, *Los mudéjares*, no 139, pp 307–11.

[155] *Ibid* no 144, pp 315–16 (27 September 1501).

[156] Pragmatic of 12 February 1502, Juan Ramírez, *Las pragmáticas del reyno* (Valladolid 1540) fols viii–ix; J. H. Elliott, *Imperial Spain, 1469–1715* (London 1963) p 40.

warm support of pope Alexander VI.[157] There was to be no going back. Indeed after Isabella died in 1504 archbishop Talavera found himself the first archbishop accused of heresy by the inquisition, an accusation of which pope Julius II cleared him just before the archbishop died in 1507.[158] On the Muslim side there was a deep and tragic irony in the fact that there was a long tradition going back to the eighth century which recommended submission to force majeure in order that the faith might secretly be preserved. Harvey has drawn attention to the fact that a decree issued from Oran in 1504,[159] if not earlier, in which Moriscos under persecution were positively advised to simulate adherence to Christianity. Nothing could have delivered them more successfully to the attentions of the inquisition.

The views of Talavera demonstrate that the Spanish church was disunited in its approach to the problem of Christians, Jews and Muslims in the same community at this crucial stage of the royal attempt to solve that problem. There was disunity among the hierarchy, and for that matter within both the Jeronimite and Dominican orders as well. It is true that it was a group of Dominicans following in the steps of the Franciscan observants of the mid-fifteenth century who pressed for the inquisition; though it was also to be the Dominicans who, when the new world had been discovered, were to produce two of the more outstanding exponents of the rights of Indians in Vitoria and Las Casas. For the moment, however, it was a Jeronimite who upheld the time-honoured concepts of *convivencia* at least between Christians and Muslims, as these were rapidly being worn away under Ferdinand and Isabella.

Merton College
Oxford

---

[157] Ladero, *Los mudéjares*, no 101 (27 March 1500).
[158] Sigüenza, 2 p 316; Azcona, *Elección y Reforma*, pp 262–5.
[159] L. P. Harvey, *Actas del primer congreso internacional de estudios árabes* (Madrid 1963) pp 163–78.

THE FLAGELLANT MOVEMENT AND FLAGELLANT CONFRATERNITIES IN CENTRAL ITALY, 1260–1400

by JOHN HENDERSON

HE 1260 movement[1] was the first widespread outbreak of popular fervour in medieval Italy to make flagellation the centre of its devotion. Together with subsequent movements it provided a general impetus to lay religious life by leading to the foundation of a large number of confraternities all over the country. In this paper I intend to describe this phenomenon and in this way examine the motivation, collective and individual, which led people to participate. I shall then outline briefly the devotional practices of flagellant companies and show how they came to institutionalise the spirit of this popular fervour.

Flagellation was not a new phenomenon to the catholic church for episcopal courts had long prescribed it as a means of punishment,[2] in particular in the process for the public reconciliation of sinners. Even after the introduction of private confession it continued to be important to the church as can be seen, for example, in the thirteenth-century conciliar edicts which ordered the discipline for the voluntary conversion of heretics.[3] But it is within the monastic context that the practice is most familiar and from the *Rule of St Benedict*[4] onwards orders such as the Cluniacs[5] and Cistercians[6] prescribed it as a means to overcome the most obdurate sinners.

---

[1] This movement was the subject of a conference held in Perugia in 1960: *Il Movimento [dei disciplinati nel settimo centenario dal suo inizio]*, B[ollettino della] R. D[eputazione di storia patria per l]'U[mbria] (Perugia 1962). See also: *Risultati [e prospettive della ricerca sul Movimento dei Disciplinati]*, BRDU(1972). I am very grateful to Brenda Bolton, Alexander Murray and professor Nicolai Rubinstein for their comments on an earlier draft of this paper.

[2] See, for example, Augustine of Hippo, *Epist* 133: *PL* 33 (1865) col 510.

[3] The councils of Tarragona (1242), Narbonne (1244) and Béziers (1246). The formula can be seen in practice in Bernard Gui's prescriptions of *c*1330: *Practica Inquisitionis pravitatis, auctore Bernardo Guidonis OFP*, ed C. Douis (Paris 1886) doct XXIX, p 54.

[4] *La régle de saint Benoit*, II, Série des Textes Monastiques d'Occident 35 (Paris 1972) cap 28, pp 550–3.

[5] See Peter the Venerable's comments in *De Miraculis*, bk II, cap 9: *PL* 189 (1854) col 919.

[6] Canivez, I pp 12–32: *statutorum annorum praecedentium prima collectio*, 1134, col 76.

147

JOHN HENDERSON

It is not so much the punitive role of flagellation which concerns us here as its function as a form of voluntary penance. This difference is important because in this second use it is the individual who recognises his own sinfulness and takes it upon himself to correct his body for the health of his soul. The origins of this concept belong properly to the ascetic tradition, for certain of the early Christian saints employed the discipline as one of the methods for mortifying the flesh.[7] It was not, however, until the eleventh century that it became a widespread monastic practice, although the way was prepared to some extent by the recently-introduced system of 'redemptions' whereby a sinner was able to condense the long drawn-out system of fixed penances, prescribed by the penitentials, into a short but more painful punishment.[8]

The first great protagonist of voluntary flagellation was Peter Damian who not only encouraged its use in his own order, the Umbrian hermits of Fonte-Avellana, but also in other religious houses and among the laity. His ideas did not meet with universal acceptance, as can be seen in his letters to the Florentine clergy and the monk Peter Cerebroso.[9] But even so the practice of self-discipline spread, Peter Damian telling us that not only was it taken up by men but noble women adopted it with enthusiasm.[10] How widespread it became as a lay practice before 1260 is difficult to tell since it appears to have been a private rather than a communal exercise and the only laymen who were recorded as having adopted it were, like St Louis of France,[11] from the highest strata of society.

Voluntary flagellation should then, as Peter Damian points out,[12] be seen within the context of traditional penances, although by the first half of the thirteenth century a more vital factor was probably the influence of the mendicants' pastoral theology and especially their emphasis on the incarnate life of Christ. It was the Franciscans in particular who encouraged their audiences to identify themselves

[7] [L.] Gougaud, [*Devotional and Ascetic Practices in the Middle Ages*] (London 1927) pp 187-9 and nn 43-7.
[8] *Ibid* p 189.
[9] *Epist ad clericos florentinos: Epist* 8: *PL* 144 (1867) cols 350-1; *Epist ad Petrum cerebrosum monachum: Epist* 27: *PL* 144, cols 414-17. See also *De laude flagellorum: Opusc* 43: *PL* 145 (1867) cols 679-81 and *Epist ad eremitas congregationis suae, Epist* 34, *PL* 144, cols 432-4.
[10] *Vita S. Rodulphi et S. Dominici Loricati: PL* 144, col 1011.
[11] Gougaud p 191.
[12] *Epist* 27, *PL* 144, cols 415-17.

with His suffering on earth[13] and this would automatically have predisposed them towards any penitential exercise associated with Christ's passion. One particular group of laymen which bears this out is the order of Penitents and it cannot be coincidental that it was one of their members, Rainero Fasani, who is supposed to have begun the flagellant movement in 1260.[14] According to legend [15] he had practised flagellation privately for eighteen years or more and was given the task by the hermit San Bevignate[16]—who appeared to him in a dream—to lead the Perugians to a proper sense of their own sinfulness and persuade them of the necessity of doing penance. He therefore delivered a series of sermons in which he emphasized the need to expiate the inumerable sins of Mankind, principally sodomy, usury and heresy, and encouraged the Perugians to participate in the sufferings of Christ by whipping themselves in public.

In order to understand the reasons which might have led people to join the movement one must consider the factors which made the situation favourable for the eruption of popular fervour in 1260. Contemporary chroniclers remain curiously silent on the subject, hailing it as an unheard-of mystery,[17] a miracle and the result of divine inspiration.[18] Historians have, however, not been slow in suggesting reasons such as the famine of 1258 and the outbreaks of plague in 1259.[19] These may have been seen by some as God's *flagelli* but their effects appear to have been localised.[20] More important was the political state of Italy which was constantly torn by the Guelph-Ghibelline struggle, culminating in the battle of Montaperti on 4 September 1260. Although the flagellants' devotion predated the battle it undoubtedly gave it an impetus which spread it beyond Perugia to

---

[13] [J.] Moorman, [*A History of the Franciscan Order from its Origins to the Year 1517*] (Oxford 1968) pp 256–7, and J. M. Cummings, *The Christological Content of the 'sermones' of St Anthony* [of Padua] (Padua 1953).

[14] See [R.] Morghen, '[Rainero Fasani e il movimento dei disciplinati del 1260]', *Il movimento*, pp 29–42. On the origins of this order see G. G. Meersseman, 'Dossier de l'ordre de la Pénitence au XIII siècle, *SpicFr*, 7 (1961).

[15] [G.] Mazzatinti: ['La Lezenda de fra Rainero Faxano'], *BRDU* (1899) 2 pp 561–3.

[16] L. Kern, 'A propos du mouvement des Flagellants de 1260: San Bevignate de Perouse', *Festschrift Gustav Schurer* (Paderborn 1930) pp 39–53.

[17] [*Annales S. Iustinae*] *Patavini*, *MGH SS* 19 p 179.

[18] [*Annali Genovesi di*] *Caffaro* [*e de' suoi continuatori dal MCCLI al MCCLXXIX*], *Fonti* [*per la storia d'Italia*] (Istituto Storico Italiano per il medio evo) (Rome 1926) 14 p 39; [*Jacopo da*] *Varagine* [*e la sua cronaca di Genova dalle origine al 1297*], *Fonti* (1941) 85, II, p 390.

[19] N. Cohn, *The Pursuit of the Millenium* (London 1970) p 128, and Morghen, p 35.

[20] [A.] Frugoni, '[Sui flagellanti del 1260]', *BISIMEAM* 75 (1963) p 227 n 1.

other parts of Italy.[21] Indicative of the effect of these years of political unrest was the flagellants' desire to spread peace from one town to another, reconcile their internal discords, open the communal prisons and free the occupants.[22]

As the result of Fasani's sermons groups of Perugians began, some time before easter, to process through the city beating themselves with whips. A measure of his impact was that the commune of Perugia issued an edict on 4 May to the effect that there should be a general holiday for fifteen days *propter utilitatem Devotionis*.[23] However, it was not for another five months that the whole population of the town took to the streets in the numbers generally associated with this devotion.

The main contemporary sources which discuss the movement were from Padua,[24] Forli,[25] Piacenza,[26] Parma[27] and Genoa[28] and all are agreed in their descriptions although the most comprehensive is to be found in the Paduan *Anonimo di S. Justina* who describes the scene in the following terms:

> Such was the fear of God engendered in them that nobles as well as the low-born, old men and young, children of only five years, processed through the *piazze* of the city stripped to the waist. Covered in shame . . . they marched two by two each one carrying a whip with which they continuously beat themselves on their shoulders until the blood began to flow, uttering groans and shrill lamentations . . . Indeed not only by day but truly also by night with lit candles and in the coldest of winters, hundreds, thousands and ten thousand processed through the cities and churches, prostrating themselves with humility in front of the altars, led by priests with crosses and banners.[29]

[21] *Ibid* pp 224–5.
[22] *Caffaro* p 40; *Patavini* p 179.
[23] V. Ansidei, *Regestrum reformationum comunis Perusini ab anno 1256 ad annum 1300* (Perugia 1935) 1 p 180. Frugoni pp 211–18 rectifies the general misconception that the flagellants did not appear until 4 May.
[24] *Patavini* p 196.
[25] [*Annales*] *Foroiulienses, MGH SS* 19 p 196.
[26] [*Annales*] *Placentini* [*Gibellini*] *MGH SS* 18 p 512.
[27] Salimbene [de Adam, *Cronica*, ed G. Scalia] (Bari 1966) 1 pp 99–101.
[28] *Caffaro* pp 39–41.
[29] *Patavini* p 179; In tantum itaque timor Domini irruit super eos, quod nobiles pariter et ignobiles, senes et iuvenes, infantes etiam quinque annorum, nudi per plateas civitatum, opertis tantum pudendis . . . bini et bini processionaliter incedebant; singuli flagellum in manibus de corigiis continentes, et cum gemitu et ploratu se acriter super scapulis usque ad effusionem sanguinis verberantes . . . Non solum itaque in die, verum etiam in

The flagellant movement in central Italy 1260–1400

The movement spread rapidly from Perugia to Rome and Bologna,[30] and in November to Modena,[31] Reggio, Piacenza and Genoa.[32] Towards the end of the year the fervour died down in Italy but crossed the Alps to France, Austria, Germany and eventually Poland.[33]

One can understand how flagellation came to be seen as the obvious method of expiation when translated into the context of a mass movement characterised by a widespread belief that God was intent on punishing mankind. It provided immediate and violent release from guilt and in the very process of beating their bodies participants could feel that they were washing away their sins. Moreover, in this exercise they saw themselves as sharing the sufferings of Christ.[34] It is surely not fanciful to suggest in these circumstances that the individual might see flagellation as leading to a personal rebirth. This in its turn could be extrapolated into a search for the salvation of mankind, for by taking the individual as a microcosm of society beating their bodies would lead to the expiation of the sins of all men.[35] One contemporary who seems to provide fuel for this argument is the chronicler of Asti, Guglielmo Ventura, who tells us that the movement was spread by hermits who, taking the prophet Jonah as their text, instructed the crowds to 'do penance because the Kingdom of Heaven is nigh'.[36]

This ideas would seem to savour of Joachimism particularly appropriate at the time because 1260 was believed by some to be the year when the age of the Holy Ghost would dawn.[37] But the only contemporary chronicler to mention Joachim in this context was Fra Salimbene of Parma,[38] although the notary Albert Milioli of

---

nocte cum cereis accensis, in hyeme asperimma, centeni et milleni, decem milia quoque per civitates et ecclesias circuibant, et se ante altaria humiliter prosternebant, precedentibus eos sacerdotibus cum crucibus et vexillis.

[30] *Placentini* p 512.
[31] *Cronaca Bolognese*, Muratori (new ed) 18, pt 1, II, p 157.
[32] *Varagine* p 389.
[33] *Annales capituli Posnaniensis*, MGH SS 29, p 461 and *Annales capituli Cracoviensis*, MGH SS 19, p 601.
[34] *Patavini* p 179.
[35] On this theme see: Brenda Bolton, 'Old wealth and new poverty in the twelfth century, *SCH* 14 pp 99–100.
[36] (Jonah 3, 4–8) [*Memoriale Guilielmi] Venturae [civis Astiensis]*, Muratori 11, col 153: 'Tunc Eremitae . . . dicebant "Poenitentiam agite, quia appropinquabit Regnum Caelorum"'. See also *Patavini* p 179.
[37] On this theme see R. Manselli, 'L'anno 1260 fu anno Gioachimitico?', *Il movimento*, pp 99–108.
[38] *Salimbene* p 677.

Reggio repeated his account verbatim.[39] However, Salimbene appears to have been dubious about a real connection suggesting that it was merely a coincidence that the flagellant movement began in 1260 and made it clear that it was others who held these views and not him.[40] Moreover, events in the preceding decade had robbed Joachimism of much of its credulity with the death of the potential Antichrist, Frederick II, in 1250 and the condemnation six years later of the spiritual Franciscan Gherardo of Borgo San Donino's introductory gloss on Joachim's *The Everlasting Gospel*.[41] Indeed other chroniclers give the impression that very different ideas were current; instead of signs indicating the dawning age of the Third Status heralded by a barefoot order of monks it was believed that God was intent on punishing mankind for their sins by consuming them with heavenly fire and swallowing them up by causing earthquakes.[42] It thus seems more probable that Joachimism helped to generate a mood rather than provide any specific influences to lead to the outbreak of fervour.[43]

In common with most popular religious movements it is difficult to distinguish between individual and mass motivation. Chroniclers usually only record the 'spirit' of the movement and all the historian can do is to assume a congruity between the individual and the many. In the 1233 *Alleluia*, for example, men and women apparently followed the lead of their neighbours and the general mood of the times took over, Salimbene describing the crowds as becoming 'drunk with heavenly joy'.[44] He tells us that in 1260 there was considerable pressure to join the processions; in Parma if anyone did not beat himself he was reputed to be of the devil, and invariably misfortune would overtake anybody thus singled out, for if he did not die he would fall gravely ill.[45]

This comment is revealing because it indicates that not all Italians were as overcome with religious fervour as the chroniclers suggest. In Genoa, for example, the first groups of flagellants to appear in the city were greeted with a mixed response, some saying 'It is a good sign', and others: 'I will never whip myself, others can do so as much as

[39] His *Liber de Temporibus* is reproduced by A. Cerlini in 'Fra Salimbene e le cronache attribuite ad Alberto Milioli), *Archivio Muratoriano* (Rome 1910) 1, fasc 8, pp 383–409.
[40] Salimbene p 677: 'Quem statum inchoatum dicunt in illa verberatione . . .'.
[41] [M.] Reeves, [*The Influence of Prophecy in the Later Middle Ages*] (Oxford 1969) pp 59–61, 187–8.
[42] *Patavini* p 179.
[43] Reeves p 55.
[44] Salimbene p 100: 'ita erant inebriati amore divino'.
[45] *Ibid* p 676.

they like',[46] On the whole, though, they were met with cries of derision and labelled as 'foolish' or 'mad'.[47] Then suddenly after three days the mood changed for, we are told, God inspired them with devotion, and those who had earlier been its most vociferous critics now became the leaders.[48] The chroniclers give no indication as to what caused this transformation except to suggest that the commotion was so great that the Genoese were inspired to follow the flagellants' example by donning habits, taking up crosses and joining the processions.[49]

There were, however, some parts of Italy where the flagellants met sustained opposition. This appears to have been for political rather than religious reasons and was directly related to the conflict between the Guelphs and Ghibellines. According to one chronicler Manfred issued an edict forbidding their entry into all those areas within his jurisdiction: Apulia, the marches of Ancona and Tuscany.[50] This explains why the movement began in a Guelph city, spread south to Rome and then turned north to the papal cities of Imola and Bologna. From there it followed the main route north-west; while some went via Tortona to Genoa, others set off for Milan and Brescia only to be turned away by the city authorities.[51] Manfred's henchmen automatically followed his example, which explains why the marquis of Cremona, Uberto Palavacino, ruled that the flagellants were not to enter his domain. He made sure they could come nowhere near the city by erecting a barricade of pitchforks on the banks of the River Po and instructed that any penitent who had the temerity to enter his lands should be hanged.[52]

It will have been noted that all these descriptions have been taken from contemporary or near-contemporary chronicles. Salimbene was the only one to say that he actually participated in the movement, but even so his account is no different in tone from his fellow chroniclers. They all remain impersonal and unemotional, and fail to conjure up any real excitement. Clearly it was not their intention to analyse the motives of the adherents but to give what might pass for an objective

[46] *Caffaro* p 40: 'alii dicebant: "bonum signum est", alii aliter. item alii dicebant: "numquam verberabo me et verberent se quantum volent", alii aliter'.
[47] *Varagine* p 389: 'tanquam fatui et deliri deridebantur a cunctis'.
[48] *Ibid.*
[49] *Caffaro* p 40.
[50] *Patavini* p 180. See also R. Davidsohn, *Storia di Firenze*, trans G. D. Klein (Florence 1972) 2, p 742.
[51] *Chronica Mediolani seu manipulus Florum*, Muratori 11, cols 690–1; *Placentini* p 512.
[52] *Salimbene* p 676; *Placentini* p 512.

view. Only occasionally does one hear the participants' attitude and even then the chroniclers merely include what is suitable to their theme, their intention being to present the movement as an orthodox phenomenon of divine inspiration. The episode in Genoa simply emphasises their point, that God's will ultimately prevails.

All the chroniclers stress that every sort of person was involved, from the *viri mediocres* to men like themselves, the *viri sapientes*.[53] In some places one finds the *podestà* himself[54] leading the processions, accompanied by the bishop[55] and the clergy holding crosses, standards and singing hymns.[56] The only participants who did not actually whip themselves during the processions were the women. According to one chronicler this was because they were too 'inexperienced' (*inexpertes*)[57] but this seems improbable when councils and monastic rules had prescribed the discipline for both sexes.[58] A more likely explanation was that because flagellation meant stripping to the waist the practice would have been regarded as unseemly for women.[59] Instead they waited until evening and retired to their rooms and included all types from 'noble matrons' to 'delicate virgins'.[60]

The membership of religious confraternities probably gives one a fair indication of the kind of people who made up the main adherents of the movement. In the same way that the excitement of a popular movement attracted a sprinkling of the upper classes so did the prestige of the larger confraternities.[61] The majority of members were lesser tradesmen and artisans,[62] reflecting the social composition of other lay

[53] *Patavini* p 179.
[54] Salimbene p 675, mentions that the Modenese were led by their *podestà* and bishop. See also *Memoriale Potestatum Regiensum*, Muratori 8, col 1122 and [*Chronicon*] *Parmense*, Muratori (new ed) 9, pt 9, p 22.
[55] At Asti for example: *Venturae* col 153, and Modena: Salimbene p 676.
[56] *Patavini* p 179 and *Venturae* col 153.
[57] *Patavini* p 179.
[58] Gougaud p 159, nn 17–18.
[59] Most chroniclers talk about flagellants being *nudi* but they probably followed the monastic example and only exposed their bodies from the waist upwards (see, for instance, *Decreta Lanfranci* 16: *PL* 150 (1880) cols 499–500). Only one witness makes this clear: Varagine pp 389–90.
[60] *Patavini* p 170: 'sed etiam matrone nobiles et virgines delicate cum omni honestate hec eadem faciebant'. See also *Foroiulenses* p 196 and Ricobaldo da Ferrara, *Historia imperatorum*, Muratori 9, col 134.
[61] See, for example, the *compagnia della Madonna d'Or San Michele* in Florence, whose membership Giovanni Villani characterised as the 'buona parte della migliore gente di Firenze': [G.] Villani, [*Cronaca*], Muratori 13, bk 7, cap 154, col 342.
[62] S. La Sorsa, *La Compagnia d'Or San Michele* (Trani 1902) pp 124–58 lists all the captains of this company from 1292 to 1347.

religious groups such as the Third Order,[63] except that in the case of flagellant companies women were excluded.[64]

The most significant legacy of the 1260 movement was therefore the inspiration it provided for the foundation of confraternities, which were, as Humbert of Romans attests, especially characteristic of Italian religious life.[65] But this type of organisation was not an isolated phenomenon because it belongs to the same tradition as communal groups such as guilds, on the one hand, and the Penitents and Third Orders on the other. It was above all in the churches belonging to the mendicant orders that one finds these new groups, and clearly the friars played an important part in founding many companies. In Tuscany, for example, the Dominican Ambrogio Sansedoni was involved in establishing the *laudesi* company at S. Domenico in Campo Regio in 1267[66] and also drew up the statutes of the flagellant company in the same church,[67] while Giordano of Rivalto reformed the Pisan *compagnia di S. Domenico*, turning it from a charitable into a flagellant company, *c*1287.[68]

Indeed the mendicants, and in particular the Dominicans, seem to have been closely associated not only with these confraternities but also the outbreaks of popular fervour. Thus a chronicler of the 1233 *Alleluia* described one particular aspect of the movement, the promo-

---

[63] Moorman pp 220–25.
[64] Although this is never actually stated by the statutes it is an underlying assumption; members are always referred to in the masculine and women never appear in membership lists.
[65] Humberti de Romani, *De eruditione religiosorum praedicatorum* (Rome 1793) p 348: 'in aliquibus nationibus, et maxime in Italia, fiunt interdum alique congregationes sive confratriae in honorem beatae Virginis vel alicuius sancti, ex quibus sequitur multiplex fructus'. The standard works on Italian confraternities are G. M. Monti's indispensable but somewhat inaccurate *Le confraternite medievali* [*dell' alta e media Italia*] 2 vols (Venice 1927) and [G. G.] Meersseman's invaluable 'Études [sur les anciennes confréries dominicaines]': 1 'Les confréries de Saint-Dominique', *AFP* 20 (1950) pp 5–113; 2 'Les confréries de Saint-Pierre Martyr', *AFP*, 21 (1951) pp 51–196; 3 'La congregation de la Vierge', *AFP* 22 (1952) pp 5–176; 4 'Les milices de Jésus-Christ', *AFP* 23 (1953) pp 275–308. Detailed surveys of many towns still remain to be done, although work has begun under the auspices of the Centro di documentazione sul movimento dei disciplinati which has published its findings in *BDRU*. For Florence see C. de la Roncière, 'La place des confréries dans l'encadrement religieux du contado florentin', *Mélanges de l'école française de Rome*, 85 (Rome 1973) fasc 1, pp 31–77, fasc 2, pp 633–71 and my forthcoming thesis for London University (Westfield College): ['The Religious] Confraternities of Florence, [*c*1250–1434: A study of the *laudesi* and *disciplinati* companies'].
[66] G. G. Meersseman, 'Nota sull'origine delle compagnia dei laudesi', *RSCI* 17 (1963) pp 395–7.
[67] Meersseman, 'Études', 1, pp 40–1.
[68] *Ibid* pp 40–1.

tion of peace, as the *devotio fratrum Predicatorum*.[69] Pacification became a standard feature of all subsequent movements as can be seen in 1260 and 1310,[70] although one cannot attribute this to direct Dominican influence since neither seem to have had identifiable leaders who spread the devotion in Italy.[71] In 1335, however, the Dominican Fra Venturino da Bergamo led a pilgrimage through Lombardy and Tuscany towards Rome. His sermons, which were straightforward and moving,[72] attracted large crowds who helped to spread his message of penitence and peace. Murderers and robbers were converted to lead a life of penance,[73] enemies were reconciled and restitution was made to injured parties.[74] Flagellant companies were founded to commemorate this devotion in, for example, Prato[75] and Viterbo.[76] The same characteristics were present at the end of the century in the 1399 Bianchi movement (so-called because its members wore white robes) when even larger crowds of Italians processed from town to town spreading their message of peace and reconciliation.[77]

However, the origins of only a few confraternities can be attributed to specific events, for their early years are usually obscured by a lack of documentation. This is partly because earlier foundations only gradually adopted flagellation as their principle exercise[78] but also because the 1260 movement gave the most immediate impetus to the foundation of *laudesi* companies, whose main function it was to sing lauds in the vernacular to their patron saints, principle of whom was Mary. Judging from the surviving documentation, in central Italy at least, these companies were founded some time before the majority of flagellant companies and it was only in the first half of the fourteenth

[69] *Parmense* p 10.
[70] *Ibid* p 117; G. Villani, *Cronaca*, bk 8, cap 122, col 444; and Ptoleomei Lucensis, *Historia Ecclesiastica*, Muratori 11, col 1233.
[71] Despite the legend, Mazzatinti pp 561-3, there is no evidence that Fasani actually led the flagellants to Bologna.
[72] Villani bk 11, cap 23, cols 767-8.
[73] *Ibid*.
[74] *Storia dal principio del secolo XIII fino al 1351 di uno Anonimo Fiorentino con annotazioni di un Anonimo Lucchese*, in Stephani Baluzii, *Miscellanae* (Lucca 1764) 4, p 114, and *Cronaca di Agnolo di Tura del Grasso*, p 514.
[75] Meersseman, 'Études' 1, pp 41-42.
[76] *Ibid* p 42.
[77] The two most detailed descriptions of this movement are: Ser Luca di Bartolomeo Dominici, *Cronaca della Venuta dei Bianchi e della moria, 1399-1400*, Società Pistoiese de storia patria (Pistoia 1933) and *Le croniche di Giovanni Sercambi Lucchese*, Fonti 20 (Lucca 1892) 2, pp 240-375. The most thorough treatment of the Bianchi is G. Tognetti, 'Sul Moto dei Bianchi del 1399, *BISIMEAM* 78 (Rome 1967) pp 205-343.
[78] Meersseman, 'Études' 1, p 27.

The flagellant movement in central Italy 1260–1400

century that they became a widespread phenomenon, as can be seen in the cases of Perugia,[79] Siena,[80] Florence,[81] Prato[82] and Lucca.[83]

What would have led somebody to join a confraternity? Clearly those companies which were founded immediately after the 1260 movement would have drawn their membership from among those of the original participants who wanted to keep alive the spirit of the devotion. One such was the Bolognese *società dei divoti*, whose statutes specifically state that they were drawn up 'at the time of the general devotion'.[84] It continued to celebrate the public nature of its origins by ordaining that members should process through the streets on Sundays and festivals 'whipping themselves in honour of the dear Christ'.[85]

This was surely the most important reason for joining a flagellant company, for by beating their bodies they were able to do reverence to Christ, and by remaining constantly aware of their own sinfulness they would be induced to strive towards self-improvement. However, there was a difference between Christ's role as envisaged by the popular imagination in 1260 and His role in confraternities. Instead of the remote deity determined to punish erring humanity, He came to be seen more as the Redeemer, the Son of God who was prepared to suffer crucifixion so that mankind could be saved. Flagellation was therefore seen less as a penance than as a way in which members of a confraternity could share His suffering, in reverence of which they would devote themselves to this exercise 'in memory of the Passion of Christ'.[86]

---

[79] The three main Perugian flagellant companies of S. Agostino, S. Francesco and S. Domenico, were founded between 1317 and 1320: R. Guèze, 'Le confraternite di S. Agostino, S. Francesco and S. Domenico di Perugia', *Il movimento*, pp 606–10.

[80] See G. M. Monti, *Le confraternite medievali* 1, pp 228–49.

[81] The earliest record of a flagellant company in Florence is that of *S. Giovanni Battista su l'arcora* founded in 1320: A[rchivio di] s[tato di] F[irenze], Cap[itoli] Comp[agnie] Rel[igiose] Sopp[resse] 354, fol 3ʳ. By the end of the fourteenth century there were at least fifteen flagellant companies in the city; see chapter 3 of my forthcoming study, *Confraternities of Florence*.

[82] Meersseman, 'Études' 1, pp 41–7.

[83] Lucca had four main flagellant companies: S. Francesco, S. Maria Maddalena, S. Lorenzo in Servi and the *confraternità della Croce*, all founded between 1300 and 1380: S. Andeucci, 'La compagnia dei Disciplinati di S. Francesco e S. Maria Maddalena in Lucca', *BDRU* 68 (1971) fasc 2, pp 233–40.

[84] A. Gaudenzi, *Statuti della società del popolo di Bologna*, 2 (Rome 1896) *Fonti* 4, p 423: 'hec sunt ordinamenta facta et conposita . . . sub annis Domini MCCLX, indictione tertia, tempore generalis devotionis'.

[85] *Ibid* cap 3, p 424.

[86] The phrase 'per memoria della passione di Cristo' recurs in the statutes of all flagellant companies. See, for example, the 1354 statutes of the Florentine [*compagnia della*] *Mis[ericordia] del Salv[atore]: I capitoli della compagnia di Gesù Pellegrinio*], ed P. Ferrato (Padua 1871) (*Nozze Carlotti-Citta della Vigodorzere*) cap 12, p 11.

JOHN HENDERSON

The way in which the fervour of the popular movements came to be contained within the practices of a confraternity can be seen clearly in the prologue to the 1335 statutes of the *compagnia di S. Domenico* in Prato:

> And the said company meets in the said place on certain ordained days to flagellate the body and commemorate the passion of our Lord Jesus Christ, crucified in remission of our sins and in utility of our souls . . .[87]

Members would thus assemble at what were essentially commemorative services not so much to do penance for the rather generalised concept of universal sin but rather for what was an even stronger motive force, in remission of their own sins and the benefit of their own souls. In this way they would build up a communal fund of merit upon which all members could draw both during this life and after death. Indeed one of the main reasons for joining a confraternity was that it provided the organisation whereby the souls of all past members would be remembered in perpetuity.[88]

Flagellation was not the only preoccupation of these companies for it was seen as a stage in the individual's spiritual development, in the same way that the days of suffering in the liturgical cycle were designed to precede the days of joy. Thus their meetings were envisaged in pairs, of either Fridays and Sundays[89] or the first and third Sunday of each month.[90] Flagellation was usually the central feature of their first meeting, while at the second they mainly sang orations, thus mirroring the transition from the passion to the resurrection.[91]

---

[87] Meersseman, 'Études' I, p 71: 'E la decta compagnia si rauna nel decto luogho certi dí ordinati a disciplinarsi lo corpo e fare memoria della passione del nostro Signore Yhesu Christo crocifisso en remissione de' peccati nostri et a utilità delle nostre anime . . .'.

[88] Each company would hold a commemorative service each month, in the case of the *compagnia della Misericordia del Salvatore* this was on the third Sunday, *Mis del Salv* (1354) cap 12, pp 11–12, and usually an annual commemorative meal. At this company it was on 2 November: *ibid* (1354) cap 43, pp 38–40.

[89] See, for example, the *compagnia di S. Andrea* at Vico: ASF, Cap Comp Relig Sopp 444, caps 7–8, fol 2ʳ; the *compagnia dei Raccomandati di Gesù Christo Crocifiso* which met under S. Maria della Scala in Siena: L. Banchi, *Capitoli della compagnia dei disciplinati di Siena* (Siena 1866) cap 15, p 17.

[90] For example, the Florentine *compagnia della Misericordia del Salvatore*, *Mis del Salv* (1354) cap 12, p 11, and the *compagnia di S. Domenico* of S. Maria Novella: Florence, Biblioteca Riccardiana, MS 3041, cap 2, fol 2ʳ. Also the *compagnia di S. Agostino* in Prato: C. Guasti, *I capitoli di una compagnia di disciplina, compilati nell'anno MCCCXIX*, *Miscellanea pratese inediti o rare, antiche o moderne*, fasc 10 (Prato 1864) cap 11, p 20.

[91] See Charles de la Roncière, 'La place des confréries dans l'encadrement religieux du contado florentin', fasc 1, p 48.

158

The flagellant movement in central Italy 1260-1400

A very strict self-contained corporate life evolved very different from the public processions of 1260. Members were forbidden from telling outsiders how the company functioned or revealing the identity of any of their fellows.[92] Indeed some companies give the impression of being almost secret organisations, borne out in the case of fifteenth-century Florence at least by the communal government setting up commissions to investigate their activities.[93] This exclusiveness was probably one of the main attractions of flagellant companies because it produced fairly small,[94] close-knit communities providing a system of both spiritual and physical support for its membership.[95] It must also have imparted a feeling of spiritual privilege for although prayers were said for people outside the membership their basic concern was for their own spiritual development.

Within a company the member was supposed to obey the wishes of the founders as laid down in the statutes.[96] If he failed to do so he was punished, standing in front of the company, each member being required to give him a blow with his whip. This done he was subjected to further humiliation for he had to walk through the city beating himself all the way, dressed in a black habit as a sign of his wickedness.[97]

Members normally wore white habits symbolising the purity of their intentions. The colour also recalled their own baptismal robes and therefore represented the member's new innocence. The words spoken by the prior of a flagellant company to a novice when giving him his new habit were taken directly from Paul's fourth letter to the Ephesians: 'Lord put on the new man which after God has been created

[92] In Florence, for example, see the *compagnia della Misericordia del Salvatore*, Mis del Salv (1354) cap 37, p 31, of S. Maria Novella and the *compagnia di S. Niccolò* of S. Maria del Carmine, ASF Cap Comp Relig Sopp 439, cap 9 fol 3ᵛ.

[93] See the prohibition of 19-20 October 1419 in ASF Prov[visione] Reg[istri] 109, fols 160ʳ-2ᵛ and two laws of February 1444 and June 1455, Prov Reg 134, fols 208ʳ-9ᵛ, and *ibid* 146, fols 147ʳ-8ᵛ.

[94] Flagellant companies could be as small as twelve members (see the *compagnia di S. Niccolò* of S. Maria del Carmine, Florence: ASF, Cap Comp Relig Sopp 439 cap 1, fol 1ᵛ, although the majority of companies were somewhat larger. For Florence see chapter 9 of my forthcoming *Confraternities of Florence*.

[95] See, for example, the prayers said in the *compagnia di S. Agostino* in Prato: C. Guasti, *I capitoli di una compagnia di disciplina*, pp 32-5.

[96] The provisions of the 1354 statute of the Florentine *compagnia della Misericordia del Salvatore* are representative of most companies: *Mis del Salv* (1354) cap 37, pp 31-2.

[97] For the punishments given to members of the Florentine *compagnia della Misericordia del Salvatore* between 1364 and 1404 see their records in ASF, Comp Relig Sopp 910 cap 7, fols 3ʳ-77ᵛ.

in righteousness and holiness of truth'.[98] The same words were said to a monk when he was taking the habit and in both cases they represent the rededication of the postulant's life to penitence.[99]

It is interesting, though, that it was precisely the wearing of a habit which Clement VI attacked in his bull of 20 October 1349.[100] The pope saw the wearing of a habit as a sign of the flagellants' rejection of the authority of the church, believing they saw their exercise as an end in itself which would lead them to their salvation unaided by the priesthood. The bull was directed principally against the activities of the groups of flagellants who swept across northern Europe during the black death period and does not seem to have effected either the later movements or confraternities in Italy which have been studied in this paper.[101] We have seen, moreover, that the motives which led people to join the processions in 1260, 1310 and 1335 were not unorthodox, but stemmed from a well-worn, recurrent fear that God was about to punish mankind for its sins. In none of these movements do we find the socially disruptive millenarian doctrines which took hold immediately the devotion crossed the Alps.[102] Even when the population of whole towns processed through the streets the impression is one of orderliness, the devotion being organised, partly at least, by members of the clergy and the mendicant orders. Even more contained was the devotion of the confraternities which was based upon the cult of Christ, for by doing reverence to Him in the form of voluntary flagellation they came to identify more closely with the incarnate Christ, the Man of Sorrows of later medieval art.

University of London
Westfield College

---

[98] Eph 4, 24. This example was taken from the *compagnia di S. Domenico* in Prato: Meersseman, 'Études' 1, pp 79–80.

[99] *Ibid* p 80, nn 11–13.

[100] Fredericq 1, nos 202, 200–1.

[101] For an account of the northern flagellants see Giles Li Muisis's *Chronica* in Fredericq 2, no 61 (194) pp 100–9, esp 108–9.

[102] For a general account of this see G. Leff, *Heresy in the Later Middle Ages* (Manchester 1967) 2, pp 485–93, and *DSAM* 5 cols 395–9.

POVERTY AND POLITICS:
THE MOTIVATION OF
FOURTEENTH CENTURY
FRANCISCAN REFORM IN ITALY

by DUNCAN NIMMO

A FTER the undoubted achievements of the thirteenth century, the fourteenth is usually considered a period of spiritual recession for the major institutions of the western church. The regular orders, on the whole, suffered along with the rest, and apparently none more so than the family of Saint Francis. Like its fellows, it experienced the general decay of discipline known as conventualism.[1] In part, however, this was but the symptom of a more fundamental malaise, a diffuse but widespread disenchantment with the ideal which, in the previous century, the order had made peculiarly and gloriously its own, that of absolute evangelical poverty;[2] and this in turn, it goes without saying, followed from the catastrophic double conflict on poverty which filled the first quarter of the fourteenth century: the 'practical' conflict over observance between the spirituals and community, which led many spirituals into heresy and revolt against the church; and the 'theoretical' conflict which embroiled pope John XXII with all shades of opinion in the order, and came likewise to a heretical and schismatic end.[3] No wonder, then, if the fourteenth century seems, for the Franciscans, an epoch peculiarly bleak.

But that is not the whole story. Amid all the gloom—and in what might be thought the heartland of ecclesiastical decadence, Italy—the period also witnessed the birth of a Franciscan reform of quintessential purity, the movement (as it came to be known) of the regular observance.[4] This was the forerunner of the great wave of renewal

---

[1] The position is described in all general accounts of the order, for example, Holzapfel, *Handbuch*, pp 80–2; Moorman, *History*, cap 28.

[2] A telling aspect is considered by A. Vauchez, 'La place de la pauvreté dans les documents hagiographiques à l'époque des spirituels', in *Chi erano gli Spirituali*, Atti del 3° Convegno Internazionale della Società Internazionale di Studi Francescani (Assisi 1976) pp 125–43.

[3] Survey of the two aspects in Moorman, *History*, caps 17, 25. For a more detailed account up to 1323: [M. D.] Lambert, [*Franciscan Poverty*] (London 1961).

[4] Outlines in such general accounts as Holzapfel, *Handbuch*; Moorman, *History*. The

that was to sweep through the order in the next century, purging it of the corruptions of conventualism, and producing such saints of European stature as Bernardino of Siena and John Capistran. And perhaps more remarkable, it set itself the same goal as the spiritual movement, and it succeeded where that had failed. Its basis was the so-called literal observance of the rule of Saint Francis—the commitment, simple and yet how demanding, to follow as closely as possible the way of life of the founder of the order and his first companions; and this observance it incorporated into the fraternity, demoralised though it was, not only without the decades of violent repression, and the ultimate condemnation, that befell the spirituals, but with the support of the highest authority in the order and the church. The outcome was thus what the spirituals had vainly struggled for, the harmonious co-existence of two different life-styles, or standards of observance, within the one institute: a situation with very few parallels among the Franciscans, and, we may suspect, not many more in other bodies. If we add that all this occurred despite the, one would have thought, invincible discredit that the spiritual schism had earned for the literal observance,[5] the foundation of the Italian reform becomes one of the most astonishing achievements of the first two Franciscan centuries. The purpose of this article is, subject to the limitations of the available evidence (particularly for the earlier part of the story), to discover how so paradoxical a development came about—that is, in a broad sense, its motivation. The answer moves between two poles, which for shorthand convenience can be labelled poverty and politics. Establish-

---

main secondary studies: F. Ehrle, 'Das Verhältniss der Spiritualen zu den Anhängern der Observanz', *ALKG* 4 (1888) pp 181–90; M. Faloci Pulignani, 'Il B. Paoluccio Trinci e i Minori Osservanti', *MF* 21 (1920) pp 65–82; [L.] Brengio, [*L'Osservanza francescana in Italia nel secolo XIV*] (Rome 1963). [M.] Sensi, ['Brogliano e l'opera di fra Paoluccio Trinci'], *Picenum Seraphicum* 12 (officially, 1975; however, the volume had not appeared at the time of writing). References here are to note, not page numbers in the author's typescript, a copy of which was kindly supplied by the Capuchin historical institute, Rome. Apart from relevant items in *AM* and *Bull Franc*, the chief early sources are: the narratives and documents collected by M. Faloci Pulignani, 'Il B. Paoluccio Trinci da Foligno', *MF* 6 (1896) pp 97–128; [*Bernardini Aquilani Chronica fratrum minorum de observantia*, ed L.] Lemmens (Rome 1902); [L.] Jacobilli, [*Vita del B. Paolo detto*] *Paoluccio* [*de' Trinci da Fuligno*] (Fuligno 1627); [L.] Jacobilli, [*Vite dei*] *Santi* [*e Beati dell'Umbria,*] 1 (Fuligno 1647). The present interpretation is based on part of the writer's PhD thesis for the university of Edinburgh, *The Franciscan Regular Observance 1368–1447 and the divisions of the Order 1294–1528* (1974); a revised version of this study is to be published by the Capuchin Historical Institute, Rome.

[5] Most evident in the failures of Philip of Majorca to have the literal observance accepted: see Brengio pp 27–37.

ing their bearing on the question of the Italian observance will lead us, in conclusion, to one or two reflections of more general application.

The stable foundation of the Italian regular observance took place fairly late in the century: in 1368 the minister general of the Minors conceded the derelict hermitage of Brugliano, situated in lonely mountains north of Foligno, to a lay brother of that town, Paoluccio, who happened to be of the Trinci family, the lords of the place; and he authorised Paoluccio to live at Brugliano in poverty and austerity with a few companions.[6] The act of foundation however—and is this a first point of general application?—marks more of an end than a beginning. For the religious aspirations of brother Paoluccio were the core of the element of poverty in the observant story, and they had been born, in the friary of his native town, more than four decades earlier. There is an important corollary. Despite first appearances, there was no real gap between the observance and the spirituals: temporally, the new movement took up where its predecessor left off; and more than that, there was, as we shall see, a direct connection between them. This may prompt a question which in concluding we shall return to: is there such a thing as a clean break, a genuine ending or beginning, in ecclesiastical affairs?

It was in 1323, at the age of fourteen, that Paoluccio dei Trinci forswore the power and pomp of his family's temporal dominion to seek a spiritual kingdom through the rule of saint Francis.[7] There is considerable irony in the date: 1323 was the year in which, with the bull *Cum inter nonnullos*, pope John XXII appeared to close the era of Franciscan total poverty.[8] Accordingly Paoluccio was, in a sense, an anachronistic figure, for from the first his aim was that of the Franciscan spirituals—to restore all the austerity and fervour of the original fraternity. Intense devotion was already, as it was to remain, the key-note, and indeed the corner-stone, of his religious life. He fasted almost perpetually, we are told, and 'his most delicate food was meditation on the passion';[9] his prayers were of such vehemence that at times he would groan or cry out aloud; so he was assigned a cell in a corner of the friary, away from his fellows, to avoid disturbing them. From such spiritual bedrock sprang characteristic Franciscan virtues. Shabbily clothed and housed, the young scion of the ruling

[6] A full account of the incident, with sources, is given later.
[7] *AM* anno 1323 no 22 (2 ed vol 7 p 9).
[8] See Lambert cap 10.
[9] Jacobilli, *Paoluccio*, p 22.

family turned out, sack on shoulder, to beg from door to door of his native town. In the friary his preference fell—at a time when it was becoming customary for the 'lesser brothers' to have servants[10]—on menial tasks: garden and kitchen work, sweeping out the church, cleaning the altar and lighting the lamps; it was then, although exceptional,[11] quite in keeping that he chose to remain a simple lay brother, rather than be advanced to the priesthood. Thus self-abased in all things, Paoluccio was a model of obedience—'the will of his superiors was the guide of his every action';[12] so much so, indeed, that he pursued his religious ends, not by direct request, still less assertion, but by prayer and patience. Given the calamitous ending of the spiritual movement it was, perhaps, as well that its would-be restorer was, above all, no dissident.[13]

This picture of Paoluccio's religious ideal in his apprenticeship can be both confirmed and complemented from the other end of his life, by what is known of his and his followers' existence at the hermitage of Brugliano. Even today the place is one of solitude; in the harsher conditions of the fourteenth century it was more nearly one of desolation.[14] The friars' rough and ready settlement stood on a hillside; below it, in all directions, stretched an enormous marsh, the haunt of frogs, which croaked incessantly, and of snakes, which used sometimes to seek out the higher ground, and would thus invade the brothers' quarters—even, on occasion, their beds (although faithful disciples of saint Francis, they were not delighted). The surrounding terrain was rough and stony; cultivation in consequence was minimal; the scattered inhabitants of the region appeared semi-barbarous, poor and uncouth, and dressed in the skins of wild animals; and the going underfoot was so hard that all, including the friars, were compelled to wear a type of clogs—wooden shoes, fitted with irons, called zoccoli (sandals were impractical, and bare feet unthinkable).

Here were poverty and austerity enough for any Franciscan: the setting for a religious life centred upon prayer, and informed with humility and a fundamental simplicity. Following their leader's

---

[10] See Moorman, *History*, p 360.

[11] *Ibid* p 352.

[12] Jacobilli, *Paoluccio*, p 23.

[13] The foregoing picture of Paoluccio is based on *MF* 6 (1896) pp 101, 104–5; Jacobilli, *Paoluccio*, pp 22–4; *AM* anno 1323 no 22 (2 ed vol 7 p 9).

[14] For the following description see: *AM* anno 1368 no 12 (2 ed vol 8 p 210); *MF* 6 (1896) pp 106–7; Brengio pp 45–6. Brugliano lies between Colfiorito and Serravalle, on the route from Foligno to Camerino.

example, few of the observants aspired to the priesthood and the cure of souls—for which their surroundings offered in any case little opportunity; similarly, they had neither the desire, nor the equipment and resources, for serious and formal study.[15] By default, then, in one sense—although fundamentally, it goes without saying, by choice— they concentrated on the elementals of the religious life, penitence and prayer. The sign of it is that, as their numbers increased, the order learnt to know them as the *fratres simplices* or *fratres devoti*, and their settlements as the *loca devota*.[16]

Poverty, humility, simplicity and prayer: these were, from first to last, the religious ideals of Paoluccio dei Trinci. They were also, of course, those of saint Francis.[17] In binding himself to them in the 1320s, brother Paoluccio was thus not merely, in a sense, a man out of his time, but a throw-back to the earliest days of the order. Just so had the spirituals been before him.

How, then, did Paoluccio's fellow-friars react to the youthful new recruit, exceptional by his birth, and more so by his aspirations? Some, it is said, viewed him with awe,[18] and others—perhaps they were the majority—with mistrust and hostility.[19] However it was not long before he was joined by two older men, who not only shared his mind, but were, like himself, destined at different times to play the decisive role in the history of the observance. These were Gentilis of Spoleto and John of Valle. All we know of the former is that, like Paoluccio, he was a lay brother; John, by contrast, was a priest, and represented the future reform's first firm contact with the hermitage at Brugliano, for he had been born and bred in the vicinity.[20] His importance to the history of the reform is however far larger on another count: although only the bare fact is attested—and by narrative sources at that—it seems beyond doubt that he was the confidant and pupil of Angelo Clareno (more properly 'of Chiarino'), one of the two great leaders of the Italian spirituals, who, defying the official suppression of his congregation in 1317, remained at large and active in central and

[15] *AM* anno 1415 no 34 (2 ed vol 9 p 382); Lemmens p 24.
[16] *AM* anno 1380 no 29 (2 ed vol 9 pp 41–2). For further terms see Sensi n 101.
[17] See J. R. H. Moorman, *Saint Francis of Assisi* (London 1963), cap 2. This is a fine short account. The nearest approach to a standard modern critical life is O. Englebert, trans E. M. Cooper, *Saint Francis of Assisi* (2 ed Chicago 1965).
[18] Jacobilli, *Paoluccio*, p 23.
[19] *MF* 6 (1896) pp 104–5.
[20] On John of Valle: Jacobilli, *Santi*, pp 371–2; *AM* anno 1334 no 24 (2 ed vol 7 p 168), anno 1351 no 40 (2 ed vol 8 p 87); Brengio pp 38–40. On Gentilis of Spoleto: *AM* anno 1350 no 15 (2 ed vol 8 p 45); Brengio pp 49–51.

southern Italy until his death in 1336.[21] Here then is the proven
channel whereby the inspiration of the first Franciscan literal observance
movement passed to its successor. Moreover Angelo, who died in
ripe old age, had joined the order around 1260, and claimed to have
known, not merely numerous friars of the second generation, but at
least three surviving intimates of saint Francis himself.[22] We can
thus say that, counting Angelo and John of Valle as intermediaries,
the reform movement begun in 1368 was linked directly with the
fraternity's original inspiration: an illuminating comment on the
authenticity and continuity of Paoluccio dei Trinci's religious ideal,
which we have encapsulated under the heading of poverty.

For the formal launching of the Italian regular observance, poverty
by itself was not enough; action was required: and that included
politics. The necessary act occurred in 1334, and was—so far as the bare
fact, which again is all that is recorded—identical, except for the
protagonists, with the event of 1368. John of Valle, and not, this time,
Paoluccio dei Trinci, obtained permission from the general minister
of the day, Gerald Odo, to retire to the derelict hermitage of
Brugliano, and there live according to the literal observance of saint
Francis' rule, together with four companions; among these was
Gentilis of Spoleto, but not Paoluccio (the reason for his absence is
not known; it may have had something to do with his youth, or with
the unassertiveness which, we saw, was characteristic).[23] Thus, at one
blow, the unheard-of was accomplished—the arrangement on which
the spirituals had spent their strength and hopes for year after year:
the literal observance was established within the Franciscan order,
and by the order's own authority. And as though this were not
remarkable enough, the prelate responsible, the general minister, has
some claim to be regarded as the symbolic father of conventualism—
that decay of discipline, and associated disenchantment with the ideal
of poverty, which is at the opposite pole to strict adherence to the rule.
    Gerald Odo was John XXII's choice to replace Michael of Cesena
as general when the latter finally broke with the pope on the question
of evangelical poverty; thus he was near the centre of the gravest

[21] A recent study of Angelo: L. Berardini, *Frate Angelo da Chiarino alla luce della storia*
(Osimo 1964).
[22] See P. Sabatier, *Speculum Perfectionis seu S. Francisci Assisiensis Legenda Antiquissima*
(Paris 1898) pp lxxix, cxxxvii; *ALKG* 2 (1886) pp 110–12.
[23] *AM* anno 1334 no 24 (2 ed vol 7 p 168), anno 1351 no 40 (2 ed vol 8 p 87); Jacobilli,
Santi, p 372; *AFH* 2 (1909) p 641; Brengio pp 40–5.

shock to its sense of purpose the order ever experienced.[24] This may partly explain why, in 1331, he proposed to John a radical simplification, but at the same time relaxation, of the order's official practice on the question of poverty:[25] the documents by which that practice was laid down, a series of papal interpretations of the rule, should be revoked; the rule's prohibition of money should be abrogated; and superiors should be given absolute discretion in all other matters relating to poverty. There was a good deal of realism in the general's proposal, as well as the merit of clarifying a highly complex code of practice; nevertheless, as is indicated by the hostile reaction of John XXII and many influential friars, it amounted to a pure sell-out as far as the order's most characteristic religious principle was concerned.

Gerald Odo's authorisation of the literal observance of the rule in 1334 was apparently then the reverse of his plan of 1331, as well as of all the traditions of the order. *A priori*, such a historical volte-face seems explicable only by the presence of some important new factor in the situation. Was there such a factor? If we consider the order's general standing and influence in the world—adopting, that is, a broadly political viewpoint—we shall see that there was: namely the challenge, spirited and sometimes all too successful, of those who claimed, with some justification, to be more authentic Franciscans— the heretical fraticelli *de paupere vita*.

These fraticelli were in effect a parallel movement to the regular observance, identical in their religious goals, separated only by their heresy—repudiation of John XXII, his successors, and their adherents.[26] They originated among those Franciscan spirituals who, during John's pontificate, forsook the church rather than renounce their ideal of the literal observance (an outstanding instance is Angelo Clareno, already mentioned). Their significance in the present context is that, following saint Francis' rule to the letter, they asserted that they, and not the official fraternity which was far from living like its founder, were the genuine Franciscans.[27] There was force in the argument, and it gained

[24] On Gerald Odo: C. V. Langlois, 'Guiral Ot', *Histoire Littéraire de la France* 36 (Paris 1927) pp 203–25; L. Bartolomé, *Gerardo de Odon* (Murcia 1928).

[25] Brengio pp 42–4; [C.] Schmitt, [*Un pape réformateur et un défenseur de l'unité de l'église,*] *Benoît* [*XII et l'ordre des frères mineurs*] (Quaracchi 1959) pp 65–6.

[26] Fundamental documentary studies: F. Ehrle, 'Das Verhältniss der Spiritualen zu den Fraticellen', *ALKG* 4 (1888) pp 64–180; L. Oliger, 'Documenta inedita ad historiam fraticellorum spectantia', *AFH* 3 (1910) pp 253–79, 505–29, 680–99; 4 (1911) pp 3–23, 688–712; 5 (1912) pp 74–84; 6 (1913) pp 267–90, 515–30, 710–47. A recent synthesis: C. Schmitt, 'Fraticelles', *DHGE* 18 (1977) cols 1063–1108.

[27] Clareno's group: *ALKG* 4 (1888) p 9 lines 12–14; other groups: *AFH* 4 (1911) pp 694, 697, 702.

the fraticelli recruits; their success was particularly marked during the 1330s, and the heart of the sect at that time was the march of Ancona, particularly the region of Camerino:[28] Camerino lies immediately to the north-east of Brugliano. There seems little doubt about the inference to be drawn: the foundation of the regular observance was the general minister's reply—and the only one with some chance of success—to the heretics' charge that he and his friars had abandoned the rule of their founder. The inference is supported by one shred of positive evidence. It is recorded that, in 1340, Gerald Odo succeeded, with the aid of the local population, in expelling a band of fraticelli from the Carceri, the hermitage high above Assisi which had been much used by Francis and his companions; and he stationed in their place a group of strict friars, brought in from elsewhere.[29] Although we are not told as much, it seems probable that these were members of the regular observance, since the Carceri was certainly in the movement ten years later;[30] but even if this was not so, and some quite separate group were involved, the incident still shows that the general's policy was to combat the austerity of the fraticelli with that of his own most zealous brothers.

Here then, we may reasonably suppose, was the major political consideration which might explain Gerald Odo's unprecedented act of favour to Franciscan literal observance. And there is a wider sense in which the arrangement can be called political: it embodied the principles—eminently the stuff of politics—of compromise and co-operation, instead of confrontation and conflict.

We can see this most easily by comparing the position of the regular observance with that of their predecessors, the spirituals. The tragic and disastrous strife between the spirituals and community arose simply from their adoption of irreconcilable basic standpoints. The former were, for good reasons, convinced of the authenticity of the literal observance of the rule, and would in the last resort go to any lengths—including separation from the order and, if necessary, the church—so as to obtain it. Conversely the community, understandably resentful of the implied criticism of their more easy-going ways, and alarmed by what they rightly saw as a potential source of rebellion—and for all that, we may think, with inadequate justification—refused point-blank

[28] See Schmitt, *Benoît*, pp 169–72.
[29] *Chronicle [of the Twenty-Four Generals]*, *AF* 3 (1897) p 530; *AM* anno 1331 no 21 (2 ed vol 7 p 126)—Wadding's dating is at fault here; Schmitt, *Benoît*, p 173; *AFH* 6 (1913) p 278.
[30] *Bull Franc* 6 (1902) p 245–6; see below.

Fourteenth century Franciscan reform

to countenance the literal observance, either within or outside the order. In such a situation, conflict, schism and heresy were the inevitable and logical outcome.

If such was confrontation, the principle of compromise depended (as it must) on the willingness of both sides to give some ground. From the side of the authorities, the crucial, and plainly very great concession was the general minister's recognition of the legitimacy of the literal observance—the very thing his predecessors had withheld.[31] In return, the observants could afford to promise everything that the spirituals eventually refused: to obey their superiors, abstain from criticising their confreres, and, above all, avoid any suggestion of a division of the order. Although we lack direct evidence, it must be assumed that Gerald Odo satisfied himself on all these points before formalising his critical concession to John of Valle.[32] The fact that the latter was only willing to proceed with the general's permission—rather than, for example, by simple secession to the fraticelli, as some friars did[33]— was already an earnest of submissiveness and orthodoxy; and the compact between the two sides reached its active and beneficial culmination in their co-operation against the fraticelli, the enemy, in their different ways, of both.

It takes the broad political perspective just outlined to disclose the full significance of the foundation of the Italian regular observance in 1334. Its essential motive—even if we judge it a response to the external threat posed by the fraticelli—was reconciliation: a readiness on the part of both the general and the reformers to abstain from extreme demands, recognise the claims of the other, and so bury the conflicts and hatreds of the past. As such it was, in the light of the order's previous history, a very great achievement—and also, we might say, a spiritual, and a characteristically Franciscan one. Moreover the achievement had a perhaps surprisingly broad base. Gerald Odo's support for the strict friars was continued by his two successors in office,[34] and also by the general chapter of 1346;[35] and when, in 1343,

[31] With the possible exception of Raymond Gaufridi, who had a hand in events leading to Celestine V's authorisation of the literal observance in 1294: see Moorman, *History*, 194.
[32] As by Brengio, p 45.
[33] *ALKG* 4 (1888) 161–2.
[34] Fortanerius Vassalis (1343–8) and William Farinier (1348–57). For the former see *AM* anno 1343 no 10 (2 ed vol 7 p 293); for the latter, a circular letter of 1349: [R.] Pratesi, ['Una lettera enciclica del ministro generale Guglielmo Farinier'], *AFH* 50 (1957) pp 348–63, at p 361.
[35] F. M. Delorme, 'Acta capituli generalis anno 1346 Venetiis celebrati', *AFH* 5 (1912) pp 698–709, at p 707.

the holy see first took cognisance of the new initiative, the pope, Clement VI, approached it with an open mind, in marked contrast to the hostility of his predecessors (save the eccentric Celestine V) towards the literal observance.[36] In this generally favourable climate, the literal observance movement made gradual if unspectacular progress; by 1350 it had gained four hermitages, besides Brugliano, in the dioceses of Assisi and Spoleto, including the already mentioned Carceri; and among those who had joined it, at a date unknown, was the young brother who had shared the aspirations of John of Valle and Gentilis of Spoleto in the friary of Foligno, Paoluccio dei Trinci.[37]

Despite these promising developments, we shall recognise, if we look closely, that the existence of the regular observance was poised on a knife-edge. Its foundation was a quite precise compromise, a delicate balance of mutual give and take between the strict friars and their superiors. Even at the best of times, the balance could be upset, and the whole structure come crashing down, through any act of ordinary clumsiness or insensitivity; and we may well judge that, in the mid-fourteenth century, the legacy of past conflict constituted a far from propitious environment for the accommodation between Franciscan authority and reform. Below the surface, then, it was always a question whether the regular observance would survive.[38]

The answer emerged in 1350. One false move upset the equilibrium of the situation, and, in a sort of chain reaction, events fell back into the old pattern of hostility—repression on the one side, disobedience and schism on the other. In 1355 the would-be reformers turned rebels were disbanded and punished, and, for all practical purposes, the reconciliation effected by John of Valle and Gerald Odo came to an end.

Overtly, the debacle was set in train by Gentilis of Spoleto, acting as leader of the four communities the reform had acquired in addition to its original home, Brugliano. Gentilis' initiative was to obtain from the pope, Clement VI, a perpetual guarantee for the principle of the literal observance—in the papal bull's memorable phrase, 'to observe inviolate now and in future the rule of [saint Francis] in that purity and primal simplicity in which he wrote it and gave it out'; and this

[36] *Bull Franc* 6 (1902) p 245.
[37] The hermitages are listed in the bull we are about to consider, *ibid* pp 245–6. Paoluccio's adherence to the movement: *AM* anno 1355 no 7 (2 ed vol 8 p 106).
[38] The question can be discerned in Clement VI's bull of 1343, *Bull Franc* 6 (1902) p 245, and Farinier's encyclical of 1349, Pratesi p 361.

notwithstanding any contrary moves from the order itself.[39] Both at the time and since, this has been seen as an act of plain separatism, unwarranted and unforgivable.[40] It is vital, in order to grasp the political nature of the affair, to appreciate that this is false. In fact, the pope's bull took every care to ensure that the literal observance should remain *within* the order, for example by insisting that the friars in the four hermitages, and their local superiors, should be chosen by the provincial minister.

Why then the guarantee for the literal observance? The bull itself, in one phrase, gives the game away: 'nor shall any superior or prelate of the said order presume to impede, perturb or molest you in the said observance.' The plain implication of these words is confirmed by the chroniclers: whether for perverse or defensible reasons, the superior of the Umbrian province had taken it upon himself to remove the strict brothers from their four hermitages, and disperse them among the remainder of his friars.[41] If we return to the reconciliation of 1334, we shall see that, consciously or unconsciously, this was to withdraw the one great concession, from the side of authority, that made the whole arrangement possible, namely the authorisation of the literal observance.

The very important conclusion follows that it was not the reformer Gentilis, but the superior of Umbria, who by accident or design first upset the delicate political relation between the regular observance and the rest of the order; and his fault was the graver because, from that point on, the situation deteriorated apace.

Gentilis of Spoleto's successful appeal to the pope was the minimum defensive response required, not to undermine, but to preserve the arrangements of 1334, by formalising the concession given *ad hoc* by Gerald Odo. And yet the order was, on the basis of its past experience, so extraordinarily touchy on the whole issue of reform and its consequences, that the bull of 1350 was immediately misinterpreted as a charter of separatism, and vilified accordingly.[42]

Perhaps extreme and unwarranted views on the one side provoked an opposite and greater reaction on the other. At any rate, as though hell-bent on completing their own tragedy, Gentilis and his followers

---

[39] *Bull Franc* 6 (1902) pp 245–6.
[40] A contemporary's view: *Chronicle, AF* 3 (1897) p 547; a modern view: Brengio pp 49–52.
[41] Jacobilli, *Paoluccio*, pp 27–8; *AFH* 3 (1910) p 302.
[42] The evidence of the *Chronicle*, above note 40, is confirmed by Wadding: *AM* anno 1350 no 15 (2 ed vol 8 p 45), anno 1355 no 7 (2 ed vol 8 p 106).

now committed an act of almost inspired folly: they did precisely what their confreres, wrongly, represented the bull of 1350 as doing, and proceeded to set themselves apart from the rest of the order—in flat defiance of the bull itself. They adopted a novel form of habit—always a tell-tale sign among religious, the Franciscans not least—and they refused to have anything more to do with the rest of the friars, or even take orders from the general minister.[43] This complete reversal of previous observant policy seems to represent a capitulation to the views of the rival fraticelli *de paupere vita*, with whom the strict friars were certainly in touch, albeit—so they said—with the laudable intention of converting them.[44] If so, it was an ironic, even tragic development: as we saw, the observance was perhaps created in the first place in order to oppose the fraticelli, with whom, apart from certain schismatic and heretical views, it had everything in common; it looks as though, in implementing this task, it found the predominant influence running in the opposite direction to what was intended. In any event, the defection of Gentilis and his followers, like the preceding over-reaction to the bull of 1350, marks the return of the order's old patterns of conflict.

It also, naturally, sealed the strict friars' fate. This, with indignation running high, was determined on by the general chapter of 1354, and secured within a year by the general minister, who till 1350 had been a firm supporter of the regular observance.[45] The ring-leader of the separatists, Gentilis, was arrested with the aid of the redoubtable Albornoz, and imprisoned; his followers were then easy prey, and were simply disbanded and dispersed; and, to finalise the operation, the pope, Innocent VI, was persuaded to revoke his predecessor's fateful bull of 1350.[46] It was a clean sweep.

Thus, after three decades of promise and new hope, did the politics of reconciliation succumb to an older politics of conflict. There is however an intriguing footnote to the story: the mystery of the reform movement's original home, Brugliano. This hermitage, it will be observed, was not mentioned in Clement VI's bull of 1350, and accordingly is absent from the revocation of five years later; and there is no other evidence to link it positively with Gentilis of Spoleto's separatist movement. Conceivably, then, it was unaffected by the

[43] *Ibid*; *Chronicle*, AF 3 (1897) p 547.
[44] *AM* anno 1355 no 2 (2 ed vol 8 p 103); *Chronicle*, AF 3 (1897) p 549.
[45] Details in Brengio pp 53–60.
[46] *Bull Franc* 6 (1902) pp 292–3.

crisis of 1350–5. The possibility is strengthened—and the puzzle much enhanced—by the intelligence that Gentilis of Spoleto, released from prison in 1362, reconciled and with not long to live, spent his last days at—Brugliano.[47] Suggestive as the matter is, it seems to have no direct bearing on the story of the observance after 1355; for when Paoluccio dei Trinci returned to Brugliano in 1368, the place, as we noted, was deserted.

The eventual return to Brugliano was, we might agree, against the odds, indeed against all human expectation; for the prospects for the literal observance within the Franciscan order were surely worse after 1355 than they had been prior to 1334. The experiment, honourably, had been tried, and it had failed—failed moreover in the way such ventures always had done; surely this was enough? Even if desirable in the abstract (which by no means all friars were agreed), was the literal observance not, in practice, simply too explosive to handle? That, despite such considerations, a further experiment was undertaken, was again due to a combination of poverty and politics: politics now of a new variety. The two factors met in the person of brother Paoluccio of Foligno, who by the dispensation of providence united an exceptional degree of religious conviction with membership of the ruling family of his native town.

Having been a follower of Gentilis of Spoleto, Paoluccio was, after the disaster of 1355, sent back in ignominy to the friary of Foligno, where, so many years before, he had been nurtured together with Gentilis and John of Valle. His reception could hardly be in doubt. Whatever feelings he had previously aroused in his confreres—and we have seen that they were probably mixed—he was now simply one of the detested schismatics; and there is no doubt that he received a rough handling.

It was at this juncture that he first proved the worth of family connection. The lord of Foligno at the time was one of Paoluccio's numerous Trinci uncles, Ugolino. The despot one day happened upon his nephew, and found him black and blue from a recent thrashing; forthwith he removed him from the friary and installed him in a tower in his own garden.[48] Since the place normally did duty as a prison, it was a secure enough refuge. And fortuitously, but much more important, it provided a fit setting for religious exercise as intense as

---

[47] *AM* anno 1362 no 4 (2 ed vol 8 p 154); Jacobilli, *Santi*, p 374.
[48] *AM* anno 1368 no 10 (2 ed vol 8 p 209); *MF* 6 (1896) p 104; Jacobilli, *Paoluccio*, p 31; Brengio pp 68–9. For some difficulties in the story see Sensi nn 79–83.

any Paoluccio had known. For, instead of being discouraged by the debacle of 1355, he was, paradoxically, only fired with greater zeal for the literal observance; and so year after year he continued, if anything more ardently, the old life of vigils and fasts, prayer and praise, and importunate intercession with God to restore the order to its pristine purity.[49]

So steadfast an example could not forever remain unregarded. Paoluccio won the admiration of his fellows, grudging perhaps at first, then without reserve; before long stories of his miracles began to circulate.[50] Gradually he built up a following among the friars of Foligno. Of a different order, and infinitely more significant, was support from another quarter: that of the new lord of the town, his own cousin Trincia.

And it is this basically political factor which is particularly commemorated by the events of 1368.[51] The setting was a provincial chapter of the Umbrian friars, which Trincia dei Trinci arranged should be held in Foligno (like any self-respecting ruler of the period, he was an ecclesiastical as well as a secular prince; Urban V had recently confirmed his title of Vicar of the Church);[52] and, to add lustre to the occasion, he secured the attendance at it of the general minister of the Minors, Thomas of Frignano, who seems to have been an acquaintance. If this was setting the trap, it was sprung by Trincia's benevolent conduct towards the assembled friars. Already reckoned a friend of the order, he now so outdid himself in generosity that the brothers were overcome with gratitude. Accordingly, once their business was concluded, an appreciative deputation—including, as was proper, the general minister—went to call upon their patron (by one account, which need not be fanciful, they were invited to a meal, and fared particularly well);[53] and, having expressed heartfelt thanks for the benefits received, they asked whether there was anything that they, in return, might do for him.

It was the supreme moment in the history of the Italian observance; and Trincia dei Trinci handled it as to the manner born. He replied that all he had done had been for the love of God and out of devotion

[49] As preceding note.
[50] MF 6 (1896) p 105.
[51] Sources for the narrative: Lemmens pp 7–8; MF 6 (1896) pp 101, 105–6; AM anno 1368 no 11 (2 ed vol 8 p 210); Jacobilli, Paoluccio, pp 33–5; Brengio pp 69–77. For a sceptical view see Sensi nn 84–6.
[52] Ibid pp 63–4.
[53] MF 6 (1896) p 106.

Fourteenth century Franciscan reform

to the order; however, since they *were* asking, he did have one small favour to request: that his nephew Paoluccio might receive the hermitage of Brugliano—which, it is worth noting, lay within the family domain[54]—there to serve God in poverty and austerity with some few companions. At this point, we are told, the local friars in the delegation (were they hand picked?) added their voices to Trincia's, beseeching that the request be granted.

The general minister gave the concession forthwith. It was only on his return to the friary that he began to have second thoughts; for a number of brothers there immediately pointed out the potentially schismatic implications of what he had done. We are assured that he passed a sleepless night; and the next day he went back to Trincia and asked to be released from his ill-considered favour (one notes that, in true medieval fashion, the unhappy general regarded even an oral concession as binding).

It was but a forlorn attempt. Hitherto Trincia had been all benevolence; now he showed the iron beneath the velvet. He flew into a rage, and insisted on the confirmation of the privilege. The general minister was no match for the violent display, and quickly submitted; and so the concession stood, and with it the second, and permanent, foundation of the Italian regular observance. All in all it may be judged one of the more remarkable monuments to the art of medieval politics.

Not that the reform movement was immediately out of the wood. It did indeed make more rapid progress than its counterpart under John of Valle—no fewer than eleven hermitages were gained in a mere five years, among them, it is interesting to note, the four involved in Gentilis of Spoleto's fall in 1355[55]—but, even so, a strong rearguard action was mounted by those who saw the general's concession as an open invitation to renewed conflict and division in the order. There was only one conclusive answer to such doubts, and it was the political one earlier arrived at by John of Valle and the general minister Gerald Odo: for the reformers to make common cause with their fellow friars against those who, more than any, embodied the schismatic tendencies of the literal observance, the fraticelli *de paupere vita*. The opportunity came, traditionally in 1374, in Perugia.[56] The town had long been one

[54] Jacobilli, *Paoluccio*, pp 26–7, but see Sensi nn 24–30.
[55] See *MF* 6 (1896) pp 112–13. The papal bulls concerned were omitted from *Bull Franc* 6. The text of one is reprinted in *AFH* 69 (1976) pp 469–71.
[56] Slightly varying accounts in: Lemmens pp 10–12; *MF* 6 (1896) pp 102–3, 107–9; *AM* anno 1374 nos 22–5 (2 ed vol 8 pp 299–300); Jacobilli, *Paoluccio*, 43. Discussion of the sources: Brengio pp 104–9, Sensi nn 104–10.

of the heretics' main centres,[57] and they grew so bold that they would pounce on passing Franciscans in the streets, expose several layers of comfortable clothing, and jeeringly ask whether that was how saint Francis had taught them to dress. The sport not only delighted on-lookers, but convincingly supported the fraticelli's claim that the friars had betrayed their founder; and matters came to such a pass that the members of the order hardly dared to show their faces. Eventually, with the support of the provincial minister, they determined on the only possible solution: to call in some of the few brothers who did observe their founder's rule to the letter, offering them the hermitage of Monteripido above the town as a base. The tangible witness of a Franciscan life as austere as that of the fraticelli, joined with fidelity instead of hostility to the church, carried the day, and before long the heretics were driven out in confusion. Although the victory was not permanent, it seems to have been decisive for the future of the observance: in 1374 they not only kept Monteripido, by gift of the provincial minister of Umbria, but also received important tokens of support from the minister general, and the see of Peter.[58]

Thereafter, with these three vital authorities behind it, the regular observance went on from strength to strength; and, until his death at a great age in 1392, it was presided over by the lay brother who had purposed it in the friary of Foligno more than half a century before. The details of the process need not concern us;[59] but one aspect of the outcome deserves to be recorded. As the observance expanded, the Franciscan authorities found it convenient to give it an increasing measure of self-government, which naturally was until his death vested in Paoluccio. He however, still the same humble lay brother, seems to have found it unwelcome, and had to be commanded to accept it.[60] Thus in the end the regular observance did introduce a degree of division into the Franciscan body: and it was the reformer who re-sisted it, his superiors who insisted on it. It is an interesting illustration of how far paradox can go in ecclesiastical affairs.

What motives, in conclusion, determined the attainment by mid-fourteenth-century Franciscans of the goal that had eluded all the

---

[57] See *AFH* 4 (1911) pp 691–2.
[58] The provincial: *MF* 6 (1896) p 108; the general: *AM* 1374 nos 20–1 (2 ed vol 8 pp 298–9); the holy see: *Bull Franc* 6 (1902) pp 533–4.
[59] The details in Brengio cap 5.
[60] Witness the tone of a letter from the provincial in 1380: *AM* anno 1380 no 29 (2 ed vol 9 pp 41–2).

efforts of their more highly reputed predecessors, namely the establishment of the literal observance? The motives were of course mixed;
something, it goes without saying, in no sense peculiarly medieval.
The *sine qua non* is however beyond doubt—the religious devotion of
Paoluccio dei Trinci, and its immediate fruit, the others whom he
inspired. Hitherto we have labelled this factor poverty; but, having
now had the chance to take its measure, we shall hardly doubt that the
appropriate term is sanctity. Thus we can concur with the tradition
that numbers brother Paoluccio of Foligno among the blessed.[61]

The specifically Franciscan character of his spirituality has already
been sufficiently illustrated, and more general interest attaches to some
of its other characteristics. In one sense, Paoluccio was a man out of, at
odds with, his time—the outsider in modern parlance. Accordingly
his essential historical role was perseverance: to wait, and go on waiting,
unmoving in purpose, until the times changed, and circumstances
propitious for his plans appeared. The evidence in fact suggests that,
from about the age of fourteen till his death at over eighty, he had only
one desire in mind, the restoration of primitive Franciscan discipline
and fervour. This might be variously described as obsessive, inflexible
or indomitable. Does it not at least represent one of the recognisable
faces of sanctity?

Persistence, then, was of the essence of Paoluccio's achievement;
and the trait is mirrored in the ideal at whose service it was placed. For
as we saw, there was, despite first appearances, no real break between
the observance and the spirituals; indeed the spirituals provided the
connection through which the observant ideal can be said to go back
directly to Saint Francis. That is to say, the particular religious
aspirations of Paoluccio dei Trinci, far from being his unique possession, were at bottom a constant and unchanging element in the order's
history from the beginning.

There is an obvious consequence. If the ideal of the literal observance
was so to speak a constant, we have to look to particular historical
circumstances to explain why it succeeded with Paoluccio and John
of Valle, and failed with Gentilis of Spoleto and, earlier, the spirituals.
The principal circumstances are what this study has termed the politics
of the situation. Most dramatically instrumental was the leverage
brother Paoluccio enjoyed by virtue of being born a Trinci; and
without this the second and permanent foundation of the observance
would not have taken place. Less specific, but more formative overall,

[61] See *MF* 6 (1896) pp 124-7.

was the influence of the fraticelli *de paupere vita*. Previously there had been two basic positions on the question of Franciscan observance, identified respectively with the community and the spirituals; the result was conflict. The advent of the fraticelli made the two-cornered debate a triangular one, and the way was opened for the deadlock between the Franciscan factions to be resolved in an alliance against the common foe—although it was also possible for the accord to go the other way, as seems to have occurred with Gentilis of Spoleto. The significance of adding the third party, we may note in passing, was to be confirmed later, for when, during the fifteenth century, the literal observance took hold in new surroundings, it was again within a triangular situation, although this time one wholly internal to the order.[62] In the fourteenth century case, the novel alliance of Franciscan authority and reform against the fraticelli was, finally, but the cornerstone of a more general political reorientation, here defined as the substitution of reconciliation for confrontation.

In summary, the foundation of the Italian observance movement reveals two principal forces at work: as a kind of substratum, an unchanging religious ideal; and the specific circumstances determining the fate of the ideal—its success or failure, and the particular institutional forms of its expression—in a given historical setting. Might not the formula be applied, *mutatis mutandis*, to almost any aspect of ecclesiastical history? If so, we should be on the way to defining the activity of the ecclesiastical historian: his normal task would be, holding religious inspiration as a constant—a historical premiss which merges into theology—to unravel, with all the available tools of social science, the manifold social forces determining the outcome of inspiration from age to age.

Department of Educational Research
University of Lancaster

---

[62] See D. B. Nimmo, 'Reform at the Council of Constance: the Franciscan case', *SCH* 14 (1977) pp 159–73, at pp 167–70.

SOME STATISTICS
OF RELIGIOUS MOTIVATION

by JOAN G. GREATREX

MOTIVES are the inner springs of action, the invisible causes which are apprehended only in their visible effects. The latter, when collected and classified as numerical data, are known as statistics, through which at least one aspect of the former can be explored and analysed. Thus, while we cannot ask them to reveal such fundamental questions as to what moved men to enter or leave the monastic life, we can legitimately seek an answer in quantitative terms to what is preliminary and, as such, vital to our understanding of the problem of religious motivation: what do statistics disclose with regard to the force of religious motivation and to its rise and decline among the black monks in England in the two centuries between the first catastrophic onslaught of the Black Death and the dissolution (AD 1350–1540)? This question encompasses a vast field and, for the purposes of this present study, our attention must be limited to the three cathedral priories of Ely, Norwich and Worcester.

A full, if not complete, answer based on an exhaustive survey of the records of the nine Benedictine cathedral monasteries will require some years of continued painstaking investigation, but it is already clear that the task is both worthwhile and important. Two points which support this conclusion will also serve to introduce the statistical approach to religious motivation.

The first is that general statements about monastic population tend to be misleading or inadequate or both. Some fifty years ago, for example, R. H. Snape compiled a table in his book on *English Monastic Finances in the Later Middle Ages*[1] showing three columns of figures, covering a period which stretched over five centuries; for some seven English Benedictine houses only three dates were given and for the other eighteen houses only two. On this slender evidence he attempted to construct a picture of decline which he judged to have begun well before 1349, although he took care to point out 'the difficulty of making any generalization as to proportions'.[2] More recently, with

[1] Cambridge (1926) p 21.   [2] *Ibid* p 22.

JOAN G. GREATREX

new evidence available in print David Knowles was able to show that
the monks and other religious increased their numbers during the
second half of the fourteenth century and in many cases, although
more slowly, during the fifteenth century as well; and he observed
that the sharp decline in numbers which occurred on the eve of the
dissolution 'has been responsible for many hasty judgements'.[3] He also
suggested in his introduction to the indispensable handbook to
Medieval Religious Houses, England and Wales that a 'study of the
causes, extent and variety of this increase in the number of religious
might lead to a valuable addition to our knowledge of the fifteenth
century'.[4] However, the 'extent and variety of this increase' is often
inadequately and unconvincingly demonstrated by the figures in this
same book. For instance, there are no figures for Worcester between
1433 and 1540, and for Ely none between 1427 and 1532.[5]

The second point is that a close examination of the manuscript
material which survives for Worcester, Ely and Norwich, and
especially of the obedientiary accounts, and their use in conjunction
with other records such as admission, profession, ordination, election
and obituary lists has revealed the feasibility of reconstructing fairly
complete lists of monks of some of the cathedral priories with
numerical and biographical data to compare favourably with, if not
to surpass, the extant medieval lists of the members of the monastic
communities at Christ Church, Canterbury and Durham.[6]

There are over 250 remaining account rolls of the obedientiaries of
Ely cathedral between 1350 and 1530, and the numbers which survive
from Worcester and Norwich are much higher. In the case of
Worcester 450 rolls are extant of which the majority also come from
the two centuries preceding the dissolution; those of Norwich and
its five dependent cells number over 1000, and these also are mainly
of the same period. From the point of view of sheer quantity there is a
formidable task involved in extracting all the pertinent information
contained in these rolls; in addition there are some difficulties in
understanding both their form and content, which reflect the
changing methods of the individual obedientiaries and their assistant

³ Knowles *RO* 2 (1961) p 257.
⁴ *MRHEW* p 47.
⁵ *Ibid* pp 81 and 65.
⁶ W. G. Searle has printed a list based on the surviving manuscript lists in *Cambridge Antiquarian Society Publications*, 34 (Cambridge 1902), pp 173–96; for the Surtees Society Joseph Stevenson in 1841 (*SS* 13) and A. Hamilton Thompson in 1923 (*SS* 136) have edited the *Liber vitae ecclesiae Dunelmensis*.

180

accountkeepers as well as the administrative reform measures which were imposed from time to time. It must also be borne in mind that these financial records and yearly statements were intended only for the inner circle of monastic auditors and senior brethren, and when necessary, the inquisitive episcopal visitor. Today's historian is not unlike the medieval diocesan in his desire to pry into the internal state of the monastery, but he is handicapped by the great gulf of centuries which separates him from the object of his study.

Numbers of monks occur in the accounts of many different obedientiaries for a variety of reasons, but most frequently to record distributions in cash or kind made to the brethren. When these payments took place twice a year on the same account or when two or three records of payments can be found for the same year the numbers fluctuate slightly; these variations undoubtedly reflect not only the comings and goings of the monks, but also the arrival of new recruits, and the departures and deaths of others. It is worth noting that the allowances paid to absent monks studying at the university are usually itemised separately and thus it will be possible to compile a fairly complete record of the numbers of monk-scholars provided by these cathedral priories in this period. Finally, an explanation of some of the fluctuations may be found by the use of additional statistical data for the same year when these can be traced in other records, as for example in some of the Norwich episcopal registers which contain copies of commissions to the prior to admit and also to profess monks who are usually listed by name, and in the Norwich chamberlain's accounts which contain receipts from the alms of deceased brethren whose names are normally entered on the roll.

The chamberlain at the three priories usually noted the number of habits and other items of clothing which he provided for the monks, or, as in the case of Ely early in the fifteenth century, of the sum of money paid to each monk for his annual clothing allowance. The precentor and sacrist also record the small payments or pittances which they distributed at the time of their respective feasts, or 'O's' as these were called after the advent antiphons which are sung each day between 16 and 23 December. These allowances were sometimes in the form of wine and spices and at other times in cash. At Worcester the chamberlain, precentor, and pittancer recorded their distributions *per capita* at the time when their 'O's' were sung; the pittancer and cellarer also gave something to each monk at the time of his periodic *minutio* or blood-letting; the almoner made distributions on certain obits or anniversaries; and two of the nine surviving rolls of the infirmarer show that he also made payments of small sums. The surviving rolls of the feretrar or shrine-keeper at Ely reveal that in the fifteenth century this obedientiary paid small amounts or *gratie* to each member of the community out of his receipts. There is an almost unbroken series of chamberlain's rolls at Norwich between 1418 and 1537, and these are complemented by a virtually complete run of account rolls for the adjacent cell of St Leonard, which lay near the summit of the wooded slope known as Thorp wood only a mile southeast of the cathedral. This dependent priory made annual payments of one or two shillings to each monk in the cathedral community. The precentor and infirmarer at Norwich also supplied spices for their brethren, but numbers are not regularly provided. It should be noted that this is not an exhaustive list of all the distributions made to the monks for two reasons: one is that in many cases the sum paid either directly to the convent or expended in purchasing spices and other items is recorded without any of the numerical details which are needed for this study. The other is that a comparative study of this kind requires constant revision in the light of the fresh insights which are gained through the assembling and arranging of numerical and other data, and the effort of interpretation leads to new problems which in turn may inspire the development of new techniques of approach to their compilation and arrangement.

It is time to turn our attention to the statistics themselves and by means of several examples to illustrate the kind of detail which the account rolls can yield.

The chamberlain of Ely was providing clothing for thirty-six or thirty-seven monks in 1353–4[7] only three years after the ravages of the Black Death, but within five years this number had risen to forty.[8] Although the sacrist reported the deaths of five brothers on his account for 1368–9[9] the chamberlain's total was thirty-nine the following year.[10] There were at least ten newcomers to the community in the years 1376 to 1385 their names being recorded on bishop Arundel's ordination lists under the section headed 'acolytes'.[11] The subsidy roll

[7] EDC 5/3/11. The Ely obedientiary accounts and episcopal registers have been deposited in the university library, Cambridge.
[8] EDC 5/3/13.
[9] EDC 5/10/16.
[10] EDC 5/3/18.
[11] EDR G/1/2 fols 117^r, 125^r, 129^v, 132^v.

of 1379 shows an even more rapid increase as it lists the names of forty-seven monks including the prior.[12] However, the chamberlain also accounts for this number in 1388,[13] thus suggesting some continuity of, or possibly an increase in, numbers in this decade depending on the number of deaths. In the next two decades the numbers dropped to just below forty, the chamberlain accounting for only thirty-nine on the first portion of his account for the year 1404–5; later the same year his total was forty-five.[14] Four years later numbers were down to thirty-six on the chamberlain's roll;[15] but another influx had taken place by 1412 as five acolytes were ordained that year,[16] and seven more are recorded in June 1419.[17] Numbers stood at forty-one in 1421 according to the feretrar's distribution of pittances;[18] thus we may deduce that half the new arrivals may have stayed, or possibly others arrived to replace them, depending on the unknown number of monks who died during this period. The chamberlain was issuing a clothing allowance to forty-four monks at 13s 6d a head in 1427–8,[19] and the precentor gave *gratie* to thirty-six in 1447–8.[20] There is a gap in the records during the next fifty years, but the feretrar's account of 1498–9 makes the total forty-two at the turn of the century.[21] The first three decades of the sixteenth century show a fall followed by an increase, there being thirty-two in 1519–20[22] and thirty-four names on the list at the time of bishop Goodrich's visitation in 1534;[23] this increase may be minimal in strictly numerical terms but not in terms of monastic vocations, since ten of the thirty-four are described as juniors. Five years later, at the final count, the total was twenty-five.[24]

The Norwich chamberlains furnish us with less detailed information of their clothing expenditures in the later fourteenth century than do their counterparts at Ely and Worcester, but the numbers of monks are given for most of the fifteenth and sixteenth centuries. Knowles

[12] PRO E 179/23/1.
[13] EDC 5/3/21.
[14] EDC 5/3/25.
[15] EDC 5/3/27.
[16] EDR G/1/3, fol 261ʳ.
[17] *Ibid*, fol 272ʳ.
[18] EDC 5/11/1.
[19] EDC 5/3/32.
[20] EDC 5/9/11.
[21] EDC 5/11/(9). The numbering and cataloguing of these rolls is in progress.
[22] EDC 5/3/34.
[23] EDR G/1/7 fols 89ᵛ–90ᵛ.
[24] *MRHEW* p 65.

and Hadcock show an increase of six (from fifty to fifty-six) in the sixty years between 1381 and 1441,[25] but in fact there were fifty-six monks in the community in 1402–3 according to the St Leonard's priory accounts.[26] In 1418–19 the chamberlain provided a clothing allowance for fifty-three monks, and although he received alms from seven of the brethren who had died during the year the number was reduced by only three on the next year's account.[27] Two entries in the register of bishop Richard Courtenay show that monastic vocations were not lacking to replace the departed for in November 1414 he commissioned the prior to profess six monks and in June 1415 he issued another commission authorising the admission of four men into the order;[28] three years later his successor bishop John Wakering recorded their profession in his register,[29] and thus the addition was made as permanent as the frailty of human nature allows. Unfortunately the ordination lists which survive at Norwich do not include the names of any religious as far as these can be identified, although several of the early pittancers' accounts make reference to the ordinands. In the first four years of Henry V's reign (1421–5) nine of the monks died according to the chamberlain's record,[30] but there were forty-nine remaining in 1428–9[31] and fifty-five three years later.[32] Numbers appear to have remained above fifty until mid-century, but between 1453 and 1456 twelve deaths were reported on the chamberlain's rolls[33] and the following year the total had dropped to forty-seven.[34] This pattern of fluctuations continued for the next two decades but a low point was reached early in Henry VII's reign when the chamberlain recorded payments to only thirty-eight monks for four consecutive years (1489–92).[35] At bishop Goldwell's visitation in 1492 forty-six names are listed,[36] and despite another drop to forty

[25] *Ibid* p 72.
[26] Roll no 1258. The Norwich obedientiary accounts and episcopal registers (institution books) are in the keeping of the Norfolk and Norwich record office.
[27] Nos 379 and 380.
[28] Institution Book 7 fol 202^v and fol 203^v.
[29] Institution Book 8 fol 23^v.
[30] Nos 382, 384 and 385.
[31] No 387.
[32] No 389.
[33] Nos 418–20.
[34] No 421.
[35] Nos 448–51.
[36] *Visitations of the Diocese of Norwich, AD 1492–1533*, ed. A. Jessop, CSer, ns 43 (1888) pp 1–8.

in 1495–6[37] there were forty-six in 1504–5.[38] A gradual but not consistent decline occurred in the years remaining before the dissolution, for numbers rose to forty-one and possibly forty-three in 1522–3[39] and after another drop were up to thirty-eight in 1533–4.[40] Five years later thirty-one remained.[41]

The Worcester chamberlain helpfully provides the number of junior monks or novices in his accounts. In 1351–2 there were nine of these, twenty-five or twenty-six monks and one *conversus*.[42] By 1360–1 the number had grown to become forty to whom the pittancer made distributions for the feast to celebrate his 'O'.[43] Bishop William de Lynn authorised the precentor to admit seven monks in 1370,[44] and the priory register known as the *Liber Albus* records the profession of two more in 1381;[45] the chamberlain and pittancer in this latter year, however, report only thirty-nine brethren,[46] although the almoner and infirmarer made payments to forty-one on their respective accounts.[47] At the election of a new prior in 1388 forty professed monks were present.[48] There were thirty-eight on the chamberlain's roll of 1392–3 of whom three were novices; and an entry in the priory register shows the date of their profession to have been 4 January 1393,[49] for until 1398 there appear to have been no more *juniores*.[50] By 1410–11 the chamberlain was supplying forty-three monks with their clothing needs and fifteen of these were juniors.[51] Five years later there were thirty-eight professed monks and seven novices,[52] but in 1419 when the total was thirty-seven monks and four novices, nine of

---

[37] No 454A.
[38] No 459.
[39] No 471.
[40] No 478.
[41] *MRHEW* p 72.
[42] C 11. The Worcester obedientiary accounts are to be found in the library of Worcester cathedral.
[43] C 305.
[44] Register William de Lynn, p 89. The Worcester episcopal registers are deposited in the Worcestershire record office (St Helen's) and have been paginated for greater accuracy of reference. This entry lacks a precise date, but occurs on a page of entries of the year 1370.
[45] Worcester cathedral muniment AV, fol 307ᵛ.
[46] C 14 and C 312.
[47] C 176 and C 242.
[48] Liber Albus, fol 334ᵛ.
[49] *Ibid* fol 366ᵛ.
[50] C 24.
[51] C 29.
[52] C 31.

the community died;[53] when three years more had elapsed the numbers were down to thirty-five, but ten of these were novices.[54] The priory continued to attract aspirants, for the next year (1423–4) the number of novices grew to fifteen.[55] Over the next six decades on the twelve extant chamberlain's rolls the number of junior monks averaged six,[56] and the ordination lists also reflect this persistent influx; for example, in 1449 there were six acolytes ordained, in 1456 four acolytes, in 1458 seven, and in 1460 three.[57] In 1498–9 numbers stood at forty monks in priests' orders and four others,[58] but three died during the year as noted by the precentor.[59] The last chamberlain's roll in 1514–5 gives the total as thirty-seven monks and five juniors,[60] one more than in 1400–1.[61] Growing uncertainty and insecurity must have marked the next few years and undermined monastic morale, although thirty-five names were entered in the register as late as 1536 at the time of the election of prior Holbech.[62]

These statistics would seem to affirm that monastic vocations, in the case of at least three cathedral priories, did not dwindle in the later middle ages, and they suggest that any lack of appreciable rise in numbers must have been due to a high incidence of departures and deaths. That deaths were frequent has also been indicated where information is available, but the records are for the most part silent about departures. It should be noted however that not all exits from these houses resulted from a loss of religious fervour, for some monks applied to transfer to a stricter house or one more conducive to prayer and quiet. In 1417, for example, John Grove requested permission to go to Syon,[63] and in 1527 William Overbury left Worcester 'to serve the most High more freely and quietly' at Winchcombe.[64] Although the Benedictine order collapsed in the face of Henry VIII's onslaught we can scarcely maintain that there had been a complete lack of religious motivation.

Carleton University
Ottawa

[53] C 32.   [54] C 34.   [55] C 35.   [56] C 36–47.
[57] Register John Carpenter, pp 524, 541, 543 and 554 respectively.
[58] C 48.   [59] C 391.   [60] C 50.   [61] C 25.
[62] Worcester cathedral muniment A VI (3) or Ledger III, fol 1r.
[63] EDR G/2/3, items 71 and 213.
[64] Worcester cathedral muniment A VI (2) or Ledger II, fol 158r.

THE PROBLEMS OF LUTHER'S
'TOWER-EXPERIENCE' AND ITS PLACE
IN HIS INTELLECTUAL DEVELOPMENT

by W. D. J. CARGILL THOMPSON

THE problem of the date and significance of Luther's so-called 'tower-experience' (*Turmerlebnis*)—the moment of illumination at which he came to his new understanding of Romans 1:17—is one of the longstanding cruces of modern Luther-scholarship. Since the problem was first raised in its modern form by German scholars at the beginning of the present century probably no aspect of Luther's biography has attracted so much attention or has been the subject of so much controversy: and even to-day, although the nature of the debate has changed considerably in recent years as new arguments and new solutions have been put forward, it still remains one of the central issues in all discussions of Luther's early intellectual development, not only because it presents the irresistible fascination of an unresolved conundrum but also because in traditional historiography it has always been closely identified with the complex question of when and how Luther arrived at his reformation theology.[1]

Considering the amount of heat that the controversy has generated, the 'tower-experience' is surprisingly well-documented. Luther himself referred to his discovery of the meaning of Romans 1:17 on numerous occasions in his *Table Talk* and in his writings, although it should be said that most of his explicit references to it date from the 1530s or early 1540s, that is between fifteen and twenty or twenty-five

---

[1] The best modern introduction to the study of the problem is *Der Durchbruch der reformatorischen Erkenntnis bei Luther*, ed B. Lohse, *Wege der Forschung* 123 (Darmstadt 1968), which contains a selection of extracts from many of the most important books and articles relating to the controversy, published between 1904 and 1966. Several of the items printed in Lohse include historiographical surveys of the development of the debate: see especially Lohse's introduction (pp ix–xxiii) and the articles by G. Pfeiffer (pp 163–202), H. Bornkamm (pp 289–383) and, for the later period, O. H. Pesch (pp 445–505). Useful surveys in English of the earlier phases of the controversy will be found in [J.] Mackinnon, *Luther and the Reformation*, 4 vols (London 1925–30) I, pp 147–56, and [G.] Rupp, [*The*] *Righteousness of God*: [*Luther Studies*] (London 1953) cap 6, pp 121–37. [O.] Scheel, *Dokumente* [*zu Luthers Entwicklung* (*bis 1519*)] (2 rev ed Göttingen 1929) contains a comprehensive collection of primary texts relating to Luther's early development.

W. D. J. CARGILL THOMPSON

years after the event. Thus in one version of a well-attested conversation which took place in 1532 Luther is reported as saying:

For these words 'righteous' (*Iustus*) and 'righteousness of God' (*Iustitia Dei*) were to me as a thunderbolt in my conscience. When I heard them I was filled with terror: for if God is righteous, then he will punish. But by the grace of God, when once in this tower and heated room (*in hac turri et hypocausto*) I was meditating on these words 'The just shall live by faith' and 'the righteousness of God', presently I came to perceive that if we as righteous men ought to live by faith and if the righteousness of God ought to be for the salvation of all who believe, then it is not our merit but the mercy of God [by which we are saved]. Thereby my spirit was cheered. For the righteousness of God is that by which we are justified and saved through Christ. And these words became more joyful to me. The Holy Spirit revealed the scripture to me in this tower (*in diesem thurn*).[2]

---

[2] *WA TR* 3, no 3232c (Lauterbach), p 228; Scheel, *Dokumente*, no 235, p 91. Other reports of the same conversation are to be found in *WA TR* 2, no 1681, p 177 (Scheel, *Dokumente*, no 238, p 94) and *WA TR* 3, no 3232a and b, p 228 (Scheel, *Dokumente*, no 235, p 91). In all these versions the phraseology in which the discovery is described is very similar, so that we may be sure that the gist of Luther's remarks is accurately recorded. The most important difference between the reports, which has given rise to considerable controversy, lies in the words used to describe the place where the discovery is alleged to have taken place. Lauterbach, quoted in the text, has *in hac turri et hypocausto* (generally interpreted as the heated room where Luther had his study) and *in diesem thurn*; Cordatus's very similar account has *in hac turri* (*in qua secretus locus erat monachorum*) and *auff diesem thurm* (*WA TR* 3, no 3232a, p 228); Schlaginhaufen has *Dise kunst hatt mir der S S* [*Spiritus Sanctus*] *auf diss Cl eingeben* (*WA TR* 2, no 1681, p 177), subsequently expanded in Rörer's version to *auf dieser cloaca*, with the words *in horto* inserted above in the MS (*Ibid*, n 1); Aurifaber's later printed version omits the reference to the place altogether (*Ibid*, p 177). On the strength of the readings *Cl* and *cloaca* and Cordatus's phrase *in qua secretus locus erat monachorum*, Grisar argued that Luther's 'tower-experience' must have taken place in the privy: see [H.] Grisar, *Luther*, trans E. M. Lamond, 6 vols (London 1913–17) I, pp 392, 396–7. Not surprisingly this view has been hotly contested by protestant scholars, chiefly on the ground that Schlaginhaufen's cryptic *auf diss Cl* is neuter and so cannot legitimately be expanded to *cloaca* which is feminine. This also rules out the suggestion of some scholars that *Cl* is an abbreviation for *cella*. For a discussion of this point, see the extract from [E.] Stracke, *Luthers grosses Selbstzeugnis* [*1545 über seine Entwicklung zum Reformator*], *SVRG* 140 (1926), in Lohse, p 111, n 9. Stracke argued that *Cl* is the standard abbreviation for *clarissimum* and that it refers not to the place where Luther's experience took place but either to the text in Paul or to the concept of *iustitia Dei*. However, this seems improbable. Perhaps the most plausible suggestion is that *Cl* is an abbreviation for *claustrum*: see [U.] Saarnivaara, *Luther Discovers the Gospel:* [*New Light upon Luther's Way from Medieval Catholicism to Evangelical Faith*] (Saint Louis 1951) p 48, n 104.

188

The problem of Luther's 'tower experience'

A very similar account is dated 12 September 1538:

That phrase 'the righteousness of God' was like a thunderbolt in my heart. For when under the papacy I read 'Deliver me in thy righteousness' [Ps 31:1] and 'In thy truth', I at once thought that that righteousness was an avenging anger, namely, of the wrath of God. I hated Paul from my heart when I read 'The righteousness of God is revealed in the Gospel' [Rom 1:16–17]. But afterwards when I saw the words that follow, namely, 'as it is written, The just shall live by faith' and when, in addition, I consulted Augustine, then was I joyful. When I understood that the righteousness of God is his mercy by which he reputes us to be righteous, then this provided a remedy for me in my affliction.[3]

A rather different version appears in the *Table Talk* for the winter of 1542/3:

For a long time I was in error and was not aware that I was. Certainly I knew something, but nonetheless I did not know what it was until I came to the passage in Romans 1, 'The just shall live by faith'. That helped me. Then I saw what righteousness Paul is speaking of when earlier in the text the word 'righteousness' appears. Then I brought the abstract and the concrete into agreement with one another[4] and became certain of my cause; I learned to distinguish between the righteousness of the law and that of the gospel. Before that I lacked nothing except that I made no distinction between the law and the gospel; I regarded them both as the same and held that Christ did not differ from Moses except in the time at which he lived and in perfection. But when I discovered that distinction, namely, that the law is one thing, the gospel another, then I broke through.[5]

These quotations could be paralleled by numerous other passages.[6] What is clear from the surviving evidence is where the experience is

---

[3] *WA TR* 4, no 4007, pp 72–3; Scheel, *Dokumente*, no 404, p 148.

[4] *da reumet ich das abstractum und concretum zusamen*: Luther means that he reconciled the abstract concept *iustitia Dei* with the concrete state of being righteous (*iustus*); in other words he perceived that 'the righteousness of God' is that by which men are made righteous (compare the two previous descriptions).

[5] *WA TR* 5, no 5518, p 210; Scheel, *Dokumente*, no 474, p 172.

[6] For example, *WA TR* 5, no 5247, p 26, September 1540 (Scheel, *Dokumente*, no 449, p 162); *WA TR* 5, no 5553, pp 234–5, winter 1542/3 (Scheel, *Dokumente*, no 476, p 173); Lectures on Genesis, *WA* 43, p 537 (Scheel, *Dokumente*, no 460, pp 166–7). The fullest description is to be found in the Preface to the 1545 edition of Luther's Latin writings, *WA* 54, pp 185–6 (Scheel, *Dokumente*, no 511, pp 191–2), quoted below pp 201–3.

supposed to have taken place. It occurred in the tower of the Augustinian house at Wittenberg—hence the term 'Luther's tower-experience'[7]—probably in the heated room (*hypocaustum*) where Luther had his study, although the alternative reading *cloaca* (lavatory), favoured by Grisar and by psychoanalysts and psychoanalytical historians like P. J. Reiter, Erik Erikson and Norman Brown, still has its supporters.[8] It is also fairly clear from Luther's accounts—although its precise theological significance is still a matter of controversy—what his discovery consisted of. It involved a new insight into the meaning of Romans 1:17, 'For therein is the righteousness of God revealed from faith to faith: as it is written, The just shall live by faith', and, in particular, into the meaning of the term 'the righteousness of God' (*iustitia Dei*). In most of his accounts Luther describes how in wrestling with this passage he came to see, as it were in a flash of illumination, that the term 'the righteousness of God' in this passage was to be understood not, as he had hitherto understood it, in the sense of the righteousness by which God judges sinners—a concept which had caused him so much spiritual anguish[9]—but rather as the righteousness by which God in his mercy justifies those who have faith. In the third of the passages from the *Table Talk*, quoted above, Luther relates his new understanding of Romans 1:17 somewhat differently to his discovery of the distinction between law and gospel; but in most of his descriptions he does not make this connection and it raises complications both about the exact nature and the date of his discovery which will have to be considered later.

What is unclear from most of Luther's descriptions of his 'tower-experience' is the date at which it is supposed to have taken place. The one exception is provided by the very long and circumstantial account of his discovery of the meaning of Romans 1:17 which he gave in the autobiographical preface which he wrote at the end of his life for the first volume of his collected Latin writings in the Wittenberg edition of his works (1545). In that account he not only presents a very full

---

[7] Grisar is generally credited with having coined the term *Turmerlebnis*: see Grisar, *Luther*, 1, p 377.

[8] P. J. Reiter, *Martin Luthers Umwelt, Charakter und Psychose sowie die Bedeutung dieser Faktoren für seine Entwicklung und Lehre. Eine historisch-psychiatrische Studie*, 2 vols (Copenhagen 1937–41) 2, pp 320–2; E. H. Erikson, *Young Man Luther: A Study in Psychoanalysis and History* (London 1959) pp 198–200; N. O. Brown, *Life against Death: the Psychoanalytical Meaning of History* (London 1959) cap 14, esp pp 202–6. For a discussion of the problem, see above p 188, n 2.

[9] See, in particular, the account in the 1545 preface, *WA* 54, pp 185–6, quoted below pp 201–3.

The problem of Luther's 'tower-experience'

description of the nature of the discovery and its impact on him, but he also appears (if one takes his words literally) to suggest a precise date for it—namely, that it took place as he was about to embark on his second course of lectures on the psalms, that is in 1519. However, that account raises a number of problems which have been at the centre of the debate and I will therefore return to it at a later stage in the discussion.[10]

The orthodox view, which held the field until comparatively recently, was that Luther's discovery took place at some point between his return to Wittenberg in the second half of 1511 and the summer of 1515 when he started to deliver his famous course of lectures on Romans. This view became established in the early years of the present century, following the discovery and publication of the manuscripts of Luther's early lectures, notably the first series on the psalms (*Dictata super Psalterium*, 1513–15) and the lectures on Romans (1515–16), which made it possible for the first time to explore the development of his theology in detail.[11] Ironically, the person who was chiefly responsible for initiating the debate over the date of Luther's breakthrough was not a Lutheran scholar but the catholic historian and polemicist, Heinrich Denifle. In the first volume of his *Luther und Luthertum*, published in 1904, Denifle argued on the basis of the newly discovered and still unpublished lectures on Romans that the crucial turning-point in Luther's development, when he broke away from the traditional teaching of the catholic church and arrived at his new understanding of justification, took place in 1515 in the early stages of the lectures on Romans and he poured heavy scorn on protestant scholars whom he accused of failing to look critically at the problem of at what period in his career Luther's new theology originated.[12] However, Denifle's challenge was soon taken up and over the next forty years a succession of (mainly protestant) scholars devoted a great deal of effort to trying to establish the precise point at which Luther arrived at his new understanding of Romans

---

[10] *WA* 54, pp 185–6: see below pp 201–3.

[11] The *Dictata super Psalterium* was published by G. Kawerau in *WA* 3–4 (1885–6); the lectures on Romans by J. Ficker in *Anfänge reformatorischer Bibelauslegung*, 1, *Luthers Vorlesung über den Römerbrief 1515/16* (Leipzig 1908). Earlier German historians had tended to place Luther's discovery very early in his career, during his Erfurt period. His most famous nineteenth-century biographer, Julius Köstlin, for example, dated it to the third and last year of his monastic life at Erfurt before his first call to Wittenberg, in other words to 1508: see J. Köstlin, *Life of Luther*, Eng trans (London 1883) pp 54–5.

[12] H. Denifle, *Luther und Luthertum in der ersten Entwickelung quellenmässig dargestellt*, 2 vols (Mainz 1904–9) 1, pp 404–15, 392–5, reprinted in Lohse, pp 1–18.

1:17. As a result, a large number of different solutions were put forward. These included: 1508-9, during his first period of residence at Wittenberg (R. Seeberg, O. Ritschl), a view soon discarded by most scholars;[13] c1512 or possibly 1511, shortly after his return to Wittenberg but before—and probably some considerable time before—the commencement of the first lectures on the psalms (Holl);[14] between October 1512 when he took his doctorate and the summer of 1513 when he began the lectures on the psalms (Scheel, Strohl, Mackinnon);[15] in April or May 1513 when he was composing the *argumenta* for the printed Latin text of the psalms which he was preparing for use in his forthcoming lectures (Boehmer);[16] early in the first course of lectures on the psalms, at psalm 31 (Hirsch);[17] half-way through the lectures on the psalms, at or before psalm 71, in other words probably in the autumn of 1514 (Vogelsang);[18] late in the lectures on the psalms or after their conclusion, but before the commencement of the lectures on Romans (Bornkamm);[19] around the

[13] R. Seeberg, *Lehrbuch der Dogmengeschichte*, 4 vols (Leipzig 1908–17) 4, *Die Lehre Luthers*, pp 68–9; O. Ritschl, *Dogmengeschichte des Protestantismus*, 4 vols (Leipzig/Göttingen 1908–27) 2, p 11. See also [H.] Boehmer, *Luther im Lichte der neueren Forschung: [Ein kritischer Bericht]* (1 ed Leipzig 1906) pp 32–3. This view has generally been held to be incompatible with Luther's statement in a sermon of 21 May 1537 that at the time he became a doctor [that is, October 1512] he was ignorant of the light—'Iterum acquisivimus lucem. Sed ego, cum doctor fierem, nescivi' (*WA* 45, p 86; Scheel, *Dokumente*, no 364, pp 135–6).

[14] K. Holl, 'Der Neubau der Sittlichkeit' in *Gesammelte Aufsätze zur Kirchengeschichte*, I, *Luther* (6 ed Tübingen 1932) pp 193–7.

[15] O. Scheel, *Martin Luther. Vom Katholizismus zur Reformation*, 2 vols (2 ed Tübingen 1917) 2, p 321; H. Strohl, *L'Évolution Religieuse de Luther jusqu'en 1515*, *Études d'Histoire et de Philosophie Religieuses publiées par la Faculté de Théologie Protestante de l'Université de Strasbourg* I (Strasbourg/Paris 1922) pp 143–6; Mackinnon, *Luther and the Reformation*, I, pp 150–1.

[16] H. Boehmer, *Der junge Luther* (Gotha 1924) p 110. This represents Boehmer's final position. In the first edition of his *Luther im Lichte der neueren Forschung* (1906) he argued against Denifle that it took place in the winter of 1508–9 during Luther's first period at Wittenberg (see above n 13). Subsequently he modified this. In the fifth edition of *Luther im Lichte der neueren Forschung* (1918) he placed it at the end of 1512 or the beginning of 1513, in the period between Luther's advancement to the professoriate at Wittenberg and the commencement of the first lectures on the psalms: see [H.] Boehmer, *Luther [and the Reformation] in the Light of Modern Research*, trans E. S. G. Potter from 5 German ed (London 1930) p 60. Finally in his monograph *Luthers erste Vorlesung, Berichte über die Verhandlungen der sächsischen Akademie der Wissenschaften*, PhK 75 (1923) pt 1 (Leipzig 1924) and in his popular biography *Der junge Luther* he narrowed the date down still further to April/May 1513.

[17] [E.] Hirsch, 'Initium theologiae Lutheri' in *Festgabe für D. Dr. Julius Kaftan* (Tübingen 1920) pp 150–69, reprinted in Lohse, pp 64–95.

[18] E. Vogelsang, *Die Anfänge von Luthers Christologie nach der ersten Psalmenvorlesung*, *Arbeiten zu Kirchengeschichte* 15 (Berlin/Leipzig 1929) esp pp 57–9.

end of 1514, while he was preparing the lectures on Romans (A. V. Müller);[20] before easter 1515 (Stracke).[21] Of these the solution which has probably attracted most support from subsequent scholars is that of Erich Vogelsang, whose argument, based on a close analysis of the language of the *Dictata*, that Luther's discovery must have taken place in 1514, at or shortly before his comments on psalm 71, was widely accepted as the authoritative answer to the problem in the 1930s, 1940s and early 1950s.[22]

Despite their differences, all these interpretations may be said to start from certain common assumptions which were shared by most early twentieth-century Luther scholars. In the first place, it was accepted more or less without question that the 'tower-experience' represented the moment at which Luther arrived at his reformation theology of justification and it was therefore frequently referred to as his 'reformation discovery' or 'reformation breakthrough' (*reformatorische Entdeckung, Erkenntnis* or *Durchbruch*). Secondly, it was generally believed that Luther's theology was in essentials complete in the lectures on Romans and this in turn led logically to the assumption that his 'reformation breakthrough' must have occurred before or, at the latest, about the time that he embarked on the lectures on Romans. In addition, running through the attempts of scholars like Hirsch and Vogelsang to establish a precise date for the 'tower-experience' was an implicit, and perhaps unconscious, assumption that his new understanding of Romans 1:17 must have been immediately reflected in his academic teaching, so that it should be possible by a close examination of the text of the early lectures to determine the exact point at which it occurred.

[19] H. Bornkamm, 'Luthers Bericht über seine Entdeckung der iustitia dei', *ARG* 37 (1940) pp 117–28; 'Iustitia dei in der Scholastik und bei Luther', *ARG* 39 (1942) pp 1–46; 'Die Frage der iustitia dei beim jungen Luther', *ARG* 52 (1961) pp 15–29, 53 (1962) pp 1–59, reprinted together in Lohse, pp 289–383. Bornkamm's views have changed slightly during the course of his career. In his 1940 article he originally argued for a date in the spring of 1515 at the time when Luther was preparing the lectures on Romans. In his 1942 article he revised his opinion and came out in favour of Vogelsang's theory. In his third article, written twenty years later, while somewhat modifying his earlier agreement with Vogelsang's arguments, he reaffirmed his belief that Luther's new understanding of Romans 1:17 dates back to his first lectures on the psalms (see Lohse, esp pp 299, 381).
[20] A. V. Müller, *Luthers Werdegang bis zum Turmerlebnis* (Gotha 1920) cap 6, esp pp 128–30.
[21] Stracke, *Luthers grosses Selbstzeugnis* in Lohse, p 114.
[22] Compare Rupp, *Righteousness of God*, p 137: 'We conclude, therefore, that, as Vogelsang suggests, the new orientation of thought seems likely to have occurred in the course of the lectures on the psalms, 1514. It is hardly likely that any closer date will be arrived at.'

One of the very few early twentieth-century scholars to dissent from the prevailing view that Luther's 'tower-experience' must have occurred by 1515 at the latest was the catholic historian, Hartmann Grisar, who argued for a late date in 1518 or at the beginning of 1519, at the time of the second lectures on the psalms, as suggested by the 1545 preface.[23] But Grisar's views were universally rejected by his protestant critics and it was not until the 1950s that the traditional interpretation began to be seriously questioned. In the past twenty-five years, however, the pendulum has swung the other way and a growing number of scholars have begun to argue that Luther did not arrive at his mature theology until around 1518/19 and that his 'tower-experience', far from occurring in his early years at Wittenberg, did not happen until about the same date, that is, probably in 1518 or early in 1519.

The first modern scholar to put forward this thesis was a Finnish-American theologian, U. Saarnivaara, in a book which originally appeared in Finnish in 1947 and was subsequently published in English in America in 1951 under the title *Luther Discovers the Gospel*. In this book Saarnivaara set out the two main lines of argument which have characterised the revisionist theory ever since. In the first place, he maintained that, contrary to the traditional view, Luther did not develop the distinctive features of his reformation theology of justification until around 1518/19. Before that, although his thought was in process of evolution, his basic conception of justification was Augustinian and even in the lectures on Romans, despite evidence of a deepening evangelical insight, it still conformed to an orthodox, pre-reformation type.[24] Secondly, Saarnivaara argued that Luther's account of the 'tower-experience' in the 1545 preface, where it is dated to about 1519, should be taken literally, for the 'tower-experience' was associated not with the beginnings of his spiritual development in his early years at Wittenberg but with the final emergence of his reformation teaching in the winter of 1518/19 and, in particular, with his second lectures on the psalms.[25]

[23] Grisar, *Luther*, I, cap 10, pp 374–404. In many respects Grisar's arguments foreshadow those of Saarnivaara and Bizer. Thus he maintains that Luther had not yet arrived at his mature doctrine of justification in the lectures on Romans; that this only occurred in 1518 or at the beginning of 1519; and that the evidence of the 1545 preface is correct in dating the 'tower-experience' to the time when he was beginning the second lectures on the psalms.

[24] Saarnivaara, *Luther Discovers the Gospel*, esp cap 6, pp 74–87.

[25] *Ibid*, esp cap 8, pp 92–120. 'Our conclusion is that Luther's tower experience took place during the time he was preparing his second course of lectures on the psalms, probably

The problem of Luther's 'tower-experience'

However, Saarnivaara's book attracted little attention when it first appeared and even in recent years its influence has largely been confined to English and American scholars.[26] Consequently, the debate did not really get under way until the publication in 1958 of Ernst Bizer's important monograph *Fides ex auditu*,[27] which reopened the question of the interpretation of Luther's early development by challenging the accepted views of Vogelsang and his followers. While Bizer does not appear to have been aware of Saarnivaara's work at the time he published the first edition of *Fides ex auditu*[28] and his own investigation into the evolution of Luther's thought between 1513 and 1519 was inspired by different principles and went considerably deeper than Saarnivaara's, their general conclusions were very similar. Like Saarnivaara, Bizer argued—though on different grounds—that Luther's 'reformation breakthrough' did not take place until 1518 or early 1519 and that Luther's account of the 'tower-experience' in the 1545 Preface was substantially correct, for the emergence of his mature doctrine of justification was closely linked with a new understanding of Romans 1:17 which is apparent in his writings from the end of 1518.[29] Where Bizer's theory differed from Saarnivaara's was, first of all, in the emphasis that he placed on *humilitas* as the key-note of Luther's theology of justification down to 1518[30] and, secondly, in the claim that the decisive element in Luther's breakthrough was his discovery of the Word as the means of grace and that it was this, not the concept of passive righteousness, that constituted the essence of his new insight into the meaning of Romans 1:17 in the 'tower-experience' of 1518.[31]

---

in the autumn or early winter of 1518' (p 108). Compare p 103: 'The only possible conclusion is that his dating of this discovery in his *Preface* of 1545 is correct.'

26 See, for example, [F. E.] Cranz, [*An Essay on the*] *Development of Luther's Thought* [*on Justice, Law, and Society*], Harvard Theological Studies 19 (Cambridge, Mass., 1959) esp p 41, n 1; A. G. Dickens, *Martin Luther and the Reformation* (London 1967) pp 25–31.

27 [E.] Bizer, *Fides ex auditu*: [*Eine Untersuchung über die Entdeckung der Gerechtigkeit Gottes durch Martin Luther*] (Neukirchen 1958, 2 rev ed 1961, 3 ed with new postscript 1966). References in this article are to the third edition, the text of which is identical with that of the second edition except for the addition of the postscript, pp 179–204. Excerpts from the third edition will be found in Lohse, pp 115–62. For a full discussion in English of Bizer's views, see the review article by G. Rupp, *ZKG* 71 (1960) pp 351–5.

28 He does not cite Saarnivaara in the first two editions and only refers to him briefly in the postscript to the third edition, p 187.

29 Bizer, *Fides ex auditu*, see esp the section 'Das Selbstzeugnis von 1545 und die Operationes in Psalmos', pp 165–71.

30 See esp his discussions of the first lectures on the psalms, *ibid*, pp 15–22, and the lectures on Romans, pp 23–52.

31 *Ibid*, esp pp 166–7. 'Was Luther entdeckt hat, ist zunächst die Theologie des Wortes und im *Zusammenhang* damit die Bedeutung des Glaubens. Das Wort zeigt nicht einfach

The significance of the revisionist theory for the interpretation of Luther's biography lies in the fact that it entails a crucial reversal of the order of events—and therefore, by implication, of cause and effect—in his early career. The traditional view, by placing Luther's 'reformation discovery' before the ninety-five theses and the indulgences controversy, encouraged historians and biographers to assume—not necessarily justifiably—that the one led logically to the other and that Luther's attack on the church was a direct, not to say inevitable, outcome of his new theology of justification. By contrast, according to the revisionist theory, Luther did not develop the distinctive features of his reformation theology until after the outbreak of the indulgences controversy, although he had, of course, been attacking scholastic theology before that. This means that the development of his mature theology and his 'tower-experience' have to be seen as taking place within the context of the debate over indulgences; and while not all the protagonists of the revisionist theory would make this connection explicitly, some, including Bizer himself, would argue that Luther's 'reformation discovery' not only occurred at the time of the indulgences controversy but was inspired, directly or indirectly, by his need to grapple with the issues that it raised,[32] so that, in effect, the traditional view is turned on its head and Luther's reformation teaching emerges not as a cause but rather as a consequence, in part at least, of his attack on indulgences.

Inevitably a theory that involves such a radical reinterpretation of Luther's early development has aroused considerable controversy. The publication of Bizer's book sparked off a heated debate which continued throughout the 1960s.[33] Not surprisingly, many scholars found it difficult at first to accept the implications of a theory which challenged so many preconceptions about the early history of the reformation[34] and it is only gradually that the revisionist thesis that

---

den Weg zur Gerechtigkeit und beschreibt diesen nicht nur, sondern es ist das Mittel, wodurch Gott den Menschen rechtfertigt, weil es den Glauben weckt' (p 167). Compare the postscript to the third edition (1966), p 180: 'Meine These ist nun, dass Luther in der Vorrede davon berichte, wie er "das Wort als Gnadenmittel" entdeckt habe.'

[32] Compare Bizer, *Fides ex auditu*, p 94.

[33] For a very full account of the development of the controversy following the publication of *Fides ex auditu*, see [O. H.] Pesch, ['Zur Frage nach Luthers reformatorischer Wende'], *Catholica* 20 (Münster 1966) pp 216–43 and 264–80, reprinted in Lohse, pp 445–505.

[34] See, in particular, R. Prenter, *Der barmherzige Richter. Iustitia dei passiva in Luthers Dictata super Psalterium 1513–15*, Acta Jutlandica 33, 2 (Aarhus/Copenhagen 1961), extract in Lohse, pp 203–42, and the extended critique of Bizer by [H.] Bornkamm, ['Zur Frage der iustitia dei beim jungen Luther'], *ARG* 52 (1961) and 53 (1962) in

The problem of Luther's 'tower-experience'

Luther did not arrive at the distinctive features of his reformation theology until around 1518/19 has begun to gain widespread, though by no means universal, acceptance.[35] Even so the debate is far from over. Not only are there still many supporters of the traditional view who remain unpersuaded by the arguments of the revisionists, but the revisionist theory itself leaves a number of loose ends and, even if one accepts (as I do) the general argument for a late date for the emergence of Luther's reformation theology, it cannot be said that the biographical problem of Luther's 'tower-experience' has yet been satisfactorily resolved.

It is this that I want to look at in the remainder of this paper. Let me say at once that I am not going to pull a new rabbit out of the hat. I cannot claim to have found the solution to the mystery that has defeated everyone else until now. In fact, I suspect that the problem is ultimately insoluble. What I want to do is simply to draw attention to a methodological confusion which, it seems to me, has bedevilled the discussion of the problem ever since it was first raised at the beginning of the century and which needs to be cleared out of the way if one is to approach the problem afresh.

This confusion lies in the fact that in modern research two quite distinct problems have been unconsciously conflated: the problem of the date of the emergence of Luther's reformation theology of justification and the problem of the date and significance of his 'tower-experience'. In discussions of Luther's early intellectual development it has generally been taken for granted that the 'tower-experience' was directly connected with the emergence of his reformation theology, either in the sense that what he discovered in the tower was the doctrine of justification by faith or in the sense that his new understanding of *iustitia Dei* was the essential insight which led him to the discovery of

---

Lohse, pp 289-383, For Bizer's reply to their criticisms, see *Fides ex auditu*, postscript (1966), pp 179-204.

[35] See [A.] Peters, ['Luthers Turmerlebnis'], *Neue Zeitschrift für Systematische Theologie* 3 (Berlin 1961) pp 203-36, in Lohse, pp 243-88; [K.] Aland, [*Der Weg zu Reformation, Zeitpunkt und Charakter des reformatorischen Erlebnisses Martin Luthers*], *Theologische Existenz Heute*, NF 123 (Munich 1965), extracts in Lohse, pp 384-412. Other notable converts to the idea of a late date include H. Jedin and E. Wolf, see Pesch in Lohse, pp 455-6. See also the important recent article by Martin Brecht, 'Iustitia Christi: Die Entdeckung Martin Luthers', *Zeitschrift für Theologie und Kirche* 74 (Tübingen 1977) pp 179-223, which appeared too late for consideration in this paper but which argues that 'Luther made the decisive discovery of his theology in the spring of 1518' (p 222). I am grateful to professor Brecht for kindly sending me a copy of his article through the good offices of Dr E. Langstadt.

justification by faith. In other words, it has generally been taken for granted that the 'tower-experience' represents what German scholars call his 'reformation discovery' or 'reformation breakthrough'. Consequently, there has been an inbuilt tendency on the part of many scholars to assume that if only one can solve the problem of the date of Luther's 'tower-experience', then one has solved the problem of when he achieved his 'reformation breakthrough', or vice-versa—if one can discover from an analysis of Luther's early writings when his 'reformation breakthrough' occurred, then one has also solved the problem of the date of his 'tower-experience'.

It is easy to understand why this assumption should have been made by the older generation of Luther scholars who first formulated the theory of a date between 1512 and 1515 for the 'tower-experience', since they started from the premiss that Luther's reformation theology was in essentials complete by the time he embarked on his lectures on Romans. Given the assumption that the lectures on Romans were to be seen as a clear statement of Luther's mature teaching on justification, it followed that his 'reformation breakthrough' must have taken place before that and it was only natural that they should have identified it with the moment of illumination that he described in his accounts of the 'tower-experience'. At the same time the tendency to treat the two problems as if they were one and the same was undoubtedly fostered by the methodological assumption made by Emanuel Hirsch and his followers that it must be possible to pin-point the precise moment in Luther's lectures at which he came to his new understanding of Romans 1:17; and one legacy of the obsessive endeavours of successive German scholars to establish such a precise turning-point in his writings has been to encourage the belief that there must be a clear-cut solution to the problem of the 'tower-experience', when probably there is not.

What is more remarkable, however, is that for the most part this basic assumption that the two problems are identical has been carried over into the revisionist theory. In part, one suspects, because it had become such a well-established tradition among Luther scholars to equate Luther's 'tower-experience' with his 'reformation breakthrough', the newer generation of scholars like Saarnivaara and Bizer, who contend that Luther did not arrive at the distinctive features of his mature theology until around 1518/19, have continued to make the assumption that the 'tower-experience' must be linked with the emergence of his mature theology and they have argued—

admittedly also partly on the basis of the 1545 preface—that it cannot have taken place until 1518 or early 1519. Similarly, again following in the tradition of earlier German Luther scholarship, they have continued to be greatly concerned with trying to detect the exact point in Luther's writings at which his new understanding of Romans 1:17 begins to emerge.

The question I want to put, therefore, is whether the two problems are necessarily identical or, at least, as closely interrelated as most scholars have tended to assume. As I see it, there are really two distinct problems which need to be kept separate. The first—and from a historical point of view the more important—problem is when did Luther arrive at the distinctive elements of his reformation theology? Was it before 1515 or only after the outbreak of the indulgences controversy, around 1518/19? The second is the much more limited biographical question, when did Luther undergo his 'tower-experience' and what precisely did it involve? Only by looking at these two questions separately can one try to establish what connection there is, if any, between Luther's 'tower-experience' and the emergence of his reformation theology.

The first is an immensely complex and technical problem which cannot be explored here. To do justice to it properly would require a detailed, step-by-step analysis of the progress of Luther's thought in his early writings of the kind provided by Bizer or by Gordon Rupp in *The Righteousness of God*. It would also involve an examination of the highly controversial question of how one defines the difference between the 'reformation' (*reformatorische*) and the 'pre-reformation' (*vorreformatorische*) elements in Luther's thought.[36] Such an analysis, even if I had the competence to undertake it, is clearly outside the scope of this paper. I will therefore confine myself to a few brief general observations. In the first place, it is now clear that the evolution of Luther's thought in the period 1512 to 1520 was a much more gradual process than used to be assumed. If the controversy has failed to produce any agreement on when Luther's breakthrough occurred, it has served to show that Luther did not formulate his new theology all at once, but rather over a period of several years, and it is significant that even those scholars who would place the decisive turning-point in his

---

[36] For the difficulty and importance of defining the terms 'reformation' and 'pre-reformation' in relation to Luther's early thought, see Bornkamm in Lohse, pp 376–7; [L.] Grane, *Modus loquendi theologicus: [Luthers Kampf um die Erneuerung der Theologie (1515–1518)]*, *Acta Theologica Danica* 12 (Leiden 1975) pp 11–12.

development relatively early would admit that on a number of important issues he did not work out his ideas in full until considerably later.[37] Secondly, again partly (although not exclusively) as a result of the controversy, there has been a marked change in the interpretation of the lectures on Romans over the past thirty years.[38] Although passions still run high over whether the lectures should be seen as a statement of his 'reformation' or his 'pre-reformation' thinking,[39] the researches of Saarnivaara, Bizer and others have demonstrated that Luther's theological position in the lectures on Romans is considerably more ambiguous, not to say transitional, than was perceived by most early twentieth-century scholars and, on balance, it seems to me that the weight of the evidence supports the revisionists' contention that at this stage his teaching on justification was still essentially Augustinian in character, and that he had not yet arrived at his distinctive reformation doctrine of justification as an instantaneous process.[40] Thirdly, a number of recent scholars have tended to argue that a general reorientation took place in Luther's thinking around 1518–19, following the outbreak of the indulgences controversy, and it is now fairly clear that certain key concepts of his mature theology, such as his teaching on law and gospel and his new understanding of the Christian as 'flesh' and 'spirit', *simul iustus simul peccator*, only began to crystallise in his thought at this period.[41] While recognising that the matter is still far from settled, I am therefore myself largely convinced by the revisionist argument that Luther did not come to a full understanding of his reformation teaching on justification until around 1518/19, and that before that his thought progressed through an Augustinian phase, represented *par excellence* by the lectures on Romans, during which he was actively engaged in attacking scholastic theology but had not yet achieved his final breakthrough.

Such a protracted view of Luther's development should not really seem surprising. On the contrary, when one reflects on the problem, it is the older belief that Luther arrived at the main principles of his reformation theology very early which makes the greater demands

[37] Compare Bornkamm in Lohse, esp pp 376, 381–2.
[38] See Grane, *Modus loquendi theologicus*, p 11. For a more detailed survey of the literature to 1966, see Pesch in Lohse, pp 445–505.
[39] Compare Bornkamm's criticisms of Bizer, Lohse, p 334.
[40] Compare, for example, the many passages in which Luther appears to treat justification in Augustine's sense as a life-long process of renewal which will not be completed until the next world, for example, *WA* 56, pp 272–3.
[41] Compare Cranz, *Development of Luther's Thought*, cap 2, pp 41–71; Peters in Lohse, pp 242–88.

The problem of Luther's 'tower-experience'

on our credulity. As he himself remarked, 'I did not learn my theology all at one time; rather I had to dig for it ever deeper and deeper where my trials took me'.[42] It makes much better sense psychologically, as well as of the evidence of his early writings, to see Luther's thought developing gradually over a period of six or seven years, as he worked out his ideas stage by stage—*scribendo et legendo*, as he put it in the 1545 preface.[43] Not only was Luther by temperament a conservative thinker, who always found it difficult (even in later years) to free himself completely from the traditional ideas in which he had been reared; but the task he was engaged on—at first unconsciously—was an immensely difficult one, since in effect it involved breaking away from one theological system and creating a new synthesis of his own. By its very nature this was bound to be a relatively long drawn out process: although the beginnings of Luther's evolution as a reformer can be traced back to the first lectures on the psalms, the final clarification of his teaching on justification almost certainly did not occur until around 1518/19, and it is only at this stage that he can properly be said to have arrived at his reformation theology.

The second problem—the problem of the 'tower-experience'—is much narrower in scope in that it concerns a particular moment in Luther's intellectual biography. Essentially it comprises three interrelated questions. First, at what point in Luther's early years at Wittenberg did it take place? Secondly, what exactly did his discovery consist of? Thirdly, what is the significance of the 'tower-experience' in the overall pattern of Luther's intellectual development?

At this point we need to turn to the famous account of his discovery which Luther gave in the 1545 preface to the first volume of his collected Latin writings. There, after describing the origins and development of the indulgences controversy and the mission of Miltitz, he writes:

> Meanwhile in that year [1519] I had returned once more to interpreting the psalms, confident that I was better trained after I had expounded the epistles of Saint Paul to the Romans and the Galatians and the epistle to the Hebrews in the schools. Certainly I had been seized by an extraordinary ardour to understand Paul in the epistle to the Romans, but what had hindered me thus far was not any coldness in my heart's blood but that one phrase in the first chapter, 'The righteousness of God is revealed in it'. For

[42] *WA TR* I, no 352, p 146.
[43] *WA* 54, p 186; Scheel, *Dokumente*, no 511, p 192.

I had hated that phrase 'the righteousness of God' (*iustitia Dei*), which by the use and custom of all the doctors I had been taught to understand philosophically in the sense of the formal or active righteousness (as they termed it) (*iustitia (ut vocant) formali seu activa*), by which God is righteous and punishes sinners and the unrighteous.

Although as a monk I lived an irreproachable life, I felt that before God I was a sinner with a most unquiet conscience, nor was I able to believe that he was appeased by my satisfactions. I did not love, nay rather I hated that righteous God who punishes sinners, and if not with silent blasphemy, then certainly with a great murmuring, I was angry with God . . . Thus I raged with a furious and troubled conscience; yet I continued to knock importunately at Paul in this passage, thirsting most ardently to know what Saint Paul meant.

Until at last, by the mercy of God, as I meditated day and night, I began to consider the connection of the words,[44] 'The righteousness of God is revealed in it, as it is written: The just shall live by faith'. Then I began to understand that the righteousness of God is that righteousness by which the righteous man lives by the gift of God, namely by faith, and that this phrase, 'The righteousness of God is revealed through the gospel', is passive, meaning the righteousness by which God in his mercy justifies us through faith, as it is written, 'The just shall live by faith'. Now I immediately felt that I had been reborn and that I had entered through open gates into paradise itself. Then forthwith the face of the whole of scripture appeared different to me. After that I ran through the scriptures, as memory served, and I found the same analogy in other phrases, such as the work of God (*opus Dei*), that which God works in us; the power of God (*virtus Dei*), by which he makes us powerful; the wisdom of God (*sapientia Dei*), by which he makes us wise; the strength of God (*fortitudo Dei*); the salvation of God (*salus Dei*); the glory of God (*gloria Dei*).

Now, just as before I had so hated that phrase 'the righteousness of God', so with equal intensity I began to love and extol it as the sweetest of words, so that that passage in Paul became for me

---

[44] *connexionem verborum*: Luther means the connection between the first phrase 'the righteousness of God is revealed in it the gospel' and the second 'the just shall live by faith'. Compare his accounts in the *Table Talk*, quoted above pp 188–9.

the very gate of paradise. Afterwards I read Augustine, *On the Spirit and the Letter*, where beyond my expectation I found that he too interprets the righteousness of God in the same manner, namely, as that with which God endues us when he justifies us. And although this is expressed somewhat imperfectly and he does not explain everything clearly about imputation, nevertheless it was pleasing to find that he taught that the righteousness of God is that by which we are justified.

Made better armed by these thoughts, I began to interpret the psalms for the second time. . . .[45]

The fullness of this account is remarkable and it contains many points of detail that are of interest. However, at the risk of oversimplifying a complex problem, it is possible to single out four points that are particularly crucial to the discussion. 1. If one interprets Luther's words literally, his chronology implies quite specifically that his discovery took place in 1519 when he was about to embark on his second series of lectures on the psalms.[46] 2. He connects his difficulties over the meaning of the term *iustitia Dei* with the personal spiritual crisis which he experienced as a monk. 3. He relates his new understanding of Romans 1:17 to the discovery that *iustitia Dei* can be interpreted not merely in an active sense as the righteousness by which God judges (and condemns) sinners, but also in a passive sense as the righteousness by which men are made righteous through faith. It is this 'passive' righteousness[47] which God bestows on men as a gift through faith that is the righteousness by which men are justified and to which Paul refers in Romans 1:17. This description is more or less identical with that which Luther gave in the first two passages from the *Table Talk*, quoted at the beginning of this paper: in the third, he suggested rather differently that it was connected with his discovery of the distinction between law and gospel.[48] 4. In the 1545 preface Luther states that after he had come to his new understanding of Romans 1:17 he read Augustine's *De spiritu et littera*, where *praeter spem* he found

---

[45] *WA* 54, pp 185–6; Scheel, *Dokumente*, no 511, pp 191–2.

[46] 'Interim eo anno iam redieram ad psalterium denuo interpretandum,' etc (*WA* 54, p 185; Scheel, *Dokumente*, p 191).

[47] E. Hirsch pointed out that the use of the term 'passive' in relation to *iustitia Dei* first occurs in Luther's writings in *De servo arbitrio* (1525) and it did not become a regular part of his theological vocabulary until the 1530s, so that the language in which he describes his discovery in the 1545 preface is that of his old age ('Initium theologiae Lutheri', Lohse, pp 71–5).

[48] See above p 189.

that *iustitia Dei* was interpreted similarly, although somewhat imperfectly.[49]

The crux arises from the fact that not only, so far as is known, were Luther's spiritual struggles as a monk over well before 1519, but that both in the 1545 preface and in most of the other accounts in the *Table Talk* and elsewhere he appears to describe his discovery in terms of a new understanding of *iustitia Dei* which he arrived at not in 1519, or even in 1518, but several years earlier—certainly by 1515 when he began the lectures on Romans and very probably at some point during the first lectures on the psalms. One has only to turn to the beginning of the lectures on Romans where Luther outlines the theme of the epistle to see that he regarded the central message of Romans as being that man is not saved by his own righteousness, but 'by an external righteousness' (*per extraneam iustitiam*)—'which does not originate from ourselves, but which comes to us from outside, which does not arise on our earth, but which comes from heaven'.[50] Moreover, if one turns specifically to Luther's exposition of Romans 1:17 in the 1515–16 lectures, one finds that he interprets *iustitia Dei* in a manner which clearly resembles the language of his later accounts of his 'tower-experience'. 'But only in the gospel', he writes, 'is the righteousness of God revealed (that is who is righteous and by what means he becomes righteous before God) through faith alone by which one believes the word of God . . . For the righteousness of God is the cause of salvation. And here again the righteousness of God is not to be understood as that righteousness by which God is righteous in himself, but that by which we are justified by him, which happens through faith in the gospel.'[51] Nor do the parallels with the 1545 preface stop there, for in the very next sentence Luther goes on to cite Augustine's *De spiritu et littera* in support of this interpretation of *iustitia Dei*;[52] and, in fact, throughout the lectures on Romans he refers to Augustine's tract on numerous occasions, so that it is evident that he was thoroughly familiar with it by the time he came to write the Romans lectures.[53]

[49] Compare the statement in *WA TR* 4, no 4007, p 73, 'Sed postea cum consequentia viderem . . . et insuper August [inum] consulerem, da wardt ich frolich' (see above p 189).

[50] *WA* 56, p 158.

[51] *Ibid* pp 171–2.

[52] *Ibid* p 172.

[53] For Luther's use of Augustine's *De spiritu et littera* in the lectures on Romans, see B. Lohse, 'Die Bedeutung Augustins für den jungen Luther', *Kerygma und Dogma* 11 (Göttingen 1965) pp 116–36; Grane, *Modus loquendi theologicus*, esp cap 1, pp 23–62.

The problem of Luther's 'tower experience'

What is one to make of these discrepancies in Luther's account? To the supporters of the traditional theory the chief source of difficulty lay in Luther's apparent dating of his discovery to 1519 and they attempted to get round this in various ways: for example, by suggesting that his use of the pluperfect tense (*captus fieram*, etc) at the beginning of the passage indicates that he was going back in time to an earlier period in his career and that the whole passage should be regarded as a digression from the main course of his narrative;[54] that he did not intend to give a precise date for his discovery here;[55] that he simply made a mistake and confused his second course of lectures on the psalms with the first;[56] or that in 1545, when the preface was written, he was a relatively old man, so that it is hardly surprising that his narrative is somewhat incoherent and rambling.[57]

However, none of these explanations is very convincing, as has frequently been pointed out. Luther's language is too precise to make it easy to accept the view that he intended the passage to be treated as a digression and there is nothing in the rest of the preface to suggest that his memory of events had become confused or that he was becoming in the least senile.[58] The revisionists would therefore argue that Luther's dating must be taken seriously: that the 'tower-experience' did occur around 1518 or early 1519 and that it was related to the emergence of his mature teaching on justification which first becomes apparent in his writings of 1518–19. In support of this Bizer quotes a number of passages from the sermon on two-fold righteousness (1519) and the second lectures on the psalms (*Operationes in Psalmos*) where Luther's ideas and the language in which he clothes them appear to parallel very closely the ideas and phraseology of the 1545 preface.[59] On the other hand, it has to be said that the revisionist argument fails to deal satisfactorily either with the major problem that in the 1545 preface and most of his other accounts

---

[54] Stracke, *Luthers grosses Selbstzeugnis*, Lohse, pp 112–13. Compare Rupp, *Righteousness of God*, p 123.

[55] Hirsch, 'Initium theologiae Lutheri', Lohse, p 86 n 62; Mackinnon, *Luther and the Reformation*, 1, p 150.

[56] F. Loofs, *Leitfaden zum Studium der Dogmengeschichte* (4 rev ed Halle 1906) p 689; O. Scheel, *Die Entwicklung Luthers bis zum Abschluss der Vorlesung über den Römerbrief*, SVRG 100 (1910) p 117.

[57] Boehmer, *Luther in the Light of Modern Research*, p 45.

[58] Compare Rupp, *Righteousness of God*, p 123; Rupp, however, followed Stracke in holding that the passage should be regarded as a digression (see above n 54).

[59] Bizer, *Fides ex auditu*, pp 10, 127–30, 165–71. Compare Saarnivaara, *Luther Discovers the Gospel*, pp 97–9.

Luther appears to describe his discovery in terms of a new under-standing of *iustitia Dei* which he had certainly acquired by 1515, and probably earlier, or with the lesser difficulty that Luther was well acquainted with Augustine's *De spiritu et littera* when he commenced the lectures on Romans. On the first point, Bizer argues that there is a crucial difference between Luther's concept of *iustitia Dei* as it appears in the lectures on Romans and the first lectures on the psalms and as he restated it in 1518/19, in that in 1518/19 he began for the first time to make justification dependent not only on faith but on the Word as the means of grace. According to Bizer, the essence of Luther's new insight into the meaning of Romans 1:17 lay in the realisation that the words *Iustitia Dei revelatur in illo* meant not merely that the righteousness of God is revealed *in* the gospel, but that it is revealed *through* the gospel. In other words, what Luther discovered in 1518/19—and this, Bizer claims, is what the 'tower-experience' consisted of—was the idea of the Word as the essential means of grace.[60] The difficulty with this is that it is not what Luther appears to be describing in his account of the 'tower-experience' in the 1545 preface where he quite specifically identifies his new understanding of Romans 1:17 with the realisation that *iustitia Dei* can be interpreted passively.[61] Even less persuasively Bizer and other supporters of the revisionist theory have tried to argue that when Luther referred to Augustine's *De spiritu et littera* in the 1545 preface he did not mean to imply that this was the first time that he had read it, since clearly he had read it before 1518/19, but that he read it again with new eyes shortly after his discovery when he was amazed to find (*praeter spem*) how closely Augustine's views corresponded to his own new conception of *iustitia Dei*.[62] No doubt it is possible to interpret Luther's words in this way, but again it is hardly the obvious impression that they convey.

---

[60] Bizer, *Fides ex auditu*, pp 165–7, 180, see above p 195 n 31. Other supporters of the revisionist theory tend to interpret Luther's discovery in the tower rather differently. Saarnivaara equates it with Luther's 'discovery of the full Reformation insight into justification, that God justifies the sinner by graciously imputing, or reckoning, the merits of Christ to him as his righteousness', though he also writes that 'from another point of view, the content of the discovery was the "Lutheran" distinction between the Law and the Gospel' (*Luther Discovers the Gospel*, p 46). Aland adheres to the traditional view that the 'tower-experience' involved the realisation that *iustitia Dei* is the passive righteousness by which God justifies man through faith and that that this righteousness is revealed in the gospel (Lohse, p 406); but he places this discovery in 1518 (p 409).

[61] See Rupp, *ZKG* 71 (1960) p 354; Bornkamm in Lohse, pp 353–6.

[62] Bizer, *Fides ex auditu*, p 184; Saarnivaara, *Luther Discovers the Gospel*, pp 109–11; Aland in Lohse, pp 399–401.

The problem of Luther's 'tower experience'

My own view is that the problem of reconciling these conflicting strands of evidence is insoluble and it is unlikely that we shall ever arrive at a satisfactory explanation that tidies up all the loose ends in Luther's account. This does not necessarily mean that no explanation of the 'tower-experience' is possible: simply that we cannot reconcile the contradictions in Luther's accounts and we ought to recognise this. In examining the problem of the 'tower-experience' we therefore need to go back to what we can be certain of.

What is beyond dispute—or almost beyond dispute[63]—is that Luther did at some period in his early years at Wittenberg experience a moment of illumination which he himself always remembered as a crucial turning-point in his spiritual life, even if its importance perhaps grew in his memory with the passage of time. In this connection, it is worth recalling that Luther's recorded reminiscences of his discovery date from the later years of his life, from the 1530s and early 1540s, and one may deduce from the verbal parallels between the different accounts that it was a story which became something of a set-piece as the years went by and which tended in consequence to take on an increasingly stereotyped form. Secondly, it is clear from all Luther's accounts that this moment of illumination involved a new understanding of Romans 1:17. More specifically, to judge by the evidence of the 1545 preface and the majority of Luther's other accounts, it appears to have been bound up with the realisation that *iustitia Dei* is to be interpreted passively as the righteousness by which God justifies men through faith, although not all modern scholars would accept this and there is the complication that in the 1542/3 passage in the *Table Talk* Luther associates his new understanding of

[63] In his article ' "Iustitia Christi" and "Iustitia Dei": Luther and the Scholastic Doctrines of Justification', *HTR* 59 (1966), pp 1–26, H. A. Oberman appears to cast doubt on the historicity of Luther's 'tower-experience' by pointing out that it belongs to a well-established literary tradition of conversion experiences, including those of Augustine and Calvin. 'This state of affairs,' he writes, 'allows us to conclude that there is a "Turmerlebnis" tradition which provides for a conceptual framework and an established language, in which and through which one can formulate one's own important discoveries' (p 9). Although Oberman does not explicitly deny that Luther's 'tower-experience' took place, the implication of his remarks is clearly that Luther's accounts of the 'tower-experience' should be treated as essentially a literary or metaphorical way of expressing his religious discovery. I find this attempt to rationalise the 'tower-experience' unconvincing. While Oberman is undoubtedly right to draw attention to the precedents in Christian literature for Luther's 'tower-experience', it does not follow from this that Luther's accounts do not relate to a genuine personal experience of his own. In view of his repeated and unequivocal statements about his discovery, I see no reason to doubt that he did experience a moment of illumination at Wittenberg, even if perhaps he afterwards magnified its importance.

Romans 1:17 with his discovery of the distinction between law and gospel. Thirdly, it is clear that the question of the date of the 'tower-experience' is inseparable from the question of its content.

It seems to me that there are two—or just possibly three—alternative solutions to the problem. The first is that Luther experienced his new understanding of Romans 1:17 relatively early in his time at Wittenberg, and that it was essentially connected not with the emergence of his final reformation theology of justification, but rather with his earlier discovery that the term 'the righteousness of God' can be understood in a passive sense as the external righteousness by which God justifies men in his mercy—a concept which is apparent throughout the lectures on Romans and which is visible in the later stages of the first lectures on the psalms. In other words, Luther's illumination must have taken place by 1515—very possibly around 1513/14 at some point during the course of the first lectures on the psalms, as favoured by many older scholars. This view would also appear to fit with Luther's statement in the 1545 preface that his discovery was linked with the resolution of his personal spiritual crisis in the monastery, for although again this cannot be dated precisely the evidence of the lectures on Romans suggests that by that time he had succeeded in overcoming the religious doubts that had tormented him earlier.[64]

On the other hand, if one accepts a relatively early date for the 'tower-experience', then one has to draw a sharp distinction between the 'tower-experience' and the emergence of his mature theology. While there is no reason to question Luther's claim that the 'tower-experience' was a momentous event in his intellectual and spiritual evolution, it is clear that far from representing the moment at which his reformation teaching suddenly came into focus, it marked only the beginning of a protracted process of development. On this view, it probably makes most sense to see it as the turning point at which he finally freed himself from the intellectual and spiritual difficulties created for him by the nominalist theology of salvation in which he had grown up and came to accept the Augustinian view that the righteousness by which man is justified is something extraneous, something which God confers on man, not something that man can

[64] Although there are few overtly autobiographical passages in the lectures on Romans referring to Luther's personal religious experiences, such as occur in some of his other lectures, the general tenor of the lectures on Romans suggests a confident assurance that men are justified through God's grace, and not through their own righteousness, which would appear to indicate that he had now found the answer to the spiritual crisis of his early years in the monastery.

achieve by his own efforts or works—a belief which enabled Luther to overcome his personal fear of God's judgement. If one accepts this solution, however, then it is evident that the 'tower-experience' was only an early step in the evolution of his theology. He had a long way to go and several years were to pass before he arrived at his mature position. Thus, though its psychological importance for Luther need not be doubted, it would be a mistake to over-estimate its significance in his intellectual development. It certainly does not represent the point at which he achieved his final 'reformation breakthrough', even though it was unquestionably a breakthrough of a kind.

The second alternative is that the 'tower-experience' did occur several years later, around 1518/19, as Saarnivaara, Bizer and others claim, and that it was closely associated with the final development of his reformation theology. On this view, it represented a moment of illumination when, so to speak, the various pieces of the jig-saw all slipped into place and it may well have been connected with his new understanding of the distinction between law and gospel which is apparent in his writings from around 1517–18.[65] If one accepts this solution, then clearly it is possible to argue that the 'tower-experience' was Luther's 'reformation breakthrough' in a literal sense, since it was associated with the emergence of some of the characteristic elements of his mature teaching. On the other hand, in that case its significance must have been a great deal less than Luther afterwards came to believe: for he had already moved a long way from traditional nominalist theology by 1518 and he had certainly arrived at his passive interpretation of *iustitia Dei* several years earlier, while he also appears to have emerged from his personal religious crisis well before this. It is quite conceivable that Luther did experience some kind of illumination around 1518/19, when he suddenly felt that he was able to see the theological problems that had occupied him for so long in a new light. But a late date would suggest that this was not so much a dramatic turning-point as a final clarification of his ideas.[66]

---

[65] See Rupp, *Righteousness of God*, pp 154–5, 195–6, 205; Bizer, *Fides ex auditu*, esp pp 148–64.

[66] This is admitted by some exponents of the revisionist theory. Compare Saarnivaara, *Luther Discovers the Gospel*, p 46, 'the "tower experience" of Luther was not the beginning, but the relative end of his development'; *ibid*, 'Luther's experience in the tower was not his conversion. It was the final exegetico-religious discovery of the evangelical way of salvation.' See also Peters in Lohse, p 255, 'In dem "Turmerlebnis" beschreibt Luther das geistige Ringen, in welchem seine systematische wie exegetische Erwägungen zu einem geschlossenen Ganzen zusammenschiessen.'

Both these solutions are psychologically quite plausible—one can imagine Luther having a moment of illumination at either point in his career—but both have their difficulties in view of the evidence. An early date runs counter to the chronology of the 1545 preface with its clear implication that Luther's new insight into the meaning of Romans 1:17 occurred as he was about to embark on his second series of lectures on the psalms: it would also not fit with the suggestion in the 1542/43 account in the *Table Talk* that his experience was associated with his discovery of the distinction between law and gospel. On the other hand, a late date would appear to conflict with Luther's repeated statements that his new understanding of Romans 1:17 involved the realisation that the righteousness by which God justified man is passive, as well as with the fact that he was certainly familiar with Augustine's *De spiritu et littera* by 1515; nor is it easy to reconcile a late date with the supposition that the 'tower-experience' was connected with the resolution of his personal spiritual crisis. So explicit is Luther's identification of his illumination with the discovery that *iustitia Dei* can be interpreted passively that it seems to me that on balance the arguments in favour of an early date outweigh those in favour of a date around 1518/19. I am therefore inclined to support the traditional view that the 'tower-experience' must have occurred by 1515 at the latest, while recognising that the evidence is by no means conclusive. However, in that case I would wish to argue, in opposition to the traditionalist theory, that it was not associated with the emergence of his reformation doctrine of justification, but belongs to an earlier phase in his intellectual development.

There is a third possibility that ought to be mentioned, although there is no concrete evidence in the sources to support it. This is that Luther, in fact, experienced two moments of illumination—one relatively early, the other around 1518—which in later years tended to get conflated in his memory. Psychologically this has much to recommend it: certainly Luther's thought progressed by stages and it is quite conceivable that the two major advances in his thinking which took place around 1514/15, when he first began consciously to attack scholastic theology, and around 1518/19, when his mature theology began to crystallise, were each preceded or accompanied by a moment of illumination when the way forward suddenly seemed to become clear. However, attractive as such a solution would be as a way round the various difficulties, it is so speculative that it would be unwise to pursue it.

The problem of Luther's 'tower experience'

To sum up, then, whichever solution one adopts, it is evident that the 'tower-experience' played a considerably less important role in Luther's overall intellectual development than most scholars have tended to assume or than he himself came to believe in his later years. The development of Luther's theology of justification was a relatively long drawn out process, which extended over several years, and it now seems probable that he did not arrive at his final position until after the outbreak of the indulgences controversy. Unless one adopts my hypothetical third possibility, the 'tower-experience' can only relate to one moment in that process. If one accepts an early date, then it only marks an early stage in Luther's development. It did not represent his 'reformation breakthrough'. If one considers a later date more probable, then it is arguable that it did constitute his 'reformation breakthrough': on the other hand, in that case it only marks the culmination of a process which had been going on for several years. It is probably true to say that, whenever it took place, the importance of the 'tower-experience' for Luther was as much psychological as intellectual. It represented a moment when doubts which had long been troubling him suddenly appeared to resolve themselves and he afterwards looked back on it as a momentous turning-point. But from a historian's point of view it is clear that one should not overemphasise the significance of what was only one incident in his intellectual biography. Equally, it is clear that in order to see Luther's intellectual development in its true perspective it is important not to confuse the problem of the date and significance of his 'tower-experience' with the broader and much more complex problem of the evolution of his reformation theology.

University of London
King's College

THE CHURCH OF ENGLAND
AND THE GREEK CHURCH
IN THE TIME OF CHARLES I

by HUGH TREVOR-ROPER

IT is well known that the church of England, in the time of
Charles I, showed a special interest in the eastern church.
Archbishop Laud patronised Greek and oriental scholarship. As
its chancellor, he enriched Oxford University with Greek and
oriental manuscripts and made plans to print them. He projected a
Greek press at Oxford and achieved one in London. He obliged the
king's printers to print three Greek texts. He also provided the learned
press at Oxford with Arabic type. He then sent qualified scholars to
the Ottoman empire in search of more manuscripts. Meanwhile he
endowed the study of the Hebrew and Arabic tongues.

The impetus behind this patronage was not humanist or scientific:
it was theological. The manuscripts which Laud sought, and the texts
which he published, were religious. He wished to encourage the study
of the Hebrew and Greek scriptures and the Greek fathers. Even his
Arabic interests had the same purpose. The tradition of the Greek
church, in the east, had often passed through Arabic channels. It seemed
reasonable to suppose that the Greek saints, like the Greek philosophers,
might reach the west in an Arab dress.

This new interest in the Greek church was well timed, for Laud's
rule over the English church happened to coincide, not only with the
revival of Greek studies in Oxford,[1] but also with the rule over the
eastern church of an equally energetic Greek archbishop who was
eager to respond to it. Cyril Lucaris, patriarch of Alexandria from 1601
to 1620 and of Constantinople—with dramatic interruptions—from

---

[1] The main centre of Greek studies since the renaissance had been Paris. Although
Henry VIII founded regius chairs at Oxford and Cambridge, the subject can hardly
be said to have flourished at Oxford until the time of Sir Henry Savile, who, as
warden of Merton College and provost of Eton, filled both places with Greek scholars.
His famous edition of St Chrysostom, in eight folio volumes, was printed at Eton
1610–12, and the Greek type, which he had obtained from Holland, was afterwards
presented by him to Oxford University and used for Laud's publications. Till then,
the university had not been equipped to print Greek texts, although it had the use of
a small type, suitable for footnotes, see Harry Carter, *A History of the Oxford University
Press* (Oxford 1975) pp 25, 30.

1620 to 1638, had good reasons to cultivate the protestant churches of the west, and he exchanged letters, gifts and emissaries with both Charles I and Laud. His gifts remain: the *Codex Alexandrinus* of the Greek bible in the British Museum; the Arabic pentateuch and many other manuscripts in the Bodleian library. Thanks to these splendid testimonies of it, and to the tragic fate which engulfed both the giver and the receivers, a special relationship seemed to unite the Greek church, defending itself against Roman aggression, with the high church party in the church of England, which was also (in spite of puritan accusations) anti-Roman. This relationship was emphasised a generation later when the documents were collected, and some of them published, by the Jacobite non-juring scholar, Thomas Smith of Magdalen College, Oxford.[2] The martyred patriarch then joined the martyred primate in the hagiography of high anglicanism.

On the face of it, this is odd, for Cyril Lucaris was certainly no Laudian. Difficult though it is to pin down and label that elusive clerical politician,[3] we can at least say that, in the end, in doctrine and in discipline, his ideas were opposed to those of Laud. Those who ultimately destroyed Laud accused him of deviating from the true faith of Calvin and selling the English church to Rome. Those who ultimately destroyed Cyril were the Romanising party in the Greek church, and they accused him of selling that church to the Calvinists. Both in fact were accused of sectarianism—but in the opposite directions. In order to resolve this difficulty, and to join the two archbishops in a common cause, the high-church defenders of Cyril have had to resort to elaborate interpretations and imputations of forgery.[4] In fact I believe that such

[2] Thomas Smith spent the years 1668–71 in Constantinople as chaplain to the ambassador Sir Daniel Harvey. He wrote, in 1672 and 1676, in Latin, two works which he afterwards translated into English as *Remarks on the Manners, Religion and Government of the Turks, together with a Survey of the Seven Churches of Asia* . . . and *An Account of the Greek Church under Cyril Lucaris with a Relation of his Sufferings and Death.* In 1707 he also published *Collectanea de Cyrillo Lucario.* These works brought him into controversy with the formidable Oratorian biblical scholar Richard Simon. See especially Simon's *Histoire Critique de la Créance . . . des nations du Levant* (Frankfort a/M 1684); *La Créance [de l'Eglise Orientale sur la Transsubstantiation]* (Paris 1687).

[3] The latest attempt to pin him down is [Gunnar] Hering, [*Ökumenisches Patriarchat und Europäische Politik 1620–1638*] Wiesbaden 1968); a work of vast cosmopolitan erudition and fine scholarship. But he remains unpinned, or at least flutters still.

[4] Almost all the crucial documents for the religious beliefs of Cyril Lucaris have been either denounced as forgeries or deliberately ignored by historians whose interpretations they might undermine. Three such documents are (1) Cyril's letter to pope Paul V, of 1608, offering to submit to his authority; (2) Cyril's 'Calvinist' confession of March 1629; (3) Cyril's letter to Bethlen Gabor, prince of Transylvania, of August 1629, repudiating as 'sin' Bethlen's proposal to impose Calvinism on the Orthodox 'Vlakhs'

The church of England and the Greek church

efforts are unnecessary. In this essay I propose to show that they are unnecessary by putting the relations of Laud and Lucaris into their historical context. This entails prior consideration of three determining factors: the Anglican need of historical justification; the ecumenical movement of the time; and the pressures of the thirty years war.

---

of Transylvania. The Greek Orthodox historian, archbishop Chrysostomos Papadopoulos, roundly declares (1) and (2) to be forgeries. See his article on Cyril in Μεγάλη Ἑλληνικὴ Ἐγκυκλοπαιδεία (1939) and his article Ἀπολογία Κυρίλλου τοῦ Λουκάρεως in Νέα Σιών (Jerusalem 1905. The Greek protestant, G. A. Hadjiantoniou ignores (1) and (3), see his Κύριλλος Λούκαρις (Athens 1954), translated as *Protestant Patriarch* (1961). The Jesuit G. Hoffmann regards only (1) as binding. (*Griechische Patriarchen und römische Päpste*, II.i. *Patriarch Kyrillus Lukaris und die römische Kirche*, OCP 17 (1929). Even Hering, who sees Cyril as a determined Calvinist, seems to me to ease his case by paraphrasing (1) and (3) into insignificance. The actual text, in each case, seems to me much stronger than his paraphrase.

In addition to these three fundamental documents, Papadopoulos has produced two further documents which, if genuine, must be allowed to support his case. They are (4) Cyril's 'orthodox' confession of 1629 (Κυρίλλου Λουκάρεως πίναξ ὁμιλιῶν Alexandria 1913) and (5) Cyril's encyclical letter of 1634 repudiating the charge of Calvinism and urging the Greek Christians of Ruthenia to stand fast in their faith. I have not seen the authenticity of these documents challenged, and Papadopoulos explicitly states that (5) has never been challenged. I therefore do not understand why Hering (p 196) says that (3) is 'the one and only document' on which the defenders of Cyril's orthodoxy rely.

Not only do historians differ among themselves: they also differ within themselves. Emile Legrand changed his mind so completely about Cyril after reading 130 privately owned letters which he was not allowed to publish, that he tore up the biographical notice which he had prepared for his *Bib[liographie] Hel[lénique] 17e siècle]*, 4 (1896) and printed his documents without commentary: an act of despair. Mr C. Th. Dimaras tells me that he too changed his mind completely about Cyril between the first and second editions of his Ἱστορία τῆς νεοελληνικῆς λογοτεχνίας; and he adds that the Greek scholar Manuel Gedeon, on discovering new documents, also destroyed what he had written about Cyril.

New documents continue to appear—and old to disappear. The 130 letters seen by Legrand have never been identified. Seven collections of sermons which Hoffmann, in 1940, wrote that he had seen in the Metochion of the Holy Sepulchre at Constantinople have since become invisible. A large volume of Cyril's draft sermons and correspondence—278 letters, mostly early—emerged in 1970 from the vast treasure-house of the Phillipps collection (MS Phillipps 7844). It is now in the Rijksuniversiteitsbibliotheek, Leiden (MS BPG 122), and has been used by Dr Keetje Rozemond for her publication, *Cyrille Lucar, Sermons 1598–1602* (Leiden 1974). The compiler of the MS (who evidently wrote in the early eighteenth century) states that Cyril's correspondence with the Cretan scholar Maximos Margounios, his teacher, who died in 1602, was then preserved in the rich library, in Constantinople, of Nicolas Mavrocordato, prince of Wallachia. The Mavrocordato library was dispersed in the mid-eighteenth century and many of its documents have also disappeared from view; but the correspondence of Cyril and Maximos was in the Metochion of the Holy Sepulchre (MS 463) at the end of the nineteenth century, when it was printed, from a copy, by Legrand, *Bib Hel* 4, ix.

The value of the Greek church as a historical justification of Anglicanism does not need to be emphasised. Roman catholic controversialists regularly denounced the church of England as an upstart church, born of schism. They made the same accusation against the Greek church which had taken the same path a few centuries earlier. To Anglicans, therefore, the Greek church was a natural ally. Moreover, because of its continuous tradition, it was an important ally. The propagandists of the English church claimed for it a continuous history going back to the apostles and by-passing, as a merely marginal episode, the Roman mission of St Augustine of Canterbury; but the earlier part of that history—the stories of Joseph of Arimathea, king Lucius, etc.—were admittedly somewhat fragile. No such weakness could be found in the Greek church whose well-documented early history eclipsed that of Rome by the glory of its fathers, and preceded the Roman claims to primacy.

If the Greek church suffered any weakness in its historical credentials, that was not in its early independence but in its later surrender of that independence. In 1439 the Byzantine emperor, in the agony of his empire, had vainly sought to purchase western aid against the Turks by accepting papal terms and submitting, at the council of Florence, to reunion with Rome. However, on his return to Constantinople, the lower clergy and people had repudiated that union, and it was never effective. The Roman church always insisted on its legal validity, but the protestants naturally, like the conquered Greeks, dismissed it as an abortive event of no significance. Nor was it of any significance—at least for the first century after the fall of the empire. Even in those parts of the empire which were under catholic rule—the Venetian colonies of Crete, the Ionian islands, Cyprus—the union was not enforced.

To the church of England, as to other protestant churches accused of schism, the Greek church was thus an encouraging example, and they naturally wished to see its independence preserved. At first their interest could only be platonic: the parties were separated by distance, had no direct communication, no common language. 'What the Grecians this day think of us', bishop Jewel wrote in his defence of the Anglican church, 'I cannot tell'.[5] In the 1570s tentative discussions took place between the patriarch Jeremiah III and German Lutheran scholars of Tübingen; but these academic interchanges had no lasting effect.

[5] John Jewel, *A defence of the Apology for the Churche of Englande* (1567).

Their most important result was the publication in 1583 of Martin Kraus', or Crusius's, *Turcograecia*: a work of propaganda which drew attention to the plight of Greece under Ottoman rule.

Meanwhile Greece was being threatened from another quarter. In the 1570s the Roman church, having recovered its strength after the shock of the reformation, was striking out to the east as well as to the west. It was now determined to end the eastern schism by enforcing the union of Florence. The foundation of the congregation for the dissemination of the faith in 1573 and of the college of St Athanasius in Rome, for the education or re-education of Greeks, in 1577 were stages in the long campaign, in which the Jesuits were the front-soldiers. Their first victory was in Poland. Under the patronage of the catholic king Sigismund III they established themselves there in strength and wrought havoc among the unprepared heretics of eastern Europe. In 1581-2 they were in Moscow, seeking to detach the Russian church from its eastern allegiance and unite it to Rome. They failed, and would resort, later, to more forcible methods. But meanwhile, in Lithuania, they had achieved a break-through. In 1596, at the second synod of Brest-Litovsk, they set up the new uniate church: a device to split the Greek church and bring it gradually under the control of Rome.

From the second synod of Brest onwards, the counter-reformation catholic church made the pace in the east, and this was the continuing background to the agitated history of the Greek church in the next half-century. In 1606 began the campaign of pope Paul V against the ecclesiastical independence of Venice: a campaign which roused Paolo Sarpi to defend the autonomy not only of the catholic church in Venice but also of the Greek church in its islands. In the following years, the Jesuits resorted to economic warfare: they sought to buy the votes of Greek bishops and so secure the election of 'unionist' patriarchs. After the outbreak of the thirty years war, spiritual and economic aggression would be reinforced by secular arms. Protestantism, already crushed in Poland, was now rooted out of Bohemia. Throughout the 1620s the Habsburg armies drove to victory. Even the entry of France into the war, on the other side, would not weaken the drive against heresy in the east. Richelieu might be the ally and patron of protestants in the west, but in the east he would compete with Austria to serve (and exploit) the imperialism of the Roman church. The French protectorate over the holy places would be at the expense of the independence of the Greek church.

The protestant churches were naturally reluctant spectators of this advance. Fortunately, by now, they too had a presence in the Ottoman empire. By the 1580s the English and Dutch had broken into the Mediterranean and had diplomatic representation in Constantinople. By the 1620s their ambassadors would be prepared to counter catholic intrigues. But before we come to that last stage of the battle, which is well-documented and well known, we must turn to a less familiar subject. This is what I have called the ecumenical movement: the movement, which coincided in time with the relatively peaceful years between 1590 and 1620, to repair and restore the universal church not by total catholic or protestant conquest but by agreement on a rational, Erasmian base. Such agreement looked forward to voluntary reunion of all those distinct national churches, or those parties within such churches, which were opposed to the extreme sectarian policies of counter-reformation Rome and Calvinist Geneva: in other words, the church of England, the 'Gallican' church of France, the moderate huguenots, the 'syncretists' of Germany, the 'Arminians' of Holland—and those earlier 'schismatics', the members of the orthodox Greek church.

The ecumenical movement of the early seventeenth century is one of those 'lost moments of history' which have been recaptured by Dame Frances Yates. It seems very remote now: an interlude between the frontal struggles of catholic and protestant, a last, ineffective dream before the final, painfully won realisation that Christendom was now irremediably plural and must settle, in despair of unity, for a diplomatic balance of power. But at the time its aims seemed not only desirable but attainable. Perhaps, but for the thirty years war, they would have been attained. The movement engaged the best spirits of the time: Richard Hooker, Justus Lipsius, J-A de Thou, Isaac Casaubon, Hugo Grotius, Lancelot Andrewes—and, in their early years, Paolo Sarpi and Cyril Lucaris. Who can say that these men might not have succeeded but for the re-polarisation, the return to fixed postures of extremity, caused by the renewal, in 1618, of ideological war: a war that was not, essentially, a war of ideas (though it drove men into opposite ideological positions), but a struggle for power?

The ecumenical programme was essentially an Erasmian programme, a programme of the centre, of moderate men, of men who were prepared to allow that many of the controversies of religion were over *adiaphora*, things indifferent. It was hated by both Tridentine catholics and stern Calvinists. The basic programme—without explicit ecumenical implications—was set out in England by Hooker. Those implications were drawn out by Hooker's most intimate disciples, George Cranmer and Edwin Sandys.

Cranmer and Sandys, the two friends who, between them, encouraged, financed and guided Hooker's *Laws of Ecclesiastical Polity*, set out together on their foreign travels in 1594. After their return, Cranmer was killed in Ireland; but Sandys wrote down his conclusions in a little book, *A Relation of the State of Religion*, which he presented to archbishop Whitgift in 1599 and which was briefly published in 1605.[6] This book was his considered plan for a reunion of the moderate catholics, moderate huguenots, and Anglicans, at the expense of the extreme Calvinists and the 'papists' of Spain and Italy, and under the presidency of the one national church which, he believed, they would all accept as a model: the historic, continuous church of England as defined by Hooker. In the course of his travels Sandys had not—as he had originally intended—visited the east, and his only direct knowledge of Greek churches was in Venice, where the most ambitious Greeks from Crete and the Ionian islands came for education and employment. But he felt, and expressed, a natural sympathy for men who had preserved the language and literature of the early church, rejected the corruptions of Rome, withstood the monarchy of the pope. Whether enslaved by the Turk, as in the former Byzantine empire, or free, as in Muscovy, the Greek churches were obvious candidates for inclusion in the new universal Anglican church.

The trouble was, the Greek churches, at that time, were so weak. Harassed or seduced in Lithuania and Ruthenia, oppressed and fleeced by their Turkish overlords, torn by the internal dissension of their own bishops, seduced by the new emissaries of Rome, they could not even help themselves, far less give useful help to distant allies. Their only educated clergy, apart from those now processed by the college of St Athanasius in Rome, came from the Venetian colonies. If the Greek church were ever to be raised up again from its fallen state, two things were essential: first education, then political alliances. These two needs were interdependent. Only if the general level of education were raised could the Greek church recover something of its old stature and qualify for alliance, against Roman aggression, with the churches of the west.

---

[6] For its publishing history see Theodore K. Rabb, 'The Editions of Sir Edwin Sandys's *Relation of the State of Religion*', *Huntington Library Quarterly* 26 (1963).

Fortunately, at precisely this time, the Greek church produced its reformer. Cyril Lucaris was a Cretan who had studied in Venice at a time when the church of Venice was defining its position in relation to the aggressive Tridentine policy of Rome. In Venice he had listened to Paolo Sarpi, already collecting material for his great work on the council of Trent, which he regarded as the fatal turning-point in the history of the reformation: the point at which the church of Rome had become sectarian and blocked the possibility of general reform. Then he had returned to Crete. In 1595 he had been sent to Lithuania, where he had vainly resisted the catholic triumph at Brest. By 1601 he was patriarch of Alexandria. There he came, perhaps for the first time, into contact with the protestant west.

One of those who discovered Cyril in Egypt was George Sandys, the younger brother of Edwin Sandys. In 1611 George Sandys fulfilled his brother's frustrated wish and travelled through the Levant. He too studied the state of religion. He particularly noted that although the patriarchs of Constantinople were in general a disreputable lot, the present patriarch of Alexandria, 'the worthy Cyril', was quite different, being 'a man of approved virtue and learning', a restorer of public works for the benefit of the Greeks in Egypt, and 'a friend to the Reformed Religion and opposing the contrary'. 'The differences between us', said this worthy patriarch, 'be but shells, but those are kernels between them and the others'.[7]

George Sandys, like his brother, was an ecumenist: he too believed in a re-united Anglo-catholic church, whose centre would be the church of England. His hero was the great Dutch scholar Hugo Grotius. Sandys would afterwards translate a tragedy of Grotius, and in the 1630s he would join that group of ecumenical admirers of Grotius who gathered to exchange their views at the young Lord Falkland's house at Great Tew.

For Grotius, though chiefly commemorated as a jurist, in fact devoted his whole life to a single, all-consuming ideal: the restoration of the universal church. He saw himself as the heir of his compatriot Erasmus, and he was soon recognised by all the ecumenists as their leader. In order to achieve his aim, he put his faith in the new 'Arminian' party in Holland and in their allies the 'Arminian' clergy in England. As he explained to his friend, the huguenot scholar Isaac Casaubon, now an *emigré* at the court of James I, the first necessity was to call a general council of all those churches which rejected the

[7] George Sandys, *Relation of a Journey begun A.D. 1610* (1615) pp 89, 105.

council of Trent. This council should draw up a public confession, leaving doubtful or indifferent matters in suspense. Then the moderate catholics should be drawn in. This should be possible when they see that good works, decent ceremonies, tradition, etc. are respected. The council should meet in Britain under the presidency of king James. If Casaubon would prepare the king, Grotius would work on the states-general of the Netherlands, then dominated by the Arminian party led by the grand pensionary Jan van Oldenbarnevelt. Invitations to attend the council should be sent to catholics and protestants alike. 'Whether the Churches of Greece and Asia should also be invited, I leave you to consider'.[8]

King James proved difficult to win over, but Grotius did not despair. In 1613 he came to England and, with the approval of Oldenbarnevelt, he worked hard for his cause. His English supporters were Lancelot Andrewes, bishop of Winchester and John Overall, dean of St. Paul's. Unfortunately he made no headway, and had no social success, with the new archbishop, George Abbot. Abbot was a patron of puritans and took a strong dislike to Grotius.

In spite of set-backs, Grotius' plans for reunion went forward. In 1614 he was at work on the French. Two years later, he welcomed an unexpected ally who visited him in the Hague. This was Marcantonio de Dominis, archbishop of Spalato, who in that year ostentatiously abandoned the Roman church, declared himself an Anglican, and set out to make a new career in Jacobean England.

De Dominis also was an ecumenist. His ideas, like those of Cyril Lucaris, had been formed in the Venice of Paolo Sarpi. Coming from Dalmatia, he knew the Greek world well. The motives of his apostasy, and of his later behaviour, were mixed; but of his fundamental ideas there can be no doubt. He expressed them next year in the first part of his book *de Republica Ecclesiastica*. He sent a copy of this book to Cyril in Alexandria. It evidently had some effect there, for ten years later the Jesuits in Constantinople complained that the heresies contained in it were being circulated in the east.[9] In his covering letter to Cyril, de Dominis commiserated with him on the plight of the Greek Christians, oppressed under a new pharaoh; but at least this Turkish pharaoh, he added, left them their religion, unlike the Roman tyrant,

[8] Grotius to Casaubon 7 January 1612. *Briefwisseling van Hugo Grotius*, ed P. C. Moelhuysen (Hague 1921–   ) I, p 219.
[9] Venier to Bailo of Venice, cited in R. J. Roberts, 'The Greek Press at Constantinople in 1627 and its antecedents'. *Bibliographical Society* 1927.

who has brought the western church to the most miserable bondage. That is why de Dominis has escaped to the land of Goshen—that is England—from which he now sends this book defending the rights of patriarchs and reducing the bishop of Rome to his right size; and he ends by urging Cyril to unite the eastern church 'with this most noble and flourishing Church of England'.[10]

Cyril was already in touch both with England and with Holland. His Dutch correspondents were, first, Cornelis Haga, who had visited him while travelling in the east in 1602, and who would afterwards play an important part in his life as Dutch ambassador at Constantinople, and, secondly, through him, Johannes Wtenbogaert, the Dutch theologian with whom the young Grotius had lived, and who was now, like him, an Arminian. Wtenbogaert sent the works of Arminius himself to Cyril, and Cyril declared himself impressed by them.[11] Cyril's English correspondent was archbishop Abbot. It seems that Cyril initiated this correspondence, probably in 1612.[12] Perhaps he was encouraged to do so by his Dutch allies, who at that time, still had hopes of the new primate; or possibly the idea had come from George Sandys. At any rate, Abbot replied suggesting, in the name of king James, that Cyril send a Greek student to study in England.

Cyril grasped the opportunity. When he received the archbishop's letter—which must have been through the English ambassador, Sir Paul Pindar—he was in Constantinople, on the way to Wallachia, Moldavia and Poland, to relieve the Greek Christians there 'who are being harassed by the tyranny of Antichrist and the subtlety and wickedness of the Jesuits'. On his return to the city, in 1615, he wrote effusively to Abbot thanking him for his letter. Above all, he said, he was delighted to hear of the friendly disposition of king James, the platonic philosopher-king whose lively image, carried by the voice of Fame, was firmly painted in the hearts of the Eastern Christians. To Cyril, as to Grotius, as to Marcantonio de Dominis, king James was the saviour in the west, destined to reunite the true church and defend it

[10] PRO MS SP 14/128. English version in [R. Neile], *M. Ant. de Dñis Arch-bishop of Spalato, his shiftings in religion* (1624) pp 85-8.

[11] Cyril to Wtenbogaert 10 Cal Oct. 1613 in *Praestantium ac Eruditorum Virorum Epistolae Ecclesiasticae et Theologicae*, ed Ph. Limborch (Amsterdam 1684) p 314.

[12] The earliest surviving letter is that of 1615 which I quote here from Bodl MS Smith 36 fol 13. (It is printed by Timotheus Themelis in Νέα Σιών 6 1909); but the previous interchange which it presupposes carries the correspondence back to 1612, when Cyril was in Constantinople as ἐπιτηρητής of the patriarchate, and Sir Paul Pindar reported his struggle against the Jesuits there (MS Smith 36 fol 32).

against those enemies who were trying to pervert it from the
Pauline model. In the east, the immediate need was a learned clergy:
'our clergy', Cyril went on, 'through ignorance, are forcibly silent,
and in the words of the Prophet, "I, even I only, am left".' But what
could he do alone? He could not be everywhere at once; even now,
he was hurrying back to his duties in Egypt; thence he would send
those whom he thought most fit to be educated in England and serve
the church.

In the same year, 1615, another Greek prelate wrote to archbishop
Abbot. This was Gabriel Severus, a well-known literary champion of
Greek orthodoxy. He too was a graduate of the university of Padua.
Forty years ago he had been consecrated as archbishop of Philadelphia
in Asia Minor; but in spite of the pleas of the clergy and people of that
diocese, he preferred—as who would not?—to live in Venice; and there
he stayed, for the rest of his life, as 'exarch' of the Greek church in
Venice and Dalmatia, collecting Greek manuscripts, corresponding
with western scholars, and assisting Sir Henry Savile with his great
edition of Chrysostom.[13] In his letter to Abbot, this epicurean and
sedentary old scholar showed at least a certain imaginary mobility.
He sighed for the wings of a dove to fly to his fellow-archbishop and
discuss not vain philosophy but the pure doctrine of Christ. However,
since intervening seas and mountains made that impossible,[14] he was
writing (he said) to send a pledge of his devotion and to urge upon his
distant colleague 'the union of the Holy Church of Christ, its true
children and its uncorrupted members'. We do not know what
response he elicited.

Meanwhile Cyril pursued his journey to Alexandria. Thence he
sent his first and most famous student to England. This was Metro-
phanes Critopoulos, a young monk whom he had picked up, in the
course of his journey, from a monastery on Mount Athos, and who
would end as patriarch of Alexandria. When Critopoulos arrived in
England, Abbot sent him to Oxford, to his own old college, Balliol.[15]

[13] See Savile's epistle to the Reader, in *S. Ioannis Chrysostomi Opera* (Eton 1610) 1.
[14] 'μεγάλοις γὰρ πελάγεσιν, ὡς εἰπεῖν, καὶ οὔρεσι μακροῖς εἰργούμεθα'. The learned archbishop
knew his Homer. The letter is in MS Smith 36 fol 33 and is dated January 1615. Thirty-
one of Gabriel's Greek MSS were brought for the Ambrosiana by cardinal Borromeo;
others are now in the Biblioteca Nazionale in Turin. Some of his works were published in Greek in Venice and would be cited by Richard Simon as evidence that the
Greek Church was doctrinally Roman Catholic—see his *Fides Ecclesiae Orientalis* (Paris
1674). On Gabriel see M. Jugie's article in *DTC* 6, and the same writer's essay in *EO* 16
(1913).
[15] On Critopoulos see especially his 'Confession', published in E. J. Kimmel, *Monumenta*

He was the first of several young Greeks whom Cyril would send to England. The last would be the Cretan, Nathaniel Conopius, who would come to Oxford in 1638, after witnessing the murder of his master, and whom Laud would similarly send to Balliol. He would be remembered as the first man to drink coffee—presumably Turkish coffee—in Oxford.

It was in 1617 that Critopoulos came to England and in the same year that de Dominis published the first part of his book. At this date it is convenient to pause and consider the whole world of the ecumenists. For this was the intellectual world of William Laud. It was also a world which was shattered before he rose to power in the English church.

The essential fact is that none of these men, with the exception of archbishop Abbot, whom Cyril Lucaris had most probably approached in view of his office rather than of his personality, could be described as puritan in any sense. All were conservative protestants seeking accommodation with moderate catholics on an Erasmian base. They were as hostile to extreme Calvinists as to 'papists'. In Holland, they were the 'Arminians', Wtenbogaert and Grotius; in England, after the Anglican Hooker and his disciples, they were the 'Arminian' clergy, Andrewes and Overall; in France, if not Gallican catholics, they were 'Arminian' huguenots like Casaubon or Pierre Daillé or Jean Hotman and Daniel Tilenus of Sedan, the friends of Grotius. Paolo Sarpi in Venice was a catholic friar; Marcantonio de Dominis was a catholic archbishop. Gabriel Severos was very critical of Lutheranism and accepted some kind of belief in transsubstantiation.[16] Cyril Lucaris himself came from the same school: though bitterly opposed to papal aggression in Poland, he would waver towards the catholic church and would even, in 1608—under what precise stress we do not know—offer his submission to Rome. Critopoulos, the disciple whom he sent to England, was, and would remain, a reunionist: he would quarrel with the puritanical archbishop Abbot on that count and leave England under something of a cloud at Lambeth.[17] Later events might

Fidei Ecclesiae Orientalis (Jena 1850), and the biography by M. Renieres, Μητροφάνης Κριτόπουλος καὶ οἱ ἐν ᾿Αγγλίᾳ καὶ Γερμανίᾳ φίλοι αὐτοῦ *1617–28* (Athens 1893). Further documents are in *Bib Hel* 5 pp 192–218. I am grateful to the Revd Colin Davey for allowing me to see his unpublished essay on Critopoulos.

[16] See Simon, *La Créance*.

[17] Abbot's complaint against Critopoulos was outwardly over his return journey: he wanted him to return direct by sea but Critopoulos insisted on going by land—and on trying to scrounge money for the purpose. Abbot's letters to Roe on this subject are

alter men's lives and thoughts, but in 1617 the advocates of alliance between east and west were not necessarily anti-catholic or puritan. Those in the west were Anglo-catholic, 'Arminian', Gallican, Erasmian. Those in the east were as yet uncommitted: for it must be emphasised that the doctrines of the Greek church had not yet been adjusted to the fierce but quisquiliary controversies of the western reformation and counter-reformation.

However, the conservative ideas which united these men depended on one necessary condition: the continuation of peace in Europe. In this too they were the heirs of Erasmus. Just as the outbreak of ideological war, by driving men into opposite postures, had destroyed the original Erasmian *via media*, so this new ecumenism, which had only been revived in the years of peace in the early 17th century, could not survive the renewal of such war. So, when the war-clouds gathered in 1618, Grotius and his 'Arminian' friends were accused of 'appeasement'; and indeed there was some truth in the charge. Irenism in the church could take root only if there was peace in the world. War would turn Erasmus into Calvin.

In fact there was to be no peace. In 1618, as the great crisis approached, the representatives of international protestantism met in general council. It was the synod of Dordt. The ecumenists had long advocated a general council which would prepare the basis of reunion and undo the schism forced upon Christendom by the perverted and sectarian council of Trent. But this was not such a council. At Dordt, favoured by events, the war-party seized the initiative. There was revolution in the Netherlands. The Arminians were routed. Oldenbarnevelt was executed, Grotius thrown into prison. Wtenbogaert had already fled abroad. Their whole international party, such as it was, crumbled. Some of its members, like Peter Bertius and the son

published in *The Negotiations of Sir Thomas Roe in his Embassy to the Ottoman Porte 1621–8* (1740) pp 102, 251. There may have been a deeper reason for Abbot's resentment. Critopoulos, by the friends whom he had made in England and by the visits which he was to make in Europe, sufficiently showed his 'Arminian', irenist views. In England, apart from Patrick Young, the king's librarian (who was known as 'the Patriarch of the Greeks', being their general patron in London), his chief friend was Meric Casaubon, the son of Isaac Casaubon, who was at Christ Church, Oxford, while Critopoulos was at Balliol. Critopoulos' correspondence with him is in BM MS Burney 369 fols 48–64. His correspondence with Young is in Bodl MS Smith 38 and is printed in J. Kemke, *Patricius Junius* (Leipzig 1898) pp 124 *seq.* On his return journey, Critopoulos was entertained in Hamburg by the family of Lucas Holstenius, the Vatican librarian; stayed in Helmstedt with the reunionist George Calixtus and in Strasbourg with Grotius' friend Matthias Bernegger; and preached general reunion at Berne and Geneva (*Bib Hel* 5 pp 202–8).

of Wtenbogaert, surrendered to the catholic church. Marcantonio de Dominis returned to Rome, to recant and die in a papal prison. Others, to avoid that fate, moved over to radicalism. Paolo Sarpi, Sir Henry Wotton, Sir Edwin Sandys became supporters of the hard line of protestantism. Sarpi and his friends had already moved in that direction under the pressure of events in Venice. Even king James now suspended his pacifism; for his daughter's inheritance was at stake. In such circumstances, the idea of an international *via media* leading peacefully to a restored universal church was clearly a chimera. And in the east, Cyril Lucaris saw that, once war had broken out, there was only one possible ally against the pressure of counter-reformation Rome. It was international Calvinism.

Cyril had already discovered the works of Calvin and had been feeling his way towards a protestant definition of the still undefined area of Greek doctrine. But now he moved further. It was in 1617–18 that he made the acquaintance of the Dutch councillor of state David Wilhelm le Leu and, through the Calvinist books supplied by him, was brought over to a firmly Calvinist position. He would become in the words of the English ambassador, 'a pure Calvinist', 'in religion a direct Calvinist; yet he dare not show it'.[18]

No doubt is was Calvinism with a difference: Greco-Calvinism. Cyril was no more willing to subject the Greek church to foreign Calvinist than to foreign catholic control. However low it had now sunk, however drastically it needed to be reformed, it must still preserve its historic identity. It was the church of St Basil and St John Chrysostom and all the great early fathers. When the Calvinist prince of Transylvania suggested that the Vlakh peasants under his rule should be absorbed into his Calvinist church, and gave sound political reasons for such a change—it would raise the level of education, it would strengthen his protestant state, the sultan had no objection, it could be done secretly, the patriarch need only stop his ears and shut his eyes as the prophet recommends (Is. XXX 15)— Cyril would repudiate the proposal indignantly. Calvinism, he agreed, was a Christian, not a pagan, religion; but it differs materially from the faith professed by the eastern church, and to support such a change, openly or secretly, would be a sin which all earthly torments would not wipe away . . . However, within this historic church, and in order to restore its power and renew its vitality, a new spirit was needed, and that spirit, he believed, must come from Calvinism. An injection

[18] *Negotiations of Sir Thomas Roe*, pp 36, 102.

of Calvinist doctrine was necessary if the Greek Church was to preserve its identity against the otherwise irresistible onslaught of the Tridentine catholic church.[19]

For the next twenty years, the Greek church, under the lead of Cyril Lucaris and the impulse of events, was dragged into European politics—the desperate, unscrupulous politics of the thirty years' war. On one side, the 'uniate' Greek bishops, headed by Cyril Contaris, metropolitan of Beroea (Aleppo), were manipulated by the French and Austrian ambassadors, on instructions from the congregation *de Propaganda Fide* in Rome. On the other side were the English ambassador, Sir Thomas Roe, an old interventionist, devoted to the cause of the dispossessed princess Palatine, queen of Bohemia, and the Dutch ambassador, Cyril's old friend Cornelis Haga. In 1620 Cyril was elected patriarch of Constantinople. The election, significantly, took place in the Dutch embassy. His reign would be stormy. In the next eighteen years he would be four times deposed and four times restored. He would be exiled to Rhodes or Tenedos after each Austro-French *coup* and brought back after each Anglo-Dutch *counter-coup*. Theoretically, deposition and election were the work of the Greek bishops; but all knew who pulled the strings. Already the rotten Turkish empire was dominated by foreign ambassadors. As Roe would write, after one of Cyril's depositions, there was no cause for alarm: the deposition would not last: it had been the work of the grand vizier—that is, of the French embassy working through the grand vizier—but the grand vizier could be removed and 'I am confident to restore him'—as he soon did.[20]

For seven years Roe and Haga sustained Cyril against his enemies. Then, in 1628, Roe was replaced, and Cyril became increasingly dependent on the Dutch. It was a crucial year. Roe's departure was a great loss—the loss of a stabilising influence. In the same year Laud obtained effective domination over the English church. Meanwhile, the thirty years war was coming to its climax: Wallenstein was on the Baltic shore and a new protestant power was looming in the east. Like so many others, Cyril would soon be looking with fascination

[19] Cyril's letter to Bethlen Gabor, in Latin, is printed in *Török-Magyarkori Történelmi Emlékek* 4 (Pest 1869) pp 137–40. Hering (pp 196–9) seems to me unreasonably to attenuate its force—and indeed to distort its meaning. He suggests that Cyril's objections were purely political. Cyril himself is quite explicit that they are not: 'non licet enim nobis ob terrena bona, etiam si illa maxima forent, fidem nostram politicis rationibus immolare; salus enim animae praecellit salutem terrenam'.

[20] *Negotiations of Sir Thomas Roe*, p 146.

towards the power of Sweden.[21] Meanwhile, the Dutch ambassador would apply to Geneva for a sound Calvinist minister to serve the patriarch as assistant and amanuensis. So from a remote valley in Piedmont there would come to Constantinople the man who was to be the *âme damnée* of the patriarch: the Calvinist enthusiast whose hand must be seen in Cyril's most dramatic gesture—his Calvinist confession of 1629, published in Latin and Greek, for east and west— Antoine Léger.[22]

It was a radical change from the old, pre-1618 days, and no man felt it more strongly than the one man who, in the general débâcle, remained consistently true to his old ideas, Hugo Grotius. In 1620, in prison in the castle of Louvestein, Grotius wrote, in Dutch, a little work of devotion which was afterwards, in its Latin form, to be a best-seller. This was his *de Veritate Religionis Christianae*, which would be for the seventeenth century what Erasmus' *Enchiridion Militis Christiani* had been for the sixteenth: an expression of rational religious philosophy for all believers, catholic and protestant alike. To Grotius, looking around him at the wreck of his hopes, Marcantonio de Dominis would be a disappointment: by his inconstancy and weakness, he had let the cause down. But Cyril was far worse: a deserter, a traitor, who had gone actively over to the opposite enemy. To him Grotius would be merciless: even after his martyrdom, he would hate him.

It is against this background, this radical change of circumstances, that we must see the attitude of Laud towards the eastern church. Moulded in the 'Arminian' tradition of Hooker and Andrewes, Laud had imbibed ecumenical views and oriental interests. He was not a *dévot* of ecumenism like Grotius, or himself an oriental scholar like Andrewes, and his intellectual views were narrowed by his somewhat insular mentality and experience, and his practical realism. But he was

---

[21] For Cyril's courting of Sweden see the letters to Gustavus Adolphus printed in *Monumenta Pietatis et Literaria Virorum illustrium selecta* (Frankfurt a/M 1702); also [Pericles] Zerlentes, [Κυρίλλου τοῦ Λουκάρεως πρὸς Ἀλέξιον Ὀξενστίερναν ἐπιστολαί] in Δελτίον τῆς ἱστορικῆς καὶ ἐθνολογικῆς ἑταιρίας τῆς Ἑλλάδος 6 (Athens 1901) pp 88–93. These letters are of 1632, but the contact began earlier: the imperial ambassador stated, in 1643, that, on his arrival in Constantinople in 1629, he had found that Cyril not only favoured Calvinism and the Dutch 'sondern selber auch Correspondenz und intelligenza hielte mit dem schwedischen König Gustavo, diesen für der Orientalisch Griechische Kirchen defensor und protector erkannte und aussruffte'. Eudoxius Hurmuzaki, *Documente privitore la Historia Romanilor IV 1600–46* (Bucharest 1882) pp 682–91. Compare also *Rikskanseleren Axel Oxenstjernas Skrifter och Brefvexeling*, I (Stockholm 1918) pp 200–1.

[22] For Léger see Samuel Baud-Bovy, 'Antoine Léger, pasteur aux vallées vaudoises du Piédmont et son séjour à Constantinople' in *Revue d'Histoire Suisse* 24 (1944).

prepared to envisage union even with Rome, if Rome should be 'other than she is now'—that is, if she would go back beyond the council of Trent; he spoke fairly of true intellectual reunionists and evidently admired Marcantonio de Dominis' book;[23] and he defended the Greek church as a true church against Bellarmine and other Roman catholics. In 1622, in his conference with the Jesuit John Fisher, Laud explicitly dealt with the position of the Greek church. It might err in particulars, like the Procession of the Holy Ghost, he said, but its foundations were sound. 'It was wrong to condemn so ample and large a Church as the Greek, especially so as to make them no Church. Heaven's gates were not so easily shut against multitudes when St Peter wore the keys at his own girdle'.[24] Several years later, a Laudian clergyman who admired the Greek church and wrote copiously in its support, Ephraim Pagitt, would send to Cyril Lucaris and all the eastern patriarchs 'a learned treatise written in defence of your Church by the most reverend William Lord Archbishop of Canterbury'.[25]

These and such ideas brought Laud to the attention of Grotius. In August 1622, three months after the conference with Fisher, hearing that Laud was the rising star among the English Arminians, Grotius sent messages to him and was told that Laud was very anxious to know him.[26] They corresponded periodically thereafter, and communicated also through third parties: Francis Junius, Meric Casaubon, and Grotius' friend, G. J. Vossius.

However, by 1628, when he came effectively to power, Laud knew well enough that all these ecumenical ideals were chimerical. In the

---

[23] Laud himself was reticent about de Dominis, but his chaplain Peter Heylin, who expressed his views, is remarkably sympathetic to de Dominis' intellectual position and describes his *de Republica Ecclesiastica* as a book 'never yet answered by the papists, and perhaps unanswerable' (*Cyprianus Anglicus*, 1668, p 108).

[24] Laud, *Works* (1847–60) 2 pp 27, 29, 385.

[25] BM MS Harl 825 contains Pagitt's letters to Cyril and other Greek and Russian patriarchs, as well as to Polish and Transylvanian protestant magnates. He sent them copies of his own book, *Christianographie or the Description of the Multitude and sundry sorts of Christians in the World not subject to the Pope, with their Unitie and how they agree with us in the principall points of difference between us and the Church of Rome* (1635), most of which is devoted to the Greek church, and also of the Anglican prayer book in Greek, as well as Laud's treatise. The treatise may have been Laud's conference with Fisher as published (pseudonymously) in 1624, and explicitly praised by Pagitt in *Christianographie* (p 119). In his book, which is dedicated to the Arminian bishop of Ely, Francis White, Pagitt refers to Laud as 'my honourable patron' and cites Sir Edwin Sandys' *Relation*. This places him in the 'Arminian', ecumenical camp, although later, at the age of seventy, he would take the covenant and support the presbyterian church as a bulwark against the sects which he catalogued in his *Heresiographie* (1645).

[26] *Briefwisseling van Hugo Grotius*, 2 p 240 (Franciscus Junius to Grotius, August 1622).

midst of the thirty years war, with the counter-reformation victorious throughout Europe, and international Calvinism the only common voice of resistance, the ecumenical dream had vanished, and Laud had no time for a lost world. It was in vain that Grotius, now Swedish ambassador in Paris, called upon him to repair the torn and dispersed body of Christ, in vain that he begged to be allowed to come from France to see him, not only on official Swedish matters but on other more private affairs—that is, undoubtedly, reunion of the churches.[27] Laud's messages to him became more and more perfunctory. He returns his compliments, praises his learning, regrets that he has no time to write back, will do what he can. He protests that it is quite out of the question to invite Grotius to England: 'as things stand here, it is un-thinkable'. He has received his poems and wishes he had time to read them[28] . . . As for the Calvinist International, which had reasserted itself and replaced the ecumenical alliance, that, of course, he repudiated altogether. He cut the church of England off from the foreign pro-testants, drove out the French and Dutch Calvinist communities, disowned the huguenot congregation in Paris, declined to countenance the candidature of Sir Thomas Roe as secretary of state, and poured cold water on the purely protestant reunionism of John Dury. He lived in a practical world. If the old programme of a universal Erasmian church was impossible, he would fall back on a more limited programme: Arminianism in one country.

That meant that there was no longer any need for immediate practical relations with the Greek church. Laud had inherited several links with that church. From his intellectual predecessors in the Arminian party he had inherited the idea of full co-operation with an ancient church, equally continuous. From his immediate predecessor in the see of Canterbury he had inherited a correspondence with the patriarch based on their common protestantism. Sir Thomas Roe was an old personal friend.[29] He had close personal relations with the great merchants of the Levant Company—Sir Paul Pindar, who advanced money to the crown and Daniel Harvey, who advised him in matters

---

[27] *Briefwisseling van Hugo Grotius* 5 pp 363-4 (Grotius to Laud), p 485 (Grotius to Axel Oxenstjerna).

[28] G. J. *Vossii . . . Epistolae* (1690) ep 158, Laud, *Works*, 6, pp 297, 299, 446. Laud's phrase, 'ut nunc res sunt apud nos, de ea re ne cogitandum quidem', shows an almost panic desire to avoid a visit from Grotius. Perhaps he was remembering Marcantonio de Dominis.

[29] Lady Roe was the daughter of Laud's first patron, Sir Thomas Cave of Stanford, Northants. On her return from the east, she brought him a cat from Smyrna.

of finance.[30] Decency required that these old links be not brutally snapped. Cyril Lucaris, in his search for allies, continued to cultivate an English alliance. He had planned to send the Codex Alexandrinus to James I: on hearing of the king's death, he re-addressed it to his successor. He sent the Arabic pentateuch to Laud, with a personal inscription.[31] He even sent his notorious 'Calvinist' confession of faith to Charles I.[32] But these courtesies implied no political or religious solidarity. That had evaporated with the ecumenical idea.

However, after the evaporation, there remained one small solid deposit. If the present Greek church was too weak to sustain the burden imposed upon it by the Arminian ecumenists in the years of peace, and was seduced by Calvinist politicians and Calvinist preachers in the years of war, at least the primitive Greek church remained as the model of an independent, continuous episcopal church, and the Anglican church of Laud, which looked back to that model, could become the repository, and the publisher, of its sacred texts. In the confusion of the thirty years war, cities were being sacked and monasteries pillaged, and there was a busy traffic in the spoils. The great collectors had their agents in Italy and the East. Laud was determined that the university of Oxford, the intellectual capital of his church, should profit from these opportunities, and he entered the competition. What he wanted was manuscripts, the documents of the church. He had his agents in Germany. He secured a monastic library from Würzburg, sacked by the Swedes. But the great opportunities, he believed, were in the Greek monasteries. There the documents of an independent church might be found; and since all things among the Greeks, including the patriarchates, were for sale, it could be no sin to buy them up. If the Greek church were to go down, swallowed up by Rome or seduced to Calvinism, at least its ancient manuscripts could be saved by its true heir, the church of England.

[30] For Laud and Daniel Harvey see Clarendon, *Life* (1760) 1 p 17. Daniel Harvey also acquired MSS—presumably oriental MSS—for Laud in 1638. See Dr R. W. Hunt's introduction to H. O. Coxe, *Bodleian Library Quarto Catalogues II Laudian Manuscripts*, reprint of 1973, p xxxiii. He was the brother of the great Dr Harvey. His son, Sir Daniel, would be ambassador in Constantinople 1668.

[31] The volume is now Bodleian Library MS Laud Or 258. The inscription, in Cyril's hand, is in both Greek and Latin: 'Cyrillus oecumenicus Patriarcha beatissimo et sapientissimo Archiepiscopo Cantuariensi Gulielmo Laud dono mittit praesentem librum in signum charitatis fraternae'.

[32] An apparently autograph MS of Cyril's confession, in Greek and Latin, is in the Bodleian Library (MS Bodley 12). It is a presentation copy, stamped with the royal arms of Great Britain. It had belonged to Thomas Smith, who had acquired it from a London bookseller after the restoration. Presumably it had left the royal library during the interregnum.

In the early seventeenth century, with the establishment of factories and embassies in the Ottoman empire, the collectors of the west had moved in. Already, by 1624, great hauls had been made. In that year, when the agent of the greatest of Jacobean virtuosi, the earl of Arundel, arrived—to be followed, hot-foot, by that of his upstart competitor, the duke of Buckingham—the English ambassador was sceptical. 'I doubt he shall find little worthy of his pains in those rude parts', he wrote, (for Mr Petty was scouring Smyrna and Milo), 'where barbarism hath spitefully trodden out all worthy relicques of Antiquity. Some few medals or coynes he may fynd rarely; but books have been so often visited that I think Duck-lane is better furnished than the Greek Church'. The only means of making bargains now, he added, was through the patriarch: he alone had the key to the real treasures of the church; and he suggested, not obscurely, that his own excellent relations with the patriarch could usefully be exploited. Would archbishop Abbot (for he was writing to him) send a personal letter to the patriarch to acknowledge 'his many favours and courtesies to me'? This would help 'my purpose of collecting Greek authors that are lost to us and not in print; of which the Patriarch is able richly to store England, and hath thereunto a good inclination'. 'This rich merchandise', he added, could easily be got with a little encouragement.

The encouragement which the patriarch most needed was printed books for the edification of his clergy, and the capacity to print suitable books for distribution in the east. This had always been a problem in the Greek church which had never known the art of printing: for the Turks would not allow that infernal machinery in their empire. Cyril's predecessors had sought to obtain printed texts in Greek from Venice and elsewhere,[33] and Cyril himself was continually begging for books from the west. Already Abbot had sent him, by the hand of Crito-poulos, 'many of the best Greek authors, and among them Chrysos-tom's eight tomes'—that is, Sir Henry Savile's great edition of the most famous of the Greek fathers.[34] Now Roe was suggesting a formal system of exchange: the patriarch was to receive a regular supply of printed books in return for a regular contribution of Greek manu-scripts. While waiting for the archbishop to respond, the ambassador

[33] J. J. Scaliger, who died in 1609, referred to these attempts: '*Graeci non habent typographiam in Graecia . . . vetitum est quidquam excudi sub Turca . . .* tant s'en faut qu'il y ait aujourd'huy des livres en Grèce que le Patriarche de Constantinople en envoye querir. Il n'y a pas long temps qu'il demandoit un Joseph', *Scaligerana* (Cologne 1667) p 98, sv *Graeci*.

[34] *Negotiations of Sir Thomas Roe* p 171.

thoughtfully lubricated the system on his own account. He presented
to the patriarch Paolo Sarpi's *History of the Council of Trent*: a work,
he explained, which illustrated to the life the arts, frauds and tricks of
the papists; and he added that the patriarch would further the same
good cause if he would ease the discovery of the books and manuscripts *quae plura latent in librariis vestris.*[35]

Archbishop Abbot took the ambassador's hint. He undertook to write
personally to the patriarch. 'I do marvellous well like of your trafficking
with him for his Greek copies, which there do no good, and may serve
for singular use here', he wrote; and he promised to send 'a good library
of books'. So the traffic began. It was no longer a mere interchange of
compliments: it was a systematic trade. Before long Roe boasted that
he had acquired through the patriarch 'the jewel of his library', an
Arabic manuscript of the first councils, and had been able to introduce
Arundel's agent 'into the best library known of Greece, where are
loads of old manuscripts', of which, 'with the help of my servants' he
abstracted twenty-two. Then came the Codex Alexandrinus: 'what
estimation it may be of', reported Roe, 'is above my skill; but he values
it as the greatest antiquity of the Greek Church'. The patriarch was by
this time deeply involved in his programme of Calvinist reform and
was prepared to part with anything. He promised Roe that before
leaving Constantinople 'I shall see what he hath, and take my choice
freely'. Then the ambassador added darkly, 'There is another business
intimated to me from the patriarch, which I dare not mention, for
his sake, without a cypher; which may bring a treasure of books into
the protection of His Majesty, and which some other states have sought;
whereof I will find means to advertise Your Grace by some safe way'.[36]
This other business was the patriarch's plan to solve his problem by
setting up a Greek press in Constantinople itself.

The Greek press was duly brought from London to Constantinople
in 1627. It created a diplomatic storm in Constantinople, and enabled
Roe to secure the expulsion of the Jesuits, who had overplayed their
hand. However, they soon returned: the press it was which went[37].
So far, therefore, the Jesuits had won. However, their triumph was
short-lived. When Roe left the city in 1628, they looked with horror
on his great haul of manuscripts, carried away under their noses 'with
the knowledge and consent of the schismatical anti-Roman Patriarch'.

---

[35] *Ibid* pp 319, 334, 414, 442.
[36] *Ibid* pp 459, 500, 618.
[37] For the Greek press, see especially the essay by R. J. Roberts cited above, note 9.

Their report (which greatly exaggerated the haul) caused horror in Rome too. The pope's nephew, cardinal Barberini, a great collector himself, was most upset. So was the librarian of the Vatican. Heretics from the ends of the earth, they complained, were carrying off the treasures of Greece which ought, of course, to have gone to Rome. First the Arundel marbles, now these Greek manuscripts, not to speak of the great Barocci collection of two hundred and forty Greek manuscripts, mainly patristic, recently sold in Venice and bought in London by the earl of Pembroke, and the incomparable art-gallery of the duke of Mantua, secretly swiped by Charles I . . .[38]

Abbot had handled the correspondence, but it was Laud who received the spoils. By the end of 1627 the archbishop was a back number. Stripped of his jurisdiction, confined to his private house in Kent, he was powerless to delay any longer the omnipotence of Laud. It was to Laud, as the instigator of the purchase, that the earl of Pembroke handed over the Barocci collection. Almost at the same time, Roe's manuscripts were brought in and were also given to Laud. It was Laud who sent the two collections down to Oxford in May 1629. They had been catalogued by two of Laud's scholarly assistants, the Grecian Augustine Lindsell and the orientalist Peter Turner—names which recur in the history of Laud's patronage of learning. Augustine Lindsell, afterwards bishop of Hereford, was the most learned of the Laudian bishops. He collected Greek manuscripts and was editor-in-chief of the Greek texts to be published by Laud's Greek press at Oxford. Peter Turner, fellow of Merton College, was a versatile and worldly don—'a thorough-paced mathematician . . . a most curious critic, a politician, statesman and what not'—who dazzled mere college codgers by his grand acquaintance and political influence. He was (says one such codger, from his own college) 'of a proud, haughty mind, because of his great parts and intimate acquaintance with archbishop Laud and the great heroes of that time'. Indeed, he was so 'much beloved of archbishop Laud, and so highly valued by him', that he could have been secretary of state or clerk of the privy council; but he preferred to stay in his college, 'entertaining hopes of being Warden thereof'.[39]

Thus already, in Abbot's time, Laud was thoroughly familiar with the means of acquiring Greek (and other) manuscripts. When he be-

[38] Lucas Holstenius to Peiresc, cited by W. D. Macray, *Annals of the Bodleian Library* (1890) p 73.
[39] A. Wood, *Athenae Oxonienses*, ed Bliss 3 p 306.

came archbishop he continued, in this at least, the policy of his predecessor. But he also carried it further, Abbot had been prepared to
receive manuscripts as payment for books, but Laud, by setting up a
Greek printing-press, proposed to convert the manuscripts which he
thus obtained into the printed texts which, in turn, would pay for
them.[40] This could be an ideological service to the Anglican church.
It was also (provided that they agreed on the texts) precisely what Cyril
wanted for the Greek church. By sending his manuscripts to England
to be printed, he was using Laud's Greek press as the unofficial
printing-house for his own church. Or rather, as one of such
printing-houses: for he was using others too. In 1632 he would send
a manuscript commentary on the Book of Job to the king of Sweden.
It was a complimentary present, but the ulterior purpose was
explicitly stated. Cyril suggested that the king submit the work to his
theologians and, if they agree, have it printed for distribution in the
east, where it would be very welcome.[41]

When Laud became archbishop in 1633, Roe had left Constantinople, but his successor, Sir Peter Wych, entered into the game. Meanwhile Laud had discovered two new agents. These were Edward
Pococke and John Greaves.[42] Laud had already used the services of
Pococke as a collector of Greek and oriental manuscripts and coins
when he was chaplain to the English factory at Aleppo from 1631 to
1636. Greaves was a fellow of Merton College, who had been brought
to his notice by the Merton activist Peter Turner, and had spent two
years in Italy, probably on Laud's account. Like Turner, he was an
orientalist, a mathematician, and an out-and-out royalist and Laudian.

In 1636 both Greaves and Pococke were back in Oxford, where
Laud appointed Pococke as his first professor of Arabic. Then both set
out to Constantinople, Pococke to perfect his knowledge of Arabic,
Greaves to make astronomical and geographical observations. They

---

[40] In planning his Greek press Laud explicitly stated that it was 'for the printing of the
library manuscripts'—that is, the manuscripts which he had given, or would give, to
the Bodleian Library.

[41] Cyril to Axel Oxenstjerna 1/11 July 1632, quoted by Zerlentes. The Codex
Alexandrinus sent to Charles I also included a series of commentaries on Job, and these
were specially printed, on Laud's orders, for the patriarch (see my *Archbishop Laud*,
p 275). It looks as if Cyril was particularly anxious to provide the Greek church with
commentaries on Job—no doubt a valuable text for a suffering church.

[42] For Pococke see L. Twells, 'The Life of Dr. Edward Pococke' prefixed to the
The Theological Works of the learned Dr. Pococke (1740); for Greaves, Thomas Smith,
Vita . . . Johannis Gravii (1699) reprinted in his *Vitae Quorundam Eruditissimorum et
Illustrium Virorum* (1707), and T. Birch, *Miscellaneous Works of John Greaves* (1737),
preface.

had letters from the archbishop and a full power to buy manuscripts at whatever price they thought fit. Naturally they found their way to the patriarch. The patriarch, as ever, was obliging. Laud had particularly instructed them—on the advice of archbishop Ussher—'Greece having been so often gleaned', to 'see what Mount Athos will afford you';[43] and the patriarch, learning of 'His Grace's honourable designs in the edition of Greek authors', was eager to help. He granted Greaves, as the more adventurous traveller, free access to all the monasteries of Mount Athos; authorised him to examine and catalogue their manuscripts; and having genially dispensed the monks from 'the anathemas which former Patriarchs have laid upon all Greek libraries, thereby to preserve the books from the Latins', bade him godspeed as he prepared to take ship for the Holy Mountain.

Unfortunately, this liberal gesture came too late. Before Greaves could set sail, the enemies of the patriarch achieved their master-stroke. They persuaded the sultan that the capture, two years ago, by the Don Cossacks, of the fort of Asad on the sea of Azov—a painful stab in the back during the Persian war—had been organised by the patriarch in alliance with the czar of Muscovy. The sultan did not wait for evidence. This time Cyril was not exiled to Rhodes or Tenedos. He was arrested, strangled, and his body thrown into the Sea of Marmara. His old enemy, the Romanising Cyril of Beroea, returned in triumph to the throne from which he had twice been deposed. He would only last a year, but it would be long enough in which to be revenged on his enemies and to repay his friends: he submitted to the church of Rome.

This dramatic revolution in the Greek church was naturally felt as a great blow in the protestant west. It was also a blow to Greaves and Laud. But for it, the remaining manuscripts of Mount Athos would now be in Oxford, protected by the stricter anathemas of the Bodleian Library. As it was, Greaves not only had to abandon his proposed expedition: he also had to surrender some of his previous gains. 'For fear of worse inconvenience', as he put it, he found it

---

[43] As Greaves put it, 'Forsan quod in Byzantio desideramus, Athos suppeditabit' (Smith, *Vita Gravii*, 8). The valuable MSS in the monasteries of Mount Athos, and the illiteracy and indifference of their monkish custodians, had been remarked by George Sandys, *Relation of a Journey*, p 64. On the other hand Pierre Belon, who had visited the monasteries half a century earlier, had found that there was nothing of value there (*Les observations de plusieurs singularités et choses memorables trouvées en Grèce*, etc. (Paris 1553). They had, in fact, been cleaned out by Janus Lascaris for Lorenzo de Medici 1491–2. But the myth died hard, as is shown by that splendid work, Robert Curzon's *Visit to the Monasteries in the Levant* (1849).

prudent to return, without compensation, 'fourteen good manuscripts of the Fathers' just acquired from 'a blind and ignorant monastery which depends upon the Patriarch'. The only consolation was that the Dutch ambassador had to disgorge even more.[44]

Laud received the news calmly. No doubt, he accurately prophesied, the new patriarch would soon come to an equally bad end. Meanwhile, he was just in time to recall a present which he was about to send to the patriarch. It was a special edition of two texts from the Codex Alexandrinus, printed by the learned press at Oxford, and personally inscribed, in Greek, to the patriarch. The inscription indicated that more was to come. No more would come. The frustrated gifts were re-directed to the Bodleian Library.

When Greaves and Pococke returned separately to England, they did not, after all, come empty-handed; but they found a revolution there too, and their own archbishop also overthrown. Greaves took his manuscripts, which included a fine text of Ptolemy's *Almagest*, 'stolen by a Spahy (as I am informed) from the king's library in the Seraglio', to Oxford, and there settled down to sustain the royal cause in college politics. His triumph would come in 1645, when, as sub-warden of Merton College, he secured the deposition of the anti-Laudian warden, Sir Nathaniel Brent, the translator of Paolo Sarpi's *History of the Council of Trent*, and the election, in his stead, of a sound royalist, the great Dr Harvey. Unfortunately that triumph did not last long: next year Oxford would fall, and when the parliamentary visitors arrived to purge the university, their president was found to be Brent. He would naturally purge Greaves, who would thus be obliged to return to oriental scholarship. It is fair to say that he returned with zest: ten considerable works would appear in his remaining six years.

Meanwhile, Pococke too had returned. On his way back, he stopped in Paris and there called on Grotius, whose ecumenical manifesto, *de Veritate Religionis Christianae*, he proposed to translate into Arabic. So Pococke was able to bring to Laud, now a prisoner in the Tower, the advice of Grotius, who had gone through the same experience twenty years before. Grotius urged Laud to escape, as he had done, from his fortress-prison, and so to preserve himself for better times in exile abroad. Thus at the end of his life, Laud was reminded, by one and the

---

[44] Greaves's own account of his adventures and misadventures is given in two letters printed, from the drafts in the Bodleian Library (MS Savile 47 fol 45), in his *Miscellaneous Works* 2 pp 434–8 and again in Kemke, *Patricius Junius* pp 83–6. The letters were probably addressed to Peter Turner.

same visitor, of his old ecumenical aspirations and their new practical application, now all alike in ruin.[45]

If we look at Laud's relations with the Greek church as a whole, we can see that they fall into three phases. First, there is the ecumenical stage, dating from the years of peace and bound up with the Erasmian ideals of the Arminians, which Laud inherited from them: ideals which embraced catholics, protestants and Greeks, excluding extremists of all kinds. Secondly, there is the period of war, in which those ecumenical ideas could not survive, but were replaced by a polarisation of ideologies, the revival of a militant international protestantism. In these years, it can be said, ecumenism shifted its base and became a purely protestant alliance, with no enemies to the left. This was a development congenial to Abbot. It was welcomed by Cyril, who thus split the Greek church; and it was repudiated by Laud, who thus split the church of England. Finally, having accepted the fact that the old ecumenism was dead and the modern Greek church captured by the Calvinist party, Laud set out to make the best of a bad job and at least secure what he could out of the spoil. For that limited purpose, he preserved relations with Cyril Lucaris; but his final judgement of him, as an ecclesiastic, would probably have been similar to that of Grotius. Grotius accused Cyril of adding to the misery of the Greeks by introducing a new schism. For purely external political reasons, he said, the patriarch had changed the rites and the faith of his church to a Calvinist form, 'without a Synod, without the consent of the Patriarchs or of his own metropolitans'. He had adulterated the Greek

---

[45] If Pococke can be seen as combining Laud's old liberal ideals with his new collector's mania in the east, the same can be said of another of Laud's protégés, Samson Johnson, in the west. Johnson was a fellow of Magdalen College, Oxford, who was appointed, in 1634, chaplain to Sir Robert Anstruther, Charles I's ambassador to the German Diet at Frankfurt. He obtained at least ten manuscripts for Laud to present to Oxford (see Bodl MS Laud Gr 39). He was then appointed chaplain to the queen of Bohemia at the Hague. However, Johnson proved too enthusiastic an advocate of ideas which Laud, by then, was seeking discreetly to disown—the ideas of Grotius. He published Grotius' *Defensio Fidei Catholicae* at Oxford in 1636; he became a personal friend of Grotius; and in 1639 being denounced as a Socinian by the puritan preacher of the English church at the Hague and by the Dutch Calvinist, Grotius' great enemy, Rivetus, he imprudently defended himself by stating that he had discussed his ideas with Grotius. This caused Grotius' brother Willem to warn Grotius (then in Paris) that the cry of Socinianism was again being raised against him. Johnson was forced to sign a recantation, but suspicion clung to him and Laud felt obliged to condemn him publicly (*Briefwisseling van Hugo Grotius* 5 pp 468, 515; 9 pp 303, 328). However, this seems to have been a tactical necessity only; for in 1640 we find Laud thanking Johnson for 'two little books you sent me, especially that of Grotius' (Bodl MS Eng Lett C 130 fol 143). Laud, by this time preferred manuscripts to ideas.

faith and usurped the rights of others. What an outcry there would have been if the pope had behaved thus! Cyril, said Grotius, was rightly condemned by the synod of Constantinople which met after his death.[46] Laud, of course, incurred exactly the same accusations and the same fate—for an opposite deviation.

However, these stages in the story of the two archbishops are not entirely distinct: each is blurred by the residue of its predecessor. The old ecumenical ideal, which dissolved in 1618, nevertheless still shed a lingering glow over the harsh reality of divergence, and the complimentary exchange of politically calculated gifts concealed the incompatibility of immediate aims. So the Anglo-catholic supporters of Laud were able to romanticise, and sought to re-forge, the links which, in truth, he had inherited only to attenuate.[47] For between Laud, the blunt undiplomatic English champion of ancient authority,

[46] H. Grotius, *Animadversiones in Animadversiones A. Riveti* (Paris 1642) p 25; *Votum pro Pace Ecclesiastica* (np 1642) p 57; *Riveti Apologetici . . . discussio* (Irenopoli 1645) pp 86–7. The condemnation of Cyril by the synods of Constantinople (1638) and Jassy (1642) repeated at Jerusalem (1672), effectively excluded Calvinist influences from the Greek church, and in 1701 a Scotch presbyterian could explain the reticence of the Book of Revelation on the subject of the Greek church by the assumption that it was 'but a limb and a branch of that great apostasy and backsliding from the truth foretold in Revelation', indistinguishable from popery, and so, 'it may very well be comprehended under the Whoor, Beast and False Prophet', *Early Letters of Robert Wodrow 1698–1709*, Scot Hist Soc (1937) pp 152–3.

[47] The continuity of high-church reunionist ideas, retrospectively associated with the name of Cyril Lucaris, can be illustrated by the activities of three men.

(1) Isaac Basire was a high-churchman who, in the 1630's, corresponded with Vossius and valued the Greek fathers only less than the bible. After the civil wars, he refused to comply with the new regime, deposited his family in London with the famous Dr Busby, and set off to convert the surprised peasantry of Greece to high Anglicanism. Among the spiritual weapons which he used, or hoped to use, was the prayer book in demotic Greek and the confession of Cyril. He returned to England, from Transylvania, in 1660 and spent the rest of his life as archdeacon of Northumberland under the congenial rule of bishop Cosin. See N. W. Darnell, *Life and Correspondence of Isaac Basire* (1831).

(2) After the restoration, Thomas Smith's studies of the eastern church in general, and of Cyril Lucaris in particular, (see above n2) were envisaged by him as part of a programme of general reunion. See his *Pacifick Discourse of the Causes and Remedies of the Differences about Religion which distract the Peace of Christendom* (1688).

(3) Paul Rycaut, who was secretary to the ambassador, Lord Winchelsea, and to the Levant Company in Constantinople from 1660 to 1667 and consul in Smyrna from 1667 to 1677, was also a general reunionist and thought that the process could begin with a union of the church of England with the Greek and Armenian churches. As precursors, he named Cassander, Melanchthon, Bucer, James I and— Cyril Lucaris. See his *Present State of the Greek and Armenian Churches* (1679), written at the suggestion of Charles II.

and Lucaris, the supple Greek enthusiast for Calvinist reform, there could be no real understanding. Their aims were not only different but opposite.

Nevertheless, beyond all differences of aim, there remains a certain similarity between these two dynamic but ill-fated contemporary primates. Both were men of resolute energy, determined to reverse the apparently irreversible slide of their churches into what they saw as disaster: into puritanism here, into Romanism there. Both relied on their personal zeal and courage, for neither of them had a solid party— only the party which they created and which depended on them. Both felt themselves isolated, struggling alone, in a corrupt age, to restore the lost integrity and the historic culture of their churches. Laud, said Sir Simonds d'Ewes, was 'the little active wheel that set the rest on work'; Cyril could say of himself that, like the prophet Elijah, he alone was left. In order to achieve their ecclesiastical aims, both involved themselves deeply in secular politics. Both, being overpowered by their enemies, were instantly abandoned by their creatures: Laud's officers deserted him and even Critopoulos, under pressure, signed the condemnation of Cyril. Both at last perished, in their old age, amid the ruin of their life's work, at the hands, one of a public, the other of a secret executioner.

Oriel College
Oxford

THE PEREGRINATIONS OF
MARCO ANTONIO DE DOMINIS, 1616–24

by W. B. PATTERSON

ON 6 December 1616, Marco Antonio De Dominis, the Roman catholic archbishop of Spalato, on the Dalmatian coast, arrived in England. According to Arthur Wilson, he was 'old and corpulent, unfit for Travel, being almost at his journies end by Nature', yet he soon began to speak out vigorously against the faith and practices of Rome.[1] Finding himself warmly welcomed by the archbishop of Canterbury and the king, he accepted several appointments in the church of England—including those of dean of Windsor and master of the Savoy—and became a prominent anti-Roman controversialist. Then, after five and a half years in England, De Dominis, like a wandering star in the Ptolemaic system, 'went Retrograde, placing himself again in the Roman Calendar.'[2] What moved De Dominis to undertake so arduous a physical and spiritual journey as that which led him to England, and why, having found an honoured place among ideological allies, did he leave it to go to the very citadel of the ecclesiastical power he had attacked?[3]

De Dominis was not reticent about his intentions. In a little book first published in Heidelberg in the course of his journey northwards the archbishop undertook to explain the motives for his departure. His decision, he said, was 'the ful-ripe fruite of ten yeeres deliberation at the least.'[4] Indeed, he found it necessary to describe his upbringing,

---

[1] Arthur Wilson, *The History of Great Britain: Being the Life and Reign of King James the First, Relating to What Passed from His First Access to the Crown, Till His Death* (London 1653) p 102. De Dominis was 56 when he entered England (born Rab, Dalmatia, 1560).

[2] *Ibid.*

[3] Recent studies of De Dominis include [Delio] Cantimori, 'Su M. A. De Dominis', *ARG* 49 (1958) pp 245–58, and 'L'Utopia ecclesiologica di M. A. De Dominis', in [*Problemi di vita religiosa in Italia nel Cinquecento*] (Padua 1960) pp 103–22; [Antonio] Russo, *Marc'Antonio De Dominis*, [*arcivescovo di Spalato e apostata (1560–1624)*] (Naples 1965); David L. Clark, 'Marco Antonio de Dominis and James I: The influence of a Venetian Reformer on the Church of England', *Papers of the Michigan Academy of Science, Arts, and Letters* 53 (1968) pp 219–30; and Dušan Nedeljković, *Marko Dominis* [*u nauci i utopiji na delu*] (Belgrade 1975). I am indebted to Professors David L. Clark, John L. Lievsay, and Michael Petrovitch, Dr John Tedeschi, and Miss Ruzica Popovitch for their assistance during the course of my research.

241

education, and early career to explain that decision adequately. He
had been educated by the Jesuits, whose order he had joined, and he
had been a lecturer in humanities at Verona before being ordained.
Subsequently, he taught mathematics at Padua, and rhetoric, logic, and
philosophy at Brescia. Only after becoming bishop of Segna, however,
did he undertake a serious study of the fathers of the church, in order to
prepare himself for preaching. 'From these lampes', he said,

> a new and strange light darted forth vpon me, the beames whereof,
> though vnwilling, and shutting mine eyes, I could not but perceiue.
> As for dogmaticall points in Diuinity, I found in the Fathers many
> passages diuers wayes repugnant to the common Tenets of the
> Schoolemen, in whom I was formerly lessoned . . . . As for Church-
> discipline, I saw, and wondered to see the spirituall gouernement
> of these times so far wide and different from the ancient.[5]

De Dominis related that he had continued these studies after being
made archbishop of Spalato and primate of Dalmatia and Croatia.
At this point in his career a practical problem intruded upon his
theological reflections. He was struck by 'the vast omnipotencie of the
Court of Rome daily encroaching, and eating vpon my Metropoliticall
rights.' Furthermore, he was disgusted by the 'Romanizing pamphlets'
which appeared during the papal interdict against Venice, pamphlets
which vilified the bishops, such as himself, within the Venetian
territories.[6] All of this had led him to dream of a church constituted, as
the ancient church had been, of more or less independent bishoprics
all sharing a common faith. He had described the way that ancient
form could be recovered in his forthcoming book on the ecclesiastical
commonwealth. In leaving Italy he had no intention of leaving the
catholic church: 'I hye me vp into some safe place, where the true
Catholique Religion holdeth vp her head, and taketh free breath.' In
such a place, 'I meane, as my dutie bindes, and as my strength affoards,
to display and publish that trueth which I haue learned, and to lay
forth the wayes for remoueall of Schismes, and reducing of the Church
to vnity.'[7]

---

[4] De Dominis [A] *Manifestation [of the Motives, Whereupon the Most Reverend Father, Marcvs Antonivs De Dominis, Archbishop of Spalato, (in the Territorie of Venice) Vndertooke His Departure Thence: Englished out of His Latine Copy]* (London 1616) p 1. De Dominis's *Consilium profectionis* had originally appeared in Heidelberg in Latin and Italian in the autumn of 1616; the text was dated at Venice, 20 September 1616.
[5] De Dominis, *Manifestation* pp 16–17. De Dominis had left the Jesuit order before becoming a bishop.
[6] *Ibid* p 19.

The peregrinations of Marco Antonio de Dominis

Contemporary documents do not necessarily contradict but they certainly add relevant information to De Dominis's own account. It is clear, for example, that De Dominis had felt himself the victim of unjust ecclesiastical procedures almost from the time he was elected archbishop in 1602. That election, made in a papal consistory, carried with it an agreement by which a certain Marzio Andreucci, dean of Udine, was to receive a pension from the new archbishop's emoluments. When Andreucci was himself elected bishop of Traù in 1604, De Dominis refused, on grounds of poverty, to pay him the required pension. The papacy insisted upon the rights of the bishop of Traù, a decision which led to a protracted dispute. In other conflicts involving relations with his cathedral chapter and the extent of his jurisdiction, De Dominis found the papacy opposing him.[8] These experiences and his associations with Venice helped to incline him to the Venetian side in the celebrated crisis of 1606–7, when pope Paul V and the republic contested the extent of papal authority within that city-state. During the crisis, De Dominis wrote in defence of Venice, though the works which he wrote for this purpose remained in manuscript.[9] By 1612, the papal nuncio in Venice had reported to Rome that the archbishop of Spalato was composing a work against the authority of the pope and of the holy see; the nuncio was repeatedly urged to use all peaceful means to dissuade the archbishop from this project.[10] Finally, there are indications that the inquisition in Venice had, by 1616, asked the dreaded council of 'the Ten' to surrender De Dominis to them for interrogation on suspicion of heresy. In a letter sent to the doge of Venice from Switzerland in October 1616, De Dominis

---

[7] *Ibid* pp 39–40. Roman catholic answers to De Dominis's *Manifestation* emphasised his pride, inconstancy, and greed. See John Floyd, *A Svrvey of the Apostasy of Marcvs Antonivs de Dominis, Sometyme Arch-bishop of Spalato* (n.p. 1617) pp 9, 20, 47, and John Sweet, *Monsig*[r]. *fate voi, or A Discovery of the Dalmatian Apostata, M. Antonivs De Dominis, and His Bookes* (St Omer 1617) pp 12–15, 29.

[8] [S.] Ljubić, 'Prilozi za životopis Markantuna de Dominisa [Rabljanina, spljelskoga nadbiskupa'[, *Starine*]*na sviet izdaje Jugoslavenska Akademija Znanosti i Umjetnosti 2*] (Zagreb 1870) pp 131–3, and 'O Markantunu Dominisu Rabljaninu, historičko-kritičko iztraživanje navlastito po izorih mletačkoga arkiva i knjižnice arsenala parizkoga', *Rad Jugoslavenske Akademije Znanosti i Umjetnosti*, 10 (Zagreb 1870) pp 44–87; Russo, *Marc'Antonio De Dominis* pp 32–9.

[9] L. Ljubić, 'Prilog krazpravi o Markantanu Dominisu Rabljaninu', *Starine* 4 (Zagreb 1872) pp 1–8; Marc'Antonio De Dominis, *Scritti giurisdizionalistici inediti*, ed Antonio Russo (Naples 1965) pp 5–22 and *passim*.

[10] Rome, A[rchivio] S[egreto] V[aticano], Fondo Borghese, series 1, vol 905, fols 63[v], 70[v], 337[v]–8, 378.

243

confided that he felt his life had been in danger from plots of the Roman curia.[11]

If De Dominis felt he was in deep trouble with the authorities of the Roman church, he seems also to have felt he would find a satisfactory position among congenial colleagues in the church of England. William Bedell, the chaplain in 1607–10 to Sir Henry Wotton, the English ambassador to Venice, was said by a contemporary biographer to have befriended De Dominis and to have given him valuable assistance in the writing of his major theological work.[12] Wotton's successor, Sir Dudley Carleton, seems to have made the initial arrangements for De Dominis's departure for England. Writing from Lambeth in December 1614, archbishop George Abbot went over these arrangements with Carleton: De Dominis was to travel to England by way of Holland and was not to expect more from his hosts than a quiet life in a university with a moderate annual stipend.[13] De Dominis's departure did not, however, take place until after Wotton arrived in Venice for his second assignment as ambassador there. Writing to king James I from Venice on 30 July 1616, Wotton said of De Dominis's plans:

> The Archbishop of Spalatro is resolved to endure no longer the idolatrous fooleries of this Church, but will within a week or such a matter begin his journey towards your Majesty; of whose favour I have given him fresh assurance, and I think his departure will breed much noise, being a person of such quality, and of singular gravity and knowledge.[14]

In addition to these theological and practical considerations, there was another which evidently influenced De Dominis profoundly. Within a short time of the archbishop's arrival in England, the first volume of his *De Republica Ecclesiastica* began to be printed there. It was, if not De Dominis's life-work, certainly an achievement by which he could reasonably hope to be remembered. Eventually published in three volumes, it contained more than 2,200 folio pages in Latin, and touched upon most of the theological disputes then

[11] Ljubić, 'Prilozi za životopis Markantunu de Dominisa' pp 148–9; Russo, *Marc'Antonio De Dominis* pp 39–40
[12] *A True Relation of the Life and Death of the Right Reverend Father in God William Bedell, Lord Bishop of Kilmore in Ireland*, ed Thomas Wharton Jones, CSer, ns 4 (1872) pp 135–9. The editor believes that the author was William Bedell, the bishop's son.
[13] *CalSPD* 9 (1858) p 262; see also p 227.
[14] *The Life and Letters of Sir Henry Wotton*, ed Logan Pearsall Smith, 2 vols (Oxford 1907) 2, p 100.

raging in Europe. There can be little doubt that, considering De Dominis's difficulties with the papacy and the argument of the book, he would have found it virtually impossible to get the work published in any Roman catholic country. In November 1616, before the *De Republica Ecclesiastica* had been published, a decree of the congregation in Rome charged with the drawing up of the index of prohibited books forbade De Dominis's book in all languages, 'whether already printed or hereafter to be printed.'[15] By the end of May 1617 cardinal Borghese had written to the papal nuncio in Paris that De Dominis had had his impious book published and that the holy Roman emperor had forbidden its circulation in Germany. He urged the nuncio to persuade the king of France to do likewise.[16] In December 1617 a committee of divines at the Sorbonne presented a list of propositions from the first volume of the work which its members considered heretical, scandalous, and injurious to the church and the holy see. The faculty of theology condemned forty-seven propositions in the book later in the same month. Not to be outdone the faculty of theology at Cologne condemned some 376 propositions from the *De Republica Ecclesiastica* at the end of March 1618.[17] England, on the other hand, seemed to welcome the work.

De Dominis's *De Republica Ecclesiastica* is a kind of Utopia, as the Yugoslavian scholar Nedeljković has recently pointed out.[18] But like many other works in that genre it is firmly rooted in an analysis of history, and is directed towards solving what seemed to be pressing contemporary problems. From one point of view those problems were ecclesiological. De Dominis's work, like Richard Hooker's, dealt with 'the laws of ecclesiastical polity',[19] and attempted to show how the

---

[15] The *Decretvm*, dated at Rome 12 November 1616, is included in De Dominis, *Manifestation of the Motives*, sig I₁-I₃.

[16] Rome, ASV, Fondo Borghese, series 1, vol 902, fol 218ᵛ. The letter to Guido Bentivoglio is dated 27 May 1617.

[17] BN MSS nouvelles acquisitions latines, vol 2456, fols 99ᵛ-100; *Censvra Sacrae Facvltatis Theologiae Parisiensis, in qvatvor priores libros De Repvblica Ecclesiastica, auctore Marco Antonio de Dominis quondam archiepiscopo Spalatensi* (Cologne nd)—the decree is dated 15 December 1617; *Censvra Sacrae Facvltatis Theologicae Coloniensis, in qvatvor priores libros De Repvbl. Ecclesiastica M. Antonij de Dominis, quondam archiepiscopi Spalatensis* (Cologne 1618). The *De Republica Ecclesiastica* was also attacked by John Sweet in advance of the book's publication (1617), Johannes Roberti (1619), Andreas Eudaemon-Joannis (1619), John Floyd (1620 and 1623), and Nicolas Coeffeteau (1623). Coeffeteau's *Pro Sacra Monarchia Ecclesiae Catholicae, Apostolicae et Romanae* is an exhaustive treatment of De Dominis's first volume, longer, in fact, than the book it answers.

[18] Nedeljković, *Marko Dominis*, pp 7-8, 74-6, 98-9. Cantimori's 'L'Utopia ecclesiologica di M. A. De Dominis', had developed this theme earlier. Nedeljković's interpretation emphasises the social aspects of De Dominis's thought.

church should be governed if it was to fulfill its divine mission and enjoy union and concord. From another point of view those problems were political. Wars were being fought on the pretext of religion and ecclesiastical leaders were not above using the temporal authorities to gain their objectives. De Dominis's work treated not only the question of the right form of the church but that of the right relation between church and state. He hoped not only to see a church restored and purified according to the apostolic pattern but a Christendom enjoying a new era of peace and stability.

Constitutionally, De Dominis considered the church to be an association of bishops, who carried out the work the apostles had been commissioned by Christ to perform. They proclaimed the gospel preserved in the scriptures, administered the sacraments by which the church was sustained, and administered such temporal goods as the ongoing life of the church required. Other orders of the ministry were dependent upon the bishops, as the ordination of priests and deacons by the bishops suggested. Among the bishops themselves there was fellowship and an administrative hierarchy. Archbishops, metropolitans, primates, and patriarchs exercised a limited jurisdiction over other bishops. But all bishops were equally the descendants of the apostles. When disputes about doctrine or discipline arose, the bishops met in regional, national, or general councils to resolve them.[20]

If this was the essential form of the church, what had happened to alter it almost beyond recognition? The alteration had come, De Dominis felt, because of the rise of the papacy. He vigorously disputed cardinal Bellarmine's interpretation of the Petrine texts of scripture and cardinal Baronius's account of the historical basis of papal authority.[21] Such an authority was, to De Dominis, an encroachment

---

[19] Compare *The Works of That Learned and Judicious Divine, Mr. Richard Hooker*, ed John Keble, 3 vols (Oxford 1836) I, pp lxxi–lxxvii. Hooker and De Dominis both defended episcopacy, the former against the puritans, the latter against the papacy, and both had an irenic point of view. Their works complement each other in that De Dominis's argument is scriptural, patristic, and historical, while Hooker's is philosophical and theological. De Dominis does not appear to have been directly influenced by Hooker.

[20] De Dominis, *De Repvblica Ecclesiastica [Libri X]* (London 1617) pp 1–2, 10–11, 25–6, 166, 194, 231–2, 472, 511–16. In spite of its title the first volume contained only books 1–4. The second contained books 5–6; the third, 7 and 9. Books 8 and 10 were not included in the published editions of the work. The first volume was published in Heidelberg as well as London.

[21] De Dominis, *De Repvblica Ecclesiastica* pp 32–4, 525–7, 676–82, 725–6. For a commentary on this part of De Dominis's work, see Joseph Turmel, *Histoire de la théologie positive du concile de Trente au concile du Vatican* (Paris 1906) pp 165, 212–15, 384–91. Abbé Turmel called De Dominis's work 'a formidable indictment' of the

upon the liberties of the church. De Dominis did not deny that Peter had enjoyed a certain primacy among the apostles and that he, along with the apostle Paul, had been associated with the foundation of the church in Rome. These circumstances, along with the fact that Rome had been the mother of many other churches, gave that see a special place of honour and respect in the Christian community. But they did not mean that the pope was justified in attempting to exercise a monarchical authority within the church. The church in every state in Christendom, De Dominis argued, was threatened by papal claims to universal jurisdiction. The archbishop made a special appeal to his fellow bishops throughout the world to unite against papal intrusions upon their episcopal rights, and to work together to bring about a genuine reconciliation of Christendom.[22] The popes, he argued further, had also attempted to exercise temporal jurisdiction over Christian princes. This, De Dominis contended in a long section directed against the Jesuit theologian Francisco Suarez, undermined the authority of the princes, led to internal rebellions, and played a conspicuous part in the fomentation of international wars.[23] In a strongly worded appeal to the princes of Europe, De Dominis called upon them to wield the authority entrusted to them by God to re-establish order by bringing a disastrous era of religious dissension to an end.[24]

This much of De Dominis's argument was contained in the first two volumes of his work, published in England by the king's printer in 1617 and 1620. But there was difficulty in publishing the third volume, which contained De Dominis's solution to the problems he recognised in the Europe of his day. His own explanation was that archbishop Abbot, a man 'most devoted' to Calvinist doctrine, was unsympathetic to De Dominis's plan for the reunion of the churches. Nor did Abbot and several other English bishops approve of the section of the work dealing with the church's use of temporal possessions, since it pointed to ways in which the English church was still insufficiently reformed.[25]

usual interpretation of the Petrine texts (p 165); on the subject of the convocation of councils he said that De Dominis's treatment 'was to be nearly the last word on a theory dear to the Protestants and, in general, to all the enemies of the papacy' (p 390).

[22] De Dominis, *De Repvblica Ecclesiastica*, 'To the Whole Order of Divine Bishops of the Holy Catholic Church', sig a1–b3ᵛ.

[23] De Dominis, *De Repvblica Ecclesiastica, pars secvnda* (London 1620) pp 877–1009. The second volume was published in Frankfort as well as London.

[24] De Dominis, *De Repvblica Ecclesiastica, pars secvnda* pp 637–9; see also pp 578–81.

[25] De Dominis, *De Pace Religionis: [Epistola ad venerabilem virum Iosephum Hallum; archipresbyterum Vigorniensem]* (Besançon 1666), pp 10–11. Book 9, dealing with tithes,

The third volume had, therefore, to be published in Germany in 1622, by which time De Dominis was preparing to leave England.[26]

In this volume De Dominis argued that the way for the schisms in the church to be healed was through a general council of all bishops. Such a council should recognise as catholic Christians all those who professed the faith of the scriptures and the historic creeds, and who wished to enter into union with their brethren. The council of Trent was not truly ecumenical since it had excluded the eastern churches, most of the German churches, and the Anglican church, and had paid scant heed to the representatives of the Gallican church. Moreover, it had been prevented from discussing and acting upon the problem of papal authority. To reunite the churches a general council would have to admit the protestants to membership and be free from papal domination. Since the papacy was almost certain to be opposed to such a council, the princes of Europe would have to act to assemble the bishops and other ecclesiastical leaders in a convenient place.[27] In De Dominis's opinion, the time for such a council as king James of England had called for had evidently arrived.[28] In 1622, of course, the time had passed, if one of the purposes of such a council was to prevent the outbreak of war. But De Dominis's conciliar solution was one which he saw as having been used from the apostles' own time and one whose usefulness was not likely to be superseded.

De Dominis's literary activity in England also included writing to the estates of the united provinces of the Netherlands to urge them to follow a moderate and conciliatory course in the controversy over Arminianism,[29] and writing to the patriarch of Alexandria to acquaint him with the ideas of the De Republica Ecclasiastica and to foster closer relations between the Anglican and Orthodox churches.[30] But along-

---

appointments, benefices, collations, and simony, is a separately paginated section of De Dominis, Repvblica Ecclesiastica, pars tertia (Frankfort 1658) pp 1–153.

[26] De Dominis, De Repvblica Ecclesiastica, pars tertia (Hanau 1622). The references which follow are to the 1658 edition, cited above.

[27] De Dominis, De Repvblica Ecclesiastica, pars tertia pp 5–68, 105–16, 126–32, 146–55, 319–22. Book 7, which deals with the problem of reunion within the context of a doctrine of the rule of faith, is analysed in detail by Russo, Marc'Antonio De Dominis, pp 97–131.

[28] De Dominis, De Repvblica Ecclesiastica, pars secvnda, Dedication to James I, p 3. De Dominis's doctrine of the church, as developed in book 7, has much in common with the views expounded by the king. See Robert Peters, 'The Notion of the Church in the Writings Attributed to King James VI & I', SCH 3 (1966) pp 223–31.

[29] Praestantium ac eruditorum virorum epistolae ecclesiasticae et theologicae, ed Christiaan Hartsoeker, (3 ed Amsterdam 1704) pp 485–90.

[30] PRO, S[tate] P[apers] 14/128/103, enclosure 16; Bibliographie hellénique, ou description

side these efforts on behalf of religious pacification, De Dominis
hammered away at Rome in a series of pamphlets which were more
explicit in their condemnation of papal abuses than his longer work
and no doubt reached a larger audience.[31] He also contributed a preface
to Paolo Sarpi's *History of the Council of Trent*, published in England
by the king's printer in 1619.[32] De Dominis's preface did not please at
least one discriminating reader. Writing to William Camden on 15
July 1619, Nicolas-Claude Fabri de Peiresc, a French catholic and a
widely known man of letters, complained that the preface, with De
Dominis's name attached, threatened to discredit a great work in the
eyes of those 'who are not of his opinion.' This preface, he feared,
would prevent the history from making its way into the hands of
catholics and even, as might otherwise have been possible, into Italy.[33]

The reputation De Dominis had earned as an outspoken opponent
of the Roman church makes his decision, in 1622, to return, not just

---

raisonnée des ouvrages publiés par des Grecs au Dix-Septième siècle, ed Emile Legrand,
5 vols (Paris 1894–1903) 4, pp 329–40. Compare Henry Newland, *The Life and Contemporaneous Church History of Antonio de Dominis, Archbishop of Spalatro* (Oxford 1859)
p 215.

[31] De Dominis, *A Sermon Preached in Italian, by the Most Reuerend Father, Marc'Antony
De Dominis, Archb. of Spalato, the First Sunday in Aduent, Anno 1617, in the Mercers
Chappel in London* (London 1617)—there were also editions in Italian (London 1617),
Latin (Leeuwarden 1618), German (Frankfort? 1618), and French (Charenton 1619).
Papatvs Romanvs: liber de origine, progressu, atque extinctione ipsius (London 1617); *The
Rockes of Christian Shipwracke, Discouered by the Holy Church of Christ to Her Beloued
Children, That They May Keepe Aloofe from Them; Written in Italian* (London 1618)—
there were also editions in Italian (London 1618), German (Frankfort 1618) and French
(La Rochelle 1618).

[32] Paolo Sarpi, *Historia del Concilio Tridentino: nella quale si scoprono tutti gl'artificii della
corte di Roma, per impedire che né la verità di dogmi si palesasse, né la riforma del Papato,
& della Chiesa si trattasse, di Pietro Soave Polano* (London 1619) sig a₂–a₄. It was thought
until fairly recently that De Dominis had brought the manuscript of this work out of
Italy to be published in England—a view this preface does much to encourage. The more
likely explanation, that Nathaniel Brent was sent to Venice to transmit the work back
to England, was indicated in documents published by Lambert B. Larking, 'Notes of
Sir Roger Twysden on the *History of the Council of Trent*', *Notes and Queries*, second
series, 4 (London, July–December 1857) pp 121–4, and elaborated in Frances A. Yates,
'Paolo Sarpi's "History of the Council of Trent" ', *Journal of the Warburg and Courtauld
Institutes* 7 (London 1944) pp 123–43, and Gaetano Cozzi, 'Fra Paolo Sarpi, l'Angli-
canesimo e la "Historia del Concilio Tridentino" ', *RStI* 68 (1956) pp 559–619. See also
Paolo Sarpi, *Opere*, ed G. and L. Cozzi (Milan–Naples 1969) pp 725–40, and John L.
Lievsay, *Venetian Phoenix: Paolo Sarpi and Some of His English Friends (1606–1700)*
(Lawrence, Kansas 1973) pp 22–73.

[33] For Peiresc see F. W. Gravit, *The Peiresc Papers* (Ann Arbor 1950), P. Gassendi, *Viri
illustris N. C. Fabricii de Peiresc . . . . vita*, 2pts (Paris 1641), and see T. Smith's *Life*
of Camden, 2pts (London 1691).

to Venice but to Rome itself, seem foolhardy or even suicidal. What could possibly have moved him to such a course of action? Once again, he wrote his own explanation, called in an English translation his *Second Manifesto*. Here he complained of the very thing it might have been concluded from the *De Republica Ecclesiastica* he would have admired: the comprehensiveness of the church of England. In this work, dated at Rome, 24 November 1622, he said that the 'milder Protestants' in England,

> although they endeauour by all meanes to free themselves ... from heresie, for that they seeme neither wholly to follow Luther nor Caluine: but the pure Doctrine of the English Church which they call reformed; yet can they not be free from the heresie both of the Puritanes, and Anabaptists; for that they communicate with them without scruple; for if any Puritane or Anabaptist come to their Ecclesiasticall assemblies, they neither auoyde, nor exclude him.[34]

Indeed, De Dominis added, 'Puritan Ministers . . . doe administer the very Sacraments of this false English Church.' As soon as he had discovered that the English church was so deeply infected with heterodoxy, he 'could not stay any longer in it.'[35] He not only repudiated his error in seeking a spiritual home in England but declared that the works he had written after he had forsaken Rome were full of heresies. These mistaken beliefs he listed and explicitly rejected.[36]

The *Second Manifesto* seems clearly to have been written as a kind of spiritual purgation by one determined to show that he was free from heresy. More revealing is a long letter written while De Dominis was still in England to the theologian Joseph Hall, who had written to dissuade the archbishop from his decision to return to Rome.

[34] De Dominis, [*The*] *Second Manifesto* [*of Marcvs Antonivs De Dominis, Archbishop of Spalatro: Wherein for His Better Satisfaction, and the Satisfaction of Others, He Publikely Repenteth, and Recanteth His Former Errors, and Setteth downe the Cause of His Leauing England, and All Protestant Countries, to Returne vnto the Catholicke Romane Church; Written by Himselfe in Latin, and Translated into English by M. G. K.*] (Liege 1623) sig C$_2$. De Dominis's *Sui reditus ex Anglia consilium exponit* (Rome 1623) was also translated into English by E. Coffin as *M. Antonius De Dominis, Archbishop of Spalato, Declares the Cause of His Returne out of England* (St Omer 1623).
[35] De Dominis, *Second Manifesto* sig C$_3$; see also sig A$_2$v.
[36] *Ibid* sig A$_2$v–C$_1$. Among the errors he acknowledged were his assertions that the pope was not the head of the visible church, that the mass was not a true sacrifice, that transubstantiation did not occur, and that auricular confession with absolution was not a true sacrament.

Hall, then dean of Worcester, pointed to the dangers which would confront De Dominis in the city of seven hills which the archbishop's thunderbolts had so often struck.[37] Assuming that De Dominis was still interested in Christian unity, he argued that Rome had shown no signs of weakening in her opposition to those outside her ranks, nor was she likely to yield to entreaties that she give up claims to spiritual and temporal authority or her own distinctive doctrines.[38] The dean seemed frankly puzzled that one whom the English church had welcomed and the king himself had bountifully entertained would now leave his newly made friends. Did the archbishop find the religion of the English, which he had once extolled, to be lacking in divine truth?[39] Hall reminded De Dominis of the inquisitorial prison in which certain English visitors in Rome had spent some seventeen years. The English theologian predicted that if De Dominis did not change his mind and remain in his adopted country, he would wish that he had never seen Britain or else that he had never left it.[40]

According to De Dominis's answer, which remained unpublished until 1666, he had come to England with several objectives: to discover the causes of dissensions and schisms in the church, to find a place where he could write freely, to work for Christian unity and concord, and to serve king James.[41]

His experience in England had, he affirmed, taught him a great deal about the causes of schism in the church. Schisms had occurred from the time of the reformation because some groups of professed Christians insisted upon considering others heretics and refused to maintain fellowship with them. Both Roman catholics and protestants were guilty of this. De Dominis maintained that, in spite of the polemical writing produced by several generations of theologians, no one had shown that Roman catholics were not sound in all the fundamental

---

[37] Joseph Hall, 'Reverendissimo viro, [D⁰. Marco Antonio De Dominis, archiepiscopo Spalatensi,] epistola [discessus sui ad Romam dissuasoria]', in *The Works of the Right Reverend Joseph Hall, D.D., Bishop of Exeter and Afterwards of Norwich*, ed Philip Wynter, 10 vols (Oxford 1863) 10, pp 208–9. The letter, which is not dated, was received by De Dominis in London on 20 February 1622. See De Dominis, *De Pace Religionis* pp 49–55.
[38] Hall, 'Reverendissimo viro epistola' pp 210–11.
[39] *Ibid* p 213.
[40] *Ibid* pp 212, 214.
[41] De Dominis, *De Pace Religionis* p 2. According to the printer, the manuscript had been obtained from an erudite Englishman who had passed through Besançon from Geneva (page opposite title page). De Dominis's letter is dated 1 March 1622 at the Savoy (p 62).

doctrines of the faith.[42] Since the English confession of faith was one of the most moderate in Christendom and seemed to be aimed at including a wide variety of Christians, he had expected to find a willingness among English churchmen to acknowledge the common ground shared by the church of England and the Roman catholic church. He had found such a willingness in king James and in a number of church leaders. The king was well aware that Roman catholics did not err in essential matters of the faith and he wished to tolerate those who were not a threat to the commonwealth. Unfortunately, the church of England was increasingly dominated by puritans, even in the episcopal ranks, who refused to have any dealings with Roman catholics, whom they condemned as heretics.[43] De Dominis argued that the recent participation of English churchmen, including Hall, in the synod of Dort showed how closely the church of England was willing to associate itself with extreme Calvinist theology. This promised to make the schism between Rome and England far more difficult to heal. Largely because of this theological state of affairs, he had not found the intellectual freedom in England he had expected. The way had been blocked, in fact, to the publication of the third volume of his theological work. As for serving king James, whose wisdom and learning so attracted De Dominis, he had been able to accomplish little. De Dominis had therefore decided to accept the invitations he had received to return home to Italy.[44]

In a letter to Gondomar, the Spanish ambassador in England, dated 9 February 1622, an extract of which was included in De Dominis's reply, the archbishop spoke of the assurances he had received from the ambassador for some eight months relative to going to Italy, and of a letter from cardinal Mellino in Rome concerning his reception on the continent.[45] He acknowledged that there were dangers in his planned journey back to Italy. But the Roman catholic church, De Dominis argued, dealt gently with those who, though disagreeing with her on some matters, were willing to be corrected. He was willing to submit his work to his fellow clerics for their judgement, and would revise it where necessary. He was confident that his faith was orthodox, and had been equally so while he had been among Roman catholics and

[42] *Ibid* pp 3–6.
[43] *Ibid* pp 13–15.
[44] *Ibid* pp 7–8, 10, 15.
[45] *Ibid* pp 16–17.

among protestants. Though he was glad to be leaving Britain, he would never cease, so long as he lived, to work for religious union and concord.[46]

Some of the ways in which De Dominis planned to work for concord are suggested by the answers he gave to questions propounded to him by ecclesiastical officials in the early part of 1622, in orders from the king.[47] In a written statement of February 11, De Dominis asserted that he was in a position to help each side in the divided Christian community to understand the other and could, perhaps, adjudicate their differences. Much, of course, depended upon the attitude of the pope:

> if the Pope would vse some moderation (as I haue formerly saide) about his supremacy, and leaue vnto Princes their intire right of regiment; that then Protestants might tolerate some abuses, (since euen themselues want not their abuses) . . . that so Schisme might be remooued, and there might issue vnion in fundamentall Faith and Charitie . . . and then afterwards there might be more regular disceptation made of dogmaticall points of controversie.[48]

If he were able to advise the pope, De Dominis said, he would recommend not only that he give up the power he claimed over princes but that

> he would approue the English Liturgie; that hee would grant them the vse of the cuppe; that hee would suffer the controuerted points of Faith to be handled by way of Councels, after the ancient vse of the Church; that in those points of the Councell of Trent, wherein the Protestants haue made good applications of their opinions, he would release his Anathematisme of them.[49]

De Dominis believed, furthermore, that many Roman practices strenuously protested against and used as a justification of schism by the protestants could be satisfactorily explained to them by reviewing the use of such practices in the ancient church. These included 'reuerencing of Reliques, vse of the Crosse, and of Images, and of Chrisme, and of annointing the sicke, Intercession and inuocation of

---

[46] Ibid pp 56–7, 62.

[47] [Richard] Neile, M. Ant. De Dñis [Arch-Bishop of Spalato, His Shiftings in Religion: A Man for Many Masters] (London 1624) sig A₂. De Dominis's interrogations were at intervals between 21 January and 30 March 1622, when he was commanded to leave the realm within twenty days. A record of these procedures is preserved in PRO, SP 14/128/103.

[48] Neile, M. Ant. De Dñis pp 44–5.

[49] Ibid p 47.

Saints, and priuate Masses.' They might then be found 'either good and holy, or laudable, or at least tolerable . . . . And thus might Schisme be taken away, and vnion reestablished.'[50] De Dominis was confident that since the accession of pope Gregory XV as Paul V's successor, the prospects for such a course of action had been much enhanced.[51]

Quite a different account of De Dominis's motives was given by archbishop Abbot, a man who had been in a position to know De Dominis well. Writing to Sir Thomas Roe, the English ambassador in Constantinople, on 20 November 1622, Abbot described De Dominis as a *bestaccio* who had accepted the honours and emoluments granted to him without a word of thanks, 'neither to the king, nor to mee, nor to any other person in England.'[52] In spite of having 'the mastership of the Savoy, the deanry of Windsor, one benefice, and another donative, besides plate given him every yeere from the kinge, to the value of 200 marks' and an additional annual contribution from the clergy of £200, he was dissatisfied with his rank and with his income. The Spanish ambassador, anxious to get De Dominis out of England, had worked upon his pride and avarice with the help of several Italians in Rome. As a result, De Dominis was promised 'a pension of 12000 crownes a yeere, or the bishopricke of Salerna in the kingdome of Naples, besides acceptation from the bishop of Rome', if he would return to his former profession. De Dominis then asked permission of the king to return to Rome 'vnder colour to seeke some reconcilement betweene the reformed and the Roman churches.' The king, in order to ascertain the archbishop's intentions more fully, prescribed a series of questions to be put to him. De Dominis's answers, in Abbot's view, showed the Italian 'to bee a meere worldly man, without conscience or religion.' Rather than being given permission to leave England, De Dominis, who now appeared 'odious both to God and man', was 'inioyned by such a day to depart the realme, and not to returne vpon his perill.'[53]

This explanation was evidently widely accepted in England. It was the basis of Thomas Middleton's play 'A Game of Chess', where 'the

[50] *Ibid* p 48.
[51] *Ibid* p 89.
[52] Thomas Roe, *The Negotiations of Sir Thomas Roe in His Embassy to the Ottoman Porte, from the Yeare 1621 to 1628 Inclusive* (London 1740) pp 102–3.
[53] *Ibid* p 102. Gondomar's brief comments to his government on De Dominis concern the archbishop's literary activities. See Diego Sarmiento de Acuña, Conde de Gondomar, *Correspondencia Oficial*, ed Antonio Ballesteros y Beretta, 4 vols (Madrid 1936–45) I, p 118; 2, p 277.

Fat Bishop' was portrayed as worldly, proud, and gullible, a fitting victim of the Black Knight's machinations, aimed at returning the prelate to the kingdom of darkness.[54] Thomas Fuller related the saga of 'that arrant Apostata' in England in much the same terms as archbishop Abbot. Later in the century John Hacket included a good deal of this material in his account of De Dominis in his life of archbishop Williams.[55] The very title of Richard Neile's collection of official documents—*M. Ant. De Dnis Arch-Bishop of Spalato, His Shiftings in Religion: A Man for Many Masters*—seems to reflect a similar view.[56]

If De Dominis aroused suspicions in England, the same was certainly the case in Rome. After receiving absolution in Brussels at the hands of the papal nuncio, according to the instructions of cardinal Mellino, for all that he had said or written contrary to the Roman catholic faith,[57] De Dominis made his way to the eternal city. There he renewed his abjuration and was given housing, provisions, servants, and a modest benefice. In January 1623 he requested a more adequate income and was accordingly raised to a standard of living which active bishops might have envied. The treatment of De Dominis by Gregory XV, a friend of his from earlier years, did not, however, suit all the members of the curia, and when pope Gregory died in the summer of 1623, the archbishop's position was rapidly undermined. By 17 April 1624, he was under suspicion of heresy, and had been conducted as a prisoner into the Castel Sant'Angelo. There he remained for several months.[58]

De Dominis seemed by this time to be bereft of supporters. His *Second Manifesto* called forth a bitter comment from Jean Hotman de Villiers, a French protestant who had worked for many years for an

[54] *The Works of Thomas Middleton*, ed A. H. Bullen, 8 vols (New York 1964—reprint of 1885 edition) 7, pp 1–135. On 12 August 1624, the Spanish ambassador protested against 'a scandalous comedy, in which his Majesty the King of Spain, Count Gondomar, and the Archbp. of Spalato are personified', a description which fits Middleton's play. See *CalSPD* 11 (1859) p 325.

[55] Thomas Fuller, *The Church History of Britain, from the Birth of Jesus Christ untill the Year M.DC.XLVIII* (London 1655) bk 10, pp 71, 93–100; [John] Hacket, *Scrinia Reserata: [A Memorial Offer'd to the Great Deservings of John Williams, D.D.]* (London 1693) pt 1, pp 98–103.

[56] Translated into Latin as *Alter Ecebolius, M. Ant. De Dominis arch. Spalatensis, pluribus dominis inseruire doctus* (London 1624).

[57] Paris, Bibliothèque de l'Arsenal, MS 4111 pp 13–25. De Dominis's deposition at the house of the nuncio, Guido di Bagno, is dated 17 May 1622.

[58] Ludwig Pastor, *The History of the Popes from the Close of the Middle Ages*, transl Ernest Graf, vol 27 (St Louis 1955) pp 106–7; Russo, *Marc'Antonio De Dominis* pp 51–3. De Dominis's journey to Rome and his reception there were reported in England by T. H., *Newes from Rome, Spalato's Doome. . . .* (London 1624) pp 24–34.

W. B. PATTERSON

amelioration of religious differences in Europe. Writing to a friend on 21 May 1623, Hotman referred to the 'retraction of this monster Spalato, considered such by both sides.'[59]

De Dominis died in prison, of a fever, on 9 September 1624. Since, however, the inquisition's proceedings had not been completed, his body remained unburied in a Roman convent. The case was finally decided on 21 December 1624, when the congregation of the holy office decreed that De Dominis had been a relapsed heretic and ordered his body and his books to be burned.[60] The summary of the proceedings of the inquisition preserved in the Arsenal in Paris indicates the grounds on which this verdict was based. The final decree cited De Dominis's communications with heretics before his flight from Italy, his refusal to obey a command to appear before pope Paul V, the writings published while he was in northern Europe, and a number of propositions which he had expounded on scripture and tradition, the sacraments, the authority of the holy see, and the nature and content of the catholic faith. But much, if not all of this had been included among the errors which De Dominis had confessed and for which he had been absolved in Brussels.[61] There was, however, an additional item in the decree which received considerable attention there. The archbishop had never, evidently, given up his design for a union of the separated members of the catholic church, that is 'the Roman, the Anglican, and all the Protestant Churches.'[62] In fact, he had written out a sketch for such a union, presumed to have been composed after his reconciliation with the church in Brussels, and in it he showed that he wished 'in every way to defend the necessity of a union with the Protestants.'[63]

De Dominis was not without worldly ambition—indeed he seems to have had more than his share of a vice considered particularly unbecoming in a cleric—but it is difficult to explain his movements on this basis alone. In his journey to England and in his journey to Rome he took great risks, and in both cases gave up a reasonably secure

[59] BN MSS nouvelles acquisitions françaises vol 5130, fol 56. For Hotman's irenic efforts, see Corrado Vivanti, *Lotta politica e pace religiosa in Francia fra Cinque e Seicento* (Turin 1963) pp 189–245.
[60] Paris, Bibliothèque de l'Arsenal, MS 4111 pp 63–73; a detailed but hardly unbiased account was published in England as *A Relation Sent from Rome, of the Processe, Sentence, and Execvtion, Done upon the Body, Picture, and Bookes of Marcvs Antonius De Dominis, Archbishop of Spalato, after His Death* (London 1624).
[61] Paris, Bibliothèque de l'Arsenal, MS 4111 pp 77–8.
[62] *Ibid* p 78.
[63] *Ibid* p 83.

256

The peregrinations of Marco Antonio de Dominis

position for one much less certain. Hacket, in the late seventeenth century, saw him not only as a place-seeker but as a man obsessed with an idea: 'He lived and died with General Councils in his Pate, with Wind-Mills of Union to concord Rome and England, England and Rome, Germany with them both, and all other Sister-Churches with the rest, without asking leave of the Tridentine Council.'[64] That judgement rings true. De Dominis would not have gone to England, in all probability, except that he saw this as his best opportunity to get his ecumenical *summa* published. But having communicated his ideas to the scholarly world he evidently concluded that his plan of union could never be realised without the support of Rome. The accession of Gregory XV seemed to promise a favourable reception there, and made the journey back a risk worth taking. De Dominis was not a martyr for Roman catholicism nor for Anglicanism—neither tradition, indeed, has wished to claim him[65]—but for an ecumenical ideal which is now, perhaps, beginning to be understood and appreciated.

Davidson College
North Carolina

[64] Hacket, *Scrinia Reserata* pt 1, pp 104–5.
[65] Note, however, the favourable comments on De Dominis by John Cosin, *The Works of the Right Reverend Father in God John Cosin, Lord Bishop of Durham*, 5 vols (Oxford 1844–55) 4, pp 160–2, and J. S. Brewer, in his edition of Thomas Fuller, *The Church History of Britain*, 6 vols (Oxford 1845) 5, pp 510–12, 529–30.

THE RELIGIOUS MOTIVATION
OF CROMWELL'S MAJOR-GENERALS

by ANTHONY FLETCHER

WHEN Oliver Cromwell sent his most trusted lieutenants into the provinces in 1655, the instructions he gave them were wide ranging and the task he set them was ·enormous. They were to oversee every aspect of local government, prevent conspiracies, remove negligent or scandalous ministers and promote godliness and virtue among the people.[1] No wonder the major-generals felt daunted. John Thurloe, who as secretary-of-state handled their correspondence, soon found himself acting as a bureau for encouragement and advice.[2] Once they were out on their own there was little to sustain the major-generals beyond their religious faith. This is not to say that their accounts of their doings should be taken wholly at face value, nor that baser motives were necessarily absent from their minds. It is hard to believe that any of the major-generals expected immediate material gain. But some at least may have been influenced by the search for power and the desire for revenge against their enemies in the civil war. Plainly, several of them still felt bitter hatred of cavaliers almost ten years after the war had ended.[3] Such attitudes can be no more than glimpsed in letters designed to give a good impression of the major-generals' performance. The motives that lay behind that performance must be assessed on the basis of what they wrote and the aspects of the Cromwellian programme upon which they concentrated. The letters to Thurloe do much to explain why the major-generals worked so hard, riding the muddy lanes of England through a hard winter; they also illuminate the nature of their vision ·of a godly commonwealth.

This paper is only concerned with the nine men who actively pursued the scheme the protector set up from the autumn of 1655 through to the following summer: Hezekiah Haynes, Thomas Kelsey

---

[1] I. Roots, 'Swordsmen and Decimators: Cromwell's Major-Generals', *The English Civil War [and After 1642–1658]*, ed [R. H.] Parry (London 1970) pp 81–2.

[2] T[hurloe] S[tate] P[apers], 4, *passim*.

[3] [*Diary of Thomas*] Burton, [ed J. T. Rutt], 1 (New York 1974) p 230; P. H. Hardacre, 'William Boteler: A Cromwellian Oligarch', H[untington] L[ibrary] Q[uarterly], 11 (1947) p 5.

and William Goffe in the south-east; John Desborough in the south-west; James Berry, William Boteler, Edward Whalley and Charles Worsley in the midlands and Wales and Robert Lilburne in the north. Like Cromwell, they were all men full of zeal, men with a desire to grasp God's purposes, to be up and doing in the world.[4] It is clear from their correspondence that they shared Cromwell's belief in providence leading them on, though some like Worsley and Whalley spent more time reflecting about it than others like 'blunt and honest' Desborough, who simply got on with the job of rounding up cavaliers.[5] The major-generals rode down to the districts allotted to them believing God had a mission for them to perform. Berry explained his mind to the fiery Welsh fifth monarchist, Vavasour Powell, whom he at once sought to conciliate: 'I told him with what confidence I came forth in this work, as sent of God; and that my heart had been towards those poor people in Wales, and particularly I did expect help and encouragement from him and his people, and did not doubt that we should come to a right understanding of each other, and I should prove useful to them for the obtaining of much good'.[6]

Once at work, the major-generals took signs of co-operation and sympathy for their purposes as proof of God's interest. 'Hitherto I may say the Lord hath been with me in making my endeavours successful', wrote Whalley from Newark on 7 November, reporting the willingness of those nominated as militia commissioners to act, and the readiness of cavaliers to submit.[7] Worsley was enthusiastic about the response of militia officers in Cheshire, Lancashire and Staffordshire: 'truly I find a spirit extraordinarily bent to the work and plainly discern the finger of God going along with it, which is indeed no small encouragement unto me'.[8] Kelsey found himself forced to reappraise the whole business in view of the positive attitude of the Kentish commissioners: 'I must confess the Lord hath given my unbelieving heart the lie, by vouchsafing unto me more of his presence and comfort in this uncouth employment than I could expect'.[9] 'Every tongue must confess it was of the Lord who is a righteous God in the execution of his judgements', declared Haynes reporting the quiet acceptance by Norfolk cavaliers of the decimation

[4] C. Hill, *God's Englishman* (London 1970) pp 217–50.
[5] M. Ashley, *Cromwell's Generals* (London 1954) p 154.
[6] *TSP*, 4, p 228.
[7] *Ibid* p 162.
[8] *Ibid* p 149.
Ibid p 225.

tax, 'and when his hand is lifted up he shall not only make them (though most unwilling) to see but also make them ashamed for their envy to his people'.[10]

The godly, in the major-generals' view, had a mission not only in every corner of England but in the wider world. Thus they absorbed with intense interest the reports they received of the progress of the expedition to the West Indies. 'God can yet raise that design out of the dust', wrote Goffe in February 1656 commenting on the latest news of reverses in Jamaica, 'and make it turn to his praise and the comfort of those that love the Lord Jesus Christ and wait for the ruin of antichrist'.[11] 'The Lord help us to know what our sin is, or what his pleasure is, that we are so crossed and visited in Jamaica', reflected Whalley. His prayer, he told Thurloe, was that 'in all things we may aim at his glory and submit to his will'.[12]

The major-generals felt a close personal attachment to the protector. Several of them had fought alongside him; they all owed their promotion to him. Whalley for instance had first attracted Cromwell's notice at the skirmish at Gainsborough in 1643, when he carried himself 'with all the gallantry becoming a gentleman and a Christian'.[13] They leaned on Cromwell, desired to emulate him, feared his disapproval. The desire to serve their master conscientiously was closely integrated with their wish to be faithful to God. 'The Lord give me a heart to answer his goodness towards me and make me able to answer the expectations of his highness and council', wrote Kelsey on 20 November.[14] Reporting his progress from Hereford on 24 November, Berry asked Thurloe to present his 'most humble service and duty to my lord', 'and tell him, that though my business be toilsome and tedious to me, and indeed somewhat chargeable, yet I shall go on with comfort and confidence, hoping for the assistance of God and his highness acceptation'.[15] He prayed for Cromwell without ceasing, Goffe told Thurloe in one of his first despatches from Sussex, 'and can I hope cheerfully sacrifice my life in the service if need be'.[16]

As the months went on, the impenetrability of local politics and the imperviousness of local society to moral reform strained even the most energetic and determined of the major-generals. The stress of the job

[10] *Ibid* p 216.   [11] *Ibid* pp 130, 153, 498.   [12] *Ibid* p 510.
[13] *Oliver Cromwell's Letters and Speeches*, ed T. Carlyle, 1 (London 1845) p 139; Ashley, *Cromwell's Generals*, pp 153–9.
[14] *TSP*, 4, p 225.
[15] *Ibid* p 237.
[16] *Ibid* p 190.

showed up the differences in their temperaments. Worsley and Whalley, both of them outstandingly dedicated from the start, grew in confidence and enthusiasm. On 3 November Worsley admitted that 'the sense of the work' and his 'unworthiness and insufficiency as to the right management of it' deterred him: 'yet however this is the ground of my hope and comfort that the Lord is able to supply my wants and will appear in weak instruments for his glory, to the perfecting of his work'.[17] Once at it, he never looked back. His letters constantly reiterated his awareness of 'the visible hand of God going along with us'.[18] Whalley was less ecstatic but equally ready to see himself and his colleagues as God's instruments. 'If the Lord give abilities to your major-generals, myself most wanting', he told Thurloe on 18 January 1656, 'it's the best way that ever was yet devised for the peace and safety of the nation'. 'I praise God I can say it', he wrote a fortnight later, 'not out of vain glory to myself but that you may take notice, God hath in a very great measure blest our endeavours'.[19]

Berry, wrestling with bad weather and the whole of Wales as well as Herefordshire and Shropshire, was generally less optimistic. 'I hope my work will go merrily on if the winter were a little over', he grumbled on 6 December. He was discouraged by the backwardness and ungodliness of the Marches: 'you had need help us with your prayers and powers. Reformation hath many enemies'.[20] He was short of money and he reckoned the least the protector should do for him was provide a decent lodging by repairing Ludlow castle, so tumbledown it would one day 'knock somebody on the head'.[21] Yet, despite all the obstacles he encountered, Berry's religious conviction did not fail him. After a busy session setting men to work in Carmarthen on 6 March, he concluded: 'I am persuaded that not only the tax but something of reformation will be carried on in poor Wales whom I seriously profess my heart pities and loves'.[22]

There were times when Goffe, timid and querulous by nature, almost lost heart. An alarming tentativeness was apparent in the postscript to his first report from Lewes on 5 November: 'I am not altogether without hope that the Lord will manifest his presence with me in this difficult affair, to me difficult because I am weak'. In another

[17] Ibid p 149.
[18] Ibid pp 179, 187, 189, 340.
[19] Ibid pp 434, 495.
[20] Ibid pp 287, 334.
[21] Ibid pp 498, 742.
[22] Ibid p 582.

letter a few days later, Goffe hoped that Cromwell did 'not repent the laying so great a trust upon so poor and inconsiderable a creature'.[23] There was more than the conventional self-denigration of the puritan in all this. Goffe was a curious mixture of messianic recklessness and temperamental weakness. During the Putney debates in 1647, he had a dream about the downfall of antichrist which he proceeded to describe to the assembled soldiers.[24] Given the opportunity to play his part in achieving the millennium, he proved anxious and vulnerable. By the summer of 1656, he was fretful and peevish about Thurloe's failure to supply him with enough money to pay the local militia troops, and about the 'want of settlement': 'I am very sensible of my great inability to manage this great trust as I ought, yet am not convinced of any unfaithfulness, and therefore may hope to be supported by my master, while I am thought worthy to be employed'. When he wrote this on 24 June, Goffe was gloomy about the future of the whole enterprise. Yet in his despondency his faith sustained him: 'when we have done all we can, it is the Lord himself that must be our support, on whom we have great reason to trust. He hath hitherto helped in all the straights we have been in and I am persuaded will yet be our helper, and notwithstanding all our unworthiness will save us and bless us for his own name's sake'.[25]

It seems then that the major-generals derived very great emotional support from their intense puritan faith. How far did they also see religious and moral reform as at the heart of their mission? It has been pointed out that they put stress on different parts of their programme.[26] Thus Boteler was keen to eliminate swearing and anxious to get the unpleasant business of decimation over so he could concentrate on 'putting down prophaneness';[27] Worsley and Whalley gave sustained and serious attention to enforcing the ordinance for the ejection of scandalous ministers;[28] others like Haynes and Goffe became pre-occupied with radical sectarianism.[29] What they shared was a concept of an ordered and godly commonwealth, a nation in which men worked hard and read the bible, heard the word of God, lived honestly,

[23] *Ibid* pp 151, 190.
[24] *Puritanism and Liberty*, ed A. S. P. Woodhouse (London 1951) pp 39–42.
[25] *TSP*, 5, pp 150–1; [A. J.] Fletcher, *A County Community [in Peace and War]* (London 1975) p 307.
[26] *The English Civil War*, ed Parry, p 86.
[27] *TSP*, 4, pp 207, 632–3.
[28] *Ibid* pp 179, 189, 211, 267, 272, 284, 315, 439, 450, 473, 495.
[29] *Ibid* pp 329, 408, 642, 687–8, 727.

ANTHONY FLETCHER

and gave obedience where it was due. Their diverging religious and
moral concerns merely reflect the priorities that occurred to them and
the particular problems they met. Thus, in his initial tour of
Lincolnshire, Leicestershire and Warwickshire, Whalley gave much
time to encouraging the clergy, on whom so much depended: 'I make
it a great part of mine to discourse with as many as I think fear God and
labour to satisfy them and to gain their affections by giving them a more
than ordinary respect, which I think they well deserve. They have and
I hope shall have as much encouragement as I can give them in the ways
of godliness. They express great affections to his highness and pray for
him in their pulpits'.[30] Berry was horrified when he reached Brecon in
February 1656 and found not a single preaching minister in the
vicinity: 'certainly if some course be not taken these people will some
of them become heathens'. His task was much harder than Whalley's
in the midlands. In the Monmouthshire market towns he found 'vices
abounding and magistrates fast asleep'.[31] Worsley's Lancashire and
Cheshire journeyings made him obsessed with alehouses. After a
session with the JPs of Blackburn hundred, when two hundred were
closed, he reported to Thurloe that they were 'the very womb that
brings forth all manner of wickedness'.[32] Boteler gave much attention
to rounding up vagrants.[33]

Recent research has emphasised the broad tolerance of the
Cromwellian church and the fluidity of the sectarian church structure
in the 1650s.[34] It would be surprising if the group of military careerists
whom Cromwell chose as his major-generals were all of like mind after
the religious controversies of more than a decade of open discussion.
Religious motivation was common to them and they agreed upon the
kind of society they were working for, but there was hardly likely to
be complete unanimity of religious belief. Whereas some of them like
Whalley and Worsley had apparently stayed in the mainstream of the
puritan tradition, others were on the radical wing of the church.
Desborough, a member of an old Cambridgeshire puritan family,
was the patron of Henry Denne who founded the gathered church at
Fenstanton in the early 1650s.[35] Berry had fallen out with his old

[30] Ibid p 273.   [31] Ibid pp 545, 565.
[32] Ibid p 450; [J. S.] Morrill, Cheshire [1630–1660] (Oxford 1974) pp 282–3.
[33] Ibid p 695.
[34] C. Cross, Church and People 1450–1660 (London 1976) pp 199–221; C. Cross, 'The
Church under the Commonwealth', The Interregnum, ed G. E. Aylmer (London 1972)
pp 99–120.
[35] M. Spufford, Contrasting Communities (Cambridge 1974) pp 227–8, 286.

friend Richard Baxter, who believed he had been led astray by the
'new light'.[36] Goffe had a history of fanatical millenarianism, but it
seems his ardour cooled after 1650, when he was one of a group of
officers who called on the godly to hold a day of seeking God to lament
the darkening of his cause.[37] Boteler campaigned for religious toleration in the early 1650s. He opposed John Owen's plan in 1652 for the
continuance of an established church on the ground that it restricted
toleration to Christians. Two years later, he was one of a group of
officers who drew up a petition for liberty of conscience, which
parliament was threatening to restrict.[38]

The establishment of the protectorate made men like Boteler ask
themselves how far social and political order depended on imposing
limits to religious toleration. Boteler proved particularly severe to
Roman catholics, whom he regarded as agents of a foreign power: 'I
look upon them as enemies', he said in parliament, 'and upon that
account would not have them have the liberties of the laws'. He was
also vigorous in suppressing quakerism.[39] The same kind of shift in
attitude, on being faced with the practical problems of governing a
turbulent populace, can be seen in the case of Kelsey. He had
previously been a member of John Simpson's fifth monarchist and
baptist congregation at Allhallows the Great in London, which was
split by Cromwell's seizure of power. Kelsey was one of those accused
of apostasy: it was alleged that he said before the congregation that 'if
any should rise up against the present power, under what pretence
soever, he would sheath his sword in their bowels though his own
brethren'.[40] Early in 1656 he reacted firmly when the preaching of the
ranter Richard Coppin, who denied 'hell or heaven to be any other
than what was within him', tainted the garrison and townsmen of
Rochester.[41] Yet, as he told Cromwell, he was sensitive to the charges
of illiberality which might follow his imprisonment of Coppin,
'knowing that many scandalous professors that have fallen off from the
worship and services of God . . . . are not backward to say it's persecution worse than in the bishops' time'.[42]

In general the major-generals were harsh opponents of quakerism.[43]
Moreover only Goffe and Berry were sympathetic to fifth monarch-

[36] R. Baxter, *Autobiography* (London 1696) p 57.
[37] [B. S.] Capp, [*The*] *Fifth Monarchy Men* (London 1972) p 54.
[38] *HLQ* 11 (1947) pp 3–4.   [39] *Ibid* p 7.
[40] Capp, *Fifth Monarchy Men*, pp 276–8.
[41] C. Hill, *The World Turned Upside Down* (London 1972) pp 177–9.   [42] *TSP*, 4, p 486.
[43] *Ibid* pp 333, 408, 642; *Burton*, 1, pp 101–4, 108–10, 153–6, 260–1.

ANTHONY FLETCHER

ism.[44] When a Welsh fifth monarchist petition accusing the government of betraying the Good Old Cause and attacking tithes was read by cornet Day at a mass meeting in December 1655, Berry advised lenience.[45] Haynes, apprehensive about fifth monarchy activity in East Anglia, represented the other pole of thought: 'surely', he wrote, 'God cannot be pleased with such horrid hypocrisy as is manifest in their approaching to him with evil purposes in their hearts and he will judge such condemners of authority; and if a special regard be not had of condign punishment of them, your friends that serve you have but little encouragement so to do'.[46]

Out in the provinces the major-generals found it hard to stay in tune with Cromwell's desire to allow all men who faithfully tried to follow Christ to do so in their own way. Yet their different conclusions about where the line should be drawn were of minor importance beside the general unanimity and coherence of their religious and moral purposes. Some achieved more than others perhaps, but some had greater personal resources than others and some were more distracted than others by mundane problems of conspiracy and security.[47] All of them believed, as Cromwell did, that their duty was to work with the godly minority for the reform of the whole of society. There must have been times when all of them felt bewilderment and dismay. There were also times for exuberance and satisfaction, such as Worsley expressed after a busy week in Lancashire in March 1656: 'we are in a very good condition in this county. This work stirs up the good people to inform us of the conversation of all men, their carriage and behaviour, so that truly I think the good sober people never were in better heart than now and so much owned'.[48] The major-generals never shrank from their task, despite the obstacles they encountered, because their vision of a better society and their belief in God's presence constantly sustained them.[49]

University of Sheffield

---

[44] Capp, *Fifth Monarchy Men*, pp 110–11.
[45] *TSP*, 4, p 359.
[46] *Ibid* pp 329–30.
[47] D. W. Rannie, 'Cromwell's Major-Generals', *EHR*, 10 (1895) pp 471–506; *The English Civil War*, ed Parry, pp 82–7; Fletcher, *A County Community*, pp 305–11; Morrill, *Cheshire*, pp 276–87.
[48] *TSP*, 4, p 595.
[49] I am grateful to my wife and to Linda Kirk for their comments on drafts of this paper.

THE SEVEN BISHOPS:
A RECONSIDERATION

by G. V. BENNETT

OR Lord Macaulay the defiance offered by the seven bishops to James II marked a turning-point in English history. It was the story of men who would not stand by as a 'harsh and inexorable prince' destroyed constitutional liberties, established a military despotism, and imposed catholicism by force. The great whig historian was not much given to praise of the clergy in general or bishops in particular, but even he could not withhold his admiration from an archbishop of Canterbury 'who was ready to wear fetters and lay his aged limbs on bare stones rather than betray the interests of the Protestant religion and set the prerogative above the laws.'[1] Macaulay's account of the seven bishops is, however, closely bound up with his view of James II as one of the great villains of English history, and recent historians, while enjoying the rich texture of Macaulay's prose, find it difficult to accept the version of classical whig historiography.[2] In their work James appears as not so much a tyrant as a peculiarly maladroit politician, not so much an absolutist with wide-ranging ambitions as an obstinate man of narrow religious perspectives. His little army was quite incapable of imposing catholicism by force on a fiercely protestant nation. James's aim was as simple as it was injudicious: to achieve civil emancipation for the small minority of his catholic co-religionists by a process of political manoeuvre and manipulation. Now, if this re-interpretation be correct, it is time to extend the process into ecclesiastical history and look afresh at the motives and policies of the seven bishops. I would suggest that what emerges is something quite different from the traditional heroic version but nonetheless an instructive study in the clerical mind of the late seventeenth century.

The great Anglican crisis of 1688 traces its origins directly back to the politics of the last four years of Charles II. After the dissolution of

---

[1] T. B. Macaulay, *History of England* (Everyman edn) 2, pp 172–3.
[2] [J. R.] Jones, [*The Revolution of 1688 in England*] (London 1972); and [John] Miller, [*Popery and Politics in England, 1660–1688*] (Cambridge 1973).

the Oxford parliament in March 1681 the king permitted, even encouraged, local tories to purge their whig opponents out of political life. An essential part of this tory reaction was the deliberate harrying and prosecution of protestant dissenters, for during the years of the exclusion parliaments not only had there been a vastly increased number of dissenting MPs, but nonconformists and occasional conformists had established themselves on grand juries and borough magistracies, and as churchwardens, constables and parliamentary voters.[3] Now the work of reversing the process and destroying whig and dissenting influence was undertaken by county benches of eager tory magistrates.[4] By the beginning of 1682 a nationwide campaign was under way, mounting to a crescendo in 1683, the year of the Rye House plot. The records of quarter sessions for these years, many of which have only recently been examined, show the severity and effectiveness of the campaign. A careful study of the Cheshire magistrates, for example, shows a dramatic rise in the annual number of prosecutions for non-attendance at church: from three hundred and ten in 1681, to five hundred and six in 1682, six hundred and twenty-two in 1683, and seven hundred and eighteen in 1684. The same bench increased the number of indictments for conventicling from eight in 1681 to one hundred and forty-four in 1683. In Norfolk recusancy convictions mounted from two hundred and thirteen in 1680 to six hundred and sixty-six in 1684, while in Middlesex and Warwickshire the evidence provides an exact parallel.[5]

It is not possible to doubt that the majority of the clergy identified themselves wholly with this severe tory reaction. Archbishop Sancroft's vast correspondence with his suffragans shows that bishops and ordinary parish priests agitated for the magistrates to initiate prosecutions and complained bitterly to higher authority if the local benches were insufficiently energetic. The church courts had neither

---

[3] See [Douglas R.] Lacey, [*Dissent and Parliamentary Politics in England, 1661–1689*] (New Brunswick 1969) cap 7.

[4] See R. G. Pickavance, 'The English Boroughs and the King's Government: a study of the Tory Reaction, 1681–85' (Oxford Univ DPhil thesis 1976). Dr Pickavance argues that the re-modelling of boroughs was an attempt by local tories to control the corporation magistracies which had protected religious dissidents.

[5] T. C. Curtis, 'Some aspects of the history of crime in seventeenth-century England, with special reference to Cheshire and Middlesex' (John Rylands univ library of Manchester, PhD thesis 1973) p 56; Miller pp 191, 265, 267; *Warwick County Records*, 8: [Quarter Sessions Records, 1682–1690, ed H. C. Johnson] (Warwick 1953) pp lxv, seq. The vast bulk of the cases, though initiated under Elizabethan recusancy statutes, were against protestant dissenters.

The seven bishops: a reconsideration

the coercive power nor the administrative machinery to sustain alone
a campaign as systematic as that of 1681–4 but they could be used in an
auxiliary role, and the more determined bishops and archdeacons
brought continual pressure to bear on churchwardens to make them
present, or formally accuse before the courts, those who absented
themselves from Sunday worship or the easter sacrament. That a
really vigorous bishop could make the system work is shown by John
Fell's visitation of the diocese of Oxford in 1682. The individual
returns of the clergy, reporting on the effects of the bishop's efforts,
indicated that his policy of a strict prosecution against all those
presented had produced record numbers of communicants and
conformity from all but the most obdurate sectaries.[6] Without doubt
the combined activities of civil and ecclesiastical courts and the
energetic endeavours of magistrates and clergy produced an impressive
appearance of Anglican uniformity. Soon Sancroft's correspondents
were reporting the virtual collapse of dissenting congregations outside
the larger towns. Bishop Lamplugh of Exeter was not untypical when
in 1682 he wrote delightedly to tell the primate of great crowds 'not
only in frequenting the Church, but in very full Communions the last
Easter; a minister in the country told me he had 700 communicants this
last Easter, whereas in previous years he had not half the number.'[7]

The work of directing and co-ordinating this ecclesiastical policy
fell to one elderly and austere man: William Sancroft, from 1677
archbishop of Canterbury. Living frugally at Lambeth, rarely venturing
away from home, solitary and valetudinarian, the primate divided his
day between chapel, private interviews, and an immense labour at
his desk. It is obvious that he carried a terrible burden of work and
anxiety, and yet his life was devoted to a single cause: that of preserving
that Anglican order, worship and piety to which he was so genuinely
and unaffectedly devoted. He was acutely aware of the weakness
behind the splendid façade of establishment. Most of his clergy were
quite desperately poor and reduced by the workings of the patronage

---

[6] See Bodl[eian Library] MS Oxford diocesan papers b. 68, fols 9–10, for Fell's careful
summary of presentations at his visitation of 1682; and *ibid* c. 430, for a volume of
incumbents' replies in June and July 1682, giving accounts of dissenters in their parishes
and measures taken to reduce them to conformity.

[7] Bodl MS Tanner 35 fol 9, Lamplugh to Sancroft, 29 April 1682. See also Bodl MS
Rawl D 372, for a volume containing the returns for Exeter diocese made to
James II's commissioners to enquire into property taken by destraint from dissenters
between 1677 and 1688. An analysis shows 1682 and 1683 as the years when convictions
were most frequent.

system to dependence on the influential laity. Inequitable endowments, pluralities and non-residence resulted in a widespread and gross neglect of pastoral care. But what was perhaps most alarming was the almost complete indifference of the ordinary people to the distinctive features of Anglican churchmanship. The letters of the archbishop's suffragans indicated only too clearly that a continual pressure had to be exerted on lay people to attend services, receive the sacrament once a year, and send their children to be catechized or confirmed. In a land which had endured many religious changes and disruptions there was fierce protestant sentiment but Anglicanism as such was very far from having won the hearts of ordinary men and women. What the old primate wanted then was time: time to initiate a programme of reforms, to raise the income and standards of the parish priests, to refurbish discipline and inculcate the ways of Anglican piety. To gain time he, like his formidable predecessor, Gilbert Sheldon, was prepared to see the penal laws rigorously enforced against dissenters who would not yield to kindness and persuasion.[8]

It must be made clear, however, that in espousing this policy of 'thorough' Sancroft was running counter to an influential body of clergy and laity who advocated an alternative Anglican strategy: that of the conciliation of moderate dissenters by offering them 'comprehension', a relaxing of the stricter terms of membership of the church by which ceremonies would be made optional and the forms of subscription attenuated so that nonconformist ministers might be admitted to benefices. Comprehension at least preserved the notion of a national church in which the morals and religious duties of all citizens came under the aegis of ecclesiastical discipline; its underlying aim was to comprehend moderate dissenters but then to continue the persecution of obstinate sectaries or admit them to the barest form of a toleration. During the exclusion crisis it had been the avowed policy of committed churchmen such as Daniel Finch, son of Lord Chancellor Nottingham, and distinguished senior divines such as Edward Stillingfleet, dean of St Paul's, and John Tillotson, dean of Canterbury. But its drawback from the Sancroftian point of view was the lengths to which some liberal churchmen were prepared to go in dismantling the Anglican beauty of holiness, and in the years of the tory reaction the archbishop set his face like a flint against the promotion of 'trimming' divines, even though these included some of the most eminent

---

[8] See R. A. Beddard, 'William Sancroft, as Archbishop of Canterbury, 1677–1691' (Oxford Univ DPhil thesis 1965) cap 5: 'The reform of the Church.'

London incumbents.[9] What, of course, virtually no Anglican was prepared to accept was a policy of 'indulgence' or general toleration, for this, they knew, would shatter the whole disciplinary machinery of the national church.

In the execution of his difficult task Sancroft was fortunate in the support of an inner group of his episcopal colleagues. Anthony Sparrow of Norwich, William Gulston of Bristol, John Fell of Oxford, Robert Frampton of Gloucester, Thomas Lamplugh of Exeter, William Lloyd of Peterborough, and his namesake, William Lloyd of St Asaph, all provided him with detailed local information and acted energetically on his advice.[10] But death created vacancies on the bench, even among his closest adjutants, and it was necessary to recruit younger men who would share his politics, churchmanship and reforming zeal. For this he required a strong interest at court and, without hesitation, he attached himself and his cause to the 'reversionary interest', the Yorkist party of James, duke of York, and the Hyde brothers, the earls of Rochester and Clarendon. When in 1681 the king set up an ecclesiastical commission to advise him on all senior appointments in the church, Sancroft and Rochester used it as an instrument to promote only divines of proven loyalism. Beddard has rightly seen this as an essential feature of the tory reaction: a parallel in the church to the purges of magistrates and the surrender of charters.[11] In the years from 1681 to 1684 three of the future seven bishops were first promoted to the episcopate: Francis Turner to Rochester in 1683, and John Lake to Bristol and Thomas Ken to Bath and Wells in 1684.

The distinctive feature of each of these men was his close personal connection with the duke of York.[12] Although a convinced and emphatic catholic convert, James drew most of his friends from among

[9] H. Horwitz, 'Protestant reconciliation in the Exclusion crisis', *JEH* 15 (1964) pp 201–17. For Sancroft's hostility to the Finch connection, see Bodl MS Tanner 36 fol 184, Nottingham to Sancroft, 2 December 1681. See also Bodl MS Rawl letters 99 fol 113, for bishop Francis Turner's notes on the 'Character of the Latitudinarian Spirit', in which he refers particularly to Stillingfleet and the London clergy.

[10] William Lloyd (1627–1717), bishop of St Asaph in 1680, had been closely concerned in the comprehension projects of 1680–1 but later recovered Sancroft's good opinion by energetic action against dissent in his diocese. See Bodl MS Tanner 35 fols 151, 162, 190; A. Tindal Hart, *William Lloyd* (London 1952) pp 48 *seq.*

[11] Robert Beddard, 'The Commission for Ecclesiastical Promotions, 1681–84: an instrument of Tory reaction', *HJ* 12 (1967) pp 11–40.

[12] For the early connections of Turner and Lake with both James and Sancroft, see *ibid* pp 23–30; for Ken's early relations with James, see E. H. Plumptre, *Thomas Ken* (2 ed London 1890) 1, p 260. John Lake had been nominated to the island-see of Sodor and Man in 1682 by the earl of Derby.

Anglicans and he maintained easy and kind relations with the Anglican members of his household. On all occasions he identified himself with the tory cause. During the time of his personal rule in Scotland he worked with and through the episcopalian party and earned the abiding gratitude and loyalty of the Scottish bishops.[13] In all this a key-figure was Dr Francis Turner whom James took to Edinburgh in 1680 as his Anglican chaplain. It is clear that Turner proved to be a natural courtier, a man of subtle intelligence who could win the trust and even affection of a master of a naturally inflexible cast of mind. Writing from Scotland in June 1681, Turner reported the substance of a number of private conversations he had had with James; he was delighted to assure Sancroft that 'he places his hopes altogether upon that interest we call the Church of England, upon the Episcopal party and mainly upon the Bishops themselves, your Grace especially.'[14] With the duke and the archbishop behind him, Turner's rise up the ladder of preferment was meteoric: in 1683 dean of Windsor, later that year bishop of Rochester, and finally in 1684 translated to the rich and important see of Ely. Already by the time of his return from the north, Turner had established himself as the primate's most direct link with the court. Living at the centre of royal power, freely admitted to the king and the duke, skilfully conveying to them the archbishop's advice and recommendations, Turner (in spite of his comparative youth) was a vital figure in the maintenance of the Anglican ascendancy.[15] On all sides it was recognized that his masterful personality and diplomatic talents marked him out as the next archbishop of Canterbury.[16]

The unexpected death of Charles II on 6 February 1685 put the whole Sancroftian strategy to the test, but in the first hours of his reign James went out of his way to affirm his adherence to the Anglican regime. Quite unprompted, at his accession council he made a formal statement, promising 'to preserve this government in Church and State as it is by law established. I know the principles of the Church of England are for monarchy and the members of it have shewed

[13] Bodl MS Tanner 35 fol 185, Alexander Burnet, archbishop of St Andrews, to Turner, 9 February 1683.
[14] *Ibid* 36 fol 31, Turner to Sancroft, 2 June 1681.
[15] Bodl MS Tanner 32 fol 37, Turner to Sancroft, 21 April 1684: he reports that he has moved the duke and the king that Lake should be given the bishopric of Bristol, and they have accepted the archbishop's motion.
[16] Bodl MS Rawl letters 94, fol 276, Dolben of York to Turner, 16 August 1684.

themselves good and loyal subjects, therefore I shall always take care to defend and support it.'[17] Throughout the country Anglicans received his words with a kind of rapture as from a man known to be obstinately firm to his promises. Sancroft himself led a rush of loyal addresses by praying James 'that you would be (what you have been ever observed to be) yourself: that is, generous and just, and true to all that you once declare.' In diocese and county, clergy and gentry joined together in compositions of sonorous prose to make an impressive demonstration of tory strength and resolve.[18]

The bishops were, of course, well aware that James would be anxious to improve the condition of his catholic co-religionists, and they were willing that the enforcement of the penal laws against them should be allowed quietly to lapse. Recusants were less than two per cent of the population, and they were mostly devoted to the Stuart cause. The problem was how to cease the prosecution of catholics without at the same time destroying the apparatus for the control of protestant dissent. This, it is clear, James himself had no wish to do. Indeed on the very evening of his accession he assured a group of bishops that 'he would never give any sort of countenance to Dissenters, knowing that it must needs be faction and not religion.'[19] In the spring royal orders were issued to the courts, civil and ecclesiastical, not to enforce the recusancy laws against those who could produce certificates of 'loyalty', and it was soon clear that such certificates were a device to distinguish catholic recusants from protestant dissenters. By May a stream of such certificates was being issued, and thereafter the bishops disregarded the presentments of recusants and instructed their legal officers not to proceed in such cases.[20] But this exception apart, the campaign against dissent went on unabated with the king's manifest consent and encouragement. In the spring individual bishops issued pastoral letters calling on the churchwardens to prosecute absentees from the easter sacrament, and in the summer old bishop Fell followed up his exhortations by conducting the last and most searching of his visitations. No less than

---

[17] *The London Gazette*, no 2006 (5–9 February 1685).

[18] Bodl MS Tanner 32 fol 214, for the text of the speech in Sancroft's hand; *ibid* fol 227, Dolben to Sancroft, 23 February 1685, for evidence of the archbishop's direction that the clergy should address with the local gentry.

[19] [Henry] Ellis, [*Original Letters*] (1 ser, London 1824) 3, p 339.

[20] See Bodl MS Tanner 31 fol 289, White to Sancroft, 9 March 1686; *The Camden Miscellany*, 2 (1853): Trelawny Papers, ed W. D. Cooper, p 14: Trelawny to Sunderland, 21 May 1686. The orders were issued on 27 February to the civil courts and 18 April to the church courts.

four hundred and twenty-four dissenters were presented in addition to those already standing excommunicate.[21]

In these halcyon days James gave his ready consent to the appointment of bishops of proven tory credentials. There was indeed one such divine whose elevation he was especially anxious to secure. The reverend Sir Jonathan Trelawny was a thirty-five year-old clergyman skilled not in theology or the pastoral care but in the coarse art of Cornish boroughmongering. In a county which returned no less than forty-four members to the house of commons the Trelawny interest commanded eleven seats. Sir Jonathan had been nursing the family boroughs since 1679, and in 1685 he succeeded to the baronetcy just in time to take charge of the royal election campaign in the west.[22] In the summer he added to his superb services by accepting the king's commission to go down to Cornwall at the time of Monmouth's rebellion to put the loyalists into a posture of defence.[23] James's initial wish was to appoint him to the bishopric of Exeter but, since bishop Lamplugh resolutely refused to vacate his see, it was decided that Trelawny must go to Bristol as the nearest thing to his home country.[24] The appointment was not entirely to the archbishop's liking. The new bishop's youth, lack of learning and squirearchical ways did not conform to the Sancroftian image of the episcopate but his politics were impeccable, and his going to Bristol co-incided with a series of episcopal moves of which the primate wholly approved. Thus John Lake was translated to Chichester; Lloyd of Peterborough went to Norwich; and Thomas White, who as archdeacon of Nottingham had been the terror of recalcitrant churchwardens, was consecrated to Peterborough. With this last promotion all the future seven bishops had reached the episcopate.

The first break in this harmony occurred in the autumn of 1685 when James began to canvass for a repeal of the recusancy laws and

[21] Bodl MS Oxf dioc papers b 68, fols 1–8, for Fell's careful summary of the churchwardens' presentments. The sixteen popish recusants returned were not proceeded against in the diocesan court: see Bodl MS Archd papers Oxon c. 23, 'joint-title' acts, 1681–1686.
[22] See G. Holmes, *British Politics in the Age of Anne* (London 1967) p 323, for a description of the Trelawny interest, which included East and West Looe, Plymouth, Liskeard and (usually) Tregony and Lostwithiel. For Trelawny's early connection with James, and his electioneering in 1679, see *Collectanea Trelawniana*, p 219, Peterborough to Trelawny, 16 Sept. 1679. I am grateful to Mr Francis T. Williams for allowing me to use these transcripts from papers once at Trelawne.
[23] *Trelawny Papers*, p 16: Trelawny to Sunderland, 14 June 1686.
[24] Bodl MS Tanner 31 fol 117, Lloyd of Peterborough to dean Simon Patrick, 20 June 1685.

the test acts of 1673 and 1678. He was acutely aware of the fact that he had no catholic heir, and he was determined to secure some statutory emancipation for his co-religionists before his death and the accession of his Anglican daughter, Mary of Orange. He assured those whom he 'closetted' that he did not thereby intend a general toleration or any breach with his tory supporters. His proposal was simply for the religious liberty and public employment of a small minority who shared the king's own religion, and this he thought a 'reasonable desire'.[25] There is no real evidence that James ever planned to impose catholicism by force. Indeed he had so absolute a conviction of the rightness of the Roman faith that he believed men would freely embrace it once its political disabilities were removed. But in this his political judgement was sadly deficient. He underestimated not only deeply-nurtured fears of secret popish machinations but tory determination that there should be no breaches in their monopoly of public office. What he did not expect was the fierce and united resistance which his proposals encountered, and in particular from the bishops. One by one, they refused point-blank to assist him, and actually began to concert a campaign against him.[26] On 19 November in the house of lords the bishop of London made a vehement attack on the employment of catholic officers in the army, 'and when he ended he said he spake the sense of the whole bench, at which they all rose up.'[27] In the following winter and spring the Sancroftian bishops led a great outburst of preaching which was clearly intended to intimidate James by whipping up popular anti-popish sentiment. Seizing on the pretext of some feeble Roman efforts at public propaganda, the pulpits in London rang with emotional denunciations of popish error and cruelty. And this was not merely the outpourings of obscure divines. The offensive was led by Turner, Frampton and, in particular, by bishop Ken of Bath and Wells, whose reputation for sanctity and whose passionate pulpit-oratory drew vast crowds. It was perhaps Turner's leading role in all this which most wounded the king. After hearing about one especially outspoken sermon, James was too upset even to speak to him at the royal levée.[28]

[25] HMC 12th Report, 9, *Beaufort MSS*, pp 89–90, James to the duke of Beaufort, 12 Feb. 1687: 'What I intend . . . is to have the two tests and penal laws repealed, that my Catholic subjects may be in the same condition the rest of my subjects are.'

[26] Dr Williams's Library, Morrice MSS, P fol 491, 7 November 1685, for the account in Roger Morrice's 'Entering Book', 1677–91.

[27] *The Autobiography of Sir John Bramston*, ed T. W. Bramston, CSer (1845) p 217.

[28] Ellis, (2 ser, 1827) 4, p 84: 5 January 1686. For sermons by Turner, Frampton and Ken, see *The Diary of John Evelyn*, ed E. S. de Beer (Oxford 1955) 4, pp 499–504.

His reaction to the situation was typical of a man well-known for his simple and authoritarian attitudes: he decided to coerce the Sancroftians by showing them that he could, if he so chose, frustrate their whole policy for Anglican uniformity and discipline.[29] On 10 March 1686 he therefore issued out a general pardon to all his subjects, and at a stroke nullified all proceedings in the civil and ecclesiastical courts. William Lloyd described pungently how at Norwich the pardon 'produced a Gaol Delivery at the Consistory' and ruined all his efforts to prosecute scandals in his diocese.[30] But the bishops were not quite so easily deterred, and with the coming of summer they journeyed down into the country to conduct visitation progresses and to urge churchwardens once again to present dissenters and all other absentees from the easter sacrament. The younger and more energetic of the archbishop's friends were given commissions to conduct metropolitical visitations within the dioceses of their decayed or negligent brethren. Thus White of Peterborough travelled the length of the vast diocese of Lincoln, reporting back to Sancroft his remorseless efforts to extract honest and full presentments from reluctant churchwardens.[31] By mid-July the ecclesiastical courts had new cases before them and were once again in full operation.[32] But the main thrust of the renewed tory campaign had to be undertaken by the magistrates, and the spring and summer of 1686 were later remembered for a severe enforcement of the conventicle acts. Indeed in Middlesex alone between February and June over three hundred certificates of conviction for conventicling were issued, and some of these included the names of twenty persons. In six months more people were convicted even than in the worst year of the popish plot.[33] By

---

[29] PRO 31/3/164 (Baschet transcripts of ambassadors' reports), Barrillon au Roi, 28 January/7 February 1686: 'Il connaît que le parti episcopal sera fort mal aisé à ramener en faveur des Catholiques: il voudra . . . tenter encore si la fermeté ne surmontera point les accoûtumer à souffrir la religion Catholique plutôt que d'être exposés à voir toutes les sectes différentes s'établir.'

[30] Bodl MS Tanner 138 fol 53, Lloyd to Sancroft, 24 March 1686.

[31] Bodl MS Tanner 31 fol 277, White to Sancroft, 1 March 1686; *ibid* 30 fol 45, 27 May; *ibid* fol 37, Lloyd of Norwich to Sancroft, 21 May; *ibid* fol 50, Trelawny to Sancroft, 1 June; *ibid* fol 63, Lake of Chichester to Sancroft, 18 June; *ibid* fol 104 Turner to Sancroft, 16 August.

[32] Morrice MSS P fol 568, 17 July 1686: 'The Spiritual Courts are open again, and they are very busy in receiving presentments, in issuing out citations and processes, etc., and injunctions are gone out from the Bps . . . to all ministers in their dioceses strictly to enjoin and require all churchwardens to present those that come not to church, or that received not the sacrament the last Easter.'

[33] Miller p 205, quoting GLC Archives, Middlesex section, MR/RC/9.

high summer that well-informed presbyterian minister, Roger Morrice, was recording not only continual disturbances of ministers and congregations but a wave of prosecutions at assizes and local quarter sessions.[34] It is perhaps not surprising that at this time the level of conformity remained high, and communicants at Easter were even larger than in the previous year. In May Lloyd of Norwich rejoiced to assure Sancroft that 'for one communicant that was in this diocese three months ago there is now three if not more in proportion through the whole diocese.' The numbers recorded by William Sampson, the bleakly disciplinarian rector of Clayworth, Nottinghamshire, rose to two hundred and eleven persons out of two hundred and thirty-six inhabitants of age and qualified to receive the sacrament.[35] Despite king James the Anglican ascendancy had reached its zenith.

Faced with such intransigence, the king passed the summer in some confusion as to what policy to adopt. In July he set up an ecclesiastical commission with the express purpose of curbing the continual anti-popish preaching of the clergy, but this produced only defiance from the bishop of London and popular demonstrations on his behalf.[36] Until this time James had rejected any idea of abandoning his Anglican alliance but gradually, as feelings became exacerbated, he listened to voices at court and among his catholic intimates which edged him towards a new and dangerous policy: a *renversement des alliances*, a joining together of catholics, dissenters, former whigs, and any tories who would serve him, into a new 'king's party'. He would exert all the influence at the crown's disposal to break the tory ascendancy and procure a new parliament which would secure catholic emancipation as part of a statutory toleration granted to all the king's subjects. It was a drastic policy; it would certainly require a stretching of prerogative power beyond its agreed limits—but it was not necessarily a mad policy. The tory regime itself had come into existence only by a vigorous purging of the personnel of public life and the Sancroftian campaign to enforce church attendance had raised up many enemies not only among protagonists for civil liberty but among the many more who were religiously indifferent.

From the beginning of August, therefore, James turned all his efforts

---

[34] Morrice MSS P fols 536, 547, 568, 572, 579, 609. For the especially harsh treatment of quakers at this time, see R. T. Vann, *The Social Development of English Quakerism* (Cambridge, Mass., 1969) p 92.

[35] Bodl MS Tanner 30 fol 37, Lloyd to Sancroft, 21 May 1686; *The Rector's Book, Clayworth, Notts*, ed Henry Gill and E. L. Guilford (Nottingham 1910).

[36] Morrice MSS P fols 602, 609–10; *The Diary of John Evelyn*, 4, p 519; Miller p 210.

to destroy the ecclesiastical strategy of his old friends among the bishops. The change came with startling suddenness. On 26 July Sancroft had an audience with the king and came away under the firm impression that he had accepted the names of two reliable tory divines for the vacant bishoprics of Chester and Oxford. But, within a fortnight, to his surprise and intense chagrin, he learned that the sees had been privately offered to two clergymen of whom he wholeheartedly disapproved: Thomas Cartwright, a servile courtier, and Samuel Parker, an unbalanced careerist with whom as archdeacon of Canterbury the primate had repeatedly clashed.[37] To be required to consecrate such a pair was a humiliation which Sancroft found it hard to forgive, and he treated them both with barely disguised distaste. But the court's principal aim was now to entice the dissenters into its new alliance by ending the church's campaign against them. On 28 August Roger Morrice noted that it was then 'taken for granted all Dissenters may have Dispensations, &c. to secure them from all Penall Statutes relateing to matters of worship &c. and to give them liberty to keepe Conventicles, and to have this so far as lyes in his Majesties power confirmed by Parliament, the like being done at the same time for Papists.'[38] For a while tory magistrates put up a vigorous rearguard action and continued to indict conventicles and prosecute absentees from church, but James's agents (and notably the catholic lawyer, Robert Brent) were active in procuring dispensations for congregations and individuals who found themselves in difficulty. At the end of November a regular dispensation-office was set up, charging fifty shillings a time for the indemnification of a whole family. Soon the magistrates were reduced to binding over or releasing dissenters who were willing to take advantage of the king's prerogative offer.

It was, however, by a revolution in the provinces that the whole Sancroftian system was finally shattered. Professor J. R. Jones has described the wholesale dismissal of lords-lieutenant, sheriffs, justices

---

[37] Bodl MS Tanner 30 fol 92, Sancroft to James, 29 July 1686, giving his recommendation of Dr Robert South ('who your Majesty mentioned') and Dr James Jeffreys for the vacant bishoprics. See also *ibid* 31 fols 166–75, for a diatribe from Parker, addressed to the king, abusing Sancroft for obstructing his promotion, *circa* July 1685. For the clandestine manner of Cartwright's appointment by the king and his subsequent career as an agent of royal policies, see *The Diary of Dr Thomas Cartwright, Bishop of Chester*, CSer (1843).

[38] Morrice MSS P fol 615. On 2 August Sir John Baber, a court agent, told Morrice that 'the Court was in great distress, finding the Church restive and uncompliant, and had therefore taken a great displeasure against it, and it should be made to feel the effects of it': *ibid* fol 594.

and mayors which took place in the early months of 1687, and their replacement by catholics, dissenters and former whigs. What has not been dealt with previously is the effect of this on the church. The evidence from the records of quarter sessions and the ecclesiastical courts shows that prosecutions for religious offences began to fall away rapidly under the impact of the dispensations but they ceased entirely in February and March, when it became known that the king intended to issue a declaration for general liberty of conscience. A few examples must suffice. At Warwick at the epiphany sessions the constables presented no less than one hundred and seventy-three absentees from church but at the following lady day sessions not a single such presentment was made. Within a few days the clerk entered the king's declaration in the court-book. At the Worcestershire quarter sessions there is nothing after 9 January.[39] In the Canterbury consistory court the last prosecution for not receiving the sacrament was on 11 February, and in the Chichester consistory the last case for absence from church was on 18 March.[40] When on 4 April 1687 the king issued out his declaration formally suspending 'all manner of penal laws in matters ecclesiastical, for not coming to church, or not receiving the sacrament, or for any other nonconformity to the religion established', the ecclesiastical courts had already ceased to exercise any jurisdiction in uniformity matters. Such a general toleration produced packed congregations in dissenting chapels both in London and the provinces, and there were alarmist reports of gravely diminished attendances at the parish churches. Well might Lloyd of Norwich bewail the situation to archbishop Sancroft and pray that 'the Lord in his mercy pity his despised Church and restore its discipline'.[41]

By the spring of 1688 it seemed that the king's policies were moving towards success. The regulation of boroughs and the replacement of

[39] *Warwick County Records*, 8, pp 198–207; Worcestershire R[ecord] O[ffice] 'Quarter Sessions Book, 1686, no 3'.
[40] Canterbury Diocesan RO, 'Consistory: Office Book, 1675–98', fol 154; West Sussex RO, 'Chichester Consistory Detection Book, 1682–1692'. In the Worcester consistory court, however, the last process for not receiving the sacrament was on 7 November 1685: Worcestershire RO, 'Consistory Detecta Act Book 33', fol 86. I am grateful to the Revd Evan Davies for these references.
[41] Bodl MS Tanner 29 fol 11, Lloyd to Sancroft, 29 April 1687. For the sudden increase of dissenting activity, see Morrice MSS Q, fol 96, 16 April; *Diary of John Evelyn*, 4, p 546; Bodl MS Tanner 29 fol 47, Trelawny to Sancroft, 1 July. For James's doubts about the wisdom of his own policies, see PRO 31/3/168, Barrillon au Roi, 24 March/3 April 1687: 'Je crois que, dans le fonds, si on ne pouvait laisser que la religion Anglicane et la Catholique établies par les lois, le roi d'Angleterre en serait bien plus content.'

local officials had reached the point where James was ready to risk calling a parliament. The managers of his campaign for repealing the test and penal laws were sending in optimistic reports that a majority would be obtained and, in spite of much anger and discontent, there was no sign of any organised opposition. Certainly the leading tory lay politicians, Rochester, Danby and Nottingham, provided neither leadership nor any focus of resistance.[42] There were many clandestine meetings and a great deal of anonymous pamphleteering but only the clergy had so far dared to expose themselves to the risks of direct opposition to the royal will. Thus the bishop of London lay under suspension for his defiance of the ecclesiastical commission, the fellows of Magdalen had incurred ejection for refusing to admit a Roman catholic president, and the leading clergy in the dioceses had organized an almost total refusal by their brethren to send up congratulatory addresses to the king. It was thus that James decided to break the resistance of the clerical order before summoning his parliament for November. The device adopted was to re-issue the declaration of indulgence and to make a formal order requiring that it should be read out in every church on two successive Sundays. The clergy had to choose whether to submit to the declaration or to disobey a direct royal command.

It was thus that James delivered himself into the hands of the Sancroftians. During the spring there had been earnest meetings at Lambeth as an inner group of bishops attempted to devise a policy. It is clear that they were searching for some way to raise up against the king an opposition so widespread that he would be forced to abandon his present policies and take refuge once again with his old friends. The anti-popery issue lay obviously to hand and the tory bishops, notably Ken of Bath and Wells, were still drawing immense crowds with sermons on the cruel sufferings of protestants at the hands of popish tyrants.[43] But this in itself was not enough, and the royal order on 4 May that the declaration should be read in all London churches on 20 and 27 May came as an opportunity that could be critical if rightly exploited. The London clergy held some hurried and inconclusive meetings; they consulted leading politicians like Rochester, Nottingham, Danby and Halifax, but their advice was either non-committal or actually to read the declaration.[44] It was at

[42] See J. R. Jones, *The Revolution of 1688 in England* (London 1972) for an excellent analysis of the campaign to pack parliament.
[43] *The Diary of John Evelyn*, 4, pp 577–8: 1 April 1688.

this point, however, that bishop Turner of Ely took matters in hand, and it is difficult not to see what followed as a triumph for his political sense and diplomatic skill. If an effective challenge were now to be offered to James, it would have to be from a united protestant front, and this would have to include not only the Sancroftians but distinguished 'moderate' divines like Edward Stillingfleet, John Tillotson, Simon Patrick and Thomas Tenison, and even (if possible) the leading dissenting ministers. And yet, if the bishops were eventually to achieve their own aims, they had to lead this resistance movement and in some measure direct its course. The task was one of great difficulty not only in view of their record against dissent but also in the light of the hostility which the Sancroftians had exhibited towards the comprehension schemes of which Stillingfleet and Tillotson had been such ardent advocates. And yet now the leading moderates were essential allies. Their influence was especially strong among the London incumbents and it was recognized on all sides that what London did on 20 May would determine the decision of the vast majority of ordinary parish priests. Only they, too, could make contact with, and even recruit, the influential dissenting ministers. To settle the terms of common action and to mobilize a solid resistance against the king required not only negotiating skill but even dissimulation of a high order.

Turner was, however, equal to the task. He held two conferences at Ely House with leading London clergymen and on 11 May a full meeting at the house of the master of the temple, at which a resolution was taken 'that the bishops should be desired to address the king, but not upon any address of ours to them'.[45] With the initiative thus fir mly in his hands, Turner could, the next day, report to a small group at Lambeth, consisting of Sancroft, Compton of London, White of Peterborough and the earl of Clarendon. That evening the archbishop sat down to summon up to town immediately the bishops with whom he wished to associate himself in this deliberate challenge to the royal authority: Mews of Winchester, Lloyd of Norwich, Frampton of Gloucester, Ken of Bath and Wells, Lake of Chichester, Trelawny of Bristol and Lloyd of St Asaph.[46] On the thirteenth Turner presided

---

[44] [*The*] *Corr[espondence of Henry Hyde, Earl of] Clarendon*, ed S. W. Singer (London 1828) 2 p 177; Morrice MSS Q, fol 255; BL Add MSS 34515, fols 67-8 (Mackintosh transcripts): James Johnston's report of 27 May 1688.

[45] ['The Autobiography of Simon] Patrick', in *Works*, ed A. Taylor (London 1858) 9 p 510; Morrice MSS Q fol 255.

[46] *Clarendon Corr*, 2 p 171; Bodl MS Tanner 28 fols 29-33.

over a meeting of about twenty of the leading London clergy: to organise the canvassing of the rest of the incumbents and the dissenting ministers, and to agree upon the actual terms of the bishops' petition. This was clearly Turner's most difficult moment. To achieve unanimity there had to be some offer of a comprehension of moderate dissenters within the ministry of the church. Then and there at the meeting a draft was worked out containing the famous phrase that an aversion to publishing the declaration did not stem from 'any want of due tenderness towards the Dissenters, in relation to whom we shall be willing to come to such a temper as shall be thought fit when that matter comes to be considered and settled in Parliament and Convocation.'[47] It was the least for which Turner could have settled. He did not agree to a toleration but only to a comprehension, the terms of which were to be worked out later and which would then be submitted to the convocation. But the formula sufficed. On 17 May Turner and White were given reports that an overwhelming majority of the London clergy would not read the petition and that, on the basis of the draft petition which they had been shown, the leading dissenters had pledged their support as well.[48]

Friday, 18 May, was the latest possible day for action, and most of it was spent in a prolonged meeting at Lambeth. By this time Sancroft, Turner, White and Compton had been joined by Ken, Trelawny and Lloyd of St Asaph. Stillingfleet, Tillotson, Patrick, Tenison and Dr Edward Grove were there to represent the London clergy. An attempt was made to insert into the petition a phrase which referred to 'this heavy burthen [which] is imposed upon them of proclaiming Liberty of Conscience to all the world (even to your Enemies)', but this could not be agreed upon and was discarded.[49] When agreement was at last reached Lake of Chichester had appeared but there was still no sign of Frampton or Lloyd of Norwich, and it was resolved that the petition should be delivered in the name of seven bishops only. Sancroft himself could not accompany his brethren, since he was forbidden the

[47] See [R.] Thomas, ['The Seven Bishops and their Petition, 18 May 1688'], *JEH*, 12 (1961) pp 64–5, for a comparison of this draft with the petition as presented. I regret that I cannot accept Dr Thomas's general thesis which, by viewing the situation through the eyes of Roger Morrice and James Johnston, seriously underrates the role of the bishops and exaggerates that of the London clergy and the dissenters.

[48] For the nonconformist reaction, see Lacey, pp 210–12. Morrice gives the draft as it was communicated to him by Dr Edward Fowler and which he describes as the 'Comprehensive Sense of the Clergy': Morrice MSS Q fol 259, 15 May.

[49] Bodl MS Tanner 28 fol 34, for the corrected draft in Sancroft's hand. For the clearest account, see 'Patrick', p 510.

court, but they, even as they set out, could not but rejoice that the mystical number of seven would itself lend significance to their protest.

The scene at Whitehall when the six handed the petition to James is too well-known to bear repetition. The king had been given no warning and it was a grievous shock to find not only that the bishops intended to disobey him but that they wished publicly to dispute the legality of his dispensing power. The wholly unexpected had occurred. The bishops, upon whose passivity he had counted, had taken the first move in what he knew only too well could easily escalate into a national movement of resistance. It is perhaps not surprising that his most reproachful words were addressed to Francis Turner: 'I did not expect this from you; especially from some of you.'[50]

From this moment on, as popular excitement mounted, James was outmanoeuvred by the bishops at every stage. On 20 May virtually none of the London clergy read the declaration, and the government had to face a situation in which its authority was openly defied. Within a few days Sancroft and his allies had a powerful letter printed and dispatched to all the country clergy, urging that the declaration should not be read since this would divide the clergy from the gentry in the face of the coming election and would lead on to 'an unlimited and universal Toleration' and teach the people 'that they need never come to church more'.[51] On 3 June there was an almost universal refusal by the ordinary parish priests. In some confusion the council hesitated over what was to be done, and when it was finally decided to prosecute the bishops for seditious libel matters were already moving out of the king's control. Now each step which the government took merely enhanced the bishops' status as protestant martyrs. When they appeared before the council on 8 June, the king assumed that they would enter into recognisances to appear at their trial but this they steadfastly refused to do, and thus manoeuvred him into a position where he had either to drop the case or send them to the Tower of London on remand.[52] As they went forth from Whitehall they were watched by vast, anxious and emotional crowds; men and

[50] See *ibid* p 511, for the bishops' report to Sancroft and for James's special reproach to Turner. Bishop Compton did not sign the petition since he was under suspension.

[51] See Bodl MS Tanner 28 fols 5–6, for a draft of 'A Letter from a Clergyman in the Citty of London to his Friend in the Country containing his reasons for not reading the Declaration'. Within two hours of the bishops' petition having been delivered what claimed to be a copy of it was hawked about the streets, and this has given rise to speculation as to who was responsible for such publication. In fact, what was printed was the earlier draft circulated among London clergy and dissenting ministers: see Thomas p 67.

women knelt in the streets to receive their blessings, and pressed forward to touch the hem of their robes. Once lodged in the Tower, they were visited by relays of nobles, other bishops, London clergy and even one superbly timed deputation of dissenting ministers. When at last they agreed to give sureties, they had ready an impressive array of aristocratic guarantors.

It is clear, then, that even before the trial of the seven bishops began the court was in grave alarm and desperately anxious to end the whole affair without too much loss of face. On the evening before, the king sent Lord Dartmouth to Turner in an endeavour to arrange some compromise which could result in a withdrawal of the prosecution, but all such overtures the bishops rejected out of hand.[53] When the trial came on 29 June Westminster Hall was packed with nobles, gentry and clergy and the streets around were filled with a large and menacing crowd. There was none of the iron grip on proceedings customary at important political trials, and the defence was allowed to move the argument on to a general attack on James for acting illegally to promote the Romish religion. Eventually the lord chief justice broke with all established legal precedent by actually putting it to the jury to decide whether in point of law the bishops' petition amounted to a seditious libel. Their acquittal had thus much of the character of a capitulation to organised public opinion, and it sparked off not only a wave of delirious rejoicing throughout the country but a massive disobedience to the efforts of the new magistrates to restore order.[54]

Now, having inflicted such a shattering blow to the king's position, the bishops set about trying to rebuild the tory system. Immediately after the acquittal Sancroft ordered his colleagues down to their dioceses with instructions to strengthen relations with the leading laity forged in the recent crisis and to keep up a friendly correspondence with dissenters.[55] It is clear that their main concern was with the parliament expected to meet in November. It was essential to encourage tory candidates to stand and to work up an interest for them, but, in

---

[52] Jones p 124. For the bishops' deliberate earlier decision not to give recognizances, see Bodl MS Tanner 28 fol 60, Turner to Sancroft, 'Friday morning' [8 June 1688].

[53] *Clarendon Corr* 2 p 179, 28 June 1688: 'Lord Dartmouth had been with the Bishop of Ely, to persuade him to make application to the King; which got air, and was like to have been very inconvenient, had not the Bishop been very steady.'

[54] For Turner's notes on the trial and the popular manifestations, see Bodl MS Rawl letters 99, fols 107–8: 'My heart bled for my Master in his Agony.' See also Miller pp 251–2, for the general breakdown of government control in the localities.

[55] Bodl MS Tanner 28 fol 121; see also Bodl MS Rawl letters 99 fol 108.

The seven bishops: a reconsideration

view of the drastically regulated state of many corporations and the probability of a strong phalanx of dissenting MPs, the obtaining of a majority was likely to be a close-run thing. Bishop Trelawny, that arch-boroughmonger, was quite cheerful about Cornwall and 'glad to find the gentry unanimous for preserving the Test and our Laws', but Lloyd of Norwich was less optimistic about the situation in Norfolk; he found 'the corporations in this county (except Norwich) are so regulated and terrified from above that I doubt I shall not be able to give your Grace so good an accompt from as I heartily wish.'[56] It was thus essential to work up a convincing tory case, and Turner busied himself in collecting from the dioceses a detailed account of the prosecutions of dissenters during the previous ten years so 'that our friends in the next Parliament may triumphantly reproach our enemies with their false accounts.'[57] During this period some of the leading London divines were allowed to meet to consider possible alterations in the book of common prayer in case comprehension became a pressing issue in parliament, but it is more than clear that the bishops regarded their activities with dire suspicion. By the beginning of September Turner was alarmed lest matters had gone further than intended. 'It grows every day plainer to me', he complained to the archbishop, 'that many of our divines, men of name and note, (I pray God there be not some Bishops with them in the design) intend upon any overture for Comprehension (which time shall serve) to offer all our ceremonies in sacrifice to the Dissenters.'[58]

The surest way, however, by which the Anglican ascendancy could be re-established was if king James could be persuaded to return again to his 'old friends' and their policies. But this he was desperately reluctant to do. During August news was received of Dutch preparations for an expedition, and his state of anxiety was apparent to all who came to him, but he seems to have been borne up by a fervent expectation that God would yet provide a miracle to rescue all his plans for catholic emancipation. Only on 18 September, when definite news was received that William of Orange intended to invade England, did he send desperate messages to the Sancroftians that he was 'resolved

---

[56] Bodl MS Tanner 28 fol 139, Trelawny to Sancroft [August 1688]; *ibid* fol 183, Lloyd to Sancroft, 26 September.
[57] Bodl MS Rawl letters 99 fol 176, George Hickes to Turner, 3 September 1688.
[58] Bodl MS Tanner 28 fol 170, Turner to Sancroft, 3 September 1688. For the clearest account of the consultations, see Robert Beddard, 'Observations of a London clergyman in the Revolution of 1688-9: being a excerpt from the Autobiography of Dr William Wake', *The Guildhall Miscellany*, 2, 9 (1967) p 414.

to support the Church of England; and that the world should see, he would not lay aside his old friends.'[59] The difficulty was that, in these critical days when something might yet have been done, the bishops had to deal with a man whom strain and religious excitement had brought to the verge of breakdown. On the evening of 26 September he insisted that Turner wait on him for an immediate private audience but even the strong-minded bishop of Ely could get no sense out of him.[60] On 30 September Sancroft himself went to plead with James that nothing would now do short of an instant re-instatement of the whole tory regime in church and state, but found himself put off with rambling general assurances.[61] At last on 3 October the archbishop and five other bishops obtained an audience in order to present the king with an itemized set of demands. It was a paper they had written and re-written to make it unmistakably clear and, if possible, acceptable. Their first, hostile references to the Roman clergy had been toned down, but it was still peremptory to the point of irritability: a demand for the full restoration of local government into its former hands, an ending of the dispensing power, the immediate summons of a free parliament, and the reversing of all measures taken against the church of England.[62] With hindsight many later saw this as the last moment when James might have preserved himself with the support of the tories and the church but, to the bishops' anguish, he merely argued, complained and procrastinated. On 12 October the bishops despaired and began to disperse to their dioceses to await what might befall.[63]

In ruining himself James ruined his old friends and their policies. William's invasion and its rapid success introduced a new era into English politics and religious life. To the horror of the Sancroftians it quickly became apparent that the prince aimed for the crown and that there were many, even among the clergy, who were willing that he should have it. It now appeared that bishop Compton had actually been among those who had signed the invitation to William, and

[59] *Clarendon Corr* 2 p 188: 22 September 1688. See also BL Add MSS 34512 fol 101, for Van Citters's dispatch of 21 September.
[60] *Clarendon Corr* 2 p 190.
[61] Bodl MS Tanner 28 fol 185, Turner to Sancroft, 'seven at night' [29 September 1688]: 'Good My Lord, press for Expedition with some such kind expression as this that otherwise the Trap will be fallen upon us ere we are aware.'
[62] Bodl MS Tanner 28 fols 187–8, for the version as delivered, and fol 189 for the archbishop's much corrected draft.
[63] See Turner's later account for his belief that if James had accepted the bishops' demands he would have created a loyalist party for himself in spite of the invasion: Bodl MS Rawl D 836 fol 87.

The seven bishops: a reconsideration

both Trelawny and Lloyd of St Asaph rapidly associated themselves with the prince's cause. Such a collapse of his world around him seems wholly to have unnerved Sancroft, and he became incapable of further action or leadership.[64] It was left to Turner of Ely to make a valiant last-ditch effort to rally support for his master but James, by his flight to France, ended what small chance this had.[65] When William was offered the throne in February 1689 the whole Sancroftian strategy of an alliance of church and state for a renewal of the church of England became a thing of the past. The toleration act of 1689 effectively ruined the cause of Anglican uniformity and discipline. Of the original seven bishops five refused the oaths to king William. They were joined by Lloyd of Norwich and Frampton of Gloucester; and in the wilderness of deprivation and bitter regrets the mystical number of seven was again made up.

New College
Oxford

[64] When on 3 January 1689 Tenison suggested that the terms of a comprehension should be prepared 'in pursuance of the petition which the Seven Bishops had given to the King', Sancroft replied 'that when there was a convocation those matters would be considered of': *Clarendon Corr* 2 p 240.

[65] See Robert Beddard, 'The Guildhall Declaration of 11 December 1688 and the Counter-Revolution of the Loyalists', *HJ*, 11 (1968) pp 403–20. For a letter bitterly critical of Sancroft's 'strange, obstinate passiveness', see Bodl MS Rawl letters 99 fols 113–16, Turner to [Thomas Turner], 17 February 1689.

'POOR PROTESTANT FLIES': CONVERSIONS TO CATHOLICISM IN EARLY EIGHTEENTH CENTURY ENGLAND

by EAMON DUFFY

THROUGH the stormy and divided history of religion in seventeenth and early eighteenth-century England runs one constant and unvarying stream—hatred and fear of popery.[1] That 'gross and cruel superstition' haunted the protestant imagination. The murderous paranoia of the popish plot was the last occasion on which catholic blood was spilled in the service of the national obsession, but the need to preserve 'our Country from Papal Tyranny; our Laws, our Estates, our Liberties from Papal Invasion; our Lives from Papal Persecution; and our Souls from Papal Superstition . . .' continued to exercise men of every shade of churchmanship, and of none.[2] Throughout the early eighteenth century zealous churchmen sought to keep alive 'the Spirit of Aversion to Popery whereby the Protestant Religion hath been chiefly supported among us', and publications poured from the press reminding men of the barbarities of the papists, ancient and modern, the fires of Smithfield and the headman's axe of Thorn.[3] Catholicism was bloody, tyrannical, enslaving, and cant phrases rolled pat from tongue and pen—popery and arbitrary government, popery and wooden shoes. The tradition was universal, as integral a part of the nation's self-awareness as beer and roast-beef,

[1] Robin Clifton, 'Fear of Popery', *The Origins of the English Civil War*, ed Conrad Russell (London 1973) pp 144–67; [John] Miller, *Politics and Popery [in England 1660–1688]* (Cambridge 1973) pp 67–90; [J. P.] Kenyon, [*The Popish*] *Plot* (Penguin ed 1974) pp 1–5.

[2] Charles Trimnell, *A Sermon Preach'd before the House of Lords . . . on Thursday Feb 17 1708* (London 1709) p 9; George Smalridge, *A Sermon Preach'd before the Queen . . . on November the 5th 1705* (London 1708) p 8.

[3] [Christ Church Oxford] Wake Papers, *Epist* 20/35, Humphrey Prideaux to William Wake, 23 February 1715/6; [Archives of the] SPCK, *Minutes and Newman's Memoranda* 6 May 1713; SPCK *Papers and Memorials* fols 109–12 Monsr Ostervald to Mr Chamberlayne 22 January 1712; (Thomas Bray), *Papal Usurpation and Persecution, As it has been Exercised in Ancient and Modern Times . . . A Fair Warning to all Protestants* (London 1712); *An Authentick Narrative of the late Proceedings and Cruel Executions at Thorn* (London 1725); Daniel Neal *The Supremacy of St Peter . . . a Sermon Preach'd at Salters Hall January 23 1734/5* (London 1735) p 38–9.

and equally above reason. There were, observed Daniel Defoe, 'ten thousand stout fellows that would spend the last drop of their blood against Popery that do not know whether it be a man or a horse'.[4]

Popery was not only evil; it was 'Affrightful to Common Sense, and Shocking to Sober Reason', a 'ridiculous and nonsensical religion'. To become a proselyte to popery was to renounce 'senses and reason, judgement and conscience', for no-one could espouse the 'Pestilent Principles of the Papists' unless 'debaucht by the base allurements of Worldly Interest, or abandoned by God to strong Delusions'.[5] And yet Englishmen did become papists. The revolution put an abrupt halt to open catholic propaganda, the machinery of James II's aggressive missionary drive was hastily dismantled,[6] yet the catholic community made a surprisingly quick recovery. By the end of the seventeenth century protestants were once more bewailing the growth of popery, and the years from the revolution to the '45 rising are marked by periodic bursts of national panic about popish growth. These fears were at their worst at moments of internal political crisis, or in the face of war with catholic powers in Europe, but there is some evidence to link such outbursts with real advances made by catholic missioners. The anti-catholic legislation of 1700 and the proclamation of 1706 recalling that it was treason to reconcile converts to the church of Rome seem to have been prompted by catholic proselytizing activity, while the nation-wide panic at the growth of popery in 1735 occurred at a time when the catholics themselves were rejoicing in the number of their converts.[7] Accounts of the 'sad enroachments' of the papists

---

[4] Quoted in M. Dorothy George, *London Life in the Eighteenth century* (Penguin ed 1966) p 125.

[5] [Solomon Lowe], *The Protestant Family Piece[; or a Picture of Popery]* (London 1716) p xvii; Kenyon, *Plot* p 1; *The Old Whig: or, the Consistent Protestant* (London 1739) 1 p 6.

[6] Miller, *Politics and Popery* pp 239–63; the statistics of catholic publications dramatically illustrate this—figures from T. H. Clancy, *English Catholic Books 1641–1700* (Loyola University Press, Chicago 1974) p xvi.

Year	Catholic books published in England
1686	104
1687	148
1688	93
1689	7
1690	4

[7] [J. Anthony] Williams, [*Catholic Recusancy in*] *Wiltshire* [*1660–1791*] C[atholic] R[ecord] S[ociety] (1968) pp 43–68; Edward Stephens *The Suppression of Popery Recommended To Her Majesty* (privately printed, dated 18 October 1704) pp 3–4; [*An*] *Account of* [*the Seducing of*] *Ann . . . Ketelbey . . .* [*to the Popish Religion Humbly Presented*

Poor protestant flies

were received by the Anglican authorities with indignation, but also with a growing sense of impotence. Archbishops might fulminate against 'the busy Zealots of the Romish Church who ungratefully employ themselves in these perversions', but there was little enough that could be done to hinder them, in the face of the pragmatism of the secular arm.[8] In 1718 bishop Chandler of Lichfield complained to archbishop Wake of the conversions being made by the chaplain of the Fitzherbert family at Norbury in Derbyshire. 'In former reigns Mr. Fitzherbert would have been convened before the privy council, to answer for this insult on the establisht religion, but what may now be done I know not'. Though he cast about for ways 'to proceed against the new converts, so as to discourage others', by May 1720 he was forced to confess his helplessness in the face of a spreading evil 'that we can't, and they that can will not give a stop to'.[9]

In the most authoritative study of the English catholic community to appear to date Bossy has shown that the years 1700 to 1770 were not, as historians had previously maintained, a time of shrinkage and decay for catholicism, but rather 'three quarters of a century of modest growth'.[10] The reversal of the older assumptions prompts some questions. In the face of the no-popery mania of the nation, who became catholics, for what reasons, and in what circumstances? To what extent were these conversions the result of a deliberately conceived strategy on the part of the leaders of the catholic mission, and by what methods was any such strategy pursued? Finally, and perhaps most obviously, what sort of numbers were involved?

The last question may be disposed of first. Bossy has estimated the rate of growth of the catholic community in this period as perhaps as much as thirty per cent, but the evidence on which his calculations are based is fragmentary, and notoriously difficult to assess. Recusancy

---

to the Lords Spiritual and Temporal, and Commons, now Assembled in Parliament] (London 1700); Edmund Gibson, The Bishop of London's Pastoral Letter . . . With a Postscript setting forth the Danger and Mischiefs of Popery (2 ed London 1745) p 17; for 1735, see below, note 12.

[8] Archbishop Herring of York, quoted in CRS 32 pp 381–8. Examples of reports of conversions, Corpus Christi College, Cambridge, Hartshorne MSS 3 fol 137 Benjamin Marshal to J. Postlethwayt 18 April 1708; E[ssex R[ecusant] 17 (London 1975) pp 35–8 Revd Alexander Jephson to bishop Edmund Gibson 11 September 1723.

[9] Wake Papers Epist 21/65 bishop Chandler to William Wake 2 December 1718; ibid 21/233 same to same 21 May 1720; further examples in E. Duffy 'Over the Wall, [Converts from Popery in Eighteenth century England'], DR 94 (1976) pp 2–3.

[10] [John] Bossy, [The English Catholic] Community [1570–1850] (London 1975) pp 278–92, and cap 8 passim.

was an offence punishable in law; the reception of converts, like any other exercise of priesthood, was a capital felony until 1700, and after that date was punishable by life imprisonment. Naturally, priests were not anxious to keep records of their activities. Nor are protestant sources any great help here, for paranoia is not the best aid to statistical accuracy, as some protestants themselves conceded.[11] We are forced therefore, at least for the time being, to content ourselves with an impressionistic approach to the subject. The fact of growth is indisputable, the catholic community was larger at the end of the period than it was at the beginning, and both protestant and catholic sources witness to the process. Bonaventure Giffard, vicar apostolic of the London district until 1733 and by no means a man given to optimism commented repeatedly on the 'daily increasing number of persons coming into the church', and in 1733 another catholic cleric wrote of 'the incredible success we have had in bringing proselytes of all ranks to our communion'.[12] Against these euphoric references must be set the Jesuit figures for conversions from 1700 to 1711. These suggest a bare and static three hundred a year, and a Jesuit commentator in 1711 spoke of flagging proselytizing zeal on the part of the society's missioners.[13] There is, in fact, no essential contradiction here, for the growth areas of catholicism were no longer in the traditional rural missions centred on gentry households, but increasingly in independent 'congregational' missions, many of them in towns. The catholic rural population was beginning its long slow decline; urban catholic numbers were increasing.[14]

The change can be illustrated, fairly crudely, in class terms. Conversions to catholicism in the seventeenth century were often associated with the university, with the high church clergy, with the court. 'Our

[11] SPCK *Papers and Memorials 1715–1729* fols 133–5.
[12] A[rchives of the] A[rchbishop of] W[estminster], *Ep[istolae] Var[iorum]* 6 no 55, Bonaventure Giffard to Laurence Mayes 5 August 1717; 6 no 117 10 July 1719 same to same 10 July 1719 (printed with minor inaccuracies and omissions in Basil Hemphill, *The Early Vicars Apostolic* (London 1954) pp 48–9; 'A' Series 40 no 3 bishops Stonor and Petre to Propaganda 25 November 1734 (this appears to be the Latin letter summarised in Edwin Burton, *The Life and Times of Bishop Challoner* (London 1909) 1 pp 79–80, but there wrongly dated 1737); [*The*] *Present State of Popery* [*in England*] (London 1733) p 15 (this hostile protestant pamphlet prints a translation of a long letter describing the English mission, sent by some unnamed member of a religious order to a cardinal in Rome. This letter is almost certainly authentic.)
[13] H. Foley, *Records* [*of the English Province of the Society of Jesus*] (London 1877–83) 5 pp 161–2.
[14] Bossy, *Community* pp 278–92; [J. C. H.] Aveling [*The Handle and the Axe*] (London 1976) p 286.

Converts', declared Roger Palmer, earl of Castlemaine, 'were and are still of Persons of Eminency both in their parts and Quality. And whereas heretical seducers ever prey upon the meanest and simplest of the land, on the contrary our Missioners had rather deal in universities than in shops . . .'[15] The eighteenth century, however, brought a marked falling away of the catholic aristocracy, and a decline among the gentry which was offset by a growing catholic middle and lower class. 'The love of the world, of greatness, of riches, has always prevailed to keep some from owning of Christ, and make others deny him,' wrote bishop Giffard in 1717, 'but as the Prince of this world has gained some few proselytes, so the powerful grace of Christ has triumphed in great numbers of the inferior, or middling sort of people, who have embraced his faith'.[16] The missionary effort in the eighteenth century, therefore, as protestant observers noticed, was 'to corrupt the meaner people especially'.[17] This transition, from a religion of deference to a religion of shop-keepers and labourers shows up most readily in the urban sprawl of London; the chief agents of the transition would appear to be the secular clergy.[18]

The reasons for this transition cannot be entered into here, but the sixteen volumes of instructional and devotional writing published by the secular priest John Gother between 1689 and 1705 stand somewhere near its centre. Himself a convert, Gother began his work in London in the early 1680s, instructing the poor in their 'cellars and garrets'.[19] Under James II he became the leading catholic controversialist; after the revolution he settled at Warkworth in Northants, as chaplain to Lady Anastasia Holman, herself a zealous proselytizer. Here he resumed his original preoccupation with catechetics. The writings which resulted became at once the backbone of the work, and the basis of the self-awareness of the secular clergy in England, 'the best helps they have for carrying on their mission'.[20] In them can be found not

[15] Aveling p 217; AAW *Ep Var* 6 no 55, Giffard to Mayes 5 August 1717.

[16] AAW *Ep Var* 6 no 55 bishop Giffard to Laurence Mayes 5 August 1717. And note the phrasing of AAW 'A' series 40 no 3 (an episcopal report to Rome), 'non pauci e *plebe* quotidie ad Fidem convertuntur' (my emphasis).

[17] John Barker, *Popery the great Corruption of Christianity. A Sermon Preached at Salters Hall, January 9, 1734–5* (4 ed London 1735) p 26.

[18] Bossy, *Community* p 285.

[19] Godfrey Anstruther *The Seminary Priests 3.1660–1715* (Great Wakering 1976) pp 81–4; John Gother [*Mr Gother's Spiritual*] *Works* (London 1718) I p iv (memoir by W. Crathorn); E. Duffy ['A Rubb-up for old soares; Jesuits, Jansenists and the] English Secular Clergy', *JEH* 28, 3 (July 1977) pp 291–317 at pp 291–4.

[20] AAW *Ep Var* I no 21 John Betham to James Gordon 16 March 1704; Bossy, *Community* p 286.

only a rationale of the new expansionist zeal of the clergy, but the perfect expression of the religious values and spirituality which those clergy offered to new converts. The dominant spiritual influence on the secular clergy during the later seventeenth century was St François de Sales,[21] and Gother's writings are permeated by a somewhat severe version of the Salesian spirit, with its emphasis on the devout life lived fully in the world. These little books were therefore ideal instruments for a missionary drive aimed at men and women engaged in ordinary occupations. 'If the hurry of necessary Business gives little opportunity for prayer or recollection yet they may find Christ present with them, even in their Business', he wrote, 'the Tradesman may find him in his Shop, the labourer at his work, the . . . Porter in the Streets . . . the Servant in the Kitchin . . . and the Afflicted in all their Distress'.[22] In sober yet impassioned prose he offered in these works a spirituality for 'all states and conditions of Christians'; thrift, honesty, social responsibility, the virtues and moral landmarks of the 'middling' and lower 'sorts' are here, in works addressed to traders, masters, workmen, apprentices. Here too as a striking and rare compassion and concern for those lower still in the eighteenth century's social scale, 'helps' for the common labourer, for 'such as cannot Read, or have not Time to Pray', and, sombre, penitential, but curiously non-judgemental, for 'Prisoners, especially . . . those who are condemned to die'.[23]

It is impossible to read these little volumes without a vivid awareness of the middle and lower-middle class enclaves of Holborn and Drury Lane, of the slums of Westminster and Southwark and Seven Dials, of the horrors of Newgate and the Fleet which are their background. But their importance in this context is not simply that they represent a deeply religious yet eminently practical body of devotional material, ideally adapted to the spiritual needs of the urban middle and lower classes. They contain also three elements which have a more immediate bearing on our concern here. The first of these is a vigorous polemic against the intrusion of reason into religious matters; the second is an insistence on the need for conversion; the

[21] It is quite wrong to talk, as Bossy does, of a 'revival' of the tradition of St François de Sales by Challoner. There were seven editions of the *Introduction to the Devout Life* published for English catholics between 1648 and 1686, and there is an almost monotonous stream of references to and praise of his works in the writings of secular clergy such as William Clifford (in the 1660s), Silvester Jenks, Christopher Tootell (in the 1690s) as well as Gother himself. Challoner stands at the end of this tradition, not its beginning.
[22] Gother, *Works* 1 p 108.
[23] *Ibid* 9 *passim*.

third is a decisive abandonment of an older, static view of the priest-hood as pacifier of feuds, channel for sacramental grace, and dispenser of charity, in favour of that of priest as teacher. Each of these elements merits a brief examination.

English catholic controversy in the later seventeenth century had been fundamentally sceptical in character, stressing the uncertainty and unreliability of human reason. Only in unswerving obedience to the teaching of the catholic church, an infallible living voice, was there any escape from total religious unbelief. This line of argument had helped convert Gother himself, and he reproduces it in his own writings. 'Reason . . . is altogether useless, except in this one Act, of judging it reasonable that man should submit to God' . . . 'For Faith is a virtue which does not directly look into the reasonableness of the thing deliver'd . . . but into the Truth of the Deliverer'. This conviction that 'Faith is the Reason of a Believer' stood starkly opposed to the mainstream of contemporary protestant apologetic. It clearly had its own dangers, but to many it seemed to possess a certain clean-cut and radical simplicity. A line of argument which could be reproduced on one side of a sheet of paper (and frequently was), but which nevertheless carried with it a call to a complete change of religious style and allegiance must have seemed a welcome relief from the endless arid moralisms of latitudinarian apologetic. Its simplicity, too, offered an escape from the 'variations of protestantism' which were so marked a feature of the age; in 1719, the year of Salters Hall, bishop Giffard thought that a major reason for the growing numbers of converts was 'the great animosityes and divisions which of late have happened among the chief Protestant Doctors'.[24]

Gother's preoccupation with conversion is evident throughout his writings. His own religion was eirenical and minimalist, hostile to the paraphernalia and excess of baroque catholicism, but he shared with his co-religionists a total rejection of the '*modern Scheme* of Religion' that a man might be saved in any church 'with a moral kind of life'. He has many strong, even harsh, things to say of those who 'unhappily Educated under the Delusion of Errors' have, when called by God 'to open their eyes', either 'wholly neglected this Offer, or [been] prevailed on by Temporal Considerations to put off this Business . . .' Much of his writing is clearly intended to encourage conversions, and his *Instructions for the Afflicted and Sick* contain death-bed prayers for

[24] L. I. Bredvold, *The Intellectual Milieu of John Dryden* (Ann Arbor 1956); Gother, *Works* 6 p 141; 2 pp 5–7, 24; AAW *Ep Var* 6 no 117 Giffard to Mayes 10 July 1719.

protestants in religious doubt 'that the Impressions of Education may not make me obstinate against thy Truth'.[25]

The most immediate and practical contribution Gother made to catechetical and proselytizing activity is to be found in his conception of the ministry. For him the priest's essential role is that of teacher, preacher and catechist. He returns to this theme again and again—behind it of course lay his own experience as a London catechist, but it was a concern he shared with many of his clerical contemporaries. It became an increasingly central part of the missionary effort in England, and in the hands of men like Richard Challoner was one of the most important factors in the growth of the community. In Gother's generation and that immediately succeeding it expressed itself in a flood of small, plainly-written, devotional and instructional works, and by the 1740s it was common for clergy to leave legacies for the distribution of such works among the poor. Protestant observers were quick to realise the importance of the pamphlets, prayerbooks and catechisms 'handed about by the Popish Emissaries'. In 1735 Samuel Chandler singled out these 'small books' as one of the chief means by which 'numerous converts are brought into . . . the Church of Rome'.[26]

Gother's writings provide both a model for the new emphases in English catholicism which lay behind the drive to make converts, and the best example of the virtues and attractions of the catholicism which drew them; it remains to consider the ways in which that drive was implemented. These can best be studied in the London mission. The clergy there, though exposed to the near scrutiny of central government, were free from the restraints which a family chaplaincy might impose, for some gentry were unwilling to antagonise neighbours or magistrates by allowing their clergy to proselytize.[27] There were other advantages. The embassy chapels allowed catholic worship to be carried on in what was, by English standards, a sumptuous style. It was common for protestants to attend these services, to hear the music or simply out of curiosity; at least one secular clergyman owed his

---

[25] Gother, *Works* 2 pp 143–50, 289; 4 pp 143–7; 7 p 303; AAW *Ep Var* 10 no 103 Robert Witham to Laurence Mayes 9 April 1735.

[26] Bossy, *Community* pp 272–7; Gother, *Works* 2 pp 102–4; Samuel Chandler, [*The Notes of the Church . . . a*] *Sermon . .* [. *Preached at Salters Hall January 16 1734–5*] (4 ed London 1735) pp 54–5. Compare SPCK *Minutes and Newman's Memoranda* 1 April 1713; SPCK *Minute Book* 16 fol 62.

[27] Bossy, *Community* p 277. This reluctance has, I think, been overestimated, and there are many examples of proselytizing gentry in the early eighteenth century.

conversion to catholicism to a sermon heard at the Sardinian embassy in Lincoln's Inn Fields.[28] Catholicism was an accepted part of London's religious pluralism, and in a city which housed the Religious Societies, the French Prophets, Orator Henley's 'gilt tub', and William Whiston's Primitive Library, catholics encountered, and were encountered by, many 'seekers'. The one documented case of a conversion made by Gother, for example, occurred in the protestant 'nunnery' founded by the eccentric high-churchman Edward Stephens, where Gother had been introduced by another priest as an expert on the treatment of the spiritual 'aridity' afflicting one of the inmates.[29] In the complex social structures of London, its lodging houses, coffee-shops, its work-shops and warehouses, its tight, village-like local communities, its slums and prisons, catholic missioners found fields white for harvest. The centre of the catholic community was the area round Lincoln's Inn Fields, Holborn and Red Lion Square, and the teeming life of Drury Lane sheltered a number of catholic clubs, inns, booksellers and houses where mass could be said. In addition to this relatively stable network of catholic meeting-places there were many less formal outlets for catholic missionary activity. A number of the London clergy were financed by funds specially allocated for 'the assistance of the poor' in designated areas. Francis Lacy worked among the poor of St Giles, Christopher Piggott in Southwark, and both were noted for the large number of their converts.[30] The poor, of course, were not converted simply by prayer and penny-catechisms. 'Their necessities are . . . relieved by the charity of the Popish nobility and gentry', complained Samuel Chandler, 'they have persons to apply to under their illnesses, and remedies freely given them, to heal their diseases; And being subdued by the kindness of those who minister to them in their necessities, How can they think ill of a religion that thus prompts men to acts of goodness?'[31] This 'loaves and fishes' aspect of conversions to

[28] *Diary of Richard Kay* (Chetham Society 1965) pp 68, 85; the priest was George Whitaker, converted 1722, for whom see Anstruther, *Seminary Priests* 4. *1716–1800* (1977) p 297.

[29] Edward Stephens, *A True Account of the Unaccountable Dealings of Some Roman Catholick Missioners of this Nation* (London 1703).

[30] John Kirk, *Biographies of English Catholics in the Eighteenth Century* (London 1909) p 184; Anstruther, *Seminary Priests 3* p 126; the Woodward fund, for example, founded in 1677 (but for which records survive only from the 1720s) had an income on £100 yearly, of which one third was for masses for the founder's repose, one third for the poor of St Giles, and one third for the priest who tended them. Christopher Piggott benefited briefly from this fund (information from the ledger books of the old brotherhood of the secular clergy, kindly supplied by Miss Elisabeth Poyser, archivist of the archbishop of Westminster): *Present State of Popery* p 18.

[31] Chandler, *Sermon* pp 54–5.

catholicism is well known on gentry missions; the Petres in Essex and the Arundells at Wardour used their influence as landlord and employer to swell their congregations.[32] Lay charity played a major role in London's missionary work also, but here it stemmed less from the nobility and gentry than from the urban middle class. In the first decade of the century there was an active club of tradesmen, bakers, cobblers, and bodice-makers who met 'in order to the relieving their poor starving neighbours'. If this is the same club described by a convert turned informer in 1719, these tradesmen employed their money not only to relieve poor catholics, but to encourage needy protestants to consider conversion.[33] Bishop Giffard reported in 1717 that the 'great charity' of lay catholics in relieving 'a vast number of prisoners', protestant as well as catholic, had 'moved many of the former to embrace our Religion'. Richard Challoner himself was 'a very able physician', and used his medical skills 'to gain the wish'd for ascendant'.[34] Samuel Chandler thought that these methods could profitably be adopted by dissenters, but they did have drawbacks. Doles to the worthy poor inevitably attracted the unworthy poor. There are many cases of priests being informed against by converts who, having exhausted the resources of catholic benevolence, sought to earn a priest-catcher's fee. In such cases one may reasonably question the use of the term 'convert' at all, but it would be a mistake to discount altogether the religious content of even these 'conversions'. One Yorkshire convert, described by the priest who reconciled him, illustrates the complexities.

> On the twelveth (sic) of December 1736, was Reconciled to the Church ... Ralph Pierceson, (Pray good Reader take notice of this Yorkshire Chap) Late Constable of Ugthorpe, from this time to December 1745, he behaved himself Exceedingly Well, and was very good and Regular ... His Wife dyed in Childbirth, and left him five small Children, I tookt one Boy from him, named Jacob, and breed him up: gave both the Boy and father Cloaths, and mony to keep him from starving, and married him for nothing to a good Careful Catholick. But in the year, 1745 ... this my Saint turnd Tail, and swore against me, ... and all this in hopes of getting

[32] SPCK *Minutes and Newman's Memoranda 11 March 1712/3; ER* 17 pp 35–8; Williams, *Wiltshire* pp 82–3, 191–2.

[33] Duffy, 'English Secular Clergy' p 305; PRO MS SP 35 19/6a, 'The Information of Mary the Wife of John Londichar . . . 8 December 1719'.

[34] AAW *Ep Var* 6 no 55 Giffard to Laurence Mayes 5 August 1717; *Present State o* j *Popery* pp 20–1.

a Reward, which was at Last but Shame and Confusion. God Pardon him: I freely forgive him.[35].

The pardonable bitterness here may well spring from disappointment and incomprehension as well as shock. Nine years is a long time to keep up a *pretence* of conversion; Pierceson's case may rightly give one pause before adopting any simplistic explanation of these 'mercenary' conversions and relapses. The London mission supplies many parallels —Deale the apothecary is one, whose career ran from debtor's prison to conversion, then to a spell abroad as apothecary in several religious institutions where 'they lookt on him as a saint', then back to London and a brief career in 1714 as a priestcatcher before he disappears once more into early Georgian London, 'skulking' from new creditors.[36] Some of these unstable converts even entered the priesthood before relapsing—the notorious priest-catcher Mottram is one of many examples.[37] This sort of episode was perhaps an inevitable side-effect of a mission directed at the poor and rootless in the city which Johnson called 'the needy Villain's gen'ral Home'.[38] It may be that some slight air of alien glamour hung round catholicism, which, with the promise it held of a new start, even an education abroad, drew such men. It may be too, that catholics exploited these things as incentives; this is, perhaps, what lies behind the report in 1708 of two catholic seamstresses persuading the youngest son of a large and needy protestant family that if he became a catholic 'he might one Day become Pope'.[39] Finally one should take account of an intrinsic weakness in the structure of the mission which may help put the overall problem of the instability of poor converts in a wider context. Many of the most successful missioners in London were priests exercising a roving ministry. Such 'itinerant' or 'free' missioners, common throughout England at the beginning of the eighteenth century, were a particular feature of the London mission, and they had certain obvious merits. An enterprising priest working on this informal basis was free to develop his own style of ministry, to form his own contacts. We have an

---

[35] CRS 14 pp 373–4.

[36] *The Letter Book of Lewis Sabran S.J.* ed Geoffrey Holt SJ, CRS 62 (1971) pp 69, 75, 79, 92, 94, 103, 111, 115, 161.

[37] Anstruther, *Seminary Priests* 3 p 154.

[38] Samuel Johnson, *London: A Poem* line 93; it is interesting to note that the commission for relieving poor proselytes, set up under royal patronage for the benefit of French converts from catholicism in England fared much worse, the vast majority of its clients turning out to be 'imposters and vagabonds . . . with no religious views'—L. W. Cowie, *Henry Newman An American in London 1708–1743* (London 1956) pp 132–53.

[39] SPCK *Papers and Memorials 1715–1729* fols 40–2.

account of one priest, 'an excellent companion and a man of humour' seeking the acquaintance of 'abundance of youths and [joining] several clubs in order to make converts'; Monox Hervey adapted one of London's most characteristic religious institutions by setting up 'several devout societies in this city and suburbs, to whom he assiduously preaches... by which means he has brought a great number of converts over to our blessed communion'.[40] These 'free missioners', then, could work with 'great fruit', but they could also produce instability and lack of continuity in pastoral care, like later 'hit and run' protestant revivalists. One lapsed convert commented shrewdly in 1689 on the fact that the missioners of his acquaintance 'if they could find one abroad that would so listen to their discourses as gave them any small hopes they were to be prevail'd upon . . . would spend hours every day with them,' but that they almost utterly neglected 'informing and instructing those under their charge'. John Gother blamed the unedifying lives of many converts on the failure of the mission clergy to consolidate conversions by long-term instruction in the obligations of the Christian life—'Truly, 'tis a way of becoming a kind of Catholick, without being a Christian'.[41] Indeed, while Gother's views on the importance of catechetics gained over an older 'magical' view of catholicism, in which the priest featured as a miracle worker, exorcist and magic doctor, nevertheless the more primitive attraction continued, particularly among the poor. The protestant girl perverted to popery in 1710 by 'tales of pretended Miracles', 'Relicques and Agnus Deis, that would cure her imediatly of all diseases', as well as the inevitable 'Books of Controversies', cannot have been untypical. Conversions of this sort were predictably unstable, and it is clear that many converts were very hazy about the faith they had embraced. Ralph Pierceson's evidence against Monox Hervey, for example, reveals an astonishing ignorance of the meaning and ceremonies of the mass for one who had been a 'Regular' catholic for nine years.[42]

It is Monox Hervey who provides us with our best picture of a

---

[40] Anstruther, *Seminary Priests* 4 p 125 (John Gunston); *Present State of Popery* p 19; Foley, *Records* 7 p 718.

[41] [Anthony Horneck *An Account of Mr . . .*] *Edward Sclater's Return* [*to the . . . Church of England*] (London 1689) pp 22–3; Gother *Works* 2 pp 102–3.

[42] Keith Thomas, *Religion and the Decline of Magic* (Penguin edition 1973) pp 239–40, 582–8; Bossy, *Community* pp 266–7; Aveling, *The Handle and the Axe* pp 299–300; SPCK, *Papers and Memorials 1715–1729*, fols 40–2; CRS 14 p 385; for the anxiety of the vicars apostolic to remedy these evils, AAW 'A' series 38 no 30, pastoral letter of bishop George Witham 19 November 1704; *Ibid* 40 no 9 circular letter of Robert Carnaby, vicar general for bishop Williams 1 February 1736/7.

successful proselytizing priest at work. In seven years of work in London
he converted ninety protestants, and entered brief details of each
reconciliation in his register. An analysis of this register enables us
to pull together much of what has already been said, and to identify
some overall trends in an admitted diversity.[43] Of the ninety converts,
by far the largest group, fifteen, were 'marriage converts', and this is
certainly true of converts to catholicism in general. Many of these
marriage conversions took place at the time of the wedding, but even
where the protestant partners retained their religious allegiance to
begin with, a high proportion subsequently made the change.
Protestant observers were unanimous that 'mixed marriages' favoured
the catholics, 'for whether the husband or wife be Papists the children
are generally brought up so'. Hervey seems to have secured a signed
promise from the protestant partner that the children should be catholic
as a matter of course; a combination of family ties and the inevitably
somewhat militant character of catholicism as a minority religion did
the rest. Many of Hervey's marriage conversions took place at the time
of the christening of a child, when contact with the priest and catholic
relatives and friends perhaps intensified. There are six cases in Hervey's
register of conversions where the convert had catholic relatives other
than a spouse, and again this is a common phenomenon. Of the seventy
one secular priests who can be firmly identified as converts between the
1640s and 1740s thirteen had catholic relatives, including John Gother,
whose maternal grandmother was Dorothy Venables, and whose uncle,
Dr John Betts, was one of the best known catholics in the city of
London.[44] As might be expected, many such converts were very young.
Gother was only fourteen at the time of his conversion, and nineteen
other of these convert clergy were in boyhood or teens when
reconciled. This should not, however, cause us to dismiss the element
of religious choice in such conversions, in favour of some vague theory
of family influence. Some were indeed the direct result of a simple
change of guardianship and education at the death of a protestant parent,
but Gother's conversion followed a consideration of the doctrinal issues
involved, and we have his own assurance that before changing churches
he was greatly exercised by fears for his popish uncle's salvation.[45]

[43] CRS 14 pp 369–72, 378–80. Hervey worked in London 1730–4, and again in 1753–6;
Anstruther *Seminary Priests* 4 pp 130–1.
[44] CRS 14 pp 332–3; SPCK *Minutes and Newman's Memoranda* 4 March 1712/13; *Papers
and Memorials 1715–1729* fols 146–7 Samuel Peploe to Henry Newman 11 May 1714;
ER 17 pp 35–8; figures on secular clergy based on analysis of Anstruther, *Seminary
Priests, 2, 3, 4.*

The ties of neighbourhood, the links of employer and employed, of landlord and tenant, are almost equally prominent in Hervey's register, and clearly played a prominent part in the process of conversion. His converts entered a tight-knit social as well as religious group. Again and again he tells us that so-and-so was reconciled 'before the congregation', and the phrase has a clear geographical and social content. The congregations in question are identified by the houses in which they met—Mr Blake's in Drury Lane, the Fleece and Dove, also in Drury Lane, Mr Wynell's at the Muzzled Bear in Little Wyld Street. Entry into such congregations was clearly an important part of conversion, and converts reconciled privately, in sickness or for some other reason[46] seem to have been required to ratify their decision 'before the congregation'. At least seven of these converts had lodged with or been employed by members of this catholic community before conversion, and other sources allow us glimpses of how such links might effect the change. The notorious Archibald Bower was a familiar figure in Little Wyld Street in his catholic days —many catholic clergy, including the Jesuit provincial, lodged in the area. Bower used the house of a protestant friend there to do his courting of a catholic maidservant, and the conversation over a dish of tea in his hostess's parlour often turned to religious topics. Bower's accounts of the *Spiritual Exercises* of St Ignatius, and 'other institutions and practices of the . . . Church of Rome' brought his hostess into the church. Her husband followed several years later.[47] The papers of the SPCK, which throughout this period exercised a watching brief on the 'practices of the Priests to pervert his Majesty's subjects', provide details of the activities of Mary Shepherd, a tailor's assistant or seamstress, in 1708. The convert daughter of a Norwich parson, Mary Shepherd was 'so very zealous for the Romish Religion' that she made it 'her principall Study and great merit to gain Proselites'. She had a number of successes among the apprentices, seamstresses and serving-girls with whom she worked, lending them 'Books of Controversies', introducing them to the worship and clergy of the embassy chapels,

---

[45] Edward Stephens *The Misrepresenter truly Represented, OR A notable Metamorphosis* . . . (privately printed, no place or date, but *c*1704/5) p 3.

[46] CRS 14 p 315; no fewer than eleven of Hervey's converts were reconciled while sick or dying.

[47] (John Douglass), *Six letters from A—d B—r to Father Sheldon . . . and the true Character of the Writer* (London 1756) pp 75–84; Archibald Bower, *The Second Part of Mr. Bower's Answer to a Scurrilous Pamphlet . . .* (London 1757) pp 27–9.

even finding 'places' for converts under pressure from protestant relatives.[48] All these activities can be paralleled elsewhere.[49]

Finally, we may note the social status of Hervey's converts—among them an engraver, a maidservant, a writing master from an anglican free school.[50] There are, in addition to these 'middling or meaner' sort, 'an antient gentlewoman', and, strikingly, Mrs Margaret Kennet, 'Daughter to the famous Doctor Brett, and Nonjuror Bishop'. The presence of these two gentlewomen serves as a reminder that it was not only the lower orders who produced converts. Throughout the period there was a small but steady stream of gentlefolk into the catholic church, some drawn by professional ties, or antiquarian sympathies, others, like Gother's protestant nun and perhaps Mrs Kennet, in search of what a hostile observer called the 'plausible artifice of austerities, and . . . ruefull show of Sanctity', a deeper spirituality and 'more eminent piety' than the high-church tradition, fighting for its political life and divided against itself by the nonjurors, seemed able to offer.[51] Christopher Piggott was so successful with seekers of this sort that he was able to form a small 'community of converted gentlewomen' at Islington, a number of whose members established funds for the maintenance of poor catholics, and for places in convents and colleges abroad.[52]

It is difficult to make any firm summary of so tentative and exploratory a survey as has been offered here. Some suggestions may be made however as to the relation of these conversions to the history of eighteenth century religion as a whole. Bossy has spoken of an unmistakeable 'general sense of effort' in the catholic mission in this period, and has contrasted this effort favourably with that of the established church. Contemporary protestant observers, anglican clergy among them, commented on the ineffectiveness of the parochial clergy in opposing the activities of proselytizing priests. Catholic gains tended to be made in areas where the parochial system was at its weakest, in the teeming urban jungles of St Martin or St Giles in the Fields, in rural parishes where the traditional alliance of squire and parson was broken by a catholic squire, or in the vast parishes of the north of

---

[48] SPCK *Papers and Memorials 1715–1729* fols 40–2.

[49] *Account of Ann Ketelbey, passim; Archbishop Herring's Visitation Returns, YAS* (1928–31) 4 pp 191; AAW 'A' series 38 no 63 'Jane Wilson's testimony'.

[50] I take the Thomas Lewis mentioned by Hervey (CRS 14 p 371) to be the same convert discussed in HMC, *Diary of the Earl of Egmont* (London 1945) 1 p 228.

[51] *The Protestant Family Piece* p xviii; *Edward Sclater's Return* pp 13, 19.

[52] *Present State of Popery* p 18.

England, where many people might have '3, 4 and 5 miles to church, while they may hear Mass at next Door'.[53] This fact prompts comparison with the later successes of methodism in similar circumstances. Other parallels might be drawn. The concern for a more intense piety, the rejection of a 'rational' form of religion in favour of one based on faith and devotion, above all the success of catholic missioners with the 'inferior or middling sort of people', all invite such comparisons. Such resemblances may well be more apparent than real. The notion of 'faith' in, say, Gother's writings is very different from any that a self-respecting evangelical could subscribe to, and catholics were as eager to dissociate themselves from enthusiasm in religion as any presbyterian or latitudinarian anglican. Catholic proselytizing activities might perhaps be just as illuminatingly considered as one manifestation of that general upsurge of religious energy which produced the religious and reformation societies, and the charitable, educative and evangelistic activities of the SPCK. As we have seen, while the missionary drive was highly successful in attaching to catholicism a growing middle and lower middle class, its hold over the 'lower sort' was precarious, and prone to slip altogether at times of political or financial stress. Yet this could surely be said of *all* missionary efforts to evangelise the labouring poor in England, and many protestants thought catholics more successful in this area than any protestant group. When all due qualifications are made, the fact remains that for the greater part of the early eighteenth century catholics were virtually the only religious group in England deliberately as a group seeking converts, and seeking them among precisely those to whom methodism would later make its appeal. There is even a certain amount of evidence to suggest some two-way traffic between methodism and catholicism, particularly in the north.[54] While acknowledging the differences in the theological character, the effects, above all the scale of the two movements, one may surely claim for the study of such catholic conversions not only an interest of its own, but a modest place among the necessary prolegomena to the study of the greatest of all eighteenth century religious movements.

University of London
King's College

---

[53] SPCK *Papers and Memorials 1715–1729* fols 139–42 Samuel Peploe to Henry Newman 29 January 1713/14.
[54] Duffy 'Over the Wall' p 22; CRS 14 p 374. (Both references to Osmotherley).

ARISTOCRATIC VOCATIONS:
THE BISHOPS OF FRANCE
IN THE EIGHTEENTH CENTURY

by JOHN MCMANNERS

' *AS III* Aristarque, Abbé de qualité, et d'un mérite distingué, sollicite un Evêché, désirant de servir utilement l'Eglise. R. Il ne peut désirer l'Episcopat dans la vue d'être élevé à une si haute dignité, sans se rendre coupable d'ambition ou de présomption; il ne peut le désirer dans le dessein d'être honoré et respecté, ou de devenir riche sans se rendre coupable d'ambition ou d'avarice. Ajoutons que ce n'est point assez d'avoir une intention pure pour pouvoir désirer sans péché l'Episcopat; il faut avoir toutes les vertus que l'Apôtre demande dans un Evêque'.[1]

Aristarcus is of distinguished merit and high birth and wishes to serve the church. Clearly he is an outstanding candidate—is he therefore entitled to solicit a bishopric? First, he would have to establish the purity of his intentions: there must be no thrill at the thought of such lofty promotion, no shadow of desire to become rich, honoured or respected. He must forget his great merits and ancestry, and ask himself if he has the episcopal virtues prescribed by St Paul: is he vigilant, sober, blameless, hospitable, apt to teach? (One might take it for granted that he would not be a brawler or striker, and the Pauline proviso about matrimonial status had been tightened up subsequently, by a presumably superior authority.) Yet, even if Aristarcus could pass these exacting tests, it is doubtful if he would be entitled to do any soliciting. By the strictest rules of the confessional, even the attempt to give a vague general impression of worthiness as a foundation for possible promotion was gravely suspect. Thus, Tronson of Saint Sulpice wrote sombrely to Fénelon to congratulate him—and call him to penitence—on being made tutor to the duc de Bourgogne. You did not seek it, your friends will tell you; true, but you may have removed obstacles, you may have taken care to show yourself in a favourable light to influential people. 'On a souvent plus de part à son élévation

[1] *Dictionnaire portatif* [*des cas de conscience*], 2 vols (2 ed Lyon 1761) 1 p 421.

qu'on ne pense ... personne ne saurait s'assurer entièrement qu'il ne se soit pas appelé soi-même'.[2] You are forbidden to call yourself; your relatives are also forbidden to engineer the invitation on your behalf. Collet's treatise of 1764 on the duties of heads of families emphasises the danger of pushing the vocations of one's children; that comfortable canonry, safe in the family for a century and ready to be handed over by 'dear uncle' may decide your son's vocation—and may also lose you your hope of eternal salvation.[3] Conversely, churchmen were forbidden to seek promotion to serve the interests of their families. A secular priest could dispose of his patrimony as he pleased, subject to the obligations of Christian charity,[4] but the income he received from the church was his only in so far as he was entitled to 'an honest subsistence'. He could give a little to his parents to rescue them from complete poverty—this was the one exception to the rule; if the sight of their misery tempted him to do more, he ought to move away from the neighbourhood and avoid seeing them.[5]

Aristarcus, the casuist's example of an episcopal aspirant, was, of course, in priest's orders already. His 'vocation' had been settled at his ordination or, rather, earlier still, when he had accepted the subdiaconate and the obligation of celibacy. What justification for his great decision did he have at that time? According to the theologians, an ordinand had to be of sound morals and of good reputation, and had to possess the appropriate abilities and temperament; he had to have the right intention, asking God to keep him in this determination *dans le fond de l'esprit*; finally, he had to be called by the bishop or his representative. This systematisation of the constituent elements of a priestly vocation (as distinct from a monastic one) was comparatively recent in France, beginning in the early seventeenth century at the time seminaries were being founded, and became clearly formulated in Godeau's *Discours sur la vocation ecclésiastique* (1651).[6] To us, something seems missing in the analysis: what of 'attraction', the impulse in the soul, the hearing of God's voice—*Magister adest et vocat te?* But we should not judge the eighteenth-century idea of vocation in the

[2] [L.] Tronson, [*Correspondance*], ed L. Bertrand, 3 vols (Paris 1904) 3 p 301.
[3] The abbé de Mangin, *Science des confesseurs, ou décisions théologiques, canoniques, domestiques et morales*, 3 vols (Paris 1757) 3 p 258. For the verdict of ten doctors concerning the sin of conferring benefices because of blood relationships, P. Feret, *La Faculté de théologie de Paris et ses docteurs les plus célèbres*, 7 vols (Besançon 1900–9) 6 p 142.
[4] Tronson p 88.
[5] Collet, *Traité des devoirs des gens du monde et surtout des chefs de famille* (Paris 1764) p 201.
[6] [A.] Degert, [*Histoire des séminaires français jusqu'à la Révolution*], 2 vols (Paris 1912) 2 pp 361–74.

context of our own social order in which the church is a marginal community, and in the light of more complex ideas of psychological motivation reached through recent controversies.[7] The eighteenth century, indeed, spoke of 'attraction', but in a prosaic fashion, for, as one theologian pointed out, there were splendid careers to be found in the service of the church, and an 'ardent desire' for ordination might owe much to self interest.[8] Even so, given the requisite qualities and being in a state of grace, a man was free to follow his impulses. *L'inclination est la principale marque de la vocation de Dieu*, said a mid-century writer.[9] The church was calling properly qualified men in general to its service and, even, to its bishoprics. There was a presumption in favour of accepting. The casuists, while banning a priest from seeking episcopal office, would not allow him to refuse it from humility, fear, or even from distrust of the worldly manoeuvres of relatives; certainly, there was an obligation to accept when 'the pope or another legitimate superior orders him to do so'.[10]

In view of the Gallican liberties the pope was not likely to order anyone to do anything in France; certainly, he could not choose the bishops, for by the concordat of 1516, that right had been confirmed to the French crown.[11] The story of the *feuille des bénéfices* (the famous list of bishoprics, abbeys and other ecclesiastical appointments at the disposal of the king) forms a sad contrast to the solemnities of the theologians concerning vocation. A man was not entitled to call himself, they said. A pamphleteer describes the scene in the antechamber of Marbeuf, bishop of Autun, minister of the *feuille* in the dozen years immediately before the revolution. 'A bizarre collection of monks, *abbés*, *curés*, soldiers, women. They all want—bread. "Pension, abbey!" Monseigneur has promises and consolations for everyone. "M. le *chevalier* . . . these are hard times, but do not get impatient, all will be arranged". "M. le *curé*, you know my intentions; use them as a pillow

---

[7] Lahitton's emphasis on the call of the ecclesiastical superior (1909); Pius XII's rehabilitation of 'attraction' (1912). See E. Farrell, *The Theology of Religious Vocation* (St Louis 1952) pp 17–18, 47, 103.

[8] L. Habert (1708), cited Degert p 374.

[9] [R. Daon] *Conduite des âmes dans la voie du salut* (Paris 1750) p 86.

[10] *Dictionnaire portatif*, 1 p 422.

[11] There were subsequent arrangements for provinces like Brittany not included in the concordat—R. Darricau, 'Louis XIV et le Saint-Siège; les indults de nomination aux bénéfices consistoriaux', *Bulletin de littérature ecclésiastique*, 66 (Toulouse 1905) pp 16–34, 107–31. The chapter of Strasbourg continued to elect its bishop, but the influence of the crown made this a formality—R. Metz, *La Monarchie française et la provision des bénéfices ecclésiastiques en Alsace, 1648–1789* (Strasbourg 1947) pp 65 seq.

for your repose, and believe me, the moment of happy awakening is not far away. I foresee . . . yes, go along, do not worry". "My dear *abbé*, you are angry, so am I; the Queen is getting hold of everything, I am master of nothing. But leave it to me, I have my plan. Good day, be discreet, and rely on me".'[12] No doubt the insistence of the applicants matched the cynicism of their reception.

Close scrutiny, of course, can make any agency for the dispensation of patronage in spiritual affairs appear unworthy, and the ministers of the *feuille*, under observation from disappointed candidates, thwarted Jansenists, severe moralists, egalitarian reformers, *philosophes* and anti-clericals, were more vulnerable than most. Memoir writers and journalists conspired to portray them as scandalous or ridiculous. Boyer, bishop of Mirepoix, who made the appointments from 1743–55, was depicted as an intolerant old monk, Jarente, bishop of Orleans (in charge from 1757–70) as a libertine and a tool of Choiseul, cardinal de la Roche Aymon, archbishop of Reims (in charge from 1771–6), as an obsequious fool, and Marbeuf as a puppet of the queen. In discussions of this kind, the devil always has the most quotable anecdotes. Jarente is doomed to be remembered by the tasteless practical jokes played on him by the king and Choiseul and gossip about an actress, rather than for his attempts to appoint tolerant bishops,[13] cardinal de la Roche Aymon by his *gaffe* after presiding over the coronation (Louis XVI asked if he was tired: *Oh non! Sire, prêt à recommencer*) rather than by the abbé Véri's testimony to his sound judgement of personalities,[14] Marbeuf by his compliance to court pressure rather than by his strict-ness about extra benefices.[15] This was an age of *bons mots* and gossip. The regent Orleans, who consulted the pious cardinal de Noailles about routine episcopal candidates, is damned for ever by his two outrageous selections for the rich see of Cambrai and by his epigram about 'pleasing the Jansenists', since he 'gave all to grace and nothing to merit'.[16] In the case of the bishop of Mirepoix, the reliability of the memoir writers can be assessed by comparison. D'Argenson accuses him of favouring the *haute noblesse*,[17] Bernis says he did not even

[12] A. Sicard, *La nomination aux bénéfices ecclésiastiques avant 1789* (Paris 1896) p 12.

[13] Louis d'Illiers, *Deux prélats d'ancien régime: les Jarente* (Monaco 1948) pp 29–32.

[14] F. Masson, *Le Cardinal de Bernis depuis son ministère, 1758–94* (Paris 1884) p 193; *Journal de l'abbé Véri*, ed J. de Witte, 2 vols (Paris nd) 2 pp 68–9.

[15] Ch. Monternot, *Yves-Alexandre de Marbeuf, ministre de la feuille des bénéfices, archevêque de Lyon, 1734–99* (Lyon 1911) pp 11, 57, 16–17.

[16] [*Mémoires et lettres de François-Joachim de Pierre, Cardinal de*] *Bernis*, [*1715–58*, ed F. Masson], 2 vols (Paris 1878) I p 40.

[17] D'Argenson, [*Journal et mémoires*, ed E. J. B. Rathéry], 9 vols (Paris 1859–64) 4 p 214.

know the names of some distinguished families, 'did not like the nobility, and preferred to be deceived by men of obscure birth',[18] while Luynes tells us how carefully he made enquiries about and imposed tests upon a prelate who was being considered for translation to the see of Paris, and how, in another case, the king collaborated in fending off the solicitations of the great.[19] It could be that, apart from the ineluctable political pressures over the wealthier sees, and in the abusive context of the social prejudices of the age, the ministers of the *feuille* came near to doing their duty.

The chief effect of social prejudice was to limit appointments to bishoprics to nobles. A few commoners were elevated in the latter years of Louis XIV,[20] but from 1743 to 1789, only one, and this was the abbé de Beauvais, the most prestigious preacher of his generation, well-known in clerical circles because his uncle had been archivist of the clergy of France, and enthusiastically supported by the king's daughters and other ladies of the court; the see given to him was Senez—thirty parishes in the Alps, a cathedral city with one hundred and seventy seven tumble-down houses and an income of only twelve thousand livres a year.[21] 'If I thought that noble birth was the principal condition required for episcopal office', said cardinal de la Roche Aymon, who appointed him, 'I would trample my pectoral cross under foot'.[22] His words, maybe, were exactly chosen, for aristocratic lineage was not the principal condition, but only an indispensable one.

In their correspondence and conversations, great aristocratic families talked of the bishoprics of France with easy, possessive familiarity. A mother would encourage a younger son to dream of pensions, abbeys, a bishopric at thirty, becoming finally 'the richest of the family', a young man of fifteen would be presented to his tutor—'he is destined to become a bishop, you have to get him through his *licence* in theology.'[23] There were one hundred and thirty nine dioceses in

[18] *Bernis* I p 82.
[19] [*Mémoires du duc de*] *Luynes* [*sur la cour de Louis XV*, ed L. Dussieux and E. Soulié], 11 vols (Paris 1860–5) 7 pp 269–70, 6 pp 418–9, 431. For the king's serious attitude in the Boyer era, M. Antoine, *Le Conseil du roi sous le règne de Louis XV* (Geneva 1970) p 605.
[20] Between 1682 and 1700, sixteen out of one hundred and ninety-four appointments—N. Ravitch, *Sword and Mitre: Government and Episcopate in France and England in the Age of Aristocracy* (The Hague 1966) pp 69–70.
[21] A. Rosne, *M. de Beauvais, évêque de Senez, 1731–90* (Paris 1883) p 13. For the diocese, M. Vovelle, *Piété baroque et déchristianisation en Provence au XVIIIᵉ siècle* (Plon 1973) pp 463 seq. In 1790, another commoner, Asseline, was made bishop of Boulogne.
[22] Sambucy, *Vie de Mgr. de Beauvais, ancien évêque de Senez* (Paris 1843) p 55.

France,[24] some huge, some tiny, some rich, some poor—size and income going together frequently, though not always. Vence, Toulon, Orange, Mirepoix and Agde had only twenty to thirty parishes and incomes from seven thousand to thirty thousand livres; Rouen had one thousand three hundred and eighty-five parishes and Cambrai six hundred, and their incomes were around the two hundred thousand livres mark. The richer the see, the greater the degree of court influence brought to obtain it. Poorer bishoprics would go to provincial nobles —sometimes to those who came to official notice by happy accident: Gabriel Cortois de Quincey, archdeacon of Dijon, became bishop of Belley because, in the coach to Paris, he out-argued a sceptic in a conversation overheard by a fellow traveller, Boyer of the *feuille*,[25] Urbain de Hercé, a *vicaire général* of Nantes, became bishop of Dol because he met the duc d'Aiguillon at the sessions of the estates of Brittany in 1765.[26] But the great court families knew their sons would be noticed; the question for the abbé de Choiseul in 1758 was, should he take Evreux, or wait for something better? Bernis and Mme de Pompadour thought he should accept what was available—'it will be a bridge', 'it's simply a stepping stone', 'the king has promised not to let him languish in a minor see.'[27] Even so, there were only a limited number of splendid promotions. The famous hold-up in Talleyrand's career was, no doubt, partly owing to his poor standing with the queen and partly to his morals, but of the twelve vacancies occurring from 1785–8, only four were high-ranking.[28]

The tribulations undergone by aspirants to a diocese of their own can be seen in the anxieties of Pierre-Augustin Godert de Belbeuf between becoming a *grand vicaire* of Verdun in 1760 at the age of thirty, and bishop of Avranches fourteen years later.[29] His brother, *procureur général* of the parlement of Rouen, was running his candidature, and re-adjusted strategy from time to time in the light of changing circum-

[23] *Mémoires du duc des Cars*, 2 vols (Paris 1890) 1 p 8; Morellet, *Mémoires* (Paris 1821).
[24] According to the *Almanach royal* of 1789. But the figure depends on decisions about what to include or exclude—see [B.] Plongeron, [*La Vie quotidienne du clergé français au XVIIIe siècle*] (Hachette 1974) pp 15–22.
[25] L'Alloing, *Le Diocèse de Belley* (Belley 1938) pp 276–7.
[26] [Ch.] Robert, [*Urbain de Hercé, dernier évêque et comte de Dol*] (Paris 1900) pp 14–15.
[27] *Bernis* 2 pp 211–12, 224, 228–9.
[28] L. S. Greenbaum, 'Ten Priests in search of a mitre: How Talleyrand became a Bishop', *Catholic Historical Review* 50 (London 1964) pp 307–31. For the emphasis on morals, however, see B. Lacombe, *Talleyrand, évêque d'Autun* (Paris 1903) pp 54–6.
[29] E. Sévestre, *Les Idées gallicanes et royalistes du haut clergé . . . Pierre-Augustin Godert de Belbeuf, évêque d'Avranches, 1762–1803* (Paris 1917) pp 29–30, 45–6.

stances—when the bishop of Verdun's goodwill became suspect, when Jarente, carefully cultivated, lost the *feuille* and sent his polished regrets, when the bishop of Lescar wrote to say that his neighbour of Tarbes had died, leaving an attractive, but distant vacancy. Finally, in 1774, cardinal de la Roche Aymon offered Avranches, suggesting it would be 'doubly agreeable' as being near the family château. The campaign for Jean-de-Dieu Raymond de Boisgelin, who became bishop of Lavaur in 1764 at the age of thirty two and archbishop of Aix six years later, was organised by his father, a magistrate of the parlement of Brittany, an operation conducted with a blend of cynicism and sincerity. 'I expect a great deal of a son who has voluntarily embraced such a respectable state; I hope that he will have religion, morals and application to the studies relevant to his profession, rather than to *belles lettres*, which adorn only the mind and which often corrupt the heart . . . The public expects edification of you. You have ambition, but it must always be subordinate to religion. You will reap the fruits in this world and the next'. Then, on one occasion, a sudden outburst: 'We must think, above all, about getting an abbey; let all other objects give place to that,' nor must it be a small one.[30]

In 1789, the affluent sees of Cambrai and Strasbourg were held by the Rohan-Guéméné family; there was a Talleyrand-Périgord at Reims and Autun (uncle and nephew); brothers held Limoges and Séez (du Plessis d'Argentré), Auxerre and Bordeaux (Champion de Cicé), Beauvais and Saintes (la Rochefoucauld), and there was another la Rochefoucauld at Rouen. As one relative rose in the church, he would lower a rope for the others to climb on. Uncles would have nephews appointed as coadjutors and successors; on the eve of the revolution, Jarente's spendthrift nephew had just succeeded him at Orleans, Loménie de Brienne's was waiting to follow on at Sens, and Barral's at Troyes. An interesting variant of the coadjutor theme was the inheritance of the see of Aire by Gilbert de Montmorin de Saint-Hêrem in 1723. His father had been a soldier who, in later life, after his wife's death, took orders and became bishop of Aire, carrying his children with him into distinguished places in the hierarchy: three daughters abbesses (one of them obtaining Jouarre and another Fontevrault, two of the most magnificent abbeys in France), one son an archdeacon in the paternal diocese, and another Gilbert, coadjutor and successor.[31] When Francois-Joseph de la Rochefoucauld-Maumont

[30] [E.] Lavaquery, [*Le Cardinal de Boisgelin, 1732–1804*], 2 vols (Angers 1920) 1 pp 24, 31,41.
[31] A. Degert, 'L'ancien diocèse d'Aire', *Revue de Gascogne*, ns 6 (Auch 1907) pp 119–69;

became bishop of Beauvais in 1772, he called on his younger brother Pierre-Louis to come as one of his *grands vicaires*. The old cardinal de la Rochefoucauld at Rouen then took over the promotion of the young man's fortunes—had him made one of the *agents* of the clergy of France when it was the turn of the Rouen province to elect, and as president of the assembly of clergy of 1780 recommended him to the crown for a bishopric, which came in the following year.[32] The career structure of this la Rochefoucauld-Maumont family was typical: the two who became bishops were third and fourth sons, the two eldest went into the army and navy. Boys of noble houses faced a routine choice between cassock and sword, 'whether they would have their heads shaved or broken'.[33] Examples of soldiers who turned to the church in later life were not infrequent; in 1789, the bishops of Soissons, Saint-Pol-de-Léon[34] and Périgueux had served in the armies, while cardinal Paul Albert de Luynes, the archbishop of Sens who died in January 1788, had been a colonel of infantry. His was an unusual case—he had been struck by a fellow officer, refused to fight a duel, and was branded as a coward and ordered into an ecclesiastical vocation by his termagant mother; thereafter, he drew a vast income from the church, but he lived austerely and became a model bishop, conducting pastoral visitations in the diocese and delighting to read to the peasants in humble parish churches the homilies of his youth, in which he warned them against luxuries like velvet cushions or ornate furnishings.[35]

Benefice holders were supposed to give no more to their aged parents than would rescue them from penury: in practice, a bishop in the family was a resource for everyone. Brothers returning from the wars, unmarried or widowed sisters, aunts, nieces and cousins found refuge in their palaces and châteaux. Bertin, the excellent bishop of Vannes, would walk after supper in the gardens of his country house discussing diocesan business with one or two ecclesiastics, and his sister, the widowed marquise de Fumel.[36] Urbain de Hercé, bishop of

---

L'Abbaye royale Notre-Dame de Jouarre, ed Y. Chaussy, 2 vols (Paris 1961) 1 pp 320–4.

[32] See L. Audiat, *Deux victimes des Septembriseurs, Pierre-Louis de la Rochefoucauld, dernier évêque de Saintes, et son frère, évêque de Beauvais* (Lille 1897).

[33] 'Vous faire tonsurer ou casser la tête', Marmontel, 'La Mauvaise mère', *Contes Moraux*, 3 vols (Paris 1765) 2 p 101.

[34] Biography by L. Kerbiriou, *Jean-François de la Marche, évêque-comte de Léon, 1729–1806* (Quimper/Paris 1924).

[35] M. Vallery-Radot, *Un Administrateur ecclésiastique à la fin de l'ancien régime: le cardinal de Luynes, archevêque de Sens, 1753–88* (Paris 1966) pp 2–3.

[36] *Vie de M. Marquis-Ducastel . . . curé de Sainte-Suzanne*, ed F. Pichon (Le Mans 1873) pp 35–9.

The bishops of France in the eighteenth century

Dol, was backed up by his elder sister, who did the housekeeping (retiring into a convent when the bishop was away from home), and administratively, by his younger brother (a virtuous parish priest who gave away everything he possessed when called to be a *grand vicaire*); one of the three went out every day to taste the soup which was dispensed to the poor in the courtyard of the *évêché*.[37] By contrast, Condorcet, bishop of Auxerre, was embarrassed by the antics of his niece, Mme Dusage, who decorated her coiffure with emblems like ships and weather vanes, and called out of her windows to strangers in the street to come in and admire her recently painted portrait.[38] Then, there were dowries to be found. On becoming bishop of Lavaur, Boisgelin gave a sister fifty thousand livres, equal to a year's income of the see and half of what his father contributed; promoted to Aix he gave his other two sisters three hundred thousand livres each, and educated his nephews. On the occasion of acquiring a rich abbey as additional income, he described his system: 'vous savez quels sont mes principes: être riche pour être utile, être riche sans rien coûter à l'Etat',[39] which might be paraphrased—the wealth of the church is available to encourage the activities of useful noble families like ours.

'To whom do they give the bishoprics? To nobles. The rich abbeys? To nobles. All the fat benefices? To nobles. What, you have to be of aristocratic birth to serve God? No, but the court uses this method to attach the nobility to itself, and military services are paid for, as well as others of less importance, with the property of the Church'.[40] So wrote Mercier on the eve of the revolution. By then, the tide of wrath against aristocratic monopoly was running high, and the *cahiers* by 1789 were to reflect the determination of the laity and of the 'disinherited' lower clergy to end this abuse.[41] The concordat, said the abbé Fauchet, in a reforming pamphlet, has instituted a 'code of brigandage', awarding honours and titles to men 'unworthy of being parish sacristans'.[42] When the national assembly in 1790 set about reforming the church, it went without saying that episcopal wealth would be reduced and all ecclesiastical promotions thrown open to talent. The abbé Lamourette

[37] Robert pp 10–11, 88.
[38] E. Esmonin, 'La société Grenobloise au temps de Louis XV d'après les *Miscellanea* de Letourneau', *Études sur la France des 17ᵉ et 18ᵉ siècles* (Paris 1964) p 490.
[39] Lavaquery 1 pp 60, 186–7.
[40] Mercier, *Tableau [de Paris,]* 12 vols (new ed Amsterdam 1782) 4 p 247 (cccxlv).
[41] [A.] Sicard, [*L'Ancien clergé de France: les évêques avant la Révolution*] (5 ed Paris 1912) pp 346–9.
[42] J. Charrier, *Claude Fauchet* (Paris 1909) pp 64–74.

313

encouraged the legislators by describing the dawn of a new golden age, when bishops, accompanied by their parish priests, would be seen walking the country lanes, their white hair and furrowed faces bearing testimony to their disciplined lives, their virile simplicity attested by the 'gnarled and rustic staff' with which they would support themselves on their journeys.[43] He was looking forward to a new era when the principle of equality had permeated society, the church included. He was also, along with the revolutionary *curés*, looking backwards to the first century of Christianity, when the apostles trudged the roads of the Roman empire, and 'not many wise men after the flesh, not many mighty, not many noble' were called; as Voltaire had said, the gospels were not written by 'Monseigneur Matthew and Monseigneur Luke'.[44]

So far removed from their apostolic predecessors, from the principles laid down by the theologians, and from the reforming aspirations of the age, how did the aristocratic bishops of the *ancien régime* defend their vocation?—or, rather, how can we interpret their subconscious mind about it, for they would not stoop to self-justification. In a sense, the answer is simple; the bishops were doing what everyone else was doing. With the exception of certain cures that were awarded by competitive examination,[45] every benefice was conferred by influence and favour; arbitrarily awarded chapels and priories supplemented the incomes of the *curés*,[46] just as abbeys supplemented those of the bishops, and the bourgeoisie, like the aristocracy, had its family policies for sending in selected emissaries to bear off the wealth of the church. The chief instrument of family policy, more certain in operation than alliances with lay patrons or contacts with chapters and monasteries with patronage rights (though these opportunities were not to be despised), was the 'resignation in favour'. One fifth of the parishes of the diocese of Lisieux[47] changed hands in this way, and probably more still in other dioceses. Not surprisingly, it was the richest cures which were thus pre-empted: the bishop of Le Mans in 1785 complained that

[43] [P.] Sage, [*Le 'Bon prêtre' dans la littérature française*] (Geneva/Lille 1951) p 379.
[44] Voltaire, *Instruction pastorale de l'humble évêque d'Alétopolis, 1763* (Moland 25 p 2).
[45] J. Mahuas, 'Le concours pour l'obtention des cures dans le diocèse de Vannes au XVIIIe siècle', *Mémoires de la Société de l'histoire et archéologie de Bretagne* 45 (Rennes 1965) pp 41–52.
[46] See my comments in *French Ecclesiastical Society under the Ancien Régime: a Study of Angers in the 18th Century* (Manchester 1960) p 140.
[47] C. Berthelot du Chesnay, 'Le clergé diocésain français au XVIIIe siècle et les registres des insinuations ecclésiastiques', *Revue d'histoire moderne et contemporaine* 10 (Paris 1963) p 245.

he was never able to reward his more virtuous clergy with one of the desirable benefices which were theoretically at his disposal.[48] The family looked after the promotion of the individual, and anyone receiving promotion naturally did his best for his family. The abbé Baston, a virtuous and scholarly canon, describes his motives in seeking ordination: he had no interest in women, he liked the duties of the ecclesiastical state, and he wanted to aid his aged parents—'Il m'était bien venu en pensée que, prêtre, je pourrais aider mes respectables parents dans leur vieillesse, mais la religion ne condamnait pas, sans doute, un sentiment si cher à la nature'.[49] He regarded the natural affections as a surer guide to religious duty than the harsh regulations of the handbooks of the confessional. Seventeenth-century attacks on the moral teachings of the Jesuits had forced the officially accepted casuistry into an uncompromisingly rigorist mould, and, by reaction, a generally accepted Christian morality had grown up outside its scope. The declamations by moral theologians against the intervention of family affections and loyalties in the conferment of benefices and the use of ecclesiastical incomes were as little regarded as their denunciations of lending at interest and, in due course, their attacks on contraceptive practices in marriage.

The voice of clerical moralists rings sternly when the imaginary Aristarcus, worthy though he is, solicits for a bishopric, but when it is the abbé Dubois, foreign minister and boon companion of the regent, lecherous and hard-swearing, making application for the *licet* to be ordained on his way to the rich see of Cambrai and the succession of Fénelon, moralising is not so easy. True, Noailles, the Jansenistically inclined archbishop of Paris, refused, but there were others to see the appointment through, including the saintly Massillon, who was one of the consecrating bishops.[50] This is an extreme case of a purely political appointment to give the son of an apothecary the standing to confront dukes and peers; how did the argument go when it was a straight-forward matter of favour, a bishopric for the son of a royal minister, with no other political overtones? Tronson, that ultra-introspective moralist, provides the formula in the letter he wrote in 1679 after testing the twenty five year old son of Colbert for fitness for the office of bishop coadjutor to the archiepiscopal see of Rouen. 'There is

[48] *Mémoires de René-Pierre Nepveu de la Manouillère, chanoine de l'Eglise du Mans*, ed G. Esnault, 3 vols (Le Mans 1877–9) 2 pp 118–19.
[49] *Mémoires de l'abbé Baston, chanoine de Rouen*, ed J. Loth and Ch. Verger, 3 vols (Paris 1897–9) 1 pp 153–4.
[50] J. Blampignon, *L'Episcopat de Massillon* (Paris 1884) pp 32–4.

nothing in him to make him unsuitable', says the superior of Saint-Sulpice, with wry exactitude, 'and he can render the Church service'.[51] 'He can render the Church service': here is the essential argument, and the thirty six bishops at the young man's consecration (there weren't any more at the council of Nicaea, said Mme de Sévigné),[52] could take comfort in the thought. An aristocrat belonged to the closed circles—at court, in the capital and in the provinces—of those who had influence, the influence without which nothing could be done in eighteenth-century France.

How did a bishop gather in the complex revenues of his see and of the supplementary abbeys which he held *in commendam*? To remain solvent, even the most unworldly or spendthrift of prelates had to know how to give orders to *fermiers* of seigneuries, lawyers and *feudistes* and to write letters to the controller general.[53] There were continual negotiations with the magistrates of the episcopal city, with royal officials, above all with the intendant, with the local parlement, with the military governor of the province—and all this in a great confusion of interlocking and overlapping jurisdictions, sometimes involving, for example, two intendants or two parlements. There were problems with other bishops over metropolitan or primatial jurisdiction, and over parishes enclaved in other dioceses or, indeed, outside France altogether; there were archbishops in France who were metropolitans over foreign sees, and foreign archbishops who were metropolitans to French ones. Patrons of livings—noblemen, chapters, monasteries—needed careful handling, more especially by those bishops who had little patronage of their own, and that subject, as always, to subversion by 'resignation in favour' or 'the rights of graduates'.[54] The lower clergy needed to be defended against the laity, powerful either by virtue of numbers or by lofty social status. When in 1777 the *curé* of La Tour Saint-Gelin faced the illwill of his parishioners, led by the baron de Chilleau, over tithe and the payment

---

[51] Tronson 3 pp 389–90.

[52] Mme de Sévigné, *Lettres*, 3 vols (Pléiade 1960) 2 p 813. Even if the six nominated but not-yet consecrated bishops she refers to are added, the figure falls far short of Nicaea.

[53] A nice example: the bishop of Lodève to the controller general about the loss of *un certain livre vert* containing information about the dues he can levy—E. Appolis, *Le Diocèse civil de Lodève . . . au milieu du XVIIIᵉ siècle* (Paris 1951) p 155.

[54] In the dioceses of Auch, Bordeaux, Tarbes, Saintes, Paris, Gap, the bishop had the patronage of numerous cures, though rarely over half. But the archbishop of Bourges had only one hundred and thirty-four out of eight hundred and two, the bishop of Dijon forty-nine out of two hundred and thirty-four, the bishop of Coutances thirty out of four hundred and eighty-nine; very few in the dioceses of Reims and Chartres also.

of a *vicaire*, the archbishop of Tours wrote to him in enheartening terms. 'Do not fear the threats which are made to you', he wrote concerning the *vicaire*, 'if any contestation is raised against you in this respect, I will defend you'. And concerning the tithe, 'whatever repugnance you may have about resorting to the law courts, I order you to do so, and I will accept the obligation myself to follow up whatever legal processes you are obliged to institute'. Two years later, the archbishop sent to the *curé* a copy of the decision of the parlement of Paris in his favour.[55] There were advantages for a parish priest in having a proud aristocrat as his diocesan.

Bishops had many extra-diocesan responsibilities, not enough to justify the more notorious cases of non-residence, but sufficient to excuse many a routine trip to Paris and Versailles. A bishop was permanently at court as the *grand aumônier*, and another as the *premier aumônier du roi*; the six who were peers worked with the lay peers to preserve their peculiar rights;[56] some, the more politically active ones, sat on the quinquennial assemblies of the clergy of France which voted clerical taxation to the crown, and all were supposed to attend (with one other representative of their diocese) at the metropolitan synods at which these deputies were elected. Above all, many bishops had huge administrative responsibilities as presidents of various provincial estates. The twenty-three prelates of Languedoc not only sat in the estates of that province, they were also in charge, individually, of the diocesan assemblies, which levied the taxation and organised local public works. The archbishop of Aix directed the deliberations of the estates of Provence, with two of his episcopal colleagues attending; bishops presided over the assemblies of the Cambrésis, Artois, Foix, Bigorre, Béarn, the Mâconnais and Bourgogne (three of them, indeed, competed for the place of honour in the latter). Prelates played an important part in the turbulent estates in Brittany; the court tried to keep them from allying with the rest of the nobility by a general policy of passing over local candidates for the Breton sees.[57] A bishop had manifold responsibilities, and in enumerating them we come as near as we can to justifying the aristocratic monopoly of high ecclesias-

---

[55] E. Millet, 'La Tour Saint-Gelin: vicissitudes d'un curé au XVIIIe siècle', *Les Amis du vieux Chinon: Bulletin*, 6 (Tours 1957–8) pp 27–32.

[56] A bishop is put forward by the peers to defend their rights—under the regency— *Journal et mémoires de Mathieu Marais*, ed M. de Lescure, 4 vols (Paris 1863) 2 p 89— and on the occasion of the marriage of the future Louis XVI to Marie Antoinette— J. Droz, *Histoire du règne de Louis XVI*, 3 vols (Paris 1839) 1 p 120.

[57] J. Meyer, *La Noblesse bretonne au XVIIIe siècle*, 2 vols (Paris 1966) 2 pp 1101–3.

tical promotion. The abuses of the social order were interlocking; to be effective, even as a figurehead, the head of a diocese had to belong to the aristocratic establishment. The abbé Lamourette's white haired patriarch, walking the lanes with his 'gnarled and rustic staff' in his hand, might have been a true apostle, but unless by an unlikely chance he happened to have the right number of quarters of nobility, he could hardly have hoped to administer a diocese of the *ancien régime*.

The vocation of a bishop of the eighteenth century ought to be considered as a vocation to what his office and work really were, rather than the theologian's ideal of what it was supposed to be. The casuists said that a churchman could not refuse episcopal consecration if ordered to accept by his legitimate superior. But, subject to an un-demanding ecclesiastical verification of a candidate's morals, it was the king, not the pope, who made the offer, and the service of the crown brought with it an intense and special compulsion, a compulsion which the concordat with the papacy could be presumed to have validated. Vocation was in the context of a social order where church and state were not only allied, but interwoven and, sometimes, indistinguishable. Theologians did not speculate about the 'attraction' theory of the call to ecclesiastical office, because a young man of any sort of education automatically thought of such a career as a possibility, and his family and society expected him to do so. If a regiment passed through town, the children played at soldiers, if a mission was held, they played at priests in processions.[58] As a child, André Chénier preached sermons and celebrated masses, lifting a toy Host made of lead at the elevation, when his nurse would take off her cap and his aunt Juliette and her friends would kneel.[59] Looking at a society in which religion is so completely a part of ordinary life, the historian tends to try to separate 'religious' actions for evaluation according to 'religious' criteria, but in so doing, he injects an element of unreality into the evidence he is considering. For example, we instinctively tend to praise the court preachers who denounced the immoral life of Louis XV. But these thunders fell within the conventional framework of 'political elo-quence' dating from the seventeenth century.[60] The preacher was just doing his duty, Louis XIV had said, and his successor said the same— sometimes. It was marginally possible to incur disgrace this way,[61]

[58] J. Brengues, *Charles Duclos* (Saint-Brieuc 1971) p 396.
[59] J. Fabre, *André Chénier* (Paris 1955) p 14.
[60] J. Truchet, *La Prédication de Bossuet*, 2 vols (Paris 1960) 2 pp 218–21.
[61] For example the Jesuit Laugier in 1754 (D'Argenson 7 pp 265–6, 8 p 784; Luynes, 13 p 228).

and more than marginally possible to qualify for promotion;[62] one school of critics talked of 'holy courage' and another of downright 'cynicism'.[63] Perhaps we end up by agreeing with the abbé Soldini: it would have been better if the preachers had not shown such an *empressement scandaleux* for drawing attention to themselves by indulging in this conventionally approved brinkmanship.[64] Similarly, we should not go all the way with the apparently morally irrefutable arguments of ecclesiastical or egalitarian reformers against nepotism in the church. The 'resignation in favour' was not just a device of family policy: it also enabled *curés* to retire with a pension and in the shadow of a friendly successor, and provided continuity of personal relationships in the parish, something important to the peasants; the aristocratic monopoly of bishoprics provided the church with active young prelates with an independent spirit and powerful connexions, as well as some scandalous timeservers.

An aristocrat ordained remained an aristocrat. A sharply defined ideal of vocation to ecclesiastical office had emerged from the precisely ordered world of the moral theologians—a world of subtle compromises, but compromises determined by clashes of principle or of scriptural interpretation, rather than by the tension between the broad religious ideal and the realities and expediences of social life. A few of the bishops walked these narrow paths,[65] a few chose their careers with worldly cycnicism, but for most, their vocation to ecclesiastical office was formulated at the point where religious duty coincided with, and adorned, the moral conventions of the class into which they were born. How should the Christian aristocrat behave? The answer began with St François de Sales' assimilation of the civility of renaissance humanism into Christian ethics. We do not renounce the world, we learn to live in it, using the principles of 'things indifferent' and of the *juste milieu* to settle the boundaries of permissible conduct. Under God, our duty is to our station in life and the office we hold in society, and we ought to pass from prayer to everyday work with untroubled minds. How then will the world be converted? By manoeuvre—if necessary we must wear 'perfumed gloves', 'but what matter if men

---

[62] For example the abbé de Beauvais, who had referred to Mme du Barry—'les vils restes de la licence publique'—E. & J. de Goncourt, *La Du Barry* (Paris 1880) p 178.

[63] L.-P. Bachaumont, *Mémoires secrets pour servir à l'histoire de la république des lettres*, 36 vols (London 1780–9) 7 pp 114, 153–4; 8 pp 78–9.

[64] P. Girault de Coursac, *L'Education d'un roi: Louis XVI* (Paris 1972) pp 251–3.

[65] See, for example, Mgr Martial Levé, *Louis-François-Gabriel d'Orléans de la Motte, évêque d'Amiens, 1683–1774* (Abbeville 1962).

are healed and, at the end, they are saved?'[66] As the old stereotype of
aristocratic conduct of the court of Louis XIV, the *honnête homme*, lost
credibility, the formula, together with some of its outward courtesies,
was taken over by the Salesian Christian civility. In the first half of
the eighteenth century, we meet *l'honnête homme chrétien* and *le chrétien
honnête homme* as a description of how Christian duties could be brought
into alliance with those of civil life.[67] My station and its duties interpreted in the light of religion: here is the key to the morality of Le
Maître de Claville's enormously influential *Traité du vrai mérite de
l'homme* (1734); this principle legitimised all moderate pleasures, and
made it unnecessary for the Christian to be odd or austere. 'If there is a
middle way between a coquette and a Carmelite, between a Capuchin
and a debauchee, it lies in the fulfilment of the duties of the state in
life which we have chosen'.[68]

In the second half of the century this view of Christian vocation was
reinforced by two currents of fashionable thought. One was the cult
of egalitarian politeness in the upper reaches of society. Its outward
effect was described by an acute observer: 'Dans le grand monde on
ne rencontre point de caractères outrés . . . Une noble familiarité y
déguise avec adresse l'amour propre, et l'homme de robe, l'évêque,
le militaire, le financier, l'homme de cour semblent avoir pris quelque
chose les uns des autres; il n'y a que des nuances, et jamais de couleur
dominante'.[69] The bishop, it will be seen, distinguishes himself from
the rest of high society only by 'nuances'. Then, there was the cult of
sensibilité and benevolence. It suited the *philosophes* to see *le bon curé*—
doctor, veterinary surgeon, reconciler of families, rescuer of star-
crossed lovers and oracle of the parish—as the representative of these
generous feelings in the church. There was an episcopal equivalent,[70]
l'évêque administrateur, much talked of in the eighties, though never
achieving the applauded status of the benevolent *curé*; an administrative bishop was anathema to respectable churchmen,[71] and would
receive only faint praise from the *philosophes* unless there was a tincture

[66] Ruth Murphy, *Saint-François de Sales et la civilité chrétienne* (Paris 1964) pp 209, 75–171.
[67] In père Buffier's *Vérités consolantes* (1710)—see F. K. Montgomery, *La Vie et l'œuvre de Père Buffier, 1661–1737* (Paris 1930) pp 28–9; and in J.-B. Morvan de Bellegarde, *Le Chrétien honnête homme, ou alliance des devoirs de la vie chrétienne avec les devoirs de la vie civile* (La Haye 1736).
[68] R. Mercier, *La Réhabilitation de la nature humaine, 1700–1750* (Villemomble 1960) p 260.
[69] Mercier, *Tableau*, 4 p 110 (cccxxii).
[70] See Sage.
[71] Especially in the *Lettres secrètes* (1781–3), see Sicard p 175.

of unbelief about him. In his memoirs,[72] Talleyrand divides the prelates of the *ancien régime* into three categories: 'very pious', 'specially administrators' and 'worldly'. He himself was in the latter two categories. But the famous apologia, 'I was lame and a younger son: there was no way of escaping my destiny', is only half the story. As an administrator he was brilliant and dedicated and served the church well as *agent du clergé*;[73] he would have served both church and state well as an effective but somewhat unedifying bishop if the revolution had not driven him into purely secular courses. Even Talleyrand had a vocation, the vocation of an aristocrat, and it was not contemptible.

Of the two hundred and ninety-six clerical deputies elected to the estates general of 1789, only forty-six were bishops. It was a measure of the rejection by the *curés*—and by the nation—of the divine right of the aristocracy to rule, and in some dioceses it was also evidence of the hatred aroused by the pride or worldliness of the governing prelate. But only in a few. Apart from their blindness at the abuses of the system which had promoted them, most bishops were estimable men. By shaking anecdotes together or by taking a few outrageous *grands seigneurs* as typical, the old fashioned composite picture of an aristocratic bishop of the *ancien régime* was created—desultory study in the charge of a tutor on the fringes of the unreformed Sorbonne (where the first five places in the *licence* were reserved for courtiers), a superficial apprenticeship to devotion in the undisciplined seminary of Saint-Sulpice with a valet in attendance, a brief spell as a nominal *grand vicaire*, consecration to the episcopate at an early age, followed by a couple of translations to wealthier sees, frequent trips to Paris and some gossip about immoralities. In fact, most bishops had to wait until about the age of forty before they were elevated, and few obtained more than one translation.[74] Most acquired enough learning, even theological, to have written their own pastoral letters if that had been necessary, though this did not take the edge off stock jokes about them being composed by authors of comedies and operas in dubious circumstances. Some had worked hard as *grands vicaires* and learned about diocesan affairs, some had served their five years as *agents* of the

[72] Talleyrand, *Mémoires*, ed le duc de Broglie, 5 vols (Paris 1891) 1 p 31.
[73] See L. S. Greenbaum, *Talleyrand Statesman-Priest* (Washington D.C. 1970).
[74] Plongeron pp 92–3. The great disparity in the size of dioceses meant that small sees were used as training grounds for large ones; some of the small sees were in isolated and difficult areas—'ne peut-on pas même regarder ces translations comme autant de récompenses d'une vie laborieuse passée dans un pays ingrat?' asked the bishop of Gap in 1790—T. Tackett, *Priest and Parish in Eighteenth-Century France* (Princeton 1977) p 30.

clergy of France and knew the whole business of central administration.[75] According to a confidential report of the papal nuncio in 1766,[76] most were of good morals, and of those of 1789, there were only twelve whose lives had given cause for scandal.[77] (If strict rules of evidence are applied to gossip, the tally might be reduced: Mgr de Conzié's 'duel' is an example of what happens to a good story when historians ask too many questions).[78] Like the aristocrats they were, bishops, even the best of them, tended to spendthrift courses, ostentatious building, and a free and easy attitude to the rules about residence; if they had any justification, it was in the reply of archbishop Dillon of Narbonne when Louis XVI asked why he hunted himself but forbade the chase to his clergy: 'Sire, my vices come from my ancestry, but the vices of my *curés* are their own'.[79] And, by contrast, ancestry had its traditional virtues. In a crisis—famine, plague, fire or flood—the bishops could be as spendthrift on behalf of others as they were usually on their own,[80] selling their plate, throwing open their palaces for hospitals, borrowing huge sums to buy grain supplies. Under the intolerant Mgr de Beaumont as under the idle Mgr de Juigné, the vast revenues of the see of Paris were a standby for the poor in bad years. Cardinal de Bernis, poetaster, courtier, professional diplomat and part-time archbishop of Albi proclaimed the rights of the labouring man as against the luxury of the rich, and when floods devastated his episcopal city, practised what he preached. A miser in a mitre was a rarity; the memory of the bishop of Grenoble who failed to leave his library to the municipality and of the archbishop of Lyons who left nothing to the hospital were execrated by the townsfolk.[81] Political ambition and the desire to exercise authority could make a prelate a more efficient diocesan administrator than piety alone. Fleury ruefully said that he was bishop of Fréjus 'by divine

[75] See E. Besnier, *Les Agents généraux du clergé de France* (Paris 1939).
[76] P. Vial, 'L'Eglise de France vue par le nonce en 1766', *Cahiers d'histoire* 8 (Grenoble 1966) pp 107 seq.
[77] According to Vallery-Radot p 136.
[78] M. G. Coolen, 'Le duel de Mgr de Conzié' *Bulletin historique de la Société des Antiquaires de la Morinie*, 16, 302 (Saint-Omer 1938) pp 46–61.
[79] G. Maugras, *La Fin d'une société: le duc de Lauzun et la cour intime de Louis XV* (Paris 1893) p 376.
[80] Sicard pp 373–421. Other examples, L. Pingaud, *Les Saulx Tavannes* (Paris 1876) p 266; J. Loth, *Histoire du cardinal de la Rochefoucauld et du diocèse de Rouen* (Evreux 1893) pp 83, 118–19.
[81] P. Vaillant, '. . . La fondation de la bibliothèque de Grenoble', *Cahiers d'histoire* 8 (Paris 1963) pp 282 seq; G. Armingon, *Banquiers des pauvres* (Lyon nd) pp 83–8.

wrath', but he was a conscientious pastor;[82] Loménie de Brienne, commonly supposed not to believe in God, and who studied 'la théologie comme un Hibernois pour être évêque et les *Mémoires* du Cardinal de Retz pour être homme d'Etat' ran a model diocese when he was archbishop of Toulouse.[83] Eighteenth-century France saw the diversification and improvement of administrative techniques, preparing the way for the revolution's over-logical reorganisation; the bishops, both as pastors and as 'administrative inspectors' of the government, played their part—surveys and maps of dioceses were produced, printed proformas for visitations were devised, collections of information about parishes and local circumstances made.[84] As presidents of provincial and diocesan estates, bishops fought for local rights against the state—more especially they negotiated reductions in taxation. Conversely, they defended the rights of the church against the local laity, as did the archbishop of Auch and the prelates of the south in the 1780s to preserve tithe against an almost universal conspiracy of refusal.[85] The entire episcopate confronted the crown with a united and successful defiance when Machault tried to tax the *clergé étranger* in the mid century—the bishop of Verdun pleaded that he was at death's door and offered to pay instead of his *curés*, while his *confrère* of Metz excommunicated the intendant.[86] In the *foi et hommage* persecution of the eighties, the crown never succeeded in extracting a *sou* from the proud and united prelates.[87] In the great affair of the *Commission des Réguliers*, set up to reform the monasteries, the bishops were seen at their worst and at their best: blind to the evil of the *commande* by which they enjoyed a slice of monastic revenues, but fair and judicious in their appraisal of local monasteries, willing to reform yet yielding as little as possible to secular clamour.[88] And, at

82 V. Verlaque, *Histoire du cardinal de Fleury* (Paris 1878) pp 29–30; M. Espitalier, 'Les évêques de Fréjus', *Bulletin de la société d'études scientifiques et archéologiques de . . . Draguignan* (1898–9) pp 124–6, 142.

83 G. Cormery, *Loménie de Brienne à Toulouse, 1763–1788* (Albi 1935).

84 Plongeron pp 101–7. In addition to the articles he cites on p 272, see R. Suadeau, *L'Evêque inspecteur administratif sous la monarchie absolue*, 2 vols (Paris 1940) and the article of Gabriel Le Bras which drew attention to the now much studied visitations— 'L'état religieux et moral du diocèse de Châlons au dernier siècle de l'ancien régime', *Nouvelle revue de Champagne et de Brie* (Reims 1935) pp 165 *seq*.

85 A. Degert, 'Les assemblées provinciales du clergé Gascon', *Revue de gascogne*, ns 20 (Bordeaux 1925) pp 87 *seq*.

86 Luynes, 10 pp 463, 466; D'Argenson, 6 p 145.

87 See, for example, *P. V. de l'Assemblée générale extraordinaire du clergé, 1782* (Paris 1783) pp 140, 225, 219–23, 232, 270.

88 P. Chevallier, *Loménie de Brienne et l'Ordre monastique, 1760–89*, 2 vols (Paris 1959) I p 72, 2 pp 210, 261–5.

the end of the *ancien régime*, they provided the most national and the most moral element in the *révolte nobiliaire*. Intelligent and well organised, they were the heart of the opposition to Calonne in the notables,[89] and in June 1788 their protest to the crown lifted the aristocratic revolt to a new plane of dignity and universality. Their right to vote taxation, they said, was a survival of the old national franchises, and these franchises should be restored. Let the king summon the estates general to consent to taxation; then, 'human nature will begin to regain its dignity, and the people will count for something', and Louis would be, not just king of France, but 'King of Frenchmen', ruling over the hearts of his subjects.

In 1776, Louis XVI made his famous jest: 'Je viens d'envoyer le Saint-Esprit en Auvergne—le saint à Clermont et l'esprit à Saint-Flour', referring to the appointment of the pious François de Bonac to the one bishopric and the frivolous Hay de Bouteville to the other.[90] There was, indeed, a vast distance between the two ends of the moral scale of the French episcopate in the latter years of the *ancien régime*, between the luxurious cardinal de Rohan of the diamond necklace scandal and the austere Lefranc de Pompignan, between the harsh and aloof Montmorency-Laval of Metz and Mgr du Tillet walking round his diocese of Orange, dog at heels and sweets in his pocket for the children.[91] But most bishops were concentrated in the middle of the scale, living decorous and useful lives in the service of crown and church, fulfilling the vocation of a Christian aristocrat, performing the public duties, and nothing loath to claim the appropriate rewards, that went with their station in life and the high office to which they had been destined. The moral theologians, for all their bleak austerity about vocation, were at least down to earth on the question of 'attraction'. They demanded no mystical internal inspiration. A duly qualified and motivated man might properly obey the call of a bishop and seek ordination, and the call of the king (as allowed by the pope) to assume the political, social and religious responsibilities of a

[89] 'Le clergé conduisit cette première assemblée des Notables. Il avait pour lui l'instruction, l'expérience, le lien de la confraternité'—and met every night at the archbishop of Narbonne's—J. Weber, *Mémoires concernant Marie-Antoinette*, 2 vols (London 1804) I p 221.

[90] Hay de Bouteville committed suicide in October 1788, according to a *curé*, because he could not account for the provincial funds—L. Berthe, 'La fin de l'ancien régime à Fosseux', *Mélanges de science religieuse. Facultés catholiques de Lille*, 12 (Lille 1955) p 54.

[91] For Montmorency-Laval, J. Eich, *Histoire religieuse du département de la Moselle pendant la Révolution*, 2 vols (Metz 1964); for Tillet, S. Bonnet, *Notice biographique sur Guillaume-Louis du Tillet, évêque d'Orange* (Paris 1880).

bishopric. In July 1776, the archbishop of Tours, after serving as royal commissioner to the chapter of the Cordeliers of Touraine, wrote to recommend père Etienne who had just been made provincial. 'Perhaps he is not very fervent, perhaps he is a freemason . . . but what I can guarantee is that he has intelligence and a very religious outward bearing', and, he added, he wishes to restore order and he has the confidence of his colleagues.[92] These were the average standards of the bishops of the *ancien régime*: père Etienne had their sort of vocation.

Christ Church
Oxford

---

[92] Ch. Gérin, 'Les monastères franciscains et la Commission des Réguliers', *Revue des Questions historiques*, 18 (Paris 1875) pp 113–14.

ASSESSING NINETEENTH-CENTURY MISSIONARY MOTIVATION: SOME CONSIDERATIONS OF THEORY AND METHOD

by STUART PIGGIN

'IT is possible that no breed of men and women can be so safely assessed as the nineteenth-century Protestant missionaries. No other breed, certainly, left more voluminous accounts of themselves to posterity.'[1] If the volume of documentation is a guarantee of safe assessment then Moorhouse's bold assertion is particularly applicable to the subject of missionary motivation in Britain in the nineteenth century. Statements of motive, explicitly requested by directors of missionary societies, prayerfully considered and copiously detailed by candidates, and lovingly preserved by missionary-society archivists, might comprise the most voluminous extant documentation on religious motivation (Moorhouse's boldness is infectious). Furthermore, this vast corpus of primary source material has been thoroughly ransacked by postgraduate students of history and sociology, so that the motives of English and Scottish missionaries for the whole of the nineteenth century have now been explored.[2]

The mere volume of primary and secondary sources, however, does not justify confidence that missionary motives have been safely assessed. Problems remain, and this paper will be addressed to three questions suggested by these problems. The first question arises from a problem which all students of motivation must face. Can we be reasonably

---

[1] G. Moorhouse, *The Missionaries* (London 1973) p 170.
[2] The four major theses on this subject of which I am aware are [D. A.] Dow, ['Domestic Response and Reaction to the Foreign Missionary Enterprises of the Principal Scottish Presbyterian Churches, 1873–1929;] 2 vols PhD, university of Edinburgh 1977; [F. S.] Piggin, ['The Social Background, Motivation, and Training of British Protestant Missionaries to India, 1789–1858'], PhD, university of London 1974; [S. C.] Potter, ['The Social Origins and Recruitment of English Protestant Missionaries in the Nineteenth Century'], PhD, university of London 1974; and [C. P.] Williams, ['The Recruitment and Training of Overseas Missionaries in England between 1850 and 1900'], MLitt, university of Bristol 1976. Other related studies include J. van den Berg, *Constrained by Jesus' Love* (Kampen 1956); [M. A. C.] Warren, [*The Missionary Movement from Britain in Modern History*] (London 1965); and [G.] Oddie, ['India and Missionary Motives, c. 1850–1900'], *JEH*, 25 no 1 (January 1974).

confident that the subjects of our research are not deceivers or deceived? The second question is prompted by the volume of the evidence and the fact that the secondary studies sometimes contradict each other. Is it possible to quantify motives in some way so that impressionism is minimised? The third question is based on the conspicuous ambivalence of nineteenth-century missionary motives. To put it crudely, is nineteenth-century missionary motivation distinguishable from missionary motivation before and since because of some unique synthesis of religious conviction and secular impulse?

Arguments which might justify scepticism of these statements of missionary motive have been advanced elsewhere.[3] Here, in an admittedly one-sided presentation, reasons will be offered for concluding that the quest for missionary motives is a hopeful enterprise. The question which all historians must ask, 'Who was this document intended to deceive?', apparently highly appropriate if addressed to French bishops of the *ancien régime*, is too cynical in this context. Accountability to God, a principal tenet of the dominant missionary theologies, moderate Calvinism and evangelical Arminianism, accentuated the importance of having right motives. Many missionary candidates, reminded on application forms that they would one day have to render an account 'in the sight of that heart-searching God', seem to have felt on the question of motive like J. T. Pattison, who wrote to the directors of the London missionary society, 'I dread the very idea of acting from impure motives, for I am persuaded that if it turn out that I am thus impelled forward, I shall most bitterly suffer.'[4] Furthermore, the prevailing conviction of innate depravity left few with the delusion that purity of motive was easily achieved. H. Dixon, a prospective missionary with the church missionary society, wrote, 'I do sincerely hope that my motives are pure. I say I hope so; for I am too well aware of the deceitfulness of the human heart not to know that our very best motives to action are not thoroughly unmixed; even though we ourselves are not aware of it.'[5] In such an atmosphere it is not even necessary to postulate, as Oddie has done,[6] that candidates would always refrain from mentioning embarrassing or unworthy

[3] Piggin pp 145–8.
[4] J. T. Pattison's answers to questions, 12 April, 1836, candidates' papers, London missionary society archives, school of oriental and african studies.
[5] H. Dixon to the committee, 23 February, 1853, church missionary society archives, C/AC1/3/496.
[6] Oddie p 64.

motives. Some seem to have suffered from what today is known as pathological candour. Robert Nesbit, who went to India with the Scottish missionary society, confessed to the committee that he was partly motivated by a desire to be first to volunteer for service in India and thus win the approval of the religious public. Although at the time of application he hoped that he was not still activated by this 'love of admiration', he confessed that his 'ruling motive' was still the desire to advance his own 'personal religion'.[7]

It seems unlikely that men, characterised by such scrupulosity, would deceive deliberately. Nor must we conclude on theoretical grounds that these earnest young men were totally deluded. The philosophers assure us that gratitude, one of the most often-mentioned missionary motives,[8] can act as a motive. Anscombe describes gratitude as a 'backward-looking'[9] motive which means in this context a candidate's explanation of why he offered himself to a society as a missionary. Schmitt denies the suggestion, frequently made by psychologists schooled in Freudian psychoanalysis, that the most vitally significant motives lie in the subconscious and are therefore inaccessible.[10] 'Insofar as desires, beliefs and intentions are among the phenomena that may function as motives,' Schmitt writes, 'it seems clearly true that some of them are known to me by introspection.'[11]

The historian, I contend, must have a very good reason for disallowing the interpretation of motives made by men after intense introspection, men unlikely deliberately to fabricate. The sociologist, Reinhard Bendix, and the historians E. P. Thompson and Otto Brunner, warn us 'against the dangers of substituting inevitably arbitrary categories for the terms in which the historical participants themselves think about the questions at issue.'[12] To accept in large measure the missionary candidates' statements of their own motives will not enable us to tell the whole story, as we shall see. But neither will it be devoid of 'explanatory force', for in this material on missionary motivation we are not far removed from 'the grain of human

---

[7] J. M. Mitchell, *Memoir of the Rev. Robert Nesbit* (London 1858) pp 27–38.
[8] Piggin p 192.
[9] G. E. M. Anscombe, *Intention* (Oxford 1957) pp 21–2.
[10] For a discussion of the relative importance attached by psychologists to conscious and unconscious motives, see [*Assessment of Human Motives*], ed [G.] Lindzey (New York 1964) pp 19–20.
[11] R. Schmitt, 'The Desire for Private Gain: Capitalism and the Theory of Motives', *Inquiry*, 16 (London 1973) p 156.
[12] [T.] Burns and [S. B.] Saul, [*Social Theory and Economic Change*] (London 1967) p 76.

experience' to which the 'historian's categories must in the end correspond'.[13]

Since missionaries said so much and so many different things about motives, how can we begin to make safe generalisations about them? Can motives be quantified in some way? In his examination of the motives of LMS missionaries in the second half of the century, Oddie attempts a quantification which appears valid. If, he explains, application papers

> are set out in chronological order and statements made by the twenty candidates during the period 1845–1858 are compared with statements made by the same number of candidates over the period 1876–1888, differences in their attitude towards eternal punishment become clearly apparent. In the earlier period a greater number of applicants refer to the 'perishing' heathen, or state explicitly their belief that all those who have not heard the Gospel will suffer in everlasting misery. During the later period, candidates were not only less inclined to state a belief in the doctrine of everlasting punishment but in a number of cases questioned its validity.[14]

By this simple procedure Oddie has corrected an impression given by Warren that 'emphasis on the heathen perishing in their blindness' was a powerful missionary motive in the second half of the century.[15] Oddie's correction, on the other hand, like all generalisations based on similar procedures, is probably too schematic. His findings have in turn been supplemented by Williams who has studied a broader cross-section of missionary societies, including the China inland mission. Williams concludes that the decline in the motive of concern for the 'perishing heathen' was both slow and uneven. 'Souls on every hand are perishing for lack of knowledge,' wrote Hudson Taylor in 1883, 'a thousand every hour are passing away into death and darkness.'[16] Williams found that Taylor 'did not wrongly judge the market and his mathematical calculations could still be a decisive motive. His constituency had not surrendered its belief in hell.'[17] Neither had those university students, pietistic and anti-intellectual, from which the

---

[13] R. Samuel, 'Local History and Oral Tradition,' History Workshop, 1 (London 1976) p 204.
[14] Oddie p 69.
[15] Warren p 48.
[16] Quoted in Williams p 195.
[17] Ibid.

Assessing missionary motivation

CMS in the 1880s drew many of its missionaries.[18] The accounts of Oddie and Williams are, of course, compatible, and consensus on the declining importance of this motive is possible.

Some motives, on which consensus has been reached, are perhaps more surprising than the demise of hell. After a review of the involvement of missionary applicants in home missions, I concluded that far from missionaries being unaware of the grave social problems of their compatriots (as is often charged) it was experience of these very problems which frequently originated the desire to be a missionary.[19] Slums, Dow reminds us, surrounded three of the four Scottish universities where most Scottish missionaries were educated, and it was quite impossible to get to the university of Glasgow without passing through 'a moral sewer of a most loathesome description'.[20] Dow, who has made a very interesting study of the place of the missionary in Scottish literature, says that it was a commonplace to compare the heathen at home with those abroad. Apparently some Scots were shocked by neither. R. L. Stevenson 'took equal delight in the elemental and savage characteristics displayed by South Sea islanders and by the submerged classes of Edinburgh'.[21] Returning to England, Williams writes of the 'conscientious reaction' to the poverty and suffering of the industrial revolution by 'the most sensitive amongst the prosperous middle class' from which the CIM and CMS drew many of their recruits.[22]

Consensus, however, has not always been reached. Both Dow[23] and Williams[24] emphasise that progressively towards the end of the century missionaries were motivated by philanthropic considerations, whereas I concluded that humanitarian motives were important from the start of the modern missionary movement, beginning with William Carey himself.[25] Uncertainty of this kind, which may result from the impressionistic, perhaps inevitably unquantified nature of our conclusions, is of some concern because it justifies historians working in other, if related, fields in continuing to select evidence which systematically supports their own theses, but in the context of

[18] *Ibid* p 196.
[19] Piggin pp 118–23.
[20] Dow p 32.
[21] *Ibid*, see also p 411.
[22] Williams p 173. See also Potter pp 134–5.
[23] Dow pp 118–28.
[24] Williams pp 245–8.
[25] Piggin pp 177–8. See Warren p 46.

the history of the missionary movement as a whole, might be rather arbitrary.

This is a great problem in considering the relationship between missions and imperialism. For example, how comprehensive and therefore valid is Wright's claim that the difference between German and British missionaries in the second half of the century was that the former rejected western materialism whereas the latter uncritically swallowed Livingstone's advice and promoted Christianity and commerce with equal zest.[26] There is, of course, no difficulty in amassing evidence of missionary enthusiasm for British imperialism. Perhaps the most topical is the picture evoked by Gairdner, trembling with emotion, as he beheld the diamond jubilee celebrations: 'I should like to serve my Queen. Can I do better than by taking Christ to her Empire? She would like that, I think.'[27] But what do we do with evidence which points in the opposite direction? Was some impact perhaps made on the crudest imperialism by the holiness movement with its asceticism and condemnation of materialism?[28] And how good a prophet was Baldwin Brown in 1878 when he said that 'from our [nonconformist] churches will come the most constant, strenuous and intelligent protest against that bastard of empire—Imperialism . . .'?[29] What criteria must we employ before we conclude that evidence of this kind is insignificant?

Although I have no answers to that question, I do want to conclude this section with the contention that distortion results if historians dismiss missionaries as uncritical supporters of imperialism or if they write on nineteenth-century ecclesiastical history as if mission was not a primary concern of British churches. A very interesting example of this distortion is found in a recent work by the historian of imperialism, Bernard Semmel. He asserts (at least seven times) that the leaders of the Wesleyan connection, particularly by the second decade of the nineteenth century when the Wesleyan methodist missionary society was founded, were so anxious about the threat of disorder posed by the evangelising enthusiasms of evangelical Arminianism that they

[26] M. Wright, *German Missionaries in Tanganyika 1891–1941: Lutherans and Moravians in the Southern Highlands* (Oxford 1971) p 3.
[27] Quoted in Williams p 239.
[28] *Ibid* p 173, but contrast A. Porter, 'Cambridge, Keswick and late nineteenth-century Attitudes to Africa,' [*The*] *J[ournal of] I[mperial and] C[ommonwealth] H[istory]*, 5 no 1 (London October 1976) pp 5–34.
[29] Quoted in C. Binfield, *So down to Prayers: Studies in English Nonconformity 1780–1920* (London 1977) p 214.

consciously diverted this potentially-disruptive energy into the ener-
vating task of converting the rest of the world.[30] Semmel's thesis is
more interesting than the old pie-in-the-sky theory and more
pleasant than E. P. Thompson's 'psychic masturbation' mechanism,
but I think it is untenable nevertheless. Why I think that I shall endeavour to explain in another place.[31] Briefly, I see no reason why the
methodists should be any different from any other denominational
group in their devotion to foreign missions for their own sake, or if
they were interested in the reflex advantages of involvement in
foreign missions, as many were, it was to make them more energetic
evangelists at home, not less.

In attempting to define the essence of missionary motivation
throughout Christian history Warren wrote:

> No doubt the man who was 'ready to be offered' was at one
> moment a Roman citizen of Jewish birth, at another a celtic
> prince, a medieval monk, a friar, or a New England minister, or
> a Baptist cobbler or even a Cambridge graduate, each the
> product and expression of the culture in which he was born . . .
> But their own self-offering was not in the name of their culture.
> It was in the name of 'Him who had died for *them*'. To grasp that
> is to grasp the essence of the missionary movement.[32]

But the nineteenth century is Latourette's 'Great Century' of missionary
endeavour, and Warren's 'essence' does not help us to explain what
made it so. Maybe it was the great century of missions because of some
unique amalgam of spiritual and secular motives, a synthesis of great
missionary genius. To enable us to detect a pattern among those
motives which did amalgamate out of all the possible combinations of
motives, we need the help of some interpretative device, some theoretical framework. In the space remaining I shall outline briefly three
promising hypotheses.

A theory which alters the traditional boundaries between spiritual
and secular is called for because frequently secular motives were
spiritualised and spiritual motives were often emptied of altruism.
Take as an example the cult of respectability. This so completely
permeated the movement that even Hudson Taylor desired to have

[30] B. Semmel, *The Methodist Revolution*, (London 1974) pp 5, 125, 137, 144–5, 147–8, 153, 171, 177.
[31] My article 'The Origins of the Wesleyan Methodist Missionary Society: an Examination of Semmel's Thesis' is due to be published in *JICH* shortly.
[32] Warren p 44.

his children educated in southern England 'as the language is spoken more softly, and the manners are more refined'.[33] But there is little doubt that many thought of the ambition for respectability as a fruit of their religion, an inspiration to greater dedication and hard work. This ostensibly secular motive was spiritualised. On the other hand the quest for holiness was sometimes so careless of worldly responsibilities, or the desire for heavenly reward so calculating, that both look selfish. In this context psychologist Gordon Allport's typology of 'intrinsic' and 'extrinsic' motivation in religion might help us to redraw the boundaries between the secular and the religious.[34] Even if the attempt by historians to use Allport's typology founders on the inadequacies of written sources,[35] his challenge to the more environmentalist theories of other social scientists remains salutary for the historian. For Allport insists that there is such a thing as an inner compulsion.[36] Human beings are not always chameleons who change in every new situation, they are sometimes leopards who cannot change their spots.

A second promising approach is to look more closely at the historical significance of conversion, central to the experience of most nineteenth-century British protestant missionaries. On the relationship between conversion and missionary motivation, I wrote:

> . . . most applicants believed that the missionary impulse was of divine origin, springing from the work which they believed Christ had performed in their hearts at, and subsequent to the time of their conversion. Their 'calling' to missionary service was implicit in their conversion . . . It was an instinct, or 'reflex' of God-given faith.[37]

In her sociological study of nineteenth-century missionaries, Potter also attached major importance to conversion which, she says, 'crystallized into the missionary calling'.[38] Because evangelical beliefs and standards were so widely accepted, and the conversion experience

[33] Quoted in Williams p 227.
[34] G. W. Allport, 'Religious Context of Prejudice,' J[ournal for the] S[cientific] S[tudy of] R[eligion] 5 (London 1966) pp 447–57. See also G. W. Allport, The Individual and his Religion (New York 1950).
[35] 'Religious motivation cannot be inferred from theological positions or external behaviour but requires some intimate knowledge of the subject. The discernment of intrinsic religious motivation can probably best be done by a judge who is well acquainted with the person in question and can understand his system of motivation.' D. R. Hoge, 'A Validated Intrinsic Religious Motivation Scale,' JSSR 11 no 4 (December 1972) p 370. The historian is not usually sufficiently informed to act as such a judge.
[36] Lindzey p 242.
[37] Piggin p 191.
[38] Potter p 142.

so normative, Potter rejects the view, prominent among sociologists, that conversion is always characteristic of the sect-mentality. 'Evidently,' she writes perceptively, ' . . . it was possible to be converted to convention.'[39] This 'peculiar pattern'[40] of religious conversion might be the synthesis of missionary genius for which we are searching, and we must therefore look at the sociological mechanism behind it. Since a significant percentage of missionaries was recruited from among skilled tradesmen, Potter explores the social and psychological effects of the apprenticeship system. The work experience of the apprentice induced a dissatisfaction with masters and peers which promoted deviance conventional in adolescents, including swearing, sabbath-breaking, card-playing and atheism. As the moral standards thus transgressed were widely accepted, this deviance created an anxiety which could be resolved by religious conversion: 'taking up a religious faith seems to have been . . . a slipway to convention and adulthood for the uneasy adolescent, and one, moreover, more easily available to the apprentice than were other adult statuses'.[41] Such 'conversions to conformity' and the consequent adoption of roles honoured in church and chapel, including that of missionary, does help to explain something of the eagerness for missionary service in the nineteenth century. The problem is that most missionaries had not been apprentices and therefore Potter's 'peculiar pattern' is too narrow to embrace the century as a whole. Realising this, Potter postulates a second pattern for the latter half of the century 'comprising a more respectable adolescence leading to a well-trodden missionary career' which 'seems to have arisen when conventional life became hedged about with protective institutions—schools, colleges, offices, suburbs, and busy churches.'[42]

So thirdly, in attempting a more broadly-based explanation, we might get a lot of mileage out of the theories of political economist Everett E. Hagen. He advances the hypotheses of 'status-withdrawal' and the increasing importance of the achievement motive to explain the dynamics of the change from traditional to industrial societies.[43] Perhaps the nineteenth century should be understood as a bridge century between the age of authority in which status is ascriptive and

[39] *Ibid* p 135.
[40] *Ibid.*
[41] *Ibid* p 141.
[42] *Ibid* p 161.
[43] E. E. Hagen, *On the Theory of Social Change* (London 1964); Burns and Saul pp 1–4, 9–34.

the achievement motive confined to a few, and the modern industrial age in which status is achieved and the achievement motive generalised. The remarkable ambivalence of missionary motives might reflect elements of both those societies. As we have seen most missionaries were influenced by a desire for respectability, and while many sought status through the traditional channel of ordination and saw missionary service as the only road to that end, others, of whom Alexander Duff is a conspicuous example, would not accept the honour of being in the home ministry. These last cared little for the approval of the old élite.[44] Nineteenth-century missionaries were also characterised by remarkably unselfish self-centredness. They had to be useful to others to be happy themselves, and evangelical utilitarianism produced men who were eager for power but who were also determined to use it responsibly.[45] These same missionaries were characterised by self-doubting confidence. 'Who is sufficient for these things?' they asked, and many answered that they were. They felt better suited to missionary work than anything else—interesting testimony to the job satisfaction which it was believed missionary work offered to men who had a deep need to exercise all their God-given talents.[46]

Romanticism was a factor in the movement, but it was a very calculating romanticism. Those drawn perhaps initially by the prospect of adventure forced themselves to count the cost and to view their future life in its worst aspects.[47] Similarly they believed that their enthusiasm was irresistibly rational. They so systematised the arguments for missionary service that they convinced themselves that it was necessary to justify staying rather than going.[48] They were prepared to work hard, but they found the creative labour afforded by missionary service more congenial than the routine tasks of their previous occupations.[49] Hence when missionary applicants aspired to be 'workmen who need not be ashamed' they may have reflected the need of an industrialising society for work-discipline plus innovation.

Evangelical religion sanctioned the climb to respectability and power of new classes against the resistance of older élites because progress for all was given the force of divine command. In an age of

[44] Dow pp 16, 23, 137.
[45] Piggin pp 249–50.
[46] Ibid 168–70; Potter p 161.
[47] Piggin p 160.
[48] Ibid p 189, Williams p 170.
[49] Potter p 143.

transition, to work for the glory of God was a more effective way to self-improvement than blatant forms of self-glorification. Hence the achievement motive released in new aspiring classes and sublimated by evangelical religion expressed itself in unprecedented evangelistic aggression. Between the rational age of Descartes (*cogito, ergo sum*) which appealed to few and today's sensuous world (*sentio, ergo sum*) which appeals to all, lay the great age of missions (*actio, ergo sum*) which appealed to many. In such an age the vast task of the Christianisation of the world was thought of as challenging and bracing rather than daunting and oppressive.

University of Wollongong

BLACK EUROPEANS, WHITE AFRICANS: SOME MISSIONARY MOTIVES IN WEST AFRICA

by A. F. WALLS

IERRA LEONE was the first success story of the modern missionary movement. The years from 1787 to 1830 saw it pass first from a green if not very fertile land supporting subsistence farmers and riverine slaving factories to Utopia in a disaster area; then transformed again as free blacks from Nova Scotia and Jamaica, full of evangelical religion and American republicanism carried out a Clapham-inspired scheme in ways the men of Clapham did not always like; and again as this population was overwhelmed by new uprooted peoples from all over west Africa, brought in from the slaveships before they had ever seen the transatlantic plantations. The new population responded, sometimes with enthusiasm and rarely with prolonged resistance, to missionary preaching; and, with those same missionaries appointed to superintend their temporal as well as their spiritual welfare, adopted the norms and characteristics of their Nova Scotian and Maroon predecessors. Contemporary British sources do not suggest that at the time Sierra Leone was regarded as a huge success; people in England tended to think of the appalling loss of missionary life in the white man's grave, and the enormous expense of the Sierra Leone mission; besides, they heard stories which suggested that the serpent still dwelt in their west African garden. Nonetheless, here was the first part of Africa, one of the very few parts anywhere in the world, where there was a mass movement towards the Christian faith, where a whole non-Christian people became Christian.[1]

Looked at from another point of view, Sierra Leone saw the birth of a new nation and a new culture. In the Krio people and Krio culture European and African elements were inextricably blended, and European institutions were adopted into an African context and

---

[1] See [C. H.] Fyfe [A History of Sierra Leone] (London 1962); [J.] Peterson, [Province of Freedom: a history of Sierra Leone 1787–1870] (London 1969); A. F. Walls, 'A Christian experiment: the early Sierra Leone colony', The Mission of the Church and the Propagation of the Faith, SCH 6 (1970) pp 107–29.

transformed by it.[2] Again, this was only partially realised at the time, since what European eyes saw was the wholesale adoption of European institutions. This self-consciously Christian community flocked to buildings looking like English parish churches in villages called Leicester, Gloucester, Kent or Sussex, or Wilberforce, Bathurst, Waterloo or Wellington. (The patronal dedication of the church in the village of Wellington is the unlikely St Arthur Wellington.) They wore European dress, as good as they could afford, for the purpose, and lived in houses influenced by European models. They were a literate community, too, and as the years went by, developed their grammar schools, for boys and for girls; and their higher educational institution at Fourah Bay college in which by the 1870s it was possible to take degrees in arts and theology.

Such things perhaps concealed the extent to which the Krio community was also an African community: maintaining indigenous rites like circumcision,[3] clinging, (though not usually with ecclesiastical approval) to forms of ancestor veneration, adapting funeral customs and friendly societies to African ideas of family solidarity and the living dead.[4] A distinctively Krio expression of Christianity emerged. If most churches, irrespective of denomination, used the Anglican liturgy, they also used the methodist class meeting. Where observers saw Krio culture and church differ from that of Britain, it was assumed that the differences were imperfections due to ignorance, which would be remedied with time and patience. The question of language affords a paradigm here. Inevitably English became the language of administration, education and worship in Sierra Leone. But a new lingua franca was growing up incorporating words from many sources, especially English, but developing a syntax which shows that it is an African language. When Englishmen heard it, they called it broken English, or bad English, or even, (with a dig at the German missionaries who formed the staple of the CMS) 'German English'. It never occurred to them that it was a new language, with an English vocabulary and an African syntax. One result is that though every Krio

---

[2] Compare [A. T.] Porter, [Creoledom] (London 1963); L. Spitzer The Creoles of Sierra Leone: responses to colonialism 1870–1945 (Madison 1974).

[3] Porter p 85.

[4] Compare Peterson esp pp 259–63; H. Sawyerr, 'Traditional sacrificial rituals and Christian worship', S[ierra] L[eone] B[ulletin of] R[eligion] 2, 1 (Freetown 1960) pp 18–27; H. Sawyerr 'Graveside libations in and near Freetown', SLBR 7, 2 (1965) pp 48–55; compare S. Rowe, 'Judas die don tidday', SLBR 7, 1 (1965) pp 1–12.

speaks Krio at home, the Krio church to this day uses English—'good English'—for liturgy and preaching.

The Krio Church was built on recaptive Africans, uprooted from coherent societies and without the means of rediscovering their former cohesion. The only identity now open to them was a new identity. They took the only viable alternative open to them, and adopted— and adapted—the package of Christianity and European civilisation.[5]

It is not surprising if both they and their European contemporaries assumed that the Sierra Leone reaction could and should be typical of African reactions to Christianity. We can see now that the recaptives were very untypical of Africa; observers in the 1840s can be forgiven for not realizing this. Critics of Sierra Leone might see it as an inferior aping of European modes; its friends could see a 'Black European' civilisation, Christian, literate, using the English language with ease, differing from Europe only in being—potentially—more religious, more moral, more literate. Here was the triumphant demonstration of the repeated missionary assertion that given the same opportunities, Africans were as capable of 'improvement' as anyone else. When the large, grave figure of Samuel Crowther, clad in immaculate clerical black, spoke convincingly on English public platforms, had audience with queen Victoria and answered all prince Albert's intelligent questions about commerce in Africa, the whole missionary enterprise seemed justified. The future operations of missions in Africa must be directed to producing more of the same. There was nothing yet to force the question whether European civilization was the only standard by which attainment could be measured; nothing to suggest that the African ministry would, apart from its colour, look any different from the English. The African ministry would have the same sort of academic training as the English: a better academic training, therefore, than most of their English missionary mentors had received.[6] Not only was Sierra Leone beginning to produce a ministry that looked like that of England (possibly a little more like it than some of the rough hewn artisan-catechists ordained via the mission field and Islington college); it was also producing a merchant class seeking culture as well as comfort, displaying godliness as well as gain. It was producing, in fact, the solid constituency reflected in the membership and leader-

5 Compare A. F. Walls, 'A colonial concordat: two views of Christianity and civilisation', D. Baker, *Church, Society and Politics*, SCH 12 (1975) pp 293–302.
6 Compare A. F. Walls, 'Missionary vocation and the ministry: the first generation', *New Testament Christianity for Africa and the World: essays in honour of Harry Sawyerr*, ed M. E. Glasswell and E. W. Fasholé-Luke (London 1974).

ship of the church missionary society itself. So when the CMS grammar school began in Freetown, under a missionary principal, the hopes of it were for more than an educated ministry. It would teach biblical history and English history, mathematics and music, geography and Greek—and Latin. Greek was part of the plan for an educated ministry but Latin was there by public insistence:[7] Sierra Leone wanted everything that would be expected in England, and they made sure they got it.

This last point is significant. Not only was it the missionary assumption that assimilation to the best norms of protestant Europe was the highest good; not only was it the missionary intention to prove that Africans could be as good Europeans as anyone else; the intention of the exponents of Krio culture was the same. Later in the century would come the conscious search for more 'African' forms of expression; in the middle years of the century, this hardly showed. As early as 1830 the government announced its intention of gradually filling 'all stations . . . by persons of colour'; in the early 1840s 'persons of colour', notably Afro-West Indians, provided the governor, chief justice and other major officials of the most important British possession in west Africa.[8]

The Krio church was to be of incalculable importance in Christian expansion in west Africa. In the first place, to a greater extent than has been commonly realized, it provided the labour force: a hundred or more ministers and missionaries in forty years for the CMS alone, and a very much larger number of schoolmasters, catechists and artisans in mission service who might also do some teaching on the side.[9] And the climax is reached when Sierra Leone can provide, in the CMS Niger mission, an all African mission, and in Samuel Crowther, its own bishop. Such missionaries reflected the values of Sierra Leone: and when they set up a training institution hundreds of miles up the Niger, they called it *Institutio Causa Preparandi.*[10]

But the Sierra Leone missionaries, important as they are, are only a fragment of the Sierra Leone influence in the diffusion of Christianity in west Africa. As clerk, railwayman, mechanic and above all as trader, the Sierra Leonean penetrated everywhere the British did, and often

[7] Fyfe p 237.
[8] Fyfe pp 178, 211, 220 seq, 229.
[9] Compare P. E. H. Hair, 'Niger Languages and Sierra Leonean Missionary linguists, 1840–1930, *Bulletin of the Society for African Church History* 2, 2 (London 1966) pp 127–38.
[10] See for example [A. F. Ade] Ajayi, [*Christian Missions in Nigeria 1841–1891: the making of a new élite*] (London 1965).

further. And wherever he went, he took his bible, his hymn singing and his family prayers. In area after area, well into the twentieth century, the first contact of African peoples with the Christian faith was through an itinerant or immigrant Sierra Leonean. And the mission to Yorubaland, which marked a turning point in bringing about a well grounded church in inland Africa, came about because Sierra Leoneans had made their way back as traders over hundreds of miles to the places from whence they had once been taken as slaves, and were missing their Sunday services.[11]

The background of the best missionary theory of the time was the conviction of the essential concomitance of Christianity, commerce and civilisation; the conviction—which seemed to have empirical evidence on its side—that it was essential for Christian expansion to abolish slave trading, and that this as an economic institution could only be overcome by economic means. Missionary theory and economic theory were thus consciously intertwined. The development of commerce will help to suffocate the slave trade and commend the gospel. And the work of preachers of that gospel is not simply to call out individual converts; it is, as the impeccably evangelical Henry Venn, secretary of the CMS, could say to missionaries as late as 1868, 'to make disciples, or Christians, of all nations . . . that all nations should gradually adopt the Christian religion as their national profession of faith, and thus fill the universal Church by the accession of national churches'.[12] To those with such a vision, Sierra Leone was a light upon the mountains.

It has often been noticed that the last quarter of the nineteenth century produced an unprecedented acceleration of the missionary movement. But not only were there throngs of eager young men to throw back the frontiers of mission: they also included a new breed of missionary. The standard product English missionary in the early part of the century had been a fairly homespun character with few formal attainments: by the end of the century the victories of the gospel were being won on the playing fields of Eton. The devotional pattern and theological influences were also different; these men felt an evangelistic imperative which required the presentation of the gospel for decision

[11] Ajayi pp 25 *seq*. There is still no full treatment of the Sierra Leone diaspora. On the nature and importance of the *Saro* in Yorubaland, see J. H. Kopytoff, *A Preface to Modern Nigeria: the 'Sierra Leonians' in Yoruba 1830–1890* (Madison 1965).

[12] Instructions of the committee of the Church missionary society, 30.6.1868. The address is reprinted in W. Knight, *The Missionary Secretariat of Henry Venn* (London 1880) pp 282 *seq*.

by every individual, and to 'lay all on the altar', a self-emptying in complete consecration to God. They had an ethic of self denial, held with the doctrine (associated with the Keswick convention) of the availability of an experience of rest and victory over sin, received by faith; and an eschatology which saw the Lord's return as following the worldwide proclamation of the gospel.[13]

Such influences bringing such men with such motives at such a time meant a revolution in African missions. The story has often been told of how the young men with their new brooms swept away the all-African Niger mission and broke Crowther's heart in the process. And it is now being seen that it is not sufficient to write the story in terms of the abandonment of the theory of the self-governing church, or of the racist assumptions of the imperialist age replacing the more tolerant theory of an earlier period.[14] The influences which made these men missionaries implicitly challenged the priorities of west African missions and the assumptions which had underlain their methods for a generation past, not only highlighting the obvious failures of such missions but calling into question their very successes.

'We feel the absence of spiritual life out here in the Church. Conversion is practically unknown, and has certainly not been required as essential for admission to baptism. A mere knowledge of the Creed, Lord's Prayer and the Ten Commandments has always been reckoned as sufficient ground for baptizing anyone who offers himself. Can anyone be surprised if under such circumstances the Church is impure and rotten through and through'.[15]

So wrote one of the young men, not long after his arrival. By this time, as the pyramids of gin bottles built up in villages and townships

[13] A full account of the background is still awaited. Some of the flavour is conveyed in the works (unfortunately undocumented) of J. C. Pollock: compare *A Cambridge Movement* (London 1953); *The Cambridge Seven* (London 1955); *The Keswick Story* (London 1964). See now also A. Porter, 'Cambridge, Keswick and late nineteenth-century attitudes to Africa', *J[ournal of] I[mperial and] C[ommonwealth] H[istory]* 5, 1 (London 1976) pp 5-34.
[14] For a variety of interpretations, compare: P. Beyerhaus, *Die Selbständigkeit der jungen Kirchen als missionarisches Problem* (Wuppertal 1959) pp 123-62; Ajayi, chapter 8; J. B. Webster, *The African churches among the Yoruba 1888-1922* (Oxford 1964); P. E. H. Hair, *The Early Study of Nigerian Languages* (Cambridge 1967) p 60; G. O. M. Tasie, *Christianity in the Niger Delta 1864-1918*, unpublished PhD thesis, Aberdeen 1969; G. O. M. Tasie, 'The story of S. A. Crowther and the CMS Niger Mission crisis of the 1880s: a reassessment', *Ghana Bulletin of Theology* 4, 7 (London 1974) pp 47-60.
[15] [*Letters of Henry Hughes*] *Dobinson* (London 1899) pp 49 seq. Dobinson, Repton and Brasenose College Oxford, had just joined the mission from an English curacy a month or two previously.

Black Europeans, white Africans

(especially, as mordant critics pointed out, in missionised areas, and very much less in Islamicised areas) it was no longer obvious that the interests of Christianity and commerce marched together. There was no Atlantic slave trade now to be counteracted by economic operations of missionary inspiration; and no place in missionary theology for such carnal activities. In symbol of the old alliance, the missionary travelled up river on a ship which put trade goods ashore:

> We have a large quantity of spirits on board, whisky and gin, and almost every place receives some. It is a frightful disgrace to our country to be daily pouring in oceans of foul liquor into a country where none is wanted . . . the [Royal Niger] Company place a very heavy duty on all goods except English goods, and so keep down very materially the supply of spirits in their Niger stations. They do, however, get rid of a good deal of their own, but are the only Company in West Africa who take any trouble at all in the matter. It certainly does make one ashamed of one's country to see this devilish trade going on . . . .[16]

But it was not only, or even principally, the Royal Niger company and that regular bugbear of the missionary, the white trader, which distressed the newcomers. It was the loose-living, gin-selling, hymn singing Sierra Leonean entrepreneur or company clerk:

> The question will face us at Onitsha, where some of the leading Church members deal largely in gin. It has been said publicly on the River and all here acknowledge, that any attack on the gin traffic will ruin utterly all the Church work. Let the Church perish then, if she is here built on gin cases; but if she is founded on the Rock, she will not fall because we fight against and pull down a rotten prop or buttress.[17]

And so the young men set off to cleanse the Augean stables and the church rolls.

This group of men has been severely criticised, not least by themselves.[18] From some charges, however, they can be absolved. They were not inconsistent with their own principles, and those who

[16] Dobinson p 40.
[17] Ibid.
[18] Dobinson, who lived longer than some of his companions (he died 'of African fever' at Asaba in April 1897) came to argue for 'more trust on God and more trust in the Africans', to deduce that 'a European missionary is of little use unless he has a native agent alongside of him to help him for a year or two at least', and to reflect that 'I certainly feel my ground more than I used to in the days of Brooke and Robinson; when I was hurried along in unknown depths of a fierce-flowing river'. Dobinson pp 166 seq.

accuse them of assumed superiority and of riding roughshod over African institutions should at least note that imperial aloofness, or the automatic assumption of the superiority of all things European over all things African,[19] did not determine their attitudes. They represented a radical criticism (though expressed principally in individualistic terms) of the nominally—but how far from really!—Christian society from which they came. And they desired identification with the life of the people with whom they now lived; to be, in fact, 'all things to all men that by all means they might save some'.

One of their instructive criticisms of the 'Black European' missionaries from Sierra Leone—not less sincere if based on a misapprehension—was their aloofness from native life:

> So far Mission compounds have been regarded by natives as absolutely sacred ground, in to which they are on no pretext to enter. We hope to break down this absurd idea.[20]

This was essential to their missionary method: the tradition of Christian life to which they belonged stressed the daily witness of the consecrated life: whether in Cambridge or Onitsha, people would be influenced not simply by preaching but by what they saw in a manner of life. If the 'Black European' clergy hid away in European type houses it was a further proof of their 'unspiritual' life style:

> The clergy have, we hear, no idea of people coming to them for help and dread having their people close at hand *to see them live*.[21]

In fact, when the missionaries, in the heyday of Christianity, commerce and civilisation introduced western style houses and developed Christian compounds in inland Africa, it was equally with the intention of demonstrating the advantages of the gospel: window frames and family worship both had a part to play in this.[22]

If the Sierra Leoneans wore European dress, the principles which the new missionaries had imbibed made them to wish to appear as

---

[19] Wilmot Graham Brooke, often singled out as the representative of these men, indicates their assumptions about the peoples of the upper Niger: 'our equals in intelligence, our superiors in courtesy, our inferiors in education'. CMS Archives G 3A3/04, 23.12.1890. Brooke, Haileybury and 'reading for Woolwich', had worked first as a freelance missionary before being accepted in 1889 as joint leader of the new Sudan mission. He was unordained, and like a number of the wealthy young men who entered missionary service, took no salary from the society. See A. Porter, 'Evangelical enthusiasm, missionary motivation and West Africa in the late 19th century: the career of G. W. Brooke, *JICH* 6 (1977).

[20] Dobinson p 39.

[21] Dobinson p 40 (italics mine).

[22] Compare Ajayi chapter 5.

Africans. Under the influence of Hudson Taylor and the China inland mission, the 'all things to all men' maxim was applied to dress.[23]

The young men on entering Hausa country adopted the tobe, and accepted the designation of *mallam*, or muslim teacher. They noted that the Hausa dress, food and houses could be adopted without serious danger to European health.

> The conditions of life thus enable the servant of Christ to live among them on equal terms, by dress and manner making himself one of them spending the day with them, learning their inner lives, their interests, their needs; showing them hourly in his own person the influence of an indwelling Christ to live among them and in such homes as their own.[24]

There was some irony in all this when one considers that the tobe was the symbol of burgeoning Islam in what was after all still a recently Islamicised area; and there were serious inconveniences in the position of Christian *mallam*. They were expected to give *saraka*, make presents, as befitted people of such status. The African missionaries, however European in appearance, had understood the custom: the newcomers, with their insistence on 'spiritual weapons' and their ethic of self denial, were written off as tight fisted.[25]

While the African clergy explicitly recommended and personified the way of the west,

> We carefully avoid praising civilization or civilised powers to the heathen, and if they themselves are extolling civilisation we tell them that they should not set their affection on things below.[26]

While the African clergy proudly accepted their designation as British subjects: the newcomers forswore British protection: they must be in the same peril as those they wished to induce to apostasize from Islam; and

> neither for them nor the converts should force or threat involving the possible use of force be employed.[27]

[23] Thus the 'Cambridge Seven', a few years earlier: 'I have been laughing all day at our grotesque appearance. Stanley, Monty and A. P.-T. have been converted into Chinamen; we put on the clothes this morning, were duly shaved and pigtailed . . . Monty, Stanley and I make huge Chinamen; it makes us very conspicuous'. C. T. Studd, quoted in N. P. Grubb, *C. T. Studd* (London 1933) p 55.

[24] *CMS Sudan Mission Leaflet* no 1 (January 1890).

[25] Compare A. C. Owoh, *CMS Missions, Muslim Societies and European Trade in Northern Nigeria, 1857–1900*, unpub MTh thesis, Aberdeen 1971, pp 297 *seq*. Owoh also describes the difficulties when the white mallams like their muslim counterparts, responded to requests for written passages of scripture. (Quranic texts were much used as charms). The problem arose from the fact that the missionaries made no charge for their passages of scripture, and thus distorted the market.

[26] *CMS Sudan Mission Leaflet* no 18 (February 1891).

A. F. WALLS

The alliance of Christianity and commerce was over: the Royal Niger company, under the leadership of the acknowledged atheist, Sir George Goldie, feared the Sudan party's potential to stir up militant Islam.[28] Crowther's longstanding policy of careful diplomacy with local rulers similarly took a new turn:

> It is our experience in this field that influence is not worth having; for it parts like a rope of sand the moment a faithful attitude is resumed.[29]

So sharp a change in motive and in method could mark a single field of a missionary society which had never wavered from its anglican or its evangelical allegiance.

University of Aberdeen.

---

[27] *CMS Sudan Mission Leaflet* no 1 (January 1890).

[28] On Goldie, see J. E. Flint, *Sir George Goldie and the Making of Nigeria* (London 1960). His alarm is indicated in letters of 22.7.1889 and 9.8.1889 appended to CMS general committee minutes of 29.10.1889. Brooke meanwhile, was equally alarmed lest the CMS committee make an agreement with the Royal Niger Company and compromise him, *ibid*, letter of 16.9.1889. The general committee resolved to forswear force or the threat of it (minutes 9.2.1889).

[29] *CMS Sudan Mission Leaflet* no 18 (February 1891). Compare Owoh p 284 *seq*.

LATE NINETEENTH-CENTURY ANGLICAN MISSIONARY EXPANSION: A CONSIDERATION OF SOME NON-ANGLICAN SOURCES OF INSPIRATION

by ANDREW PORTER

ORE than a decade ago, Max Warren suggested that the nature of protestant missionary expansion in the last quarter of the nineteenth century presented 'some of the most perplexing features in the history of the modern missionary movement'; but the extensive 'painstaking research' which he called for into the metropolitan roots of that movement has hardly yet been forthcoming.[1] Historians have more usually preferred to direct their attention to the impact of western missions outside Europe, and to consider their contribution to the modernisation of the non-European world. This growing body of published research unquestionably aids the would-be historian of metropolitan motives, but—for reasons requiring too much space for elucidation here—also makes his own work the more necessary if the expansive forces within western society are to be clearly understood and placed in perspective.[2]

It is worth remarking first of all upon the idea that the expansion of its foreign missionary activity reflects an increase in the vigour, unity, wealth and strength of conviction of a religion or church. This has long been almost a commonplace, and anglicanism in the period 1860–1914 felt to be no exception.[3] It would be foolish to say that there is no truth in this assertion, but it is the purpose of this paper to suggest

---

[1] M. A. C. Warren, *Social History and Christian Mission* (London 1967) p 143 and cap 7. This book and his other equally suggestive work, *The Missionary Movement from Britain in Modern History* (London 1965), are based on lectures delivered in Cambridge during 1964 and 1965.

[2] Some historians of Africa have recently begun to press for a much wider examination of missionaries' theological backgrounds; see J. D. Hargreaves, 'Imperialist Religion', unpubl seminar paper (university of Ibadan 1971), and T. O. Beidelman, 'Social Theory and the Study of Christian Missions in Africa' *Africa* 44 (London 1974) pp 235–49. I am very grateful to professor Hargreaves for showing me a copy of his paper.

[3] S. C. Neill *A History of Christian Missions, The Pelican History of the Church* 6 (Harmondsworth 1964) cap 10 and p 323; also [E.] Stock, [*The History of the Church Missionary Society. Its Environment, Its Men and Its Work*], 3 vols (London 1899) 2 p 337 and passim.

that such an 'optimistic' view of missionary expansion frequently rests on a superficial understanding of both its roots in the metropolitan society, and its relation to opposing forces in the field. An examination of these wider dimensions of anglican missionary activity in the late nineteenth century illustrates the extent to which missionary expansion may equally be related to uncertainty of conviction, and mark the defensive reaction of a church conscious of its own weaknesses and relatively declining fortunes in the face of more vigorous rivals, both secular and religious. I would like to argue that this self-consciousness is closely related to the fact that for the Victorian church some extremely powerful, even perhaps the most important, sources of inspiration to sustained missionary activity came not from within but from outside the church itself.

This suggestion inevitably leads us on to consider the relation between anglicans with their motives for expanding missionary endeavours, and the wider secular urge to empire-building in this period. Discussion of this theme has followed several lines. Some have argued that missionaries' sense of moral and cultural superiority inevitably involved the wish to dominate, that missionary work is inherently imperialistic, and that the two imperialisms therefore naturally combined. Others believe that this parallel advocacy of expansion shows the anglican church for what it is, an arm of the state, and would suggest that religious belief in general with its inspiration to missionary activity simply expresses the imperatives of socio-economic structures. A third possibility is that in its attitude to the expansion of western influence, as in other spheres, the anglican church's record has always been one of mere conformity to the secular ideology of the time—a congruence arising from its lack of any real source of authority, from the facts of establishment, and an education common to lay and ecclesiastical leaders alike.[4] Here my hypothesis would be that not only were important sources of anglican missionary inspiration external to the church, but that where such impulses derived from secular society they were based on an awareness of the *division* of sympathy between the church and society at large, and on a desire to reassert anglican conceptions of the right order. Many anglicans initially looked to foreign missionary expansion not as the expression of mutual sympathy which already existed, but as a way of reconciling secular and religious differences in joint action.

[4] Compare E. Norman, *Church and Society in England 1770–1970. A Historical Study* (Oxford 1976).

Late nineteenth-century anglican missionary expansion

When they looked at their own society, anglicans shared in the widespread uneasiness created by the spread of secular disciplines and materialistic values, whether embodied in changing habits of church-going, positivist propaganda, in the frequent necessity for 'non-denominational' compromises, or the rise of anthropology and the appearance of a mechanistic psychology. Many churchmen felt that theirs was a society which still often heard but rarely listened to or accepted the Christian message, and this frequently strengthened their wish to leave for the mission field. Some, for example, through the universities' mission to central Africa, but also in the church missionary society and the 'faith' missions, sought relief for their disquiet in attempts to reach those elsewhere whose religious sensitivity was thought still to be very real; others simply hoped to find for themselves a less materialistic environment.[5] These reservations about British society were often associated with revived fears for the impact of one's own civilisation on the wider non-European world. Unless that impact could be softened or moderated by an infusion of explicitly Christian values, unless missionary influence kept pace with, and preferably even preceded, other forms of contact, then British expansion might prove corrupting for all concerned (as it was felt to have been in the days when Britain had dominated the European slave trade). Occasional intimations that such might be the case had not been lacking in certain settler colonies, but it was only after 1875, for example, that the developmental philosophy of Henry Venn was replaced in CMS minds in part by spreading concern with the dangers of European commercial expansion. Missionary motivation thus became closely bound up with the desire to prevent contact between western and non-European societies from bringing out the worst in each other. This was of particular relevance in the years immediately before the first world war, as growing experience of European expansion and rule stimulated nationalist resistance; it became increasingly necessary, through changes in methods and the extension of missionary work, to maintain the allegiance of nationalist movements to Christianity in order to prevent them driving back the church.[6]

[5] For the fullest recent study of the UMCA, D. R. J. Neave, 'Aspects of the Universities Mission to Central Africa 1858–1900', unpubl MPhil thesis (university of York 1975) and esp cap 6.
[6] For earlier examples see, for example, W. M. Macmillan, *Bantu, Boer, and Briton. The Making of the South African Native Problem* (2 ed Oxford 1963). The trade in opium, liquor, and firearms was of great concern to missionaries even by 1870, and see speeches at the open conference on commerce and Christian missions in [*Report of*

Criticism of the societies and cultures of others could also act as a spur. Some missionaries and their supporters, whose reservations about their own countrymen were inhibited by nationalistic sentiments, invoked stereotypes of continental rivals whose imperialistic ambitions they felt required forestalling by the establishment of a prior English missionary presence.[7] Towards the end of the century, as the disintegrating effects of western culture on the non-European world became more widely recognised, still others actually encouraged this destruction in order partly that new fields might be opened for effective missionary work, the only answer to the social and moral degradation with which they felt themselves confronted.[8] Resentment ran high in the 1890s at the sight of resistance to evangelism and the physical exclusion of missionaries or their converts by peoples looked upon as culturally and often racially inferior.

Adding to the intensity of such resentment was the view, quite widely shared and warmly welcomed in a period of religious and doctrinal uncertainty, that missionary expansion might provide a means of placing the rational arguments in defence of the faith on a surer footing. At a certain level, increasing numbers of converts and missionaries were pointed to as proof of the truth, efficacy, and vigour of anglicanism. More intellectually sophisticated, but, it would seem, largely overlooked by historians, was the encouragement of missionary enterprise which might reinforce the scholarly bases of Christianity. It has been suggested that although 'the British missionary movement produced scholarship . . . it was never integrated into theological scholarship'.[9] But if very few missionaries either contributed signifi-

---

the Centenary Conference on the Protestant Missions of the World, ed [as] Johnston, 2 vols (London 1888) 1 pp 111–37. Alongside these themes, the nationalist question emerged, and all permeate many papers delivered at the pan-anglican congress in 1908; see esp A. G. Fraser, 'The Problem before Educational Missions in Ceylon', and L. Byrde, 'The Evangelical Method. China', Pan-Anglican Papers [Being Problems for consideration at the Pan-Anglican Congress, 1908] (London 1907–8). The bibliography is immense.

[7] See, for example, Stock 3 pp 420–1. Directed in turn at French, German and Portuguese, such sentiments were naturally bound up closely with issues of religious rivalry and, through missionary desires for protection in their work, with the hopes for national unity touched on below.

[8] See the examples cited in H. A. C. Cairns, Prelude to Imperialism. British Reactions to Central African Society 1840–1890 (London 1965) pp 235–6 and passim; A. Holmberg, African Tribes and European Agencies. Colonialism and Humanitarianism in British South and East Africa 1870–1895 (Göteborg 1966) pt 2, 'The Conquest and Division of Zambezia'; also the debate on British policies in Nigeria during the 1890s, [E. A.] Ayandele, [The Missionary Impact on Modern Nigeria 1842–1914] (London 1966) caps 2–3.

[9] Andrew Walls, 'The nineteenth-century missionary as scholar', Misjonskall og forsker-

cantly to such studies, or themselves shewed that missionary experience might enrich theological understanding, it seems that there were others—at least within the anglican fold—anxious to take advantage of missionaries' findings, and supporting the expansion of their endeavours to that end. Philologists, students of comparative religion, scholars devoted to old testament or patristic studies, looked especially in the last quarter of the century to the islamic world for useful data. Many in their search for the most reliable manuscripts, their attention to linguistic and textual criticism, and in their concern with the history of the early church, sought to reconcile the highest standards of scientific scholarship with defence of their own faith. Such were many supporters of the Hausa association, founded in 1891 in memory of John Alfred Robinson, late scholar of Christ's College Cambridge and CMS missionary, with the purpose of furthering both his work amongst the Hausa people and his study of their language. As one of the most extensively-used languages of west Africa, Hausa had obvious potential as a vehicle for the gospel; it was hoped that its study would give scholars access to religious traditions and even written sources, of importance not least for their understanding of the old testament and the course of early church history. On the association's general committee, alongside archbishop Benson, there sat the Norrisian and Lady Margaret professors from Cambridge, Robertson Smith, Max Muller, and John Wordsworth then bishop of Salisbury, whose writings had included the Bampton lectures of 1881.[10]

From reactions to social and economic change or to rationalism, one may turn to the incentive to greater effort provided by religious rivalry. Logically, there is a case for considering this theme from two standpoints, the responses first to awareness of the headway being made by other Christian denominations, and, secondly, to the expansive powers of other faiths. Yet it is perhaps still more important to stress the extent to which these worries became intertwined and fed upon each other especially after 1885. The CMS, for example, had

---

glede. Festskrift til Professor Olav Guttorm Myklebust, ed N. E. Bloch-Hell (Oslo 1975) p 220.

[10] For the general committee of the association in 1892 and 1896, see London, University College Library, Francis Galton MSS, file 77, and C. H. Robinson, *Hausaland or Fifteen Hundred Miles through the Central Sudan* (London 1896) app 2. For the association see my 'The Hausa Association: Sir George Goldie, the Bishop of Dover, and the Niger in the 1890s', *JICH* (forthcoming); the only existing study is very brief, A. H. M. Kirk-Greene, 'Cambridge and the Hausa Language', *West Africa* 2056 (London 1956) p 675.

always been acutely conscious that the annual statistical indices of its progress provided amongst other things a basis for comparison with other protestant bodies, but these rivalries were somewhat over-shadowed from about 1880 by confrontation with Roman catholics. Expansion of missionary efforts of course brought all missions into closer physical contact with each other, but, whether it was in Buganda or on the Niger, resentment steadily grew at Roman catholic prosely-tising, their refusal to respect or enter 'comity' agreements, and at what were in protestant eyes their insufficient conditions for church membership.[11] In such circumstances, changes of method adopted by a mission might carry every appearance of intensified aggression aimed at its rivals. This was the view taken of the Holy Ghost fathers' abandonment in eastern Nigeria of the 'Christian village' strategy in favour of evangelisation through the schools.[12]

Such a Roman catholic strategy which appeared to exacerbate divisions within Christendom was all the more damnable when Christians everywhere seemed to be faced with the increasingly rapid expansion of islam. Its importance was such that one may fairly portray the reaction to islam as dominating the pattern of anglican missionary activity between 1870 and 1914. From west Africa, CMS sources for the 1840s and 1850s reveal the first real awareness of this problem, and show it as one which came rapidly to be seen as a challenge; by 1860, anglican attitudes had hardened accordingly.[13] Between 1873 and 1880, at the church congresses and in a series of missionary conferences, sustained attention was given to the question and a missionary strategy gradually evolved. Of especial importance was the CMS conference on missions to Mohammedans held in 1875,

[11] See for example *Letters of Henry Hughes Dobinson Late Archdeacon of the Niger* (London 1899) pp 73–4, 120–1; also [*The*] *M[ission] F[ield]* (London July 1894) p 271, for comment on discussion of the issue at the 1894 anglican missionary conference. For recent studies throwing light on such tensions between protestants and Roman catholics before 1914, G. O. M. Tasie, 'Christianity in the Niger Delta 1864–1918', unpubl PhD thesis (university of Aberdeen 1969), C. M. Cooke, 'The Roman Catholic Mission in Calabar 1903–1960', unpubl PhD thesis (university of London 1977).
[12] [P. B.] Clarke, ['The Methods and Ideology of the Holy Ghost Fathers in Eastern Nigeria 1885–1905'], *JRA* 6 (1974) pp 81–108.
[13] See G. O. Gbadomosi, 'The Growth of Islam among the Yoruba 1841–1908', unpubl phD thesis (university of Ibadan 1968) esp cap 4, 'The Zenith of Islamic Expansion 1895–1908'; P. D. Curtin, *The Image of Africa. British Ideas and Action, 1780–1850* (London 1965) pp 256, 405–6; J. D. Holway, 'C.M.S. contact with Islam in East Africa before 1914', *JRA* 4 (1971–2) pp 200–12. I am grateful to Mr Martin Lynn of the university of Ilorin for information on these and related points.

which not only led to an intensification of work in long-established areas, but endorsed plans for advances in Palestine and the west African Soudan.[14] The British invasion of Egypt in 1882 enabled the CMS to resume work there, and up until 1914 anglican pressure on the islamic heartlands steadily mounted.[15] Opinions were for a long time divided as to whether islam's revival was evidence of vitality or 'a sign that Islam feels itself put on the defensive, and is trembling for its existence'. But two fundamental propositions secured widespread assent, that in Africa the crucial problem for all missions lay in stemming the tide of islam, and that in a victory there lay the key to the world-wide confrontation between Christians and the followers of the prophet.[16]

However, the conviction that the defeat of islam in Africa was either necessary or even likely aroused considerable criticism. Indeed, the anglican missionary attack, while occasionally inspired to greater efforts by a death such as Hannington's, received more sustained impetus from the periodic denunciations of missionary work by defenders of islam. Here, three principal lines of argument were developed. From the mid-1860s, under the influence of Richard Burton and Winwood Reade, the idea gained currency that Christianity was a religion unsuited to the negro races, who were better able to comprehend and benefit from the truths of Mohammedanism.[17] A decade later, Bosworth Smith's lectures on *Mohammed and Mohamme-*

---

[14] For a record of the principal landmarks, Stock 3 pp 117–18 and *passim*; west African plans were set out and early work described in the C[*hurch*] M[*issionary*] I[*ntelligencer*] (London March, April, December 1876). For a different and potentially conflicting strategy developed by British government officials in India, R. J. Gavin, 'The Bartle Frere Mission to Zanzibar, 1873', *HJ* 5 (1962) pp 122–48.

[15] Stock 3 cap 94; [W. H. T.] Gairdner, [*D. M. Thornton. A Study in Missionary Ideals and Methods*] (London 1908); [C. E.] Padwick, [*Temple Gairdner of Cairo*] (2 ed London 1930). Much attention was devoted to the need for combating islam at both the Lambeth conferences and the pan-anglican conference congress of 1908.

[16] W. Gray, 'Missions to Mohammedans', *CMI* (Jan 1888). The debate may be followed in such works as *Methods of Mission Work Among Moslems. Being those Papers read at the first Missionary Conference on behalf of the Mohammedan World held at Cairo* (London 1906); [*Report of the World Missionary*] *Conference 1910*, 9 vols (London 1910) I pp 20–1, 243 and *passim*; *Islam and Missions. Being Papers read at the Second Missionary Conference on behalf of the Mohammedan World held at Lucknow*, ed E. M. Wherry, S. M. Zwemer, C. G. Mylrea (London 1911); W. H. T. Gairdner, *The Reproach of Islam*, (London 1910).

[17] R. F. Burton, *A Mission to Gelele, King of Dahome*, 2 vols (London 1864) 2 p 192; W. Winwood Reade, *Savage Africa* (London 1863) esp pp 578–87, and *The African Sketch Book*, 2 vols (London 1873) I pp 314–15. These themes continually recur in Burton's and Reade's work; for a brief description and introduction, C. Bolt, *Victorian Attitudes to Race* (London 1971) cap 4.

danism was only the most illustrious of several works which awoke the ire of evangelicals and high church men,[18] and a still greater outburst of anger followed in the late 1880s on the heels of Joseph Thomson's articles and canon Isaac Taylor's address at the Wolverhampton church congress of 1887.[19] These commentators suggested not only that the positive values of islam were almost everywhere grossly under-rated, but that conversion of the African to that faith might provide for him an acceptable preparation, or even substitute, for Christianity. At a time when islam appeared to be experiencing a powerful resurgence, notably in the shape of the mahdi's activities in the Sudan, missionaries felt that they could have done without this additional onslaught on their position, and hastened to put out their own counter-statements.[20]

What anglicans, particularly evangelicals, failed to realise was that their own disquiet at such advocacy and their fears of islam's advance were fully shared by the Roman catholic missions. It was this fear which had largely prompted in many parts of east and west Africa that change of missionary tactics on the part of the catholics which anglicans, in common with other denominations, interpreted not as a Christian offensive against a common enemy but merely as renewed aggression directed at themselves.[21] Instead of taking heart in a joint

---

[18] Reginald Bosworth Smith, *Mohammed and Mohammedanism* (London 1874), subsequently revised and enlarged (2 ed 1876, 3 ed 1889). In fact a firm supporter of the anglican church and its missionary work, his writings culminated in *The British Empire and its Missionary Responsibility. A Speech . . . at the Annual Meeting of the S.P.G.* (London 1903) and *Mohammedanism and Christianity. A Paper read at the Weymouth Church Congress, 1905* (Derby/London 1905). Changes in reactions to his work, and the growth of his acceptability to anglican missionaries over thirty years, are of interest not least as a pointer to the shift in attitudes explored below.

[19] Isaac Taylor, 'Mohammedanism', *The Official Report of the Church Congress 1887* (London 1887) pp 325–31; R. B. Smith, 'Mohammedanism in Africa', *The Nineteenth Century* (London December 1887); for Thomson's writings and attitudes, R. I. Rotberg, *Joseph Thomson and the Exploration of Africa* (London 1971) is indispensable. For reactions, *CMI* throughout 1887–89; the tone of the SPG was less strident, but arguments in its periodicals were equally dismissive, see *MF* (London January 1888) p 19, (February 1888) pp 71–2, (May 1888) pp 161–9, (December 1888) p 460, (June 1889) pp 238–9.

[20] For example, when reviewed, *CMI* (May 1881), C. E. Sell's *The Faith of Islam* (London 1880) was seen as a very necessary corrective to Smith's work, and was republished in new editions in 1896 and 1907; later, the lengthy article by G. Knox, 'A Rejoinder to Canon Taylor on missions to Mohammedans', *CMI* (Dec 1887), was specially reprinted in pamphlet form by the society; Stock 3 pp 345–8.

[21] See Clarke *JRA*, and [J. A. P.] Kieran, ['The Holy Ghost Fathers in East Africa 1863–1914'], unpubl PhD thesis (university of London 1966). The development of the Holy Ghost fathers' attitudes to islam and then secular authority, while compressed into a shorter period, essentially mirrors that of the anglicans outlined here, compare Kieran pp 358–63.

endeavour, anglican missionaries and their supporters felt the more beleaguered, and tended instead to see in the forces which opposed them a larger and in some respects more sinister pattern. The spread of rationalism, the increase in numbers of Mohammedan adherents, and Roman catholic aggression were ranked alongside other remarkable events of the late nineteenth century, such as the decline of the Turkish empire, and recognised collectively as the 'signs of the times'.[22] Such signs, widely felt to herald Christ's second coming, were at once grounds for both fear and hope, preliminaries to the final battle for the faith and heralds of the millennium. As such their tendency was strongly to encourage the aggressive defence of Christianity. The expansion of missionary endeavour in obedience to Christ's last command received a new prominence and urgency, as both a necessary response to the signs of the times and as a means whereby the second coming itself would be hastened.

It is neither easy to explain this revival of millennial preoccupations nor perhaps possible, until further work has been done, to argue convincingly that renewed study of the books of Daniel or Revelation generally either prompted or followed from widespread disquiet with the world's state. The historian's task is the harder in the case of anglicans, many of whom preferred to keep their own counsel on such controversial topics.[23] That such preoccupations were rife, and were progressively reinforced by reference to the non-European world, is, however, unquestionable. They seem to have gained ground in the mid-1870s, paralleling the developing missionary strategy referred to above, and were contemporaneous with major changes in Europe, with the developing conviction that the Turkish empire was on the verge of collapse, the development of the eastern question, and the renewed determination to suppress the Arab-dominated slave trade of east and central Africa. They appear to have been confirmed in part by growing acquaintance with islam's own religious chronology, for, if it pointed in the right direction, evidence derived even from comparative religious studies was acceptable to many who would otherwise have dismissed them.[24] Certainly, they were widely

---

[22] As illustrations of this tendency, 'On Missions to Mohammedans', *CMI* (January 1876); 'C.M.S. Work among Mohammedans', *ibid* (January 1882); 'Aden as a Mission Station', *ibid* (December 1882).

[23] Stock 3 pp 817–18, or *CMI* (January 1876) pp 6–7.

[24] See 'Imam Mahdy, and Dajjal, the Muhammadan Antichrist' *CMI* (October 1883) pp 596–601, or passage from CMS *Niger and Yoruba Notes* (London January 1900) in Ayandele p 128. It would be interesting to know how much these ideas contributed

popularised among anglicans, by speakers on the annual circuit of evangelical gatherings, by the Mildmay second advent conferences, and by the persuasive advocacy of influential teachers such as H. C. G. Moule in Cambridge.[25] The early nineteenth-century notion that conversion of the world was the prerequisite for Christ's return steadily gave way to that which saw the only necessity as—in the words of the student volunteer movement—'the evangelization of the world in this generation'. Invocation of an imminent apocalypse was thus for many anglicans one way in which they felt able to explain the rapidly changing world in which they lived; while of hermeneutic value, the concept was also found to provide additional inspiration for foreign missionary activity.

Prompted or at least largely encouraged by religious opposition, millenarian beliefs of this kind flourished alongside and became intertwined with other external stimuli to missionary activity, one of the strongest being that combination of perfectionist ideas and revivalism derived from American sources and associated above all with the annual Keswick convention.[26] The revivalist practices of Charles Finney, Moody, and Sankey, together with the 'higher life' precepts of W. E. Boardman and the Pearsall Smiths, found amongst anglican evangelicals an extremely receptive audience. There were many whom Keswick's message led straight to the mission field. From the early 1880s onwards, the argument was ever more frequently advanced that amongst the clearest indications of the true willingness to conform with God's Will, and the surest routes to present sanctification, was the offer of oneself for foreign missionary service. Linked with the debate on the place of asceticism in missions, the task of evangelist to the non-Christian world was felt to call for complete surrender and unselfishness, and to constitute the highest form of service both to man and God. It involved hardships which could most easily be overcome by those who had experienced that complete peace of mind, the indwelling of the Holy Spirit and that truly Christian

---

to the conflicts of opinion treated by R. T. Shannon, *Gladstone and the Bulgarian Agitation, 1876* (London 1963).

[25] *Mildmay Second Advent Conference Report* (London 1876, 1878, 1886); W. T. Waddington and J. T. Inskip, *Charles Vickery Hawkins. Memorials of His Life* (London 1896) pp 52, 72, *passim*; on Moule, [A. N.] Porter, ['Cambridge, Keswick and late nineteenth-century attitudes to Africa'], *JICH* 5 (1976) pp 5–34; leading article by H. Rickard, 'The Historical Preparation for the Second Advent', *MF* (October 1894) pp 361–4.

[26] This is explored in Porter; see also the fuller treatment of themes touched on here in my 'Evangelical enthusiasm, missionary motivation, and West Africa in the late nineteenth century: the career of G. W. Brooke', *JICH* 6 (1977) pp 23–46.

fulfilment which Keswick aimed to promote.[27] If the offer for missionary service was held to be evidence of that strength of character upon which Keswick came to lay so much stress, there were also those who, after having imbibed the spirit of Keswick, then felt themselves strong enough to devote their lives to the heathen. All alike sought by more aggressive means to recreate abroad the intense fellowship characteristic of Keswick circles.

Those most receptive to the Keswick message and its association with missionary enterprise were largely of student age. Alongside more traditional types of recruit new graduates, the freshly ordained, and their female contemporaries, all flocked to join the missions—especially from the universities and above all from Cambridge. Between 1884 and 1894, bodies such as the UMCA or CMS experienced an unprecedented period of growth. Just as this increase in numbers originally owed a great deal to north American inspiration, so fresh influences from across the Atlantic helped sustain it into the twentieth century. Reinforced in its turn by Scottish revival and the work of professor Henry Drummond, R. P. Wilder's influence and his visit to Cambridge in January 1892 set in motion the development of the student volunteer movement in this country, thus bringing together Christians of all denominations in the task of world-wide evangelisation.[28]

If, for evangelicals in particular, Keswick and American revivalism reinforced the pressures to missionary involvement created by the general sense of embattlement, for other higher churchmen it was their acquaintance with the history of the church which in part performed a similar function. The interplay between the historical scholarship of such men as Lightfoot and Westcott has often been commented upon.[29] The place of missions in their schemes has by comparison received little attention. Visiting Tunis in search of St Cyprian, archbishop Benson was grieved at the thought that 'all these are children of Christians—that the Christian Church *lost* them—that

---

[27] For Keswick teaching, *The Keswick Convention. Its Message, Its Method and Its Men*, ed C. F. Harford (London 1907); Porter, *passim*.

[28] T. Tatlow, *The Story of the Student Christian Movement of Great Britain and Ireland* (London 1933) esp cap 1 pp 17–21.

[29] For example D. L. Edwards, *Leaders of the Church of England 1828–1944* (London 1971) caps 6–7; H. Chadwick, *The Vindication of Christianity in Westcott's Thought*, (Cambridge 1961) p 10 and *passim*; L. E. Elliott-Binns, *English Thought 1860–1900: the theological aspect* (London 1956) caps 4–5; for an interesting contemporary demonstration, J. Wordsworth, *The Bearings of the Study of Church History on some Problems of Home Reunion, The Murtle Lecture 1902* (London 1902).

it lost them through the dissent which is daily gaining ground among us.'[30] Impressed by first-hand experience of islam's vigour, Benson was strongly confirmed in his enthusiasm (widely shared amongst anglicans, even while they differed over practicalities) for the revival of the decayed churches of the east—churches which, it was often also suggested, had themselves declined for want of missionary zeal.[31] So in yet another way were missions to be propagated and bulwarks in defence of Christianity to be strengthened, particularly against the islamic world.

Benson's observation and the question of the eastern churches together highlight another anglican preoccupation. Awareness of external threats encouraged on all sides a heightened consciousness of the anglican community's lack of ability to meet them. Abroad, periodic occurrences such as the conflict between bishop Blyth and the CMS in Palestine threatened vigorous missionary work, and were clearly rooted in anglicanism's own divisions. The advice of Benson's committee of inquiry in the Blyth controversy is only one sign that many men, sensing the gravity of the external situation, were beginning to ask whether the internal disputes of anglicans were not after all of comparatively little importance.[32] By banding together in defence of the very principle of missions men came to see in the expansion of missionary activity a route to renewed ecclesiastical unity. Benson, ex-officio president of the SPG, felt very strongly that full support for the CMS was essential if he was to keep 'the Puritan party faithful to the Church of England'.[33] His organisational reforms, designed to link the anglican hierarchy and the missionary societies more closely, and particularly his 'intelligent sympathy' with CMS problems, were widely appreciated. Evangelicals, although feeling that it was not they who were in danger of being isolated, also tried to bridge the gap between the parties with proposals for common missionary enterprise.[34]

---

[30] [A. C.] Benson, [*The Life of Edward White Benson*] (abr ed London 1901) p 441.

[31] For example S. A. Donaldson, 'The Obligation of the Church to Foreign Missionary Work generally among Non-Christian Peoples', *Pan-Anglican Papers*; also Florence Robinson, *Charles H. Robinson. A Record of Travel and Work* (London 1928).

[32] Compare F. J. A. Hort to Benson 26 December 1882, A. F. Hort, *Life and Letters of Fenton John Anthony Hort*, 2 vols (London 1896) 2 p 90; for the Blyth controversy and the advice, Stock 3 pp 523–7.

[33] Benson p 432; also A. J. Mason, 'Edward White Benson', *DNB*; for an interested view of Benson's contacts with the CMS, Stock 3 *passim*; compare *Life and Letters of Mandell Creighton By His Wife*, 2 vols (London 1905) 2 pp 446–7.

[34] See for example Gairdner (3 ed London 1909) pp 30–44, 52–3, *seq.*

Late nineteenth-century anglican missionary expansion

This impetus to anglican missionary work, whether as a means of drawing closer to other churches or to bind factions more tightly within a single communion, was further reinforced by the ecumenical vision of a reunified Christendom.[35] The progress of this vision can be traced partly in the reports and even the titles of the great missionary conferences of this period. Between the centenary conference on the protestant missions of the world, convened at Exeter Hall in 1888, and the world missionary conference held at Edinburgh in 1910, ecumenical sentiments were visibly extended. This is witnessed, for example, by the presence in Edinburgh of the archbishop of Canterbury, of high anglicans, and by the greater moderation of statements made there about Roman catholicism.[36] However, this progress towards mutual tolerance and co-operation was, for all anglicans in some degree, born less of optimism and generous tolerance than of disquiet out of dashed hopes.

Expressive of the apprehension and the element of disappointment associated for anglicans with these movements towards unity, is the following passage by the CMS missionary who acted as official chronicler of the Edinburgh conference. Emphasising that the present marked an historical turning-point in which men faced a crisis equivalent to that which had preceded Christ's first coming, he continued:

> Once more has the World, nay, Nature, the Universe itself smashed ruthlessly into the conventionalised theology of Christendom: it needs no seer standing on the sand of the shore of any Patmos to see The Beast rising from the world-tide and presenting once more the immemorial alternative 'Naturism, or, Deeper into God'. The spectacle of the East, with half a worldful of men suddenly drawn into the full current of world-thought is one scene in the vision of the modern Apocalypse. The spectre of the West rapidly surrendering to a radically atheist philosophy of Nature is the other.[37]

By any standards a dramatic description, it reflected for anglicans, as

[35] For the early nineteenth century, see the very suggestive article by S. Piggin, 'Sectarianism versus Ecumenism. The Impact on British Churches of the Missionary Movement to India c. 1800–1860', *JEH* 27 (1976) pp 387–402.

[36] Johnston; the SPG, SPCK, and UMCA refused invitations to this conference. *Conference 1910*. For a general survey of ecumenical developments which mentions missionary work in a much wider context, *A History of the Ecumenical Movement 1517–1948*, ed R. Rouse and S. C. Neill (London 1954).

[37] W. H. T. Gairdner, *'Edinburgh 1910'. An Account and Interpretation of the World Missionary Conference* (London 1910) p 152.

for others albeit in different ways, the alteration for the worse which many saw as having taken place in their position since the mid-1880s. Then, as the partition of Africa began, even if as mentioned above reservations existed as to the impact of private European enterprise on 'primitive society', missionaries at least felt able to look forward to productive co-operation with their secular contemporaries in the process of official, formal colonisation. In the introduction to the centenary conference report, ecumenism was qualified by confinement to 'the Saxon race', and the prospect held out that in the common task of conquest and administration of colonies men of all shades of religious opinion or even none might reconcile their growing differences.[38] That secular responsibility and deep religious conviction might equally join hands, and promote missions overseas, seemed at the time to be borne out in the career of general Gordon, who was elevated as model or hero well before his death at Khartoum.[39] In the late 1880s and early '90s the future still looked promising. Co-operation seemed to be envisaged by administrators like H. H. Johnston, and effected by Lugard, Portal and Rosebery in Uganda. The Hausa association promoted a lectureship at Cambridge in part to provide interpreters for a colonial administration. Here perhaps lie important roots of that comparative lukewarmness in practice if not in principle towards 'comity' within the mission field, which historians of the ecumenical movement have noted as characteristic of the anglican response in the years up to the end of the south African war in 1902.[40] Some historians have suggested that missionaries gave little thought to their relations with the colonial authorities before 1914, but in anglican minds at least clear expectations existed as to the high degree of religious influence and national unity of purpose that would arise from partnership between colonial officials and churchmen. This expectation in turn led the latter for some time to harbour hopes of dominating ecclesiastical rivals through influence with the secular powers.[41]

[38] Johnston introduction pp xv-xviii.
[39] Gairdner pp 114-15; Padwick pp 65-9; R. Sinker, *Memorials of the Hon. Ion Keith-Falconer* (new ed London 1903) pp 100-1; of particular importance and influence was *Colonel Gordon in Central Africa 1874-1879 from Original Letters and Documents*, ed G. B. Hill (London 1881) which inspired, amongst others, G. W. Brooke of the Niger mission; Stock 3 *passim*.
[40] [R.] Oliver, *Sir Harry Johnston and the Scramble for Africa* (London 1957) pp 128-9; Oliver, [*The*] *Missionary Factor* [*in East Africa*] (London 1952) cap 3; M. Perham, *Lugard. The Years of Adventure 1858-1898* (London 1956) pt 3; R. P. Beaver, *Ecumenical Beginnings in Protestant World Mission. A History of Comity* (New York 1962) pp 29-30, 39, 78, 274-81.

Late nineteenth-century anglican missionary expansion

However, if the mythical Gordon reflected the ideal, flesh-and-blood administrators increasingly fell short of it; for the missionary interest, the administrators' final symbolic act of rejection came with Cromer's stringent criticisms of Gordon, published in 1908.[42] Cromer's own administration in Egypt, his attitude to missionaries in the Sudan, and British rule in northern Nigeria especially under Girouard, were widely condemned for their deference to muslim susceptibilities, and destroyed anglican hopes of close co-operation. In geographical areas of crucial importance to the missionary strategist, and in the field of education which lay at the heart of missionary methods, British administrators seemed instead to be favouring the opponents of anglican missions, and so were formally censured in the report of the Edinburgh conference.[43] The experience of colonial rule, despite a continuing preference for that of a British rather than a French or German authority, had slowly raised doubts in many minds as to whether formal colonial rule would in fact make the missionaries' task any easier than it had been in the days of uncontrolled European penetration. The colonial situation by 1910 no longer held out the prospect of healing through concerted action the nation's ideological divisions.

Of course, precedents for such tensions were not hard to find, and had they been better students of *modern* history many anglicans might initially have been less optimistic, and so less prone to a certain sense of disappointment and isolation on the eve of the first world war.

[41] Compare Oliver *Missionary Factor* p 246. In cap 5 'Mission, Church and State 1914–49', Oliver, on a much grander scale, argues that for the missions as a whole, both protestant and Roman catholic, it was the 1914–18 war which led to significant changes in their thinking and the decline of missionary influence. In the anglican case, however, there would seem reason to believe that many missionary sympathisers were never as self-confident as Oliver seems to suggest, and that consciousness of their weakened position was evident well before 1914.

[42] For the persistence of Gordon as the standard against which all were measured, E. Stock, 'Missionaries in Egypt', *CMI* (September 1900); high church anglican attitudes to episcopacy may have prompted some disillusionment in their ranks rather earlier than in those of the evangelicals, to judge from the anti-erastian tone of, for example, the leading article in *MF* (October 1894) pp 361–4. Cromer's views on Gordon appear in his *Modern Egypt*, 2 vols (London 1908) esp 1 pp 427–31, 438–9, 559–74; this was reviewed in a leading article, 'Modern Egypt. Western Education and Eastern Morals', C[hurch] M[issionary] R[eview] (London July 1908) pp 385–93. For the archbishop's fruitless interview with Lord Cromer, G. K. A. Bell, *Randall Davidson Archbishop of Canterbury* (3 ed Oxford 1952) pp 567–8. From another quarter, Lord Salisbury's speech at the bi-centenary of the SPG on relations between missions and governments formally marked a turning point for the anglican community.

[43] For a summary of such attitudes, *Conference 1910, Report of Commission VII: Missions and Governments*, pp 51–60, 73–7, 113, 152, 157, 167.

Had they been so, however, it seems likely that more of the earlier religious sectarianism would have persisted and been exported; even the modest ecumenical advances achieved after 1908 would have been lost to many anglicans if they had not first seen their opportunities and attempted their own experiment in nationalist harmony. Only when this failed was the way opened for a greater degree of direct co-operation both amongst Anglicans and between them and other denominations, whether in the missionary field or in other forms of ecumenical activity.[44] Anglican churchmen's renewed sense of separation from secular officials and forces, and the weakening of Anglo-Saxon racial exclusiveness (itself fostered by these same internal conflicts), did much to pave the way for full anglican participation in the world missionary conference of 1910.[45] Anglican confrontation with islam was important throughout. At first this had stimulated missionary activity and raised the prospect of greater national harmony even at the price of some continued sectarian strife. Subsequently, it underlay the revived tension between church and state, and thereby encouraged steps towards greater anglican unity and ecumenical co-operation. This was signified by archbishop Davidson's presence at Edinburgh, which, while it symbolised anglicans' renewed commitment to the expansion of missionary efforts, was also indicative of the growing insistence by all parties on the centrality of foreign missions to the life of the anglican church.

Perhaps there is a certain artificiality in examining 'anglicans' in this way. There are obvious problems of nomenclature and periodisation, and it is not intended for one moment to deny either that influence and inspiration have moved in the opposite direction, or that other religious

[44] As illustrations of what churchmen felt had been achieved, archbishop Cosmo Gordon Lang, 'The Difference in the Attitude of the Church towards Missions in the last fifty years', and 'World Missionary Conference 1910. II Further Impressions', by a CMS delegate, *CMR* (August 1910). In moves towards anglican unity and a wider view of non-anglican work, the pan-anglican congress of 1908 was felt to have played a large part.

[45] This shift of attitudes may be sensed, for example, in debates on relations between missions and governments in both 1908 and 1910; see *Official Report of the Pan-Anglican Congress*, 7 vols (London 1908) 5 pp 85–102, and the *Report of Commission VII* in 1910. It is explicit in archbishop Davidson's speech at the SPG anniversary meeting, *MF* (June 1910) pp 171–6, and is evident in the writings and comments of lay administrators themselves, for missionaries were frequently their own worst enemies. These perspectives need to be added to the otherwise full discussion of the anglican decision to participate at Edinburgh, in W. R. Hogg, *Ecumenical Foundations. A History of the International Missionary Council and its Nineteenth-Century Background* (New York 1952) cap 3 esp pp 110–15.

groups were sometimes similarly affected. However, evidence from a variety of sources seems to show that reactions to the secular and religious forces of the non-anglican world were often appealed to as justification for, or seem directly to have prompted, the interest in and commitment to the mission field of ever increasing numbers of anglicans in this period. It may be the case that anglicanism, with an established church and a tendency towards comprehensiveness, was not well-adapted for inspiring or initiating its own missionary enterprise. Perhaps this is one reason why in the late nineteenth century, anglicanism, unlike many other denominations, seems often to have owed its extensive missionary activity far less to any positive internal dynamic of its own than to what were perceived as external threats, the fears engendered by them, and the inspirational offerings of non-anglicans. In conclusion, it is perhaps enough to reiterate the plea from Max Warren with which this paper began. The study of missionary motivation in this period still has much to offer—not simply for the history of the missionary movements of the west, but also in the light it throws on the interaction of British and non-western societies. Moreover, at a time when interests in missionary activity probably excited a larger number of anglicans than ever before or since, study of their motivation can also help to deepen our understanding of the Victorian church.

University of London
King's College

DR HENRY COOKE: THE ATHANASIUS
OF IRISH PRESBYTERIANISM

by R. F. G. HOLMES

D R Henry Cooke, the Athanasius of Irish presbyterianism, who might fairly be described as the archetypal Ulster unionist political parson, is an obvious subject for a study in religious motivation. Emerging in the 1820s as a vigorous champion of trinitarian orthodoxy, he led a relentless campaign against Arianism in the Belfast Institution, the college in which at that time the majority of Irish presbyterian ordinands were educated, and in his church, until the Arians had withdrawn from the synod of Ulster and, ultimately, the link had been broken between his church and the college. During the campaign he made clear his opposition, not only to theological liberalism, but also to the political radicalism which had characterised the outlook of many Ulster presbyterians in the eighteenth century.

After the synodal conflict he became increasingly identified with conservative interests in politics and with the promotion of political protestantism and anti-catholicism in response to the challenge of the catholic Irish nation which was emerging under the leadership of Daniel O'Connell. In this paper we shall consider a question which has been often asked but to which no completely satisfying answer has yet been given—what motivated Henry Cooke?

Cooke himself claimed that he was actuated by the purest religious motives. Justifying his campaign against Arianism and his policy of bringing about a separation in the synod he claimed: 'It is the blessed light of God which has opened my eyes to the danger and which directs me to withdraw from those men whose views are not my views and whose hopes of salvation do not rest on the same rock as mine.'[1] His political activities, he insisted, were dictated by religious considerations. 'I confess I am a party man', he said on one occasion, 'some there are who cry woe to a political parson, but only when he is not on their side. If I renounce my politics I must renounce my religion'.[2]

---

[1] [The] N[orthern] W[hig] 26 July 1827.
[2] B[elfast] N[ews] L[etter] 21 July 1840.

Cooke wrote no autobiography and his professed reason for not doing so may be revealing: 'No man can be trusted with a full and honest development of his own character, thoughts and acts. There are secret springs and motives within him which he dare not reveal—which, indeed, it would be folly to attempt to expose to the world's eye'.[3] It was left to his son-in-law, J. L. Porter, to provide an extended apologia for Cooke in his *Life and times of Henry Cooke*, published three years after Cooke died in 1868. Porter was an able man, a distinguished president of the Belfast Queen's College,[4] but the continuous strain of panegyric that runs through the book arouses the suspicion that he has not painted his father-in-law 'warts and all'.

Porter's answer to our question is simple: it repeats Cooke's own. In the preface to the first edition he states his theme, which resounds throughout the entire work: 'Dr Cooke's Life, therefore, is not the history of an individual man merely, it is rather the history of a great work undertaken on behalf of pure religion, of sound education, and of constitutional government—a work prompted by ardent patriotism, prosecuted with consummate ability, and crowned with distinguished success'.[5]

Porter's assumptions are simple and obvious—the superiority of protestantism, particularly 'sound Calvinism', over catholicism; the splendid liberty of the British constitution; the evil self-deluding character of Irish nationalism and the menace of anything that can be castigated as 'radicalism'.[6] He was an exponent of what might be called the Ulster protestant myth, which Cooke himself did so much to create, and which understood and depicted the Irish situation in terms of a conflict between light and darkness, God and the devil, with Britain and protestantism in the vanguard of the forces of light, and Irish nationalism, popery and radicalism in the hosts of darkness. Again and again one can detect the editorial hand in Porter's biography of Cooke, arranging his material so that his hero will appear in the best possible light. Thus when he quotes a tribute by a contemporary writer to Cooke's powers of oratory he conveniently omits those sentences which balance praise with criticism.[7] Clearly we cannot be completely satisfied with Porter's answer to our question.

[3] [J. L.] Porter, [*Life and times of Henry Cooke*] (Belfast 1875) p 26.
[4] T. W. Moody and J. C. Beckett, *Queen's Belfast, 1845–1949: the history of a university* 2 vols (London 1959) I p 320.
[5] Porter p ix.
[6] Porter pp 344–5 illustrates these assumptions splendidly.
[7] Porter pp 434–5; T. Witherow, *Three prophets of our own* (Londonderry 1880) pp 51–2.

Of course, not all Cooke's contemporaries, even within orthodox presbyterianism, shared Porter's view. Many seem to have believed that Cooke had served their church well in his leadership of the party of orthodoxy in the synodal conflict, but regarded his political activities as, at best, open to criticism, and, at worst, disastrous. Reviewing Porter's book Richard Smyth, a presbyterian theological professor, commented, 'Dr Cooke's real life's work began and ended with the purgation of the synod of Ulster from the leaven of Arianism, but for this great achievement, it would scarcely be worthwhile to write his life at all'.[8]

This was the view of the chief interpreters of Cooke within the Irish presbyterian tradition in the nineteenth century, of contemporaries like James McKnight, the presbyterian journalist, and James Morgan, the pious minister of Fisherwick church, Belfast, and historians like W. D. Killen, Thomas Witherow and W. T. Latimer, although it is only fair to recognise that all of them, like Richard Smyth, were liberals in politics and supporters of the tenant-right movement which Cooke opposed.[9] The official minute of the general assembly, recording his death, expressed gratitude 'that one so highly gifted was raised up, strengthened and sustained (with others whose memories are dear to this church) for the purpose of leading back one important section of this assembly to the 'old paths' of evangelical presbyterianism'.[10] The general assembly was, of course, the body resulting from the union of the general and secession synods and it is usually agreed that it was made possible by the withdrawal of the Arians from the general synod, as J. E. Davey has written: 'There can be no shadow of doubt that the schism of the Arians led directly to the union with the seceders and so to a new age of quickened enthusiasm for the common evangelical inheritance of the Irish churches sprung out of the Scottish reformation'.[11]

It was also widely believed that the apparent prosperity, material and spiritual, that Irish presbyterianism enjoyed after 1830 was the

[8] R. Smyth, 'Review of J. L. Porter, Life and times of Henry Cooke', *British and Foreign Evangelical Review*, 21 no 70 (April 1872) p 210.
[9] W. D. Killen completed the third volume of J. S. Reid, *History of the Presbyterian Church in Ireland*, 3 vols (Belfast 1867). T. Witherow wrote a brief appreciation of Cooke in *Three prophets of our own*, cited above; he also contributed the main address when the centenary of Cooke's birth was celebrated, see *The Cooke Centenary* (Belfast 1888) pp 9 seq [W. T.] Latimer was the author of two brief lives of Cooke, [*A history of the life and times of*] *Henry Cooke* (Belfast 1888) and *A champion for the faith* (Belfast 1899).
[10] Minutes of the general assembly, 1869.
[11] J. E. Davey, *The story of a hundred years* (Belfast 1940) p 12.

R. F. G. HOLMES

result of the controversy and schism. The historian, Killen, judged: 'The attention of the people all over the land was drawn to the great discussion and a marked improvement in regard to things spiritual was everywhere visible. Family prayer revived, sabbath schools increased in numbers and efficiency, new congregations were gathered, churches were rebuilt and repaired and missionary movements were undertaken on a scale which had never before been attempted'.[12] James Morgan, in his address at Cooke's funeral, declared: 'Our church extension in the great increase of congregations, our missions, home, foreign, continental, colonial; along with our daily and Sunday schools, and our colleges and professors. All these were the issues of the one great measure of which Dr Cooke was the originator.'[13]

Undoubtedly the vitality of Irish presbyterianism after 1840 owed much to the evangelicalism with which Cooke had identified himself but not everyone accepted him as simply the champion of evangelicalism. 'Few of his best friends', wrote Crozier, the son-in-law and biographer of Cooke's great opponent, Henry Montgomery, 'will be prepared to maintain that, in the great contests of his public life, he was actuated by no other motive than purely and solely the desire for the propagation of Calvinistic principles, and that the gratification of a great personal ambition did not at least keep pace with it in the direction of the leading actions of his life'.[14]

'Nothing will so avail to divide the church as love of power,'[15] said Chrysostom, and Greenslade, in his study of schism in the early church, has judged that: 'Without the leadership of some strong personality, it is scarcely likely that any group will have the force or courage to divide the church, and few men, especially powerful men, are free from some taint of ambition or pride, jealousy or pique'.[16]

Few could claim that Cooke escaped that taint. His friend, James Morgan, described Cooke's most striking quality as his 'purpose to conquer'[17] and we can be certain that this played its part in determining his conduct of his campaign against Arianism. Yet it is too simple to suggest that ambition was the sole driving force of his life. Witherow was not an uncritical admirer of Cooke, but, speaking on the occasion

---

[12] W. D. Killen, *Reminiscences of a long life* (London 1901) p 46.
[13] *BNL* 19 December 1868.
[14] [J. A.] Crozier, [*The life of the Rev. Henry Montgomery* (London 1875)] I p 86. Only the first volume of Crozier's biography of Montgomery was ever published.
[15] S. L. Greenslade, *Schism in the early church* (London 1964) p 37.
[16] *Ibid.*
[17] [J.] Morgan, *Recollections [of my life and times]* (Belfast 1874) p 48.

370

of the celebration of the centenary of Cooke's birth, he said: 'Had Dr Cooke been guided by no higher motive than ambition of worldly success, he would have sought a more conspicuous field than a remote province of Ireland for the exercise of his great and varied powers—a Scottish pulpit, a London congregation, a seat in the house of commons were positions quite within his reach at an early period of his career'.[18]

Personal ambition and genuine conviction can go hand in hand, of course, and in Cooke's case the crucial question seems to be the question of the relationship between his politics and his religion. It is clear that, from an early stage in the conflict in the synod, its political overtones and implications were apparent. The divisive political issue in Ulster in the 1820s was the question of catholic emancipation and when Cooke, giving evidence as moderator of synod before select committees of both houses of parliament investigating Irish affairs, stated that he and, he believed, the majority of his fellow presbyterians, were opposed to full emancipation, he immediately became a hero with the 'no-popery' party.[19] His great Arian opponent Henry Montgomery, who was an ardent supporter of the catholic claims, considered that this contributed enormously to Cooke's popularity and power: 'Orthodoxy in all its phases hailed him as its champion. Thus uniting evangelicism with Orangeism and the countenance of the aristocracy with the applause of the multitude, in a few months from the publication of his evidence he had acquired extraordinary popularity and influence'.[20]

During the synodal debates the galleries of the meeting-houses in which they were held were crowded with political partisans, who gave Cooke and his party vocal support and to whom, on occasion, Cooke appealed, in spite of rebukes from the moderatorial chair.[21] Crozier claimed that in Strabane, where the crucial 1827 synod was held, the cries, 'No surrender' and 'Down with the Arians', were the same,[22] and William Porter, the Arian clerk of synod, insisted that it was his 'advocacy of catholic emancipation' that was 'the real cause of the crusade the orthodox were mounting against him!'[23] A writer in the unitarian periodical, *The Christian Reformer*, expressed the opinion that, 'The unchristian and hateful temper of the majority in the Synod

[18] *The Cooke Centenary* (Belfast 1888) p 21.
[19] Porter pp 65–6; *NW* 14, 21 April 1825.
[20] *Irish Unitarian Magazine* 2 no 2 (Belfast 1847) p 360.
[21] *NW* 7 July 1825.
[22] Crozier pp 108–9.
[23] *NW* 5 July 1827.

of Ulster, has, we believe, been nurtured by the Orange faction in Ireland.'[24] Is it possible, then, that the conflict that split the synod of Ulster in the 1820s was really a political conflict in disguise and, that, in attacking the Arians in the Belfast Institution and in the synod, Cooke was already serving the tory political interests which he espoused so enthusiastically during the rest of his life?

Affirmative answers have been given to these questions, unequivocally by the late John Jamieson, the historian of the Belfast Institution,[25] and more guardedly, by J. M. Barkley.[26] Jamieson is quite certain that Cooke's motives in attacking Arianism were political and selfish: 'Cooke's championship of religious orthodoxy after 1821 turned out, as his evidence to the parliamentary committees in 1825 and his activities after he had gained supremacy in the synod proved, to be chiefly a cloak beneath which he sought to conceal his real objective, which was the destruction of political liberalism in his church because it stood for the negation of his own political convictions'.[27] Barkley is more judicious; he considers that 'there was a greater consistency in Cooke's theological outlook than some of his critics have been prepared to admit', but that, 'while there is no reason to doubt Cooke's theological integrity, as some have done, the evidence is rather against his primary motive being theological'.[28]

Certainly the evidence, both in its general coherence, and in its particular details, is impressive. The presbyterians of Ulster occupied, as Cooke was fond of pointing out, a strategic position in the Anglo-Irish political situation. They were in Ireland as the result of waves of immigration from Scotland, chiefly in the seventeenth century. Then they had originally been encouraged to come to augment and support the crown garrison and they were cast in the role of allies for the minority protestant establishment, a fact which was recognised by the payment, from 1672, of *regium donum* for their ministers. In the crisis of 1688–90 they played their part but in the eighteenth century, disappointed by their failure to share in the fruits of the Williamite victory, shut out as dissenters from office and influence, they became

[24] *The Christian Reformer* 13 (London 1827) p 376.
[25] [J.] Jamieson, 'The influence [of the Rev. Henry Cooke on the political life of Ulster',] MA thesis (Queen's University Belfast 1950); [*The history of the Royal Belfast Academical*] *Institution* (Belfast 1959).
[26] [J. M.] Barkley, 'The Arian schism [in Ireland, 1830'], *SCH* 9, *Schism, Heresy and Religious Protest* (1972) p 335.
[27] Jamieson 'The influence' p 78.
[28] Barkley, 'The Arian schism' p 335.

increasingly disenchanted with their role as second-class citizens. Many emigrated to America, where they became involved in the colonists' fight for independence, while some who remained, inspired to some extent by the American example, were leaders in the united Irish radical reform movement, which sought to transform the Irish political scene by uniting Irishmen of all creeds and winning independence from England, and which led to the rebellion of 1798.[29]

It was obviously very much in the interests of the British government, particularly in the context of the Napoleonic war, to counteract and reverse this trend in Ulster presbyterian political sympathies and Castlereagh, the Ulster tory statesman, himself baptised a presbyterian, took the lead in implementing a policy of discouraging radicalism and encouraging loyalism in the synod of Ulster.[30] In 1792 and again in 1803 the *regium donum* was substantially increased, but, after 1803, the minister who was responsible for distributing the payment became a salaried government official and a system of differentiation in the amount of grant according to the size of congregation was introduced.[31]

A study of Castlereagh's correspondence on this subject provides many illustrations of his policy but one item is of special interest in view of the schism which divided the synod of Ulster in the 1820s. In July 1802 Castlereagh wrote to Addington, the prime minister, enclosing a letter he had received from Black, the *regium donum* agent:

> ... the enclosed sketch will show you how much there is in the body which requires amendment and how much may be done by an efficient protection and support given on the part of government to those who have committed themselves in support of the state against a democratic party in the synod, several of whom, if not engaged in the rebellion, were deeply infected with its principles. In our church [Castlereagh had become an anglican]

---

[29] For the eighteenth-century radical movement in Irish presbyterianism see A. T. Q. Stewart, 'The transformation of presbyterian radicalism in the north of Ireland, 1792–1825', MA thesis (Queen's University Belfast 1956); R. F. G. Holmes, 'Eighteenth century Irish presbyterian radicalism and its eclipse', *The Bulletin of the Presbyterian Historical Society of Ireland*, no 3 (Belfast January 1973) pp 7–14.

[30] For Castlereagh's policy of discouraging radicalism in the synod of Ulster see especially Black to Castlereagh, 26 April 1800 and 28 February 1801, [*Memoirs and Correspondence of*] *Castlereagh*, [ed Marquess of Londonderry,] 8 vols (London 1848–53) 3, pp 287–91 and 4, pp 65–6; Knox to Castlereagh, 5 February 1802 and 15 July 1803, *ibid*, 4, pp 216–18 and 284–90.

[31] *Records of the General Synod of Ulster*, 1691–1820, 3 vols (Belfast 1890–8) 3, pp 270–2.

which is naturally attached to the state, I should dread schism as weakening its interests; but in such a body as the presbyterians of Ireland, who . . . have partaken so deeply first of the popular and since of the democratic politics of the country as to be an object much more of jealousy than of support to the government, I am of opinion that it is only through a considerable internal fermentation of the body . . . that it will put on a different temper and acquire better habits.[32]

So remarkably did the schism of 1829 realise Castlereagh's hopes and bring about what was in his mind in 1802 that one can scarcely resist the conclusion that in Cooke the effective agent of his policy had been found. Black of Derry, the *regium donum* agent, who was Castlereagh's great ally in the synod, was himself an Arian and therefore unable to ride the rising tide of evangelicalism in his church but Henry Montgomery later claimed that, before his death in 1817, Black had begun to cultivate the friendship of rising evangelicals like Cooke.[33] Certainly it looks as though Black's mantle as 'prime minister of the general synod', as he was called by the veteran presbyterian radical, William Drennan,[34] passed eventually to Cooke and in both cases the party label tory might properly have been added.

There was, of course, a discernible correlation between radicalism in theology and politics in the synod, though the correlation was not absolute, as the case of Black shows.[35] It is clear that Montgomery and his friends, forthright advocates of full catholic emancipation, stood firmly in the eighteenth-century presbyterian radical tradition and Cooke did not scruple to arouse political hostility against them during the theological conflict in the synod. In Strabane in 1827, for example, replying to the charge that he was interfering with man's liberty of opinion, he declaimed: 'Opposed to liberty. It is a calumny. We are the determined friends of the British constitution. We were so in days past when some of those who now oppose us set up the standard of rebellion'.[36]

The fact that Cooke opened his campaign against Arianism with an

---

[32] Castlereagh to Addington, 21 July 1802, *Castlereagh* 4, p 224.
[33] Montgomery, speaking at the first meeting of the remonstrant synod, set up after the schism of the general synod, *NW* 27 May 1830. See also [T.] Witherow, [*Historical and literary memorials of presbyterianism in Ireland*,] 2 vols (London/Belfast 1879–80) 2, p 271.
[34] Drennan to Mrs McTier 7 June 1816, *The Drennan Letters*, ed D. A. Chart (Belfast 1931) p 392.
[35] Black was a radical turned tory. For Black's career see Witherow pp 266–75.
[36] Porter, 1872 edition, p 107.

attack upon the Belfast Institution appears to support the suggestion that he had taken Black's place as the agent of Castlereagh's policy, for Castlereagh and Black had done all they could to prevent the presbyterian synods forming a relationship with the college. The Institution was founded by the liberal intelligentsia of Belfast, personified by William Drennan, who gave the address at the opening of the college in 1814,[37] and it was intended to provide opportunities for higher education for, among others, students for the presbyterian ministry, who had hitherto to go to Scotland for academic training. Castlereagh saw in this 'a deep laid scheme again to bring the presbyterian synod within the ranks of democracy' by giving 'Dr Drennan and his associates . . . the power of granting certificates of qualification for the ministry in that church'.[38] He urged Peel, the Irish chief secretary to warn the synod that a university degree might be made an obligatory qualification before a minister could receive *regium donum* and he himself tried to dissuade the synod from forming a relationship with the Institution.[39] In spite of his advice the synod appointed a divinity professor to teach their students in the college and recognised its general certificate as the equivalent of a university degree, while Peel considered that to do as Castlereagh suggested would be too draconian at that stage though he, too, disapproved the arrangement.[40] He chose to put pressure on the Institution by refusing to continue the £1500 annual grant which the government had grudgingly given the college, unless they abandoned their intention of providing an education for presbyterian ordinands.[41] This the Institution authorities would not do and so, in 1816, church and college had stood together in defence of ecclesiastical and academic freedom, and the reverend Henry Cooke was one of those who had supported this stand and the arrangement between the synod and the Belfast Institution.[42]

The fact that, six years later, Cooke should have attacked the Institution, admittedly on theological grounds, and raised doubts about the link between it and the synod, is interpreted by Jamieson as

[37] Jamieson, *Institution*, pp 203–7.
[38] Castlereagh to Peel, 9 November 1816 BM Add MS 40181 fols 225–6.
[39] *Ibid.*
[40] *BNL* 2 July 1816, Peel to Castlereagh, 13 November 1816 BM Add MS 40181, fols 225–6.
[41] Peel to Castlereagh, 2 December 1816, *ibid* fols 241–5; Castlereagh to Peel, 10 December 1816, *ibid* fols 249–50; N. Gash, *Mr Secretary Peel* (London 1961) pp 143–4.
[42] *BNL* 2 July 1816.

clear evidence that he was really continuing the old tory hostility under a theological cloak.[43] Jamieson argues that the rest of Cooke's career—his partisan support for conservative political causes, often in opposition to the majority opinion in his church—corroborates this interpretation. Cooke's opposition to the national education system, introduced in Ireland by a whig government in 1831 on the principle of non-sectarian secular education for Roman catholic and protestant alike is explained as a piece of tory politics to embarrass the whigs. 'Nothing,' wrote Jamieson, 'shows Cooke more clearly as the ally of the ascendancy tories'.[44] His enthusiasm for protestant union—his celebrated publication of the banns of marriage between presbyterian and episcopalian—is seen as 'an attempt to hitch the presbyterian waggon to the ascendancy star'.[45]

Cooke's political activities, in particular his opposition to full catholic emancipation and his attacks on the tenant-right movement, are presented as different aspects of his service to his masters, the protestant ascendancy landlords, and a coherent and credible picture is painted of a 'blustering bigot'[46] who served his own interests by serving a selfish ruling class.

Clearly Jamieson was out of sympathy with everything that Cooke stood for—orthodoxy in theology, puritanism in religion, conservatism and unionism in politics. One is reminded of Edwin Muir's admission about his own book on John Knox: 'I came to dislike him more and more . . . my book was not a good one, it was too full of dislike for Knox and certain things in Scottish life'.[47] Jamieson's obvious dislike of Cooke and certain things in Ulster life may be justified, but it arouses suspicion about some of his judgements. His portrait of Cooke, like Porter's, is too simple. If Cooke was such a time-serving hypocrite, how did he win the admiration of so many of his contemporaries,[48] and how could the historian, W. T. Latimer, who disapproved of his politics, have written: 'with all his faults he was a good man, an able minister of Jesus Christ'?[49] Jamieson built

[43] Jamieson, *Institution*, p 38.
[44] Jamieson, 'The influence', p 108.
[45] *Ibid* p 29.   [46] *Ibid* p 17.
[47] E. Muir, *An Autobiography* (London 1954) p 231.
[48] For example James Morgan, the devout evangelical who was the first minister of the Fisherwick congregation in Belfast, whose autobiography and journal are full of references to his friendship with Cooke and who wrote: 'there never has been a misunderstanding between us, we have lived in the closest personal friendship'. Morgan, *Recollections*, p 67.
[49] Latimer, *Henry Cooke*, p 43.

up an impressive *prima facie* case against Cooke, but it is necessary for us to examine *alteram partem*.

In the first place, we cannot ignore Cooke's prodigious labours as a minister of his church. He was always preaching, opening new churches, supporting old ones, serving the interests of innumerable charities as well as bible societies and Sunday schools. On 20 April 1841 the reverend John Dill of Clonmel wrote to his brother James: 'Dr Cooke has been with me a good part of a week. He addressed the annual meeting of the Tipperary protestant orphan society and outdid himself. He preached for me in the evening to a crammed house ... After dinner he and I set out by posting to Cork where we arrived at six in the morning. That day, Friday, he preached twice, two long sermons for Edward [Dill], at the opening of his new church. Then on Sunday two others . . .'[50] Jamieson seems to dismiss this kind of activity too easily when he describes Cooke's preaching as 'little more than an exercise for keeping himself in good voice for the vaster projects on which he deliberately embarked'.[51] He also ignored his demanding but often unspectacular religious literary work: for example his edition of Brown's bible, with notes, and his concordance of scripture.[52]

We have considerable evidence of Cooke's personal sincerity and pastoral zeal as a minister. During the cholera epidemic of 1832, when some of the protestant ministers of Belfast were accused of failing to visit those stricken with the disease, Cooke did not fail to do so and served on the board of health set up to combat the epidemic.[53] In 1829, as he approached the climax of his conflict with the Arians, he wrote some letters to a young minister who had sought his advice on the problems he had to face in his parish. Two of them have survived and they breathe a genuine spirit of piety.[54] No reference is made either to the synodal controversy or to the catholic emancipation question.

Cooke has sometimes been portrayed as a caricature of some of the worst features of reactionary toryism, a man without any social conscience. It is true that, as an evangelical, he believed that the ills of society were spiritual in origin and required spiritual solutions but

[50] J. R. Dill, *Autobiography of a country parson* (Belfast 1888) p 49.
[51] Jamieson, 'The influence', p 17.
[52] *Brown's Self-interpreting Bible*, ed H. Cooke (Glasgow 1846).
[53] *BNL* 20 March and 28 August 1832.
[54] Cooke to W. Campbell 20 March and 23 April 1829. Belfast, Presbyterian Historical Society MS.

it is wrong to suggest that he had no concern for the poor and no interest in social evils. Many examples of his social concern could be given, one must suffice: he supported the bakers of Belfast in their fight for better working conditions. In their published expression of gratitude they thank him 'for his benevolent assistance in putting down the cruel and unjust system of incessant night work'.[55]

Cooke's toryism, as outlined in his 1834 Hillsborough speech, was the reformist conservatism of Peel's Tamworth manifesto and, in any case, the tories were not always the villains of the peace in nineteenth-century Ireland. That great liberal Sharman Crawford admitted that Peel and the tories had done more for the Irish tenant farmers than the whigs had ever done.[56]

The fact that Cooke was the friend of men of the landlord class like lords Roden and Mountcashel and captain Sidney Hamilton Rowan is sometimes used to support the idea that he was serving their interests, which are assumed to be political and tory, in driving the Arians out of the synod.[57] But these men were fervent evangelicals in religion belonging to that society of aristocratic pietists among whom the 'Brethren' movement developed, with its strong emphasis on 'separation'. When Mountcashel urged Cooke to 'bring about a separation'[58] in the synod he was most probably doing so for religious reasons. Certainly *The Northern Whig*, no friend of landlords and tories, considered that Mountcashel's opposition to catholic emancipation was for 'principally religious'[59] reasons.

Undoubtedly religion, politics and economics were tortuously intertwined in nineteenth-century Ireland (as they still are) and it is almost impossible to disentangle them.[60] Cooke, Porter and the mainstream Irish presbyterian tradition have seen the conflict which divided their church in the 1820s as essentially religious in character while Jamieson and some recent interpreters have seen it as essentially political and personal. We can be sure that it was neither purely religious nor simply political. To recognise the importance of politics in the conflict does not mean that we must consider the theological

[55] *The Banner of Ulster* 14 October 1842.
[56] NW 20 July 1847. For Cooke's Hillsborough speech see *Authentic report of speech at the great protestant meeting at Hillsborough 30 October 1834* (Belfast 1834).
[57] Barkley, 'The Arian schism' pp 335–7. For S. H. Rowan see A. Breakey, *A discourse occasioned by the death of Sidney Hamilton Rowan 28 November 1847* (Belfast 1847).
[58] Porter p 110.
[59] NW 14 December 1829.
[60] R. B. McDowell, *Public Opinion and Government Policy in Ireland 1801–46* (London 1952) p 110.

issues trivial or artificial. A question which has always been of crucial importance in Christian doctrine was at issue, the question of the relationship of Jesus to God. As Maurice Wiles has written: 'to deny the full divinity of Christ . . . is the thing that more decisively than any other has been understood to set a man outside the Christian fellowship'.[61] And when we examine the theological exchanges and positions of the two parties we can see that their differences went deep, it is not too much to say that two fundamentally different understandings of Christianity were in conflict.[62]

There is not time, in a paper of this length, to examine particular questions about Cooke's actions in detail but something must be said about his attack upon Arian influences in the Belfast Institution. The occasion of his attack was the election of William Bruce to the chair of Hebrew and Greek, which involved him in teaching all students for the ministry. The records of the election make it quite clear that Bruce was elected to try to disarm the suspicions of Castlereagh and the tories (his father was a great friend of Castlereagh).[63] He was supported by Sir Robert Bateson, a leading tory politician so it is hard to see what political motive Cooke could have had for his attack but there was certainly a theological motive, for Bruce's Arianism was well known and was indeed made the basis of objections to him at the election.[64]

It is significant that none of the 'establishment' figures who gave evidence during the government's inquiry into the Institution's affairs in 1825—the marquesses of Donegall and Downshire, the bishop of Down and Connor, Sir Stephen May—expressed any political suspicion against the college. Sir Stephen May affirmed: 'There was a time, I think, when there was an impression against it but really I cannot say upon what, particularly, that impression was grounded, further than that some people had a lead in it who were considered inimical to the government, but I think that feeling has entirely gone off'.[65] Certainly Cooke was not riding a wave of political hostility against the Institution when he launched his attack upon Arian influences in it.

If Cooke was seeking primarily to serve the tory and protestant ascendancy interests there were other ways in which he could have used his talents more dramatically than in combating Arianism in his church.

---

[61] M. Wiles, *The Christian Fathers* (London 1966) p 53.
[62] See, in particular, H. Montgomery, *The creed of an Arian* (Belfast 1830).
[63] *BNL* 6 November 1821. For Bruce senior see Crozier p 77.
[64] *Ibid.* John Barnett, one of the electors, admitted in 1825 that he had written to Cooke urging him to do what he could to prevent an Arian being elected, *NW* 7 July 1825.
[65] *Fourth Report of the Commissioners of Irish education inquiry*, H.C. 1826–7 (89) 13 p 184.

Hereward Senior in his history of Orangeism in this period has suggested that what the protestant cause needed during the emancipation crisis particularly in 1826 when British government and public opinion were outraged by O'Connell's proposed invasion of Ulster by his 'Liberators' was 'a demagogue of genius' who might have marshalled Orange strength to 'force a wavering government to suppress the Catholic Association without granting emancipation', but 'no such leader could be found in the ultra tory camp' and the opportunity passed.[66] Yet this was a role Cooke could have played admirably but his own public opposition to emancipation was late and low-key. Indeed he never was an Orangeman; strange as that may seem to some.

The overwhelming impression made by the evidence we have surveyed is ambivalence. The general case for political motivation is strong but it is often contradicted by particular evidence, for example, the fact that political hostility to the Belfast Institution seems to have been declining when Cooke began his attack upon Arianism in it. What is required is precise evidence of collusion between Cooke and, say, Castlereagh, but we have none. We do have correspondence between Cooke and Peel. In 1825 Cooke wrote to Peel asking for guidance on the Institution question, promising that negotiations with the college 'so far as I have any influence, would be managed according to your wishes'.[67] This looks as though Cooke were offering himself as the tory government's obedient servant but his aim in writing is clearly to obtain government support for what he himself wanted, a college under his church's control. Again the evidence is ambivalent.

The late Cyril Connolly once wrote: 'In reading biographies and autobiographies, one is sadly conscious of the point of no return, the moment when the life shaping forces begin to recede, when the actors are acted upon'.[68] I am inclined to the view that Cooke's primary motive in attacking Arianism may have been religious but that he quickly became a prisoner of the forces with which he allied himself in his victorious campaign. Having tasted the heady wine of popular acclaim he became an addict for the remainder of his life. I do not believe that he was consciously a hypocrite, but, like most of us, he was often the victim of self-deception.

The Presbyterian Colleges
Belfast.

[66] H. Senior, *Orangeism in Ireland and Britain 1795–1836* (London 1966) p 230.
[67] Cooke to Peel, 20 July 1825. BM Add MS 40380 fol 151.
[68] *The Sunday Times* 23 October 1966.

THE FAILURES OF SUCCESS:
WORKING CLASS EVANGELISTS
IN EARLY VICTORIAN BIRMINGHAM

by GEOFFREY ROBSON

UTOBIOGRAPHY and statistics appear at first sight to be incompatible sources in any study of religious motivation. The former rarely hint at the sociological factors governing religious commitment. The latter are difficult to interpret in terms of individual conviction. Yet the evangelical revival produced an abundance of both. John Wesley in the *Arminian Magazine* set a fashion which was followed by evangelicals of every brand who published spiritual autobiographies to edify the faithful. Wesleyan methodism also kept careful membership statistics on which scholars like A. D. Gilbert[1] can base a sociological explanation of the rise and fall of denominational religion. Placed side by side the inward and outward evidence gave the impression that statistical success, in terms of ever increasing membership, depended on intense individual conviction in preacher and convert. The Liverpool minutes of 1820 are but the Wesleyan example of a general pattern. Nevertheless this recipe did not guarantee success. It would seem that the challenge to the individual conscience needed to be combined with a strong appeal to a sense of group or class solidarity for any lasting impression to be made. Unfortunately the places where evangelical religion was successful do not always coincide with available autobiographical sources. Birmingham, however, provides an illuminating example of the failure of the individualistic approach to the urban working class.

Long before the 1851 census of religious worship showed that it had one of the lowest church attendances in England[2] Birmingham was notoriously inhospitable to revivalist religion. Wesleyan superintendents in the first quarter of the century bemoaned their lack of conver-

---

[1] A. D. Gilbert, 'The growth and decline of nonconformity in England and Wales', Oxford DPhil thesis 1973.

[2] K. S. Inglis, 'Patterns of religious worship in 1851', *JEH* 11, 1 (April 1960) pp 74–86. D. H. Mcleod, 'Class, community and religion', *A Sociological yearbook of religion in Britain* 6 (London 1973) pp 29–72.

381

sions and longed for 'a little bit of Yorkshire zeal.'[3] Aspiring working class preachers found little support and although they lived in Birmingham relied on the religiously more fertile ground of the black country to sustain their ministry. Nevertheless efforts were made, along the lines described by H. D. Rack,[4] to evangelise the teeming courts and alleys of the town centre. Tract societies had existed for some years before the most sustained onslaught by district visiting began in 1837.[5] The interdenominational Birmingham town mission was first in the field followed speedily by the independents of Carrs Lane and the Wesleyans. All had full time lay agents and their surviving journals provide a fascinating glimpse into the motives of the missionaries and their clientele. The evangelical revival had revealed to working men the possibility of a quasi-professional career as an itinerant evangelist. Failure in business or lack of settled employment spurred on those who felt a divine call and wished to emulate the more successful preachers of the respectable churches. Such a person was Henry Fowler who came to Birmingham from Devon in 1813, received a call after three weeks and became minister to a Calvinistic congregation of a hundred 'labouring poor' who could not afford to support him.[6] Another was William Cope who records forty years spent supplying various black country congregations when they had no settled minister and who eventually preached regularly at the countess of Huntingdon's chapel in Birmingham until silenced by a paralytic stroke.[7] The town missionaries also did their share of open air preaching, often in competition with others, but with equal lack of success in producing conversions.[8]

What led them to persevere in preaching and visiting despite the evident fruitlessness of their labours? One factor was a conviction, not simply of their own call, but of their spiritual superiority as agents of divine judgement on sin.

[3] Manchester John Rylands Library MS methodist church archives. J. Entwhistle to Miss Tooth, 20 September 1823. G. Morley to J. Bunting 28 October 1815.

[4] H. D. Rack, 'Domestic visitation; a chapter in early nineteenth century evangelism', *JEH* 24, 4 (October 1973) pp 357–76.

[5] B[irmingham] C[entral] H[all] MS Cherry Street Wesleyan tract society minutes 1828–84, 1 (25 October 1836) claimed that the society had been 'established upwards of twenty years.'

[6] H. Fowler, *Travels in the wilderness of my life* (London 1839).

[7] W. Cope, *A Faithful and particular account of God's gracious dealings with William Cope of Birmingham, Itinerant preacher of Jesus Christ forty years* (Birmingham 1830).

[8] B[irmingham] R[eference] L[ibrary] MS Carrs Lane deposit 64, journal of E. Derrington (2 August 1840).

Failures of success in early Victorian Birmingham

I had a long conversation with a family in Litchfield Street. It was the first house I entered this day Monday 24th July. 'Sir, said the woman, 'it is no use to talk to us for we be working folk and we must work of a Sunday for other people, as we are bakers and pieclate makers and until all the other folk of our trade give over working on a Sunday we cannot give up our living'. 'My dear friends', said I, 'you may as well say that until all the people of your trade in Birmingham made up their minds to flee from the wrath to come you would make no attempts to escape the firy indignation of an Angry God, who enforces His command by a word which He has not employed in giving any of the other commandments, that is *Remember* which is almost saying, should you be such a slave to sin and to Hell as to violate any or all of my other commandments, *Remember* this one, That thou keep Holy the Sabbath Day, and again', said I, 'hear the words of Christ, what doth it profit a man if he gain the whole world and lose his own soul.' I followed up these observations with others in allusion to the terrors of the Lord . . . and I was much encouraged to notice a marked degree of attention paid to all my observations.[9]

Encouraging though this activity may have been it was unlikely to be much in demand among the labouring poor. The poor had other priorities and saw the missionaries as potential ministers to their own needs. Even this could sometimes supply a strong motive for continuing service amongst them.

The people in the district around the chapel to whom in the various streets I am pretty well known are frequently applying to me . . . to visit cases of affliction and distress. This interests me in as much at it shows that many who cannot be persuaded to attend regularly the house of God nonetheless regard me as their best friend.[10]

William Jackson who wrote these words was a particularly insensitive agent of Carrs Lane who did not realise why he was constantly called upon to visit the sick and dying. Another Carrs Lane man, the self educated Edward Derrington, was more aware of the real motives of his clients.

Friday 9th November 1838 I was sent for to visit the case of a poor woman who had fallen down in the street and discharged a great quantity of blood. As I entered the room she said; 'Oh I

[9] BRL MS 312749, journal of T. A. Finegan 24 July 1837.
[10] BRL MS Carrs Lane deposit 69, journal of W. Jackson 28 January 1846.

did want to see you.' 'And what did you want to see me for?'
'That you might send me to heaven.' 'That's more than I am able
to do, it doesn't lie in my power to send people to heaven.'
'Don't it?' 'No it does not. There's no going to heaven but through
Jesus Christ. The Bible tells us what he is the way, the truth and
the life.' 'Well I pray to my sweet Jesus that he would save me.'
'What has Jesus Christ done to save sinners?' 'I don't know, I am
no scholar.' She repeated the words, my sweet Jesus many times
but nothing further could I learn. . . . Thus the poor wretched
creature must be left to her ignorance and her sin with little
prospect of doing her any good. We have succeeded in removing,
to a very considerable degree, the delusion of sending sinners to
heaven by the administration of the Lord's Supper and have
instead substituted our prayers. Not that this was intended but so
it is. These poor ignorant creatures think that if they can but
obtain the attendance of some servant of Jesus Christ they may
safely soar to heaven on the breath of his prayers.[11]

This is only one illustration of the gulf which separated popular
religion from Calvinist evangelicalism and made the task of conversion
so difficult. In these circumstances the missionary was tempted to take
one of two courses. He could allow his work to be dictated more by
the demands of his clients than by the rules of the mission. Alternatively
his admiration for such pulpit orators as J. Angell James could divert
him into becoming pastor of a small chapel rather than a missionary to
the poor. Derrington, who constantly reiterates his preference for the
service of the sanctuary over open air evangelism, followed the latter
course.[12]

The most colourful of the missionaries whose journals survive was
led into social work as much by his origins as by the destitution he
encountered on his visits. Thomas Augustin Finegan was an Irish
convert from Roman catholicism who spoke the language of the most
unpopular group of immigrants in Birmingham. The town mission
wisely employed him in the Irish quarter without bargaining on his
becoming a leader in the cause of relief for the Irish poor. He presented
one case after another to the managers of the mission, the general
hospital and the overseers of the poor. Finegan claimed 'he had sent
fifty persons the other day to the workhouse because they were in
distress and they were denied relief and turned away with disdain

[11] *Ibid* 62, journal of E. Derrington 9 November 1838.
[12] *Ibid* 63, journal of E. Derrington 4 August 1839.

because they were Irish.'[13] The town had a deliberate policy not to levy poor rates on houses valued at less than ten pounds a year.[14] Thus most of the seasonally unemployed could claim no relief from the parish having been born beyond its boundaries and having paid no rates within them. Such a policy naturally provoked popular discontent and the occasional riot. In response, from the 1760s, collections were taken in churches and chapels during the Christmas season, subscriptions were raised and a town relief committee co-ordinated the provision of tickets for food, clothing and fuel. Half of these were distributed by the churches, the remainder were kept in the hands of the committee for individual applicants.[15] The missionaries were regularly used both to distribute tickets and to check the credentials of applicants. Many of the most needy failed to apply, preferring the dignity of silent starvation. Finegan and others were engaged in a hopeless but persevering attempt to bring them some relief through visitation, appeals in the press and personal application to charities. In addition Finegan found himself helping young women to escape from prostitution. Visiting brothels was a distasteful but regular part of his duties and the Magdalen hospital received several new inmates as a result.[16] Such activities brought him a sense of personal fulfilment and gave him a secure place in local slum society. Finegan was also sustained by a convert's zeal to refute the errors of Rome. Despite regular cautioning from the mission managers to avoid controversy he obviously relished a brush with a catholic on a theological issue.[17] Deists of course were fair game for all evangelicals and Owenites were particularly prominent in the period around 1840. The Wesleyans regularly attended their meetings and distributed tracts, arguing in public against the follies of the rational religionists.[18]

This raises the corporate aspect of motivation. The personal convictions of the missionaries were nevertheless serving the institutional church. Finegan was expected to encourage attendance at public worship in any evangelical church or chapel. His eventual break with the town mission came when he accused dissenters on the com-

---

[13] B[irmingham] J[ournal] 17 February 1838 (report of the statistical committee).
[14] *VCH Warwickshire* (London 1964) 7 p 321.
[15] J. A. Langford *A Century of Birmingham Life* (1868) 1 pp 119–20; 2 pp 41, 51, 57, 323.
[16] BRL MS 312749, journal of T. A. Finegan, Jane Osborn 24 August 1837, Mary Robinson 9 October 1837, Jane Gibson 12 October 1837, Ann Bevens 14 October 1837, Elizabeth Martin 4 November 1837 and *passim*.
[17] *Ibid* 27 July 1837, 18 August 1837, 31 August 1837, 6 September 1837, 27 October 1837, 2 November 1837, 17 November 1837 and *passim*.
[18] BRL MS Carrs Lane deposit 71, journal of P. Sibree 10 October 1838.

mittee, especially baptists, of trying to take over the undenominational
Sunday school and evening preaching which he, an episcopalian, had
established in the Gullett, a notorious alley which females and
respectable males avoided whenever possible.[19] Unlike the town
mission, which they imitated, the independents and Wesleyans had a
deliberately sectarian motive and saw each other as rivals in wresting
souls from Satan, deism, Owenism and chartism. Of the two the
Wesleyan town mission was the shorter lived. Its agent, referred to in
the circuit quarterly meeting minutes simply as brother Bakewell,
began work in September 1839 and was dispensed with, on financial
grounds, in December 1844. The circuit took another three years to
liquidate the debt.[20] Bakewell was specifically instructed to encourage
those whom he visited to join classes connected with the town
chapels. Their membership, during his years of labour, did not
significantly increase. That of Cherry Street the old central chapel,
actually declined whilst two of the other three on the growing fringes
of the town had increased by seventy members each and the third by
thirty five.[21] Despite this apparent failure the independents saw the
Wesleyans as their chief rivals. Again and again fascinated and
horrified Calvinists noted the attraction of methodism for the working
man.[22] Derrington, in his desire for a respectable chapel to preach in,
threatened Carrs Lane with the success of the Wesleyans.[23]

> The state of the cause is encouraging but I think much more
> might have been done had we better accomodation. . . . Must it
> be [that] the success of the cause of God must be confined in the
> narrow bounds of our place of worship? No for the Wesleyans
> have a scent of what we are doing and they have entered my
> district and will catch the birds now the bushes are bent. I say not
> this from sectarian feeling but I am not willing that they should
> take away the materials that should build up our own cause.[24]

The Wesleyans were not necessarily more effective open air preachers.
Finegan accused them of a grave tactical error in preaching against
Roman catholicism as idolatry.[25] That was not the way to gain a

[19] BRL MS 312749, journal of T. A. Finegan 3 May 1838.
[20] BCH MS Cherry Street West Circuit quarterly meeting minutes 24 September 1838,
23 December 1839, 18 March 1844, 23 September 1844, 27 December 1847.
[21] Ibid 18 March 1844.
[22] BRL MS Carrs Lane deposit 64, journal of E. Derrington 9 October 1839, 65 journal of
E. Derrington 15 December 1841.
[23] Ibid 63, journal of E. Derrington 4 August 1839.
[24] Ibid 61, journal of E. Derrington 29 July 1838.
[25] BRL MS 312749, journal of T. A. Finegan 19 November 1837.

hearing among the Irish. Their strength lay in exploiting those aspects of popular religion which Calvinism condemned. Following the teaching of J. Angell James[26] the Carrs Lane missionaries attacked the roots of popular religion in ecstatic experience and corporate feeling.

'Mrs W. wants to see you, she has been so happy she couldn't rest but must rise to praise God for his mercy'. . . . Mrs W. entered, 'Oh Sir' said she (stretching out her hand) 'I am in a new world, everything seems new to me this morning. I have had such a night as I never before spent. I have been so happy. I prayed twice before I could get it, at last after praying hard I did get it. I heard a voice say to me "Go and sin no more." I asked my husband if he heard it but he said, "No, I am too wicked to hear such things" For sure I heard it.' 'Now I do not give up to these things and had the very day before cautioned this woman against it . . . neither visions, dreams nor revelations are to be depended upon. These persons want the evidence of believing before they exercise faith. They are in danger of trusting to a mere impression, a sight or a sound instead of the testimony of the word . . . but I find it very difficult to deal with these favoured persons so as to disabuse their minds of what appears to me to be a delusion.'[27]

The Wesleyans could appeal to emotional experiences quite openly and encouraged corporate fellowship instead of attempting to train up self reliant saints. The clash of religious styles sheds light on the motives of that element of the working class which attended church and chapel. The innumerable lapsed Wesleyans who still boasted of their former spiritual experiences contrasted with the few whom Derrington, after a year of conscientious instruction, still felt unable to present for membership at Carrs Lane.

I sometimes think I might write a chapter 'Tales of Methodism.' I was called for in haste after the service this evening to visit a man who was very ill. I hastened to the spot and enquired for my guide. She led me to the chamber of the sick man whom I found fast hastening to the tomb. After some introductory remarks I said, 'Well my man, you appear fast sinking under the pressure of disease.' 'Yes Sir I am.' 'And what is the state of your mind on the prospect of your removal from time to eternity?' 'It is far from being happy.' 'Have you ever paid attention to religion?' 'Yes

[26] R. W. Dale, *Life and Letters of J. Angell James* (London 1861) pp 353-4, letters to Mr Hart 17 December 1838.
[27] BRL MS Carrs Lane deposit 63, journal of E. Derrington 17 November 1840.

sir, I believe I once knew the love of God, but I am a backslider.'
'You once knew the love of God!' 'Yes Sir, I did.' 'Tell me what
you mean by that expression will you.' It is a phrase Wesleyans
often make use of but I cannot get them to tell me what they
mean by it. I pressed the question. At last he said, 'I think I had
peace . . .' 'It is a strange thing,' said I, 'but I suppose that on my
visits I find ten backsliders of the Wesleyan denomination to two
of all the sects of the Christian Church and I know not how to
account for it except it is that they take conviction for
conversion. We seldom hear much of backsliders among us.'[28]

Delivered an address to those in a state of concern about their
souls. About twenty attended . . . there were some who had been
in the class of enquirers as much as twelve months. I know nothing
that I could bring against them in a charge of inconsistency but
there is such an inaptness to receive instruction . . . that it appears
like labour in vain. They are constant in their attendence on the
means of grace and appear to enjoy them but they still seem unable
to give a reason for the faith that is in them. I have no more
reason to doubt of their sincerity than I have of those already
received into the church. Yet I know that they would not appear
so satisfactory to those who could only judge of them by
conversation with them.[29]

His own ineffectiveness was revealed when visiting a dying woman
who had regularly attended his chapel but could not produce the
approved formula of trust in the atoning work of Christ.[30] Like other
poor folk she relied for salvation on prayer and good works. One
conclusion seems to emerge from these journals. <u>The chance of a ticket
for food or clothing may occasionally have increased the missionary's
hearers. It did not increase his converts.</u> In fact Derrington is indignant
that their neighbours should accuse a poor family of attending chapel
for charity.

There is a family that I have induced to attend the chapel and
there is one of the neighbours, more bold than the others (and one
that I have been the means of helping on in reading and cyphering)
who dares to call after them 'Ah, if I was ready I would go and
get half a crown.' I never gave this family but one shilling and that
while the wife was ill and the man had long been out of work.[31]

[28] *Ibid* 65, journal of E. Derrington 15 December 1841.
[29] *Ibid* 63, 21 September 1840.   [30] *Ibid* 62, 27 September 1838.
[31] *Ibid* 61, 27 July 1838.

Whether the missionary discovered it or not the neighbours could be relied on to expose hypocrisy with brutal directness.

William Jackson's failure to attract working class followers was not surprising when we learn how he dealt with his own adherents.

> I had been informed that a father and mother who had formerly lived in Allison Street and attended the preaching room were now mourning over a departed infant. I went to visit them . . . to render them spiritual benefit. I reminded the father of the painful affliction from which he had sometime before been raised up. . . . I reminded both parents that former impressions and resolutions had evidently been forgotten and disregarded, but nevertheless God in his mercy had spared them and visited them with another warning . . . by taking their infant to Himself, I also faithfully reminded them that God's gracious dealings in the event of continued rebellion might be turned into manifestations of wrath . . . My fidelity was received in silence by these poor wanderers from the paths of peace.[32]

Derrington, however, despite his more sympathetic approach did not see the relevance of novel methods of evangelism in capturing the popular imagination. He regularly supplied the pulpit at Brierley Hill where his sermons and appeals for conversion produced no response. But he noted the activities of the local primitive methodists who disturbed him 'at half past six-o-clock, sabbath morning, singing and praying. After breakfast they marched their children through the streets and so they brought the people together and so managed to keep a crowded place during the day'.[33] Their disturbance of the 'sanctity of the sabbath' impressed him more than the effectiveness of their missionary methods. In Birmingham itself he actually preached for the primitives whose cause was disastrously weak[34] and who do not seem to have followed the advice of Hugh Bourne about open air evangelism.[35] The statistical contrast between the success of methodism in all its varieties in several black country townships and its relative failure in Birmingham is indeed striking.[36] Even the Wesleyans could

---

[32] *Ibid* 67, journal of W. Jackson 26 July 1843.

[33] *Ibid* 63, journal of E. Derrington 18 July 1838; 64, 13 June 1841.

[34] *Ibid* 61, 11 February 1838.

[35] P[rimitive] M[ethodist] M[agazine] (London 1835) p 72 (journal of Hugh Bourne 24 November 1834).

[36] G. Robson, 'Methodists and the 1851 census of religious worship in Birmingham and the Black Country' *Bulletin of the Wesley Historical Society*, West Midlands Branch (Birmingham) 2, nos 10, 11 (1975).

command massive working class support in some areas. One factor was certainly the employment of intensive methods of mass evangelism which could have a profound effect on a compact industrial village.[37] Some awareness of the need for popular emotional involvement in religion is revealed in the journal of Henry Clay, employed by Carrs Lane from 1837 to 1840, who constantly re-iterates 'there wants a little more excitement among the people, without this we shall not see the desire of our hearts for the salvation of the ungodly.'[38]

It was not merely lack of excitement which led the poor to reject the missionaries' appeal. Their rigid sabbatarianism and insistence on the reality of hellfire for the ungodly offended a public not scrupulous about legalistic interpretations of scripture and optimistic about the next life whatever their situation in this one. Suffering, in fact, was seen as expiatory and a guarantee of a better life hereafter.[39] The sheer struggle to carry on any sort of existence was recognised by all the missionaries as deadening the mind to higher things. While to some it seemed as though politics had taken over from religion in the minds of the working man.

> I was somewhat shocked in this case to discover the influence which political subjects had over the mind of an individual given up by medical advisers in the immediate prospect of death.
>
> After conversing with him in the most solemn manner on the subject of faith and repentence he said, without anything to lead to such an observation, 'Do you think the present ministers will go out?' On my wishing to evade the subject he said he had been a Reformer and really did not think a Tory could be saved and evidently comforted himself with the hope that it would fare better with him in another world because he had always voted against the abuses of government and church rates.[40]

The Birmingham town mission was undoubtedly seen by chartist sympathisers as part of an establishment plot to subdue the working class. The suspicion was mutual though it did not prevent one chartist sending an illiterate warning to an anglican clergyman of a plot against the churches.[41] Birmingham chartism is revealed in the spies' reports as a political movement with a markedly religious tone. Throughout 1839 and 1840 meetings of chartists with hymns and sermons, though

[37] Compare PMM (1840) pp 226–8 (Salvation meetings in Dudley circuit 1839).
[38] BRL MS Carrs Lane deposit 72, journal of H. Clay 11 December 1838.
[39] *Ibid* 61, journal of E. Derrington 10 October 1838.
[40] *Ibid* 71, journal of P. Sibree 8 April 1839.
[41] PRO Home Office papers H040/50.

with fewer attenders, took place on Sunday evenings in Allison Street alongside the mission room of Carrs Lane. Their attitude to each other's motives is revealed in the following quotations. First from Henry Clay, '27th November 1839. Made fifteen visits in New Canal Street. Came into contact with a Socialist and Chartist. The object of the chartists is to have the majority of the House of Commons composed of working men and that of the socialists to destroy the Christian religion. These two parties are combined. There is a most determined spirit infused into their mind. My opinion is there will be much secret plunder'.[42] In June 1839 the annual meeting of the town mission became the scene of a chartist demonstration. An editorial rebuke in the *Birmingham Journal* provoked in reply a more spirited appeal to working class solidarity than anything the town mission could produce.

The chartists, like other friends of freedom, regard priestcraft as a hostile power; they know very well that our saints are not the men who can face the foes of the people and that every man who is changed into a wretched looking, meek and sanctified quietist, content to bear his cross, in hopes of paradise in the clouds, in addition to being made a poor, unhealthy, miserable and degraded being, is totally lost to the cause of patriotism, altogether unsuited to aid in either moral or physical struggle for the rights of the people . . . the meeting, which proved so offensive to you Mr. Editor, assembled and the people saw before them in the phalanx of 'pious ministers' their deadliest political foes; there was the soldier of the *Church militant*, the advocate of the church rate imposition, the resolute opponent to the education of the people. Then there was the Tory-Methodist, the rival of the church in hostility to enlightenment, and the subtle Whig-Calvinist, more fearful because of his crafty, deceptive and treacherous pretensions to liberalism. All these parties are intolerants, are the known advocates of the 'bitter observance views' and would doubtless force the people to attend their places of worship by law; and their objects were to collect funds and send these booby-missionaries about the town, or maintain that other most pestiferous and annoying nuisance, the delivery of tracts at the houses of the poor. The rich man is not molested in this way . . .[43]

Westhill College
Birmingham

[42] BRL MS Carrs Lane deposit 72, journal of H. Clay 27 November 1839.
[43] BJ 29 June 1839.

THE RELIGIOUS REVIVAL OF 1857-8 IN THE UNITED STATES

by RICHARD CARWARDINE

I N August 1858 an American minister described the current revival in that country as a 'Fourth Great Awakening' to be likened to pentecost, the sixteenth-century reformation and the eighteenth-century awakening in colonial America.[1] His historical judgment was weak, but his euphoria typified the mood of American evangelicals after a year of mass conversions. Particularly through denominational 'protracted meetings' and inter-denominational or 'union' prayer meetings, all the protestant churches throughout the country shared in the excitement. Even many of the more cautious episcopalians, unitarians and universalists showed sympathy for a wave of revivals which seemed remarkably well-ordered and free of the 'enthusiasm' and 'human machinery' of earlier 'ingatherings'.[2] By the end of *annus mirabilis* each of the evangelical denominations could report huge accessions: of the largest bodies, the presbyterians (old and new schools) added almost thirty thousand members by examination, the major baptist churches baptised almost one hundred thousand new members, while the two main branches of methodism reported a staggering net increase of nearly one hundred and eighty thousand, a growth of sixteen per cent over the previous year.[3] What had moved

---

[1] There is no definitive study of the revival of 1857–8. The most helpful treatment is provided by [Timothy L.] Smith, [*Revivalism and Social Reform: American Protestantism on the Eve of the Civil War*] (New York 1965) pp 63–79. William G. McLoughlin, Jr, *Modern Revivalism: Charles Grandison Finney to Billy Graham* (New York 1959) pp 163–4 is too dismissive. See also Russell E. Francis, 'Pentecost: 1858. A Study in Religious Revivalism', unpublished PhD thesis (University of Pennsylvania 1948) and [Carl L.] Spicer, ['The Great Awakening of 1857 and 1858'], unpublished PhD thesis (Ohio State University 1935).

[2] Charles P. McIlvaine, *Bishop McIlvaine's Address to the Convention of the Diocese of Ohio on the Revival of Religion* (Cincinnati 1858); Frederic D. Huntingdon, *Permanent Realities of Religion and the Present Religious Interest* (Boston 1858); [Adoniram J.] Patterson, [*A Discourse on the Revival* . . .] (Portsmouth, New Hampshire 1858).

[3] Herman C. Weber, *Presbyterian Statistics through One Hundred Years 1826–1926* (The General Council, Presbyterian Church in the U.S.A. 1927) pp 18, 44; J. Edwin Orr, *The Second Evangelical Awakening in Britain* (London 1949) p 36; [*Minutes of the Annual Conferences of the*] M[ethodist] E[piscopal] C[hurch] (1858) ; P. A. Peterson, *Handbook of Southern Methodism* (Richmond, Virginia 1883) p 115.

Americans to flock to revival meetings and 'get religion' in these numbers?

By the 1850s a pattern of evangelical church growth through periodic country-wide revivals was well established in the United States. On several occasions in the first half of the century a gathering momentum of conversions and special revival services had produced peaks of religious excitement—most recently in 1832-3 and, as the climax of the so-called 'Second Great Awakening', in 1843-4.[4] After the moderate growth of the late 1840s and early 1850s the evangelical community considered another revival to be in some sense 'due'. The demand of a New York minister in the autumn of 1856 for 'a revival . . . deeper and more powerful than we have seen for years' was echoed in other parts of the country throughout the ensuing winter by those anxious that 1857 should be 'marked in the history of the church as the great revival year.'[5]

When that 'great revival' eventually developed in the following autumn, its converts were drawn very largely from a group that had become the most likely and dependable source of new members— young persons belonging to the denominational Sunday schools, often children of church members. Since the 1820s, as recruitment from the wider society had become more difficult, the evangelical churches had come increasingly to view Sunday schools, whose 'grand object' was not secular education but 'the salvation of the soul', as the 'nurseries' where '[o]ur revivals begin'.[6] It seemed crucial that during America's 'national adolescence' (one minister noted that in 1850 over half the white population was under twenty years old) evangelicals should use the Sunday schools 'to Christianize America in the bud'.[7] By 1857 there were over eleven thousand such schools in the United States; from their ranks had come in recent years four out of every five methodist converts, and—in parts of New England—five out of every six new members of congregational churches.[8] This general pattern

---

[4] Charles C. Goss, *Statistical History of the First Century of American Methodism* (New York 1866) p 110; Samuel W. Dike, 'A Study of New England Revivals', *The American Journal of Sociology* 15 no 3 (Chicago 1909) pp 361–78.

[5] C[hristian] A[dvocate and] J[ournal] (New York) 2 October 1856; S[outhern] C[hristian] A[dvocate] (Charleston, South Carolina) 8 January 1857.

[6] *CAJ* 19 June, 30 October 1856, 19 November 1857; *SCA* 14 May 1857.

[7] *CAJ* 15 January 1857; [James W.] Alexander, [*The American Sunday School and Its Adjuncts*] (Philadelphia 1856) pp 70, 327.

[8] Spicer, p 57; *CAJ* 30 October 1856; N[ew] Y[ork] O[bserver] 11 September 1856; Addie G. Wardle, *History of the Sunday School Movement in the Methodist Episcopal Church* (New York 1918) p 89.

The American religious revival of 1857-8

persisted into the revival year of 1857–8, when all denominations shared the experience of the old school presbyterian church, in which 'the great body of [converts are] from the ranks of the young, from the Sabbath school and the Bible class'.[9]

The evidence of this revival thus conforms closely to Laqueur's findings for British Sunday schools in the late eighteenth and early nineteenth centuries, and Argyle's summary of twentieth-century data: conversion was most expected during the middle and late teens, 'a period of intense inner turmoil'.[10] David O. Mears of Massachusetts was just one fourteen-year-old who felt a powerful sense of 'duty to take a decided stand upon the subject of religion.'[11] His decision, and those of many others, owed much to the influence of church-going parents who had presented their infants for baptism and had brought them up 'in conformity to the word of God', impressing on them their responsibility ultimately to 'be saved from their sins'. During adolescence, a time of growing guilt over inadequate Christian commitment and developing fear of 'the wrath to come', pressures from within the family and Sunday schools intensified until 'many a glad parent was seen embracing his converted children [and] brothers and sisters were rejoicing over each other'.[12] This search for salvation grew not only out of a sense of religious duty, however; occasionally it represented a recognition of secular responsibility. Young persons had been taught to see their conversion as a patriotic step towards becoming good evangelical citizens who would help 'get the start of error, infidelity, Socialism, anti-marriage, anti-property, anti-legal fanaticism, anti-Sabbath and anti-Christ'; one of the Sunday school's foremost tasks was to produce the nation's 'future statesmen and patriots'.[13]

The revival of 1857–8 drew on more than dutiful American youths. Sunday schools were central to the life of churches across the country, yet revival converts were drawn disproportionately from urban areas and from the northern states: methodist growth during the revival year in Boston, New York city, and Cincinnati, for example, ranged

[9] *NYO* 3 June 1858. There were extensive revivals in schools and colleges in 1857–8. See, for example, *CAJ* 26 November 1857, 8 and 15 April 1858, 17 February 1859.

[10] Thomas W. Laqueur, *Religion and Respectability: Sunday Schools and Working Class Culture 1780–1850* (London 1976) pp 166–7; Michael Argyle, *Religious Behaviour* (London 1958) pp 59–65.

[11] David O. Mears, *An Autobiography 1842–1893* (Boston 1920) pp 12–14.

[12] *CAJ* 5 June 1856; *SCA* 24 September, 10 December 1857. For parental opposition to Sunday school conversions, see John A. Roche, *The Life of Mrs. Sarah A. Lankford Palmer* . . . (New York 1898) pp 50–3.

[13] *CAJ* 17 January 1856; Alexander, p 327.

from twenty-two to twenty-six per cent at a time when overall denominational growth in the north was nearer to sixteen per cent and stood at about seven per cent in the south.[14] Moreover, report after report from individual churches told of a revival beginning—as at Morrisville, Pennsylvania—'with married persons and heads of families'; at Bridgeton, New Jersey, the minister reported that 'the proportion of adults has been very unusually large'; of the one hundred and seventy seven who joined the methodist church in Steubenville, Ohio, all but half a dozen were adults.[15] Very often, too, 'the majority of the converts [were] males'. This was the case at Burlington, New Jersey, for example, and in the New York city region generally.[16] Frequently these converts were 'persons of great influence in the community': in the Bridgeton revival just noted many of the two and a half thousand converts in the district were 'highly respected . . . for established moral character and great social worth.'[17]

The revival was thus eccentric in both geography and much of its recruitment. Earlier nineteenth-century revivals had generally looked to rural areas and small towns for their momentum; they had drawn their converts disproportionately from the ranks of the female population. The shift in emphasis is best explained as a product of the shattering financial panic of September 1857 and the gruelling economic depression of the ensuing winter. The south and the rural north escaped the worst of the poverty, unemployment and social strain of those months: it was urban America, particularly the financial centres of the north-east, that was most seriously affected. And it was here that the most novel and distinctive feature of the revival, the special inter-denominational midday prayer meetings for businessmen, germinated and took firmest root. From October 1857 merchants and their clerks from the financial district of New York crowded into brief daily meetings in Fulton Street; by the following spring similar male-dominated services in other parts of New York, and in the downtown areas of Baltimore, Boston, Chicago, Philadelphia and other cities were attracting variegated audiences that included 'leading capitalists, prominent lawyers and judges, eminent physicians, merchants, bankers, mechanics [and] tradesmen'.[18]

[14] *MEC* (1857, 1858).
[15] *CAJ* 11 and 25 March, 22 April 1858.
[16] *Ibid* 11 February, 4 March 1858.
[17] *Ibid* 14 January, 25 March 1858.
[18] *NYO* 27 May 1858.

The American religious revival of 1857-8

Earlier religious revivals in America had not necessarily depended on economic recession for their occurrence, but there is little doubt that the mass conversions of the winter of 1857-8 owed much to the sudden jolt out of prosperity; indeed, contemporaries themselves were convinced of '[t]he connection between the prostration of business and the revival of religion'.[19] But why, in the words of a Maine Calvinist minister, should 'the depressed state of business [have] proved a most favourable circumstance'?[20] For some, the answer was that business stagnation gave men more 'time to reflect'; or, as a more jaundiced observer put it—'religious demonstrations are only made when business is so flat that nobody can find anything to do.'[21] But this hardly goes to the heart of the matter. More fundamentally, we need to ask: what was the psychological motivation that drew Americans in hard times into the evangelical churches? The answer is at least threefold.

First, evangelical churchmen were able to capitalise on a prevalent feeling of guilt within the business community for its 'departure from God'.[22] With increasing urgency during the previous decade ministers had pressed on American businessmen their duty to deal honestly with their customers and employees, and to make, at a time of burgeoning national prosperity, socially responsible use of their wealth. A flood of publications in 1856 and 1857 encouraged Christian stewardship and methodical giving to charitable organisations (particularly through the newly-established American systematic beneficence society), denounced the ostentatious American pursuit of the 'almighty dollar', and warned that 'upstart prosperity, . . . walk[ing] on stilts, . . . in due time will stumble.'[23] While accepting that there were discoverable economic causes for the financial collapse, most men recognised that in September 1857 God had intervened directly in human affairs: 'In the very heart of a land abounding with elements of wealth, he lays his hand upon it,

[19] *Ibid* 1 April 1858; *O[berlin] E[vangelist]* (Oberlin, Ohio) 24 March 1858; Heman Humphrey, *Revival Sketches and Manual* (New York 1859) pp 278-9.
[20] *NYO* 25 March 1858.
[21] *Ibid* 1 July 1858; *CAJ* 18 March 1858, 28 July 1859.
[22] Francis Wayland and H. L. Wayland, *A Memoir of the Life and Labors of Francis Wayland, D.D., LL.D.,* 2 vols (New York 1867) 2 p 213.
[23] [James W. Alexander and others, *The] Man of Business [Considered in his Various Relations]* (New York 1857); Henry C. Fish, *Primitive Piety Revived* . . . (Boston 1855), especially pp 34-64; William Arthur, *The Duty of Giving Away a Stated Proportion of our Income* (Philadelphia 1857); William Arthur, *The Successful Merchant* (London 1852), which went into numerous American editions in the 1850s; *Gold and the Gospel* (New York 1855).

and locks it up for a season.'[24] The 'paralysis' was God's punishment for moral disease, for 'violated laws, and forgotten precepts of social and individual morality', for the adulteration of goods and the deceptions of advertising, for 'artifice' and 'tricks of the trade' in selling, and for Sabbath-breaking in the course of business. Racked with guilt over these sins and over their 'wicked speculation' and *'monomaniacal haste to get rich'*, men who had lost all or part of their wealth rushed to find forgiveness.[25] The 'hardware manufacturer' who confessed at the Fulton Street meeting to overcharging his retailers exemplified those who accepted their responsibility for the economic collapse.[26]

Secondly, a number attended revival services as a means of finding what the universalist Adoniram Patterson described as 'strength and consolation'.[27] The noon prayer meetings offered considerable comfort to one New York businessman, representative of many others, who unequivocally claimed:

> Prayer was never so great a blessing to me as it is in this time! I should certainly either break down or turn rascal, except for it! When one sees his property taken from him every day, by those who might pay him if they were willing to make sacrifices in order to do it, but who will not make the least effort, even for this end, and by some who seem designedly to take advantage of the times, in order to defraud him—and when he himself is liable to the keenest reproaches from others if he does not pay money, which he cannot collect and cannot create—the temptation is tremendous to forget Christian Charity, and be as hard and unmerciful as anybody. If I could not get some half hours every day to pray myself into a right state of mind, I should certainly either be overburdened or disheartened, or do such things as no Christian man ought.[28]

Thirdly, evangelical religion offered hope. An omnipotent God had intervened to punish American wickedness; surely, then, he would intervene to restore prosperity if Americans supplemented the standard recipes for economic recovery—contraction of the credit system,

[24] *NYO* 29 October, 24 December 1857.
[25] *Ibid* 19 March, 24 December 1857; *CAJ* 2 July, 15 October, 12 November 1857; James W. Alexander, 'The Merchant's Clerk Cheered and Counselled', p 20, in *Man of Business*; *SCA* 24 December 1857.
[26] *NYO* 29 July 1858.
[27] Patterson p 8.
[28] [William C.] Conant, [*Narratives of Remarkable Conversions and Revival Incidents . . .*] (New York 1858) p 357.

restraints on the expansion of banks, and so on—with a return to the paths of righteousness?[29] George Peck, methodist minister at the 'small and greatly depressed station' of Scranton, Pennsylvania, where unemployment and poverty had crippled the community, injected a sense of purpose and hope through special services that directed attention 'to the one infallible source of help in the time of need.' Significantly, most of the forty who had 'professed faith' by late January were 'heads of families in the prime of life', men and women desperate to fulfil the needs of their hungry dependents.[30] Similar hope was nourished in Henry Ward Beecher's regular services in Plymouth church, Brooklyn: in emotional prayer meetings businessmen who had lost heavily in the crash 'sobbed and laughed and told their dreams.'[31]

Broadly speaking, then, the revival of 1857–8 drew its recruits from two quite separate groups which manifested two quite different sorts of motivation: children and adolescents who sought salvation to fulfil their secular and religious duty; and adults, very often men, who turned in their anxiety and muted hope to religion at a time of financial crisis. Additionally, if less obviously, some evangelical Americans hoped to fulfil two further objectives: the inauguration of an era of harmony in the churches and in society at large; and the creation of a perfect protestant republic freed from the taint of catholicism, socialism and infidelity.

1856 and 1857 had been years of occasionally bitter dispute within and between churches. The three great ecclesiastical separations of the 1830s and 1840s, when presbyterians, methodists and baptists suffered schisms that grew largely out of north–south sectionalism, had not ended the wrangling over the churches' relationship with slavery. In the summer of 1857, after the new school presbyterian general assembly had declared slavery a sin in the sight of God, the southern presbyteries of the church withdrew.[32] The two branches of the methodist episcopal church, one advocating slavery's moral and permanent propriety and the desirability of its extension, the other firmly convinced of its immorality, came to sometimes physical blows in the border states, where their jurisdiction overlapped—particularly in the Virginia and Baltimore conferences and in Missouri, where northern methodists

[29] *CAJ* 15 October 1857; *SCA* 15 October, 5 November 1857.
[30] *CAJ* 21 January 1858.
[31] Spicer pp 102–3.
[32] *NYO* 11 June 1857.

were tarred and feathered by sympathisers of the southern church.[33]
More damaging was the division within the northern branch between
the 'ultra abolition party', whose leading lights included Hiram Mattison
and William Hosmer of upstate New York, together with the more
temperate Daniel Wise of New England, and the larger party of
moderates, led by the bishops, who put revivals and soul-saving before
antislavery agitation. The major question of dispute was: should
slaveholders be allowed to continue as members in good standing
within the church? At the general conference at Indianapolis in 1856
the ultras failed in their bid to exclude the several thousand slave-
holding members in the border states—but only after a protracted and
acrimonious debate that persisted into the following year.[34] Similar
battles between firm abolitionists and more conservative evangelicals
marked other northern denominations and the major benevolent
organisations, the American home missionary society, the American
bible society and the American tract society.[35]

In this context non-abolitionist evangelicals in the north came to
regard the preserving of church unity as one of their major tasks. The
methodist editor, Abel Stevens, gave expression to their determination
to avoid the slavery issue when he wrote: 'The Church needs peace in
all her borders; the sigh is heard and the prayer goes up for . . . an
evangelical peace . . . . Let us then . . . turn universally to our great
ostensible work—the evangelization of the land and of the world.'[36]
For these men the revival of 1857–8 represented a substantial victory.
In cultivating and sustaining it they had inaugurated a brief period of
church harmony. Old school presbyterians in the summer of 1858
reflected on 'a year marked by unusual peace, concord, unanimity,
co-operation, and brotherly kindness among our churches', the Dutch
reformed church told of 'divisions . . . healed', congregationalists of
'disturbing influences . . . greatly lessened', and not even the Rochester
antislavery convention of northern methodists in December 1857 could
shake the growing and 'gratifying tone of conservative good sense and

[33] *CAJ* 10 July, 7 and 21 August, 6 November 1856, 22 January, 10 September 1857.
[34] Arthur E. Jones, Jr, 'The Years of Disagreement 1844–61' in *The History of American Methodism*, ed Emory S. Bucke and others, 3 vols (Nashville, Tennessee 1964) 2 pp 196–9; *CAJ* 5, 12 and 19 June, 7 August, 9 October, 25 December 1856, 22 January, 5 February, 30 July 1857.
[35] *NYO* 12 and 19 March, 2, 9 and 30 April, 21 May, 11 June, 2 July 1857; *CAJ* 11 June, 3 December 1857; Clifford S. Griffin, 'The Abolitionists and the Benevolent Societies, 1831–1861', *Journal of Negro History* 44 no 3 (Washington, D.C., 1959) pp 195–216.
[36] *CAJ* 26 June 1856.

good temper' in that denomination.[37] Equally significant, much greater inter-denominational co-operation prevailed than in any previous revival. Union meetings became the order of the day, some held in churches under denominational or YMCA auspices, others in theatres, music halls or huge mobile 'union tabernacles' associated with no single denomination. The extent of union varied from place to place— the revival in Boston, for example, developed primarily within the individual churches—but everywhere the general absence of sectarian argument occasioned remark.[38]

At the same time many saw the revival as a means of soothing tensions in society at large. During 1856 and 1857 sectional bitterness reached a new pitch over the violence in 'Bleeding Kansas', the Sumner–Brooks affair in congress and the Dred Scott decision. Even northern evangelicals of a cautious temperament generally questioned the southern position on slavery, maintained the benefits of free labour, and advocated colonisation or compensated emancipation as a means of ending the peculiar institution. They upheld the duty of all citizens to fulfil their political duty and vote according to their conscience; indeed Formisano has argued that in Michigan during the 1850s the whig and republican parties, the political agencies of antislavery, relied heavily on evangelical protestantism.[39] Nevertheless, most evangelicals were anxious to curb sectionalism, 'to inculcate reverence for authority', and preserve the union from a threatened conflict and even civil war stimulated by southern disunionists and the 'idio-sin-crazi-ness' of northern 'fanatics'.[40] Only through religion would harmony come. As one Baltimore methodist argued, 'the perpetuity of the country depend[s] upon a higher power than the mere politician looked to as a security against threatened evils. Righteousness alone exalts and saves a nation.'[41]

At the time that he spoke, in October 1856, the immediate prospects for a revival were poor. The country was in an 'almost continual uproar' from 'the sirocco of political excitement' of the presidential election campaign: a Philadelphian complained that ' "Buchanan", "Fremont", "Fillmore", "Kansas", "Buck and Breck", "Hurrah!",

[37] *Ibid* 7 January, 4 February 1858; *NYO* 3 and 24 June, 1 July, 5 August 1858; *SCA* 13 May 1858.
[38] Spicer pp 87–9, 132, 210–11; *OE* 17 March 1858.
[39] *CAJ* 30 October 1856; Ronald P. Formisano, *The Birth of Mass Political Parties: Michigan, 1827–1861* (Princeton, New Jersey 1971).
[40] *CAJ* 9 October 1856, 2 April 1857; *NYO* 31 January, 13 November 1856, 2 July 1857.
[41] *CAJ* 30 October 1856.

"Yankee Doodle", etc., etc., are to be heard at nearly every corner'.[42] Further, the intensity and moral fervour of the campaign made conventional religious practice less than relevant. Men carried their religion into politics. According to one view 'the present political contest is a religious movement, a revival of religion, "a great awakening" to be classed among the moral reformations of the world'; certainly the national convention of the republican party that preceded the election 'had assumed the character of a great revival meeting, filled with camp-meeting fervor and a crusading enthusiasm'.[43]

Evangelicals, who were in consequence quite unsurprised by the absence of any general revival movement in the winter of 1856–7, found two sources of comfort. First, they could point to a number of local revivals in individual churches suggestive of better times to come. The methodist minister in Burlington, Connecticut, for example, explained that attending political meetings had 'got the inhabitants in the habit of being "out at nights" and was seized upon . . . as an argument for holding religious meetings' to which oxteams and sleds brought penitents through storm and snow.[44] More importantly, evangelicals were well used to regular political distractions, and had come to appreciate the concept of oscillation between political and religious excitement. In both spheres periods of activity were followed by periods of lull. As the excitement of the election winter declined, ministers and laymen were confident that religious activity would increase.[45]

The revival of 1857–8 was thus related to the evangelical drive 'to harmonise sectional differences',[46] and to the relative cooling of the political temperature during that year. 'The revival is the great event of the times', exulted one presbyterian minister. 'Kansas, Cuba, or even the Russian War . . . fade in comparative importance.'[47] The radical abolitionist and disunionist, William Lloyd Garrison, was well aware of the diversionary aspect of the revival, labelling it an 'emotional contagion' which turned attention from reform and 'practical righteousness' into 'a pharisaical piety and sectarian narrow-

[42] *Ibid* 2 and 16 October 1856.
[43] *NYO* 30 October 1856; [Russell E.] Francis, ['The Religious Revival of 1858 in] Philadelphia', *Pennsylvania Magazine of History and Biography* 70 no 1 (Philadelphia 1946) p 57.
[44] *CAJ* 5 February 1857.
[45] *Ibid* 6 and 13 November, 11 December 1856, 5 February 1857, 20 December 1860; *SCA* 23 October 1856.
[46] Philadelphia *Press* 6 March 1858, quoted in Francis, 'Philadelphia', p 64.
[47] *NYO* 6 May 1858.

ness'.[48] The slavery issue did not go away, of course; but even in Kansas, where the storm over the Lecompton constitution raged during the early part of 1858, some methodist preachers reported 'a great work'.[49] Elsewhere, to maintain the harmony that generally prevailed, posters carried the injunction 'no controverted points discussed'; others carefully avoided singling out politicians for special mention for fear of giving offence.[50] Some politicians, in fact, recognising the soothing effects of the revival, came to its support; president Buchanan himself became a daily attender of the meetings at Bedford Springs, Pennsylvania, and took 'a deep and solemn interest in knowing all that he could of the progress of the great revival.'[51] Most significantly, it was the northern business community, particularly of New York, economically tied to the south and aware that it had much to lose from disunion and civil war, that rallied most enthusiastically to a movement that offered hope of sectional peace.

Southern evangelicals, too, sought to preserve the union through the spread of 'conservative christian influence'; for example, various members of the methodist episcopal church south proposed a less sectional name and urged an aggressive campaign that would check the 'tide of Freeloveism, Fannywrightism and Abolitionism' and would recruit anti-abolitionist converts as far north as Boston.[52] But there was a further stimulus to the south's pursuit of revival, deriving from her growing sense of isolation and embattlement over the slavery issue. When northerners claimed that southern religion was 'severed from morality' and British churches in 'pious horror' refused to receive her preachers on a formal basis, she defiantly pursued a revival to vindicate an institution she considered compatible with 'right and the Bible'.[53] During the winter, when the revival gathered pace in the north, there was little sign of a similar movement in the southern states; indeed such opponents of slavery as Charles Finney believed that '[t]he people there were in such a state of . . . vexation, and of committal to their peculiar institution . . . that the Spirit of God seemed to be grieved away from them.'[54] What such observers ignored was that

---

[48] William L. Van Deburg, 'William Lloyd Garrison and the "Pro-Slavery Priesthood": The Changing Beliefs of an Evangelical Reformer, 1830–1840', *Journal of the American Academy of Religion* 43 (Tallahassee 1975) p 235n.

[49] *CAJ* 4 February 1858.

[50] Spicer, appendix B; *NYO* 15 April 1858.

[51] *NYO* 26 August 1858.

[52] *SCA* 21 May, 3 September, 8 October 1857.

[53] *Ibid* 15 January, 27 August, 10 September 1857.

[54] Charles G. Finney, *Memoirs* (New York 1876) p 444.

in the south winter was not, as in their own section, the season of revivals: meeting houses were not equipped to deal with the colder weather, while the methodist convention of changing preachers' stations during these months worked against successful protracted services. But from March 1858 onwards southern churches threw themselves urgently into the task of copying northern successes and cultivating their missions to the blacks, so that they could point to divine blessing on their social institutions and say: 'God prospers us as a church.'[55]

Finally, many Americans turned to the revival as a means of achieving a better, perhaps even perfect society. The optimistic millennialism of the 1820s and 1830s, if now more muted, had not been entirely undermined by the second adventist disappointments of the 1840s. There was no shortage of evangelicals who saw in the gathering religious excitement a means of combating the 'corruption' and crime of growing city populations and the 'infidelity' of the 'Socialism, Owenism, Fourierism, Abolitionism, and all the various *isms* and schemes for the reform of the great evils of society' that ignored the need for individual regeneration.[56] Most heartening of all, the revival would challenge Roman catholicism, much strengthened in the 1840s and 1850s by waves of Irish and German immigrants, and by the domestic missions of such groups as the redemptorists. To protestant eyes these missions—held not just in New York, Cincinnati, Baltimore and Pittsburgh, but also in the deep south—were sinister and dangerously competitive imitations of evangelical protracted meetings.[57] They spread a code of beliefs and practices which was held in New York, for example, to be 'mostly responsible for the moral degradation and the criminal and pauper expense of our city; [Roman catholics] fill our prisons and almshouses, eat up the resources of our voluntary charities, and crowd our doorsteps with their beggaries.'[58] Popery unchecked would undermine the fundamental American values of individualism, republicanism and enlightenment. Through its 'music, and candles, and pictures, and romantic humbuggery', through its 'priestcraft' and its enslavement of women in convents by 'priestly ghouls', it encouraged unthinking emotion, 'superstition', dependence, conspiracy and 'despotism'.[59]

[55] *SCA* 10 September 1857.
[56] *NYO* 10 January 1856.
[57] 'Protestant Revivals and Catholic Retreats', *Brownson's Quarterly Review* 15 (New York 1858) pp 289–322.
[58] *CAJ* 8 January, 27 August 1857, 4 February 1858.

The American religious revival of 1857–8

Protestants saw the revival that began in 1857 as an excellent opportunity to prove that 'Popery, except in the stagnant populations of southern Europe, is a thing of the past [and] is out of place amid the new ideas and aims of the new world.'[60] It was no accident that the first major religious movement since the great influx of Irish catholics should be marked by unprecedented protestant co-operation; nor that during the revival a methodist deputation from Ireland (*'the pope's nursery for English-speaking priests'*) should return home after two years' work with seventy thousand dollars to 'unseat the hoary despotism of the Italian priest in the Celtic mind.'[61] Proportionately the number of converts from the catholic community was small,[62] but evangelicals achieved enough for many to believe that the death of popery was not far distant.

Elsewhere, too, there seemed to be abundant signs of the moral transformation of society. The penitent owners of gambling saloons made them available for daily prayer meetings; southern grocery keepers rolled out their barrels, poured their contents on the ground, and 'abandoned the traffic in ardent spirits'; the chief of police in Atlanta, Georgia, maintained that the revival had so reduced the rate of crime that he could dispense with half his force; in the fourth ward of New York city many 'haunts of sin and shame' were shut up and 'hundreds' of prostitutes allegedly 'rescued'.[63] That such reports may have been exaggerated is less significant than that they were believed. They reinforced the conviction that evangelical protestant morality, the morality of small-town and rural America, would inevitably triumph. At the same time the revival saw the broadening of the influence of perfectionism, the doctrine that regenerate men and women must aspire to a second and higher stage of Christian experience, and a doctrine which, as T. L. Smith has argued, had potent social implications: sanctified Christians had a duty to work for the perfection of society.[64] Taken together, the evidence of multiplying conversions, the influence of perfectionist teaching, and reports of fundamental improvement in social morality prompted the question: 'Why should such a work cease till the Millennial dawn?'[65]

[59] *Ibid* 3 and 31 January, 7 February 1856, 18 June 1857.
[60] *Ibid* 5 November 1857.
[61] *Ibid* 15 May 1856, 2 April 1857.
[62] See, for example, *CAJ* 14 January, 18 February, 4 March 1858; *NYO* 1 April, 23 September 1858; *SCA* 15 July 1858.
[63] *CAJ* 22 April 1858; *SCA* 17 June, 15 July, 14 October 1858; *NYO* 5 August 1858.
[64] Smith pp 154–62.   [65] *SCA* 25 March, 26 August 1858.

RICHARD CARWARDINE

The motivation of converts in the 1857-8 revival was, inevitably, complex and varied. By no means all the motives suggested here were at work in every case. Moreover, some individuals were moved, at least in the first instance, by separate considerations. Many undoubtedly were drawn to meetings out of a curiosity fed by the extraordinary enthusiasm of the secular press and by the rapid spread of information through the new national telegraph system.[66] In tightly-knit communities some went to meetings to avoid offending accepted notions of correct behaviour; in towns such as Fairfield, Connecticut, where there were reckoned to be less than a dozen who were unconverted, there were intense pressures on the conspicuous minority to attend.[67] Others were moved by a sense of apostasy: one young man who had come to New York from a neighbouring village fifteen years earlier told the Fulton Street meeting that he had betrayed his 'pious' upbringing; for him, as for so many others, the revival offered a chance to make good his 'backsliding'.[68] In Charleston, South Carolina, one stimulus to revival was an epidemic of yellow fever; in the Tampa district of Florida the defeat of the Indians in the seminole war brought the local population into the churches out of relief and gratitude; in Pennington, New Jersey, one convert attributed his religious awakening to 'the sudden death of a beloved friend', another to 'the solemn charge of a dying mother' and a third to 'being brought through wasting sickness "nigh unto death" '.[69] Yet cases of this kind do not in themselves explain the mass turning to religion in 1857 and 1858. That dramatic and extensive revival is most usefully seen as the product of the search by a primarily protestant and evangelical society for a panacea that would cure economic disaster, heal sectional conflict and carry God's chosen people one large step closer to the millennium.

University of Sheffield

[66] Smith pp 64-5.
[67] *CAJ* 1 and 15 April 1858.
[68] *NYO* 19 August 1858. See also Conant pp 376, 380.
[69] *SCA* 23 and 30 September 1858; *NYO* 11 March 1858.

'THE ONLY TRUE FRIEND': RITUALIST CONCEPTS OF PRIESTLY VOCATION

by W. N. YATES

THE title of this paper was inspired by a piece of ecclesiastical doggerel published in the *Hensal-Cum-Heck Church Monthly* for November 1895:

They may call me a Papist, and laugh at my creed,
'Tis the Faith that will save in the hour of need;
Let them talk, let them laugh, but when death is at hand
The priest is the only true friend in the land.

It is not the only ritualist concept of priestly vocation; in a somewhat earlier tract on confession priests are described as 'the spiritual police of Almighty God; they must hunt out, track, pursue, and arraign sinners, as the police pursue and apprehend thieves and rascals'.[1] Although both concepts are to be found elsewhere in ritualist literature, and both would have been accepted by many ritualist priests as not being mutually exclusive, it would seem that the concept of the priest as 'friend' was the dominant one.

It has already been made clear that very great changes took place in the social role of the Anglican clergyman during the course of the nineteenth century.[2] Equally important changes also took place in his spiritual role. Much of this was the obvious result of the gradual disappearance of the non-resident, pluralist clergyman for whom ordination had been the means to an income rather than the sealing of a vocation. The gross disparity, in financial terms, between one benefice and another, remained, of course, until well into the present century, but by the last quarter of the nineteenth century, and in many places well before this, it was clear that most clergy would have claimed a vocation to the ministry, and for most the claim would have been sincere. Many aspects of this general concept of vocation were common to clergy of all parties within the church; the strong emphasis on parochial visiting, which grew throughout the nineteenth century,

---

[1] Both quotations will be found in W. Walsh, *Secret History of the Oxford Movement* (London 1899) p 388.
[2] See especially G. S. R. Kitson Clark, *Churchmen and the Condition of England* (London 1973).

is an obvious example. Many clergy, again of all parties within the church, felt that their vocation necessitated their taking a strong line on local political and social issues. The growing popularity of work in difficult urban parishes, particularly inner-city slums, attracted evangelicals as well as 'high churchmen'. The desire to make the liturgical services of the church more meaningful to those who participated in them, and to involve the laity more fully in the work of the church, were also generally supported. Above all, clergy of all parties agreed that it was essential to bring as many people as possible to church, particularly in the towns where the provision of ecclesiastical accommodation had not generally kept pace with the growth of population. Those controversial campaigns to abolish church rates and pew rents were also supported by churchmen whose theological and liturgical opinions were very different from one another.

The supporters and disciples of the Oxford movement did, however, bring a number of their own individual ingredients into this growth of a common concept of vocation, ideas which were certainly not shared by many of their contemporaries within the church of England, and ideas which many anglicans would still find difficult to accept. One of the great problems in discussing concepts of vocation is that the historian has to rely on the problematical evidence of written opinions. Many clergy never committed their views to paper. Yet there is so much obvious common ground in what does survive that one can have a fair idea of what both more moderate tractarians and more advanced ritualists felt on many of these matters. Looking at the views expressed, there would appear to be three very important issues on which the tractarian or ritualist clergyman felt that his vocation required him to give a lead to the laity to whom he ministered. The first was in the general area of the church's liturgy, and it involved the need to offer in every way—architecturally, devotionally, musically—a more elaborate form of worship than the rather drab and tedious services which had become the accepted norm in most churches. The second issue was the nature of the church itself, and in particular the relationship of the church of England to the rest of catholic Christendom. The third, and perhaps, most interesting issue was the role of the priest as confessor and the importance of the sacrament of penance as an ecclesiastical discipline.

On the first of these issues the tractarian or ritualist clergyman would have found some common cause with clergy of a different outlook. A distinction has to be made between the period before and that after about 1860. In the earlier period architectural improvements to churches tended to be the hallmark of the 'high church' clergyman, and there was a good deal of early opposition to the work of the ecclesiologists. This opposition was fairly short-lived; the tastes of the age largely determined that aesthetic considerations should outweigh theological scruples, and evangelicals were as active as anybody else in restoring and rebuilding churches in the later Victorian period. Even the dissenters jumped on the bandwagon and built their chapels in high Gothic. The reverse was the case with anglican church services. In the earlier period evangelical and tractarian reformers made very similar suggestions for the reform of the prayer book. One can, for instance, compare the informal evening services introduced by the evangelical John Knapp at a former circus building in Portsmouth, in which a communion service with hymns and sermon alternated with an intercessory service based on the litany,[3] with the similar services introduced by 'high churchmen' like Hook and Jackson at St Peter's and St James', Leeds.[4] Evening communion was specifically encouraged on the grounds that it was popular with working people. Later 'high churchmen' discouraged it, regarding the traditional fast from midnight as more important. The rapid increase in evening communion services among evangelicals after about 1860 looks almost like a deliberate attempt to provoke ritualist outrage. The gulf could be seen elsewhere. Evangelicals concentrated on trying to do away with as much as possible of the prayer book's liturgical structure; tractarians and ritualists, to a greater or lesser degree, turned towards a vigorous effort to clothe that structure with the ceremonial of the English medieval or the modern Roman catholic mass, according to taste.

What motivated the tractarian or ritualist clergyman coming to a new parish? The first priority was usually to deal with the fabric of the church before attempting to alter its services. It was in any case likely that one would have less opposition to liturgical changes if they could be made part of the opening of a new or substantially altered building. Sometimes, however, it might not be possible to carry out one's architectural plans immediately. At Farlington, near Portsmouth, the 'high church' Edward Tew Richards was appointed to the rectory in 1826, but he ran foul of his vestry in his attempts to rebuild the church and this was not finally completed until fifty years later. Richards had,

[3] J. Knapp, *The Church in the Circus* (London 1858).
[4] [W. N.] Yates, ['Leeds and the Oxford Movement'], *Thoresby Society Publications* 55 (Leeds 1975) pp 18, 27.

nevertheless, attempted to improve the liturgy of the church despite the limitations of the building.[5] By the later nineteenth century, when restoration or rebuilding had already been undertaken, the advanced ritualist appointed to a non-ritualist parish had to implement his liturgical changes more blatantly. Most tended to introduce their ideas gradually, in the hope, frequently disappointed, that this would lead to a greater degree of acceptance. Others acted swiftly, like W. H. Baker of St Silas', Hull, who sent a list of the new services, with Sunday mattins replaced by 'Holy Sacrifice and Sermon', to his churchwardens a week before his institution, prefaced by a slight concern 'that just during this next fortnight or so the newness of some of our ways may disturb some of us a little bit'.[6] After a sustained campaign against him in the local press and a petition to the archbishop of York for his removal, the parish settled down to accept the 'new ways' and Baker remained there for forty-three years.

There was a good deal of variety in the way individual tractarian and ritualist clergymen interpreted the liturgical aspect of their vocation. Many 'high churchmen' followed the example of Leeds and Portsea in maintaining dignified but very moderate ceremonial. At Leeds under E. S. Talbot (vicar 1889–95) 'we had the surplice and black stole and nothing more. We had two lights upon the altar; and we took the eastward position'.[7] Portsea was even more moderate liturgically, despite firm tractarian teaching from the pulpit. C. G. Lang (vicar 1896–1901), afraid of public protest, even resisted his natural inclinations to light the altar candles.[8] Twenty years later his successor expressed the view that any 'further advance in the ritual . . . might not be followed by a serious reduction in the numbers who attended the services, but it would undoubtedly mean the quiet withdrawal from active work of a number of the best and most faithful of the laity, and an atmosphere of prejudice and suspicion would be created which would hinder the work of the parish for many years to come'.[9] But from 1860 the more advanced ritualists felt that their teaching could only be effective if accompanied by elaborate ceremonial. Some argued that this was particularly attractive to working class congregations but the point has never been proved. The likelihood is that working class congregations were built up more by strong preaching and devoted

[5] [*Royal Commission on*] *Ritual, First Report* (London 1867) pp 63–70, 115–19.
[6] St Silas, Hull, *Parish Paper*, July 1894.
[7] *Royal Commission on Ecclesiastical Discipline, Minutes of Evidence* (London 1906) 3, p 99.
[8] J. G. Lockhart, *Cosmo Gordon Lang* (London 1949) p 121.
[9] C. F. Garbett, *The Work of A Great Parish* (London 1915) pp 59–60.

pastoral care than by liturgical extravagance, and that liturgical extravagance had an appeal to the middle classes who frequently dominated the eclectic congregations of inner city parishes by the late nineteenth century. Liturgical extravagance included a devotion to good church music; the so-called 'cathedral service' and the revival of plainsong were the result of tractarian innovations. The later ritualists, like J. L. Fish of St Margaret Pattens[10] or Nicholas Greenwell of St Barnabas', Holbeck,[11] preferred high masses to Schubert in F with full orchestra. Like the late medieval writers of parish priests' manuals, several ritualist scholars devoted themselves to both the academic study of liturgy and, from this, the publication of practical handbooks showing their contemporaries how to inject medieval English or modern Roman catholic ceremonial into the prayer book services: the *Directorium Anglicanum*, first published in 1858, *Ritual Notes*, first published in 1894, and the *Parson's Handbook*, first published in 1899, were the most popular of many. Just as their congregations were frequently eclectic, so many early ritualists tended to be eclectic in their liturgical borrowings. George Nugée of Wymering and Widley explained to the ritual commissioners in 1867 that his own ceremonial usage in two country parishes was a mixture of the best in the pre-reformation English and modern Roman catholic traditions.[12]

It is not surprising, therefore, that Nugée was an ecumenical idealist and possibly one of the negotiators of an ill-fated scheme for corporate reunion with the Roman catholic church in 1877. But as the public furore, in which most 'high churchmen' took part, showed, he and his collaborators were in a small minority. The ritualist clergyman, labelled a Romaniser by his critics, had to consider very carefully the second issue raised by his concept of priestly vocation, the role of the church of England as a part of catholic Christendom. Most tended to take a strongly anti-Roman catholic stand and state a firm belief in the branch theory of catholic Christendom whereby the national church, if it retained the apostolic succession, as was claimed for the church of England, was the true representative of catholic orthodoxy. For them the Roman catholic church was what it was for Bruce Cornford of St Matthew's, Southsea, the 'Catholic Church of Italy' or the 'Italian Mission':

[10] G. Huelin, 'St. Margaret Pattens: A City Parish in the Nineteenth Century', *Guildhall Miscellany* 3 (London 1971) pp 277–86.
[11] Yates pp 32–4.
[12] *Ritual, First Report* pp 50–63.

Supposing our English Catholic Church were to come to the conclusion that Italians sadly needed the Gospel, and the Archbishop of Canterbury sent to Italy a number of Bishops and Priests to build churches and proclaim the Faith, suppose also that they called this development "the London Catholic Church", and named these Bishops after the chief towns in Italy. How would the Italian nation generally or particularly regard such a scheme?[13]

The implication was clear. If the church of England did not proselytise in Italy, why should the Roman catholic church proselytise in England? George Huntington of Tenby was horrified to learn that some of his parishioners had been seen attending services at a new Roman catholic chapel in the town and were known to have subscribed towards the cost of its erection.[14] Bruce Cornford claimed that 'in obedience to his Ordination Vow' he had 'attacked Heresy and Schism' by publishing six attacks on 'the Italian Mission' and twenty-one on 'Dissenters and Protestants' in a period of four years:[15]

In England the Italian Mission wears its best clothes and brightest aspect, things which we commonly see in France or Italy would not be tolerated here for a moment. There are no vulgar china spittoons on the steps of the altars at Brompton Oratory! But the system and the doctrine are the same. Alike fatal to truth, and life, and progress . . . May I say once again what I have often said before? One of the best protests against Romanism is Ritualism—not a cold dreary spiteful Protestantism.[16]

After the papal condemnation of anglican orders as null and void in 1896 there was even less anglican clerical support for rapprochement with Rome and many 'high churchmen', including advanced ritualists, would have agreed with Bruce Cornford privately, even if publicly they might have expressed their feelings rather less violently.

The third area of discussion in this paper is the tractarian and ritualist view of the role of the priest as confessor. In a way it was perhaps the element in their concept of priestly vocation which most clearly distinguished them from their evangelical contemporaries. Evangelicals and 'high churchmen' both had liturgical concerns, both had to have a view about the nature of the church, even if they came to take a different view of what their vocation demanded. The tractarian

[13] [St Matthew], Southsea, [Parish Magazine], November 1906.
[14] G. Huntington, Romish Aggression (Tenby 1893).
[15] [E. B.] Cornford, [Parish Book] (Southsea 1908) p 235.
[16] Southsea, February 1904.

and ritualist view of confession was, in many cases, a challenge to traditional anglican theology and to contemporary public opinion. Yet it was also an answer to contemporary needs. Victorian churchmen were dominated by a sense of sin which is not shared by most Christians today. The 'high church' emphasis on confession and on the penitential practices associated with it, such as the use of the discipline, the wearing of hair shirts, and other personal mortifications were a means of trying to cope with this sense of sin, just as much as the evangelical conversion experience. For the clergy it had the advantage of making them full priests in the traditional catholic sense; it was the one thing that the pre-Victorian clergyman had not attempted. Although 'high church-men' frequently quoted the prayer book passage about receiving 'the benefit of absolution' in defence of their confessional practice, there is no doubt that they were departing very substantially from the practice of the church since the reformation. Indeed the departure was not welcomed by the more moderate 'high churchmen'. Hook took the view that 'Confession was a means of comfort, not of grace. As an extreme exception it was allowed in the Church of England'.[17] He considered that it was his duty to make his penitents do without the need for confession to a priest, just as the modern psychiatrist would presumably hope that his patients could eventually manage without his services. Very many of the more advanced ritualists, however, laid great emphasis upon regular confession in this form, and there is no doubt that some practised and encouraged others to practise some form of self-mortification. The use of the discipline seems to have been fairly widespread in religious communities, and even prominent lay-men like Gladstone made use of one. It became common for ritualist clergy to hear confessions in the 1840s, and they were publicly adver-tised as being heard in some churches by the 1860s. Nicholas Greenwell at St Barnabas', Holbeck, regarded systematic confession as of the greatest use in the moral training of working-class youths, and the reception of communion without confession beforehand as com-munion on the cheap.[18] Robert Dolling also found regular confession an essential discipline in the conversion of a working-class population.[19] In an area of rather less pressing social need, Bruce Cornford of St

[17] J. H. Pollen, *Narrative of Five Years at St. Saviour's, Leeds* (Oxford 1851) pp 83–4, 89–90. There was a major confessional scandal at St Saviour's in 1850 which led to the resignation of the incumbent.
[18] Yates pp 35–6, 57–8. Greenwell himself published a pamphlet entitled *Priesthood, Confession and Absolution* (Leeds c1874).
[19] R. R. Dolling, *Ten Years in A Portsmouth Slum* (London 1896) p 142.

Matthew's, Southsea, regarded confession once a year as a reasonable minimum.[20]

This emphasis on sacramental confession provoked considerable public hostility. There was a widespread feeling that the practice was an invasion of personal privacy, was somehow un-English and possibly indelicate, particularly in the case of a young woman confessing to a man, in private. This revulsion was not assisted by the incompetence of some early confessors, who had very little idea of how to hear a confession and frequently questioned penitents about their moral lapses. An enormous furore was caused when Lord Redesdale exposed a confessional manual entitled *The Priest in Absolution* in 1877; it had been circulated widely among ritualist clergy having been privately published in two parts, in 1866 and 1872. The furore was caused precisely because it dealt with sexual issues and it was condemned as an obscene book even by the bishops. How successful ritualist clergy were in persuading their congregations to accept confession it is impossible to estimate, but their constant reiteration of the need to confess suggests that they were not getting as many penitents as they would have liked. It was not for want of trying. In this way especially they felt the priest could be the laity's 'only true friend', and assist them on the road to salvation.

The aim in this paper has been to look at the principal ways in which the tractarian or ritualist clergyman attempted to implement his concept of his priestly vocation. There were many who had specific motives that do not come within the scope of this paper. W. H. Baker of St Silas', Hull, for instance, was particularly concerned to brighten up the drab Victorian Sabbath, and brought upon himself the wrath of the Hull primitive methodist council for advising all Christians to communicate in their respective churches and to spend the rest of Sunday in various kinds of innocent recreation, such as visiting museums and art galleries, playing cricket or football, attending open-air concerts and even theatres.[21]

There is a popular view, promoted to a large extent by anglo-catholic folklorists, of the ritualist priest as a quiet saintly man, leading his people to God according to the rites and traditions of the catholic church, and persecuted by his bishop for doing so. It is a myth. There were a few priests of this type and some clergymen found themselves the victims of episcopal displeasure. Most were quite capable of coping

[20] Cornford p 97.
[21] *Hull Daily Mail*, 4 November 1897.

with it. The average ritualist clergyman tended to be a very strong-willed individual, some would say bloody-minded, who believed firmly in the rightness of his cause and was determined to see it prevail. It was the ritualists who broke the bishops, not vice-versa, though it could be argued that ritualism by eventually becoming almost respectable lost its full dynamism. Ritualism, and ritualist priests, thrived on conflict. Nevertheless in his relations with his own laity, who attended his services, who listened to his teaching and who sought his spiritual advice, the ritualist priest did, I believe, see himself as their 'only true friend' and acted accordingly. The role of 'spiritual policeman' he reserved for those who disagreed with him, and thereby seemed to challenge his priesthood.

Portsmouth

GLADSTONE, VATICANISM, AND THE QUESTION OF THE EAST[1]

by H. C. G. MATTHEW

T HAT Gladstone was religious is obvious enough, and to state it does not get us very far, but this remains as far as most historians get. The aim of this paper is to show by exposition the religious motivation behind two of the greatest Gladstonian and Victorian outbursts—the clutch of writings on the Vatican council published in 1874–5[1a] and the pamphlet and articles on the 'Bulgarian Horrors' in 1876.[2] These two expostulations, though they occurred within twenty two months of each other, are usually treated by historians as quite unrelated. Moreover, although attention has been paid to their proximate causes, they have not been placed in the complex and long-drawn out process of Gladstone's religious development. I hope to show that both groups of pamphlets, though written in passion spurred by proximate causes, reflected long standing and interrelated intellectual, theological and political interests, an understanding of which illuminates both Gladstone and his age. If this paper ranges from idealism to cabinet diplomacy, this reflects the range of influences on Gladstone who consistently and deliberately tried to place himself at the cross-roads of Victorian culture, society, religion and politics.

Rome and Constantinople; what more dramatic and, one might add, traditional subjects could be found for the man whom Pusey described in his *Eirenicon*[3] as 'a statesman and a theologian, earnest for the cause of

---

[1] I am indebted to Perry Butler and David Nicholls for their comments on an earlier draft of the first part of this paper which was read to the Newman conference in Dublin 1975.

[1a] 'Ritualism and ritual', *Contemporary Review*, October 1874; *The Vatican Decrees in their bearing on civil allegiance: a political expostulation*, [November] 1874; 'Speeches of Pope Pius IX', Q[uarterly] R[eview], January 1875; *Vaticanism: an answer to replies and reproofs*, 1875; 'Italy and her church', *Church Quarterly Review*, October 1875.

[2] *Bulgarian Horrors and the Question of the East*, [September] 1876, *A speech delivered at Blackheath . . . September 9th, 1876; together with letters, on the Question of the East*, 1876; 'Russian policy and deeds in Turkistan', *Contemporary Review*, November 1876, 'The Hellenic factor in the Eastern Problem', *Contemporary Review*, December 1876.

[3] E. B. Pusey, *An Eirenicon* (London 1865) p 260. For the *Eirenicon*, see B. and M. Pawley, *Rome and Canterbury through four centuries* (London 1974) cap eight, and H. R. T. Brandreth, *The Œcumenical ideals of the Oxford Movement* (London 1947) cap 4.

Christ and zealous for His truth and His Church'. The cause of Christ is in principle straightforward enough for those who believe themselves called to it; the difficulties come, as always, from 'His truth' and 'His Church'.

Gladstone's religious views in his early manhood must be our starting point. It used to be the case that Gladstone's literary products of the 1830s, *The State in its relations with the Church*, (1838, 4 ed 2 vols 1841) and *Church Principles considered in their results* (1840), could be seen as peripheral aberrations, inconsequential to Gladstone's development as man and politician, significant only in their short-term consequences and as regards dissenters, memorable only for stimulating Macaulay to respond. Gladstone's first book, in my view, raised important questions about the nature of the state, which need not concern us, except incidentally, here.[4] The book also refocused attention on the central feature of institutional anglicanism: its relationship to nationality, and its compatibility, or incompatibility, with a plural society. This was really the central point of Gladstone's interest in his first book, and it is through an exploration of his discussion of these themes, though not only in his first book, that I hope to illuminate the origins of his pamphlets on Vaticanism and the 'Bulgarian Horrors'.

There were, Gladstone believed, two forms of universal association, the family and the nation.[5] 'The nation is the realised "unity of the people" ';[6] the state is the institutionalised form of the nation, 'the self-governing energy of the nation made objective'.[7] Religious belief, not necessarily Christian, was a necessary defining feature, amongst others, of a nation; Mahometans were therefore to be commended because 'the Mahometan creed is distinguished among the religions of the East for its hostility to indifferentism, because it is a definite though false belief in revelation' manifested in an identifiable nation.[8] 'National life' was therefore 'curtailed of its moral fulness' in proportion as there was any diminution from 'the clear and intelligible profession of unity in faith and in communion'.[9]

But of course it was not that easy. There were few countries where

---

[4] These are discussed in my introduction to M. R. D. Foot and H. C. G. Matthew, *The Gladstone Diaries* (Oxford 1974) 3, pp xxiii *seq*.
[5] *The State*, 1 pp 73–6.
[6] *Ibid* 1 p 78, quoting Coleridge.
[7] *Ibid*.
[8] *Ibid* 1 p 126.
[9] *Ibid* 1 p 124, 1 pp 296–7. It is interesting that in his Bulgarian pamphlet Gladstone specifically disavowed an attack on Islam.

'national religion' or 'religious nationality' existed in a pure form, in
the sense that no substantial group disputed the tenets of the national
religion. Perhaps only the Iberian peninsula could be so regarded, and
Gladstone does not discuss it. It is characteristic that he does not, for
much of his interest necessarily lay, for he wrote of course as an anglican, in the dilemma posed to a nation and to its national church by the
existence of dissident groups. I will not describe here the complex
process by which Gladstone uses utilitarian arguments which he had
excoriated in his justification of an ideal nation, to justify the existing
state of affairs in the United Kingdom in the 1830s. But we may notice
two points. First, Gladstone conceded the exceptional nature of his
claim: 'I am free to admit that, on any other than specifically Christian
principles, the human understanding would probably incline to the
theory of a plurality of establishment';[10] in other words Providence
prevented the exercise of rationality. Second: Gladstone's justification
of the 1830s position was contained in an adroit move from theoretical
to practical considerations. 'Our nationality is yet entire. And in
particular, the national estate of religion embodies, in its present form,
the convictions of the numerical majority, as well as the yet greater
moral preponderance of the people'.[11] It is not therefore surprising to
find buried in this book a remark of explosive consequence for the
Victorian age: 'it is desirable to avoid attempting to tighten the bonds
of a merely secular connection whenever it has been found impracti-
cable to cement and dignify the union by a brotherhood in the
Christian faith'.[12]

In his book Gladstone had in fact prepared the way for his escape
from its arguments. The book contains a persistent ambivalence
between idealism and empiricism, an ambivalence which remained
with Gladstone throughout his life and which goes far to explain his
behaviour in the 1870s. Faced with what he saw as the failure in the
secular sphere of the great movement to moral and religious anglican
progress which he believed to have begun in the 1830s and which his
books were designed to encourage, Gladstone in the 1840s moved
regretfully[13] but dramatically away from the support of the institutional consequences of his idealism. In 1845 he had resigned from the

[10] *Ibid* 1 p 123.
[11] *Ibid* 1 p 301.
[12] *Ibid* 1 p 109.
[13] Manning later correctly noted the difference between himself and Gladstone on this
point: 'he saw his theory to be impossible, and I saw it to be false', [E. S.] Purcell,
[*Life of Cardinal Manning*] (London 1896) 2 p 491.

cabinet over the Maynooth grant, the last man on a sinking ship as he said of himself, though he was more accurately the last man to try to represent at cabinet level an unrelenting view of national religion.[14] But by 1847 he was able to support the Jewish disabilities bill, and in 1851 he was able energetically to oppose Russell's ecclesiastical titles bill in a famous speech, a classic defence of religious pluralism.[15] In 1869 he disestablished the Irish church, the most effective assault on national religion since the Hanoverian succession.

It was not easy for Gladstone to abandon the position of his formative years, and the struggle to salvage something of 'national religion' from the ruins of the experience of Peel's government involved him in moments of extreme sexual and psychological tension. However, the remedy was to hand. If 'national religion' could not be maintained entire, perhaps pluralism could be accompanied by a general movement towards that vision of a reunited apostolic Christendom which Gladstone had discussed in his second book *Church Principles* (1840),[16] in significant respects a precursor to Pusey's *Eirenicon*. For if religious nationality, in its less elevated but unavoidably plural form was to embrace separate elements of Christianity, then a clear means of re-elevation would be a movement of oecumenicalism. This raised the question of the relation of anglicanism to other churches not merely in its church-state form, but in its more general theological context.

Here we at last arrive at the direct rather than implied starting point of the origins of our two pamphlets.

'Looking on the one hand to Protestant, on the other to the Roman bodies, and to the complexion and practice of the churches of the East' is there 'any spot along the whole line at which they may more probably, or could more equitably meet, than at that very spot . . . of the Reformed English Church . . . the Church of England appears to be placed in the very centre of all the conflicting forms of Christianity.'[17] Other protestant churches presented formidable problems of the validity of orders and of fundamental questions about institutional

---

[14] I have discussed the details of Gladstone's resignation in *The Gladstone Diaries*, 3, pp xxx seq.

[15] *Hansard*, third series, 115 p 565, 25 March 1851.

[16] C[hurch] P[rinciples], cap 7.

[17] *CP* pp 506–7. This goes a good deal further than W. Palmer of Worcester's branch church theory, which saw anglicanism merely as part of an apostolic triangle; though his own interests centred on Roman and eastern relations, Gladstone maintained his position, as, for example in the case of Scandanavia and the 1867 Lambeth conference; see A. M. G. Stephenson, *The first Lambeth Conference, 1867* (London 1967) p 221.

arrangements[18]—the Roman and eastern churches much less so, and we may now examine Gladstone's attitude to each.

Gladstone made a sharp though fairly common distinction between what he regarded as the catholic attributes of the Roman catholic church, and what he called 'Romanism'.[19] Its catholic attributes were, broadly speaking, those attributes the Roman church shared with anglicanism and Orthodoxy; 'Romanism' constituted false and illegitimate accretions to catholicity. If, as Gladstone told Manning in 1850, it was possible to argue that on the question of whether 'the Church of England must be understood really to deny that the Church of Rome is a true Church', he found that the Roman catholic and anglican churches did not differ 'on essential points', including transubstantiation and penance (he did not mention purgatory), then questions of church organisation and government, and therefore of history, must be crucial.[20] After 1840, Gladstone's religious publications dealt very largely with religious history, especially the nature of the sixteenth or seventeenth century settlement. Gladstone's aim was to demonstrate that the reformation in England could not be classed as an act of 'private judgment', and that a national and constitutional decision about the form of religion differed in kind from an individual's decision to change his denomination.[21]

He noted in a memorandum of 1885 on Palmer's *Treatise on the Church of Christ*

> great numbers of those who have abandoned the Anglican for the Roman Communion have taken that unhappy step without examining this great historic argument, and often indeed on principles of mere private judgment in the sense of personal preference.[22]

[18] From the 1860s onwards Gladstone developed a wary working relationship with English nonconformity, but though it commanded his political respect and in individual cases affection, he remained unable in principle to find theological justification for it: 'If in the abstract it be difficult to find justification for English Nonconformity, yet when we view it as a fact, it must surely command our respect and sympathy'; 'The place of heresy and schism in the modern Christian Church' (1894), in *Later Gleanings* (London 1897) pp 288–9; see also G. I. T. Machin, 'Gladstone and Nonconformity in the 1860s', *HJ* 17, 2 (1974) p 347.

[19] *CP* p 327, and *ibid* p 390: 'those Catholic or primitive principles not only do not naturally lead into Romanism, but are the one barrier which effectually closes the way thither . . .' He noted that even in Italy 'Romanism' was an unnatural imposition, often resisted at a local level, where sermons were often 'much more Catholic than specifically Roman'; *ibid* p 349.

[20] Gladstone to Manning, 1 June 1850, in [*Correspondence on Church and Religion of W. E. Gladstone*, ed D. C.] Lathbury (1910) 2 p 26.

[21] Many of the papers are collected in W. E. Gladstone, *Later Gleanings* (London 1897).

[22] Memorandum of 17 April 1885, BM Add MS 44769 fol 77.

In view of all this, it is not surprising to find that the papacy does not figure favourably in Gladstone's writings, public or private. His direct experience[23] with Roman catholicism was confined to France, Italy, to a lesser extent Germany, to recusants and to his tortuous relationships with friends contemplating or defending 'perversion'. His diary shows that while consistently impressed when abroad with the idea of a universal church, he always regarded the papacy as the stumbling block to its achievement.

Thus on first entering St Peter's in 1832:

> In entering such a Church as this, most deeply does one feel the pain and shame of the schism which separates us from Rome—whose guilt (for guilt I at least am well persuaded there always is where there is schism), surely rests not upon the Venerable Fathers of the English Reformed Church, but upon Rome itself . . .[24]

Revisiting St Peter's in 1838, he recalls:

> Here I remember almost to have experienced the first conception of unity in the Church—acquired alas! by the existing contrasts—and first to have longed for its visible attainment . . . But alas how much yet more sad is the frightful association which forces itself upon the mind between the gorgeous magnificence of St. Peter's . . . and the fearful corruptions ingrained by long practice in that portion of the Church of which this is the master-temple.[25]

Observation of Romanism might lead to intellectual criticism and reflection: personal experience of its success was far worse. Loss of faith, not a common occurrence in the circles in which Gladstone moved, led to pity, but apostasy to horror, revulsion and torment. The first two great sexual crises of Gladstone's life were directly related to apostasy; first to that of his sister through his attempts to assist her in 1845, second, to the apostasies of Manning and James Hope in 1851.

In the 1851 crisis 'the two friends whom I might call the only supports for my intellect have been wrenched away from me, leaving me lacerated, and I may say barely conscious morally.'[26] 'They were my two props. Their going may be to me a sign that my work is gone with them . . . One blessing I have: total freedom from doubts. These dismal events have smitten but not shaken'.[27] But the shock of the 1851

---

[23] Gladstone put considerable stress on observation of traditional religious practices as a necessary means of making sense of written material; see CP p 354n.

[24] Diaries, 1 p 462, 31 March 1832.

[25] Ibid, 2 p 429, 8 October 1838.

[26] Ibid, 4 pp 352–3, 19 August 1851.

[27] Diary, 19 August 1851.

crisis, 'my saddest year',[28] a year of physical and psychological debasement, to which Gladstone referred on a number of occasions, was not purgative. Three years later he told Samuel Wilberforce on the occasion of the apostasy of Robert Wilberforce:

> For could I, with reference to my own precious children, think that one of them might possibly live to strike, though in sincerity and thinking he did God service, such a blow, how far rather would I that he had never been born.[29]

Although in public Gladstone was often accused of being a Roman catholic, and of encouraging apostasy, it is clear that his private emotional response to the 'Scarlet Woman' was not unusual, seen in terms of the early nineteenth-century Scottish and Liverpudlian protestantism in which he was reared, though it was unusual in the form of its expression.

'Are there no Tunstals, and no Erasmuses?' asked Gladstone in 1840.[30] In 1845 on a visit to Munich to his apostate drug-ridden sister, he found one: Döllinger.[31] Döllinger's work appealed to Gladstone because of its historical basis, and in their first meeting Gladstone found Roman catholic authority to set at rest his mind on the chief theological difficulty which he then perceived between the Roman and anglican churches, purgatory. In 1850 he noted in his diary during a visit to a Neapolitan church:

> I often think of Dr. Döllinger's assurance to me—expressing I am sure his own conviction—that the Church had no judicial function, no authority beyond the grave. I wish this were the real Roman doctrine.[32]

Gladstone's meeting with Döllinger and their subsequent friendship coincided with Gladstone's growing awareness and denunciation of ultramontanism.

Believing in the possibility of a reconciled Christendom—and, as he wrote, 'By unity I mean of course visible unity'[33]—then ultra-

---

[28] *Ibid* 4 p 322, 7 April 1851. See also *ibid* 3 pp xliii-xlviii.
[29] Gladstone to S. Wilberforce, 17 October 1854, Bodleian Library, MS Wilberforce d. 36, fol 25. For similar views and emotional denunciation of Rome see Gladstone's review of [Elizabeth Harris], *From Oxford to Rome*, in QR 81 (June 1847) p 131.
[30] *CP* p 509.
[31] See Lathbury, 2 p 383 for Gladstone's account of this meeting. At the same time as meeting Döllinger, Gladstone familiarised himself with the Ronge movement, which attacked the pope, initially from within Roman catholicism. See *Diaries*, 3 pp 488-9, 10 October 1845 ff.
[32] *Diaries*, 3 p 275, 22 November 1850.
[33] *CP* p 506.

montanism, 'alike needful and dangerous to the Roman system',[34] was a chief and growing barrier to the possibility of that reconciliation. Gladstone confronted ultramontanism directly though anonymously in a review in 1852 of Montalembert's Des Intérêts Catholiques au XIXe siècle, a review which in many respects presages the arguments and sometimes even the phrasing of the Vatican pamphlets of 1874–5. Gladstone deplored 'the change of spirit that has come over the Papal See' and anticipated worse to come. He argued that Montalembert's position of being both liberal and ultramontane was wholly untenable: 'Ultramontanism and liberty may coexist: Ultramontanism and the true love of liberty stand in a reciprocal repulsion never to be over-come'.[35]

By ultramontanism Gladstone meant not merely institutional developments, but 'above all a frame of mind, a tone and direction of thought, which, continually exalting the hierarchical elements of the Christian system, and the mystical next to them, and, on the other hand, continually depressing those counterbalancing ingredients which are so fully exhibited in Holy Scripture and in the early history of the Church ... has at length well-nigh reduced the latter elements of the Christian system to zero, and installed the first in exclusive possession of the sacred domain'.[36] Gladstone pointed particularly to the resurgence of the Jesuits and to Mariolatry.

These fears were confirmed during the 1850s and 1860s. Gladstone was involved in as yet not fully documented discussions with Sir William Heathcote on unity with Rome[37] and in 1856 he was an enthusiastic contributor to Meyrick's Anglo-Continental society, though declining actually to join its executive committee.[38] But like its other members his view towards the Latin church was both con-ciliatory and pessimistic, as the consequences of ultramontanism became clear. Those elements of Romanism such as Mariolatry, which Glad-stone and others like him had hitherto excluded from ecumenical consideration by regarding them as traditional peculiarities of Italian national religion, were being codified into official Roman doctrine.

[34] Gladstone's comment on De Maistre in 'Remarks on the royal supremacy' (1850, rep 1865, 1877), in Gleanings, 5 p 288. This passage was quoted by E. B. Pusey at the culmination of his argument in his Eirenicon pp 260–1.
[35] QR 92 p 137 (December 1852). Gladstone re-read this review in 1873, commenting 'the pope was a worm in the gourd all through'; Morley 2 p 476.
[36] QR 92 p 150.
[37] Diaries, 27 March 1855.
[38] Gladstone to Meyrick, 8 October 1856, Pusey House, Oxford, Meyrick MSS 30.

The bull of 1854 defining the immaculate conception raised a large new barrier, and the syllabus of 1864 seemed even worse, for while the 1854 bull might be seen as merely self-regarding, the syllabus was clearly combative. It struck at the heart of Gladstone's belief 'in a reconciliation between Christianity and the conditions of modern thought, modern life, and modern society'.[39]

Like many of his generation, Gladstone was dismayed by the church of Rome well before 1870; he had laboured to refurbish his national church for catholicy, only to find the conditions for its full achievement had become impossible. But Gladstone does not seem to have asked himself the question, could the church of Rome be expected not to respond to the nationalism which his own enthusiasm for autonomy and 'national religion' necessarily encouraged?

Gladstone's attitude to Orthodoxy was, like most anglicans', less emotional and less urgent. Whereas the relationship with Rome was a persistent and historic problem, relations with Orthodoxy involved no immediate social or civil crisis and were entirely confined to a self-conscious élite. Orthodoxy fitted well into Gladstone's analysis of national religion. Moreover he believed that the Greeks had a special place in what he called the 'providential order of the world'.[40] His Homeric studies were dedicated to proving the dual revelation to Hebrew and Hellene, the first examples of 'religious nationality'.

Thus 'If Abraham when he was blessed by Melchisedec carried Levi in his loins so Homer carried in his mind the features and qualities which in historic times made up the portraiture of the Greek nation.'[41] Greek 'religion was . . . intimately associated with the preservation of their national life during their degradation'.[42]

'It was the Greek mind . . . in which was shaped and tempered the original mould of the modern European civilization . . . civilization as a thing distinct from religion, but designed to combine and coalesce with it.' Whereas the Mosaic books represent human nature in 'one master-relation', Homer shows 'the entire circle of human action and experience' and so 'may be viewed, in the philosophy of human nature, as the complement of the earlier portion of the Sacred Records'; [43] thus together they show, in their different ways, aspects of the divine

[39] Gladstone to Manning, 16 November 1869, in Purcell, 2 p 408.
[40] See *Gleanings* 7 p 31.
[41] *Diaries*, 7 September 1863.
[42] *Ibid*, 19 March 1862.
[43] W. E. Gladstone, 'The place of Homer in classical education and in historical inquiry', *Oxford Essays* (London 1857) pp 4–5.

revelation. It is therefore not surprising to find Gladstone relying mainly on the Greek tradition of political theory in his analysis of the nature of society in *The State in its Relations with the Church,* while at the same time claiming an ultimately divinely given legitimacy for it.

As lord high commissioner in the Ionian islands in 1858–9 he had an early taste of episcopal politics of the sort familiar to British imperial governors in the Mediterranean in the twentieth century, but there, and on a visit to Greece, he formed a favourable opinion of the Orthodox church, observing favourably of an Orthodox monastery 'I have not in the Latin countries seen any monastery like this'[43a] and telling father Tosti in 1860: 'As a member of the western church not in the Latin Communion I perhaps feel a special interest in the Church of the East; but in many points of view it is a subject of the greatest importance. It is more odious to the ultra-protestants of this country than the Church of Rome: its temporal depression and the low estate and limited acquirements of its clergy in general incite the contempt of superciliousness and bigotry: but surely it has its own works to perform, and in its own place, that too no small one, in the Counsel of God for mankind.'[44]

He encouraged Greek Orthodox priests to an actively anti-Roman policy, telling the reverend J. N. Valettas, a Greek professor:

> The aggressive tendencies of the See of Rome towards the Eastern Church have been a source of great evil, & I cannot wonder that they should be resented by those who are the object of them. They are the result of the Exclusive claims of Popedom wound up to a higher pitch, & urged seemingly with greater tenacity than ever. My first wish would be a better mind for those who push them thus unwisely & injuriously to the whole Christian world. My second is that failing such better mind their endeavour may be baffled by firm, mild, & judicious resistance.[45]

He had meetings with the archpriest Wassilieff, the leading Russian advocate of closer links with anglicanism, during his London visit of 1865[46] and, though he was not a member of the eastern churches association, founded in 1863, he was familiar with many of its leading members.

Gladstone was thus an important figure in the 1860s in ecumenical

---

[43a] *Diaries,* 2 December 1858.
[44] Gladstone to Tosti, 20 August 1860, printed in *Nuova Antologia,* January 1937, p 163.
[45] Gladstone to Valettas, 5 September 1865, BM Add MS 44535, fol 192.
[46] *Diaries,* 15 February 1865.

initiatives towards both the Roman and the Orthodox churches. His real significance, however, was that he had moved from being an author and minor politician in the 1840s to being one of the dominant forces in British politics from the 1860s onwards. How much as chancellor and prime minister would he use his power and influence for oecumenical ends?

From the start of his membership of Palmerston's cabinet in 1859 he pressed for the diminution of the pope's temporal power partly for diplomatic reasons, for Gladstone wished to involve protestant as well as Roman catholic powers in ensuring a monarchic not republican solution for the papal states, and foresaw that 'if the Roman question is left to the Pope and his people, the Pope will be forthwith expelled: a republic will be almost of necessity established: the cause of temperate freedom must be discredited',[47] partly because the pope's authority should be seen in spiritual terms, separated from his Italian role. He commented on a letter by Marliani: 'to say . . . that the question of the Papal States is not Italian but Catholic, is simply to establish a war of life and death between human nature and religion, with human nature in the right. If we take narrower ground, and consider the effect on the Roman Church as Roman, then I firmly believe Exeter Hall has invented no such weapon of offence against it as that which Pope, Cardinals & the whole kit are now wielding with such zeal and effect.'[48] He therefore argued for a solution of temporal suzerainty, pointing out to the cabinet how much more how much better the eastern churches and anglican churches had managed their primates.[49]

In his involvement in the 'Italian triumvirate' of Palmerston's ministry, he found his worst fears about ultramontanism practically confirmed. He warned the cabinet in 1860 of the potential hazards if ultramontanists transferred their campaign for the preservation of the papal states to domestic questions:

> I cannot but think that the recent conduct and declaration of the Papal party throughout Europe, and particularly the declaration and threats in this country from the Roman Catholics generally to be governed in their conduct upon civil and domestic questions by our conduct if we presume to concur in any measure of interference with the Papal states (except of course keeping him by

[47] *Diaries*, 30 June 1859.
[48] Gladstone to Clarendon, 26 November 1859, Bodleian Clarendon MSS dep. c. 523, on Marliani's letter forwarded to Gladstone by Clarendon.
[49] *Ibid* and 27 March 1863, in Lathbury, 2 p 391.

force upon his throne) constitute something of a challenge to all Governments as such.[50]

In the 1860s therefore Gladstone became more pessimistic about anglican relationships with Roman catholicism, and more aware of the possibility of open conflict with the papacy on civil questions. A visit to Rome in 1866 after the debacle of his reform bill did not dispel this view. The preparations for the visit had included if not a reconciliation at least a renewal of contact with Manning, a move required more by reasons internal to the liberal party than oecumenicity. Manning set up the Rome visit carefully[51] but, though Gladstone had two interviews with Pio Nono, in which Fenianism and the Irish university question were scouted rather than discussed,[52] his impression was that 'Romanism' was everywhere, 'Catholicity' nowhere: he later recalled: 'the atmosphere of Antonelli's room stifles me. Every question, Turco-Greek, Italo-French, Anglo-Irish, or be it what it may, means one thing and one thing only, the Pope's power and especially his temporal power.'[53]

On becoming prime minister in December 1868, Gladstone was neither optimistic nor sympathetic towards Rome, but almost wherever he turned, Roman issues loomed: Ireland, elementary and university education, convents, the Vatican council. In all these Gladstone's ambivalence between pluralism and religious nationalism had an important influence. [53a]

As regards the council, that influence was spectacular but delayed. Throughout the 1860s, Gladstone took the view that if there was to be a solution to the papal question, it would have to be a European solution: no one power could hope to effect it, nor should it be left to the Roman catholic powers: 'the destiny of Rome will I suppose come before not the "Catholic Powers" but Europe.'[54] The complex diplomacy surrounding the council has been described elsewhere;[55] but we

[50] Diaries, 7 January 1860.
[51] Purcell, Life of Manning, 2 p 398.
[52] Diaries, 22 October 1866, and Lathbury, 2 p 395.
[53] Gladstone to Clarendon, 11 January 1869, Bodleian Clarendon MSS dep. c. 497. Antonelli was Gladstone's chief link with the papal court during his 1866 visit.
[53a] For an interesting view of Gladstone's pluralism, differing from mine, see D. Nicholls 'Newman, Gladstone and the politics of pluralism', paper read to the 1975 Newman conference in Dublin, whose proceedings are expected to be published.
[54] Gladstone to Clarendon, 7 November 1867, Bodleian Clarendon MSS dep. c. 523; see also his memoranda quoted earlier.
[55] There is much new detail in F. W. Cwickowski, The English bishops and the first Vatican Council (Louvain 1971).

may glance here at its effect on Gladstone. From his view-point the following were immediately involved: Clarendon his foreign-secretary; Odo Russell, the unofficial British emissary to the papacy, who was both earl Russell's nephew and Clarendon's son-in-law, son of a Roman catholic mother, and described by Pio Nono as 'a very bad Protestant'; Acton, step-son of Granville, which last succeeded Clarendon as foreign secretary on the latter's death in July 1870, just as the council was adjourned. Acton was in Rome as a journalist and as a lay-observer.

With the exception of Gladstone, these family relationships constituted a classic example of English whiggery in action. All, including Gladstone, were in principle opposed to a definition of infallibility; all, with the possible exception of Acton, believed the calling of the council made definition inevitable. Gladstone, Clarendon and Russell however disagreed as to the amount of opposition the British government should offer. The whigs, characteristically, thought definition would be silly rather than appalling: solid erastianism was undisturbed by barriers to pecumenicalism. Indeed the whigs thought definition might do good: 'I hope that the dogmas and doctrines to be propounded will be to the last degree extravagant as the common sense of mankind may thereby be awakened and *possibly* impelled to revolt.'[56] Believing this, and agreeing with Russell that 'the Sovereigns of the world will allow themselves to be sat upon by the Pope, that the independent bishops will accept their defeat in all humility and that the triumph of the Italian Jesuits will be complete for the time being',[57] Clarendon came to see little point in empty hostile gestures; his visit to Napoleon in Paris in September 1869 showed that the emperor would do nothing about the council before it began.[58]

Gladstone's position was that Britain could only assist, not initiate, opposition, but that the council should not pass wholly unchallenged. He stated his position to Clarendon in May 1869.

About the Oecumenical Council I should like much to converse with you. My ideas briefly indicated are these
(a) not to discourage a combined action of the Governments for

[56] Clarendon to O. Russell, 28 June 1869, Bodleian Clarendon MSS dep. c. 475.
[57] O. Russell to Clarendon, 22 December 1869, *ibid* c. 487.
[58] Clarendon altered his position on a protest at Rome. On 11 September 1869 he told Gladstone that despite its futility 'It will not be difficult to state at Rome your apprehension about the Council in which I entirely concur'. On 17 October 1869 he wrote 'Odo Russell and I have discussed the practicability of a collective or single growl against the Council. He, well knowing the ground at Rome, sees difficulties in the way of remonstrance . . .'; Bodleian, Clarendon MSS dep. c. 501.

it might strengthen the hands of the more moderate and right-minded Bishops.

(b) to plead for ourselves that on account of our want of direct relations both to the Pope and to the Roman Catholic Churches in H.M.'s dominions we naturally fall into the rear though without *renouncing* absolutely.

(c) to suggest for consideration whether one or more of the Roman Catholic powers might not submit to the Court of Rome that they should submit to the respective Governments of Christendom, some time before the Council meets, a statement of such of the subjects intended to be brought before it as bear *upon civil rights* or upon *the relation of Church and State.*

It seems to me that a representation would be reasonable; might act as a salutary check; and is such as even we, in case of need, might join in or support.

... The Syllabus was a great outrage: and there may be an opportunity of helping to do what the Reformation in many things did—to save the Pope and the Roman Church from themselves.[59]

Thus when Clarendon's enthusiasm for protest flagged, Gladstone encouraged him:

I quite agree that it is but little we can do in the affair of the Council but I shall be glad if you think proper to do it. And I think the Queen, who is full of the Roman Catholic extravagances, would like it.[60]

But Gladstone would not attempt an initiative: 'I could not press or ask you [Clarendon] to attempt an isolated movement: we are not strong enough in that quarter.'[61]

Three occasions for protest did occur.

Firstly there was the Bavarian initiative of the spring of 1869. This

---

[59] Gladstone to Clarendon, 21 May 1869, Bodleian, Clarendon MSS dep. c. 497. Clarendon's visit to cardinal Grassellini and to Paris in August and September 1869 was intended to discover whether the basis for such action existed. He went enthusiastically anti-papal: 'You may be sure of the pleasure I shall have in taking every opportunity legitimate and the reverse of throwing dirt on the Council. I believe that will best be done through the Emperor . . . if within the next two months there is a tolerable unanimous expression of opinion on the Pope and his jesuits may think it expedient to put much water in their wine'; Clarendon to Gladstone, 31 August 1869, Bodleian, Clarendon MSS dep. c. 501.

[60] Gladstone to Clarendon, 14 September 1869, Bodleian, Clarendon MSS dep. c. 498.

[61] Gladstone to Clarendon, 19 October 1869, Bodleian, Clarendon MSS dep. c. 498.

was 'addressed to the Governments of those States of Europe which have a mixed population of Protestants and Catholics, suggesting the expediency of an understanding between them with reference to the Decision which may be come to by the Oecumenical Council', Britain not being officially included since Hohenlohe, the Bavarian foreign minister, 'assumed, as a matter of course, that the negotiation by his Circular was one in which Her Majesty's Government would not be disposed to take an active part'.[61a] On the basis of Manning's recollections and Purcell's report of them, there has been much confusion about this initiative: Purcell stated there had been 'a formal proposal to the English Government' as a result of which, Manning recollected, Gladstone, briefed by Acton, 'after a hot discussion . . . was defeated in the Cabinet . . .' In his copy of Purcell, Gladstone annotated opposite this passage: 'totally untrue', 'false', and 'false'.[62] Gladstone's memory was better than Manning's who had clearly confused Hohenlohe in 1869 with Daru in March 1870. First: the Hohenlohe initiative was sent officially to all European governments with 'a mixed population of Protestant and Catholic subjects, suggesting that an understanding should be come to between them as to the course to be taken with reference to the decision, which may result from the Oecumenical Council . . . and which may be in contradiction with the internal legislation of the Country . . .',[63] but Britain was not officially included.[64] Second: there is no evidence that the initiative was discussed in cabinet, let alone that Gladstone was overruled.[65] The second

[61a] Howard (minister in Munich) to Clarendon, 4 May 1869, PRO FO 9/194.

[62] Purcell, *Life of Manning*, 2 p 436; I am obliged to Sir E. W. Gladstone for lending me Gladstone's copy. Manning's recollections, long after the event, clearly misdate the Hohenlohe initiative placing it by implication in 1870, during the council. The Manning-Purcell account is followed by E. C. Butler, *The Vatican Council* (London 1930) I p 10, and by others, for example, E. R. Norman, *The Catholic Church and Ireland in the Age of Rebellion* (London 1965) p 411, which otherwise has much useful information on the council. In 1896, on the publication of Purcell's *Manning*, Gladstone wrote to Acton: 'Have you any recollection of keeping me by letter steadily or frequently informed of what was going on? I have no such recollection. You are represented as having been to me what Odo Russell was to Manning . . . You will find that Manning gives with undoubting confidence the account of a hot debate in the Cabinet of 1870 on Prince Hohenlohe's application to the British Government. According to my recollection and belief, there is not one word of truth in it'; Acton MSS, Cambridge University Library, uncatalogued.

[63] Loftus (ambassador in Berlin) to Clarendon, 24 April 1869, PRO FO 64/662.

[64] Howard to Clarendon, 4 May 1869, PRO FO 9/194; governments officially included were: Würtemberg, Baden, Hesse Darmstadt, Austria, Prussia, France and Belgium; Britain was informed unofficially.

[65] There is no mention of the initiative in Gladstone's cabinet minutes for 1869; BM Add MS 44637. The initiative did prompt Gladstone's letter to Clarendon of 21 May 1869,

occasion was in December 1869 when Acton asked permission to publicise Gladstone's opinions.[66] Gladstone instructed Clarendon to telegraph his approval in cipher through Odo Russell, and he stated those opinions to refer to 'the effect in this country of Ultramontane doctrines and proceedings upon legislation, policy and feeling, with respect to Ireland, and to the Roman Catholic subjects of the Crown generally', especially mentioning education;[67] this was therefore a personal warning not about definition itself, but about its secular consequences.

Acton followed his success in involving Gladstone personally by attempting in January 1870 to involve him officially.[68] Gladstone swiftly withdrew; as he told Clarendon, 'Acton . . . must know how difficult it is for England to take any ostensible initiative'.[69]

The third and most probable chance for intervention came with the memorandum in March 1870 from Daru, the French foreign minister, proposing joint representations: Gladstone and Clarendon agreed that British support should be given verbally: they disagreed on whether verbal support should be accompanied by a note, Gladstone being for a note, Clarendon against, the latter getting his way after consulting the cabinet.[70] This was the maximum extent of disagreement. But by then Daru had resigned on another question, Ollivier's ministry was in confusion, and the question had become academic.

What emerges, from Gladstone's point of view, from these exchanges, is an acute sense of frustration: 'It is by threats and threats alone that the Court of Rome as to its Roman and Church policy is influenced: its whole policy is based on the rejection of reason . . .',[71]

---

quoted above. Clarendon was by no means opposed, sending the letter to O. Russell, commenting 'letter c. might be advantageous if practicable'; Clarendon to O. Russell, 31 May 1864, Clarendon MSS dep. c. 475.

[66] Acton to Gladstone, 24 November [1869], in [J. N.] Figgis and [R. V.] Laurence, [*Selections from the correspondence of the first Lord Acton*] (London 1917) 1 p 84.

[67] Gladstone to Acton, 1 December 1869, BM Add MS 44093, fol 96, in Lathbury, 2 p 49 and Gladstone to Clarendon, 1 December 1869, Clarendon MSS dep. c. 498.

[68] See Figgis and Laurence, 1 p 96.

[69] Gladstone to Clarendon, 13 January 1870, Clarendon MSS dep. c. 498.

[70] See Clarendon to O. Russell, 2 May 1870, in N. Blakiston, *The Roman Question* (London 1962) p 430. Manning's recollections confused this incident with the Hohenlohe initiative a year earlier. Apart from its comments on the council, Britain could not accept Daru's memorandum in full because it expected continued French occupation of the papal states. Acton's note on 7 December 1869 is a misunderstanding of the exchange between Gladstone and Clarendon in October 1869; *Lord Acton and the First Vatican Council,* ed E. Campion (Sydney 1975) p 26.

[71] Gladstone to Clarendon, 13 March 1870, Clarendon MSS dep. c. 498. Gladstone's cabinet minute of 19 March 1870 (BM Add MS 44638, fol 51) reads: 'Ecumenical

frustration increased by relations with the Irish, for the more the liberals conciliated the Irish catholics, the more they found themselves limited by Irish constraints.

In the debacle of the Irish universities bill of 1873, these constraints fell away: 'we are no longer hampered by Irish consideration in the direction of our general policy, and Ultramontanism should for us, wherever our orbits touch, stand or fall upon its merits'.[72]

For Gladstone, of course, ultramontanism fell by its merits decisively. He had been encouraged to say so by Clarendon once out of office: indeed the government's silence in 1869–70 had been partly based on the assumption that the decrees would lead to a public outcry. In fact, though there had been a spate of hostile leaders and press letters, protest had not been clearly focused. Nothing comparable to the 1850–1 explosion had occurred.[73] Newdegate's inquiry into convents was balanced by the government's successful repeal of the 1851 ecclesiastical titles act. Nor had there been much public movement by English catholics opposed to the council's definition. In his draft manifesto for the 1874 election Gladstone included a passage warning of ultramontanist dangers, but later struck it out:

> Our institutions & habits of Government in a great degree exempt us from contact with the Ultramontanist movement now widely and injuriously felt on the Continent of Europe. No British Administration can regard that movement with sympathy or approval: but we shall continue to guard with vigilance, for the sake not of individuals only but of the entire community, the civil rights and equality of all irrespective of the religious belief.[74]

In Germany, of course, the situation was quite different, and it is in Germany that the proximate causes of 'Vaticanism' are to be found. Döllinger was excommunicated in 1871, and in 1874 organised the first Bonn conference which marked the institutional beginning at an international level of the Old Catholic movement. Döllinger himself never actually became an Old Catholic, but he lent intellectual authority to the movement.

The importance of the Bonn conferences of 1874 and 1875 was that they included anglicans and Orthodox representatives. The anglican

---

Council: conversation on concurrence in possible French move. HM Govt. to stand in 2d rank'.
[72] Gladstone to Acton, 18 November 1873, Figgis and Laurence, I p 175.
[73] The disarray of dissenters and anglicans over the 1870 education act may have accounted for this.
[74] BM Add MS 44762, fol 14.

representatives were mostly members of the eastern churches association, including Gladstone's close liberal tractarian friends Liddon, Malcolm MacColl and T. T. Carter, warden of the House of Mercy to which Gladstone sent redeemed prostitutes. We may today see the Bonn conferences as a dead end which by circumventing the problem of the papacy ignored the central question of European apostolic oecumenicalism, but at the time it seemed the only possible way of asserting the idea of 'Catholicity' in the face of papal 'Romanism'. It was also seen by many tractarians as the best means of buttressing their position, under assault from the bishops, the tory party and sections of the liberal party, in the form of the 1874 public worship act, a clearly erastian measure of the sort which Gladstone had always deplored.[75]

Soon after the 1874 conference Gladstone visited Döllinger in Bavaria; they discussed the conference and the position of the English catholics, and Gladstone proposed to work for the next conference. Döllinger raised in Gladstone's mind the following line of thought: 'It strikes me that it is in principle far less anarchic to seek for Christian ordinances at the head of a provisional but orthodox organization such as the *alt-Catholische* than to claim the title at once to be within the pale and privileges of a certain communion and to exercize the power of annulling by private judgment its solemn and formal ordinances of faith'.[76] The sentence seems directly aimed at Acton. While in Bavaria, Gladstone learnt of the apostasy of his cabinet colleague, the earl of Ripon.

Before seeing Döllinger, Gladstone had written an article for the *Contemporary Review* mutedly defending the ritualists without condoning their behaviour. After meeting Döllinger he inserted in it at proof stage a notorious passage attacking British Roman catholics for their subservient reaction to the decrees.[77] Gladstone told Acton of his addition to the article and mentioned a possible subsequent expansion; Acton strongly encouraged him to go on: 'I can easily believe you will find it necessary to say more. In such matters it is best to be as definite and explicit as possible. No reproach can be too severe.'[78] Acton was

---

[75] See P. T. Marsh, *The Victorian church in decline* (London 1969) cap 7.

[76] Gladstone to Döllinger, 23 September 1874, in Lathbury, 2 p 57. See also Gladstone's memorandum of 30 September 1874, in Lathbury, 2 p 400. For a useful account of this visit and of the proximate causes of the pamphlet, see J. L. Altholz, 'Gladstone and the Vatican Decrees', *The Historian*, 25 May 1963) pp 312–24; see also E. R. Norman, *The Catholic Church and Ireland in the Age of Rebellion 1859–1873* (London 1965 pp 457–9 and Norman, *Anti-Catholicism in Victorian England* (London 1968).

[77] *Contemporary Review*, 24 p 674.

[78] Gladstone to Acton, 19 October 1874, and Acton to Gladstone, 21 October 1874, BM Add MS 44093, fols 154–6.

summoned to Hawarden to see the final draft of the pamphlet, *The Vatican Decrees in their bearing on civil allegiance: a political expostulation.* He was appalled, and tried to stop publication.[79] The cosmopolitan Acton had clearly failed to comprehend the extent and vehemence of Gladstone's 'religious nationality'.

Seen as a tract on civil allegiance, Gladstone's claim was that the Vatican decrees flew in the face of all that had been achieved in establishing a plural state in Britain by asserting the temporal power of the pope in the area of civil allegiance:

> All other Christian bodies are content with freedom in their own religious domain. Orientals, Lutherans, Calvinists, Presbyterians, Episcopalians, Non-conformists one and all, in the present day, contentedly and thankfully accept the benefits of civil order; never pretend that the State is not its own master . . . never are in perilous collision with the State.[80]

By not accepting toleration and freedom of speech as civil virtues justifiable in themselves, ultramontanism struck at the basis of Victorian political development—a development in which Roman catholics had hitherto shared and of which they had been beneficiaries. This view was quite consistent with the utilitarian line Gladstone had taken in the passages in his early works defending toleration and which he had supported politically since 1845.

The rational aims of the pamphlet—to stir up English inopportunists, to drive a wedge between them and the ultramontanists, to get a catholic reassertion of civil allegiance, to force others to take up theologically what Gladstone had raised politically, perhaps to prepare the basis for some sort of Old Catholic movement in England—these aims accorded with this political theory. But the ambivalence noted earlier persisted. The first *Vatican* pamphlet began and ended with apostasy: Gladstone wrote as a betrayed anglican, not a political scientist, and the form of pluralism which existed in Britain was, after all, pluralism on anglican terms, a semi-plural solution, in which the national church conceded no more than necessary.

Moreover, the uncharacteristically intemperate, even sarcastic tone of the pamphlet revealed the frustration of thirty years reticence. This became clearer in the subsequent pamphlet warfare. It was apostasy and its affront to religious nationality which really moved Gladstone

[79] Acton to Simpson, 4 November 1874, in J. L. Altholz, D. McElrath and J. C. Holland, *The correspondence of Lord Acton and Richard Simpson* (London 1975) 3 p 318.
[80] W. E. Gladstone, *The Vatican Decrees* (London 1874) p 10.

emotionally: 'The Roman Army, which confronts our Church and nation . . . has been strangely but very largely recruited from the ranks of the English Church, and her breasts have, for thirty years, been pierced mainly by the children whom they fed'.[81] 'Vaticanism' was Gladstone's real 'Chapter of Autobiography': his first substantial public comment on the apostasies of the 1840s—which had contributed to the failure of his great experiment of anglican resurgence. This was a quarrel in which Acton had no part and little understanding. Beneath the earlier restraint, the diplomacy of the 1869–70 period, the dissection of the imperial and political defects of ultramontanism, lay the still-remembered wounds of 1851—'the rending and sapping of the Church, the loss of its gems'. Indeed, the pamphlets led quickly first to a public row about the nature of the break between Gladstone and Manning in 1851, then to the subsequent breaking off of their relationship for the second time.[82]

If the 'expostulation' was a rhetorical success publicly, and a psychological success privately, it was a failure in terms of its stated objectives: it caused no general disavowal by British Roman catholics of Rome's newest fashions: it came too late to do so. Newman had already decided that Birmingham was not to be Munich: his *Letter to the duke of Norfolk* offered reconciliation but not rebellion. Publicly Gladstone had to admit that Newman's criticism of 'the chronic extravagances of Catholics here and there', with their 'wild words and overbearing deeds', was as good as he was going to get; privately he told Döllinger 'in my opinion, if he [Newman] had possessed will and "character" enough, he ought to have been at this moment on the same standing ground with you, engaged in the same noble conflict for the truth'.[83]

The pamphlets, well though they sold, were generally regarded as a traditional piece of papist-bashing, but even, as such, they evoked no great reaction, although the protestant press made its expected comments. As in 1870, the 1850–1 popular protest did not reappear. Gladstone had sent his pamphlet to Bismarck, and the Germans naturally enough tried to equate the pamphlets with the Falk laws of May 1873. Bismarck replied in a splendid pastiche of Gladstonian language: 'It affords me a deep and hopeful gratification to see the two nations,

[81] W. E. Gladstone, 'Vaticanism: an answer to reproofs and replies', February 1875, in *Rome: and the newest fashions in religion* (London 1875) p 6. In view of the nature of Gladstone's sexual crisis of 1851, the imagery is significant.
[82] See Purcell, *Life of Manning*, 2 pp 475–9.
[83] Gladstone to Döllinger, 7 March 1875, quoted in D. McElrath, *The Syllabus of Pius IX: some reactions in England* (London 1964) p 316.

which in Europe are the champions of liberty of conscience, encountering the same foe, stand henceforward shoulder to shoulder in defending the highest interests of the human race'.[84] Münster, the German ambassador, told Gladstone that Bismarck admired 'the manly courage and great lucidity with which you expose the false doctrines of Rome and treat a question that has such vivid interest for Germany at this moment.'[85] But Hawarden was not Friedrichsruh: the British *Kultur Kampf*—the 1851 ecclesiastical titles act—had just been repealed by Gladstone himself, and he emphasised the rhetorical nature of his campaign by withdrawing from political leadership shortly after its publication: a fact which emphasised the retrospective nature of his expostulation.

Gladstone concluded his second Vatican pamphlet with a brief review of the effect of the decrees on the church seen as a whole, and ended with a quotation from Homer. The quotation from Homer was apt enough geographically, for the consequence of the council, Döllinger's excommunication, the Old Catholics and the anti-ritualist campaign in England, had been an intensification of interest and activity with regard to the Orthodox churches, which has been in general terms well documented.[86] Gladstone had commented in his second Vatican pamphlet on the role of the eastern church in providing 'an authentic and living record' of the primitive church's 'early provisions for a balance of Church-power, and for securing the laity against sacerdotal domination',[87] always a strong Gladstonian theme from his *Letter on the functions of laymen in the Church* of 1851 and his mistrust of the bishops' handling of the Gorham judgment onwards.

As we have already seen, Gladstone was well informed about the Orthodox church in the 1860s, and well in touch with some of its leading figures. As prime minister, he used his position to try to prevent proselytization in Wolverhampton by the archimandrite Timotheos Hatherley, an anglican convert to orthodoxy ordained by the patriarch of Constantinople. The incident, trivial in itself, as Gladstone said, was important because it showed his concern that nothing should occur to prevent closer contacts between anglicans and

---

[84] BM Add MS 44446 fol 293.

[85] Münster to Gladstone, 25 November 1874, BM Add MS 44445, fol 106. Münster addressed ultra-protestant societies in the same vein.

[86] C. B. Moss, *The Old Catholic Movement, its origins and history* (London 1948); *Anglican initiatives in christian unity*, ed E. G. W. Bill (London 1967); *A history of the Ecumenical Movement 1517–1948*, ed R. Rouse and S. C. Neill (2 ed London 1967).

[87] *Rome and the newest fashions in religion*, p 119.

Orthodox. Gladstone always believed proselytization dangerous as encouraging anarchic private judgment.[88]

Gladstone told Musurus, the Turkish ambassador in London and a Greek Orthodox Christian:

> The English Churchman . . . comprehends and respects the position and the character of the Eastern Church on its own ground: appreciates its merits and makes allowance for its weaker points, dealing out to it the liberal consideration, which he is aware that he much needs for himself and his own Church. But it is just this body, the *only* body in this country that has any sympathy with the Eastern Church, which Mr. Hatherley seeks to wound and to estrange . . . I have never known a proceeding more causeless and more foolish, or which united so much significance with as much mischief . . .[89]

Also during his first administration, he was host to archbishop Alexander Lycurgus of Syros and Tenos. As the archbishop pointed out in his report on his visit, it was only after Gladstone's hospitality that he began to receive invitations from the anglican bishops.[90] Gladstone subsequently corresponded with Lycurgus with the aim of 'advancing still further the object of a brotherly approximation',[91] Döllinger being kept in touch with this correspondence through Acton.[92] Lycurgus was involved in the Bonn conferences, strongly encouraged by Gladstone, who went further than most anglicans in conceding the Orthodox case on the vexed question of the *Filioque*.[93] The aim of the conferences, Gladstone believed, was that 'of establishing the voice of the undivided Church as the legitimate traditional authority',[94] that is, the conferences were both anti-Vatican and also constructive in their own right, and in 1875 Gladstone encouraged both Döllinger and Lycurgus to continue the momentum built up in 1874 and 1875.[94a]

---

[88] The Anglo-Continental society's constitution explicitly disavowed proselytization; see F. Meyrick, *Memories of life at Oxford and elsewhere* (London 1905) p 178.

[89] Gladstone to Musurus, 2 January 1872, BM Add MS 44541, fol 27. For the remarkable Hatherly, see P. Anson, *Bishops at Large* (London 1964) cap 2.

[90] *Occasional paper of the Eastern Church Association Number XIV*, ed George Williams (London 1872) p 9.

[91] *Ibid* p 11.

[92] See Gladstone to Acton, 8 December 1851, copy in Add MS 44541, fol 3.

[93] Gladstone to Lycurgus, October 1875, in D. C. Lathbury, *Correspondence on Church and religion of W. E. Gladstone* (London 1910) 2 p 64.

[94] Gladstone to Döllinger, 29 August 1875, in *ibid* 2 p 62.

[94a] Gladstone to Döllinger, 8 April 1875, BM Add MS 44140, fol 384.

The question of the eastern church was thus one of those in the forefront of Gladstone's mind in his retirement from politics in 1875. Even as he was discussing with Hartington and Forster the early reports in 1876 of the Bulgarian atrocities,[95] he was entertaining father Hyacinthe Loyson, the maverick and married French priest, and presiding over his conference held in London to further his ecumenical mission.[96] Hyacinthe was a prominent camp follower of the Old Catholic movement, and equally active in the discussions on the Orthodox church.[96a] Though by 1878 Gladstone 'had some doubt about the [Hyacinthe] movement, fearing it would become exotic',[97] in 1876 he was impressed by Hyacinthe's 'brilliant and most honest speech'.[98]

Gladstone's pamphlet on the Bulgarian atrocities was published on 6 September 1876.[99] It was designed for the working people whom Gladstone claimed had 'in the first instance raised the flag under which we are now marching'.[100] The pamphlet was in the tradition of his 'pale of the constitution' speech of 1864, that is, it made a bold popular appeal combined with careful but not over-obtrusive qualifications, and was subsequently supplemented by explanations in the newspapers.

The pamphlet was designed to appeal to a Popular Front of moral outrage: the movement of protest was founded 'on grounds, not of political party, not even of mere English nationality, not of Christian faith, but on the largest and broadest ground of all—the ground of our common humanity',[101] a coalition from Ambrose Phillips de Lisle[102]

---

[95] *Diaries*, 28 June 1876.

[96] *Ibid.* See also A. Houtin, *Le Père Hyacinthe, Réformateur Catholique 1869–1893* (Paris 1922) p 199.

[96a] See, for example, Gladstone to Döllinger on Hyacinthe, the Old Catholics and Orthodoxy, 29 May 1876, BM Add MS 44140, fol 416.

[97] 'Memorandum' by F. A. White, 11 December 1878, on a meeting with Gladstone to prepare for a mission in London by father Hyacinthe; Gladstone said 'he might subscribe again, but could not move actively. But I might use his name'; Lambeth Palace Library MS 1472, fol 25. See also Gladstone to Döllinger, 29 May 1876, in Lathbury, 2 p 314.

[98] See *Diaries*, 28 June 1876.

[99] For the atrocities and the agitation, see R. W. Seton-Watson, *Disraeli, Gladstone and the Eastern Question* (London 1935) and [R. T.] Shannon, [*Gladstone and the Bulgarian Agitation 1876*] (London 1963) with an introduction by G. Kitson Clark. Shannon stresses the delay between the start of the serious agitation and Gladstone's intervention, but at the most this was not more than two weeks in the summer recess.

[100] W. E. Gladstone, 'A speech delivered at Blackheath', 9 September 1876.

[101] *Ibid.* To achieve this, Gladstone had to withhold strongly felt anger at Vatican exploitation of the eastern question; see Gladstone to Acton, 16 October 1876, in Shannon p 192.

to Bradlaugh. A deliberately popular pamphlet was not the place to discuss the complexities of ecumenicalism, whose interest was confined to a small group of tractarians, particularly when the popular mis-conceptions about the Vatican pamphlets of some twenty two months previously are remembered.

Moreover, the Bulgarian atrocities were, in one respect inconvenient, for Gladstone believed that, while undoubtedly the victims of disgrace-ful atrocities, Bulgarian Christians were at the same time clearly in the wrong, encouraged by the Russians, in the vexed question of the Bul-garian schism of 1872 from the see of Constantinople.[103] Gladstone always by inclination sided with the Greeks, but in this case he also be-lieved the Bulgarians had transgressed one of the cardinal virtues of Orthodoxy, in demanding 'that wherever there were Bulgarians, con-stituting a local majority, the jurisdiction of the national Church should extend. This claim directly traverses the principle of local distribution, in which the Oriental Church claims, in conformity with the Ante-Nicene Church, to be founded'.[104] Thus, when he dealt with the reli-gious side of the question, as he did soon after his pamphlet was publi-shed, his aim was to broaden the question to include consideration of Hellenic as well as Slav national ecclesiastical grievances.[105]

The failure of the British government to act against the Turks put paid to any future Bonn conferences:[106] the Slavs would not attend a conference with anglicans while the British government was the chief defender of their persecutors. It also broke the unity of the tractarians: liberals, Gladstone, Liddon and MacColl, led the agitation; most tories would not follow. As Liddon told Döllinger in 1878, a conference was impossible, 'so many good Churchmen (—for instance Mr. Beresford Hope—) are political allies of Lord Beaconsfield'.[107] Problems about

[102] de Lisle, the foremost Roman catholic ecumenical layman, assisted in the preparation of the first Vatican pamphlet, and was requested by Gladstone, while writing his Bulgarian pamphlet, to influence Manning.
[103] When prime minister, Gladstone had discouraged intemperate action by the Greeks which might have formalised the schism; see Gladstone to archbishop Lycurgus, 18 August 1872, in Lathbury, 2 p 304.
[104] W. E. Gladstone, 'The Hellenic factor in the Eastern problem', published December 1876, reprinted in *Gleanings*, 4 p 298. See also his previously quoted letter to Lycurgus of October 1875.
[105] *Ibid.* In this article Gladstone does comment on Vatican attempts to 'profit by the quarrel'.
[106] The 1876 conference was abandoned in June 1876 because of disagreements about the *Filioque*; the 1877 conference and Döllinger's proposal of one in 1878 came to nothing because of British support for Turkey; see J. O. Johnston, *Life and letters of H. P. Liddon* (London 1904) p 190.
[107] Liddon to Döllinger, Trinity Sunday 1878, Liddon Papers, Keble College, Oxford.

the *Filioque* could be bypassed; the immediate political situation in the Balkans could not. Beaconsfield had thus contributed to snapping off a promising development in ecumenicalism, as Pius IX had earlier broken a much more important growth.[108] The inner passion of a Gladstonian pamphlet was always religious, however political the content, and Gladstone's hatred of the Turk and his frustration of national religion in the Balkans was the same as his bitterness against the papacy and its perversion of catholicity. Both pamphlets sprang from a long, complex and interrelated development which, because of the proximate causes of their publication, was not immediately apparent in their content.

For the Balkans Gladstone offered a solution of suzerainty, as he had for the temporal papacy in the 1860s and as he was to do for South Africa and Ireland in the 1880s. This solution was a halfway house between central control and local autonomy, a compromise of the same sort advocated for the churches in England, an ill-defined balance between imperialism and pluralism.

What light does all this shine on 'religious motivation'? From Gladstone's own point of view, the adjective would have been redundant; motivation, regardless of the area of activity, meant the desire to do God's will: for *ein Gott-betrunken Mann* such as Gladstone, taken on his own terms, this had to be the case.

Looked at historically, Gladstone's religion can be seen to be intricately and essentially linked to his sense of organic nationality, hence his horror of apostasy. It can also be seen to be developing into something definably 'religious' in its motivation, a change less in Gladstone than in his times.

'I seemed to see the old dream of organic unity surviving where moral unity is lost' wrote Manning in 1865 of the 1840s.[109] For both Gladstone and Manning this vision faded quickly in the late 1840s. Manning found his alternative in rigid ultramontanism, Gladstone, first in ecumenical activities and later, after the 1870-4 debacle, in crusades to reconstruct 'moral unity' through the humanitarianism of the 'party of progress', in which his personal motivation was 'religious' but a religious motivation veiled because of the need to preserve unity over a wide front—a tacit acceptance of secularisation.

A. J. Beresford-Hope had been, with Gladstone, the chief layman involved. See also Liddon's notes of a conversation with Döllinger, 11 June 1880, Liddon MSS.

[108] See Gladstone's 'Soliloquium and Postscript' of 1896 in his *Later Gleanings* (London 1897) p xiii.

[109] H. E. Manning, *The temporal mission of the Holy Ghost* (6 ed London 1909) p 31.

In the 1830s, anglicanism was an undifferentiable element of English society and of the English identification of the nature of the state. The development and political success of nonconformity and of English Roman catholicism outside anglicanism, and of the Oxford movement within it, forced the anglican church to accept a degree of pluralism. It was to forestall this development that Gladstone's early books had been written. But this had been a pluralism of branches of Christianity; paganism had been a regret but not an intrusion. But by the 1870s, the 'religious' aspect of public campaigns of the Gladstonian sort had become self-conscious and was beginning to look anomalous; the anglican church recognised that 'religious nationality' had become a dream, even supposing it had ever been a reality.

Christ Church
Oxford

OTTO DIBELIUS:
A MISSING PIECE IN THE
PUZZLE OF DIETRICH BONHOEFFER?

by HADDON WILLMER

OTTO Dibelius is missing in our interpretations of Dietrich Bonhoeffer's development in the sense that though well-known, the Berlin general superintendent has been little thought of in this role. Eberhard Bethge in his life of Bonhoeffer and in the collected writings gives enough evidence of their social and ecclesiastical connections throughout Bonhoeffer's career to provoke enquiry.[1] That Bethge and others have not pursued the enquiry is due in part to the fluctuations of Dibelius's reputation, especially in the tradition of the Berlin theologians who were young around 1930. Bonhoeffer's life was written in the shadows of the last period of Dibelius's life, when he was a prince of the restored evangelical church, the 'NATO-bishop' taking a different line in the cold war from many who were finding their prophet in Bonhoeffer.

Another reason for neglect is that the study of Bonhoeffer has been primarily theological, not historical. Theologians tend to regard the personal development of the theologian as of little value in understanding his work.[2] So, Bonhoeffer scholarship notes those connections made explicit by Bonhoeffer himself as of theological importance—most of all, the relation with Barth—but they ignore those which require to be uncovered by historical exploration. In this respect, even Bethge's life is only partially an exception.

It is possible that Dibelius was unimportant to Bonhoeffer, and that this is why he mentioned him little. In that case interpreters of Bonhoeffer are right to neglect him, but only as it were by luck. For we may make little explicit mention not only of those who are unimportant to us, but also of those who are close to us, in a relation that goes

---

[1] [E.] Bethge, [Dietrich Bonhoeffer] (Munich 1967) pp 122, 207, 178 (compare O. Dibelius in Der Tag, 27 February 1927; 19 February 1933 and [O.] Dibelius, [Die] Verantwortung [der Kirche] (Berlin 1931); Bethge pp 870, 915; [D. Bonhoeffer], G[esammelte] S[chriften] (Munich) 2, p 441; Bonhoeffer Gedenkheft, ed E. Bethge (Berlin 1947) pp 34-5.

[2] K. Scholder, 'Neuere deutsche Geschichte und protestantische Theologie', Evangelische Theologie, 23, 10 (Munich 1963) pp 510-11.

without saying, or that generates oblique and inhibited references only, because comment of any other sort may be embarrassing. A study of motivation must look for what is so important that it has to be concealed. Whether Bonhoeffer's relation with Dibelius was such cannot be decided on Bonhoeffer's explicit references to Dibelius, nor on what later traditions incline us to think must have been. Only imaginative reflection on the evidence, ready to entertain, as one hypothesis, positive relation between them can bring us nearer the truth. Of course, the relation may turn out to have merely anecdotal, human interest. Against that view, I wish to argue that it was important for Bonhoeffer's formation as a theologian and so for our understanding of him and his times.

It was not easy to be neutral about Dibelius, who in the ten years after *Das Jahrhundert der Kirche* (1926) was one of the most controversial figures in German protestantism. Communists and nazis, church bureaucrats and academic theologians all found him provocative—often enough because he seemed to be too close to their opponents.[3] By the early 1930s Dibelius had roused many of the younger theologians of Berlin, especially those attracted by Barth.[4] When in January 1931 Barth lectured in Berlin on *Die Not der Evangelischen Kirche* and a week later, Dibelius replied on *Die Verantwortung der Kirche*, the battle standards had been raised. A major theological and practical issue for many in Berlin was identified. Even though it occurred while he was in America it had similar significance for Bonhoeffer.[5] Apparently, he had not got involved in the earlier controversy about *Das Jahrhundert der Kirche*—perhaps he was too young, perhaps still too taken up with purely academic theology. Just as cultured Germans declined to take *Mein Kampf* seriously, because of its barbarous style, so theologians dismissed Dibelius's book because it lacked theology. But Bonhoeffer's view of the task of the theologian became more churchly around 1930,[6] and the Dibelius who answered Barth in 1931 became for him not a teacher but at least a problematic reference point. As late as 1936 he was explicitly arguing that protestants in Germany were beset by two dangers in their conflict about the place of the church in the world: on one hand they could fall for an 'idealistic-docetic' ecclesiology, which he characterised as a 'misunderstood Barthian theology', and

[3] For example, [O. Dibelius,] *Nachspiel* (Berlin 1928) p 89.
[4] Compare my paper on the controversy between Dibelius, Barth and Heinrich Vogel (forthcoming).
[5] Bethge pp 178, 208.
[6] *Ibid* pp 268 *seq.*

on the other, be taken in by a 'materialistic-secular or magical-sacramental' ecclesiology, which was Dibelius's theology 'rightly understood'.[7]

The controversy of 1931 was an occasion where Bonhoeffer's deepening attachment to Barth issued in antipathy to Dibelius. There may, however, have been more in his attitude than suspicion and hostility. Bonhoeffer probably first heard of the lectures through a letter from his mother, who told him she had been at a party where someone from the evangelical church press spoke in an unmannerly way about Barth's lecture, and was rebuked by Dibelius who did not think Barth was so lightly to be dismissed.[8] He was aware, then, that Dibelius took a more sober and open view, feeling no need to radicalise the argument into an uncompromising alternative. Bonhoeffer always had a natural tendency to radicalise conflicts; and at this period especially, the growing sense of crisis in Germany reacted with his own youthful impatience and intellectual-cum-spiritual intensity to lead him to side with Barth against Dibelius. But Bonhoeffer was not a simple character. Like Dibelius he was a Prussian, a Lutheran and a pupil of Harnack's. His home was the single most important influence on him.[9] Good manners, a dislike of pathos and a commitment to objectivity were all parts of his character. (Later his *Ethics* were to show how he valued the normality of an ordered and modest life even while he accepted that the abyss had opened and a revolution made by the good was called for.)[10] Bonhoeffer came close to fanaticism especially in the earlier 1930s, but the tinge of embarrassment when he explained himself to his family shows that it was still put under question at the boundary by his objectivity.[11] Indeed the cultivation of objectivity was deliberate and self conscious because it was not the commonplace objectivity of secularism or positivism. Like Barth, he sought *Sachlichkeit* theologically, as attention and obedience to the Word of God. The theological quest, pursued so radically, could easily appear to be fanaticism; but despite the danger that objectivity might become merely fanaticism's camouflaged self-assertion, it was in fact more than that in Bonhoeffer. His theological quest, however irrational it could appear, was on one side the necessary working out of what he had by natural inheritance.[12]

[7] GS 3, p 325.
[8] Bethge p 207.
[9] Bethge pp 159 *seq.*
[10] [D. Bonhoeffer] *Ethics* (Fontana 1964) pp 64 *seq*, 263 *seq.*
[11] Bethge p 249.   [12] *Ibid* p 246; *Ethics* pp 55, 64 *seq.*

Bonhoeffer, then, was not only aware of Dibelius's openness, but shared with him qualities which prevented a relation of simple anti-pathy. Bonhoeffer was a critic of Dibelius, but that did not rule out paying him serious attention, and to some extent he shared his concerns and spoke his language. Bonhoeffer's commitment to Ger-many, to Berlin, and to the church there made him as close to Dibelius on those matters as he was on others to Barth. For example, although he sometimes went to the church of Günther Dehn, Bonhoeffer did not share Dehn's Barthian unwillingness to relate the sacrifices men make for others in society with the sacrifice of Christ.[13] That Bonhoeffer was never a straightforward Barthian may be symbolised, if it is not explained by, what he shared with Dibelius.

There can be no denying that Bonhoeffer, especially in the early 1930s, attempted to distance himself from Dibelius, sometimes by impatient scepticism about him.[14] But Bonhoeffer's later reconsidera-tion of his development suggests this evidence should not be taken merely at face value. At the end of his life Bonhoeffer came to accept himself and ceased to be worried by the fact that he had never experienced any drastic break in the continuity of personal develop-ment (at least after 1930).[15] But in the 1930s, when the Barth-Dibelius confrontation, like so many other disturbing changes, seemed to place Berlin theologians before an *Either-Or*, the younger Bonhoeffer was looking for such a break from his past, a transformation of his being, just as Germans generally were 'under the very definite impression that they are standing at a tremendous turning point in world history'.[16] Bonhoeffer's discontent with himself and his feeling of the redundancy of the German past expressed itself in hostility to Dibelius, precisely because so much of himself and that past was represented by Dibelius. We must try to interpret this relationship with the finesse of Bonhoeffer's own later comments on his development in the 1930s. He experienced some kind of determinative conversion around 1930-1, and never regretted it.[17] But as his later views on *The Cost of Discipleship* show, he could affirm the general direction of his growth

[13] Dehn had argued that John 15:13 should not be used on war memorials, since the death of soldiers could never be likened to the death of Jesus; theology and politics have to be separated. See G. Dehn *Kirche und Volkerversammlung* (Berlin 1932). Compare *GS* 3, pp 259-69. 'Das Recht auf Selbstbehauptung', and Bethge p 161.
[14] See his letter to his Barthian friend Sutz on Dibelius's lecture, Christmas 1931, *GS* 1 p 26.
[15] [D. Bonhoeffer] *Letters [and Papers from Prison]* (London 1953) 22 April 1944.
[16] *GS* 1, pp 23 *seq.*
[17] Bethge pp 246 *seq.*

without feeling bound to every act and attitude which it had involved.[18] Earlier, he had not been aware how deep the opposition was between Lasserre's wishing to be a saint and his own desire to learn to believe. At the end he accepted that they were very different, and faith meant declining *aus sich selbst etwas zu machen*, so as to live fully in the world, in the sufferings of God in the world. Dibelius also understood and expressed his Lutheran spirituality in a similar way. In 1935, for instance, Dibelius had made a remarkable speech in the court case he brought to clear himself from the widely spread charge of high treason, in which he said that faith in Luther's sense meant, *der Mensch darauf verzichtet aus sich selber etwas zu machen . . .*[19] The wording may be that of a Lutheran commonplace, but for both Dibelius and Bonhoeffer it was the clue to the true way of the Christian in the world before God.

At least for the sake of argument, then, it is not frivolous to look for positive aspects of the relation between these two men, without denying the differences of age, of politics and of theology. Another suggestive piece of evidence is to be found in Bonhoeffer's lectures of 1931–2 on the history of twentieth-century systematic theology.[20] Barth is the central figure: only in him did the human spheres of religion and culture cease to be basic categories of theological conversation and give way to those of God and man. In this historical perspective Dibelius was identified as a pre-Barthian. The independence of the church he so much prized was no more than a creation of cultural development, (*Geschenk der Kultur*), an outcome of the shattering of a unified culture which took political form at the end of the war in 1918–19. Barth's theology, by contrast, came from God's word—it was not *Kriegspsychose sondern Hören auf Gottes Wort. Barth kommt nicht aus dem Schützengraben, sondern von einer Schweizer Dorf Kanzel.* So Bonhoeffer would not allow that the new leadership of the church (that is, Dibelius) might be seen in parallel with Barthian theology, as Dibelius himself wanted—a renewed theology for a church in renewal. They were incompatible, for one was the outcome of merely human development, the other came from God.

After this negative judgement on Dibelius, however, Bonhoeffer listed in his final lecture some questions which had to be faced along

[18] *Letters*, 5 December 1943, 21 July 1944. Compare note 12.
[19] O. Dibelius, *Die Kraft der Deutschen, in Gegensätzen zu leben* (Berlin 1936) F. Gollert, *Dibelius vor Gericht* (Munich 1959) pp 160–71.
[20] GS 5, pp 181–226, esp pp 215–16.

the road opened by Barth. The last of these stemmed from his well known concern that Barth hindered any concrete ethic.[21] And here Bonhoeffer's similarity with Dibelius becomes evident, for Dibelius had asked whether Barth was able to speak to the concrete situation in Germany. Bonhoeffer concluded:

> Unsere kirchlichen Botschaften sind dadurch so kraftlos, dass sie auf der Mitte bleiben zwischen allgemeinen Prinzipien und konkreter Lage. Die Not der Kirche ist stets auch die Not der theologischen Fakultäten. Nur dass diese dafür in der Regel blind sind! Luther konnte de servo arbitrio und die Schrift vom Zinsgroschen gleichzeitig schreiben. Warum können wir das nicht mehr? Wer zeigt uns Luther?

Talk of *die Not der Kirche* in Berlin in early 1932 would be heard as an allusion to Barth's lecture there in 1931. But Bonhoeffer's definition of the distress echoed Dibelius rather than Barth. And it is not impossible that Bonhoeffer is deliberately quoting Dibelius, thus making a significant response to Dibelius's criticism of Barth. In his lecture, Dibelius had said that the concentration on theology threatened to make the life and work of the church abstract and doctrinaire. Recent research gave the impression, he complained, that Luther wrote little more than a book *über den unfreien Willen: Dass er auch von Kaufhandlung und Wucher, von der Ordnung des gemeinen Kastens, vom Türkenkreig und von der Bauernrevolte geschrieben hat, davon hört man selten.* Comparing the sermons of dialectical theologians and Luther, he found *dort theologische Auseinandersetzungen, zeitlose und vielfach blutleere Abstraktionen; und bei Luther alles hineingestellt in das Leben, wie es seine Wittenberger Gemeinde führt, überall ein kraftvolles Anpacken äusserer Fragen.*[22]

Bonhoeffer wanted the concrete ethic, to know how law could be preached as well as gospel. And he was always prepared to understand that in an historical way, related to the specific situation in German and world history,[23] whereas Barth even in the church conflict spoke with such Christological purity that it could too easily be taken as *zeitlos*.[24] Bonhoeffer's commitment to the visible church[25] was the result of a development not unlike Dibelius's in some respects, for the latter had

---

[21] *Ibid* p 227.
[22] Dibelius, *Verantwortung*, pp 5–6.
[23] *Ethics* pp 85 seq.
[24] Karl Barth, *The German Church Conflict* (London 1965) pp 30 seq.
[25] *GS* 1, pp 61–3. These letters to Rössler become clearer when read in the context of the Barth-Dibelius debate of 1931.

become a churchman out of faith in Jesus and of ethical responsibility together.[26] The church for Dibelius was no *Selbstzweck*; the test of the church was the effectiveness of its obedience to the command to love neighbour. Bonhoeffer was unwilling theologically to follow the pre-Barthian liberalism of Dibelius, and disliked many practical features of Dibelius's church, but he too wanted an ethically responsible ecclesiology. We may conclude that Bonhoeffer, in part, perceived his theological task to be given by his place between Barth and Dibelius. This situation helps to explain why, so often, Bonhoeffer gives the impression of being constricted—it was not easy to criticise Barth without getting closer to Dibelius than he wished. In theology, there is not an infinity of wave bands. The obvious options had been stated by others, and there was little room for manoeuvre to develop a distinctive third way.

Another example of Bonhoeffer's critical yet respectful relation to Dibelius is hidden in the *Ethics*.[27] In the course of a discussion of the ways in which 'calling' might limit 'responsibility', he gives an example. In 1931 (the English translation of the *Ethics* wrongly says 1831) nine young negroes in the USA were sentenced to death for the rape of a white girl of doubtful reputation.[28] 'There arose a storm of indignation which found expression in open letters from some of the most authoritative public figures in Europe. A Christian who was perturbed by this affair asked a prominent cleric (*einer führender Kirchenmann*) whether he, too, ought not to raise his voice on this matter, and on the grounds of the "Lutheran" idea of vocation, that is to say, on the grounds of the limitation of his responsibility, the clergyman refused . . .'

The leading churchman was, I think, Dibelius. In 1933, writing almost the last of his Sunday articles in *Der Tag* before his frankness was found unacceptable, Dibelius recalled how he had declined to

---

[26] *Nachspiel* pp 46 *seq*.

[27] *Ethics* p 260. How close Bonhoeffer got to Dibelius on the subject of responsibility and service is suggested implicitly by Dorothee Sölle's criticism of Bonhoeffer in *Christ the Representative* (London 1967) pp 96–7.

[28] I am grateful to the members of the Ecclesiastical History Society who, in the discussion of this paper, directed my attention to the Scottsboro Case which began its terrible course at the end of March 1931, while Bonhoeffer was in America. Nine negroes in all were charged with the rape of two white girls. The discrepancies in numbers between the different accounts mentioned in the text may well arise from the complications of the case and are unimportant here. There can be little doubt that it is this case to which Bonhoeffer refers. See Dan T. Carter, *Scottsboro: A Tragedy of the American South* (Louisiana 1969) pp 59, 142, 146.

intercede for two blacks falsely condemned in America, which would have put the evangelical church alongside protesters like Einstein and Thomas Mann.[29] Dibelius had acted on the principle that he should not interfere without knowledge of the situation or a request from the church of the land unless the local Christian church had been prevented from speaking, and he quoted this case in 1933 to rebuff the protest from the anglican bishop Manning of New York about the 'so-called persecution of the Jews' in Germany.

If Dibelius was 'the leading churchman', it is more than likely that Bonhoeffer was the 'perturbed Christian'. If not, why the Kierke-gaardian anonymity? That he remembered this incident a decade later indicates perhaps how seriously he was engaged with Dibelius in the early 1930s. The story makes clear what sharp disagreements existed between them. But there was also a respect from Bonhoeffer's side grounded in an ethical humility he shared with Dibelius. For under the cloak of anonymity he could easily have condemned 'the churchman's' conduct outright, had he wished. Instead he moved on with the comment: 'We do not say this in order to pass judgement in the particular case. . . . We say it in order to keep open the boundary'. Perhaps the truth was that Bonhoeffer knew Dibelius (and others like him) well enough to be aware that it was not cowardice or gross ethical blindness that conditioned his action so much as concern that action be responsible. Bonhoeffer could still have had Dibelius in mind when, in the next paragraph, he quoted cases from the church conflict of pastors who had refused to intervene where their own flocks were not affected, but did so with 'free responsibility' when they were. Kurt Scharf tells of an encounter between Dibelius, Stupperich, Bonhoeffer and himself in 1933.[30] Dibelius had written brave and clear words about nazism and the German Christians, but the young pastors

---

[29] *Der Tag*, 26 March 1933. To pass judgement on Dibelius's political stance, and especially on his conduct in the early months of Hitler's regime, is not the purpose of this paper. Dibelius is hardly to be defended, except against simplified condemnations, in which, for example, he is contrasted with Bonhoeffer, as black from white.

Bonhoeffer's article on 'The Church and the Jewish Question', (GS 2, pp 44–53, 1933) makes the crucial concessions to supposed political necessity in principle which Dibelius, given his official position and consistency, acted on. Bonhoeffer, like Barth, was concerned primarily with the theological issue, of what put the church *in statu confessionis*. He was then impatient with men like Dibelius who did not see the church situation immediately in such extreme terms, not because they were blind or crypto-nazis, but because they had a very similar political analysis and ethic to Bonhoeffer's. And on many points it was politics not theology that was determinative—as Bonhoeffer allowed, it was the state not the church that made history.

[30] *Die Stunde der Kirche, Festschrift* for Dibelius (Berlin 1950) p 35.

thought Dibelius was too objective and careful in his judgement. They failed to persuade him to a radical rejection of the teaching and methods of the German Christians. They accused him of indulging in historical relativism, when uncompromising prophetic decision was called for. Scharf comments: *Wir haben später gelernt, dass man solche Grundsätze als ein christlicher Streiter haben und dennoch in der sachlichen Entscheidung unerbittlich konsequent und vor der Übermacht der Gewalt unerschrocken tapfer sein kann, ja dass nur durch solche Haltung der Kampf rein bleibt und zum Zeugnis für Gottes Ehre wird.*

Bonhoeffer might well have agreed. When at the end of 1942, he made the moral reckoning, *After Ten Years*, he showed himself deeply sensitive to the problems of keeping the struggle pure, and saw it as essential if he and his friends were to be usable.[31]

Dibelius's person, his deeds and words, are then a neglected aid to our interpretation of Bonhoeffer and may throw light on much that has not been mentioned here. I am not concerned to argue that Dibelius explains Bonhoeffer's growth, if that means claiming that he exercised a significant causal influence on him. Not influence but character, not act so much as being, is disclosed. Dibelius enables us to see something of what was in Bonhoeffer, because he drew it out from him. When the relation of these two is discussed we get beyond abstract talk of Bonhoeffer's Germanness and Lutheranism to deal with their concrete historicity. And we become aware of the complexities of the personal, tactical and theological problems of the younger Bonhoeffer. In his positive and negative relation with Dibelius, in tension with his commitments to the church in Germany and to Barth, we are made aware of some of the bewildering and powerful motivations at play in Bonhoeffer's development.

University of Leeds

[31] In *Letters.*

THE SOCIALIST COMMITMENT
IN KARL BARTH

by W. R. WARD

T HE young Karl Barth is not an easy man to assess. It is not just that he covered a major theological revulsion by violent polemics, nor even that in the second world war he became a cult figure with hard-pressed protestants everywhere, overwhelmed by the need to save their churches from the destructive compromises of the church leaders, and subsequently, more briefly, a cult figure with a new theological establishment. More recently the young Karl Barth has been the victim of disputes over the uses to which Barthianism can be put. In the German student revolt the need to unify thought and action in politics and theology exposed a generation gap; a burning concern to many theological students, it embarrassed many of their teachers. At the Kirchliche Hochschule in Berlin, a bastion of Barthianism, Friedrich-Wilhelm Marquardt, a pupil of Hellmut Gollwitzer, sought to bridge the gap by showing that from beginning to end the core of Barth's theology was a socialist commitment. (The first paragraph of this book reads starkly, 'Karl Barth was Socialist'.)[1] The perspective first opened by the student movement was confirmed by Marquardt's editorial work on Barth's Safenwil remains, and especially on forty three socialist speeches. Marquardt worked out his view systematically in a *Habilitationschrift* which was rejected at the Kirchliche Hochschule as *unwissenschaftlich*. Gollwitzer made a public scene, got the book published, and took the whole argument further in a long essay of his own.[2] The clinching evidence (if that is what it really is) of the speeches is not available under the terms on which Karl Barth's unpublished remains are being edited until the volume in which they are to be incorporated is published. Yet most of the voluminous material ever likely to be available for the young Barth is now in print, and it is worth examining in its own right, as distinct from being expounded in the light of the *Church Dogmatics* with Marquardt.

[1] [F.-W.] Marquardt, [*Theologie und Sozialismus, Das Beispiel Karl Barths*] (Munich 1972) p 39.
[2] [Helmut] Gollwitzer, [*Reich Gottes und Sozialismus bei Karl Barth*], Theologische Existenz heute no 169 (Munich 1972).

Marquardt's argument is that the socialist practice of Barth's years as a parish minister at Safenwil (1911–21) shaped not merely his social theory but his understanding of God. If Barth's socialism was in a sense pre-Marxist, apocalyptic, his conception of the unity of theory and practice was very Marxist indeed, notwithstanding current allegations from the DDR that Barth represented 'a genuine bourgeois position'.[3] For the only practice corresponding to the kingdom of God must be a practice aiming to overthrow social conditions which radically contradicted the kingdom. The living God who fetched up in the last volume of the *Church Dogmatics* as 'the partisan of the poor and finally . . . revolutionary'[4] had been the great overthrower from the beginning. As Marquardt puts it, Barth's development had been 'from "God" as a hall-mark of revolution interpreted in the religious-socialist way, to "revolution" as the hall-mark of God understood in revelation.'[5] If revolution implies radical discontinuity, so also do justification and the new birth as understood in the reformed tradition. The bourgeoisie had the material and moral resources to benefit by reform. The only hope for the proletariat was in a total up-heaval in their inward and outward circumstances; but in its desperate helplessness the proletariat was close to the kingdom of God. The socialist understanding of the proletarian lot was a parable of the human predicament; the will to revolution was a parable of God's response. To admit, as eventually Brunner came to do, even a point of contact between natural man and the living God, was not merely an erroneous concession to humanism, it was bourgeois reformism. Indeed natural theology, an attempt by human resources to lay some hold on the riddle of existence, and to domesticate revelation by laying a foundation for it, was simply the *Verbürgerlichung des Evangeliums*, the process of making the gospel respectable.[6] No discontinuity could be more discontinuous or revolutionary than the resurrection, understood not so much Christologically as apocalyptically, the secret force of God in the history of the world, the beginning of a messianic history on earth, of a new people of God who grasp the act of God and are grasped by it.[7] How do all these claims look in the light of Barth's voluminous early correspondence, the scores of sermons and addresses, and the first two editions of his *Romans* (1919 and 1921)?

[3] Robert Steigerwald, *Marxismus-Religion-Gegenwart* ([East] Berlin 1973) p 157.
[4] [Karl] Barth, [*Church*] *Dogmatics* (Edinburgh 1936–69) 4/2 p 180.
[5] Marquardt p 27.
[6] *Ibid* pp 117–18, 293–4: Gollwitzer p 30: E. Brunner and K. Barth, *Natural theology* (London 1946): Barth, *Dogmatics* 2/1 p 141.   [7] Marquardt p 192.

The socialist commitment in Karl Barth

Even as a student Barth had written a paper for the Zofingia society embodying conventional religious-social views, and like so many others, in Switzerland as well as England, found a way into the social question through the Blue Cross teetotal movement. He made no secret of his socialist views from the moment of his arrival in Safenwil, and was certainly considering joining the party as early as midsummer 1913.[8] The jolt Barth received from the patriotic stance of his German teachers at the outbreak of war, he steadily embroidered into one of the most famous legends of recent church history, even claiming that it justified turning against the whole theological tradition stemming from Schleiermacher,[9] a blanket condemnation from which only Schleiermacher's rough handling by the Prussian government earned him exoneration in Barth's extreme old age.[10] It ought to have been as important to Barth as it was to Ragaz that the leaders of the second international had behaved as badly as the theologians, but instead he joined the party early in 1915, explaining that 'just because I set such emphasis Sunday by Sunday on the last things, it was no longer possible for me personally to remain suspended in the clouds above the present evil world'. This eschatological gesture was, however, one of qualified solidarity. Barth limiting his party activity to paying sub-scriptions and giving lectures,[11] in which, among other things, he explained what was wrong with the party. 'I do it without enthusiasm', he reported in 1916, 'because it is necessary and because I cannot as yet get on to the one thing necessary with them in the way it must be done'.[12] There was also some trade union activity, and in the autumn of 1917, he became involved in a clash between fifty five women knitters in his parish who organised and were threatened with dismissal by their employer. Barth interceded with the employer who gave him a polite reception and then declared war, adding that Barth 'was the worst enemy he has had in his whole life'. Barth claimed to have shown that the gospel was behind the knitters, and the village also backed them up; but he reported, 'I have contributed *nothing* directly other than a statement of facts to the factory workers, on which

---

[8] [K. Barth, *Gesamtausgabe* 5] *Barth-Thurneysen Briefwechsel* (Zurich 1973–4) I, pp 4–5.
[9] [Eberhard] Busch, [*Karl Barths Lebenslauf: nach seinen Briefen und autobiographischen Texten*] (Munich 1975) pp 93–4.
[10] *Schleiermacher-Auswahl. Mit einem Nachwort von Karl Barth*, ed H. Bolli (Munich/Hamburg 1968) pp 293–4.
[11] *Barth-Thurneysen Briefwechsel* I, p 30, partly translated into English in [J. D.] Smart, [*Revolutionary theology in the making*] (London 1964) p 28.
[12] *Ibid* I p 122, Smart p 36.

I . . . reported in the meeting, in order to make clear to them the seriousness of their position'.[13] No more indeed is heard of the united knitting workers. In all this there is something less than the practitioner of revolution being led to the God of revolution and back again. So far from the hostile mill-owner opposing Barth's re-election to the parish in 1917, he got him an increase in pay, and the relief measures Barth organised during the influenza epidemic of November 1918 were generously supported by the employers of the village. The truth is that the vast correspondence with Thurneysen is strikingly unpolitical, overwhelmingly dominated by ecclesiastical concerns, exchanges of sermons, the preparation of the commentary on Romans, professional reading and so forth. For a man preaching an eschatological hope, perceiving the breaking through of the kingdom of God, Barth's silence about the events of the time is deafening. He seems to have had a perverse sympathy with the German offensive in March 1918,[14] and his sneers against the league of nations were even more offensive than the barbs he usually directed against Ragaz whose pro-league sympathies were doubtless what really provoked him. 'The good-boy Anti-Christ in Wilson is now coming to light and the League of Nations will surely become the great whore of Babylon.'[15] Thurneysen enthused over Barth's reports of the strength of old-fashioned pietism in Württemberg, rejoiced that Germany 'did not have to be transformed into a red army camp like Hungary! And [held that] despite everything I would rather stand by Germany than by Wilson who wants to attend the peace settlement with his wife and children, apparently in high moral spirits.'[16]

The argument from silence to the conclusion that Barth was basically unpolitical is clinched by what he does not say on the theme he claimed to take seriously, that of socialism. There is not the least suggestion that he knew or cared that the party he had joined was at the centre of important developments in the world of international labour; still less that he appreciated that the labour troubles in his own parish were part of the wider resentments that led to the Zürich riots in November

[13] *Ibid* 1 pp 98, 208, 223, 227, 229 (Smart p 42), 230 (Smart pp 42–3—included in wrong letter) 233.

[14] *Ibid* 1 p 271, Smart p 44 (This paragraph is misleading as it does not indicate the omission of two sentences).

[15] *Ibid* 1 p 327.

[16] *Ibid* 1 p 335, compare [K. Barth and E. Thurneysen], *Suchet Gott*, [*so werdet ihr leben*] (2 ed Zollikon 1928) p 64: 'We [that is, sinful men] are President Wilson and would like to proclaim peace to half the world—and have ourselves to set the other half alight.'

The socialist commitment in Karl Barth

1917. The year between the riots and the general strike was still more tense; Barth, the man who proclaimed from the pulpit that 'God is! signifies a revolution', had absolutely nothing to say.[17] While Ragaz was puzzling out the drift of the times from Burckhardt and Alexander Herzen, and even Thurneysen was seeking illumination from Carlyle's *French Revolution*,[18] Barth, who throughout the year had been applying himself intensively to the Württemberger pietists, was pinning his faith to the apocalyptic Bengel.[19] Thurneysen indeed reminded him that there were reactionary pietists who had interfered in politics too much, but then, as Switzerland teetered on the edge of revolution, Thurneysen was not willing to make a public proclamation, for he was not sure whether events portended bolshevism, the last things, or a revival of the age of Metternich.[20] None of this can be reckoned a moral failing in Barth. He had his *Romans* to finish, and the pietist literature seemed one road to that goal. Nor did his literary labour exclude assisting his parishioners, as distinct from his core-congregation in their temporal necessities. Nevertheless the record seems threadbare as evidence for a Marxist union of theory and praxis, and it suggests that when Barth talked about socialism, he sometimes did so in a rather special sense.

That this is the case is the tenor of the utterances from Thurneysen's side of the partnership (whence most of the references to the affairs of the day come) and of the sermons of the two friends so far published. In 1914 Thurneysen had to prime Barth about Naumann,[21] on whom he had published a substantial paper in 1910.[22] Naumann is here perceived as significant in the sharpness of the antithesis which he discovered between Christianity and the autonomous power-state, and the way he exemplified the more general problem posed to Christianity by modern openness to autonomous culture. It was this which led to the everlasting discussions of the day on Christianity and culture, ethics and business, religion and socialism, all those things which Barth was to put under the blanket condemnation of 'hyphenated

[17] [K. Barth, *Gesamtausgabe* 1] *Predigten 1914* p 168: *Suchet Gott*, p 102. Barth was prepared to explain the strike when it was all over: *Barth – Thurneysen Briefwechsel* I p 321.
[18] *Ibid* 1 p 302.
[19] *Ibid* 1 pp 196, 201–2, 205, 214–16, 300, 307, 320, 327.
[20] *Ibid* 1 pp 221, 303, 323.
[21] *Ibid* 1 pp 5–7.
[22] E. Thurneysen, 'Ethik und Politik in ihrem gegenseitigen Verhältnis bei Friedrich Naumann', *Centralblatt des Schweizerischen Zofingervereins* 21 (Basel? 1910–11) pp 138–60.

Christianity'. In 1910 Thurneysen could find no ethical basis for the state, though he was prepared to argue with Troeltsch that the state must provide for the good life according to the current level of cultural achievement, once the physical basis of existence had been met. Thus the separation of political and religious values was not as complete as was affirmed by Naumann from the side of the state, or by Tolstoy from the side of the kingdom of God. There was a positive Christian ethic distinct from all *Kulturseligkeit*, from which the achievements, crises and catastrophes of public life could not be withdrawn, but a manifold reality was not to be conceived in simple formulae; it must be laid hold of and mastered in personal act and decision. At this point Thurneysen was already fitted to absorb Barth's later doctrine that language about God and man could not proceed on the same level, and their common addiction to Russian spirituality, and especially Dostoievsky.[23] It was also significant that Thurneysen responded with genuine enthusiasm to Naumann's early period, quoting a long passage from *Was heisst christlich-sozial?* (1894): 'We feel the Christian-social cause as a force and power. It hovers over us as a new power of thought, it moves us, raises up, bears us. . . . The gospel is to us as a melting glow, the power of a new epoch.' Here in the young Naumann at his most unpolitical was the rhetoric needed by Kutter and the young Barth to express the action of the living God. It was perhaps too close for comfort to the stark irrationalism of the life-philosophy and was not politics at all in the ordinary sense of the word.

Echoes of the Naumann discussion recur in Barth's sermons for 1914. Jesus had fought for social justice, but now men supposed the fight could go on without him. Barth replies 'it is to stand the matter on its head if one says: indeed . . . we want Socialism, but not the source from which it flowed and must flow, if it wishes to be something genuine or deep.' And the conclusion is doubly unpolitical. 'Yes, Jesus has proclaimed a new, righteous world, the Kingdom of God, but only those will enter it, only those will see it, who are of a pure

---

[23] *Barth-Thurneysen Briefwechsel* I pp 25, 72, 167, 324, 404. In the secular Russian tradition revolution was transformed from being the means to an end into a way of life—Theodor Schieder, *Staat und Gesellschaft im Wandel unserer Zeit* (3 ed Munich 1974) pp 42–6; it was fitting that theologians given to equating resurrection and revolution should turn back to the Russian religious tradition. On the theological and political debate on revolution in Russia, see Bastiaan Wielenga, *Lenins Weg zur Revolution. Eine Konfrontation mit Sergei Bulgakov und Petr Struve im Interesse einer theologischen Besinnung* (Munich 1971).

heart and a good will . . . whoever wants a better world must become a better man'. The conclusion of November 1914 was predictable: 'Others expect salvation from a general *revolution*, from a rising of peoples against their governments . . . [But] in reality every nation has the government it deserves.'[24] To right wrong by revolution was to cast out devils by Beelzebub. The socialists had failed to stop the war, and the moral was, 'put not your trust in men (compare Ps 146 3) whatever their names may be'.[25] In six hundred and fifty pages of sermons the momentous politics of 1914 receive a handful of banalities of this kind, banalities on the whole derogatory to socialism. The later sermons published as *Suchet Gott, so werdet ihr leben* (1917) show equally little evidence of the concurrent reading of the bible and newspaper with which Barth is credited, though the anti-establishment tone is sharper,[26] and there is the acute feeling of social break-up which had been with the religious-socialist movement from the beginning. Yet the social movements in Russia and elsewhere were 'not the full powerful, certain wind of the spirit as it happened at Pentecost',[27] and the earth tremors 'powerfully rattling at our churches' did not alter the fact that efforts to reorder the world of work or education, politics and social relations must take second place to 'the great turn from death to life, waiting to break forth from heaven upon earth'.[28] The role of the socialist party was that of an eschatological 'sign', it was a pointer to the Christian hope. That was why Blumhardt and Barth had joined it, and that was why Barth concluded of himself what he had elsewhere concluded of Blumhardt, that 'to hope upon God is something unpolitical and supra-political, and coincides with no party, be it socialist, conservative or liberal.'[29] Barth like Kutter was pressing the *analogia fidei*, the view that social unrest, socialism, was the earthly analogy of the action of the living God in judgement and redemption. There were two problems here. The first was that the closer socialism resembled an idea in the mind of God, the less connexion it could have with any working system of politics. The second was that the closer Barth came to Kutter in insisting on the indispensability of the *analogia fidei*, the less they could agree on what it amounted to. For in 1914 Kutter had become a violent

[24] *Predigten 1914* pp 38, 42, 591.
[25] *Ibid* pp 435–6. Compare pp 526, 531.
[26] For example *Suchet Gott* p 65.
[27] *Ibid* p 93.
[28] *Ibid* pp 133–4, 150.
[29] *Ibid* pp 170–2.

pro-German, was reported to be singing the 'Watch on the Rhine' all day and publicly maintaining that God demonstrated his purposes for mankind in the history of a particular people or state, specifically at present the German people and state, whose very authoritarianism was intended to nurture a culture of humanity for the human race at large.[30] Not for the last time, the *analogia fidei* seemed capable of producing results to order. But Kutter, counselling his young friends against destroying 'the inner processes of growth' by too much clarity,[31] encouraged work on the *Romans*, to the early editions of which we must now turn.

Barth's exposition of Romans 13. 1–7 ('Let every soul be subject to the higher powers. For . . . the powers that be are ordained of God') turned into a political tirade, but was not more singular than Marquardt's exposition of Barth. On Marquardt's view ' "Revolution" becomes . . . the basic concept of his understanding of God, his eschatology, his ethics',[32] and Barth's doctrine of the state is structured like Lenin's *State and Revolution* which had recently appeared. The state embodies no values, it is simply a power organisation existing for purposes of exploitation. The difference is that while Lenin was prepared to proceed to the dictatorship of the proletariat without waiting for better men to sustain it, Barth criticized the presumption of revolutionary individuals, and called for the 'absolute revolution of God'. No Christian revolutionary cadre has the fate of the kingdom of God in its hands, but the Christian revolutionary, unlike Lenin's comrades, is in some sense already 'a new creation'. Hence Barth's throw-away phrase which matters so much to Marquardt, that his revolution (or God's) is 'more than Leninism'.[33]

The unpolitical Barth of the war years did not of course suddenly metamorphose into a protestant Lenin. The keynote to his discussion is given at the very beginning—it is 'intended in the *Spirit* and must be understood in the *Spirit*. Only to the pure in heart will the path to be trod be and remain a *straight* path.'[34] It is a homily to the saints. History after the fall, declared Barth, is under the wrath of God, and the normal management of earthly relations through the righteousness of God can only be restored in Christ. So far from the powers that be being

[30] Hermann Kutter jun, *Herman Kutters Lebenswerk* (Zürich 1965) p 63. Compare *Barth-Thurneysen Briefwechsel* 1 p 339.
[31] *Ibid* 1 p 41.
[32] Marquardt pp 126–7.
[33] *Ibid* pp 126–41.
[34] K. Barth, *Der Römerbrief* (1 ed Bern 1919) p 375.

The socialist commitment in Karl Barth

ordained of God in the common place sense of the words, 'the power-state of the present day is diametrically opposed to the intentions of God; it is intrinsically evil'.[35] The state indeed achieved a certain interlocking balance in the affairs of fallen men, and as such is one of God's devices for keeping men in hand; but the overwhelming weight of Barth's rhetoric is directed to the point that the Christian as such has 'nothing to do with the power state,' any kind of power state or political party, with 'Gustavus Adolphus or Napoleon, Cromwell or Frederick the Great, Windthorst or Bebel . . . with monarchy, militarism, patriotism [or] liberalism.' 'All politics, as the struggle for power, as the diabolical art of legitimation, is *basically dirty*' and any Christian who goes into it, particularly bearing 'the banners of God' deserves all he gets, for he abandons the analogy of the sufferings of Christ.[36] The Christian has no fatherland, he still seeks one. 'The decisive struggle between the old and the new world will never be fought out in the political arena', and the absolute revolution of God is not to be hastened by individual initiative. 'Only through the quiet other-worldly construction of a new man according to the order of God' and through alienating the affections of the flock from this world to another, is the Christian 'to starve out the state religiously'. Right at the end of his treatment Barth returns with his left hand a little of what he has so violently taken away with his right, allowing that running away from politics has as little merit as deifying them. But the limit is 'illusionless fulfilment of duty without song-and-dance . . . *no* combinations of throne and altar, *no* Christian patriotism, no beating-up of democratic crowds. Strike and general-strike and street fighting if it must be, but *no* religious justification and glorification of it. Military service as soldier or officer, if it must be, but under *no* circumstances as chaplain'.[37] It was in this context that Barth uttered his now famous slogan, 'social-democratic but not religious-socialist.'[38] Barth had defended himself against the commonplace political idolatry of Germany, both protestant and catholic, but if pushed hard he might have had to concede at least a provisional autonomy to politics of the kind he so bitterly resented in Naumann. And the main tenor of his message, like so much of Barth in those years was pietism accompanied by an unpietist gnashing of teeth. It was not just that he gave no guid-

---

[35] *Ibid* p 376.
[36] *Ibid* pp 377–8, 381–2, 384, 386.
[37] *Ibid* pp 379, 380–1, 382, 388, 391.
[38] *Ibid* pp 387–90.

ance to the Christian caught up in street-fighting to decide on which side to fight, and approved only a minimum stake in a temporal order hastening to dissolution; it is that a man who can use the word 'penultimate' as a term of abuse[39] with an abandon perhaps only possible to one committed to the ethos of an endowed establishment, feels no need for discrimination among penultimate things and does not appreciate the ingenuity required to maintain a supply of them. There may be some virtue in this position; there is none in regarding it as the theological counterpart to Lenin, the exemplar of the terrifying potentialities of political decision.

A few months after the appearance of the *Romans*, Barth resumed his struggle for a transcendent view-point in his address on the 'Christian in Society' at the religious-socialist conference at Tambach.[40] Disenchantment with the state, now extended to other social institutions which claimed to grasp the riddle of existence—'authority in itself', especially academic authority, 'the family in itself . . . the voracious idol of the bourgeoisie', and, worst of all, 'religion as such . . . this power of death in its catholic and protestant form'.[41] Barth came within an ace of denying the possibility of policy,[42] but fetched up by saying that in Christ lay 'the overcoming of the false *denial of the world* and the unconditioned assurance against all *false* affirmation of the world'. The resurrection included God's 'Yes' and his 'No' to the world, just as socialism showed how it was impossible to say 'No' to the world without entering it.[43] The conclusion was that of Thurneysen in 1910: 'We will neither burn up and go mad about affirmation with Naumann until it becomes nonsense, nor go with Tolstoy into rejection until it becomes absurd'.[44] Once again Barth had, in the hottest possible language, advised the radical to play it cool.

The Tambach address opened the German market to Barth for the first time, literally as well as metaphorically, for it enabled him to find a German publisher; this in its turn led to the decision completely to rewrite the *Romans* and to twelve months of furious literary effort to

---

[39] *Ibid* pp 381, 391.
[40] Given, September 1919; published, 1920. Conveniently reprinted in [*Anfänge der dialectischen Theologie*, ed J.] Moltmann (Munich 1962-3). The fact that the English translation of Moltmann—James M. Robinson, *The beginnings of dialectical theology* (Richmond, Va., 1968)—omits the piece gives some colour to Marquardt's charge that a theological Barth has been invented *ex eventu*.
[41] Moltmann I pp 15-16.
[42] *Ibid* I pp 6, 8.
[43] *Ibid* I pp 21, 28.
[44] *Ibid* I pp 32-4, 36.

which even his parish preaching took second place. Marquardt who grossly exaggerates the significance of radical political decision in Barth's earliest theology, exaggerates again in seeing in the second Romans 'a sensational anti-revolutionary turn',[45] but has certainly got the direction right, and may well be correct in his supposition that the new stance contributed to the book's success in Germany on its appearance in 1922. It is not quite clear why the new turn took place. At the crucial time Thurneysen was writing his paper on 'Socialism and Christianity'[46] which showed little advance on the line of Kutter and Blumhardt; the doctrine was still the unpolitical one that socialism mattered because it taught the church about justification by faith.[47] But Barth now affirmed 'too broken a position towards Socialism' to be put on the list of party speakers, and found his curate, Frau Thurneysen's cousin, Fritz Lieb, reporting him as holding that 'the social question would be the next to come off the order of the day.'[48] It is hard to believe that Barth was not tempted by the very success of the Russian revolution to take it down a peg; and he suspected he had misled the German religious-socialists by the blunt certainties of the first edition.[49] Above all he had to cope in the most domestic sense with Fritz Lieb, who had gone over from Syriac to Karl Marx without acquiring discretion in transit. When the Swiss socialist party split in December 1920 on the issue of affiliation to the third international, and the minority withdrew to form a communist party, Lieb was one of the hardest hardliners among them; Barth was on the other side, and subsequently had to take time off from the second Romans to sort out Lieb's behaviour in both pulpit and parish.[50]

The new treatment bore the marks of the Tambach address, for it

[45] Marquardt p 142.

[46] Barth - Thurneysen Briefwechsel 1 pp 364–5. The paper was first published in Zwischen den Zeiten, 2 (Munich 1923) and republished in Moltmann 2, pp 221 seq, and E. Thurneysen Das Wort Gottes und die Kirche. Aufsätze und Vorträge (Munich 1971) pp 159 seq.

[47] Moltmann 2, pp 233–4. This may be what Thurneysen meant when late in life he said that Barth's socialism was to be understood theologically. [E.] Thurneysen, [Karl Barth, 'Theologie und Sozialismus' in den Briefen seiner Frühzeit] (Zürich 1973) p 31.

[48] Barth - Thurneysen Briefwechsel 1 pp 402, 404, 430, 449 (compare p 453).

[49] Ibid 1 p 436.

[50] Busch pp 117–18, 120, 131: Barth-Thurneysen Briefwechsel 1 pp 454, 486, 493, 495–6. Lieb (1892–1970) became a professor of systematic theology at Bonn 1931 (dismissed 1933) and Basel 1937. During the second world war he was connected with the French resistance movement to which he dedicated the French translation of his book, Russland Unterwegs (Bern 1945: translations into French, Dutch and Czech) advocating a positive approach to the Soviet Union. In 1947 he received a chair in East European church history at Berlin.

was directed not narrowly to the state and revolution, but to the whole range of great social institutions which limited the rights of individuals by virtue of their claim to solve the riddle of life. To admit their authority was to concede legitimation, to reject it was to accept the principle of revolution. Barth proposed to deny both in the name of the honour of God. But on the somewhat implausible ground that no-one was likely to be won for reaction reading Romans, he was specially concerned 'to wrest from . . . [the Radical's] hands the principle of revolution . . . a sacrifice of quite peculiar dignity.'[51] The revolutionary sees clearly that all human authority is fraudulently acquired, but so far from overcoming evil with good 'he too usurps a position which is not due to him, . . . an authority which, as we have grimly experienced in Boshevism, but also in the behaviour of far more delicately-minded innovators! soon displays its essential tyranny.' The rebel stands near to God for 'he really means that Revolution which is the impossible possibility. He means forgiveness of sins and the resurrection of the dead. He means Jesus Christ—He that hath *over-come*!' He substitutes doing for 'not-doing', and establishes the old order in more powerful form by contriving revolution in the Leninist fashion with men as they are.[52] The basically unpolitical conclusion of the first *Romans* was necessarily reaffirmed more starkly. 'A political career . . . becomes possible only when it is seen to be essentially a game'. Tax-paying, the most passive of political actions, now appeared as the type of that 'not-doing' by which the man saved by grace and that not of himself signified his allegiance to the righteousness of God.[53]

There was perhaps more truth than Thurneysen knew in his conclusion of February 1923 that socialism and Christianity had passed each other to a distance which made dialogue almost impossible.[54] Barth became a professor at Göttingen and in his own phrase 'had better things to do than follow German politics' until the time came when paying taxes to a nazi government seemed a not very striking testimony to the revolution of God,[55] not least because that

[51] K. Barth, *Der Römerbrief. Zweite Auflage in neuer Bearbeitung* (Munich 1922) p 462. As the text did not change in subsequent editions it is convenient to use the English translation made by Sir Edwyn Hoskyns from the 6 ed, Karl Barth, *The Epistle to the Romans* (London 1972) pp 476–8.

[52] *Ibid* pp 480–4.

[53] *Ibid* pp 487–8, 491–2.

[54] *Barth-Thurneysen Briefwechsel* 2, pp 146–7, Eng tr Smart p 136.

[55] Karl Barth, *Letzte Zeugnisse* (Zürich 1969) p 43. Thurneysen (p 8) says Barth achieved a real understanding of politics only after he went to Germany.

The socialist commitment in Karl Barth

government refused to accept them any longer. Marquardt emphasises that Barth was now a guest on foreign soil, and had to acquire the formidable technical equipment of his teaching office.[56] But the truth was that he aspired to a view point too Olympian for politics, and this must make him attractive to conservatives. To say with Gollwitzer that 'Barth, as the Christian theologian he was, always kept clear of everything built on a closed ideological system; his options always remained pragmatic, practical-political,'[57] is to put too flattering a construction on the mid-twenties. Bultmann was nearer the truth in 1924 when he reported that at a lecture by Siegmund-Schultze, 'K. Barth's followers get up with the Brethren [Gemeinschaftleute] as men who emancipate themselves from social obligations.'[58] Real politics began with the expulsion of Barth from the country in 1935,[59] but that is another story.[60]

University of Durham

[56] Marquardt p 45; Gollwitzer pp 8–10. Compare Busch p 162.
[57] H. Gollwitzer in Marquardt, p 8.
[58] K. Barth, Gesamtausgabe 5, Karl Barth—Rudolph Bultmann Briefwechsel, ed B. Jaspert (Zürich 1971) pp 24–5.
[59] A useful commentary is Daniel Cornu, Karl Barth et la Politique (Geneva 1967).
[60] Since this paper was delivered Ulrich Dannemann has published his Theologie und Politik im Denken Karl Barths (Munich 1977) in which he confirms the view here taken of the young Barth's inadequacies as a political thinker, but attempts to sustain Marquardt's main line of argument by ascribing them to Barth's theological immaturity.

THEOLOGICAL AND SOCIOLOGICAL
APPROACHES TO THE MOTIVATION
OF THE ECUMENICAL MOVEMENT

by DAVID M. THOMPSON

'ECUMENICALISM is assumed to be the will of God, and is less discussed than eulogized. . . . In belittling old conflicts and veiling new, the ecumenical movement obscures past and present alike'.[1] This assertion from the introduction to Robert Currie's study of division and reunion in methodism constitutes a challenge to historians of the modern church which cannot be ignored. The significance of the ecumenical movement is acknowledged by both its protagonists and its critics, but the issue raised here is essentially one of integrity, primarily on the part of ecumenical advocates, but also indirectly on the part of those who study the movement historically. As such it is directly related to questions of religious motivation, whether treated theologically or sociologically.

Historical accounts of the ecumenical movement thus far have been largely either commissioned by ecumenical bodies, or written by individuals sympathetic to the movement's aims.[2] Alongside these, however, there is a critical sociological appraisal represented particularly by the work of Bryan Wilson and Robert Currie, an appraisal which has aroused remarkably little response from the supporters of the ecumenical movement. Recent historical writing, particularly from those anxious to use sociological insights into church history, suggests that the Wilson thesis may be accepted by default as the standard objective assessment;[3] and this paper therefore seeks to raise some questions about the validity of the assumptions made by Wilson and Currie and to suggest alternative approaches.

Although it is difficult to do justice to Wilson's thesis in a short space, the main points may be briefly stated. Firstly, the ecumenical movement is seen as a reflection of the weakness of religion in an

---

[1] [R.] Currie, [*Methodism Divided*] (London 1968) pp 11–12.
[2] For example, in the former category, *A History of the Ecumenical Movement, 1517–1948*, ed R. Rouse and S. C. Neill (London 1954); in the latter, N. Goodall, *The Ecumenical Movement* (London 1961).
[3] For example, A. D. Gilbert, *Religion and Society in Industrial England* (London 1976) p 59; S. Yeo, *Religion and Voluntary Organisations in Crisis* (London 1976) p 25.

increasingly secularised society: 'the spirit has descended on the waters and brought peace between churchmen of different persuasions only as those churchmen have recognised their essential marginality in modern society.'[4] Secondly, it is regarded as a primarily clerical phenomenon—'a defence mechanism, mounted for professional survival'—though he admits that it would be going too far to suggest that it is only that.[5] Thirdly, actual church unions are seen as involving compromise or surrender of principles and are therefore a further sign of weakness: 'the ecumenical tendency illustrates then the extreme weakness of religious commitment and belief, since much more markedly than organisations which have purely instrumental ends, amalgamation must mean the surrender of basic principles or their attenuation'.[6]

So far the analysis does not entail any particular view of the motivation behind the movement. But the stress laid on ministerial initiative and the extended discussion of the reasons why clergy support the ecumenical movement strongly suggest that Wilson sees a close link between his analysis and his view of clerical motivation. He lists the following main reasons for clerical support: a desire not to lose identification with national institutions, which in a secular society means the abandonment of distinctive religious values; the desire, particularly among nonconformist ministers, to compensate for loss of status by gaining equality with the clergy of larger churches; an increasing sense of professional identity between the ministers of different denominations, accentuated by the development of similar patterns of professional training; and greater claims for ministerial prerogatives even in denominations which historically protested against priestly power, seen particularly in the liturgical movement which in Wilson's view emphasises the role of the minister. Free church sacramentalism, he writes, is 'a stepping stone on the way to reabsorption in the Established Church'.[7] It may be noted in passing that the last point is somewhat surprising in view of the fact that one of the key emphases of the liturgical movement has been that worship is the activity of the whole people of God and not just the clergy. The history of the Weber thesis indicates that a sociological hypothesis may be analytically fruitful even though it was inspired by

---

[4] [B. R.] Wilson, [*Religion in Secular Society*] (London 1966) p 128.
[5] *Ibid* pp 85, 138.
[6] *Ibid* pp 126–7.
[7] *Ibid* p 161.

evidence which is now known to be insufficient to substantiate it:[8] nevertheless questions of empirical truth cannot be evaded.

How adequate is this assessment of the motivation behind the ecumenical movement? There are two main issues: one is the extent to which the appraisal of the historical nature and origins of the movement (and therefore, indirectly, of religious divisions) is justified; the other is the relationship between sociological and theological appraisals of ideas behind ecumenical action.

The definition of what constitutes the ecumenical movement is obviously fundamental. Wilson's terminology includes 'ecumenism' and 'ecumenicalism' as well as 'the ecumenical movement'. It is not clear why he invented the term 'ecumenicalism', nor what exactly it means. A concept cannot be created simply by adding 'ism' to an adjective, even though this is a popular pastime. (I have a similar doubt about the term 'ecumenism', though in this case the second Vatican council did attempt a definition.)[9] In practice the main difference between the two seems to be that 'ecumenism' usually represents a positive and 'ecumenicalism' a negative evaluation. For my own part I would prefer to use 'ecumenicity', because that suggests an attitude rather than an ideology. A related point is the question of whether the ecumenical movement should be defined as a movement primarily for the organisational amalgamation of churches or more widely. In view of the actual history it is arguably more sensible to define it as a movement for closer relationships between separated churches in which in certain circumstances organisational amalgamation is seen as the appropriate action to take. In practice even organisational amalgamation turns out not to have a simple and self-evident meaning as soon as negotiators for union begin to try and work out how it can be achieved. The clarification of definition is not just an intellectual exercise.

The problem of origins is also related to that of definition. It is generally agreed that the origin of the modern ecumenical movement lies in the missionary movement of the nineteenth century, though Wilson only turns to this after his chapter on 'The Clergy and Ecumenicalism'. Currie, however, implies that this view is misleading. 'Ecumenical projects are interpreted in lofty terms of "mission", with little reference to their specific motivation and origin. Much emphasis is placed on enthusiastic international conferences, while the practi-

---

[8] K. Samuelsson, *Religion and Economic Action* (Stockholm/London 1961) pp 137–50.
[9] Second Vatican ecumenical council, *Decree on Ecumenism* (1964) para 4.

calities of everyday church life are often overlooked.'[10] This is the justification for his study of methodism. Yet it might be argued that the story of division and reunion in methodism has scarcely anything to do with the ecumenical movement as it is conventionally understood. The United Methodist Church was formed before the Edinburgh world missionary conference of 1910, and by the time of the Lambeth appeal of 1920 and the faith and order movement of the 1920s the plans for wider methodist union were well under way. Currie says practically nothing about the significance of the world methodist ecumenical conferences after 1881, nor about the effects of methodist unions in Ireland and the dominions. In any case since methodist reunion involved only the members of a single denominational family it may be questioned how significantly ecumenical it was; but that is probably going too far. Nevertheless it is far from clear that a study of methodism shows that the emphasis on international conferences is misplaced (though there may be other reasons why it is), or that discussion of the ecumenical movement in terms of mission is to misunderstand its origin.

It can also be argued that the Edinburgh conference was very much concerned with the practicalities of everyday church life in the mission field. The very detailed discussion of practical matters in various parts of the world in the eight volumes of preparatory reports for the conference may be one reason why they are so seldom read or referred to. Wilson acknowledges the missionary origins of the ecumenical movement: yet in a reference to the communion service at the Kikuyu conference of 1913 he remarks that it is not surprising to find ecumenicalism expressing itself 'in Africa—and India—rather than in London, *at the periphery rather than the centre of the movement*'.[11] No reason is given, however, for supposing that London was the centre of the ecumenical movement at that time, or indeed at any time. It seems a curious assumption, though it may be just chance that no significant gathering in the history of the ecumenical movement has ever taken place in London—the Lambeth conferences, of course, are not inter-denominational. It is odd to find Wilson taking such an anglocentric, even an anglican-centred, view; though it is interesting to ponder how much of Wilson's analysis remains convincing if applied to the Scottish, rather than the English, scene. Currie has a similar blind spot in not even considering a comparison between the methodist

[10] Currie p 11.
[11] Wilson p 144 (italics mine). He mistakes the date of the Kikuyu Conference.

experience and presbyterian reunion in Scotland, which has been studied in some depth.[12] Wilson does discuss the powerful motivation for cooperation in missionary areas; but although he notes that denominational divisions were, and were seen to be, irrelevant to missionary endeavour, he seems reluctant to mention that this might have led missionaries to query the relevance of denominational divisions in a more fundamental way.

The reason for this probably lies in the way Wilson understands the historical and sociological significance of division in the church. Church historians now have no difficulty in recognising that such division involves more than theology, but it is sometimes difficult to be sure exactly what the role of theology is. Wilson is explicit about the social reasons for the emergence of nonconformity: 'Nonconformity in England was the expression of much more than *mere* ideological disagreement about transcendental verities. It was the social expression of divergent values, divergent life-styles and hence of social strata whose claims to status rested on quite different grounds from the criteria of distinction in the existing status hierarchy'.[13] Despite the give-away word 'mere', such a description does not exclude genuine theological motivation; but in a later passage socio-economic determinism is much clearer. In explaining the changes in nonconformity, he refers to 'the disappearance of the social and economic conditions *which had made Nonconformists express themselves as a distinct people with a different approach to the transcendental*'.[14] A whole paper could be written on the difficulties surrounding such an assumption, but one or two may be briefly mentioned. What denominations stand for socially and economically does not remain constant: the social transformation of the quakers in the eighteenth century is one of the most striking examples. Unless society is static the simple passing of time is likely to produce change. Thus a distinction should be made between the reasons for division and the reasons for the continuance of division. It may well be that social differences are a more powerful obstacle to reunion than they are a cause of division, because in so far as religious division disrupts society the ability of the social groups thus created to transcend the division is diminished. Thus division might be triggered theologically, but reinforced and perpetuated sociologically.

[12] For example, R. Sjölinder, *Presbyterian Reunion in Scotland, 1907–1921* (Edinburgh nd ? 1962).
[13] Wilson p 99 (italics mine).   [14] *Ibid* p 121 (italics mine).

Theological perceptions also change over time, however, and it is doubtful whether theology and sociology can be so easily separated. The development of unitarianism in the eighteenth century, for example, affected most denominations, and eventually even methodism. But it became focused in English presbyterianism, and theological rebels in other churches, such as Theophilus Lindsey, allied themselves with the presbyterians. This might suggest that there was a tendency for theological divisions to approximate to social divisions: it does not show that theological divisions reflected social divisions, let alone that they were determined by them. It is, of course, true that continuing religious division in Victorian England was justified in social terms: thus congregationalists were apt to speak of their mission to the middle classes, the primitive methodists of their mission to the working classes and so forth. But the historian should beware of taking such statements as faithful indicators of social reality. It is notoriously difficult to make universally valid correlations between denominations and social class, and it is as plausible to see these nineteenth-century denominational defences as accommodation to the prevailing ideology of the age. The language of class is as much a part of ideology as it is of scientific observation.[15] All this is not to deny the force of Wilson's observations on the social changes which have weakened English nonconformity; but it is to deny that the development of ecumenical attitudes can be explained in sociological terms alone, without reference to accompanying theological developments.

This leads to the second area of discussion: how adequate is the sociological appraisal of the theological ideas behind the ecumenical movement? Both Wilson and Currie argue that the ecumenical movement involves the surrender or compromise of distinctive principles. To use such terminology, however, is to take sides in the argument. 'Compromise' is a slightly less abject position than 'surrender', but both terms have clear evaluative as well as descriptive connotations. 'Surrender' derives its power from its original context of war and conflict. If this is the way in which the issues are perceived, the context is not propitious for talk of unity. The old testament prophets who cried peace when there was no peace were rightly dismissed as false prophets.[16] The parallel is illuminating because in Jeremiah's time the critical issue was whether people perceived what

[15] See Asa Briggs, 'The Language of "Class" in early nineteenth-century England', *Essays in Labour History*, ed A. Briggs and J. Saville (London 1960) pp 43–73.
[16] Jer 6:14, 8:11, compare Ezek 13:16.

the true situation was. Those who are opposed to church union schemes either in general or in particular are likely to see the issues in conflict terms: those who favour union schemes either will not see the issues in this way, or will believe that the issues should not be seen in this way. Such difference cannot easily be resolved by an appeal to what is the case, because that is exactly what is in dispute: here as so often happens it is more important for the historian to understand how people see the situation and what they think about it, than for him simply to understand the situation.

The term 'surrender' also involves an over-simplification. A war is between two sides, and only one side can win: the other side is either defeated or surrenders. But the theological differences involved in religious divisions can rarely be reduced to a single issue where one side takes one position and the other another. Anyone who has taken part in union negotiations knows that discussion takes place at different levels and that a whole range of issues is involved. Nor is it the case that some people believe in unity for one kind of reason and others for another: the same person may believe for different kinds of reasons. How does such a negotiator relate his various motives when speaking or writing in discussion or advocacy? Judgment of the significance of particular principles thus becomes a complex matter, more like calculus than arithmetic. In such a situation there may be a temptation to appeal to matters of expediency rather than principle (such as the possibility of greater evangelistic success) in order to simplify a complex question. Yet if such a problem exists for the ecumenical negotiator, how much more does it exist for the historian who seeks to analyse retrospectively the negotiator's motives. Given that the modern historian's problem is often too much evidence rather than too little, the temptation for abbreviation to lead to reductionism is almost overwhelming. If moreover the historian begins with certain assumptions about human motivation, whether derived from sociology, economics, psychology or whatever, which are of a materialist or semi-materialist nature, then the chances of avoiding reductionism are virtually nil. It should be emphasised that the problem of method here is more fundamental than the question of bias. It is too simple to dismiss the analyses of Wilson and Currie as biased: the real question is whether they do justice to the evidence.

Even matters of expediency depend upon implicit theological assumptions. This can be illustrated by reference to the relationship between attitudes to church union and attitudes to evangelism. At the end of his chapter on the clergy Wilson refers to the argument for the better use of facilities and the elimination of wasteful competition between churches. He suggests that this argument is derived from 'the rational economic thinking of the modern world', citing the fact that some clergy are trained in the methods of modern business: 'economic rationalism becomes one important strand in ecumenism'.[17] Yet just as economic rationalism depends upon certain assumptions about the nature of man and is not self-evident truth, so here economic rationalism in the use of religious facilities depends upon prior theological assumptions. If the theological difference between two churches is not felt to be significant, then it may be economically rational to amalgamate: but if the theological difference is felt to be significant, then amalgamation will be economically irrational as well as theologically unacceptable. It is not that in one case economic rationalism is the motive, and in the other the motive is religious. It is rather that the theological perception of the state of affairs differs. Currie's discussion of the difficulties faced by the methodist church after 1932 in eliminating overlapping circuits (which was one of the main advantages hoped for by advocates of union) shows that residual theological differences are not easily overcome, though clearly there were other factors involved as well.

Wilson cites the methodist experience as evidence for the effects of ecumenical compromise: 'The laity who remain committed to their various denominations appear markedly less enthusiastic for assimilation with other bodies than do the clergy. Nor does ecumenism achieve much in the way of increasing the influence of reunited bodies. Currie has shown how reunions in Methodism, far from stemming the tide of falling membership, made no visible impact upon the rate at which loss occurred. *If compromise means the loss of distinctive purpose and particular commitment, it may also be that for those who remain, something of their previous ardour will disappear.* Ecumenism may be a policy not only induced by decline, but one encouraging decline'.[18] The logic of this passage deserves careful attention. It is not clear whether the relative clause in the first sentence is an assertion that the laity do remain committed to their various denominations, or whether it is a definition of those laity who are less enthusiastic for assimilation with other bodies. If it is the latter, then the statement is a tautology and only becomes significant if such laity are compared with the clergy who

[17] Wilson pp 139–41.
[18] *Ibid* p 176 (italics mine).

remain committed to their denominations. The statistical evidence cited by Currie certainly shows that advocates of methodist union who predicted an increase in numbers were mistaken: but it does not show that union caused the continuing decline—it would rather suggest that union was irrelevant; it does not show that the union policy was mistaken; and it will never be known whether without union the trend would have been different—though comparison with other nonconformist denominations might suggest that it would have been rather worse. The penultimate sentence about loss of ardour does not therefore stand in any logical relation to the previous two, but is rather a plausible speculation about human nature. Nevertheless it does require to be tested against evidence: why, for example, should it be assumed that it is impossible for members of a united church to acquire a new loyalty and a new commitment to replace the old?

The passage does, however, illuminate Wilson's understanding of what constitutes religious vigour. He seems to use the existence of social tension or division as a criterion for the strength of religious feeling. Thus elsewhere he writes that 'the whole direction of Protestant dissent in the days in which religion was a vigorous force, *providing expression for social and economic tensions*, was away from the sacerdotalism and sacramentalist elements of the Established Church'.[19] It is easy to see why such an understanding of religion should appeal to a sociologist: by concentrating on the social implications of religious belief he is enabled to avoid questions of theological truth but still to treat religion seriously. The theologian, however, dare not avoid the question of truth, and the historian has to be aware that one of the questions posed by supporters of the ecumenical movement is whether a united or a divided church more properly represents the mind of Christ. It is not necessary for the historian to reach a judgment on that question, though it will probably be helpful for himself and his readers if he does so and is explicit about it. But at least there should be an awareness that there is a question here, and that the question is open. To assume that division is a sign of religious vigour is bound to lead to the conclusion that union is a sign of weakness: the argument therefore becomes deductive rather than inductive and its force as an historical (and, one might have thought, as a sociological) analysis disappears.

There is another reason why the historian has a special responsibility to avoid the language of betrayal in interpreting changes in outlook.

[19] *Ibid* p 157 (italics mine).

It is that historical study itself is relevant to the process. Christian reflection finds itself in a tension between faithfulness to the past and openness to the present. Study of the bible has often been a stimulus to reformation and renewal in the church; and the study of church history has sometimes had similar effects for similar reasons. Thus Wilson refers to the decision by the society of friends in the 1920s to stop recording the names of ministers. Elizabeth Isichei has shown how this represented the reversal of a trend and was partly due to the historical study of quaker origins.[20] Wilson's comment comes in the course of a discussion of how difficult it is even for sects to avoid the emergence of religious professionalism. Elsewhere he comments (approvingly?) on the 'genuine lay character' of quakerism.[21] Yet was the sense of history which led to the quaker decision in 1924 so strikingly different from the sense of history among some congregationalists and baptists in the 1930s—the so-called 'Genevan' school—which produced the tendencies towards a stress on the calling of the minister which Wilson condemns as the revival of sacerdotalism?[22] If motivation is being analysed, should one stress the common interest in the seventeenth-century origins of dissent—which would also remind us of the theological differences between the various strands? or should one stress the twentieth-century reassertion of lay power in the one and ministerial power in the other (though the use of the word 'lay' does not really do justice to the quaker view of ministry)? It is immediately clear that the two possible interpretations are not mutually exclusive, but as the kind of explanation involved in each is different, it is not so clear by what criteria one interpretation is to be preferred to the other. Presumably Wilson regards the quaker development as sociologically authentic and the congregationalist development as artificial, because of his view of the direction of social development generally and his understanding of the sociological origins of dissent in particular. But by what criteria is a sociological interpretation preferred to a theological one?

The same problem can be illustrated from the history of the church of England. Wilson's book was written before the introduction of synodical government in the church of England in 1969, which has given the laity an official standing in the government of the church which they did not previously possess. It is a step which might qualify

[20] E. Isichei, 'From Sect to Denomination among English Quakers', *Patterns of Sectarianism*, ed B. R. Wilson (London 1967) p 169: compare E. Isichei, *Victorian Quakers* (Oxford 1970) pp 97–9, Wilson p 209.
[21] Wilson p 132.
[22] J. W. Grant, *Free Churchmanship in England, 1870–1940* (London nd) pp 325–55.

slightly some of Wilson's observations about the development of sacerdotalism. Synodical government, however, is but the latest stage in a development which goes back nearly a century, to archbishop Benson's institution of a house of laity attached to the convocation of Canterbury in 1886. The idea was pressed upon Benson by Westcott and other Cambridge dons, and it might be plausible to interpret it as an accommodation to democracy at Christian socialist instigation. Yet in opening the house's first session Benson cited St Peter and Cyprian as authorities for the proper and necessary role of the laity in the life of the church.[23] Is it possible to say that Benson's motivation was primarily theological or primarily sociological? Surely both elements must be acknowledged.

If therefore this paper has been rather negative about a particular sociological approach, it is not through any wish to put up a notice saying 'Sociologists keep out!' It is precisely because they cannot be kept out that church historians must concern themselves with the questions of method which they raise. Matters of church polity and ministry will always have a sociological as well as a theological dimension. Such issues are central in ecumenical discussions because theological divisions usually end up by being articulated in some way which involves polity or ministry, if only to excommunicate the dissentients. The development of centralised and bureaucratic organisation in the main denominations in the last hundred years also means that organisational amalgamation becomes a more complicated exercise and one in which sociological analysis is relevant, as the world council of churches has itself recognised.[24] It is worth noting in passing that much opposition to ecumenical schemes is opposition to centralised bureaucracy even though this is not a unique characteristic of the ecumenical movement. The relevance of sociological analysis to the ecumenical movement, however, should not become a pretext for sociological reductionism.

There are already signs of more promising analyses which have isolated the same themes as Wilson and Currie but in a different perspective. Significantly this perspective is not unrelated to a theme present in the biblical material—the difference between local and more-than-local experiences of religion. David Clark has used R. K.

[23] A. C. Benson, *The Life of Edward White Benson*, 2 vols (London 1900) 2 pp 73, 110–11.
[24] In 1955 the commission on faith and order established a study commission on 'Institutionalism', some of the findings of which are contained in N. Ehrenstrom and W. G. Muelder, *Institutionalism and Church Unity* (London 1963).

DAVID M. THOMPSON

Merton's distinction between the 'local' and the 'cosmopolitan' to show that those who support ecumenical development are likely to be people with 'cosmopolitan' experience. Similarly Robert Towler has observed that people who have experienced some kind of mobility —social or geographical—are more inclined to support ecumenical projects, and this regardless of whether they are ministers or laity.[25] It is not, however, that such people are less strongly committed; they are committed in a different way: their commitment arises out of a different experience. It remains significant that ministers are relatively more committed ecumenically than laity, and this is due to their position as ministers: but it is not primarily related to sacerdotalism or a desire for higher status: it is because in the nature of their position they are more likely to be exposed to the sort of experience which stimulates ecumenical attitudes. Preoccupation with the local is what hinders ecumenicity. Thus itinerancy in methodism gave the ministers a greater sense of identification with each other than with their congregations, and this influenced their attitudes to reunion. But this situation was virtually unique to the methodist denominations since in both the church of England and the older dissent it was more natural for ministers to identify with their localities, even though there were still differences between ministers and laity. In the twentieth century more people have been exposed to the kind of social experience implicit in methodist itinerancy.

Such a perspective also illuminates the crucial significance of other aspects of the ecumenical movement—the missionary background and international conferences. Both of these broadened people's outlooks and exposed them to new experiences. This is also why organisations such as the SCM and events such as the first world war (by taking so many people, both clergy and laity, away from home) had similar effects. The international dimension of the ecumenical movement is not an optional extra: Sir Henry Lunn was probably inspired in taking his church leaders off to Grindelwald in the 1890s.

Nor has theology been forgotten. Another sociologist, Roland Robertson, has suggested that Barthian neo-orthodoxy in theology may have played an important role in providing an anti-relativist basis for ecumenical endeavour in the 1930s and 1940s.[26] Certainly

---

[25] D. B. Clark, 'Community, Membership and the Church'; R. Towler, 'Inter-Church Relations: a Sociological Comment': both in *Church Membership and Intercommunion*, ed J. Kent and R. Murray (London 1973) pp 181–225.
[26] R. Robertson, *The Sociological Interpretation of Religion* (Oxford 1970) pp 212–14.

478

The motivation of the ecumenical movement

the decline of that theology, together with the increasing involvement of the Orthodox and Roman catholic churches, has changed the atmosphere of the world council of churches considerably since 1960. But Robertson's view, based on the history of the Consultation on Church Union in the USA, that the administrative concerns of church leaders have become the main inspiration for ecumenical development, leaving the theologians to play with radical theology, does not look as plausible now as it did in 1970. Progress in the Consultation on Church Union has proved impossible without further theological discussion as well as the consideration of other problems such as racism. Theology still keeps on bursting in. This example also serves as a reminder of how difficult it has been to make progress in church union negotiations. Both Wilson and Currie wrote at a time when it was widely expected that the anglican-methodist union scheme would succeed. The failure of that scheme does weaken the force of some of the points in their analyses: it also illustrates the complexity of motivation in both supporters and opponents of the ecumenical movement. Wilson and Currie may be right in their assessment of the motivation of some ministers, but it is not the whole story. The history of the ecumenical movement certainly shows how difficult it is in matters of religion to start again without taking something of the past as well; but perhaps at least the ecumenical movement may be allowed the opportunity of attempting a fresh start without being accused of betraying the past.

Fitzwilliam College
Cambridge

BECOMING A SECTARIAN:
MOTIVATION AND COMMITMENT

by BRYAN R. WILSON

URING the period of their emergence and growth, sects are generally discussed in terms of opprobrium, perhaps because most of those who have written about them have been people not only of other theological persuasions, but often people with vested professional interests in sustaining their own theology against that of others, or, occasionally, they have been men of decidedly rationalistic temper, eager to condemn all religion by reference to what they take to be the latest and most patent religious outrage to common sense. By the time a sect becomes a historical phenomenon it is likely that those still interested in it will discuss it with a measure of detached objectivity: for contemporary sects, only sociologists are likely to espouse the same canons of ethical neutrality and objectivity that are, perhaps so much more easily, endorsed by historians in their treatment of things past.

Objective as he may be, the historian knows that much of his source material about sectarianism in the past is likely, in the nature of its provenance, to be biased. With such sources, it becomes difficult to make judgments about sectarian motivation. Sectarians themselves have not usually been men capable of putting down the considerations that entered into their decision to adopt a particular religious persuasion: and when they have done so, their comments have often been regarded as too slanted or fanatical to merit serious attention. Commonly, sectarian converts have been more concerned to set out the proofs of their principles, almost in rejection of the idea that a right-thinking man, specifically a member of his own sect, could have any motives at all but that of discovery and acceptance of the truth. Much of the internal written source material on sects has come from leaders, but even these sources have sometimes been subject to editing, censorship, or restriction of access by their faithful followers: so it was with the papers of Mary Baker Eddy, such has been the practice of the Mormons, the Exclusive Brethren, and in some measure of Jehovah's Witnesses.

For historical sects, then, neither the writings of the sectarians themselves, nor the evidence of commentators (including apostates, whose motives for writings, let alone the substance of what they write, must always occasion suspicion), can take us far towards an under-standing of motivation and commitment. Nineteenth-century sects, however, sometimes offered us another resource: they sometimes produced a periodical literature entirely for internal consumption, which not infrequently dealt with issues in which differences, policies, and strategies were at stake, and from which something could be gleaned about motives and the mechanisms for eliciting commitment. In the twentieth century, even this source has deteriorated in quality if not in quantity: much of the sectarian literature written in recent years is written with the consciousness that the world is leaning over the writer's shoulder. As sects have grown, and particularly where they have acquired hierarchic and even bureaucratic centralised administra-tive structures, internal differences tend to be glossed over, controversy muted, or presented in a form in which only those thoroughly conversant with the context can read between the lines to discover just what issues are really at stake. As sects have become large, international movements, so their literature has become, in consequence, impersonal, official, and remote from the rank-and-file believer and his motivations. In an inflationary age, even smaller sects that are unaffected by bureaucratic impersonalism, can no longer put their concerns so readily into print as they could in the nineteenth century, and for them the less durable cyclostyled sheet, the news-letter, ignored by libraries (even when not positively rejected by librarians) comprise the ephemera in which, if anywhere, revelations are made about individuals, about motives, procedures, and disputes.

In contrast with these disadvantages which the study of historical sects presents, research into contemporary sects offers distinct and perhaps unique advantages. Ideally without any theological *parti pris* (although there are some prominent exceptions), the sociologist may do what the historian cannot do—involve himself in the life of a sectarian movement. Tactfully approached, some sects, even the most intense and rigorous such as Witnesses and the Children of God, may admit a neutral observer into their religious and communal life. He may not only observe and participate, but he may ask direct questions of the people whom he is studying. The method is time-consuming and may induce considerable emotional stress, and the information that is gained is often incommensurate with the time expended, but as information it is of a high order of authenticity. These procedures suffer from drawbacks of their own, but they do yield direct information, and information that is much less seriously subject to selectivity and pre-meditated secondary elaboration than is normally the case with the written word, whether in the form of published articles, or diaries and letters (which, among sectarians, are in any case rare commodities). The interviewer or the participant may always seek additional elucidation. He may double-check his impressions or his records. He may seek a clarification of ambiguities. He may question the relationship of one statement to another. And he may elicit important information about the background and context of the information that he is given. In some circumstances he may be able to interview two or more members of the same family and get two or more versions of particular events and experiences.

The advantages of studying sects accrue not merely from the opportunities for enquiry afforded by sociological methods, but also from some of the intrinsic qualities of the sect itself. Sects offer a unique field of enquiry in a variety of respects, but of particular importance for an understanding of religious motivation is the fact that within those groups that we designate as sects religious commitment is a value that utterly transcends all other obligations and relationships. If a man is an anglican or a methodist, this is but one among many of his attributes— he is also a lathe-turner, a pigeon-fancier, a trades unionist, a harmonica-player, and so on. If a man is one of Jehovah's Witnesses, a Seventh-day Adventist, or even a committed Pentecostalist, this is the single most significant fact about him. His religious commitment is supposed, by him, by his co-religionists, and even by his workmates, kinsfolk, and acquaintances, to influence in very high degree, not only his attitudes but the choice and quality of performance of all his social roles, and perhaps even to determine them.[1] It follows, that if religious motivation is so much superordinate to all other motivations, so the motivation for becoming religious in this way must have been unusually powerful and distinctive. Here we have a conundrum: were the primary motives that lead an individual to become religiously committed and that lead him to espouse religious motivations for the conduct of his life in themselves essentially non-religious? Or are we

---

[1] It is difficult to agree with William James when he wrote, 'Converted men as a class are indistinguishable from natural men; some natural men even excel some converted men in their fruits . . .' *The Varieties of Religious Experience* (New York: New American Library of World Literature edn, 1958) p 192. Sectarians generally are readily distinguishable from 'natural men', although that is generally more completely the case of those who belong to sects where conversion is (as it was in the cases to which James principally referred) a sudden experience.

to presuppose a religious disposition in the first place, which, at some point, simply found powerful and distinctive expression?

Sectarian commitment is of course, from the perspective of the wider society, deviant in both kind and degree, with respect to beliefs, practices, and social comportment. The sect establishes an alternative *Lebenswelt* for its adherents, both in their intellectual apprehensions of reality and in their social relationships. The sect is exclusive, tolerating no dual allegiances, no compromise with its principles, no defections from the standards of conduct that it endorses, and no infringement of the taboos that it maintains. It is a bounded community, ideally allowing no ambiguity, and in actuality allowing very little, with respect to the status of adherents, its claim to a monopoly of truth, and an exclusive warrant for its practice. Above all it claims the transcendent allegiance of all those who belong, and it does so on the basis of its own supernatural legitimation.

Undoubtedly sects have attracted investigation because they are deviant minorities, but in its assertion of totality and in its emphasis on distinctive boundaries a sect approximates the anthropologist's tribe. It is a culture, or at least a sub-culture in itself, but in this lies a difficulty for those interested in religious motivation. The very totalism of the sect induces a high degree of conformity in which individual motivation is often subsumed in corporate purposes. Thus, although in sectarians we have people who are profoundly motivated by religious considerations, we have the difficulty that their common religious commitment is supposed to motivate them in much the same way. Once in the movement, the individual's motivations are supposed to be those of the ideal member. There is a premium on conformity and there are standard tests—of social behaviour; of performance in recruitment service; of volubility in prayer or in speaking in tongues; of being able to pursue a line of doctrinal exegesis; of abstinences, and so on—by which conformity is measured and in accordance with which behaviour is regulated. In particular, any unauthorised exercise of spirituality (such as being a vegetarian among Christian Scientists, or being a teetotaler among Christadelphians, or practising meditation among Jehovah's Witnesses) would meet at least with surprise and vague disapproval, as an implicit intimation that the individual concerned regarded the sect's own behavioural directives as in some way less than adequate. Divergences do exist among members of the same sect, of course, but with respect to so basic a matter as motivations, the differences are difficult to discern, and might be most fully visible at the point at which individuals *become* sectarians.

Why, then, does an individual join a sect? What induces him to abandon an existing pattern of life, and an existing state of belief or unbelief (however vague it may be) for a commitment that is so totally at variance with that of the generality of men in his society, and which in some measure must set him over against other men, at least as a man apart, if not as a man at odds with the wider society? One is asking, then, not merely about religious motivations and religious commitment, but about how such strongly religious dispositions were first summoned.

In putting this question, one may note in passing that although almost all sects insist on the individual's personal and voluntary decision to seek fellowship, and insist on the maintenance of rigorous standards, none the less, a distinction may be made between those who enter the sect as the children of parents who are already members and the first-generation converts. Although formally all enter on the same terms, and all are subject to the same continuing tests of eligibility, and the same sanctions for misconduct, the individual who comes to the sect without having had what might be called a 'sectarian up-bringing', experiences a much more radical reorientation of values. We might ask, then, of these people—the converts—what exactly induced them not merely to abandon, but also to renounce their former way of life, and to accept religious considerations as the determinants of all actions and decisions in all other departments of life.

To ask converts why they were attracted to the sect to which they now belong is, initially, to get a response that validates the decision by reference to the ideological terms in which the sect as a collectivity seeks legitimation. Such legitimations may be primarily intellectual, primarily experiential (in the sense of emotional experience); they may, (and in the Christian world they usually do) include direct reference to scripture as a source of knowledge, and sometimes as source of specific prophecy that forecasted the events of recent history and in particular the emergence of the sect itself. 'The Truth' as a sectarians of many kinds commonly refer to the message of their own particular movement, is a self-evident and sufficient reason for their allegiance. But why, behind the slogans and the stereotypes, do sectarians take the message of their movement as the sufficient and convincing 'truth', which not only explains life, the world, and the purposes of God in history, but which also establishes principles in the light of which to organise their own lives? The answers to questions about what attracted them to the movement, and elicited statements about their lives, reveal, understandably, a wide variety of personal circumstances. Motivation is not completely and clearly uncovered even by protracted interview, but a sample of responses (in this case from a number of Jehovah's Witnesses in a congregation in the south of England) provide statements of conscious motives, and indicate some background circumstances and perhaps some unconscious predispositions.[2]

Case no 1 is that of a married bricklayer's labourer of nineteen, of no previous religion, who had been introduced to the movement by his father-in-law. He said of his conversion:

I became interested in the Truth through my father-in-law. When he came to the Kingdom Hall and asked for a [Bible] Study for himself, I thought he was mad, and when the two Witnesses used to come to their house, I was often there. I was impressed, and I began sitting in on the Study, and I developed a conscience. I got to thinking that smoking was wrong, and I stopped, and from there on I progressed. My father-in-law was just coming into the Truth himself, and it was seeing what a change it made in him that impressed me, because he used to be a bad person the same as myself. I told my father about it and I told my probation officer. They told me a lot about Jehovah's Witnesses—they were lies. I asked why do people tell these lies, and this stimulated my interest. My probation officer told me that they had sex within their families, and he professed to be a Christian, though he used to swear and smoke himself . . . My friends were surprised—they couldn't believe it and didn't think it was going to last. One of my friends actually came into the Truth himself, and he married my wife's sister, which astonished my friends a lot more. I still like to see them, and regard them as good friends, and I think that they respect me a bit because of my conduct. My mother herself said, if it weren't for being in the Truth, I'd be in prison. That is all finished now. I've never been in trouble since I've been in the Truth. My conscience wouldn't allow it. I've got a happy marriage:

[2] These responses were elicited by asking people to relate, in the course of recounting how they came to join the movement, 'What, apart from the Truth itself [the movement's teachings], first attracted you to Jehovah's Witnesses?'; 'Have you experienced any blessings?'; 'Did you have any difficulties in becoming a Witness?'; and 'Has being a Witness occasioned any changes in your life?'

it wouldn't have been as good as it is if I hadn't been in the Truth. My wife thinks that but for the Truth we wouldn't be together, because of the way I used to act before—because we came into the Truth together. . . . I stole a car and lots of other things. I was in court for actual bodily harm, for threatening behaviour, driving without insurance and without passing a test, theft—all different cases—drinking under age, lots of other things, and lots of things I got away with. All of this is a thing of the past. I've given up getting drunk. This makes it clear why my mother [who is not a Witness] thinks it a good thing, because she was a bag of nerves when I went out—and this was why she recommended to my father that the younger brothers should come to Kingdom Hall ['but my father doesn't see it'].

It is perhaps not appropriate here to subject a statement of this kind to extended analysis, and ultimately the idiosyncracies of individual cases are of less interest than general patterns, but we may note the underlying themes: pride in having acquired a conscience; the possible stimulation arising from the opposition of his father (with whom his relations have always been bad) and his probation officer; the pleasure in having become a celebrity as a bad character reformed. In the background is the importance of the reinforcement of family ties with the family into which he is marrying—a family which itself is at that moment undergoing conversion and a reintegration of values.

Case no 2 is that of the father-in-law of the young man in the preceding case: a married semi-skilled manual worker, who had been a Roman catholic. He had become for a time one of Jehovah's Witnesses while in the forces, and after refusing to wear his uniform had then been put into prison: after his release, and on getting married, he 'fell away', but after twenty years he returned to his sectarian faith. Recounting his experience, he said:

I'd been wondering about things and wondering if there was a God. Suddenly the world situation became tense—with the Arab oil business, and things were getting worse, and suddenly I could see it. So I came to Kingdom Hall and asked for a Bible Study. I was unhappy. My marriage was dodgy. I was chasing women, leading a worldly life, everything others would do, terrible things —encouraged by TV. You become detestable to yourself. You look at society and ask where is it going to go. I feel a lot better for looking forward to a new system of things. I'm motivated to do things. I did things out of selfishness before: now there's no greed. It doesn't worry me any more . . . the money will be worth nothing. I've always wondered why we are here. You see people dying. Why are we here? They are told—Evolution, but if they examine it carefully, and the teachings of religion, when I studied with Jehovah's Witnesses, I could see for myself. God has a purpose. You are being used at present. If you lead a nice life at present—you've got to work nine hours a day. What is there? Too much materialism. Man is bogged down with factories and cars and is not really free.

. . . I'm really grateful to have come back, because if Armageddon had come in the twenty years I was out of the Truth, I'd have been gone. When I returned I was really depressed, and wept—and the TV showing starving children, and I've wept. I can't understand why man does this to man—there must be something driving man on. Now I realize what the Bible says is true, about Satan being the God of this system.

. . . Now I consider everything a blessing—earning a living. I've been self-employed—car-dealing. My conscience wouldn't let me repair cars as I used to do. I owed taxes. I earn more money than anyone in the factory—I earn big bonuses. I keep working. It upsets some men in the factory. They smoke and say 'Why keep on?'. They want all that goes in society except the work that goes with it. I consider my family coming in the Truth as a blessing. My two girls were going out with two notorious characters—trouble-makers, in the the police courts. Today, it's all changed. One was notorious—he's changed and still changing . . . I had difficulties: the opposite sex. You have to watch your eyes, your thinking, and what you read: you don't have to go for girlie magazines. These things give me a bad conscience and a bad life. I can't turn that away, but the Scriptures tell me how to be forgiven providing I don't persist in them . . . [But people] don't want to change their ways. If you've found the easy way of making money, you don't want to change. You can understand people not wanting to know. I feel sorry for people who've been deceived [by different religions]. They'll die at Armageddon—we've got to get out and save them. I'm doing no more than I should. I feel so motivated, I've got to tell people what is true. Eventually they may pick up a seed . . . people have had enough of the system. Things still trouble me. I even feel I'm not worthy, though one shouldn't feel that way. I'm getting a clean conscience, and I've got to guard it. Jehovah has given me that conscience—and I'll not do the wrong things that I was doing. I've got to make sure and come to meetings and think about others instead of myself. I must think of fellow man first. I've always worked pretty hard. I've become honest. Before I took things I considered perks. I've got a better marriage: I'm not deceiving my wife as I used to. I used to have inferiority complex (or guilt). I no longer suffer embarrassment when talking to people like you. I feel a better person than I was—no violent temper, which I had. I'm not me no more.

The theme of conscience occurs again, which is not entirely usual as an expressed emphasis in this way among Jehovah's Witnesses, whose religion does not dwell on guilt, and indeed this convert said that he ought not to feel unworthy, which is in accordance with the movement's teachings. In this case, and we shall notice it in others, and perhaps it is more appropriate for a middle-aged man than for his young son-in-law, there is despair about the state of the world. There is the emphasis on new beginnings, and there is the process of externalising one's rottenness. The insistence on the need to act to save others is perhaps a justification of one's own decision and certainly a reinforcement of newly chosen values.

Case no 3 is that of a once-divorced remarried man of thirty-seven, working as a radio and TV service manager, who had formerly been an agnostic. He said:

I had just come out of prison as a conscientious objector on humanitarian grounds, during National Service. I was classed as anti-religious and therefore I went to prison. I had a three months' sentence. The Jehovah's Witnesses called on me about a week after my release. I said, 'Don't talk to me about religion', and he said, 'Many of us have been in prison, too'. . . . The Jehovah's Witnesses did not interest me, but my mother became interested. [We may suppose that this was about 1958 or 1959.] In 1971, I started to study [the Witnesses' literature]. Originally, I was interested because it seemed a good thing for myself and my fiancee, but she said don't do anything about it. After ten years she went off with my best mate and my three-year-old daughter, who I discovered wasn't even mine. The Witnesses had called in this period, but she wouldn't listen. I didn't want what they said to become a crutch for me. It took a lot [of thought] to make me accept. [This appears to have been after his wife had left him.] I met my present wife at the meetings here in Kingdom Hall.

[What attracted me was] the harmony among the congregation —and their unitedness throughout the world. How can God be partial to some and not to others?

I used to lose my temper a lot and swear. I used to chuck the [radio and TV] sets about a bit: my temper is better now. I used to have quite a problem with masturbation—this is now totally controlled. I used to tell bad jokes, but this is now completely controlled.

The message of the Witnesses and the benefits of social involvement in their well-integrated group life became available for this respondent (after some early acquaintance and attraction) just at a time of personal crisis. The individual accepts the sect, as he was tempted to do before his first marriage, when that marriage has broken down. There is a measure of self-awareness in not wanting 'what they said to become a crutch for me'.

Case no 4 is of a married woman of forty-eight, working as a part-time home-help, herself the mother of four sons, the youngest dead from drowning, and with a husband much opposed to her membership of Jehovah's Witnesses. She said:

I was attracted by their answering Bible questions that I couldn't get any answer to [elsewhere] . . . When they came to the door they were able to answer my questions. My husband was amenable at first, till he found they were Jehovah's Witnesses: then he wouldn't let them come again. So I went to them. The more I studied, the more it made sense. One saw why there was suffering in the world. I couldn't find out what I'd done to deserve so much suffering—and I saw it wasn't from God. It became clear that whereas some people have all the good fortune and others none—why if God was love should there be a differ-ence? It looked as if there wasn't a God, but I couldn't accept evolution. When I came to realize that it was Adam who wrote the first five chapters of Genesis, it began to make sense—that was the simplicity, honesty, and truth of the whole thing. I had questioned vicars and priests who said I had to believe and one said that it wasn't for the likes of me to know. The Witnesses could answer the questions.

My husband had made me feel incompetent and unable to be a proper mother and I developed an inferiority complex. We were

not allowed to have friends to the house unless they were people
he knew. He had been a sergeant-major and he expected them
[the children] to be men before they were boys. I could never see
the end of it. There was a gap between the boys [of about fifteen
years] and I prayed for strength to stay with him till all the boys
were old enough. None of the boys are at home now—the two
middle ones were turned out at sixteen: the youngest was made
such a fuss of till he died. I am still living with my husband, and
the two oldest boys are now married.

At first I wasn't allowed to mix [with the Witnesses] and sometimes I used to come when he was at work. When I did come, it
felt as if I was coming home, and everyone was so friendly. This
feeling of belonging and everyone in the same boat, and understanding the purpose of life—giving a purpose to life. It is everything about it [that attracts me]—knowing the whys and where-
fores. I can't imagine what life would be without it. I had tried
suicide before coming into the Truth. I thought it would be
better if I was out of the way. It was a help when my son died:
I knew he had only gone to sleep. He was drowned, and three
weeks before they found the body. It was a help even to my
husband: he asked a Jehovah's Witness to conduct the service,
although he had nothing good to say of them before or since.
But the blessing is that I know I shall see Tony again.

I now have a wide range of friends that I never had before,
and a purpose. I never feel alone, helpless, or useless. I feel that I
can do something. It has given me life . . . My husband does object
—he's locked me out and hit me at times. But no matter, I
still come. He is away today, but when he is at home I go to the
Central [a more conveniently timed meeting] so I can be home the
rest of the day with him.

For this woman, the Witnesses provided an alternative *Lebenswelt*,
gave her purpose and restored self-confidence in an apparently scarcely
tolerable marriage situation. There is an intellectual emphasis in the
initial attraction that the movement exerted, and both emotional and
intellectual elements in the factors that sustained her commitment.

Case no 5 is that of thirty-five year old married driver-salesman,
formerly a lapsed anglican, with a wife who was not one of Jehovah's
Witnesses. He said:

I was going to emigrate to Australia. I had done National Service
abroad and I was restless. I wondered a lot about life and death,

and I wanted to emigrate to do something with my life. I went to Perth, Western Australia in 1970. I had a few problems—I didn't have my car—it was held up in the dock strike. Having no car, two jobs proved inconvenient, and I went to work close by, at some seedling nurseries. There I came in contact with the Truth: I was labouring at the nurseries and there was a young pioneer working there. He refused to touch the blood and bone manure for the plants.[3] Everyone laughed. I didn't: I ask him why. He told me about the Bible. He witnessed to me, and placed the Truth book with me. With the many problems I had—we had no car and things were not going right—I used to read the Truth book, and it was like giving a donkey strawberries: it was like dragging me from darkness to light. . . . There was a terrific friendship among the Witnesses. There were no barriers. The man who gave me the Bible Study was the top architect in Perth, and there was no side—the hours he would spend, all free of charge of course. It surprised me to see so many walks of life with no barriers, myself being just ordinary educated. And there were Italians and Yugoslavs, and you would go round to their homes with no barriers at all. I came back at the beginning of 1973 for the sole reason to get my family to listen. I'd tried with letters. If your Mum and Dad's life are in danger, you'd come back. It cost a lot —£4,000 at least—a mortgage to try to get the family to listen. It hasn't worked yet—not even with my wife. She is friendly with Jehovah's Witnesses but there is no desire [on her part to join]. She didn't want to come back from Australia, but being head of the family I made the decision. I've known Italians go back from Australia for the same reason. Many people have said, 'You didn't like it in Australia', but I've said that if I thought there were many years left for this system, I would go back.

[The Truth is] an answer to life. I've always had the feeling there was something greater than man. Many times I'd think, 'You will die one day'. I could never understand: a vicar once went abroad and while he was away his family were killed: that was puzzling. I'd think of things like that. Death used to shake me a lot. The wife's father died suddenly: it disturbed me a lot. I saw my two sons born in the room. [The Truth] was the answer to life. It was not so much that the system was coming to an end: it was the answers in the Truth book. Biggest thing now is why

[3] Jehovah's Witnesses consider that the bible proscribes the ingestion of blood.

the wife and I divide on this . . . She has no desire and that worries me a lot. After four and a half years in the ministry, once a week speaking to all walks of life from doctors to dustmen, and all different religions, I've not come against anything to show me that we don't have the Truth. I changed my ways of thinking a lot. I was thirty-four years of age: I'd done all the bad things. I had to put on a new personality. I've got reason for living, and hope for the future. World events and problems don't get me down any more. Death doesn't worry me any more . . . I have the free feeling. I've come out of a dark tunnel.

Clearly, the sect has a strong intellectual appeal for this man: the sect answers questions. It also breaks down barriers: the eradication of differences in social status is clearly of some importance to this respondent.

Case no 6 is that of a married woman of forty-four with five children, formerly anglican, and the wife of a disabled skilled manual worker. She said:

[Apart from the Truth itself, I was attracted by] the friendliness and genuineness of the Jehovah's Witnesses who came to the house, and the welcome that I received at Kingdom Hall. I used to feel terribly shy, but the Witnesses did not make me feel small or laugh at me. I used to be serious and deep. The Truth really brought me out. They are genuine friends. I have never wanted for anything, although I have had many trials. The children have plenty of clothes: we help one another. I have a real hope for the future: I don't seek to associate frequently with worldly people.

Poverty and difficult circumstances lie in the background for this respondent who is impressed by the friendship of the Witnesses and by her own acquisition of confidence from being among them.

Case no 7 is that of another married woman, the wife of a carpenter, with four sons, the youngest of whom was spastic: she and her husband had both been Witnesses since 1952. She said:

One Sunday morning a Witness called. I was in the middle of cooking and very angry. I questioned her, 'Why do you keep calling when we want nothing to do with you?' She was little and quiet, and she shamed me. They called back by arrangement. My husband said, 'Anyone but them': he carried on working [when they came] and made a lot of noise. After he said, 'I deliberately made the noise, but what you've said in this last half hour has made more sense than I've ever heard from the Methodists—may I come in and listen?'

[I was attracted by] the meekness of the Witness who called on me—she was only eighteen. I was so rude to her. The Witnesses' attitude was marvellous. They said, 'The reason why we come round is because we love our neighbours'. It took us about two years to really get the message. Previously, I had been awkward—no one could get on with me. I used to beat my children—but it changed. The house became happy and full of laughter—a greater unity. The children began to respect us and show love. [What is impressive is] the love. We can go and pop in, and they are really glad to see you—the love is absolutely marvellous.

When I had my youngest son [the spastic], the doctor said, 'This should never have happened'. The sister in charge hated Witnesses. Nobody came when the baby was born, although I rang and rang—and the child's brain was damaged because of no oxygen. My treatment was not good in hospital, even the doctor recognized that the treatment was bad. However, I left a marvellous witness behind me. I am always being praised at the way in which I bring up and manage to help raise him [the spastic child].

The husband of this woman also asserted, in a separate interview, that the love experienced in associating with Witnesses was something that 'you couldn't get outside'. In this case again, there is evidence of both the communal support gained from the movement and the appeal of the attitudes and dispositions which the movement encourages. In this case, the serious trauma comes much later, long after the respondent became a Witness, but being Witnesses is clearly important for them during this trial, allowing them to re-interpret events and to remain contented despite family misfortune.

In *Case no 8*, family tragedy appears to be a much more significant element in prompting conversion. This case is that of a married woman, the wife of a press reader and the mother of four children, and formerly a Methodist Sunday School teacher, whose husband was not one of Jehovah's Witnesses. She said:

My husband had contracted polio; mother had died; and at this time the Belgian Congo problems had arisen which really broke my heart, because of the situation of the children. I asked the minister about it but he said, 'They don't know any different', which was surprising because the Methodists were doing what they could. Then came the house-call [by Jehovah's Witnesses]. I was very rude to the Witnesses. She returned the following week, and I asked why they were called 'Jehovah's Witnesses'. She quoted the Bible, Matthew 6, and I asked about the Belgian Congo. The [account of the] Kingdom was the first thing that made an impact on me.

When my husband became completely paralysed, the Methodist minister asked his congregation of seven hundred and fifty if anyone would offer to fetch him from hospital for the weekend: only one volunteered. He had been attached to the church since the age of nine, and was a scoutmaster, and was known to all the congregation. This surprised me.

When I had been studying with the Jehovah's Witnesses for about a year, I became very ill with malignant cancer, and had a breast, womb, and ovaries removed. This Kingdom Hall had a rota to visit my house and did all the house-work, etc., and at this time I was not even baptised. They really practised what they preached. This also impressed my husband. [One blessing is] peace of mind—against all the odds, with my husband still in a wheel-chair and four children to look after. My husband now comes to the Sunday meeting—although he was very anti. He had actively worked against my becoming a Jehovah's Witness. He [now] says, 'If everyone behaved as they do the world would be a wonderful place'. My husband and [our] friends can see a difference between those sons who are and those who are not Witnesses.

This already religiously commited woman apparently changed her religious allegiance and accepted her sectarian faith following personal tragedies and in a period of concern about world affairs—towards all of which her own church had shown indifference.

But not all conversions occur in circumstances of severe personal upset. Thus, in *Case 9*, that of a married roofing contractor of twenty-nine, with two young children, who had been a nominal member of the church of Scotland, there are no such traumatic events to relate. He said:

[Apart from the Truth itself] at the very first meeting, the friendliness of the members impressed me most. An elderly gentleman [had] called and offered literature. The day was wet and I was feeling down in the dumps. I couldn't afford the book, so I took the magazines. He arranged to call back and see me for my opinion—but I wasn't in. When I came home, mother told me that he had called and kept the appointment. He had left an invitation to a public talk. That day I attended my first public meeting, and I've been going ever since. This happened in Glasgow. I joined the book study and have attended regularly ever since. I met my wife here on holiday at the Kingdom Hall. A week later, I came down here to live. The person who originally showed interest [presumably in conducting a bible study] was disabled—that she had time to visit me was very attractive.

I am happily married and I think a lot of this, because I have generally a fiery temper, but knowledge of the Truth quells this feeling. Many things I avoid: friends in Glasgow are in all sorts of trouble, but the Truth helps me to avoid this and protects me. To be able to bring my children up as Jehovah's Witnesses helps me to protect them also. My mother and father—my mother, although she at first encouraged me—raised objections. She accosted one brother and sister [that is, sect brother and sister, Jehovah's Witnesses] on the bus and on the street: these were the people who were studying with me. My parents argued and raved, but the brother and sister said, 'Don't let that stand in your way'. It made no difference to their attitude. About three months afterwards, I managed to get my mother to come to the Kingdom Hall, and the first person who spoke to my mother was the Jehovah's Witness she had shouted at . . . It has made me a lot more placid, helped me to understand other people's feelings and given me a greater interest in all other men—makes me more outgoing. I feel I am raising my children properly. I have reasonably nice home, a good business, and this I put down to Jehovah.

The easy and unproblematic acceptance of a radically different religious position—at least as recounted by this respondent, stands in sharp contrast to the stories of bereavement, a criminal past, and the striving for intellectual certainty recounted by others. He is impressed by the people, their concern and conscientiousness, as if this were his first acquaintance with a consciously moral community, association with which has added a dimension of moral control to his own life.

Case no 10 is that of thirty-six year old married driver-salesman with four children, who had formerly been a Roman catholic who had lapsed about three years before becoming interested in the Witnesses. He said:

Becoming a sectarian: motivation and commitment

I've always believed in God. When the Witnesses called, I said to my wife, 'Get rid of them', but she talked to them. My inclination was to go and tell them what was right (from my Roman Catholic upbringing). I chatted about an hour. They told me things the church had never told me: the new system on earth, and they showed me Scriptures. I said I'd have to look into it. It aroused my interest, and having a neighbour who was a Witness, I went to talk to her. My wife was expecting, and I thought that if there was going to be destruction [at Armageddon], I had to look into it from their point of view. The neighbour came often to chat, and she gave me the Bible Study. It took her two years to convince me. I stopped completely in 1968. I realized I had to do something positive. I had a spell in which to think, and we were unsettled by not doing anything. After a year, I came back again to the meetings, to the Ministry Service and so on. I was very reserved, and I wouldn't read aloud. I was nervous of doing things that you had to do to be one of Jehovah's Witnesses. Once you realized that they were not there to pick holes, it became different. The main thing [that attracted me] was their friendliness, and the open way of going on with each other. In church you didn't know anyone, you didn't know the priest. There was the association [among Witnesses], and once I started coming here everyone was friendly, and this made it more social—we hadn't had that at church. Because I was reserved, I needed someone to come to me because I wouldn't have made the approach to them. In a little time there was nothing that they wouldn't do for you. I would sooner ask Jehovah's Witnesses than my parents, although my parents would do anything for me.

Life is a lot more peaceful now. I don't have problems. I've not had a lot of experiences. Life has run smoothly, and what I've prayed about has been answered in one way or another. Presenting material in public [giving short talks] was the biggest problem [in becoming a Witness]. It was put to me gradually and in a nice way [that I ought to do this]. If it had been said at the beginning, all I'd have to do, it would have frightened the life out of me. You feel you are not qualified till you learn slowly. They put me in charge of the accounts and this was frightening and a worry, but I've done it for a year now. They do have a good system which is virtually foolproof. I do it in my head now—I've given up the calculator.

497

One becomes more law-abiding. Before I'd adhere to the thirty mile an hour limit only when the police were there—now you keep it. God can see what you're doing, and so there is no point in trying to deceive anyone. Certainly, the Scripture helps a lot with the children. When correcting them, you can align Scripture with your correction: they appreciate that Jehovah is in a close relation.

Before, at work, there were underhand things going on, which I wouldn't tolerate once I started studying [the Truth]. Drawing stock from stores, and they thought you were soft for not picking up trivial items in a dishonest way. The organization makes you aware that there is no difference between taking a packet of paperclips and a £5 note. What isn't yours, isn't yours.

The benefits of a warm, supportive community is evident, in this case providing not only moral regulation and the satisfactions of assured rectitude, but also in providing the individual with a context in which to develop his talents and for the encouragement to learn new skills. Diffidence and embarrassment are overcome—'I do it in my head now —I've given up the calculator.'

The ten accounts that we have examined differ in expectable ways from one another, although there are recurrent elements and shared assumptions and emphases. They indicate what the respondents *now* consider were the motives that brought them to a specific religious commitment, and the subsequent experiences that reinforced it. There is an evident tendency in these accounts to indicate the functions of religious commitment. Perhaps the questions themselves may have stimulated certain types of response, yet in none of these responses, nor in any of the others that I have collected, is there from anyone a denial of the positive functions of believing. No one has said: 'I realized that it was the truth and that therefore I must believe it, although I experienced only suffering from doing so, and realize that it would be much better for me were I not to believe it, or were it to be shown untrue.' Perhaps such a response defies too explicitly the logic that all (sane) men assume to be operative in their decisions. Yet, it is clear that for those for whom religious motivation is transcendent, there is the implicit and apparently unvarying assumption that what is true will also be good, that what one believes to be true will also be beneficial. Some of the functions of believing are evident and manifest to the respondents themselves: the sense of intellectual certainty; the acquisition of a sense of purpose; the benefits of mutual help within a segregated and totally committed group; the attainment of self-confidence; the development of certain talents; the prospects of a better future; unequivocally stated moral standards. Others may be only implicit, or hypothesised by the external observer: —the opportunity to acquire status; compensation for misfortune; even social support for socially inadequate people.

The functional benefits of sect adherence become apparent to converts only slowly, however, and even though the process of becoming a Jehovah's Witness is itself a slow process, without any dramatic or sudden change of heart, thus allowing the convert to become gradually aware of the benefits of adherence, none the less, functions cannot bear the whole weight of explanation of conversion, particularly if we are concerned with the initial attraction of religious commitment. Nor can the entire burden of explanation be shifted to a more general and abstract level, although this is the level at which sociologists, no doubt in contrast to historians, have often sought to make their contribution. The two most frequently invoked general theses about the causes of sect emergence, and thus implicitly about collective dispositions to accept religious commitment are offered with different degrees of refinement. The first such general theory, if it can be flattered by the description, is that of anomie: sects are said to arise in social conditions in which there is uncertainty about mores, norms and values, and the groups most prone to religious solutions are, correspondingly, said to be those that are particularly exposed to the disrupting process of social change. I propose to say little about anomie: in so far as it is true it is also trite, and as a thesis it is too ill-defined to lend itself to adequate empirical specification.

The second thesis demands more attention because it has acquired wider acceptance, and because in some respects it had been given greater specificity. This thesis is that of relative deprivation. Perhaps it is an indication of the lack of specificity of each of these theses— both anomie and relative deprivation, that they are not set forth with the rigour that makes it apparent at what points they might contradict each other (which, if they were properly grounded theories they would certainly do). Nor do they—although I leave this point until later—seem to me to address the central question of determining just *who* in a given population will become religiously committed, who, in the case we have under review, will become sectarians.

Relative deprivation refers 'to any and all of the ways in which an individual or group may be, or feel disadvantaged in comparison either to other individuals or groups or to an internalized set of standards'.[4] The thesis is a modification of older assumptions, not always graced by the term 'relative deprivation', that sects began with individuals who suffered economic disadvantage. In Glock's formulation, deprivation is not regarded as necessarily economic in origin, and Aberle provides additional comparative reference for present deprivation, by extending it to include not only other groups, but also the past conditions (real or imagined) of particular individuals, and the legitimate expectations that they might have entertained about the present.[5] In practice the formulation that is employed is that of 'felt deprivation', which is intended to indicate that the sense of deprivation may or may not be objectively warranted, and further that even where the sense of deprivation is objectively justified its causes may not be perceived. Initially, Glock sought to use the concept in explanation of the origins of new movements, both religious and secular: subsequently, he came to suggest that the concept explained not only new movements but all religious dispositions: religious commitment was itself a response to a sense of deprivation.[6] People became religious because in some way they felt deprived and were unable to perceive the real causes of their condition, or, if perceiving these causes, were unable by rational action to affect them. Religion then became an agency of compensation. Thus, the implication is that religious motivation and commitment stem from the lack either of information or intellectual capacity; from frustration because the causes of deprivation are not perceived or cannot be eradicated; or from delusions. Thus, religion is in effect reduced to an irrational response. It becomes an agency by which a change is produced in the way in which deprivation is regarded and its causes understood: only in very limited cases is a shift to a religious commitment in any sense an adequate response to the feelings of relative deprivation (and these, as I view the matter, are the cases in which the concept of 'deprivation' is least appropriately used).

It is unnecessary here to discuss the refinement that Glock has

[4] C. Y. Glock, 'The Role of Deprivation in the Origin and Evolution of Religious Groups', in Robert Lee and Martin E. Marty (editors), *Religion and Social Conflict* (New York 1964) p 27.

[5] David F. Aberle, 'A note on Relative Deprivation Theory as applied to Millenarian and other cult movements', in Sylvia L. Thrupp, *Millennial Dreams in Action*, Comparative Studies in Society and History, supplement 2 (The Hague 1962) pp 209–14.

[6] The later formulation is to be found in C. Y. Glock and R. Stark, *Religion and Society in Tension* (Chicago 1965) cap 13.

introduced into the concept of deprivation, extending it from essentially
economic causes to social, organismic, ethical, and psychic causes of
deprivation, or to consider the types of collective agencies that he
believes arises in response to each of these. Nor need we consider in
any detail the research in which he sought to demonstrate that among
a representative sample of the membership of the Episcopal Church
in the United States, those who, as measured by objective indices,
might be described as more deprived were precisely those whose
church commitment was greatest.[7] We need only note that with respect
to conversion to religion, the thesis indicates some general probabilities
about what sorts of people might be 'at risk'. But we may also observe
that the subjective element in the deprivation thesis seriously impairs
its rigour. Just which people will *feel* deprived, and just which of these
will seek religious compensation? Some, whose objective circumstances
would warrant feelings of deprivation, may not entertain them, or
doing so may not seek or accept religious solace for those feelings.
Why, we may ask, do some people not feel deprived when, by all
objective criteria, they are deprived, and why, even of those who feel
deprived, do only a proportion become absorbed by religious groups?
Do none of the undeprived become religious? Here, then, we have
an important intervening variable: the religiosity, or the openness to
religion, of those who are converted. Perhaps implicitly the relative
deprivation thesis assumes that with the increase of cause-and-effect
thinking and of rational action, men who are objectively deprived
will, more and more, take appropriate, empirically justified, steps to
eliminate the causes of their deprivation—or will have such action
taken for them by the welfare state.

Only the relentless problems of personal anguish, the need to cope
with the untoward, and the search for ultimate meanings, will then
be sources for religious dispositions. The idea of relative deprivation
as such might be seen as an iconoclastic challenge to pure religious
motivation. Yet, at least in Christianity, the appeal to the deprived is
quite explicit: religion is offered as a compensation. 'Come unto me,
all ye that labour and are heavy laden, and I will give you rest'
(Matt. 11. 28). Compensation and reassurance are the rewards of
faith, and the deprived in this world may take further pleasure,
relatively, in the idea that the rich man will hardly enter the kingdom
of heaven. In Christianity, if not in all the higher religions, compen-

[7] C. Y. Glock, B. B. Ringer and E. R. Babbie, *To Comfort and to Challenge* (Berkeley/
Los Angeles 1967).

satory benefits are an explicit part of religious ideology, offered as a distinct stimulus to faith, sometimes as an almost crude exchange principle. Let us, then, not cavil at the relative deprivation thesis on the grounds that it seeks to uncover unworthy motives for religious commitment. We may, however, aver that there is no evidence that only those who feel relatively deprived become religious, unless we cause that conclusion to follow from our definitions or unless we posit a general condition of relative deprivation for mankind.

We may keep in mind the postulation of relative deprivation and of the social conditions of moral uncertainty that is called anomie, when seeking to uncover the mechanisms of religious conversion. From our life-histories we can obtain some idea of those mechanisms, and we can augment this information by taking account of the range and availability of religious solutions that are proffered to meet men's needs. We must ask just what types of sect exist. Men choose among sects in some respects, and neither the concept of anomie nor the relative deprivation thesis, even after Glock's distinction of types of deprivation, provide cogent evidence about just which individuals will respond to particular sectarian solutions to their daily life problems. Becoming a sectarian is a voluntary choice: it implies exposure to sect ideology and practice; some sort of conscious decision or set of decisions; and a subsequent process of socialisation that leads the individual to express his needs, and to meet his needs, in ways different from those of the majority of men.

At best, we may hope to uncover recurrent patterns, the incidence of which may differ with different age groups, sexes, social classes, ecological contexts, cultures, and historical periods. Just possibly they may differ with different basic personality types, but evidence of psychological differences that is independent of, for example, allegiance to the sect itself, is perhaps impossible to collect on any significant scale. (Perhaps, too, there is in such an approach an implicit assumption, which I should regard as gratuitous, that deviant religious movements necessarily mobilise people who suffer basic personality disorders.) If we remain at what might be called the emergent level of the social, we need perhaps to take into account the fact that divergent patterns of religious commitment are to a considerable degree institutionalised in western societies. If we take sects alone, we have already a wide choice of patterns of organisation of religious life. The cases that we have examined are drawn from only one sect, and we should expect to find different ways of accounting for the conversion process, and indeed different processes, were we to examine converts to other persuasions. I do not wish here to propose a typology of patterns of sectarian commitment, but we should need to distinguish, to complete our task, at least those sects, such as Jehovah's Witnesses, the rationale of which is intellectual, from sects that are emotionally-oriented, expressive and consummatory.[8] We might construct other variables: sects concerned with recruitment explicitly contrasted with those preoccupied with the in-group's own sanctity; rationalistic sects and those essentially therapeutic, subjective, and mystic; sects that are world-renouncing and those that are world-embracing. In these various groups, the language of religious commitment, and the experience of induction would be variable phenomena. Sects are differentially available, and each mobilises its following by a unique set of recruiting techniques which differ from the house-canvass of the Witnesses to the revival meetings of the Pentecostals, and the social programme of the Mormons. Each creates its own context in seeking to awaken men to their discontents or in providing an articulation for discontents already felt. All have their own arrangement and procedures for the incorporation of the individual and for his socialisation to group mores, norms, and values. All of them, with varying degrees of emphasis, offer new meanings for life, whether couched in primarily intellectual or emotional terms.

Clearly, there is no one pattern of conversion, or of awakening in an individual a superordinate sense of religious motivation. The profound change of values (implicit or explicit) may occur from a variety of circumstances and according to various procedures. Thus, if we were to generalise from what we know already of sects, we might, for instance, characterise Jehovah's Witnesses as an authoritarian movement, in which dogmatic certainty is a cardinal value. It is ideologically and intellectually well insulated from the wider society, emphasising formal learning procedures of socialisation, and a predominantly intellectual, if literal, commitment. It demands a high degree of clearly specified participation in sect activities, and the purposes that become part of God's new world order. It offers a minimum of ritual, emotional involvement and worship. The sect is a community of work.

Were we to consider Christian Scientists, by way of comparison,

---

[8] For a typology of sects, albeit not specifically directed towards the problem of religious motivation, see B. R. Wilson, *Religious Sects* (London 1970) pp 36–47, and for some reflections on the use of such a typology, B. R. Wilson, *Magic and the Millennium* (London 1973) pp 9–30.

we should again see an intellectual, but in this case a highly abstract, orientation. The sect provides a metaphysical philosophy to which a votary must become intellectually committed for his own advantage rather than as a participating member of a group with collective purposes. The advantage is his own rather than that of the group or of the wider society. Communal involvement is low, and insulation from evil is operative only at a mental level for each individual. There is little demand for participation, and there is scarcely any opportunity, and then of a very formalised kind, for individual initiative within the religious context. There is no real community, only a mental hygiene and therapy.

With Pentecostals, we should in general find very low intellectual commitment and an emphasis on the experiential, with much less effective insulation from the wider society except for the actual time demanded by participation in the meetings. Emotional intensity in a pattern of ritualised spontaneity would be the chief evidence of participation. Initiative within a given framework of expressive activity is encouraged in the repetitive creation of a community of love.

For these, and many other, groups there is no one pattern of conversion, no one way of articulating the way in which religious motivation has been summoned. Whatever may be the differences in background circumstances, in patterns of deprivation, if we accept that proposition (and sectarians themselves, in telling of the benefits of their new faith, often imply that there has been deprivation), we should certainly find differences in accounting for the acquisition of present compensations. Thus, a Jehovah's Witness would tell, as we have seen, a story of gradual intellectual conviction about the meaning of contemporary world events. He would emphasise the acquisition of a coherent authoritative intellectual comprehension acquired by study. As Beckford has said, there is a sense in which he might be claiming to have achieved his own salvation.[9] There is little discussion of faith, and not much of guilt, which indeed is in some respects what they must overcome to be Witnesses. The process is slow not sudden, and sudden conversion would be, for Witnesses, a matter for suspicion. For them there is a rational account of a cumulative process revealing a better life and better social relationships which

[9] James A. Beckford, 'Accounting for Conversion' unpublished paper, 1977; for a critique of the relative deprivation thesis in accounting for conversion among Jehovah's Witnesses, see Beckford, *The Trumpet of Prophecy: A Sociological Study of Jehovah's Witnesses* (Oxford 1975) pp 154–8.

are themselves an earnest of the better things of the new world order that is to come.

The Christian Scientist would also emphasise gradual intellectual attainment, but with a much less specific application to the contemporary scene. The acquisition of abstract metaphysical principles has a more egocentric, therapeutic, and manipulative significance, even though it claims to stand on universal and objective premises. Salvation is a highly individuated phenomenon, a progressive, this-worldly experience. The pace may not be forced, even though the process is sustained by study. People 'come when they are ready', and make their demonstrations progressively. There is no emphasis on faith, nor on guilt, but only on understanding. Salvation is an expression of independence, it is 'ours by right', with physical and material benefits serving as proofs of advanced spiritual thinking.

For the Pentecostals, conversion is sudden and radical, a 'heart experience', in which the individual is 'born-again'. It occurs usually in an emotionally charged atmosphere, with emphasis on sin and guilt, grace and faith: salvation is individual but as one of a body of sinners. The event is recalled, recounted, re-enacted, and relived in the routines of the meeting, as guilt and sin are recurrently transformed, at least in recollection, and in the conversion of newcomers into 'saved' people. The emotional relation with Jesus is paramount, and dependence and gratitude are the appropriate responses. The experience is intense, and it often defies verbal articulation, and is to be communicated only emotionally.

Each sect has its own conception of conversion and of religious motivation: each specifies the terms in which experience must be understood and recounted (although they differ in the importance that they attach to the activity of recounting their own histories).[10] In a sense, sectarians learn of their own motives subsequently, or at least they learn subsequently how to articulate them in an appropriate way—in a way satisfactory both to themselves and their fellow religionists. They bring their reasons for conversion into conformity with group expectations, gradually eliminating idiosyncratic elements and reiterating in-group justifications. There may be, for many, pre-

---

[10] Thus, while Christian Scientists are encouraged to offer 'testimonies' both in their regular meetings and in their journals (usually of specific experiences of healing), and while Pentecostalists have ample opportunity to recount their own conversion experiences, Jehovah's Witnesses have no such institutionalised provision. Some of those whom I interviewed told me that they had never before recounted their own experience of joining the sect.

disposing events—bereavements, illness, intellectual or emotional confusion—but the sect has to find those who are thus afflicted, and, finding them, to convince them of its offer to make all things new by the transformation of values that it proposes. For those it reaches, some find the sect re-kindles old dispositions, learned perhaps in Sunday school, for others it awakens hidden doubts, or challenges unexamined propositions about life and the world. It offers a context of concern and fellowship for people who, once experiencing life in the sect, become conscious that formerly there was something missing in their lives. Just as recounting conversion experience involves learning a language, so undergoing conversion is itself a process of learning (and unlearning). Individuals are socialised to conversion, and subsequently they learn how to express, in appropriate language, just what has happened. If this leaves us in some doubt about the motivations that have prompted men to accept a sectarian commitment, that is perhaps because we do not accept entirely at its face value the explanations which sectarians themselves offer us or the language and the concepts in which these explanations are uttered. Perhaps the most that we can hope to do is to note certain patterns of background experience and certain sequences of experience and decision. Such patterns may be of varying incidence from one sect to another, since in each sect men will learn to organise mentally and verbally their recollection of their own experience.

All Souls College
Oxford

ABBREVIATIONS

AASRP	*Associated Archaeological Societies Reports and Papers*
AAWG	*Abhandlungen der Akademie [Gesellschaft to 1942] der Wissenschaften zu Göttingen*, (Göttingen 1843–)
AAWL	*Abhandlungen der Akademie der Wissenschaften und der Literatur* (Mainz 1950–)
ABAW	*Abhandlungen der Bayerischen Akademie der Wissenchaften* (Munich 1835–)
Abh	Abhandlung
Abt	Abteilung
ACO	*Acta Conciliorum Oecumenicorum*, ed E. Schwartz (Berlin/Leipzig 1914–40)
ACW	*Ancient Christian Writers*, ed J. Quasten and J. C. Plumpe (Westminster, Maryland/London 1946–)
ADAW	*Abhandlungen der Deutschen [till 1944 Preussischen] Akademie der Wissenschaften zu Berlin* (Berlin 1815–)
AF	*Analecta Franciscana*, 10 vols (Quaracchi 1885–1941)
AFH	*Archivum Franciscanum Historicum* (Quaracchi/Rome 1908–)
AFP	*Archivum Fratrum Praedicatorum* (Rome 1931–)
AHP	*Archivum historiae pontificae* (Rome 1963–)
AHR	*American Historical Review* (New York 1895–)
AKG	*Archiv für Kulturgeschichte* (Leipzig/Münster/Cologne 1903–)
AKZ	*Arbeiten zur kirchlichen Zeitgeschichte*
ALKG	H. Denifle and F. Ehrle, *Archiv für Literatur- und Kirchengeschichte des Mittelalters*, 7 vols (Berlin/Freiburg 1885–1900)
Altaner	B. Altaner, *Patrologie: Leben, Schriften und Lehre der Kirchenväter* (5 ed Freiburg 1958)
AM	L. Wadding, *Annales Minorum*, 8 vols (Rome 1625–54); 2 ed, 25 vols (Rome 1731–1886); 3 ed, vol 1– , (Quaracchi 1931–)
An Bol	*Analecta Bollandiana* (Brussels 1882–)
Annales	*Annales: Economies, Sociétés, Civilisations* (Paris 1946–)
Ant	*Antonianum* (Rome 1926–)
APC	*Proceedings and Ordinances of the Privy Council 1386–1542*, ed Sir Harris Nicolas, 7 vols (London 1834–7)
—	*Acts of the Privy Council of England 1542–1629*, 44 vols (London 1890–1958)
—	*Acts of the Privy Council of England, Colonial Series (1613–1783)* 5 vols (London 1908–12)
AR	*Archivum Romanicum* (Geneva/Florence 1917–41)
ARG	*Archiv für Reformationsgeschichte* (Berlin/Leipzig/Gütersloh 1903–)
ASAW	*Abhandlungen der Sächsischen Akademie [Gesellschaft to 1920] der Wissenschaften zu Leipzig* (Leipzig 1850–)
ASB	*Acta Sanctorum Bollandiana* (Brussels etc 1643–)
ASC	*Anglo Saxon Chronicle*
ASI	*Archivio storico Italiano* (Florence 1842–)
ASL	*Archivio storico Lombardo*, 1–62 (Milan 1874–1935); ns 1–10 (Milan 1936–47)
ASOC	*Analecta Sacri Ordinis Cisterciensis [Analecta Cisterciensia* since 1965] (Rome 1945–)

ABBREVIATIONS

ASOSB	*Acta Sanctorum Ordinis Sancti Benedicti*, ed L' D'Achery and J. Mabillon (Paris 1668–1701)
ASP	*Archivio della Società* [*Deputazione* from 1935] *Romana di Storia Patria* (Rome 1878–1934, 1935–)
ASR	*Archives de Sociologie des Religions* (Paris 1956–)
AV	Authorised Version
AV	*Archivio Veneto* (Venice 1871–): [1891–1921, *Nuovo Archivio Veneto*; 1922–6, *Archivio Veneto-Tridentino*]
B	*Byzantion* (Paris/Boston/Brussels 1924–)
Bale, *Catalogus*	John Bale, *Scriptorum Illustrium Maioris Brytanniae Catalogus*, 2 parts (Basel 1557, 1559)
Bale, *Index*	John Bale, *Index Britanniae Scriptorum*, ed R. L. Poole and M. Bateson (Oxford 1902) *Anecdota Oxoniensia*, medieval and modern series 9
Bale, *Summarium*	John Bale, *Illustrium Maioris Britanniae Scriptorum Summarium* (Ipswich 1548, reissued Wesel 1549)
BEC	*Bibliothèque de l'École des Chartes* (Paris 1839–)
Beck	H-G Beck, *Kirche und theologische Literatur im byzantinischen Reich* (Munich 1959)
BEHE	*Bibliothèque de l'École des Hautes Études: Sciences Philologiques et Historiques* (Paris 1869–)
Bernard	E. Bernard, *Catalogi Librorum Manuscriptorum Angliae et Hiberniae* (Oxford 1697)
BF	*Byzantinische Forschungen* (Amsterdam 1966–)
BHG	*Bibliotheca Hagiographica Graeca*, ed F. Halkin, 3 vols + 1 (3 ed Brussels 1957, 1969)
BHI	*Bibliotheca historica Italica*, ed A. Ceruti, 4 vols (Milan 1876–85), 2 series, 3 vols (Milan 1901–33)
BHL	*Bibliotheca Hagiographica Latina*, 2 vols + 1 (Brussels 1898–1901, 1911)
BHR	*Bibliothèque d'Humanisme et Renaissance* (Paris/Geneva 1941–)
Bibl Ref	*Bibliography of the Reform 1450–1648, relating to the United Kingdom and Ireland*, ed Derek Baker for 1955–70 (Oxford 1975)
BIHR	*Bulletin of the Institute of Historical Research* (London 1923–)
BISIMEAM	*Bullettino dell'istituto storico italiano per il medio evo e archivio muratoriano* (Rome 1878–)
BJRL	*Bulletin of the John Rylands Library* (Manchester 1903–)
BL	British Library, London
BM	British Museum, London
BN	Bibliothèque Nationale, Paris
Bouquet	M. Bouquet, *Recueil des historiens des Gaules et de la France. Rerum gallicarum et francicarum scriptores*, 24 vols (Paris 1738–1904); new ed L. Delisle, 1–19 (Paris 1868–80)
BQR	*British Quarterly Review* (London 1845–86)
Broadmead Records	*The Records of a Church of Christ, meeting in Broadmead, Bristol 1640–87*, HKS (London 1848)
BS	*Byzantinoslavica* (Prague 1929–)
Bucer, *Deutsche Schriften*	*Martin Bucers Deutsche Schriften*, ed R. Stupperich and others (Gütersloh/Paris 1960–)
Bucer, *Opera Latina*	*Martini Buceri Opera Latina*, ed F. Wendel and others (Paris/Gütersloh 1955–)
Bull Franc	*Bullarium Franciscanum*, vols 1–4 ed J. H. Sbaralea (Rome 1759–68) vols 5–7 ed C. Eubel (Rome 1898–1904), new series vols 1–3 ed U. Hüntemann and J. M. Pou y Marti (Quaracchi 1929–49)

ABBREVIATIONS

BZ	*Byzantinische Zeitschrift* (Leipzig 1892–)
CA	*Cahiers Archéologiques. Fin de L'Antiquité et Moyen-âge* (Paris 1945–)
CaF	*Cahiers de Fanjeaux* (Toulouse 1966–)
CAH	*Cambridge Ancient History* (Cambridge 1923–39)
CalRev	Calumy Revised, ed A. G. Mathews (Oxford 1934)
CalLP	*Calendar of the Letters and Papers (Foreign and Domestic) of the Reign of Henry VIII*, 21 vols in 35 parts (London 1864–1932)
CalSPD	*Calendar of State Papers: Domestic* (London 1856–)
CalSPF	*Calendar of State Papers: Foreign*, 28 vols (London 1861–1950)
Calvin, *Opera*	*Ioannis Calvini Opera Quae Supersunt Omnia*, ed G. Baum et al, Corpus Reformatorum, 59 vols (Brunswick/Berlin 1863–1900)
Cardwell, *Documentary Annals*	*Documentary Annals of the Reformed Church of England*, ed E. Cardwell, 2 vols (Oxford 1839)
Cardwell, *Synodalia*	*Synodalia*, ed E. Cardwell, 2 vols (Oxford 1842)
CC	*Corpus Christianorum* (Turnholt 1952–)
CF	*Classical Folia*, [*Folia 1946–59*] (New York 1960–)
CGOH	*Cartulaire Générale de l'Ordre des Hospitaliers de St.-Jean de Jerusalem (1100–1310)*, ed J. Delaville Le Roulx, 4 vols (Paris 1894–1906)
CH	*Church History* (New York/Chicago 1932–)
CHB	*Cambridge History of the Bible*
CHistS	*Church History Society* (London 1886–92)
CHJ	*Cambridge Historical Journal* (Cambridge 1925–57)
CIG	*Corpus Inscriptionum Graecarum*, ed A. Boeckh, J. Franz, E. Curtius, A. Kirchhoff, 4 vols (Berlin 1825–77)
CMH	*Cambridge Medieval History*
CModH	*Cambridge Modern History*
COCR	*Collectanea Ordinis Cisterciensium Reformatorum* (Rome/Westmalle 1934–)
COD	*Conciliorum oecumenicorum decreta* (3 ed Bologna 1973)
Coll Franc	*Collectanea Franciscana* (Assisi/Rome 1931–)
CR	*Corpus Reformatorum*, ed C. G. Bretschneider and others (Halle etc. 1834–)
CS	*Cartularium Saxonicum*, ed W. de G. Birch, 3 vols (London 1885–93)
CSCO	*Corpus Scriptorum Christianorum Orientalium* (Paris 1903–)
CSEL	*Corpus Scriptorum Ecclesiasticorum Latinorum* (Vienna 1866–)
CSer	*Camden Series* (London 1838–)
CSHByz	*Corpus Scriptorum Historiae Byzantinae* (Bonn 1828–97)
CYS	*Canterbury and York Society* (London 1907–)
DA	*Deutsches Archiv für [Geschichte, –Weimar 1937–43] die Erforschung des Mittelalters* (Cologne/Graz 1950–)
DACL	*Dictionnaire d'Archéologie chrétienne et de Liturgie*, ed F. Cabrol and H. Leclercq (Paris 1924–)
DDC	*Dictionnaire de Droit Canonique*, ed R. Naz (Paris 1935–)
DHGE	*Dictionnaire d'Histoire et de Géographie ecclésiastiques*, ed. A. Baudrillart et al (Paris 1912–)
DNB	*Dictionary of National Biography* (London 1885–)
DOP	*Dumbarton Oaks Papers* (Cambridge, Mass., 1941–)

509

ABBREVIATIONS

DR	F. Dölger, *Regesten der Kaiserurkunden des oströmischen Reiches* (*Corpus der griechischen Urkunden des Mittelalters und der neueren Zeit*, Reihe A, Abt I), 5 vols: 1 (565–1025); 2 (1025–1204; 3 (1204–1282); 4 (1282–1341); 5 (1341–1453) (Munich-Berlin 1924–65)
DSAM	*Dictionnaire de Spiritualité, Ascétique et Mystique*, ed M. Viller (Paris 1932–)
DTC	*Dictionnaire de Théologie Catholique*, ed A. Vacant, E. Mangenot, E. Amann, 15 vols (Paris 1903–50)
EcHR	*Economic History Review* (London 1927–)
EEBS	Ἐπετηρὶς Ἑταιρείας Βυζαντινῶν Σπουδῶν (Athens 1924–)
EETS	*Early English Text Society*
EF	*Études Franciscaines* (Paris 1899–1938, ns 1950–)
EHD	*English Historical Documents* (London 1953–)
EHR	*English Historical Review* (London 1886–)
Ehrhard	A. Ehrhard, *Uberlieferung und Bestand der hagiographischen und homiletischen Literatur der griechischen Kirche von den Anfängen bis zum Ende des 16. Jh*, 3 vols in 4, *TU* 50–2 (=4 series 5–7) 11 parts (Leipzig 1936–52)
Emden (O)	A. B. Emden, *A Biographical Register of the University of Oxford to 1500*, 3 vols (London 1957–9); *1500–40* (1974)
Emden (C)	A. B. Emden, *A Biographical Register of the University of Cambridge to 1500* (London 1963)
EO	*Echos d'Orient* (Constantinople/Paris 1897–1942)
ET	English translation
EYC	*Early Yorkshire Charters*, ed W. Farrer and C. T. Clay, 12 vols (Edinburgh/Wakefield 1914–65)
FGH	*Die Fragmente der griechischen Historiker*, ed F. Jacoby (Berlin 1926–30)
FM	*Historie de l'église depuis les origines jusqu'à nos jours*, ed A. Fliche and V. Martin (Paris 1935–)
Foedera	*Foedera, conventiones, litterae et cuiuscunque generis acta publica inter reges Angliae et alios quosvis imperatores, reges, pontifices, principes vel communitates*, ed T. Rymer and R. Sanderson, 20 vols (London 1704–35), re-ed 7 vols (London 1816–69)
Franc Stud	*Franciscan Studies* (St Bonaventure, New York 1924–, ns 1941–)
Fredericq	P. Fredericq, *Corpus documentorum inquisitionis haereticae pravitatis Neerlandicae*, 3 vols (Ghent 1889–93)
FStn	*Franziskanische Studien* (Münster/Werl 1914–)
GalC	*Gallia Christiana*, 16 vols (Paris 1715–1865)
Gangraena	T. Edwards, *Gangraena*, 3 parts (London 1646)
GCS	*Die griechischen christlichen Schriftsteller der erste drei Jahrhunderte* (Leipzig 1897–)
Gee and Hardy	*Documents illustrative of English Church History* ed H. Gee and W. J. Hardy (London 1896)
GEEB	R. Janin, *La géographie ecclèsiastique de l'empire byzantin*; 1, *Le siége de Constantinople et le patriarcat oecumenique*, pt 3 *Les églises et les monastères* (Paris 1953); 2, *Les églises et les monastères des grands centres byzantins* (Paris 1975)
Golubovich	Girolamo Golubovich, *Biblioteca bio-bibliografica della Terra Santa e dell' oriente francescano*:
	series 1, *Annali*, 5 vols (Quaracchi 1906–23)
	series 2, *Documenti* 14 vols (Quaracchi 1921–33)
	series 3, *Documenti* (Quaracchi 1928–)
	series 4, *Studi*, ed M. Roncaglia (Cairo 1954–)

ABBREVIATIONS

Grumel, Regestes	V. Grumel, *Les Regestes des Actes du Patriarcat de Constantinople,* 1: *Les Actes des Patriarches,* I: 381–715; II: 715–1043; III: 1043–1206 (Socii Assumptionistae Chalcedonenses, 1931, 1936, 1947)
Grundmann	H. Grundmann, *Religiöse Bewegungen im Mittelalter* (Berlin 1935, 2 ed Darmstadt 1970)
HBS	Henry Bradshaw Society (London/Canterbury 1891–)
HE	*Historia Ecclesiastica*
HistSt	*Historical Studies* (Melbourne 1940–)
HJ	*Historical Journal* (Cambridge 1958–)
HJch	*Historisches Jarhbuch der Görres Gesellschaft* (Cologne 1880–, Munich 1950–)
HKS	Hanserd Knollys Society (London 1847–)
HL	C. J. Hefele and H. Leclercq, *Histore des Conciles,* 10 vols (Paris 1907–35)
HMC	Historical Manuscripts Commission
Holzapfel, Handbuch	H. Holzapfel, *Handbuch der Geschichte des Franziskanerordens* (Freiburg 1908)
Hooker, Works	*The Works of . . . Mr. Richard Hooker,* ed J. Keble, 7 ed rev R. W. Church and F. Paget, 3 vols (Oxford 1888)
Houedene	*Chronica Magistri Rogeri de Houedene,* ed W. Stubbs, 4 vols, RS 51 (London 1868–71)
HRH	*The Heads of Religious Houses, England and Wales, 940–1216,* ed D. Knowles, C. N. L. Brooke, V. C. M. London (Cambridge 1972)
HS	*Hispania sacra* (Madrid 1948–)
HTR	*Harvard Theological Review* (New York/Cambridge, Mass., 1908–)
HZ	*Historische Zeitschrift* (Munich 1859–)
IER	*Irish Ecclesiastical Record* (Dublin 1864–)
IR	*Innes Review* (Glasgow 1950–)
JAC	*Jahrbuch für Antike und Christentum* (Münster-im-Westfalen 1958–)
Jaffé	*Regesta Pontificum Romanorum ab condita ecclesia ad a. 1198,* 2 ed S. Lowenfeld, F. Kaltenbrunner, P. Ewald, 2 vols (Berlin 1885–8, repr Graz 1958)
JBS	*Journal of British Studies* (Hartford, Conn., 1961–)
JEH	*Journal of Ecclesiastical History* (London 1950–)
JFHS	*Journal of the Friends Historical Society* (London/Philadelphia 1903–)
JHI	*Journal of the History of Ideas* (London 1940–)
JHSChW	*Journal of the Historical Society of the Church in Wales* (Cardiff 1947–)
JIntH	*Journal of Interdisciplinary History* (Cambridge, Mass., 1970–)
JLW	*Jahrbuch für Liturgiewissenschaft* (Münster-im-Westfalen 1921–41)
JMH	*Journal of Modern History* (Chicago 1929–)
JMedH	*Journal of Medieval History* (Amsterdam 1975–)
JRA	*Journal of Religion in Africa* (Leiden 1967–)
JRH	*Journal of Religious History* (Sydney 1960–)
JRS	*Journal of Roman Studies* (London 1910–)
JRSAI	*Journal of the Royal Society of Antiquaries of Ireland* (Dublin 1871–)
JSArch	*Journal of the Society of Archivists* (London 1955–)

ABBREVIATIONS

JTS	*Journal of Theological Studies* (London 1899–)
Knowles, MO	David Knowles, *The Monastic Order in England, 943–1216* (2 ed Cambridge 1963)
Knowles, RO	, *The Religious Orders in England*, 3 vols (Cambridge 1948–59)
Knox, *Works*	*The Works of John Knox*, ed D. Laing, Bannatyne Club/Wodrow Society, 6 vols (Edinburgh 1846–64)
Laurent, *Regestes*	V. Laurent, *Les Registes des Actes du Patriarcat de Constantinople*, 1: *Les Actes des Patriarches*, IV: *Les Regestes de 1208 à 1309* (Paris 1971)
Le Neve	John Le Neve, *Fasti Ecclesiae Anglicanae 1066–1300*, rev and exp Diana E. Greenway, 1, St Pauls (London 1968); 2, Monastic Cathedrals (1971)
	Fasti Ecclesiae Anglicanae 1300–1541 rev and exp H. P. F. King, J. M. Horn, B. Jones, 12 vols (London 1962–7)
	Fasti Ecclesiae Anglicanae 1541–1857 rev and exp J. M. Horn, D. M. Smith, 1, St Pauls (1969); 2, Chichester (1971); 3, Canterbury, Rochester, Winchester (1974); 4, York (1975)
Lloyd, *Formularies of faith*	*Formularies of Faith Put Forth by Authority during the Reign of Henry VIII*, ed C. Lloyd (Oxford 1825)
LRS	*Lincoln Record Society*
LQR	*Law Quarterly Review* (London 1885–)
LThK	*Lexikon für Theologie und Kirche*, ed J. Höfer and K. Rahnes (2 ed Freiburg-im-Breisgau 1957–)
LW	*Luther's Works*, ed J. Pelikan and H. T. Lehman, American edition (St Louis/Philadelphia, 1955–)
MA	*Monasticon Anglicanum*, ed R. Dodsworth and W. Dugdale, 3 vols (London 1655–73); new ed J. Caley, H. Ellis, B. Bandinel, 6 vols in 8 (London 1817–30)
Mansi	J. D. Mansi, *Sacrorum conciliorum nova et amplissima collectio*, 31 vols (Florence/Venice 1757–98); new impression and continuation, ed L. Petit and J. B. Martin, 60 vols (Paris 1899–1927)
Martène and Durand, *Collectio*	E. Martène and U. Durand, *Veterum Scriptorum et Monumentorum Historicorum, Dogmaticorum, Moralium Amplissima Collectio*, 9 vols (Paris 1729)
Thesaurus	*Thesaurus Novus Anecdotorum*, 5 vols (Paris 1717)
Voyage	*Voyage Litteraire de Deux Religieux Benedictins de la Congregation de Saint Maur*, 2 vols (Paris 1717, 1724)
MedA	*Medium Aevum* (Oxford 1932–)
Mendola	*Atti della Settimana di Studio*, 1959– (Milan 1962–)
MF	*Miscellanea Francescana* (Foligno/Rome 1886–)
MGH	*Monumenta Germaniae Historica inde ab a.c. 500 usque ad a. 1500*, ed G. H. Pertz etc (Berlin, Hanover 1826–)
AA	*Auctores Antiquissimi*
Ant	*Antiquitates*
Briefe	*Epistolae* 2: *Die Briefe der Deutschen Kaiserzeit*
Cap	*Leges* 2: *Leges in Quart* 2: *Capitularia regum Francorum*
CM	*Chronica Minora* 1–3 (=*AA* 9, 11, 13) ed Th. Mommsen (1892, 1894, 1898 repr 1961)
Conc	*Leges* 2: *Leges in Quart* 3: *Concilia* [*regum*
Const	4: *Constitutiones et acta publica imperatorum et*

ABBREVIATIONS

DC	*Deutsche Chroniken*
Dip	*Diplomata in folio*
Epp	*Epistolae 1 in Quart*
Epp Sel	4: *Epistolae Selectae*
FIG	*Leges 3: Fontes Iuris Germanici Antique,* new series
FIGUS	4: , *in usum scholarum*
Form	2: *Leges in Quart 5: Formulae Merovingici et Karolini Aevi*
GPR	*Gesta Pontificum Romanorum*
Leges	*Leges in folio*
Lib	*Libelli de lite*
LM	*Ant 3: Libri Memoriales*
LNG	*Leges 2: Leges in Quart 1: Leges nationum Germanicarum*
Necr	*Ant 2: Necrologia Germaniae*
Poet	1: *Poetae Latini Medii Aevi*
Quellen	*Quellen zur Geistesgeschichte des Mittelalters*
Schriften	*Schriften der Monumenta Germaniae Historica*
SRG	*Scriptores rerum germanicarum in usum scholarum*
SRG ns	, new series
SRL	*Scriptores rerum langobardicarum et italicarum*
SRM	*Scriptores rerum merovingicarum*
SS	*Scriptores*
SSM	*Staatschriften des späteren Mittelalters*
MIÖG	*Mitteilungen des Instituts für österreichische Geschichtsforschung* (Graz/Cologne 1880–)
MM	F. Miklosich and J. Müller, *Acta et Diplomata Graeca medii aevi sacra et profana,* 6 vols (Vienna 1860–90)
Moorman, History	J. R. H. Moorman, *A History of the Franciscan Order from its Origins to the year 1517* (Oxford 1968)
More, Works	*The Complete Works of St Thomas More,* ed R. S. Sylvester et al, Yale edition (New Haven/London 1963–)
Moyen Age	*Le moyen âge. Revue d'histoire et de philologie* (Paris 1888–)
MRHEW	David Knowles and R. N. Hadcock, *Medieval Religious Houses, England and Wales* (2 ed London 1971)
MRHI	A. Gwynn and R. N. Hadcock, *Medieval Religious Houses, Ireland* (London 1970)
MRHS	Ian B. Cowan and David E. Easson, *Medieval Religious Houses, Scotland* (2 ed London 1976)
MS	Manuscript
MStn	*Mittelalterliche Studien* (Stuttgart 1966–)
Muratori	L. A. Muratori, *Rerum italicarum scriptores,* 25 vols (Milan 1723–51); new ed G. Carducci and V. Fiorini, 34 vols in 109 fasc (Città di Castello/Bologna 1900–)
NCE	*New Catholic Encyclopedia,* 15 vols (New York 1967)
NCModH	*New Cambridge Modern History,* 14 vols (Cambridge 1957–70)
nd	no date
NEB	*New English Bible*
NF	Neue Folge
NH	*Northern History* (Leeds 1966–)
ns	new series
NS	New Style
Numen	*Numen: International Review for the History of Religions* (Leiden 1954–)

OCP	*Orientalia Christiana Periodica* (Rome 1935–)
ODCC	*Oxford Dictionary of the Christian Church*, ed F. L. Cross (Oxford 1957), 2 ed with E. A. Livingstone (1974)
OED	*Oxford English Dictionary*
OS	Old Style
OHS	*Oxford Historical Society*
PBA	*Proceedings of the British Academy*
PG	*Patrologia Graeca*, ed J. P. Migne, 161 vols (Paris 1857–66)
PhK	Philosophisch-historische Klasse
PL	*Patrologia Latina*, ed J. P. Migne, 217+4 index vols (Paris 1841–64)
Plummer, Bede	*Venerabilis Baedae Opera Historica*, ed C. Plummer (Oxford 1896)
PO	*Patrologia Orientalis*, ed J. Graffin and F. Nau (Paris 1903–)
Potthast	*Regesta Pontificum Romanorum inde ab a. post Christum natum 1198 ad a. 1304*, ed A. Potthast, 2 vols (1874–5 repr Graz 1957)
PP	*Past and Present* (London 1952–)
PPTS	*Palestine Pilgrims' Text Society*, 13 vols and index (London 1896–1907)
PRIA	*Proceedings of the Royal Irish Academy* (Dublin 1836–)
PRO	Public Record Office
PS	Parker Society (Cambridge 1841–55)
PW	*Paulys Realencyklopädie der klassischen Altertumswissenschaft*, new ed G. Wissowa and W. Kroll (Stuttgart 1893–)
QFIAB	*Quellen & Forschungen aus italienischen Archiven und Bibliotheken* (Rome 1897–)
RAC	*Reallexikon für Antike und Christentum*, ed T. Klauser (Stuttgart 1941–)
RB	*Revue Bénédictine* (Maredsous 1884–)
RE	*Realencyclopädie für protestantische Theologie*, ed A. Hauck, 24 vols (3 ed Leipzig, 1896–1913)
REB	*Revue des Études Byzantines* (Bucharest/Paris 1946–)
RecS	Record Series
RGG	*Die Religion in Geschichte und Gegenwart*, 6 vols (Tübingen 1927–32)
RH	*Revue historique* (Paris 1876–)
RHC,	*Recueil des Historiens des Croisades*, ed Académie des Inscriptions et Belles-Lettres (Paris 1841–1906)
Arm	*Historiens Arméniens*, 2 vols (1869–1906)
Grecs	*Historiens Grecs*, 2 vols (1875–81)
Lois	*Lois. Les Assises de Jérusalem*, 2 vols (1841–3)
Occ	*Historiens Occidentaux*, 5 vols (1844–95)
Or	*Historiens Orientaux*, 5 vols (1872–1906)
RHD	*Revue d'histoire du droit* (Haarlem, Gronigen 1923–)
RHDFE	*Revue historique du droit français et étranger* (Paris 1922–)
RHE	*Revue d'Histoire Ecclésiastique* (Louvain 1900–)
RHEF	*Revue d'Histoire de l'Église de France* (Paris 1910–)
RHR	*Revue de l'Histoire des Religions* (Paris 1880–)
RR	*Regesta Regum Anglo-Normannorum*, ed H. W. C. Davis, H. A. Cronne, Charles Johnson, R. H. C. Davis, 4 vols (Oxford 1913–69)
RS	*Rerum Brittanicarum Medii Aevi Scriptores*, 99 vols (London 1858–1911). *Rolls Series*
RSR	*Revue des sciences religieuses* (Strasbourg 1921–)
RTAM	*Recherches de théologie ancienne et médiévale* (Louvain 1929–)

RSCI	*Rivista di storia della chiesa in Italia* (Rome 1947–)
RStI	*Rivista storica italiana* (Naples 1884–)
RV	Revised Version
Sitz	*Sitzungsberichte*
SA	*Studia Anselmiana* (Rome 1933–)
sa	*sub anno*
SBAW	*Sitzungsberichte der bayerischen Akademie der Wissenschaften*, PhK (Munich 1871–)
SCH	*Studies in Church History* (London 1964–)
ScHR	*Scottish Historical Review* (Edinburgh/Glasgow 1904–)
SCR	*Sources chrétiennes*, ed H. de Lubac and J. Daniélou (Paris 1941–)
SF	*Studi Francescani* (Florence 1914–)
SGre	*Studi Gregoriani*, ed G. Borino, 7 vols (Rome 1947–61)
SGra	*Studia Gratiana*, ed J. Forchielli and A. M. Stickler (Bologna 1953–)
SMon	*Studia Monastica* (Montserrat, Barcelona 1959–)
Speculum	*Speculum, A Journal of Medieval Studies* (Cambridge, Mass 1926–)
SpicFr	*Spicilegium Friburgense* (Freiburg 1957–)
SS	*Surtees Society* (Durham 1835–)
SSSpoleto	*Settimane di Studio sull'alto medioevo*, 1952– , Centro Italiano di studi sull'alto medioevo, Spoleto (Spoleto 1954–)
STC	*A Short-Title Catalogue of Books Printed in England, Scotland and Ireland and of English Books Printed Abroad 1475–1640*, ed A. W. Pollard and G. R. Redgrave (London 1926, repr 1946, 1950)
Strype, *Annals*	John Strype, *Annals of the Reformation and Establishment of Religion . . . during Queen Elizabeth's Happy Reign*, 4 vols in 7 (Oxford 1824)
Strype, Cranmer	John Strype, *Memorials of . . . Thomas Cranmer*, 2 vols (Oxford 1840)
Strype, *Grindal*	John Strype, *The History of the Life and Acts of . . . Edmund Grindal* (Oxford 1821)
Strype, Memorials	John Strype, *Ecclesiastical Memorials, Relating Chiefly to Religion, and the Reformation of it . . . under King Henry VIII, King Edward VI and Queen Mary I*, 3 vols in 6 (Oxford 1822)
Strype, *Parker*	John Strype, *The Life and Acts of Matthew Parker*, 3 vols (Oxford 1821)
Strype, Whitgift	John Strype, *The Life and Acts of John Whitgift*, 3 vols (Oxford 1822)
sub hag	*subsidia hagiographica*
sv	*sub voce*
SVRG	*Schriften des Vereins für Reformationsgeschichte* (Halle/Leipzig/Gütersloh 1883–)
TCBiblS	*Transactions of the Cambridge Bibliographical Society* (Cambridge 1949–)
THSCym	*Transactions of the Historical Society of Cymmrodorion* (London 1822–)
TRHS	*Transactions of the Royal Historical Society* (London 1871–)
TU	*Texte und Untersuchungen zur Geschichte der altchristlichen Literatur* (Leipzig/Berlin 1882–)
VCH	*Victoria County History* (London 1900–)

ABBREVIATIONS

VHM	G. Tiraboschi, *Vetera Humiliatorum Monumenta*, 3 vols. (Milan 1766–8)
Vivarium	*Vivarium: An International Journal for the Philosophy and Intellectual Life of the Middle Ages and Renaissance* (Assen 1963–)
VV	*Vizantijskij Vremennik* 1–25 (St Petersburg 1894–1927), ns 1 (26) (Leningrad 1947–)
WA	D. *Martin Luthers Werke*, ed J. C. F. Knaake (Weimar 1883–) [*Weimarer Ausgabe*]
WA Br	*Briefwechsel*
WA DB	*Deutsche Bibel*
WA TR	*Tischreden*
WelHR	*Welsh History Review* (Cardiff 1960–)
Wharton	H. Wharton, *Anglia Sacra*, 2 parts (London 1691)
Wilkins	*Concilia Magnae Britanniae et Hiberniae A.D. 446–1717*, 4 vols, ed D. Wilkins (London 1737)
YAJ	*Yorkshire Archaeological Journal* (London/Leeds 1870–)
Zanoni	L. Zanoni, *Gli Umiliati nei loro rapporti con l'eresia, l'industria della lana ed i communi nei secoli xii e xiii, Biblioteca Historica Italica*, 2 series, 2 (Milan 1911)
ZKG	*Zeitschrift für Kirchengeschichte* (Gotha/Stuttgart 1878–)
ZOG	*Zeitschrift für osteuropäische Geschichte* (Berlin 1911–35) = *Kyrios* (Berlin 1936–)
ZRG	*Zeitschrift der Savigny-Stiftung für Rechtsgeschichte* (Weimar)
GAbt	*Germanistische Abteilung* (1863–)
KAbt	*Kanonistische Abteilung* (1911–)
RAbt	*Romanistische Abteilung* (1880–)
ZRGG	*Zeitschrift für Religions- und Geistesgeschichte* (Marburg 1948–)
Zwingli, *Werke*	*Huldreich Zwinglis Sämmtliche Werke*, ed E. Egli and others, *CR* (Berlin/Leipzig/Zurich 1905–)